Using and Administering Linux: Volume 1

Zero to SysAdmin: Getting Started

Second Edition

David Both

Apress®

Using and Administering Linux: Volume 1: Zero to SysAdmin: Getting Started

David Both
Raleigh, NC, USA

ISBN-13 (pbk): 978-1-4842-9617-2
https://doi.org/10.1007/978-1-4842-9618-9

ISBN-13 (electronic): 978-1-4842-9618-9

Managing Director, Apress Media LLC: Welmoed Spahr
Acquisitions Editor: James Robinson-Prior
Development Editor: Jim Markham
Editorial Assistant: Gryffin Winkler

Cover image designed by the author

Distributed to the book trade worldwide by Springer Science+Business Media New York, 1 New York Plaza, 1 FDR Dr, New York, NY 10004. Phone 1-800-SPRINGER, fax (201) 348-4505, e-mail orders-ny@springer-sbm.com, or visit www.springeronline.com. Apress Media, LLC is a California LLC and the sole member (owner) is Springer Science + Business Media Finance Inc (SSBM Finance Inc). SSBM Finance Inc is a **Delaware** corporation.

For information on translations, please e-mail booktranslations@springernature.com; for reprint, paperback, or audio rights, please e-mail bookpermissions@springernature.com.

Apress titles may be purchased in bulk for academic, corporate, or promotional use. eBook versions and licenses are also available for most titles. For more information, reference our Print and eBook Bulk Sales web page at http://www.apress.com/bulk-sales.

Any source code or other supplementary material referenced by the author in this book is available to readers on GitHub (https://github.com/Apress). For more detailed information, please visit https://www.apress.com/gp/services/source-code.

Paper in this product is recyclable

This book is dedicated to all

Linux and open source developers, system administrators, course developers, and trainers.

:(){ :|:& };:

Table of Contents

About the Author

David Both is an open source software and GNU/Linux advocate, trainer, writer, and speaker. He has been working with Linux and open source software for more than 25 years and has been working with computers for over 50 years. He is a strong proponent of and evangelist for the "Linux Philosophy for system administrators."

He worked for IBM for 21 years and, while working as a course development representative in Boca Raton, FL, in 1981, wrote the training course for the first IBM PC. He has taught RHCE classes for Red Hat and has taught classes on Linux ranging from Lunch'n'Learns to full five-day courses.

David's books and articles are a continuation of his desire to pass on his knowledge and to provide mentoring to anyone interested in learning about Linux.

David prefers to purchase the components and build his own computers from scratch to ensure that each new computer meets his exacting specifications. Building his own computers also means not having to pay the Microsoft tax. His latest build is an ASUS TUF X299 motherboard and an Intel i9 CPU with 16 cores (32 CPUs) and 64GB of RAM in a Cooler Master MasterFrame 700.

David is the author of *The Linux Philosophy for SysAdmins* (Apress, 2018) and co-author of *Linux for Small Business Owners* (Apress, 2022) and can be found on Mastodon @linuxgeek46@LinuxRocks.online.

About the Technical Reviewers

Branton Brodie started his Linux journey last year while attending All Things Open 2022. Getting into the IT world was something he wanted to do for a while but didn't know where to start until he went there and saw all the opportunities shown. Linux stood out to him the most, and he is now studying to become a SysAdmin. He enjoys reading about tech and how the future of tech will shape the world around us. He lives in the calming town of Wake Forest, NC.

Seth Kenlon is a Unix and Linux geek, SysAdmin, open source and free culture advocate, music producer, Java and Lua programmer, game designer, and tabletop gamer. He arrived in the computer industry by way of film production.

Acknowledgments

Writing a book – and especially a three-volume second edition – is not a solitary activity, and this massive Linux training course required a team effort much more so than most.

The most important person in this effort has been my awesome wife, Alice, who has been my head cheerleader and best friend throughout. I could not have done this without your support and love. Again!

I owe many thanks to my editors at Apress, James Robinson-Prior, Jim Markham, and Gryffin Winkler, for seeing the need for a second edition and especially for being supportive as I worked my way through some major restructuring and a significant amount of new material. I especially thank you for your immediate support when I suggested having a student as second technical editor.

Seth Kenlon, my amazing technical reviewer, and I have worked together before on previous books as well as many of the articles I wrote for the now defunct Opensource.com website. I am grateful for his contributions to the technical accuracy of all three volumes of this course. Seth also made some important suggestions that improved the flow and accuracy of this course. I once said that Seth was on the "ragged edge of being brutally honest" in his editorial tasks; he responded that he had been aiming for "completely brutal," but had apparently failed. You still have my ongoing gratitude for the work you do.

I also owe many thanks to Branton Brodie, my second technical editor for all three volumes. Branton and I met as part of his desire to learn about Linux at a time when I was just starting on this second edition. I thought that having a student who wanted to take the course anyway act as a technical editor could provide me with some insight into how students view the course. His contributions have been valuable to my work as I was able to revise descriptions and explanations that made sense to me but not necessarily to anyone who has never been exposed to Linux or system administration.

Of course any remaining errors, omissions, and poor explanations are my responsibility alone.

Introduction

This Linux training course, *Using and Administering Linux – Zero to SysAdmin*, is significantly different from other courses. It consists of three volumes. Each of these three volumes is closely connected, and they build upon each other.

This Linux training course differs from others because it is a complete self-study course. You should start at the beginning of Volume 1 and read the text, perform all of the experiments, and do all of the chapter exercises through to the end of Volume 3. If you do this, even if you are starting from zero knowledge about Linux, you can learn the tasks necessary to becoming a Linux system administrator, a SysAdmin.

Another difference this course has over others is that all of the experiments are performed on one or more virtual machines (VMs) in a virtual network. Using the free software VirtualBox, you will create this virtual environment on any reasonably sized host, whether Linux or Windows. In this virtual environment, you are free to experiment on your own, make mistakes that could damage the Linux installation of a hardware host, and still be able to recover completely by restoring the Linux VM host from any one of multiple snapshots. This flexibility to take risks and yet recover easily makes it possible to learn more than would otherwise be possible.

These course materials can also be used as reference materials. I have used my previous course materials for reference for many years, and they have been very useful in that role. I have kept this as one of my goals in this set of materials.

Not all of the review exercises in this course can be answered by simply reviewing the chapter content. For some questions you will need to design your own experiment in order to find a solution. In many cases there will very probably be multiple solutions, and all that produce the correct results will be the "correct" ones.

The Process

The process that goes with this format is just as important as the format of the course – really even more so. The first thing that a course developer must do is generate a list of requirements that define both the structure and the content of the course. Only then can the process of writing the course proceed. In fact, many times I find it helpful to write the review questions and exercises before I create the rest of the content. In many chapters of this course, I have worked in this manner.

These courses present a complete, end-to-end Linux training course for students like you who know before you start that you want to learn to be a Linux system administrator – a SysAdmin. This Linux course will allow you to learn Linux right from the beginning with the objective of becoming a SysAdmin.

Many Linux training courses begin with the assumption that the first course a student should take is one designed to start them as a user. Those courses may discuss the role of root in system administration, but ignore topics that are important to future SysAdmins. Other courses ignore system administration altogether. A typical second course will introduce the student to system administration, while a third may tackle advanced administration topics.

Frankly, this baby step approach did not work well for many of us who are now Linux SysAdmins. We became SysAdmins, in part at least, due to our intense desire to learn as much as possible as quickly as possible. It is also, I think in large part, due to our highly inquisitive natures. We learn a basic command and then start asking questions, experimenting with it to see what its limits are, what breaks it, what using it can break. We explore the man(ual) pages and other documentation to learn the extreme usages to which it might be put. If things don't break by themselves, we break them intentionally to see how they work and to learn how to fix them. We relish our own failures because we learn more from fixing them than we do when things always work as they are supposed to.

In this course we will dive deep into Linux system administration almost from the very beginning. You will learn many of the Linux tools required to use and administer Linux workstations and servers – usually multiple tools that can be applied to each of these tasks. This course contains many experiments to provide you with the kind of hands-on experiences that SysAdmins appreciate. All of these experiments guide you one step at a time into the elegant and beautiful depths of the Linux experience. You will learn that Linux is simple and that simplicity is what makes it both elegant and knowable.

Based on my own years working with Unix and Linux, the course materials contained in these three volumes are designed to introduce you to the practical, daily tasks you will perform as a Linux user and, at the same time, as a Linux system administrator – SysAdmin.

But I don't know everything – that's just not possible. No SysAdmin does. Further, no two SysAdmins know exactly the same things because that, too, is impossible. We have each started with different knowledge and skills; we have different goals; we have different experiences because the systems on which we work have failed in different ways, had different hardware, were embedded in different networks, had different distributions installed, and many other differences. We use different tools and approaches to problem solving because the many different mentors and teachers we had used different sets of tools from each other; we use different Linux distributions; we think differently; and we know different things about the hardware on which Linux runs. Our past is much of what makes us what we are and what defines us as SysAdmins.

So I will show you things in this course – things that I think are important for you to know, things that, in my opinion, will provide you with the skills to use your own curiosity and creativity to find solutions that I would never think of to problems I have never encountered.

I have always found that I learn more from my mistakes than I ever have when things work as they are supposed to. For this reason I suggest that, rather than immediately reverting to an earlier snapshot when you run into trouble, you try to figure out how the problem was created and how best to recover from it. If, after a reasonable period of time, you have not resolved the problem, that would be the point at which reverting to a snapshot would make sense.

What This Course Is Not

This course is not a certification study guide. It is not designed to help you pass a certification test of any type. This course is intended purely to help you become a good or perhaps even great SysAdmin, not to pass a test.

There are a few good certification tests. Red Hat and Cisco certifications are among the best because they are based on the test-taker's ability to perform specific tasks. I am not familiar with any of the other certification tests because I have not taken them. But the courses you can take and books you can purchase to help you pass those tests are designed to help you pass the tests and not to administer a Linux host or network. That does not make them bad – just different from this course.

Content Overview

This quick overview of the contents of each volume should serve as a quick orientation guide if you need to locate specific information. If you are trying to decide whether to purchase this book and its companion volumes, it will give you a good overview of the entire course.

Using and Administering Linux: Volume 1 – Zero to SysAdmin: Getting Started

Chapters 1 through 3 of Volume 1 introduce operating systems in general and Linux in particular and briefly explore the Linux Philosophy for SysAdmins in preparation for the rest of the course.

Chapter 4 then guides you through the use of VirtualBox to create a virtual machine (VM) and a virtual network to use as a test laboratory for performing the many experiments that are used throughout the course. In Chapter 5, you will install the Xfce version of Fedora – a popular and powerful Linux distribution – on the VM. Chapter 6 shows you how to use the Xfce desktop, which will enable you to leverage your growing command-line interface (CLI) expertise as you proceed through the course.

Chapters 7 and 8 will get you started using the Linux command line and introduce you to some of the basic Linux commands and their capabilities. In Chapter 9 you will learn about data streams and the Linux tools used to manipulate them. And in Chapter 10 you will learn a bit about several text editors, which are indispensable to advanced Linux users and system administrators. You will also learn to use the vim text editor to create and modify the many ASCII plain text files that Linux uses for configuration and administrative programming.

Chapters 11 through 13 start your work as a SysAdmin and take you through some specific tasks such as working as root and installing software updates and new software. Chapters 14 and 15 discuss more terminal emulators and some advanced shell skills. In Chapter 16 you will learn about the sequence of events that take place as the computer boots and Linux starts up. Chapter 17 shows you how to configure your shell to personalize it in ways that can seriously enhance your command-line efficiency.

Finally, Chapters 18 and 19 dive into all things files and filesystems.

1. Introduction
2. Introduction to Operating Systems
3. The Linux Philosophy for SysAdmins
4. Preparation
5. Installing Linux
6. Using the Xfce Desktop
7. Using the Linux Command Line

Using and Administering LInux: Volume 2 – Zero to SysAdmin: Advanced Topics

Volume 2 of *Using and Administering Linux* introduces you to some incredibly powerful and useful advanced topics that every SysAdmin must know.

In Chapters 20 and 21, you will experience an in-depth exploration of logical volume management – and what that even means – as well as the use of file managers to manipulate files and directories. Chapter 22 introduces the concept that, in Linux, everything is a file. You will also learn some fun and interesting uses of the fact that everything is a file.

In Chapter 23 you will learn to use several tools that enable the SysAdmin to manage and monitor running processes. Chapter 24 enables you to experience the power of the special filesystems, such as /proc, which enable us as SysAdmins to monitor and tune the kernel while it is running – without a reboot.

Chapter 25 will introduce you to regular expressions and the power that using them for pattern matching can bring to the command line, while Chapter 26 discusses managing printers and printing from the command line. In Chapter 27 you will use several tools to unlock the secrets of the hardware in which your Linux operating system is running.

Chapters 28 and 29 show you how to do some simple – and not so simple – command-line programming and how to automate various administrative tasks. In Chapter 30 you will learn to use Ansible, a powerful tool that makes automating tasks for thousands of computers just as easy as for one. Chapter 31 discusses the tools you will use to perform repetitive and automated tasks at specific times.

You will begin to learn the details of networking in Chapter 32, and Chapter 33 covers use of the powerful NetworkManager tool.

Chapter 34 introduces the BTRFS filesystem and covers its very interesting features. This chapter also informs you why BTRFS is not an appropriate choice for a filesystem in most use cases.

Chapters 35 through 37 allow you to explore systemd, the modern tool for starting Linux at boot time and which is also used to manage system services and tools. Chapter 38 discusses dbus and udev and how Linux uses them to treat all devices as plug and play. Chapter 39 explores the use of the traditional Linux log files.

Chapter 40 covers the tasks required to manage users, while Chapter 41 introduces you to some basic tasks needed to manage the firewall. You will use the firewalld command-line tool to create and manage zones to which the network interfaces will be assigned based on various security needs such as internal and external networks.

Using and Administering Linux: Volume 3 – Zero to SysAdmin: Network Services

In Volume 3 of *Using and Administering Linux,* you will start by creating a new VM on the existing virtual network. This new VM will be used as a server for the rest of this course, and it will replace some of the functions performed by the virtual router that is part of our virtual network.

Chapter 42 begins this transformation from simple workstation to server by adding a second network interface card (NIC) to the new VM so that it can act as a firewall and router and then changing its network configuration from DHCP to static IP addressing. This includes configuring both NICs so that one is connected to the existing virtual router so as to allow connections to the outside world and so that the other NIC connects to the new "inside" network that will contain the existing VM.

Chapter 43 discusses Domain Name Services (DNS) in detail both from client and server standpoints. You'll learn to use the /etc/hosts file for simple name resolution and then create a simple caching name server. You will then convert the caching name server into a primary name server for your internal network.

In Chapter 44 you will convert the new server into a router using kernel parameters and a simple firewall configuration change.

Chapter 45 shows how to use SSHD to provide secure remote access between Linux hosts. It also provides some interesting insights into using commands remotely and creating a simple command-line program to back up specific directories of a remote host to the local host.

Although we have incorporated security in all aspects of what has already been covered, Chapter 46 covers some additional security topics. This includes physical hardening as well as further hardening of the host to provide enhanced protection from network intrusions.

In Chapter 47 you will learn techniques and strategies for creating backups that use easily available open source tools, which are easy to use for both creating backups and restoring complete filesystems or individual files.

You will learn to install and configure an enterprise-class email server that can detect and block most spam and malware in Chapters 48 through 50. Chapter 51 takes you through setting up a web server, and in Chapter 52 you will set up WordPress, a flexible and powerful content management system.

In Chapter 53 you return to email by setting up a mailing list using Mailman.

Sometimes accessing a desktop remotely is the only way to do some things, so in Chapter 54 you will do just that.

Chapter 55 discusses package management from the other direction by guiding you through the process of creating an RPM package for the distribution of your own scripts and configuration files. Then Chapter 56 guides you through sharing files to both Linux and Windows hosts.

Finally, Chapter 57 will get you started in the right direction because I know you are going to ask, "Where do I go from here?"

Taking This Course

Although designed primarily as a self-study guide, this course can be used effectively in a classroom environment. This course can also be used very effectively as a reference. Many of the original course materials I wrote for Linux training classes I used to teach as an independent trainer and consultant were valuable to me as references. The experiments became models for performing many tasks and later became the basis for automating many of those same tasks. I have used many of those original experiments in parts of this course, because they are still relevant and provide an excellent reference for many of the tasks I still need to do.

You will see as you proceed through the course that it uses many software programs considered to be older and perhaps obsolete like Sendmail, Procmail, BIND, the Apache web server, and much more. Despite their age, or perhaps because of it, the software I have chosen to run my own systems and servers and to use in this course has been well-proven and is all still in widespread use. I believe that the software we will use in these experiments has properties that make it especially valuable in learning the in-depth details of how Linux and those services work. Once you have learned those details, moving to any other software that performs the same tasks will be relatively easy. In any event, none of that "older" software is anywhere near as difficult or obscure as some people seem to think that it is.

Who Should Take This Course

If you want to learn to be an advanced Linux user and even a SysAdmin, this course is for you. Most SysAdmins have an extremely high level of curiosity and a deep-seated need to learn Linux system administration. We like to take things apart and put them back together again to learn how they work. We enjoy fixing things and are not hesitant about diving in to fix the computer problems that our friends and co-workers bring us.

We want to know what happens when some computer hardware fails so we might save defective components such as motherboards, RAM, and storage devices. This gives us defective components with which we can run tests. As I write this, I have a known defective hard drive inserted in a hard drive docking station connected to my primary workstation and have been using it to test failure scenarios that will appear in this course.

Most importantly, we do all of this for fun and would continue to do so even if we had no compelling vocational reason for doing so. Our intense curiosity about computer hardware and Linux leads us to collect computers and software like others collect stamps or antiques. Computers are our avocation – our hobby. Some people like boats, sports, travel, coins, stamps, trains, or any of thousands of other things, and they pursue them relentlessly as a hobby. For us – the true SysAdmins – that is what our computers are. That does not mean we are not well-rounded and don't do other things. I like to travel, read, go to museums and concerts, and ride historical trains, and my stamp collection is still there, waiting for me when I decide to take it up again.

In fact, the best SysAdmins, at least the ones I know, are all multifaceted. We are involved in many different things, and I think that is due to our inexhaustible curiosity about pretty much everything. So if you have an insatiable curiosity about Linux and want to learn about it – regardless of your past experience or lack thereof – then this course is most definitely for you.

Who Should Not Take This Course

If you do not have a strong desire to learn about how to use or administer Linux systems, this course is not for you. If all you want – or need – to do is use a couple apps on a Linux computer that someone has put on your desk, this course is not for you. If you have no curiosity about what superpowers lie behind the GUI desktop, this course is not for you.

Why This Course

Someone asked me why I wanted to write this course. My answer is simple – I want to give back to the Linux community. I have had several amazing mentors over the span of my career, and they taught me many things – things I find worth sharing with you along with much that I have learned for myself.

This course – all three volumes of it – started its existence as the slide presentations and lab projects for three Linux courses I created and taught. For a number of reasons, I do not teach those classes any more. However, I would still like to pass on my knowledge and as many of the tips and tricks I have learned for the administration of Linux as possible. I hope that with this course I can pass on at least some of the guidance and mentoring that I was fortunate enough to have in my own career.

About Fedora Releases

The first edition of this self-study course was originally written for Fedora 29, and we are now up to Fedora 38. As I have worked through the second edition of this course, I have added new materials I thought appropriate and incorporated as many errata corrections as possible.

Where it was necessary, I have also included revised graphics such as screenshots used for illustrative purposes. In many cases the graphics for earlier releases of Fedora are still applicable although the background images and some non-essential visual elements have changed. In those cases I have retained the original graphics.

I have only replaced older graphics with newer ones where necessary to ensure the accuracy and clarity of the illustrated points. Some of the illustrations in this course are from Fedora 29. If you are using later releases of Fedora, such as Fedora 37, 38, or later, the background and other cosmetic elements may be different from Fedora 29.

CHAPTER 1

Introduction

Objectives

After reading this chapter, you will be able to

- Define the value proposition of Linux.

- Describe at least four attributes that make Linux desirable as an operating system (OS).

- Define the meaning of the term "free" when it is applied to open source software.

- State the Linux Truth and its meaning.

- Describe how open source software makes the job of the system administrator (SysAdmin) easier.

- List some of the traits found in a typical SysAdmin.

- Describe the structure of the experiments used throughout this course.

- List two types of terminal environments that can be used to access the Linux command line.

About Linux

The value of any software lies in its usefulness not in its price.

—Linus Torvalds[1]

---

[1] Wikipedia, *Linus Torvalds*, https://en.wikipedia.org/wiki/Linus_Torvalds

© David Both 2023
D. Both, *Using and Administering Linux: Volume 1*, https://doi.org/10.1007/978-1-4842-9618-9_1

The preceding quote from Linus Torvalds, the creator of Linux,[2] perfectly describes the value proposition of free open source software (FOSS) and particularly Linux. Expensive software that performs poorly or does not meet the needs of the users can in no way be worth any amount of money. On the other hand, free software that meets the needs of the users has great value to those users.

Most open source software[3] falls in the latter category. It is software that millions of people find extremely useful, and that is what gives it such great value. I have personally downloaded and used only one proprietary software application in over 25 years that I have been using Linux.

Linux itself is a complete, open source operating system that is open, flexible, stable, scalable, and secure. Like all operating systems, it provides a bridge between the computer hardware and the application software that runs on it. It also provides tools that can be used by the system administrator, the SysAdmin, to monitor and manage the following things:

1. The functions and features of the operating system itself

2. Productivity software like word processors; spreadsheets; financial, scientific, industrial, and academic software; and much more

3. The underlying hardware, for example, temperatures and operational status

4. Software updates to fix bugs

5. Upgrades to move from one release level of the operating system to the next higher level

The tasks that need to be performed by the system administrator are inseparable from the philosophy of the operating system, both in terms of the tools that are available to perform them and the freedom afforded to the SysAdmin in their performance of those tasks. Let's look very briefly at the origins of both Linux and Windows and explore a bit about how the philosophies of their creators affect the job of a SysAdmin.

---

[2] Wikipedia, *History of Linux*, https://en.wikipedia.org/wiki/History_of_Linux

[3] Wikipedia, *Open source software*, https://en.wikipedia.org/wiki/Open-source_software

The Birth of Windows

The proprietary DEC VAX/VMS[4] operating system was designed by developers who subscribed to a closed philosophy, that is, that the user should be protected from the internal "vagaries" of the system[5] because the users are afraid of computers.

Dave Cutler[6] who wrote the DEC VAX/VMS operating system is also the chief architect of Windows NT, the parent of all current forms of Windows. Cutler was hired away from DEC by Microsoft with the specific intention of having him write Windows NT. As part of his deal with Microsoft, he was allowed to bring many of his top engineers from DEC with him. Therefore, it should be no surprise that the Windows versions of today, however far removed from Windows NT they might be, remain hidden behind this veil of secrecy.

Black Box Syndrome

Let's look at what proprietary software means to someone trying to fix it. I will use a trivial black box example to represent some hypothetical compiled, proprietary software. This software was written by a hypothetical company that wants to keep the source code a secret so that their alleged "trade secrets" cannot be stolen.

As the hypothetical user of this hypothetical proprietary software, I have no knowledge of what happens inside the bit of compiled machine language code to which I have access. Part of that restriction is contractual – notice that I do not say "legal" – in a license agreement that forbids me from reverse engineering the machine code to produce the source code. The sole function of this hypothetical code is to print "no" if the number input is 17 or less and to print "yes" if the input is over 17. This result might be used to determine whether my customer receives a discount on orders of 17 units or more.

Using this software for a number of weeks/months/years, everything seems normal until one of my customers complains that they should have received the discount but did not.

---

[4] Renamed to OpenVMS circa late 1991.
[5] Gancarz, Mike, *Linux and the Unix Philosophy*, Digital Press, 2003, 146–148
[6] ITPro Today, *Windows NT and VMS: The Rest of the Story*, www.itprotoday.com/management-mobility/windows-nt-and-vms-rest-story

Simple testing of input numbers from 0 to 16 produces the correct output of "no." Testing of numbers 18 and up produces the correct output of "yes." Testing of the number 17 results in an incorrect output of "no." Why? We have no way of knowing why! The program fails on the edge case of exactly 17. I can surmise that there is an incorrect logical comparison in the code, but I have no way of knowing, and without access to the source code, I can neither verify this nor fix it myself.

So I report this problem to the vendor from whom I purchased the software. They tell me they will fix it in the next release. "When will that be?" I ask. "In about six months – or so," they reply.

I must now task one of my workers to check the results of every sale to verify whether the customer should receive the discount. If they should, we assign other people to cut a refund check and send that along with a letter explaining the situation.

After a few months with no work on a fix from the vendor, I call to try and determine the status of the fix. They tell me that they have decided not to fix the problem because I am the only one having the problem. The translation of this is, "Sorry. You don't spend enough money with us to warrant us fixing the problem." They also tell me that the new owners, the venture capital company who bought out the company from which I bought the software, will no longer be selling or supporting that software anyway.

I am left with useless – less than useless – software that will never be fixed, and I cannot fix it myself. Neither can anyone else who purchased that software fix it if they ever run into this problem.

Because it is completely closed and the sealed box in which it exists is impenetrable, proprietary software is unknowable. Windows is like this. Even most Windows support staff have no idea how it works inside. This is why the most common advice to fix Windows problems is to reboot the computer – because it is impossible to apply reason and logic to a closed, unknowable system of any kind.

Operating systems like Windows that shield their users from the power they possess were developed starting with the basic assumption that the users are not smart or knowledgeable enough to be trusted with the full power that computers can actually provide. These operating systems are restrictive and have user interfaces – both command line and graphical – that enforce those restrictions by design. These restrictive user interfaces force regular users and SysAdmins alike into an enclosed room with no windows and then slam the door shut and triple-lock it. That locked room prevents them from doing many clever things that can be done with Linux.

The command-line interfaces (CLIs) of such limiting operating systems offer a relatively few commands, providing a de facto limit on the possible activities in which anyone might engage. Some users find this a comfort. I do not, and, apparently, neither do you to judge from the fact that you are taking this course.

The Birth of Linux

The short version of this story is that the developers of Unix, led by Ken Thompson[7] and Dennis Ritchie,[8] designed Unix to be open and accessible in a way that made sense to them. They created rules, guidelines, and procedural methods and then designed them into the structure of the operating system. That worked well for system developers, and that also – partly, at least – worked for SysAdmins. That collection of guidance from the originators of the Unix operating system was codified in the excellent book *The Unix Philosophy*, by Mike Gancarz, and then later updated by Mr. Gancarz as *Linux and the Unix Philosophy*.[9]

Another fine book, *The Art of Unix Programming*,[10] by Eric S. Raymond, provides the author's philosophical view of programming in a Unix environment. It is also somewhat of a history of the development of Unix as it was experienced and recalled by the author. This book is also available in its entirety at no charge on the Internet.[11]

In 1991, in Helsinki, Finland, Linus Torvalds was taking computer science classes using Minix,[12] a tiny variant of Unix that was written by Andrew S. Tanenbaum.[13] Torvalds was not happy with Minix as it had many deficiencies, at least to him. So he wrote his own operating system and shared that fact and the code on the Internet. This little operating system, which started as a hobby, eventually became known as Linux as a

---

[7] https://en.wikipedia.org/wiki/Ken_Thompson

[8] https://en.wikipedia.org/wiki/Dennis_Ritchie

[9] Gancarz, Mike, *Linux and the Unix Philosophy*, Digital Press – an imprint of Elsevier Science, 2003, ISBN 1-55558-273-7

[10] Raymond, Eric S., *The Art of Unix Programming*, Addison-Wesley, September 17, 2003, ISBN 0-13-142901-9

[11] Raymond, Eric S., *The Art of Unix Programming*, http://www.catb.org/esr/writings/taoup/html/index.html/

[12] https://en.wikipedia.org/wiki/MINIX

[13] https://en.wikipedia.org/wiki/Andrew_S._Tanenbaum

tribute to its creator and was distributed under the GNU GPL (General Public License) 2 open source license.[14]

Wikipedia has a good history of Linux[15] as does DigitalOcean.[16] For a more personal history, read Linus Torvalds's own book, *Just for Fun*.[17]

The Open Box

Let's imagine the same software as in the previous example but this time written by a company that open sourced it and provides the source code should I want it. The same problem occurs. In this case, I report the problem, and they reply that no one else has had this problem and that they will look into it but don't expect to fix it soon.

So I download the source code. I immediately see the problem and write a quick patch for it. I test the patch on some samples of my own customer transactions – in a test environment of course – and find the results to show the problem has been fixed. I submit the patch to them along with my basic test results. They tell me that is cool and to insert the patch in their own code base, run it through testing, and determine that the fix works. At that point they add the revised code into the main trunk of their code base, and all is well.

Of course, if they get bought out or otherwise become unable or unwilling to maintain the software, the result would be the same. I would still have the open source code, fix it, and make it available to whoever took over the development of the open source product. This scenario has taken place more than once. In one instance I took over development of a bit of shell script code from a developer in Latvia who no longer had the time to maintain it, and I maintained it for several years.

In another instance, a large company purchased a software firm called StarOffice who open sourced their office suite under the name OpenOffice.org. The new organization decided they would create their own version of the software starting from the existing code. That turned out to be quite a flop. Most of the developers of the open source version migrated to a new, open organization that maintains the

---

[14] https://en.wikipedia.org/wiki/GNU_General_Public_License

[15] https://en.wikipedia.org/wiki/History_of_Linux

[16] Juell, Kathleen, *A Brief History of Linux*, https://www.digitalocean.com/community/tutorials/brief-history-of-linux

[17] Torvalds, Linus, and Diamond, David, *Just for Fun: The Story of an Accidental Revolutionary*, Harper Business, 2001

reissued software that is now called LibreOffice. OpenOffice now languishes and has few developers, while LibreOffice flourishes.

One advantage of open source software is that the source code is always available. Any developers can take it over and maintain it. Even if an individual or an organization tries to take it over and make it proprietary, they cannot, and the original code is out there and can be "forked" into a new but identical product by any developer or group. In the case of LibreOffice, there are thousands of people around the world contributing new code and fixes when they are required.

Having the source code available is one of the main advantages of open source because anyone with the skills can look at it and fix it and then make that fix available to the rest of the community surrounding that software.

In the context of open source software, the term "open" means that the source code is freely available for all to see and examine without restriction. Anyone with appropriate skills has legal right to make changes to the code to enhance its functionality or to fix a bug.

For one release of the Linux kernel, version 4.17, on June 3, 2018, over 1,700 developers from a multitude of disparate organizations around the globe contributed 13,500 changes to the kernel code. That does not even consider the changes to other core components of the Linux operating system, such as core utilities, or even major software applications such as LibreOffice, the powerful office suite that I use for writing my books and articles as well as spreadsheets, drawings, presentations, and more. Projects such as LibreOffice have hundreds of their own developers.

This openness makes it easy for SysAdmins – and everyone else, for that matter – to explore all aspects of the operating system and to fully understand how any or all of it is supposed to work. This means that it is possible to apply one's full knowledge of Linux to use its powerful and open tools in a methodical reasoning process that can be leveraged for problem solving.

The Linux Truth

Unix was not designed to stop its users from doing stupid things, as that would also stop them from doing clever things.

—Doug Gwyn

This quote summarizes the overriding truth and the philosophies of both Unix and Linux – that the operating system must trust the user. It is only by extending this full measure of trust that allows the user to access the full power made possible by the operating system. This truth applies to Linux because of its heritage as a direct descendant of Unix.

The Linux Truth results in an operating system that places no restrictions or limits on the things that users, particularly the root[18] user, can do. The root user can do anything on a Linux computer. There are no limits of any type on the root user. Although there are a very few administrative speed bumps placed in the path of the root user, root can always remove those slight impediments and do all manner of stupid and clever things.

Non-root users have a few limits placed on them, but they can still do plenty of clever things as well. The primary limits placed on non-root users are intended to – mostly – prevent them from doing things that interfere with others' ability to freely use the Linux host. These limits in no way prevent regular users from doing great harm to their own user accounts.

Even the most experienced users can do "stupid things" using Linux. My experience has been that recovery from my own not so infrequent stupidity has been made much easier by the open access to the full power of the operating system. I find that most times a few commands can resolve the problem without even a reboot. On a few occasions, I have had to switch to a lower runlevel to fix a problem. I have only very infrequently needed to boot to recovery mode in order to edit a configuration file that I managed to damage so badly it caused serious problems including failure to boot. It takes knowledge of the underlying philosophy, the structure, and the technology of Linux to be able to fully unleash its power, especially when things are broken. Linux just requires a bit of understanding and knowledge on the part of the SysAdmin to fully unlock its potential.

Knowledge

Anyone can memorize or learn commands and procedures, but rote memorization is not true knowledge. Without the knowledge of the philosophy and how that is embodied in the elegant structure and implementation of Linux, applying the correct commands as

---

[18] The root user is the administrator of a Linux host and can do everything and anything. Compared with other operating systems, non-root Linux users also have very few restrictions, but we will see later in this course that there are some limits imposed on them.

tools to resolve complex problems is not possible. I have seen smart people who had a vast knowledge of Linux be unable to resolve a relatively simple problem because they were unaware of the elegance of the structure beneath the surface.

As a SysAdmin, part of my responsibility in many of my jobs has been to assist with hiring new employees. I participated in many technical interviews of people who had passed many Microsoft certifications and who had fine resumés. I also participated in many interviews in which we were looking for Linux skills but very few of those applicants had certifications. This was at a time when Microsoft certifications were the big thing but during the early days of Linux in the data center and few applicants were yet certified.

We usually started these interviews with questions designed to determine the limits of the applicant's knowledge. Then we would get into the more interesting questions, ones that would test their ability to reason through a problem to find a solution. I noticed some very interesting results. Few of the Windows certificate owners could reason their way through the scenarios we presented, while a very large percentage of the applicants with a Linux background were able to do so.

I think that result was due in part to the fact that obtaining the Windows certificates relied upon memorization rather than actual hands-on experience combined with the fact that Windows is a closed system that prevents SysAdmins from truly understanding how it works. I think that the Linux applicants did so much better because Linux is open on multiple levels and that, as a result, logic and reason can be used to identify and resolve any problem. Any SysAdmin who has been using Linux for some time has had to learn about the architecture of Linux and has had a decent amount of experience with the application of knowledge, logic, and reason to the solution of problems.

Flexibility

Flexibility means the ability to run on any platform, not just Intel and AMD processors. Scalability is about power, but flexibility is about running on many processor architectures.

Wikipedia has a list of central processing unit (CPU) architectures supported by Linux,[19] and it is a long one. By my automated count, there are over 100 CPU

---

[19] Wikipedia, *List of Linux-supported computer architectures*, https://en.wikipedia.org/wiki/List_of_Linux-supported_computer_architectures

architectures on which Linux is currently known to run. Note that this list changes and CPUs get added to and dropped from the list. But the point is well taken that Linux will run on many architectures. If your architecture is not currently supported by Linux, with some work you can recompile it to run on any 64-bit system and some 32-bit ones.

This broad-ranging hardware support means that Linux can run on everything from my Raspberry Pi[20] to my television, to vehicle entertainment systems, to cell phones, to DVRs, to the computers on the International Space Station[21] (ISS), to all 500 of the fastest supercomputers back on Earth,[22] and much more. A single operating system can run nearly any computing device from the smallest to the largest from any vendor.

Stability

Stability can have multiple meanings when the term is applied to Linux by different people. My own definition of the term as it applies to Linux is that it can run for weeks or months without crashing or causing problems that make me worry I might lose data for any of the critical projects I am working on.

Today's Linux easily meets that requirement. I always have several computers running Linux at any given time, and they are all rock-solid in this sense. They run without interruption. I have workstations, a server, a firewall, and some that I use for testing, and they all just run.

This is not to say that Linux never has any problems. Nothing is perfect. Many of those problems have been caused by my own misconfiguration of one or more features, but a few have been caused by problems with some of the software I use. Sometimes a software application will crash, but that is very infrequent.

If you read my personal website, you know that I have had some problems with the KDE GUI (graphical user interface) desktop over the years and that it has had two significant periods of instability. In the first of these instances, which was many years ago around the time of Fedora 10, KDE was transitioning from KDE 3 to the KDE Plasma 4 desktop, which offered many interesting features. In this case most of the KDE-specific applications I used had not been fully rewritten for the new desktop environment so

---

[20] Raspberry Pi website, https://www.raspberrypi.org/

[21] ZDNet, *The ISS just got its own Linux supercomputer*, https://www.zdnet.com/article/the-iss-just-got-its-own-linux-supercomputer/

[22] Wikipedia, *TOP500*, https://en.wikipedia.org/wiki/TOP500

lacked required functionality or would just crash. During the second instance, the desktop just locked up, crashed, or failed to work properly.

In both of these cases, I was able to use a different desktop to get my work done in a completely stable environment. In the first case I used the Cinnamon desktop, and in the second instance I used the LXDE desktop. However, the underlying software, the kernel, and the programs running underneath the surface – they all continued to run without problem. So this is the second layer of stability; if one thing crashes, even the desktop, the underlying stuff continues to run.

I currently use the Xfce desktop and like it very much.

Scalability

Scalability is extremely important for any software, particularly for an operating system. Running the same operating system from watches to phones (Android), laptops, powerful workstations, servers, and even the most powerful supercomputers on the planet can make life much simpler for the network administrator or the IT manager. Linux is the only operating system on the planet today that can provide that level of scalability.

Since November of 2017, Linux has powered all of the fastest supercomputers in the world.[23] One hundred percent (100%) – all – of the top 500 supercomputers in the world run Linux of one form or another, and this is expected to continue. There are usually specialized distributions of Linux designed for supercomputers. Linux also powers much smaller devices such as Android phones and Raspberry Pi single-board computers (SBC). Supercomputers are very fast, and many different calculations can be performed simultaneously. It is, however, very unusual for a single user to have access to the entire resources of a supercomputer. Many users share those resources, each user performing their own set of complex calculations.

Linux can run on any computer from the smallest to the largest and anything in between.

---

[23] Top 500, https://www.top500.org/statistics/list/

Security

We will talk a lot about security as we proceed through this course. Security is a critical consideration in these days of constant attacks from the Internet. If you think that they are not after you, too, let me tell you that they are. Your computer is under constant attack every hour of every day.

Most Linux distributions are very secure right from the installation. Many tools are provided to both ensure tight security where it is needed and allow specified access into the computer. For example, you may wish to allow Secure Shell (SSH) access from a limited number of remote hosts, access to the web server from anywhere in the world, and email to be sent to a Linux host from anywhere. Yet you may also want to block, at least temporarily, access attempts by crackers – the bad guys – attempting to force their way in. Other security measures provide your personal files protection from other users on the same host while still allowing mechanisms for you to share files that you choose with others.

Many of the security mechanisms that we will discuss in this course were designed and built into Linux right from its inception. The architecture of Linux is designed from the ground up, like Unix, its progenitor, to provide security mechanisms that can protect files and running processes from malicious intervention from both internal and external sources. Linux security is not an add-on feature; it is an integral part of Linux. Because of this, most of our discussions that relate to security will be embedded as an integral part of the text throughout this book. There is a chapter about security, but it is intended to cover those few things not covered elsewhere.

Freedom

Freedom has an entirely different meaning when applied to free open source software (FOSS) than it does in most other circumstances. In FOSS, free is the freedom to do what I want with software. It means that I have easy access to the source code and that I can make changes to the code and recompile it if I need or want to.

Freedom means that I can download a copy of Fedora Linux or Firefox or LibreOffice and install it on as many computers as I want to. It means that I can share that downloaded code by providing copies to my friends or installing it on computers belonging to my customers, both the executables and the sources.

Freedom also means that we do not need to worry about the license police showing up on our doorsteps and demanding huge sums of money to become compliant. This has happened at some companies that "over-installed" the number of licenses that they had available for an operating system or office suite. It means that I don't have to type in a long, long "key" to unlock the software I have purchased or downloaded.

Our Software Rights

The rights to the freedoms that we have with open source software should be part of the license we receive when we download open source software. The definition for open source software[24] is found at the Open Source Initiative website. This definition describes the freedoms and responsibilities that are part of using open source software.

The issue is that there are many licenses that claim to be open source. Some are and some are not. In order to be true open source software, the license must meet the requirements specified in this definition. The definition is not a license – it specifies the terms to which any license must conform if the software to which it is attached is to be legally considered open source. If any of the defined terms do not exist in a license, then the software to which it refers is not true open source software.

All of the software used in this book is open source software.

I have not included that definition here despite its importance because it is not really the focus of this book. You can go to the website previously cited, or you can read more about it in my book *The Linux Philosophy for SysAdmins*.[25] I strongly recommend that you at least go to the website and read the definition so that you will more fully understand what open source really is and what rights you have.

I also like the description of Linux at Opensource.com[26] as well as their long list of other open source resources.[27]

[24] Opensource.org, *The Open Source Definition*, https://opensource.org/docs/osd

[25] Both, David, *The Linux Philosophy for SysAdmins*, Apress, 2018, 311–316

[26] Opensource.com, *What is Linux?*, https://opensource.com/resources/linux

[27] Opensource.com, *Resources*, https://opensource.com/resources

Longevity

Longevity – an interesting word. I use it here to help clarify some of the statements that I hear many people make. These statements are usually along the lines of "Linux can extend the life of existing hardware" or "Keep old hardware out of landfills or unmonitored recycling facilities."

The idea is that you can use your old computer longer and that by doing that you lengthen the useful life of the computer and decrease the number of computers you need to purchase in your lifetime. This both reduces demand for new computers and reduces the number of old computers being discarded.

I have written about how Linux can keep old computers running and out of landfills or recycling streams. My most recent article is *How Linux rescues slow computers (and the planet)*[28] at Opensource.com, and it discusses one of my computers that has a BIOS (Basic I/O System) date of 2010, so is about 13 years old.

I now have an old Dell I am working on that has a BIOS date of 2005, which makes it at least 18 years old. According to the Intel website, the Pentium 4 processor was released in the first quarter of 2004, so that BIOS date is probably as good as anything to estimate the age of the computer.

You can see the specs for this system, which are pretty minimal:

```
################################################################
# MOTD for Thu Sep  1 03:23:02 AM EDT 2022
# HOST NAME:            test1.both.org
# Machine Type:         physical machine.
# Host architecture:    X86_64
#--------------------------------------------------------------
# System Serial No.:    CXXXXXY
# System UUID:          44454c4c-5900-1051-8033-c3c04f423831
# Motherboard Mfr:      Dell Inc.
# Motherboard Model:    0F8098
# Motherboard Serial:   ..Cxxxxxxxx00TQ.
# BIOS Release Date:    05/24/2005
#--------------------------------------------------------------
```

---

[28] Both, David, Opensource.com, *How Linux rescues slow computers (and the planet)*, https://opensource.com/article/22/4/how-linux-saves-earth

```
# CPU Model:          Intel(R) Pentium(R) 4 CPU 3.00GHz
# CPU Data:           1 Single Core package with 2 CPUs
# CPU Architecture:   x86_64
# HyperThreading:     Yes
# Max CPU MHz:
# Current CPU MHz:    2992.644
# Min CPU MHz:
#-----------------------------------------------------------------
# RAM:                3.142 GB
# SWAP:               3.142 GB
#-----------------------------------------------------------------
# Install Date:       Wed 31 Aug 2022 09:26:13 PM EDT
# Linux Distribution: Fedora 36 (Thirty Six) X86_64
# Kernel Version:     5.19.4-200.fc36.x86_64
#-----------------------------------------------------------------
# Disk Partition Info
# Filesystem    Size  Used Avail Use% Mounted on
# /dev/sda2     298G  9.8G  287G   4% /
# /dev/sda2     298G  9.8G  287G   4% /home
# /dev/sda1     974M  226M  681M  25% /boot
###################################################################
```

It has a single 3GHz Pentium 4 processor with hyperthreading, so the equivalent of two CPUs. It originally had 2GB of DDR 533 RAM (random-access memory), so I added 2GB for a total of 4GB, which is the maximum amount of RAM supported by this system.

Naturally, I installed Linux on it just to see how it would work. This old computer works just fine with the most recent version of Fedora. My next test is to see how well it runs a Linux virtual machine (VM) using VirtualBox.

So yeah, when I say that Linux keeps old computers running, it is absolutely the truth. Linux keeps these old computers safe from malware and bloatware, which are what really cause them to slow down.

Linux prevents the planned obsolescence continually enforced by the ongoing requirements for more and faster hardware required to support upgrades. It means I do not need to add more RAM or hard drive space just to upgrade to the latest version of the operating system.

Until it died I had an old Lenovo Thinkpad W500 that I purchased in May of 2006. It was old and clunky and heavy compared with many of today's laptops, but I liked it a lot and it was my only laptop. I took it with me on most trips and used it for training. It had enough power in its Intel Core 2 Duo 2.8GHz processor, 8GB of RAM, and 300GB hard drive to support Fedora running a couple virtual machines and to be the router and firewall between a classroom network and the Internet, to connect to a projector to display my slides, and to use to demonstrate the use of Linux commands. I used Fedora 37 on it, the very latest. That is pretty amazing considering that this laptop, which I affectionately called vgr, was a bit over 12 years old.

The Thinkpad died of multiple hardware problems in October of 2018, and I replaced it with a System76[29] Oryx Pro with 32GB of RAM, an Intel i7 with six cores (12 CPU threads), and 2TB of SSD (solid-state drive) storage. I expect to get at least 15 years of service out of this new laptop.

And then there was my original Eee PC 900 netbook with an Intel Atom CPU at 1.8GHz, 2G of RAM, and an 8GB SSD. It ran Fedora up through Fedora 37 for ten years before it, too, started having hardware problems.

Linux can most definitely keep old hardware useful.

Data

Another aspect of longevity is the open source software that stores data in open and well-documented formats. Documents that I wrote over a decade ago are still readable by current versions of the same software I used then, such as LibreOffice and its predecessors, OpenOffice and before that StarOffice. I never need to worry that a software upgrade will relegate my old files to the bit bucket.

Resist Malware

Another reason that I can keep old hardware running longer is that Linux is very resistant to malware infections. It is not completely immune to malware, but none of my systems have ever been infected. Even my laptop that connects to all kinds of wired and wireless networks that I do not control has never been infected.

---

[29] System76 home page, `https://system76.com/`

Without the massive malware infections that cause most peoples' computers to slow to an unbearable crawl, my Linux systems – all of them – keep running at top speed. It is this constant slowdown, even after many "cleanings" at the big-box stores or the strip mall computer stores, that causes most people to think that their computers are old and useless. So they throw them away and buy another.

Linux eliminates those problems.

Should I Be a SysAdmin?

Since this book is intended to help you become a SysAdmin, it would be useful for you to know whether you might already be one, whether you are aware of that fact or not, or if you exhibit some propensity toward system administration. Let's look at some of the tasks a SysAdmin may be asked to perform and some of the qualities one might find in a SysAdmin.

Wikipedia[30] defines a system administrator as "a person who is responsible for the upkeep, configuration, and reliable operation of computer systems, especially multiuser computers, such as servers." In my experience, this can include computer and network hardware, software, racks and enclosures, computer rooms or space, and much more.

The typical SysAdmin's job can include a very large number of tasks. In a small business, a SysAdmin may be responsible for doing everything computer related. In larger environments, multiple SysAdmins may share responsibility for all of the tasks required to keep things running. In some cases, you may not even know you are a SysAdmin; your manager may have simply told you to start maintaining one or more computers in your office – that makes you a SysAdmin, like it or not.

There is also a term, "DevOps," that is used to describe the intersection of the formerly separate development and operations organizations. In the past this has been primarily about closer cooperation between development and operations, and it included teaching SysAdmins to write code. The focus is now shifting to teaching programmers how to perform operational tasks.[31] Attending to SysAdmin tasks makes these folks SysAdmins, too, at least for part of the time. While I was working at Cisco, I had a DevOps type of job. Part of the time I wrote code to test Linux appliances, and the

---

[30] Wikipedia, *System administrator*, https://en.wikipedia.org/wiki/System_administrator

[31] Charity, *Ops: It's everyone's job now*, https://opensource.com/article/17/7/state-systems-administration

rest of the time I was a SysAdmin in the lab where those appliances were tested. It was a very interesting and rewarding time in my career.

I have created this short list to help you determine whether you might have some of the qualities of a SysAdmin. You know you are a SysAdmin if…

1. You think this book might be a fun read.

2. You would rather spend time learning about computers than watch television.

3. You like to take things apart to see how they work.

4. Sometimes those things still work when you are made by someone else to reassemble them.

5. People frequently ask you to help them with their computers.

6. You know what open source means.

7. You document everything you do.

8. You find computers easier to interact with than most humans.

9. You think the command line might be fun.

10. You like to be in complete control.

11. You understand the difference between "free as in beer" and "free as in speech" when applied to software.

12. You have installed a computer.

13. You have ever repaired or upgraded your own computer.

14. You have installed or tried to install Linux.

15. You have a Raspberry Pi.

16. You leave the covers off your computer because you replace components frequently.

17. Etc.

You get the idea. I could list a lot more things that might make you a good candidate to be a SysAdmin, but I am sure you can think of plenty more that apply to you. The bottom line here is that you are curious, you like to explore the internal workings of devices, you want to understand how things work – particularly computers – you enjoy helping people, and you would rather be in control of at least some of the technology that we encounter in our daily lives than to let it completely control you.

About This Course

If you ask me a question about how to perform some task in Linux, I am the Linux guy that explains how Linux works before answering the question – at least that is the impression I give most people. My tendency is to explain how things work, and I think that it is very important for SysAdmins to understand why things work as they do and the architecture and structure of Linux in order to be most effective.

So I will explain a lot of things in detail as we go through this course. For the most part, it will not be a course in which you will be told to type commands without some reasoning behind it. The preparation in Chapter 4 will also have some explanation but perhaps not so much as the rest of the book. Without these explanations the use of the commands would be just rote memorization, and that is not how most of us SysAdmins learn best.

UNIX is very simple, it just needs a genius to understand its simplicity.

—Dennis Ritchie[32]

The explanations I provide will sometimes include historical references because the history of Unix and Linux is illustrative of why and how Linux is so open and easy to understand. The preceding Ritchie quote also applies to Linux because Linux was designed to be a version of Unix. Yes, Linux is very simple. You just need a little guidance and mentoring to show you how to explore it yourself. That is part of what you will learn in this course.

Part of the simplicity of Linux is that it is completely open and knowable and you can access any and all of it in very powerful and revealing ways. This course contains many experiments that are designed to explore the architecture of Linux as well as to introduce you to new commands.

Why do you think that Windows support – regardless of where you get it – always starts with rebooting the system? Because it is a closed system and closed systems

---

[32] Wikipedia, *Dennis Ritchie*, https://en.wikipedia.org/wiki/Dennis_Ritchie

cannot ever be knowable. As a result, the easiest approach to solving problems is to reboot the system rather than to dig into the problem, find the root cause, and fix it.

About the Experiments

As a hands-on SysAdmin, I like to experiment with the command line in order to learn new commands, new ways to perform tasks, and how Linux works. Most of the experiments I have devised for this book are ones that I have performed in my own explorations with perhaps some minor changes to accommodate their use in a course using virtual machines.

I use the term "experiments" because they are intended to be much more than simple lab projects, designed to be followed blindly with no opportunity for you, the student, to follow your own curiosity and wander far afield. These experiments are designed to be the starting points for your own explorations. This is one reason to use a VM for them, so that production machines will be out of harm's way and you can safely try things that pique your curiosity. Using virtualization software such as VirtualBox enables us to run a software implementation of standardized hardware. It allows us to run one or more software computers (VMs), in which we can install any operating system, on your hardware computer. It seems complex, but we will go through creating a virtual network and a virtual machine (VM) in Chapter 4 as we prepare for the experiments.

All SysAdmins are curious, hands-on people even though we have different ways of learning. I think it is helpful for SysAdmins to have hands-on experience. That is what the experiments are for – to provide an opportunity to go beyond the theoretical and apply the things you learn in a practical way. Although some of the experiments are a bit contrived in order to illustrate a particular point, they are nevertheless valid.

These enlightening experiments are not tucked away at the end of each chapter, or the book, where they can be easily ignored – they are embedded in the text and are an integral part of the flow of this book. I recommend that you perform the experiments as you proceed through the book.

The commands and sometimes the results for each experiment will appear in **EXPERIMENT** sections as shown in the following. Some experiments need only a single command and so will have only one experiment section. Other experiments may be more complex and so are split among two or more experiments.

SAMPLE EXPERIMENT

This is an example of an experiment. Each experiment will have instructions and code for you to enter and run on your computer.

Many experiments will have a series of instructions in a prose format like this paragraph. Just follow the instructions, and the experiments will work just fine.

1. Some experiments will have a list of steps to perform.

2. Step 2.

3. Etc.

Code that you are to enter for the experiments will look like this:

```
[root@testvm1 ~]# echo "This is a command you enter for experiments"
```

This is a command you enter for experiments:

```
[root@testvm1 ~]#
```

This is the end of the experiment.

Some of these experiments can be performed as a non-root user; that is much safer than doing everything as root. However, you will need to be root for many of these experiments. These experiments are considered safe for use on a VM designated for training such as the one that you will create in Chapter 4. Regardless of how benign they may sccm, you should not perform any of these experiments on a production system whether physical or virtual.

There are times when I want to present code that is interesting but which you should not run as part of one of the experiments. For such situations I will place the code and any supporting text in a **CODE SAMPLE** section as shown in the following.

CODE SAMPLE

Code that is intended to illustrate a point but which you should not even think about running on any computer will be contained in a section like this one.

```
echo "This is sample code which you should never run."
```

Warning   Do not perform the experiments presented in this book on a production system. You should use a virtual machine that is designated for this training.

What to Do If the Experiments Do Not Work

1. These experiments are intended to be self-contained and not dependent upon any setup, except for the USB thumb drive, or the results of previously performed experiments. Certain Linux utilities and tools must be present, but these should all be available on a standard Fedora Linux workstation installation or any other mainstream general-use distribution. Therefore, all of these experiments should "just work." We all know how that goes, right? So when something does fail, the first things to do are the obvious.

2. Verify that the commands were entered correctly. This is the most common problem I encounter for myself.

3. You may see an error message indicating that the command was not found. The bash (Bourne again shell) shell shows the bad command; in this case I made up badcommand. It then gives a brief description of the problem. This error message is displayed for both missing and misspelled commands. Check the command spelling and syntax multiple times to verify that it is correct.

    ```
    [student@testvm1 ~]$ badcommand
    ```

    bash: badcommand: command not found...

    Use the man command to view the manual pages (man pages) in order to verify the correct syntax and spelling of commands.

    Ensure that the required command is, in fact, installed. Install them if they are not already installed.

For experiments that require you to be logged in as root, ensure that you have done so. There should be only a few of these, but performing them as a non-root user will not work.

There is not much else that should go wrong – but if you encounter a problem that you cannot make work using these tips, contact me at LinuxGeek46@both.org, and I will do my best to help figure out the problem.

Terminology

It is important to clarify a bit of terminology before we proceed. In this course I will refer to computers with multiple terms. A "computer" is a hardware or virtual machine for computing. A computer is also referred to as a "node" when connected to a network. A network node can be any type of device including routers, switches, computers, and more. The term "host" generally refers to a computer that is a node on a network, but I have also encountered it used to refer to an unconnected computer.

How to Access the Command Line

All of the modern mainstream Linux distributions provide at least three ways to access the command line. If you use a graphical desktop, most distributions come with multiple terminal emulators from which to choose. I prefer Krusader, Tilix, and especially the xfce4-terminal, but I recommend that you use the xfce4-terminal because it is the default for the Xfce desktop. After completing all three volumes of this course, you can use any terminal emulator that you like.

Linux also provides the capability for multiple virtual consoles to allow for multiple logins from a single keyboard and monitor (KVM[33]). Virtual consoles can be used on systems that don't have a GUI desktop, but they can be used even on systems that do have one. Each virtual console is assigned to a function key corresponding to the console number. So vc1 would be assigned to function key F1 and so on. It is easy to switch to and from these sessions. On a physical computer, you can hold down the Ctrl and Alt keys and press F2 to switch to vc2. Then hold down the Ctrl and Alt keys and press F1 to switch to vc1 and the graphical interface.

The last method to access the command line on a Linux computer is via a remote login. Secure Shell (SSH) is used for remote terminal access. SSH is not a shell but rather a secure communications protocol. We will explore it in Chapter 45 of Volume 3.

---

[33] Keyboard, Video, and Mouse.

For some of the experiments, you will need to log in more than once or start multiple terminal sessions on the GUI desktop. We will go into much more detail about terminal emulators, console sessions, and shells as we proceed through this book.

Chapter Summary

In this chapter we have explored some of the failings of the Windows operating system and the greatly different philosophies that underlie the designs of both Windows and Linux. While Windows is closed and unknowable, Linux is open and can be explored in detail and understood by anyone who wishes to do so.

Linux was designed from the very beginning as an open and freely available operating system. Its value lies in the power, reliability, security, and openness that it brings to the marketplace for operating systems and not just in the fact that it can be had for free in monetary terms. Because Linux is open and free in the sense that it can be freely used, shared, and explored, its use has spread into all aspects of our lives.

The tasks a SysAdmin might be asked to do are many and varied. You may already be doing some of these or at least have some level of curiosity about how Linux works or how to make it work better for you. Most of the experiments encountered in this book must be performed at the command line. The command line can be accessed in multiple ways and with any one or more of several available and acceptable terminal emulators.

Exercises

Note that a couple of the following questions are intended to cause you to think about your desire to become a SysAdmin. There are no right answers to these questions, only yours, and you are not required to write them down or to share them. They are simply designed to prompt you to be a bit introspective about yourself and being a SysAdmin.

1. From where does open source software derive its value?

2. What are the four defining characteristics of Linux?

3. As of the time you read this, how many of the world's top 500 supercomputers use Linux as their operating system?

4. What does the "Linux Truth" mean to Linux users and administrators?

5. What does "freedom" mean with respect to open source software?

6. Why do you want to be a SysAdmin?

7. What makes you think you would be a good SysAdmin?

8. How would you access the Linux command line if there were no GUI desktop installed on the Linux host?

CHAPTER 2

Introduction to Operating Systems

Objectives

In this chapter you will learn to

- Describe the functions of the main hardware components of a computer.

- List and describe the primary functions of an operating system.

- Briefly outline the reasons that prompted Linus Torvalds to create Linux.

- Describe how the Linux core utilities support the kernel and together create an operating system.

Choice – Really!

Every computer requires an operating system. The operating system you use on your computer is at least as important as – or more so than – the hardware you run it on. The operating system (OS) is the software that determines the capabilities and limits of your computer or device. It also defines the personality of your computer.

The most important single choice you will make concerning your computer is that of the operating system, which will create a useful tool out of it. Computers have no ability to do anything without software. If you turn on a computer that has no software program, it simply generates revenue for the electric company in return for adding a little heat to

27

the room. There are far less expensive ways to heat a room. The operating system is the first level of software that allows your computer to perform useful work. Understanding the role of the operating system is key to making informed decisions about your computer.

Of course, most people do not realize that there even *is* a choice when it comes to operating systems. Fortunately, Linux does give us a choice. Some vendors such as EmperorLinux, System76, and others are now selling systems that already have Linux installed. Others, like Dell, sometimes try out the idea of Linux by selling a single model with few options.

We can always just purchase a new computer, install Linux on it, and wipe out whatever other operating system might have previously been there. My preference is to purchase the parts from a local computer store or the Internet and build my own computers to my personal specifications. Most people don't know that they have either of these options and, if they did, would not want to try anyway.

What Is an Operating System?

Books about Linux are books about an operating system. So what is an operating system? This is an excellent question – one that most training courses and books I have read either skip over completely or answer very superficially. The answer to this question can aid the SysAdmin's understanding of Linux and its great power.

The answer is not simple.

Many people look at their computer's display and see the graphical (GUI[1]) desktop and think that is the operating system. The GUI is only a small part of the operating system. It provides an interface in the form of a desktop metaphor that is understandable to many users. It is what is underneath the GUI desktop that is the real operating system. The fact is that for advanced operating systems like Linux, the desktop is just another application and there are multiple desktops from which to choose. We will cover the Xfce desktop in Chapter 6 of this volume because that is the desktop I recommend for use with this course. We will also explore the window manager (wm), a simpler form of desktop, in Chapter 16 of this volume.

---

[1] Graphical user interface.

In this chapter and throughout the rest of this course, I will elaborate on the answer to this question, but it is helpful to understand a little about the structure of the hardware that comprises a computer system. Let's take a brief look at the hardware components of a modern Intel computer.

Hardware

There are many different kinds of computers from single-board computers (SBC) like the Arduino and the Raspberry Pi to desktop computers, servers, mainframes, and supercomputers. Many of these use Intel or AMD processors, but others do not. For the purposes of this series of books, I will work with Intel X86_64 hardware. Generally, if I say Intel, you can also assume I mean the X86_64 processor series and supporting hardware and that AMD X86_64 hardware should produce the same results and the same hardware information will apply.

Motherboard

Most Intel-based computers have a motherboard that contains many components of the computer such as bus and input/output (I/O) controllers. It also has connectors to install RAM and a CPU, which are the primary components that need to be added to a motherboard to make it functional. Single-board computers are self-contained on a single circuit board and do not require any additional hardware because components such as RAM, video, network, USB, and other interfaces are all an integral part of the board.

Some motherboards contain a graphics processing unit (GPU) to connect the video output to a monitor. If they do not, a video card can be added to the main computer I/O bus, usually PCI[2] or PCI Express (PCIe).[3] Other I/O devices like keyboard, mouse, and external storage devices and USB memory sticks can be connected via the USB bus. Most modern motherboards have one or two Gigabit Ethernet network interface cards (NICs) and four or six SATA[4] connectors for storage devices.

---

[2] Wikipedia, *Conventional PCI*, https://en.wikipedia.org/wiki/Conventional_PCI

[3] Wikipedia, *PCI Express*, https://en.wikipedia.org/wiki/PCI_Express

[4] Wikipedia, *Serial ATA*, https://en.wikipedia.org/wiki/Serial_ATA

Random-access memory (RAM) is used to store data and programs while they are being actively used by the computer. Programs and data cannot be used by the computer unless they are stored in RAM from where they can be quickly moved into the CPU cache. RAM and cache memory are both volatile memory; that is, the data stored in them is lost if the computer is turned off. The computer can also erase or alter the contents of RAM, and this is one of the things that gives computers their great flexibility and power.

Storage devices are magnetic media used for long-term storage of data and programs. Magnetic media is non-volatile; the data stored on a disk remains even when power is removed from the computer. DVDs and CD-ROM store data permanently and can be read by the computer but not overwritten. The exception to this is that some DVD and CD-ROM disks are rewritable. ROM means read-only memory because it can be read by the computer but not erased or altered. Storage devices and DVD drives are connected to the motherboard through SATA adapters.

Solid-state drives (SSDs) are the solid-state equivalent of storage devices. They have the same characteristics in terms of the long-term storage of data because it is persistent through reboots and when the computer is powered off. Also, like storage devices with rotating magnetic disks, SSDs allow data to be erased, moved, and managed when needed. However, the data stored on SSDs can begin to degrade if the power is removed from the device for extended periods of a year or more. That makes HDDs more appropriate for long-term archival backup storage than SSDs.

Printers are used to transfer data from the computer to paper. Sound cards convert data to sound as well as the reverse. USB storage devices can be used to store data for backup or transfer to other computers. The network interface cards (NICs) are used to connect the computer to a network, hard-wired or wireless, so that it can communicate easily with other computers attached to the network.

The Processor

Let's take a moment to explore the CPU and define some terminology in an effort to help reduce confusion. Five terms are important when we talk about processors: *processor*, *CPU*, *socket*, *core*, and *thread*. The Linux command lscpu, as shown in Figure 2-1, gives us some important information about the installed processor(s) as well as clues about terminology. I use my primary workstation for this example:

```
[root@myworkstation ~]#lscpu
Architecture:          x86_64
CPU op-mode(s):        32-bit, 64-bit
Byte Order:            Little Endian
CPU(s):                32
On-line CPU(s) list:   0-31
Thread(s) per core:    2
Core(s) per socket:    16
Socket(s):             1
NUMA node(s):          1
Vendor ID:             GenuineIntel
CPU family:            6
Model:                 85
Model name:            Intel(R) Core(TM) i9-7960X CPU @ 2.80GHz
Stepping:              4
CPU MHz:               3542.217
CPU max MHz:           4400.0000
CPU min MHz:           1200.0000
BogoMIPS:              5600.00
Virtualization:   -x   VT
L1d cache:             32K
L1i cache:             32K
L2 cache:              1024K
L3 cache:              22528K
NUMA node0 CPU(s):     0-31
Flags:                 <snip>
```

Figure 2-1. *The output of the lscpu command gives us some information about the processor installed in a Linux host. It also helps us understand the current terminology to use when discussing processors*

The first thing to notice in Figure 2-1 is that the term "processor" never appears. The common usage for the term "processor"[5] refers generically to any hardware unit that performs some form of computations. It can refer to the CPU[6] – central processing unit – of the computer, to a graphics processing unit (GPU[7]) that performs calculations relating to graphical video displays, or any number of other types of processors. The terms *processor* and *CPU* tend to be used interchangeably when referring to the physical package that is installed in your computer.

Using Intel terminology, which can be a bit inconsistent, the processor is the physical package that can contain one or more computing cores. Figure 2-2 shows an Intel i5-2500 processor that contains four cores. Because the processor package is plugged into a socket and a motherboard may have multiple sockets, the lscpu utility numbers the sockets. Figure 2-1 shows the information for the processor in socket number 1 on the motherboard. If this motherboard had additional sockets, lscpu would list them separately.

Figure 2-2. *An Intel Core i5 processor may contain one, two, or four cores. Wikimedia Commons, CC by SA 4 International*

---

[5] Wikipedia, *Processor*, https://en.wikipedia.org/wiki/Processor

[6] Wikipedia, *Central processing unit*, https://en.wikipedia.org/wiki/Central_processing_unit

[7] Wikipedia, *Graphics processing unit*, https://en.wikipedia.org/wiki/Graphics_processing_unit

A core, which is sometimes referred to as a compute core, is the smallest physical hardware component of a processor that can actually perform arithmetic and logical computations, that is, it is composed of a single arithmetic and logic unit (ALU)[8] and its required supporting components. Every computer has at least one processor with one or more cores. Most modern Intel processors have more – two, four, or six cores – and many processors have eight or more cores. They make up the brains of the computer. They are the part of the computer that is responsible for executing each of the instructions specified by the software utilities and application programs.

The line in the lscpu results that specifies the number of cores contained in the processor package is "Core(s) per socket." For this socket on my primary workstation, there are sixteen (16) cores. That means that there are 16 separate computing devices in the processor plugged into this socket.

Hyperthreading

The line "CPU(s)" shows that there are 32 CPUs on this socket. How can that be? Look at the line with the name "Thread(s) per core," and the number there is 2, so $16 \times 2 = 32$. Well, that is the math but not the explanation. The short explanation is that compute cores are really fast. They are so fast that a single stream of instructions and data is not enough to keep them busy all the time even in a very compute-intensive environment. The details of why this is so are beyond the scope of this book, but suffice it to say that before hyperthreading, most compute cores would sit waiting with nothing to do while the slower external memory circuitry tried to feed them sufficient streams of program instructions and data to keep them active.

Rather than let precious compute cycles go to waste in high-performance computing environments, Intel developed hyperthreading technology that allows a single core to process two streams of instructions and data by switching between them. This enables a single core to perform almost as well as two. So the term *CPU* is used to specify that a single hyperthreading core is reasonably close to the functional equivalent of two CPUs.

But there are some caveats. Hyperthreading is not particularly helpful if all you are doing is word processing and spreadsheets. Hyperthreading is intended to improve performance in high-performance computing environments where every CPU compute cycle is important in speeding the results.

---

[8] Wikipedia, *Arithmetic Logic Unit*, https://en.wikipedia.org/wiki/Arithmetic_logic_unit

P- and E-Cores

But wait – there's more!

Most Intel processors typically contain identical cores, no matter how many there are. But newer processors may now have two different types of cores.[9]

P-cores are for overall performance and usually include hyperthreading. E-cores are aimed at providing efficient computing for low CPU loads and can save energy when working with those loads. P- and E-cores are only a few years old, and not all Intel processors use them. They are typically found in high-end i5, i7, and i9 processors.

Peripherals

Peripherals are hardware devices that can be plugged into the computer via the various types of interface ports. USB devices such as external storage devices and thumb drives are typical of this type of hardware. Other types include keyboards, mice, and printers.

Printers can also be connected using the very old parallel printer ports, which I still see on some new motherboards, but most are USB capable of being attached using USB or a network connection. Displays are commonly connected using HDMI, DVI, DisplayPort, or VGA connectors.

Peripheral devices can also include such items as USB hubs, disk drive docking stations, plotters, and more.

The Operating System

All of these hardware pieces of the computer must work together. Data must be gotten into the computer and moved about between the various components. Programs must be loaded from long-term storage on the hard drive into RAM where they can be executed. Processor time needs to be allocated between running applications. Access to the hardware components of the computer such as RAM, disk drives, and printers by application programs must be managed.

---

[9] Help Desk Geek, https://helpdeskgeek.com/reviews/what-are-intels-e-cores-and-p-cores/

It is the task of the operating system to provide these functions. The operating system manages the operation of the computer and of the application software that runs on the computer.

The Definition

A simple definition of an operating system is that it is a program, much like any other program. It is different only in that its primary function is to manage the movement of data in the computer. This definition refers specifically to the kernel of the operating system.

The operating system kernel manages access to the hardware devices of the computer by utility and application programs. The operating system also manages system services such as memory allocation – the assignment of specific virtual memory locations to various programs when they request memory – the movement of data from various storage devices into memory where it can be accessed by the CPU, communications with other computers and devices via the network, display of data in text or graphic format on the display, printing, and much more.

The Linux kernel provides an API – application programming interface – for other programs to use in order to access the kernel functions. For example, a program that needs to have more memory allocated to its data structures uses a kernel function call to request that memory. The kernel then allocates the memory and notifies the program that the additional memory is available.

The Linux kernel also manages access to the CPUs as computing resources. It uses a complex algorithm to determine which processes are allocated some CPU time, when, and for how long. If necessary, the kernel can interrupt a running program in order to allow another program to have some CPU time.

An operating system kernel like Linux can do little on its own. It requires other programs – utilities – that can be used to perform basic functions such as create a directory on the hard drive and then other program utilities to access that directory, create files in that directory, and then manage those files. These utility programs perform functions like creating files, deleting files, copying files from one place to another, setting display resolution, and complex processing of textual data. We will cover the use of many of these utilities as we proceed through this book.

Typical Operating System Functions

Any operating system has a set of core functions, which are the primary reason for its existence. These are the functions that enable the operating system to manage itself, the hardware on which it runs, and the application programs and utilities that depend upon it to allocate system resources to them:

- Memory management

- Managing multitasking

- Managing multiple users

- Process management

- Interprocess communication (IPC)

- Device management

- Error handling and logging

Let's look briefly at these functions.

Memory Management

Linux and other modern operating systems use advanced memory management strategies to virtualize real memory – random-access memory[10] (RAM) and swap memory (disk) – into a single virtual memory space that can be used as if it were all physical RAM. Portions of this virtual memory[11] can be allocated by the memory management functions of the kernel to programs that request memory.

The memory management components of the operating system are responsible for assigning virtual memory space to applications and utilities and for translation between virtual memory spaces and physical memory. The kernel allocates and deallocates memory and assigns physical memory locations based upon requests, either implicit or explicit, from application programs. In cooperation with the CPU, the kernel also manages access to memory to ensure that programs only access those regions of

---

[10] Wikipedia, *Random-access memory*, https://en.wikipedia.org/wiki/Random-access_memory
[11] Wikipedia, *Virtual Memory*, https://en.wikipedia.org/wiki/Virtual_memory

memory that have been assigned to them. Part of memory management includes managing the swap partition or file and the movement of memory pages between RAM and the swap space on the hard drive.

Virtual memory eliminates the need for the application programmer to deal directly with memory management because it provides a single virtual memory address space for each program. It also isolates each application's memory space from that of every other, thus making the program's memory space safe from being overwritten or viewed by other programs.

Multitasking

Like most modern operating systems, Linux can multitask. That means that it can manage two, three, or hundreds of processes at the same time. Part of process management is managing multiple processes that are all running on a Linux computer.

I usually have several programs running at one time such as LibreOffice Writer that is a word processor, an email program, a spreadsheet, a file manager, a web browser, and usually multiple terminal sessions in which I interact with the Linux command-line interface (CLI). Right now, as I write this sentence, I have multiple documents open in several LibreOffice Writer windows. This enables me to see what I have written in other documents and to work on multiple chapters at the same time.

But those programs usually do little or nothing until we give them things to do by typing words into the word processor or clicking an email to display it. I also have several terminal emulators running and use them to log into various local and remote computers for which I manage and have responsibility.

Linux itself always has many programs running in the background – called daemons – programs that help Linux manage the hardware and other software running on the host. These programs are usually not noticed by users unless we specifically look for them. Some of the tools you will learn about in this course can reveal these otherwise hidden programs.

Even with all of its own programs running in the background and users' programs running, a modern Linux computer uses a few compute cycles and wastes most of its CPU cycles waiting for things to happen. Linux can download and install its own updates while performing any or all of the preceding tasks simultaneously – without the need for a reboot. Wait – what?! That's right. Linux does not usually need to reboot before, during, or after installing updates or when installing new software. After a new kernel or glibc (General C Libraries) is installed, however, you may wish to reboot the computer to activate it, but you can do that whenever you want and not be forced to reboot multiple times during an update or even stop doing your work while the updates are installed.

Multiuser

The multitasking functionality of Linux extends to its ability to host multiple users – tens or hundreds of them – all running the same or different programs at the same time on one single computer.

Multiuser capability means a number of different things. First, it can mean a single user who has logged in multiple times via a combination of the GUI desktop and the command line using one or more terminal sessions. We will explore the extreme flexibility available when using terminal sessions a bit later in this course. Second, multiuser means just that – many different users logged in at the same time, each doing their own thing and each isolated and protected from the activities of the others. Some users can be logged in locally and others from anywhere in the world with an Internet connection if the host computer is properly configured.

The role of the operating system is to allocate resources to each user and to ensure that any tasks, that is, processes, they have running have sufficient resources without impinging upon the resources allocated to other users.

Process Management

The Linux kernel manages the execution of all tasks running on the system. The Linux operating system is multitasking from the moment it boots up. Many of those tasks are the background tasks required to manage a multitasking and – for Linux – a multiuser environment. These tools take only a small fraction of the available CPU resources available on even modest computers.

Each running program is a process. It is the responsibility of the Linux kernel to perform process management.[12]

The scheduler portion of the kernel allocates CPU time to each running process based on its priority and whether it is capable of running. A task that is blocked – perhaps it is waiting for data to be delivered from the disk or for input from the

---

[12] Process management is discussed in Chapter 4 of Volume 2.

keyboard – does not receive CPU time. The Linux kernel will also preempt a lower-priority task when a task with a higher priority becomes unblocked and capable of running.

In order to manage processes, the kernel creates data abstractions that represent that process. Part of the data required is that of memory maps that define the memory that is allocated to the process and whether it is data or executable code. The kernel maintains information about the execution status such as how recently the program had some CPU time, how much time, and a number called the "nice" number. It uses that information and the nice number to calculate the priority of the process. The kernel uses the priority of all of the processes to determine which process(es) will be allocated some CPU time.

Note that not all processes need CPU time simultaneously. In fact, for most desktop workstations in normal circumstances, usually only two or three processes at the most need to be on the CPU at any given time. This means that a simple quad-core processor can easily handle this type of CPU load.

If there are more programs – processes – running than there are CPUs in the system, the kernel is responsible for determining which process to interrupt in order to replace it with a different one that needs some CPU time.

Interprocess Communication

Interprocess communication (IPC) is vital to any multitasking operating system. Many programs must be synchronized with each other to ensure that their work is properly coordinated. Interprocess communication is the tool that enables this type of inter-program cooperation.

The kernel manages a number of IPC methods. Shared memory is used when two tasks need to pass data between them. The Linux clipboard is a good example of shared memory. Data that is cut or copied to the clipboard is stored in shared memory. When the stored data is pasted into another application, that application looks for the data in the clipboard's shared memory area. Named pipes can be used to communicate data between two programs. Data can be pushed into the pipe by one program, and the other program can pull the data out of the other end of the pipe. A program may collect data very quickly and push it into the pipe. Another program may take the data out of the other end of the pipe and either display it on the screen or store it to the disk, but it can handle the data at its own rate.

Device Management

The kernel manages access to the physical hardware through the use of device drivers. Although we tend to think of this in terms of various types of storage devices, it also manages other input/output (I/O) devices such as the keyboard, mouse, display, printers, and so on. This includes management of pluggable devices such as USB storage devices and external USB and eSATA storage devices.

Access to physical devices must be managed carefully, or more than one application might attempt to control the same device at the same time. The Linux kernel manages devices so that only one program actually has control of or access to a device at any given moment. One example of this is a COM port.[13] Only one program can communicate through a COM port at any given time. If you are using the COM port to get your email from the Internet, for example, and try to start another program that attempts to use the same COM port, the Linux kernel detects that the COM port is already in use. The kernel then uses the hardware error handler to display a message on the screen that the COM port is in use.

For managing disk I/O devices, including USB, parallel and serial port I/O, and filesystem I/O, the kernel does not actually handle physical access to the disk, but rather manages the requests for disk I/O submitted by the various running programs. It passes these requests on to the filesystem, whether it be EXT[2,3,4], VFAT, HPFS, CDFS (CD-ROM File System), NFS (Network File System), or some other filesystem types, and manages the transfer of data between the filesystem and the requesting programs.

We will see later how all types of hardware – whether they are storage devices or something else attached to a Linux host – are handled as if they were files. This results in some amazing capabilities and interesting possibilities.

Error Handling

Errors happen. As a result the kernel needs to identify these errors when they occur. The kernel may take some action such as retrying the failing operation, displaying an error message to the user, and logging the error message to a log file.

---

[13] A COM (communications) port is used with serial communications such as a serial modem to connect to the Internet over telephone lines when a cable connection is not available.

In many cases the kernel can recover from errors without human intervention. In others, human intervention may be required. For example, if the user attempts to unmount[14] a USB storage device that is in use, the kernel will detect this and post a message to the umount program that usually sends the error message to the user interface. The user must then take whatever action necessary to ensure that the storage device is no longer in use and then attempt to unmount the device.

Utilities

In addition to their kernel functions, most operating systems provide a number of basic utility programs that enable users to manage the computer on which the operating system resides. These are the commands such as cp, ls, mv, and so on, as well as the various shells, such as bash, ksh (Korn shell), csh (C shell), and so on, which make managing the computer so much easier.

These utilities are not truly part of the operating system; they are merely provided as useful tools that can be used by the SysAdmin to perform administrative tasks. In Linux, often these are the GNU core utilities. However, common usage groups the kernel together with the utilities into a single conceptual entity that we call the operating system.

A Bit of History

Entire books have been written just about the history of Linux[15] and Unix,[16] so I will attempt to make this as short as possible. It is not necessary to know this history to be able to use Unix or Linux, but you may find it interesting. I have found it very useful to know some of this history because it has helped me understand the Unix and Linux Philosophy and formulate my own philosophy, which I discuss in my book *The Linux Philosophy for SysAdmins*[17] and a good bit in the three volumes of this course.

---

[14] The Linux command to unmount a device is actually umount.

[15] Wikipedia, *History of Linux*, https://en.wikipedia.org/wiki/History_of_Linux

[16] Wikipedia, *History of Unix*, https://en.wikipedia.org/wiki/History_of_Unix

[17] *The Linux Philosophy for SysAdmins*, Apress, www.apress.com/us/book/9781484237298

Starting with UNICS

The history of Linux begins with UNICS, which was originally written as a gaming platform to run a single game. Ken Thompson was an employee at Bell Labs in the late 1960s – before the breakup[18] – working on a complex project called Multics. Multics was an acronym that stood for Multiplexed Information and Computing System. It was supposed to be a multitasking operating system for the GE (yes, General Electric) 645[19] mainframe computer. It was a huge, costly, complex project with three very large organizations, GE, Bell Labs, and MIT, working on it.

Although Multics never amounted to much more than a small bump along the road of computer history, it did introduce a good number of then innovative features that had never before been available in an operating system. These features included multitasking and multiuser capabilities.

Ken Thompson,[20] one of the developers of Multics, had written a game called *Space Travel*[21] that ran under Multics. Unfortunately, due at least in part to the committee-driven design of Multics, the game ran very slowly. It was also very expensive to run at about $50 per iteration. As with many projects developed by committees, Multics died a slow, agonizing death. The platform on which the *Space Travel* game was run was no longer available.

Thompson then rewrote the game to run on a DEC PDP-7 computer, similar to the one in Figure 2-3, that was just sitting around gathering dust. In order to make the game run on the DEC, he and some of his buddies, Dennis Ritchie[22] and Rudd Canaday, first had to write an operating system for the PDP-7. Because it could only handle two simultaneous users – far fewer than Multics had been designed for – they called their new operating system UNICS for UNiplexed Information and Computing System as a bit of geeky humor.

---

[18] Wikipedia, *Breakup of the Bell System*, https://en.wikipedia.org/wiki/Breakup_of_the_Bell_System

[19] Wikipedia, *GE 645*, https://en.wikipedia.org/wiki/GE_645

[20] Wikipedia, *Ken Thompson*, https://en.wikipedia.org/wiki/Ken_Thompson

[21] Wikipedia, *Space Travel*, https://en.wikipedia.org/wiki/Space_Travel_(video_game)

[22] Wikipedia, *Dennis Ritchie*, https://en.wikipedia.org/wiki/Dennis_Ritchie

UNIX

At some time later, the UNICS name was modified slightly to UNIX, and that name has stuck ever since, because – well – "X" is just so much cooler than "CS."

In 1970, recognizing its potential, Bell Labs provided some financial support for the Unix operating system, and development began in earnest. In 1972 the entire operating system was rewritten in C to make it more portable and easier to maintain than the assembler it had been written in allowed for. By 1978, Unix was in fairly wide use inside AT&T Bell Labs and many universities.

Due to the high demand, AT&T decided to release a commercial version of Unix in 1982. Unix System III was based on the seventh version of the operating system. In 1983, AT&T released Unix SystemV Release 1 (SVR1). For the first time, AT&T promised to maintain upward compatibility for future versions. Thus, programs written to run on SVR1 would also run on SVR2 and future releases. Because this was a commercial version, AT&T began charging license fees for the operating system.

Also, in order to promote the spread of Unix and to assist many large universities in their computing programs, AT&T gave away the source code of Unix to many of these institutions of higher learning. This caused one of the best and one of the worst situations for Unix. The best thing about the fact that AT&T gave the source code to universities was that it promoted rapid development of new features. It also promoted the rapid divergence of Unix into many distributions.

Figure 2-3. *A DEC PDP-7 similar to the one used by Ken Thompson and Dennis Ritchie to write the UNICS[sic] operating system. This one is located in Oslo, and the picture was taken in 2005 before restoration began. Wikimedia, CC by SA 1.0*

SystemV was an important milestone in the history of Unix. Many Unix variants are today based on SystemV. The most current release is SVR4, which is a serious attempt to reconverge the many variants that split off during these early years. SVR4 contains most of the features of both SystemV and Berkeley Software Distribution (BSD). Hopefully they are the best features.

The Berkeley Software Distribution (BSD)

The University of California at Berkeley got into the Unix fray very early. Many of the students who attended the school added their own favorite features to BSD Unix. Eventually only a very tiny portion of BSD was still AT&T code. Because of this it was very different from, though still similar to, SystemV. Ultimately the remaining portion of BSD was totally rewritten as well, and those using it no longer needed to purchase a license from AT&T.

The Unix Philosophy

The Unix Philosophy is an important part of what makes Unix unique and powerful. Because of the way that Unix was developed, and the particular people involved in that development, the Unix Philosophy was an integral part of the process of creating Unix and played a large part in many of the decisions about its structure and functionality. Much has been written about the Unix Philosophy. And the Linux Philosophy is essentially the same as the Unix Philosophy because of its direct line of descent from Unix.

The original Unix Philosophy was intended primarily for the system developers. In fact, the developers of Unix, led by Thompson and Ritchie, designed Unix in a way that made sense to them, creating rules, guidelines, and procedural methods and then designing them into the structure of the operating system. That worked well for system developers, and that also – partly, at least – worked for SysAdmins (system administrators). That collection of guidance from the originators of the Unix operating system was codified in the excellent book *The Unix Philosophy* by Mike Gancarz and then later updated by Mr. Gancarz as *Linux and the Unix Philosophy*.[23]

Another fine and very important book, *The Art of Unix Programming*,[24] by Eric S. Raymond, provides the author's philosophical and practical views of programming in a Unix environment. It is also somewhat of a history of the development of Unix as it was experienced and recalled by the author. This book is also available in its entirety at no charge on the Internet.[25]

I learned a lot from all three of those books. They all have great value to Unix and Linux programmers. In my opinion, *Linux and the Unix Philosophy* and *The Art of Unix Programming* should be required reading for Linux programmers, system administrators, and DevOps personnel. I strongly recommend that you read these two books in particular.

I have been working with computers for over 45 years. It was not until I started working with Unix and Linux, and started reading some of the articles and books about Unix, Linux, and the common philosophy they share, that I understood the reasons many things in the Linux and Unix worlds are done as they are. Such understanding can be quite useful in learning new things about Linux and in being able to reason through problem solving.

[23] Gancarz, Mike, *Linux and the Unix Philosophy*, Digital Press – an imprint of Elsevier Science, 2003, ISBN 1-55558-273-7

[24] Raymond, Eric S., *The Art of Unix Programming*, Addison-Wesley, September 17, 2003, ISBN 0-13-142901-9

[25] Raymond, Eric S., *The Art of Unix Programming*, www.catb.org/esr/writings/taoup/html/index.html/

A (Very) Brief History of Linux

Linus Torvalds, the creator of Linux, was a student at Helsinki University in 1991. The university was using a very small version of Unix called Minix for school projects. Linus was not very happy with Minix and decided to write his own Unix-like operating system.[26]

Linus wrote the kernel of Linux and used the then ubiquitous PC with an 80386 processor as the platform for his operating system because that is what he had on hand as his home computer. He released an early version in 1991 and the first public version in March of 1992.

Linux spread quickly, in part because many of the people who downloaded the original versions were hackers like Linus and had good ideas that they wanted to contribute. These contributors, with guidance from Torvalds, grew into a loose international affiliation of hackers dedicated to improving Linux.

Linux is now found in almost all parts of our lives.[27] It is ubiquitous, and we depend upon it in many places that we don't normally even think about. Our Android mobile phones, smart televisions, automobile infotainment systems, the International Space Station, all of the 500 largest supercomputers and probably most of the rest as well, the backbone of the Internet, and most of the websites on the Internet all utilize Linux.

For more detailed histories of Linux, see Wikipedia[28] and its long list of references and sources.

Core Utilities

Linus Torvalds wrote the Linux kernel, but the rest of the operating system was written by others. One key portion is the GNU core utilities developed by Richard M. Stallman (a.k.a. RMS) and others as part of their intended free GNU Operating System. All SysAdmins use these core utilities regularly, pretty much without thinking about them. There is also another set of basic utilities, util-linux, that we should also look at because they also are important Linux utilities.

---

[26] Torvalds, Linus, and Diamond, David, *Just for Fun*, HarperCollins, 2001, 61–64, ISBN 0-06-662072-4

[27] Opensource.com, *Places to find Linux*, https://opensource.com/article/18/5/places-find-linux?sc_cid=70160000001273HAAQ

[28] Wikipedia, *History of Linux*, https://en.wikipedia.org/wiki/History_of_Linux

Together, these two sets of utilities comprise many of the most basic tools – the core – of the Linux system administrator's toolbox. These utilities address tasks that include management and manipulation of text files, directories, data streams, various types of storage media, process controls, filesystems, and much more. The basic functions of these tools are the ones that allow SysAdmins to perform many of the tasks required to administer a Linux computer. These tools are indispensable because without them it is not possible to accomplish any useful work on a Unix or Linux computer.

GNU is a recursive algorithm that stands for "Gnu's Not Unix," the GNU Utilities developed by the Free Software Foundation (FSF) to provide free software to programmers and developers. Most distributions of Linux contain the GNU Utilities.

GNU Coreutils

To understand the origins of the GNU core utilities, we need to take a short trip in the Wayback machine to the early days of Unix at Bell Labs. Unix was originally written so that Ken Thompson, Dennis Ritchie, Doug McIlroy, and Joe Ossanna could continue with something they had started while working on a large multitasking and multiuser computer project called Multics. That little something was a game called *Space Travel.* As is true today, it always seems to be the gamers that drive forward the technology of computing. This new operating system was much more limited than Multics as only two users could log in at a time, so it was called UNICS. This name was later changed to UNIX.

Over time, UNIX turned out to be such a success that Bell Labs began essentially giving it away to universities and later to companies, for the cost of the media and shipping. Back in those days, system-level software was shared between organizations and programmers as they worked to achieve common goals within the context of system administration.

Eventually the PHBs[29] at AT&T decided that they should start making money on Unix and started using more restrictive – and expensive – licensing. This was taking place at a time when software in general was becoming more proprietary, restricted, and closed. It was becoming impossible to share software with other users and organizations.

---

[29] PHBs: pointy-haired bosses. A reference to the boss in the *Dilbert* comics.

Some people did not like this and fought it with free software. Richard M. Stallman[30] led a group of rebels who were trying to write an open and freely available operating system that they call the "GNU Operating System." This group created the GNU Utilities but did not produce a viable kernel.

When Linus Torvalds first wrote and compiled the Linux kernel, he needed a set of very basic system utilities to even begin to perform marginally useful work. The kernel does not provide these commands or even any type of command shell such as bash. The kernel is useless by itself. So Linus used the freely available GNU core utilities and recompiled them for Linux. This gave him a complete operating system even though it was quite basic.

You can learn about all of the individual programs that comprise the GNU Utilities by entering the command **info coreutils** at a terminal command line. The utilities are grouped by function to make specific ones easier to find. Highlight the group you want more information on and press the Enter key.

There are 102 utilities in that list. It does provide many of the tools necessary to perform some basic tasks on a Unix or Linux host. However, many basic utilities are missing. For example, the mount and umount commands are not in this list. Those and many of the other commands that are not in the GNU Coreutils can be found in the util-linux collection.

util-linux

The util-linux package of utilities contains many of the other common commands that SysAdmins use. These utilities are distributed by the Linux Kernel Organization, and virtually every distribution uses them. These 107 commands were originally three separate collections, fileutils, shellutils, and textutils, which were combined into the single package, util-linux, in 2003.

These two collections of basic Linux utilities, the GNU core utilities and util-linux, together provide the basic utilities required to administer a basic Linux system. As I researched this chapter, I found several interesting utilities in this list that I never knew about. Many of these commands are seldom needed. But when you do, they are indispensable. Between these two collections, there are over 200 Linux utilities. Linux

---

[30]Wikipedia, *Richard M. Stallman*, https://en.wikipedia.org/wiki/Richard_Stallman

.has many more commands, but these are the ones that are needed to manage the most basic functions of the typical Linux host. The **lscpu** utility that I used earlier in this chapter is distributed as part of the util-linux package.

I find it easiest to refer to these two collections together as the Linux core utilities.

Copyleft

Just because Linux and its source code are freely available does not mean that there are no legal or copyright issues involved. Linux is copyrighted under the GNU General Public License Version 2 (GPL2). The GNU GPL2 is actually called a copyleft instead of a copyright by most people in the industry because its terms are so significantly different from most commercial licenses. The terms of the GPL allow you to distribute or even to sell Linux (or any other copylefted software), but you must make the complete source code available without restrictions of any kind, as well as the compiled binaries.

The original owner – Linus Torvalds in the case of parts of the Linux kernel – retains copyright to the portions of the Linux kernel he wrote, and other contributors to the kernel retain the copyright to their portions of software no matter by whom or how much it is modified or added to.

Games

One thing that my research has uncovered and which I find interesting is that right from the beginning it has been the gamers that have driven technology. At first it was things like *Tic-Tac-Toe* on an old IBM 1401, then *Space Travel* on UNICS and the PDP-7, *Adventure* and many other text-based games on Unix, and single-player 2D video games on the IBM PC and DOS and now first-person shooter (FPS) and massively multiplayer online games (MMOGs) on powerful Intel and AMD computers with lots of RAM, expensive and very sensitive keyboards, and extremely high-speed Internet connections. Oh, yes, and lights. Lots of lights inside the case, on the keyboard and mouse, and even built into the motherboards. In many instances these lights are programmable.

AMD and Intel are intensely competitive in the processor arena, and both companies provide very high-powered versions of their products to feed the gaming community. These powerful hardware products also provide significant benefits to other communities like writers.

For me, having many CPUs and huge amounts of RAM and disk space makes it possible to run several virtual machines simultaneously. This enables me to have two or three VMs to represent the ones you will use for the experiments that will help you explore Linux in this book and other, crashable and disposable VMs that I use to test various scenarios.

Chapter Summary

Linux is an operating system that is designed to manage the flow and storage of programs and data in a modern Intel computer. It consists of a kernel, which was written by Linus Torvalds, and two sets of system-level utilities that provide the SysAdmin with the ability to manage and control the functions of the system and the operating system itself. These two sets of utilities, the GNU Utilities and util-linux, together consist of a collection of over 200 Linux core utilities that are indispensable to the Linux SysAdmin.

Linux must work very closely with the hardware in order to perform many of its functions, so we looked at the major components of a modern Intel-based computer.

Exercises

1. What is the primary function of an operating system?

2. List at least four additional functions of an operating system.

3. Describe the purpose of the Linux core utilities as a group.

4. Why did Linus Torvalds choose to use the GNU core utilities for Linux instead of writing his own?

CHAPTER 3

The Linux Philosophy for SysAdmins

Objectives

In this chapter you will learn

- The historical background of the Linux Philosophy for SysAdmins
- A basic introduction to the tenets of the Linux Philosophy for SysAdmins
- How the Linux Philosophy for SysAdmins can help you learn to be a better SysAdmin

Background

The Unix Philosophy is an important part of what makes Unix[1] unique and powerful. Much has been written about the Unix Philosophy, and the Linux Philosophy is essentially the same as the Unix Philosophy because of its direct line of descent from Unix.

The original Unix Philosophy was intended primarily for the system developers. Having worked with Unix and Linux for over 25 years as of this writing, I have found that the Linux Philosophy has contributed greatly to my own efficiency and effectiveness as a SysAdmin. I have always tried to follow the Linux Philosophy because my experience has been that a rigorous adherence to it, regardless of the pressure applied by a legion of pointy-haired bosses (PHBs), will always pay dividends in the long run.

---

[1] https://en.wikipedia.org/wiki/Unix

D. Both, *Using and Administering Linux: Volume 1*, https://doi.org/10.1007/978-1-4842-9618-9_3

The original Unix and Linux Philosophy was intended for the developers of those operating systems. Although system administrators could apply many of the tenets to their daily work, many important tenets that address things unique to SysAdmins were missing. Over the years I have been working with Linux and Unix, I have formulated my own philosophy – one which applies more directly to the everyday life and tasks of the system administrator. My philosophy is based in part upon the original Unix and Linux Philosophy, as well as the philosophies of my mentors.

My book *The Linux Philosophy for SysAdmins*[2] is the result of my SysAdmin approach to the Linux Philosophy. Much of this chapter is taken directly from that book.

The Structure of the Philosophy

There are three layers to the Linux Philosophy for system administrators in a way that is similar to Maslow's hierarchy of needs.[3] These layers, shown in Figure 3-1, are also symbolic of our growth through progressively higher levels of enlightenment.

The bottom layer is the foundation – the basic commands and knowledge that we as SysAdmins need to know in order to perform the lowest level of our jobs. The middle layer consists of those practical tenets that build on the foundation and inform the daily tasks of the SysAdmin. The top layer contains the tenets that fulfill our higher needs as SysAdmins and that encourage and enable us to share our knowledge.

In the first and most basic layer of the philosophy is the foundation. It is about the "Linux Truth," data streams, Standard Input/Output (STDIO), transforming data streams, small command-line programs, and the meaning of "everything is a file," for example.

The middle layer contains the functional aspects of the philosophy. Embracing the command line, we expand our command-line programs to create tested and maintainable shell programs that we save and can use repeatedly and even share. We become the "lazy admin" and begin to automate everything. We use the Linux filesystem hierarchy appropriately and store data in open formats. These are the functional portions of the philosophy.

---

[2] Both, David, *The Linux Philosophy for SysAdmins*, Apress, 2018, ISBN 978-1-4842-3729-8
[3] Wikipedia, *Maslow's hierarchy of needs*, https://en.wikipedia.org/wiki/Maslow%27s_hierarchy_of_needs

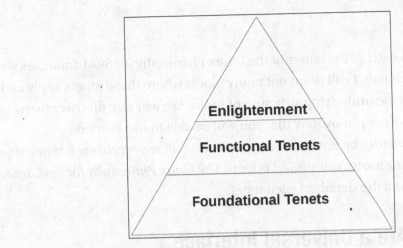

Figure 3-1. *The hierarchy of the Linux Philosophy for SysAdmins*

The top layer of the philosophy is about enlightenment. We begin to progress beyond merely performing our SysAdmin tasks and just getting the job done; our understanding of the elegance and simplicity in the design of Linux is perfected. We begin striving for doing our own work elegantly, keeping solutions simple, simplifying existing but complex solutions, and creating usable and complete documentation. We begin to explore and experiment simply for the sake of gaining new knowledge. At this stage of enlightenment, we begin to pass our knowledge and methods to those new to the profession, and we actively support our favorite open source projects.

In my opinion it is impossible to learn about many Linux commands and utilities without learning about the structure and philosophy of Linux. Working on the command line requires such knowledge. At the same time, working on the command line engenders the very knowledge required to use it. If you use the command line long enough, you will find that you have learned at least some about the intrinsic beauty of Linux without even trying. If you then follow your own curiosity about what you have already learned, the rest will be revealed.

Does that sound a bit Zen? It should because it is.

The Tenets

Here we look briefly at each of the tenets of the Linux Philosophy for SysAdmins. As we proceed through this course, I will point out many places where these tenets apply and what they reveal about the underlying structure of Linux. We will also discover many practical applications of the philosophy that you will be able to use every day.

This list must necessarily be terse, and it cannot cover all aspects of each tenet. If you are interested in learning more, you should refer to *The Linux Philosophy for SysAdmins*[4] for more information and the details of each tenet.

Data Streams Are a Universal Interface

Everything in Linux revolves around streams of data – particularly text streams. In the Unix and Linux worlds, a stream is a flow of text data that originates at some source; the stream may flow through one or more programs that transform it in some way, and then it may be stored in a file or displayed in a terminal session. As a SysAdmin your job is intimately associated with manipulating the creation and flow of these data streams.

The use of Standard Input/Output (STDIO) for program input and output is a key foundation of the Linux way of doing things and manipulating data streams. STDIO was first developed for Unix and has found its way into most other operating systems since then, including DOS, Windows, and Linux.

> *This is the Unix philosophy: Write programs that do one thing and do it well. Write programs to work together. Write programs to handle text streams, because that is a universal interface.*
>
> —Doug McIlroy, Basics of the Unix Philosophy[5,6]

---

[4] Both, David, *The Linux Philosophy for SysAdmins*, Apress, 2018, ISBN 978-1-4842-3729-8

[5] Raymond, Eric S., *The Art of Unix Programming*, www.catb.org/esr/writings/taoup/html/ch01s06.html

[6] Linuxtopia, *Basics of the Unix Philosophy*, www.linuxtopia.org/online_books/programming_books/art_of_unix_programming/ch01s06.html

STDIO was developed by Ken Thompson[7] as a part of the infrastructure required to implement pipes on early versions of Unix. Programs that implement STDIO use standardized file handles for input and output rather than files that are stored on a disk or other recording media. STDIO is best described as a buffered data stream, and its primary function is to stream data from the output of one program, file, or device to the input of another program, file, or device.

Data streams are the raw materials upon which the core utilities and many other CLI tools perform their work. As its name implies, a data stream is a stream of data being passed from one file, device, or program to another using STDIO.

Transforming Data Streams

This tenet explores the use of pipes to connect streams of data from one utility program to another using STDIO. The function of these programs is to transform the data in some manner. You will also learn about the use of redirection to redirect the data to a file.

Data streams can be manipulated by using pipes to insert transformers into the stream. Each transformer program is used by the SysAdmin to perform some transformational operation on the data in the stream, thus changing its contents in some manner. Redirection can then be used at the end of the pipeline to direct the data stream to a file. As has already been mentioned, that file could be an actual data file on the hard drive or a device file such as a drive partition, a printer, a terminal, a pseudo-terminal, or any other device connected to a computer.

I use the term "transform" in conjunction with these programs because the primary task of each is to transform the incoming data from STDIO in a specific way as intended by the SysAdmin and to send the transformed data to STDOUT for possible use by another transformer program or redirection to a file.

The standard term for these programs, "filters," implies something with which I don't always agree. By definition, a filter is a device or a tool that removes something, such as an air filter removing airborne contaminants so that the internal combustion engine of your automobile does not grind itself to death on those particulates. In my high school and college chemistry classes, filter paper was used to remove particulates from a liquid. The air filter in my home HVAC system removes particulates that I don't want to breathe. So, although they do sometimes filter out unwanted data from a stream, I much prefer

---

[7]Wikipedia, *Ken Thompson*, https://en.wikipedia.org/wiki/Ken_Thompson

the term "transformers" because these utilities do so much more. They can add data to a stream, modify the data in some amazing ways, sort it, rearrange the data in each line, perform operations based on the contents of the data stream, and so much more. Feel free to use whichever term you prefer, but I prefer transformers.

The ability to manipulate these data streams using these small yet powerful transformer programs is central to the power of the Linux command-line interface. Many of the Linux core utilities are transformer programs and use STDIO.

Everything Is a File

This is one of the most important concepts that makes Linux especially flexible and powerful: everything is a file. That is, everything can be the source of a data stream, the target of a data stream, or in many cases both. In this course you will explore what "everything is a file" really means and learn to use that to your great advantage as a SysAdmin.

> The whole point with "everything is a file" is… the fact that you can use common tools to operate on different things.
>
> —Linus Torvalds in an email

The idea that everything is a file has some interesting and amazing implications. This concept makes it possible to copy a boot record, a disk partition, or an entire hard drive including the boot record, because the entire hard drive is a file, just as are the individual partitions. Other possibilities include using the **cp** (copy) command to print a PDF file to a compatible printer, using the **echo** command to send messages from one terminal session to another, and using the **dd** command to copy ISO image files to a USB thumb drive.

"Everything is a file" is possible because all devices are implemented by Linux as these things called device special files, which are located in the /dev/ directory. Device files are not device drivers; rather, they are gateways to devices that are exposed to the user. We will discuss device special files in some detail throughout this course as well as in Volume 2, Chapter 22.

Use the Linux FHS

The Linux Filesystem Hierarchical Standard (FHS) defines the structure of the Linux directory tree. It names a set of standard directories and designates their purposes. This standard has been put in place to ensure that all distributions of Linux are consistent in their directory usage. Such consistency makes writing and maintaining shell and compiled programs easier for SysAdmins because the programs, their configuration files, and their data, if any, should be located in the standard directories. This tenet is about storing programs and data in the standard and recommended locations in the directory tree and the advantages of doing so.

As SysAdmins our tasks include everything from fixing problems to writing CLI programs to perform many of our tasks for us and for others. Knowing where data of various types are intended to be stored on a Linux system can be very helpful in resolving problems as well as preventing them.

The latest Filesystem Hierarchical Standard (3.0)[8] is defined in a document maintained by the Linux Foundation.[9] The document is available in multiple formats from their website as are historical versions of the FHS.

Embrace the CLI

The Force is with Linux and the Force is the command-line interface – the CLI. The vast power of the Linux CLI lies in its complete lack of restrictions. Linux provides many options for accessing the command line such as virtual consoles, many different terminal emulators, shells, and other related software that can enhance your flexibility and productivity.

The command line is a tool that provides a text-mode interface between the user and the operating system. The command line allows the user to type commands into the computer for processing and to see the results.

The Linux command-line interface is implemented with shells such as bash (Bourne again shell), csh (C shell), and ksh (Korn shell) to name just three of the many that are available. The function of any shell is to pass commands typed by the user to the operating system, which executes the commands and returns the results to the shell.

---

[8] The Linux Foundation, *The Linux Filesystem Hierarchical Standard*, http://refspecs. linuxfoundation.org/fhs.shtml
[9] The Linux Foundation maintains documents defining many Linux standards. It also sponsors the work of Linus Torvalds.

Access to the command line is through a terminal interface of some type. There are three primary types of terminal interface that are common in modern Linux computers, but the terminology can be confusing. These three interfaces are virtual consoles, terminal emulators that run on a graphical desktop, and an SSH remote connection. We will explore the terminology, virtual consoles, and one terminal emulator in Chapter 7. We look at several different terminal emulators in Chapter 14.

Be the Lazy SysAdmin

Despite everything we were told by our parents, teachers, bosses, well-meaning authority figures, and hundreds of quotes about hard work that I found with a Google search, getting your work done well and on time is not the same as working hard. One does not necessarily imply the other.

I am a lazy SysAdmin. I am also a very productive SysAdmin. Those two seemingly contradictory statements are not mutually exclusive; rather, they are complementary in a very positive way. Efficiency is the only way to make this possible.

This tenet is about working hard at the right tasks to optimize our own efficiency as SysAdmins. Part of this is about automation, which we will explore in detail in Chapter 29 of Volume 2, but also throughout this course. The greater part of this tenet is about finding many of the myriad ways to use the shortcuts already built into Linux.

These are things like using aliases as shortcuts to reduce typing – but probably not in the way you think of them if you come from a Windows background. Naming files so that they can be easily found in lists, using the file name completion facility that is part of bash, the default Linux shell for most distributions, and more all contribute to making life easier for lazy SysAdmins.

Automate Everything

The function of computers is to automate mundane tasks in order to allow us humans to concentrate on the tasks that the computers cannot – yet – do. For SysAdmins, those of us who run and manage the computers most closely, we have direct access to the tools that can help us work more efficiently. We should use those tools to maximum benefit.

In Chapter 8 of *The Linux Philosophy for SysAdmins*,[10] I state, "A SysAdmin is most productive when thinking – thinking about how to solve existing problems and about how to avoid future problems; thinking about how to monitor Linux computers in order to find clues that anticipate and foreshadow those future problems; thinking about how to make their job more efficient; thinking about how to automate all of those tasks that need to be performed whether every day or once a year."

SysAdmins are next most productive when creating the shell programs that automate the solutions that they have conceived while appearing to be unproductive. The more automation we have in place, the more time we have available to fix real problems when they occur and to contemplate how to automate even more than we already have.

I have learned that – for me at least – writing shell programs, which are also known as scripts, provides the best single strategy for leveraging my time. Once having written a shell program, it can be rerun as many times as needed.

Always Use Shell Scripts

When writing programs to automate, well, everything, always use shell scripts rather than compiled utilities and tools. Because shell scripts are stored in plain text[11] format, they can be easily viewed and modified by humans just as easily as they can by computers. You can examine a shell program and see exactly what it does and whether there are any obvious errors in the syntax or logic. This is a powerful example of what it means to be open.

A shell script or program is an executable file that contains at least one shell command. They usually have more than a single command, and some shell scripts have thousands of lines of code. When taken together, these commands are the ones necessary to perform a desired task with a specifically defined result.

Context is important, and this tenet should be considered in the context of our jobs as SysAdmins. The SysAdmin's job differs significantly from those of developers and testers. In addition to resolving both hardware and software problems, we manage the day-to-day operation of the systems under our care. We monitor those systems for potential problems and make all possible efforts to prevent those problems before they impact our users. We install updates and perform full release-level upgrades to the

---

[10] Both, David, *The Linux Philosophy for SysAdmins*, Apress, 2018, 132, ISBN 978-1-4842-3729-8

[11] Wikipedia, *Plain text*, https://en.wikipedia.org/wiki/Plain_text

operating system. We resolve problems caused by our users. SysAdmins develop code to do all of those things and more; then we test that code; and then we support that code in a production environment.

Test Early and Test Often

There is always one more bug.

—Lubarsky's Law of Cybernetic Entomology

Lubarsky – whoever they might be – is correct. We can never find all of the bugs in our code. For every one I find, there always seems to be another that crops up, usually at a very inopportune time.

Testing affects the ultimate outcome of the many tasks SysAdmins do and is an integral part of the philosophy. However, testing is not just about programs. It is also about verification that problems – whether caused by hardware, software, or the seemingly endless ways that users can find to break things – that we are supposed to have resolved actually have been. These problems can be with application or utility software we wrote, system software, applications, and hardware. Just as importantly, testing is also about ensuring that the code is easy to use and the interface makes sense to the user.

Testing is hard work, and it requires a well-designed test plan based on the requirements statements. Regardless of the circumstances, start with a test plan. Even a very basic test plan provides some assurance that testing will be consistent and will cover the required functionality of the code.

Any good plan includes tests to verify that the code does everything it is supposed to. That is, if you enter X and click button Y, you should get Z as the result. So you write a test that does create those conditions and then verify that Z is the result.

The best plans include tests to determine how well the code fails. The specific scenarios explicitly covered by the test plan are important, but they may fail to anticipate the havoc that can be caused by unanticipated or even completely random input. This situation can be at least partially covered by fuzzy testing in which someone or some tool randomly bangs on the keyboard until something bad happens.

For SysAdmins, testing in production, which some people consider to be a new thing, is a common practice. There is no test plan that can be devised by a lab full of testers that can possibly equal a few minutes in the real world of production.

Use Commonsense Naming

The lazy SysAdmin does everything possible to reduce unnecessary typing, and I take that seriously. This tenet expands on that, but there is much more to it than just reducing the amount of typing I need to do. It is also about the readability of scripts and naming things so that they are more understandable more quickly.

One of the original Unix Philosophy tenets was to always use lowercase and keep names short,[12] an admirable goal but not one so easily met in the world of the SysAdmin. In many respects my own tenet would seem a complete refutation of the original. However, the original was intended for a different audience, and this one is intended for SysAdmins with a different set of needs.

The ultimate goal is to create scripts that are readable and easily understood in order to make them easily maintainable and then to use other simple scripts and cron jobs to automate running those scripts. Keeping the script names reasonably short also reduces typing when executing those scripts from the command line, but that is mostly irrelevant when starting them from another script or as cron jobs.

Readable scripts depend upon easily understandable and readable variable names. Sometimes, as with script names, these names may be longer but more understandable than many I have encountered in the past. Variable names like $DeviceName5 are much more understandable than $D5 and make a script easier to read.

Note that most of the historical Linux command names are short but they also have meaning. After working at the command line for a while, you will understand most of these. For example, the **ls** command means list the contents of a directory. Other commands contain the "ls" string in their names, such as **lsusb** to list the USB devices connected to the host or **lsblk** to list the block devices – storage drives – in the host.

Many newer commands such as those relating to logical volume management (LVM), NetworkManager, and the systemd init system are longer but meaningful. You will encounter them as you proceed through this course.

---

[12] Early Unix systems had very little memory compared with today's systems, so saving a few bytes in a name was important. Unix and Linux are case sensitive, so an extra keystroke to hit the Shift key was extra work.

Store Data in Open Formats

The reason we use computers is to manipulate data. It used to be called "data processing" for a reason, and that was an accurate description. We still process data although it may be in the form of video and audio streams, network and wireless streams, word processing data, spreadsheets, images, and more. It is all still just data.

We work with and manipulate text data streams with the tools we have available to us in Linux. When there is a need to store data, it is always better to store it in open file formats than closed ones.

Although many user application programs store data in plain text formats including simple flat plain text and XML, this tenet is mostly about configuration data and scripts that relate directly to Linux. However, any type of data should be stored as plain text if possible.

"Open source" is about the code and making the source code available to any and all who want to view or modify it. "Open data"[13] is about the openness of the data itself.

The term *open data* does not mean just having access to the data itself; it also means that the data can be viewed, used in some manner, and shared with others. The exact manner in which those goals are achieved may be subject to some sort of attribution and open licensing. As with open source software, such licensing is intended to ensure the continued open availability of the data and not to restrict it in any manner that would prevent its use.

Open data is knowable. That means that access to it is unfettered. Truly open data can be read freely and understood without the need for further interpretation or decryption. In the SysAdmin world, *open* means that the data we use to configure, monitor, and manage our Linux hosts is easy to find, read, and modify when necessary. It is stored in formats that permit that ease of access, such as plain text. When a system is open, the data and software can all be managed by open tools – tools that work with plain text.

Use Separate Filesystems for Data

There is a lot to this particular tenet, and it requires understanding the nature of Linux filesystems and mount points.

---

[13] Wikipedia, *Open Data*, https://en.wikipedia.org/wiki/Open_data

Note   The primary meaning for the term "filesystem" in this tenet is a segment of the directory tree that is located on a separate partition or logical volume (LV) that must be mounted on a specified mount point of the root filesystem to enable access to it. We also use the term to describe the structure of the metadata on the partition or volume such as EXT4, XFS, or some other structure. These different usages should be clear from their context. These meanings will be covered in more detail in Chapter 19.

There are at least three excellent reasons for maintaining separate filesystems on our Linux hosts. First, when storage devices crash, we may lose some or all of the data on a damaged filesystem, but, as we will see, data on other filesystems on the crashed hard drive may still be salvageable.

Second, despite having access to huge amounts of hard drive space, it is possible to fill up a filesystem. When that happens separate filesystems can minimize the immediate effects and make recovery easier.

Third, upgrades can be made easier when certain filesystems such as /home are located on separate filesystems. This makes it easy to upgrade without needing to restore that data from a backup.

I have frequently encountered all three of these situations in my career. In some instances there was only a single partition, the root (/) partition, and so recovery was quite difficult. Recovery from these situations was always much easier and faster when the host was configured with separate filesystems.

Keeping data of all types safe is part of the SysAdmin's job. Using separate filesystems for storing that data can help us accomplish that. This practice can also help us achieve our objective to be a lazy Admin. Backups do allow us to recover most of the data that would otherwise be lost in a crash scenario, but using separate filesystems may allow us to recover all of the data from unaffected filesystems right up to the moment of a crash. Restoring from backups takes much longer.

Make Programs Portable

Portable programs make life much easier for the lazy SysAdmin. Portability is an important consideration because it allows programs to be used on a wide range of operating system and hardware platforms. Using interpretive languages such as Bash, Python, and Perl that can run on many types of systems can save loads of work.

Programs written in compiled languages such as C must be recompiled at the very least when porting from one platform to another. In many cases, platform-specific code must be maintained in the sources in order to support the different hardware platforms that the binaries are expected to run on. This generates a lot of extra work, both writing and testing the programs.

Perl, Bash, and many other scripting languages are available in most environments. With very few exceptions, programs written in Perl, Bash, Python, PHP, and other languages can run unchanged on many different platforms.

Linux runs on a lot of hardware architectures.[14] Of course Linux supports Intel and AMD 64-bit processors. Most Linux distributions no longer support 32-bit AMD and Intel processors, but there are still a few specialized distros that do. Linux also supports 32- and 64-bit ARM architectures that are found in practically every mobile phone on the planet and devices such as the Arduino and Raspberry Pi.[15] Most mobile phones use a form of Linux called Android.

Use Open Source Software

This tenet may not mean exactly what you think it does. Most times we think of open source software as something like the Linux kernel, LibreOffice, or any of the thousands of open source software packages that make up our favorite distribution. In the context of system administration, *open source* also means the scripts that we write to automate our work and the scripts and programs we obtain from other SysAdmins who also share their work.

> *Open source software is software with source code that anyone can inspect, modify, and enhance.*[16]

—Opensource.com

---

[14]Wikipedia, *List of Linux-supported computer architectures*, https://en.wikipedia.org/wiki/List_of_Linux-supported_computer_architectures

[15]Raspberry Pi Foundation, www.raspberrypi.org/

[16]Opensource.com, *What is open source?*, https://opensource.com/resources/what-open-source

The web page from which the preceding quote was taken contains a well-written discussion of open source software including some of the advantages of open source. I suggest you read that article and consider how it applies to the code we write – our scripts. The implications are there if we look for them.

The official definition of *open source* is quite terse. The annotated version of the open source definition[17] at opensource.org contains ten sections that explicitly and succinctly define the conditions that must be met for software to be considered truly open source. This definition is important to the Linux Philosophy for SysAdmins. You do not have to read this definition, but I suggest you do so in order to gain a more complete understanding of what the term *open source* really means. However, I can summarize a bit.

Open source software is open because it can be read, modified, and shared because its source code is freely available to anyone who wants it. This "free as in speech" approach to software promotes worldwide participation by individuals and organizations in the creation and testing of high-quality code that can be shared freely by everyone. Being a good user of open source also means that we SysAdmins should share our own code, the code that we write to solve our own problems, and license it with one of the open source licenses.

Strive for Elegance

Elegance is one of those things that can be difficult to define. I know it when I see it, but putting what I see into a terse definition is a challenge. Using the Linux **dict** command, WordNet provides one definition of *elegance* as "a quality of neatness and ingenious simplicity in the solution of a problem (especially in science or mathematics); 'the simplicity and elegance of his invention.'"

In the context of this book, I assert that elegance is a state of beauty and simplicity in the design and working of both hardware and software. When a design is elegant, software and hardware work better and are more efficient. The user is aided by simple, efficient, and understandable tools.

Creating elegance in a technological environment is hard. It is also necessary. Elegant solutions produce elegant results and are easy to maintain and fix. Elegance does not happen by accident; you must work for it.

---

[17] Opensource.org, *The Open Source Definition (Annotated)*, https://opensource.org/osd-annotated

Find the Simplicity

The quality of simplicity is a large part of technical elegance. The tenets of the Linux Philosophy helped me solidify my understanding of the truth that Linux is simple and that the simplicity is illuminated by the philosophy.

> *UNIX is basically a simple operating system, but you have to be a genius to understand the simplicity.*[18]
>
> —Dennis Ritchie

In this tenet we search for the simplicity of Linux. I cringe when I see articles with titles like "77 Linux commands and utilities you'll actually use"[19] and "50 Most Frequently Used UNIX / Linux Commands (With Examples)."[20] These titles imply that there are sets of commands that you must memorize or that knowing large numbers of commands is important.

I do read many of these articles, but I am usually looking for new and interesting commands, commands that might help me resolve a problem or simplify a command-line program. I never tried to learn all of those Linux commands, regardless of what numbers you might come up with as the total for "all."

I just started by learning the commands I needed at any given moment for whatever project was at hand. I started to learn more commands because I took on personal projects and ones for work that stretched my knowledge to the limit and forced me to find commands previously unknown to me in order to complete those projects. My repertoire of commands grew over time, and I became more proficient at the application of those commands to resolve problems. I began finding jobs that paid me more and more money to play with Linux, my favorite toy.

As I learned about piping and redirection, about standard streams and STDIO, as I read about the Unix Philosophy and then the Linux Philosophy, I started to understand how and why the command line made Linux and the core utilities so powerful. I learned about the elegance of writing command-line programs that manipulated data streams in amazing ways.

---

[18] azquotes.com, www.azquotes.com/quote/246027?ref=unix

[19] TechTarget.com, http://searchdatacenter.techtarget.com/tutorial/77-Linux-commands-and-utilities-youll-actually-use

[20] The Geek Stuff, www.thegeekstuff.com/2010/11/50-linux-commands/?utm_source=feedburner

I also discovered that some commands are, if not completely obsolete, then seldom used and only in unusual circumstances. For this reason alone, it does not make sense to find a list of Linux commands and memorize them. It is not an efficient use of your time as a SysAdmin to learn many commands that may never be needed. The simplicity here is to learn what you need to do the task at hand. There will be plenty of tasks in the future that will require you to learn other commands.

When writing our own administrative scripts, simplicity is also key. Each of our scripts should do only one thing and do it well. Complex programs are difficult to use and to maintain.

> *Fools ignore complexity; pragmatists suffer it; experts avoid it; geniuses remove it.*
>
> —Alan Perlis[21]

Use Your Favorite Editor

Why is this a tenet of the Linux Philosophy for system administrators? Because arguing about editors can result in a great deal of wasted energy. Everyone has their favorite text editor, and it might not be the same as mine. So what!

I use vim as my editor. I have used it for years and like it very much. I am used to it. It meets my needs more than any other editor I have tried. If you can say that about your editor – whichever one that might be – then you are in editor nirvana.

I started using vi when I began learning Solaris over 20 years ago. My mentor suggested that I start learning to edit with vi because it would always be present on every system. That has proven to be true whether the operating system is Solaris or Linux. The vi editor is always there, so I can count on it. For me, this works. Vim is the new vi, but the **vi** command is a link that launches vim.

The vi editor can also be used as the editor for bash command-line editing. Although the default for command editing is EMACS-like, I use the vi option because I already know the vi keystrokes. Other tools that use vi editing are the crontab and visudo commands; both of these are wrappers around vi. Lazy developers use code that already exists, especially when it is open source. Using existing editors for these tools is an excellent example of that.

---

[21] Wikipedia, *Alan Perlis*, https://en.wikipedia.org/wiki/Alan_Perlis

It does not matter to me what tools you use, and it should not matter to anyone else, either. What really matters is getting the job done. Whether you use vim or EMACS, systemd or SystemV, RPM or DEB, what difference does it make? The bottom line here is that you should use the tools with which you are most comfortable and that work best for you.

Document Everything

Real programmers don't comment their code, if it was hard to write, it should be hard to understand and harder to modify.

—Unknown

I, too, would want to remain anonymous if I had written that. It might even have been meant to be sarcasm or irony. Regardless, this does seem to be the attitude of many developers and SysAdmins. There is a poorly disguised ethos among some developers and SysAdmins that one must figure everything out for themselves in order to join the club – whatever club that might be. If you cannot figure it out, they imply, you should go do something else because you don't belong.

First, that is not true. Second, most developers, programmers, and SysAdmins that I know definitely do not subscribe to this view. In fact, the best ones, some of whom have been my mentors over the years, exemplify the exact opposite. The best of the best make documentation – good documentation – a high priority in everything they do.

I have used a lot of software whose creators subscribed to the philosophy that all code is self-explanatory. I have also been required to fix a lot of code that was completely uncommented and otherwise undocumented as well. It seems that many developers and SysAdmins figure if the program works for them, it does not need to be documented. I have been the SysAdmin assigned to fix uncommented code on more than one occasion. That is one of the least enjoyable tasks I have ever had to do.

Part of the problem is that many PHBs do not see documentation as a high priority. I have been involved in many aspects of the IT industry, and fortunately most of the companies I worked for believed that documentation was not only important but that it was crucial to the task at hand, regardless of what that task was.

And yet there is a lot of really good documentation out there. For example, the documentation for LibreOffice is excellent. It includes several documents in multiple formats including HTML and PDF that range from "Getting Started" to a very complete user's guide for each of the LibreOffice applications.

The documentation for Red Hat Enterprise Linux (RHEL) and CentOS and that for Fedora – which are all very closely related distributions – are also among the best I have seen in my more than 50 years of working in the IT industry.

Good documentation is not easy and takes time. It also requires an understanding of the audience – not only in relation to the purpose of the documentation but also the technical expertise of the intended readers as well as the languages and cultures of the readers. Rich Bowen covered that quite nicely in his fine article at Opensource.com, "RTFM? How to write a manual worth reading."[22]

There is also the question of what constitutes good documentation for a SysAdmin. We explore these things in this tenet, which is mostly about documenting the scripts we write.

Backup Everything – Frequently

Nothing can ever go wrong with your computer and you will never lose any data. If you believe that, I have a bridge you might like to buy.

I have experienced data loss for a myriad of reasons, many of them my own fault. Keeping decent backups has always enabled me to continue with minimal disruption. This tenet is concerned with some of the more common reasons for data loss and methods for preventing data loss and facilitating easy recovery.

Recently, very recently, I encountered a problem in the form of a hard drive crash that destroyed the data in my home directory. I had been expecting this for some time, and it came as no surprise. The first indication I had that something was wrong was a series of emails from the SMART (Self-Monitoring, Analysis, and Reporting Technology)–enabled hard drive on which my home directory resided.[23] Each of these emails indicated that one or more sectors had become defective and that the defective sectors had been taken off-line and reserved sectors allocated in their place. This is normal operation. Storage devices are designed intentionally with reserved sectors for just this event, and the data is stored in a reserved sector instead of the intended one.

---

[22] Bowen, Rich, Opensource.com, *RTFM? How to write a manual worth reading*, https://opensource.com/business/15/5/write-better-docs

[23] Your host must have a mail transfer agent (MTA) such as Sendmail installed and running. The /etc/aliases file must have an entry to send root's email to your email address.

When the hard drive finally failed – I left it in my computer until it failed as an experiment – I replaced the drive, partitioned and formatted the new one appropriately, copied my files from the backup to the new drive, did a little testing, and was good to go.

Backups save time, effort, and money. Don't be caught without backups. You will need them.

Follow Your Curiosity

People talk about life-long learning and how that keeps one mentally alert and youthful. The same is true of SysAdmins. There is always more to learn, and I think that is what keeps most of us happy and always ready to tackle the next problem. Continuous learning helps keep our minds and skills sharp no matter what age.

I love to learn new things. I was fortunate in that my curiosity led me to a lifetime of working with my favorite toys – computers. There are certainly plenty of new things to learn about computers; the industry and technology are constantly changing. There are many things on Earth and in this universe to be curious about. Computers and related technology just seem to be the thing I enjoy the most.

I also assume that you must be curious because you are reading this book. Curiosity got me into Linux in the first place, but it was a long and winding road. Over a period of many years, my curiosity led me through many life events that led me to a job at IBM, which led to writing the first training course for the original IBM PC, which led to a job at a company where I was able to learn Unix, which led me to Linux because Unix was too expensive to use at home, which led to a job at Red Hat, which... you get the idea. Now I write about Linux.

Follow your own curiosity. You should explore the many aspects of Linux and go wherever your curiosity leads you. It was only by following my curiosity, first about electronics, then computers, programming, operating systems, Linux, servers, networking, and more, that I have been able to do so many fun and interesting things.

There Is No "Should"

This tenet is about possibilities. It is also the most Zen of all the tenets. It is more about how our minds work to solve problems than it is about specific technology. It is also about overcoming or at least recognizing some of the obstacles that prevent us from fully utilizing the potential we have in ourselves.

In *The Wrath of Kahn*, Spock says, "There are always possibilities." With Linux there are always possibilities – many ways to approach and solve problems. This means that you may perform a task in one way while another SysAdmin may do it in another. There is no one way in which tasks "should" be done. There is only the way you have done it. If the results meet the requirements, then the manner in which they were reached is perfection.

I believe that we Linux SysAdmins approach solving Linux problems with fewer constraints on our thinking than those who appear to think more in terms of "harnessing" and "restrictions." We have so many simple yet powerful tools available to us that we do not find ourselves constrained by either the operating system or any inhibitive manner of thinking about the tools we use or the operational methods with which we may apply them.

Rigid logic and rules do not give us SysAdmins enough flexibility to perform our jobs efficiently. We don't especially care about how things "should" be done. SysAdmins are not easily limited by the "should's" that others try to constrain us with. We use logical and critical thinking that is flexible and that produces excellent results and that enables us to learn more while we are at it.

We don't just think outside the box. We are the ones who destroy the boxes that others try to make us work inside. For us, there is no "should."

Mentor the Young SysAdmins

I have taken many training courses over the years, and most have been very useful in helping me learn more about Unix and Linux as well as a host of other subjects. But training – as useful and important as it is – cannot cover many essential aspects of performing SysAdmin duties. Some things can only be taught by a good mentor in a real-world environment, usually while you are under extreme pressure to fix a critical problem. A good mentor will allow you to do the actual work in these situations so you can have a valuable learning experience while keeping the wolves at bay, taking the heat while you work uninterrupted. A great mentor will also be able to create a learning opportunity from every situation no matter how critical.

This tenet is also about teaching the young SysAdmins critical thinking and application of the scientific method to the art of solving problems. It is about passing on what you have received.

Support Your Favorite Open Source Project

Linux and a very large proportion of the programs that we run on it are open source programs. Many of the larger projects, such as the kernel itself, are supported directly by foundations set up for that purpose, such as the Linux Foundation, and/or by corporations and other organizations that have an interest in doing so.

As a SysAdmin I write a lot of scripts and I like doing so, but I am not an application programmer. Nor do I want to be because I enjoy the work of a SysAdmin, which allows for a different kind of programming. So, for the most part, contributing code to an open source project is not a good option for me. There are other ways to contribute, such as answering questions on lists or websites, submitting bug reports, writing documentation, writing articles for websites like Opensource.com, teaching, and contributing money. And I use some of those options. This tenet is about exploring some of the ways in which you might contribute. As in mentoring, this is an excellent way to give back to the community.

Reality Bytes

The Linux Philosophy for SysAdmins is a technical philosophy that would not normally be considered to be very practical. But there is "truth" here. Reality imposes itself upon SysAdmins every day in a multitude of ways. It is possible always to be able to follow each of the tenets – but it is quite improbable. In the "real" world, we SysAdmins face some incredible challenges just to get our assigned work completed. Deadlines, management, and other pressures force us to make decisions many times a day about what to do next and how to do it. Meetings usually waste our time – not always but usually. Finding time and money for training is unheard of in many organizations and requires selling your SysAdmin soul in others.

Adhering to the philosophy does pay high-value returns in the long run. Still, reality always intrudes on the ever so perfect philosophical realm. Without room for flexibility, any philosophy is merely doctrine, and that is not what the Linux Philosophy for system administrators is about. This tenet explores how reality may affect us as system administrators.

Computers are easy – people are hard.

—Bridget Kromhout

SysAdmins must work and interact with people. It can be difficult, but we do need to do so from time to time. We SysAdmins must interact with other people whether they be users, technical professionals on other teams, our peers, or management. We need to discuss our work with other people who have differing levels of knowledge. Knowledge is not a binary condition; it is analog. People have a wide disparity in the amount of knowledge that they have about computers and technology. This ranges from seemingly less than none to very knowledgeable. Their level of knowledge is important in how we interact with them.

I have been accused of overexplaining things, but I would rather overexplain than under-explain. Some have even called it "mansplaining," but that is not really my intent. I have found that all technical people, regardless of gender, gender preference or identification, or other identifying characteristics, all have the same tendency to explain things from the ground up when asked a simple question. That is because the answers are never as simple as the questions.

Chapter Summary

This chapter is a brief overview of the Linux Philosophy for SysAdmins. The philosophy is my mental framework for how I work as a SysAdmin. It has been a useful tool for me, and as we proceed through this course, I will point out and explain why and how these tenets apply to certain situations or tasks. Working in accordance with the tenets of the philosophy will enhance our productivity and efficiency as we perform our work.

Exercises

Perform the following exercises to complete this chapter:

1. Why do *you* think that the Linux Philosophy for SysAdmins is important?

2. In your opinion, what is the most important of these tenets? Why?

3. Do any of the tenets discussed in this chapter suggest doing things differently for you?

CHAPTER 4

Preparation

Objectives

In this chapter you will

- Choose a computer host on which to install VirtualBox and a virtual machine (VM) on which you can perform the experiments.

- Install VirtualBox on the hardware you chose.

- Create a small VM with which to safely perform experiments.

- Configure the virtual network adapter as needed for this course.

Overview

There are some tasks that need to be accomplished in order to prepare for the experiments in this Linux training course. Most lab environments use physical machines for training purposes, but this course will ultimately use at least two Linux hosts in a private network in order to enable a realistic environment for learning about being a SysAdmin. It is also helpful for these hosts to be left untouched during the times between one course and the next or in case of long breaks while in the middle of any of the courses. So a normal classroom environment is not optimal for learning Linux.

Also, most people who want to learn Linux do not usually have that many physical hosts and a private network available. Even if you work for a company that supports your training with money – a very big consideration for many people – and the time to take classes, usually an even more scarce commodity, I have never seen a company or public training center that can dedicate multiple computers to a single student during a class and keep them untouched between classes, which may be scheduled months apart.

75

© David Both 2023
D. Both, *Using and Administering Linux: Volume 1*, https://doi.org/10.1007/978-1-4842-9618-9_4

Because of these factors, this series of three volumes that make up our training manual – which is what this is – uses virtual machines (VMs) in a virtual network that can be installed on a modest system with a set of specifications to which nearly everyone should have access. Thus, the VMs can be used for this volume and saved for use in the next two volumes. Of course they can always be restored from snapshots, which we will take at one or two checkpoints, or even recreated from scratch if necessary. This is one advantage of VMs over physical hosts because it is easy to recover from really bad mistakes.

Hopefully the use of multiple VMs to create a virtual network on a single physical host will provide a safe virtual computing and network environment in which to learn by making mistakes.

In this chapter you begin to do the work of the SysAdmin. One of the many tasks that SysAdmins do is install Linux, and that is what you will do in the next chapter – in this chapter, we install VirtualBox visualization software. I will try to explain as much as I can as we go through this chapter, but there are probably some things you won't yet understand. Don't worry – we will get to them.

You will also begin to use some Linux commands, most of which you may not yet know or understand. For now I will explain a little about some of the commands that we will encounter, but so long as you enter them as they are given in the experiments, you should have no problems. In many cases, if you make an error when typing the command, the system will respond with an error message that should help you understand what is wrong.

Got Root?

Root is the primary user account on a Linux system. Root is the god of Linux, the administrator, the superuser, the SysAdmin, the privileged user. Root can do anything. There is an entire chapter a bit later in this book about root and the powers available to root that go far beyond those of mere mortals and non-privileged users.

This course is intended to enable you to safely use those root privileges, but we are not going to start by having you merely dip your toes into the water and wade in deeper a little bit at a time. I was always told to just dive into the water and get wet all over. That is what we do in this chapter – dive right in. So I hereby declare that you are now root. Much of what we do from this point on will be performed as root, and you are the SysAdmin.

Hardware Specifications

In order to perform the experiments contained in this course, you must have access to a single physical computer that can run a single virtual machine for this volume and at least two virtual machines for the next volume in this series. These hardware specifications are intended to provide you with some guidance for selecting a computer for use with this course and the second course in this series as well.

Because the VMs will not be running large complex programs, the load on them in terms of CPU and RAM will be relatively low. Disk usage may be somewhat high because virtual disks for the VMs may take up a significant amount of disk space after some of the experiments, and you will also make occasional snapshots of the virtual disk in order to make recovery from otherwise catastrophic failures relatively simple. This course uses a single VM, but the hardware specifications listed here for the host machine should be enough to handle at least three virtual machines because at least two and possibly three will be required for the next course. You should nevertheless consider these hardware specifications as a *minimum* for use during this course. More is always better.

The motherboard, processor, and memory should be 64-bit. Many of the 32-bit versions of Linux are no longer supported, and there are few 32-bit computers left in any event. Table 4-1 is a list of the minimum physical hardware requirements for this course. More is always better.

Table 4-1. *Physical system minimum hardware requirements*

Component	Description
Processor	The Intel i5 or i7 processors or an AMD equivalent; at least four cores plus hyperthreading with support for virtualization; 2.5GHz or higher CPU speed.
Motherboard	Capable of supporting the Intel processor you selected previously; USB support for a keyboard and mouse; video output that matches the video connector your display (see the following) such as VGA, HDMI, or DVI.
Memory	I recommend at least 16GB of RAM for your host system. This will allow sufficient memory for multiple VMs and still have enough available for the host itself. As little as 8GB will work although somewhat slowly.
Hard drive	Internal or external hard drive with at least 300GB of free space for storage of virtual machine disk drives.
Network	One Ethernet network interface card (NIC) that has support for 1GB connections.
USB keyboard and mouse	Seems obvious but just being thorough.
Video display	Any decent flat-screen monitor will do so long as it is at least HD resolution.
Internet connection	The physical host should have an Internet connection with at least 200Mb/s download speeds. Greater download speed is highly recommended and will make downloading faster and result in less waiting.

Host Software Requirements

In all probability the computer you use will already have an operating system installed and it will most likely be Windows. Preferably you will have the latest version, which, as of this writing, is Windows 11 with all updates installed.

The preferred operating system for your physical lab host would be Fedora 37 or the most recent version of Fedora that is currently available. I strongly recommend using the most recent version of Fedora because that is what I am using in these books and you won't need to make any adjustments for other distributions in this chapter. You will be using Fedora on the virtual machines anyway, so this makes the most sense.

Regardless of which operating system is installed as the host OS on your lab system, you should use VirtualBox as the virtualization platform for these experiments because it is open source and free of charge. All of the procedures for creating the VMs and the virtual network are based on VirtualBox, so I strongly suggest that you use it for virtualizing your lab environment. Other virtualization tools would probably work, but it would be your own responsibility to install and configure them and the VMs you create.

No other software is required for the physical system that will host the virtual environment.

Installing VirtualBox

The VirtualBox virtualization software can be downloaded from web pages accessible from the URL `www.virtualbox.org/wiki/Downloads`.

Note   You must have root access, that is, the root password, on a Linux host or be the administrator on a Windows host in order to install VirtualBox. You will also need to have a non-root user account on the Linux host.

If your host computer runs Linux, install VirtualBox as described in the next section. When finished go directly to the section "Creating the VM."

If your host computer runs Windows, skip the next section and go to the section "Install VirtualBox on a Windows Host."

Install VirtualBox on a Linux Host

This section covers the steps required to install VirtualBox on a Fedora Linux host. If you have a Windows host, you can skip to the next section.

For this book we will download the files from the VirtualBox website. If you are using a different Linux distribution, the steps will be mostly the same, but you should use the VirtualBox package and the package manager commands for your own distribution.

In the following steps, the # character is the command prompt for root. Do not enter it. It is displayed on the console or terminal screen to indicate that the command line is waiting for input. You will type the commands that are shown in boldface type in the following instructions. After typing each command and ensuring that it is correct, then press the **Enter** key to submit the command to the shell for processing.

Don't worry if you don't yet understand what these commands are doing. If you enter them just as they are, they will all work just fine. You are doing tasks that are typical of those you will be doing as a SysAdmin, so you might as well jump right in. However, if you do not feel that you can safely do this, you should have the SysAdmin who has responsibility for this host do it for you.

Your entries are shown in **bold**. Press the Enter key when you see **\<Enter\>** if there is no data to enter such as when you might take a default that requires no keyboard input.

Note   Although VirtualBox 6.0.6 is shown in many of the graphics and commands in this section, Version 7.0.2 is current as of January 2023. The version available when you read this will also likely be more recent than either of those.

Warning   When trying to install VirtualBox on a Linux host, you may encounter the following error:

```
nothing provided python (abi) = 3.8 needed by virtualBox-
6.1-6.1.18_142142_fedora32-1.x86_64.
```

This is a relatively new problem and can occur when some older Python libraries don't get updated and get out of step with VirtualBox requirements. I have started using the "All distributions" (AMD) version of VirtualBox, which is at the bottom of the Linux distributions list of the VirtualBox Linux download page. This version seems to work well and has resolved the error shown.

I have not experimented with installing VirtualBox on a Windows host since this book was originally written, so I do not know if the same error will occur.

---

1. Log into your Linux host GUI desktop as a non-root user. In the example in Figure 4-1, I use the student user ID. You may need your SysAdmin to create an account for you and set the password.

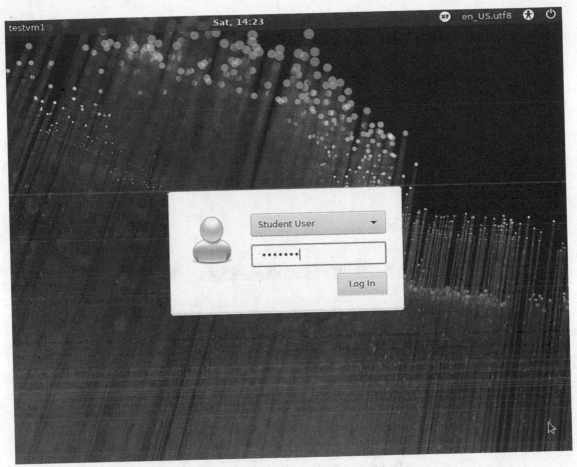

Figure 4-1. *Select a non-root user account and type the password for that account*

Note   The login GUI may look a little different on the release of Fedora you are using, but it will have the same elements that will enable you to select a user account and enter the password.

---

2. After the GUI desktop has finished loading, open your favorite web browser.

3. Enter the following URL to display the Linux download page: www.virtualbox.org/wiki/Linux_Downloads. If this download page does not appear, you can go to the VirtualBox homepage and click through to the download section.

4. Download the most recent VirtualBox package suitable for your Linux distribution into the /Downloads directory. As of my writing of this second edition, VirtualBox-6.1-6.1.38_153438_fedora36-1. x86_64.rpm is current for Fedora. Be sure to use the most recent Fedora version of VirtualBox as in Figure 4-2.

The AMD version is the 64-bit version of VirtualBox and can be used for both AMD and Intel processors. I only use the AMD version when a Fedora-specific version is not available or has a problem.

Do not use the i386 version.

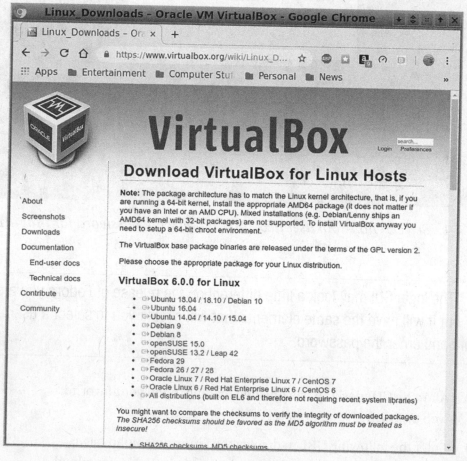

Figure 4-2. *Download the most recent VirtualBox package appropriate to your distribution. The VirtualBox version will probably be more recent than the one shown here*

5. When the **Save file** dialog pops up, be sure to verify the directory location to which your browser saves the file. This might be ~/Downloads for browsers like Chrome, and other browsers may ask you to specify the location. If you have a choice, use ~/Downloads.

6. Click the **Save** button.

7. Click the Downloads link on the left of the web page.

8. Under the section " ... **Oracle VM VirtualBox Extension Pack**," select the **All supported platforms** link to download the Extension Pack.

9. When the Save file dialog pops up, be sure to select ~/Downloads as the destination directory.

10. Click the **Save** button.

11. Now that both files we will need have been downloaded, we can install VirtualBox.

12. Launch a terminal session on the desktop and use the su command to switch to the root user:

```
[student@myworkstation ~]$ su -
Password: <Enter the password for root>
[root@myworkstation ~]#
```

13. Make ~/Downloads the present working directory (PWD) and verify the files just downloaded are located there:

```
[root@myworkstation ~]# cd /home/student/Downloads/ ; ls *Virt*
Oracle_VM_VirtualBox_Extension_Pack-6.1.38.vbox-extpack
VirtualBox-6.1-6.1.38_153438_fedora36-1.x86_64.rpm
```

14. We need to install all the current updates and some RPMs that are needed for VirtualBox to work. They may be already installed on your Fedora computer, but attempting to install them again will not cause a problem. The dnf command is the package manager for Fedora Linux and can be used to install, remove, and update packages:

```
[root@myworkstation Downloads]# dnf -y update
```

15. Reboot the physical computer after installing the latest updates.
    It is not always necessary to reboot after installing updates on a
    Linux computer unless the kernel has been updated. I suggest
    do it here in case the kernel has been updated. It is important
    for the next steps that the kernel be the most recent one, or the
    installation of VirtualBox may not properly complete.

16. As the root user, install some required utilities:

```
[root@myworkstation Downloads]# dnf -y install elfutils-libelf-devel
kernel-devel
```

> I did not include any of the output from these commands in order
> to save some space.

17. As the root user, make /home/student/Downloads the PWD:

```
[root@myworkstation ~]# cd /home/student/Downloads/
```

18. Now install the VirtualBox RPM with the following dnf command.
    Note that the command needs to be entered on a single line. It
    can wrap on your screen if there are not enough columns in your
    terminal, but just don't press the **Enter** key until you have entered
    the entire command. Be sure to use the correct name for your
    VirtualBox installation file, which probably will be different from
    this one:

```
[root@myworkstation Downloads]# dnf -y install VirtualBox-6.0-6.0.0_127566_fedora29-
1.x86_64.rpm
Last metadata expiration check: 0:04:17 ago on Tue 18 Dec 2018 04:40:44 PM EST.
```

Dependencies resolved.

```
=================================================================
 Package      Arch     Version                   Repository    Size
=================================================================
Installing:
 VirtualBox-6.0  x86_64   6.0.0_127566_fedora29-1   @commandline  130 M
Installing dependencies:
 SDL          x86_64   1.2.15-33.fc29            fedora        202 k

Transaction Summary
=================================================================
Install  2 Packages

Total size: 130 M
Total download size: 202 k
Installed size: 258 M
Downloading Packages:
SDL-1.2.15-33.fc29.x86_64.rpm             112 kB/s | 202 kB   00:01
-----------------------------------------------------------------
Total                                      58 kB/s | 202 kB   00:03
Running transaction check
Transaction check succeeded.
Running transaction test
Transaction test succeeded.
Running transaction
  Preparing        :                                            1/1
  Installing       : SDL-1.2.15-33.fc29.x86_64                  1/2
  Running scriptlet : VirtualBox-6.0-6.0.0_127566_fedora29-1.x86_64   2/2
  Installing       : VirtualBox-6.0-6.0.0_127566_fedora29-1.x86_64   2/2
  Running scriptlet : VirtualBox-6.0-6.0.0_127566_fedora29-1.x86_64   2/2

Creating group 'vboxusers'. VM users must be member of that group!

  Verifying        : SDL-1.2.15-33.fc29.x86_64                  1/2
  Verifying        : VirtualBox-6.0-6.0.0_127566_fedora29-1.x86_64   2/2
```

```
Installed:
  VirtualBox-6.0-6.0.0_127566_fedora29-1.x86_64        SDL-1.2.15-33.fc29.x86_64
Complete!
```

19. We now install the Extension Pack, which provides some additional functionality for the guest operating systems. Note that the command needs to be entered on a single line. It can wrap on your screen if there are not enough columns in your terminal, but just don't press the **Enter** key until you have entered the entire command:

```
[root@myworkstation Downloads]# VBoxManage extpack install
Oracle_VM_VirtualBox_Extension_Pack-6.0.0.vbox-extpack
VirtualBox Extension Pack Personal Use and Evaluation License (PUEL)
<Snip the long license>
```

20. Press the Y key when asked to accept the license:

```
Do you agree to these license terms and conditions (y/n)? y

License accepted. For batch installation add
--accept-license=56be48f923303c8cababb0bb4c478284b688ed23f16d775d729b89a2e8e5f9eb
to the VBoxManage command line.

0%...10%...20%...30%...40%...50%...60%...70%...80%...90%...100%
Successfully installed "Oracle VM VirtualBox Extension Pack".
[root@myworkstation Downloads]#
```

Do not close the root terminal session. It will be used to prepare an external USB hard drive on which we will store the virtual storage devices and other files required for the virtual machines that we will create.

If your host computer runs Linux, skip the next section and go directly to the section "Creating the VM."

Install VirtualBox on a Windows Host

This section covers the steps required to install VirtualBox on a current host with a currently supported version of Windows. This procedure downloads the VirtualBox installer and then installs VirtualBox and the VirtualBox Extension Pack. If you have never worked as the administrator before, just follow the directions as given, and everything should work. However, if you do not feel that you can safely do this, you should have the SysAdmin who has responsibility for this host do this for you.

1. Log into your Windows host as an administrative user.

2. Install all current updates.

3. Open your browser.

4. Enter the following URL in the browser: www.virtualbox.org.

5. Click the big large "Download VirtualBox" button in the middle of the screen to continue to the download page.

6. Locate the section heading **VirtualBox X.X.X platform packages** where X.X.X is the most current version of VirtualBox.

7. Locate the **Windows hosts** link and click that.

8. When the **Save As** window opens, as in Figure 4-3, ensure that the download target is the Downloads directory, which should be the default.

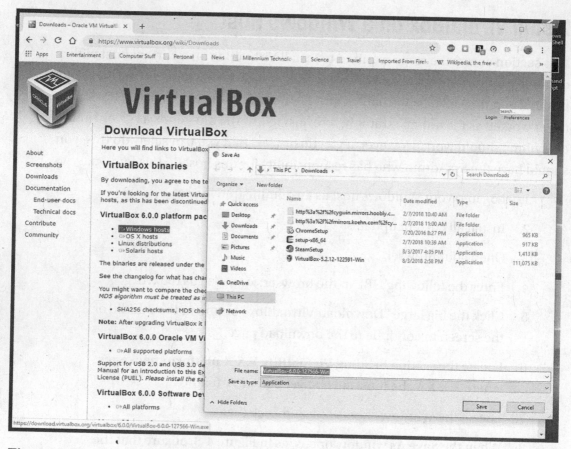

Figure 4-3. *The **Save As** window. Be sure to download the VirtualBox installer for Windows into the Downloads directory*

9. Click the **Save** button.

10. When the file has finished downloading, open the **File Explorer** and click **Downloads**.

11. Locate the VirtualBox installer and double-click to launch it.

12. When the setup wizard welcome dialog shown in Figure 4-4 appears, click the **Next** button. This will take you to the Custom Setup dialog. Once again, the version of VirtualBox will be more recent than the one in Figure 4-4, but it will otherwise look and work the same.

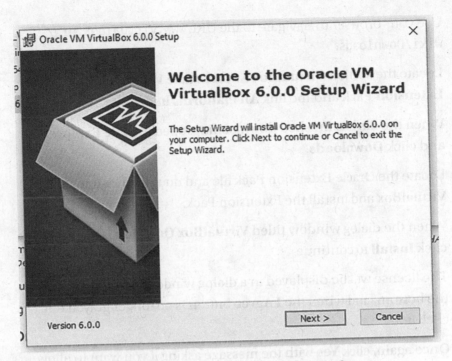

Figure 4-4. *The Oracle VirtualBox setup wizard for Windows*

13. Do *not* make any changes to the **Custom Setup** dialog and click **Next** to continue.

14. Again, do *not* make any changes to the second **Custom Setup** dialog and click **Next** to continue.

15. If a dialog appears with a warning about resetting the network interfaces, just click **Yes** to continue.

16. When the **Ready to install** window is displayed, click **Install**.

17. You will see a dialog asking whether you want to allow this app to make changes to your device. Click **Yes** to continue.

18. When the completion dialog is displayed, remove the check from the box to start VirtualBox after the installation.

19. Click the **Finish** button to complete the basic installation. You should now have a shortcut on your desktop to launch VirtualBox. However, we still need to install the "Extension Pack," which helps integrate VMs more closely into the Windows desktop.

20. Use your browser to navigate to the URL `www.virtualbox.org/wiki/Downloads`.

21. Locate the section **VirtualBox X.X.X Oracle VM VirtualBox Extension Pack** and the link **All Platforms** under that.

22. When the file has finished downloading, open the **File Explorer** and click **Downloads**.

23. Locate the Oracle Extension Pack file and double-click it to launch VirtualBox and install the Extension Pack.

24. When the dialog window titled **VirtualBox Question** is displayed, click **Install** to continue.

25. The license will be displayed in a dialog window. Scroll down to the bottom, and when the **I Agree** button is no longer grayed out, click it.

26. Once again, click **Yes** with the message asking if you want to allow this app to make changes. You will receive a verification dialog window when the Extension Pack software has been installed.

27. Click **OK** to close that dialog, and this leaves the VirtualBox Manager welcome window displayed on the screen.

28. From this point on, using the VirtualBox Manager GUI is the same whether you are running Windows or Linux.

Creating the VM

Resume with this section regardless of whether the host computer is running Windows or Linux.

Before setting up the VM itself, we want to create a virtual network that has a specific configuration. This will enable the experiments in this course to work as designed, and it will provide the basis for the virtual network in the next course. After the virtual network has been configured, we will create the virtual machine and configure it properly for use in the experiments. This VM will also be used in the follow-on course.

VirtualBox Manager

Both tasks, configuring the virtual network and creating the VM, are accomplished using the VirtualBox Manager, which is a GUI that is used to create and manage VMs.

Start by locating the Oracle VM VirtualBox item in the application launcher on your desktop. The icon should look similar to Figure 4-5.

Figure 4-5. *The VirtualBox icon*

Click this icon to launch the VirtualBox Manager. The first time the VirtualBox Manager is launched, it displays the VirtualBox welcome shown in Figure 4-6.

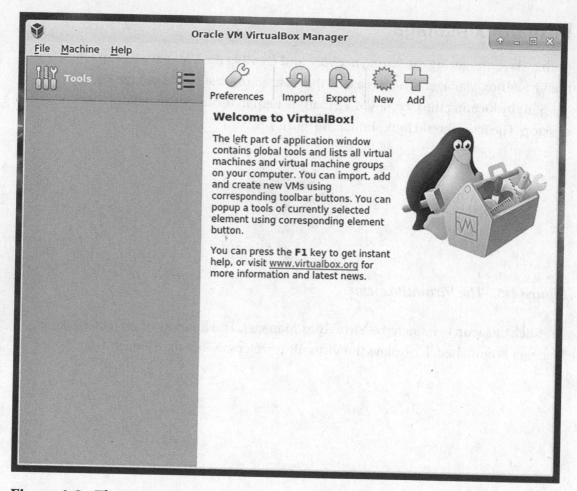

Figure 4-6. *The VirtualBox Manager welcome is displayed the first time it is launched*

The VirtualBox Manager is identical in both Windows and Linux. The steps required to create your VMs are the same. Although VirtualBox can be managed from the command line, I find that, for me, working with the GUI is quick and easy. Although I am a strong proponent of using the command line, I find that using the VirtualBox Manager GUI is easy and quick enough for the type of work I am doing. Besides, for the purposes of this book, it will probably be easier for you. Using the GUI will certainly enable you to more easily find and understand the available options.

Configuring the Virtual Network

Before creating the virtual machine, we need to configure the virtual network. The virtual network is a private network that exists only on the VirtualBox host. It is designed to allow the user to manage access to the outside world. The virtual router that is created also provides services such as DHCP and name services for the VMs that are created on the virtual network.

VirtualBox has a number of interesting options for connecting the VM hosts to a network. The Oracle VM VirtualBox User Manual[1] lists these options with excellent descriptions of the capabilities of each as well as their limitations.

The simplest is the default, which is using Network Address Translation[2] (NAT), which allows the VM to talk to the Internet but which does not allow multiple VM hosts to talk to each other. Because we will need our VM to be able to communicate with at least one more host in the next volume of this course, this option won't be appropriate for us. We will instead use the NAT Network option, which allows hosts to communicate with each other on the virtual network as well as the outside world through a virtual router. The limitation of the NAT Network option is that it does not allow communication from the physical host into the virtual network. That limitation can be overcome if necessary, but the NAT Network option gives us the virtual network environment that most closely resembles most real networks, so that is what we will use for this course.

We will discuss networking in more detail later in this course, but for now, the folks at whatismyipaddress.com, referenced in footnote 2, have the best short description of NAT, while Wikipedia[3] has an excellent, if somewhat long and esoteric, discussion of NAT. We will use the VirtualBox Manager to create and configure the virtual NAT Network.

Tip   Be sure you are using the most recent version of VirtualBox, which is 7.0.x as of this second edition.

---

[1] The Oracle VM VirtualBox User Manual (PDF), `https://download.virtualbox.org/virtualbox/UserManual.pdf`, 128–140

[2] `https://whatismyipaddress.com/nat`

[3] Wikipedia, *Network Address Translation*, `https://en.wikipedia.org/wiki/Network_address_translation`

1. The VirtualBox Manager should be open. If it is not, start the VirtualBox Manager now.

2. In the VirtualBox Manager shown in Figure 4-6, click the **Tools** list icon to open the tools window. This has changed from earlier versions of VirtualBox.

3. Click the Network folder on the right side of the pop-up menu and select **Network** as shown in Figure 4-7.

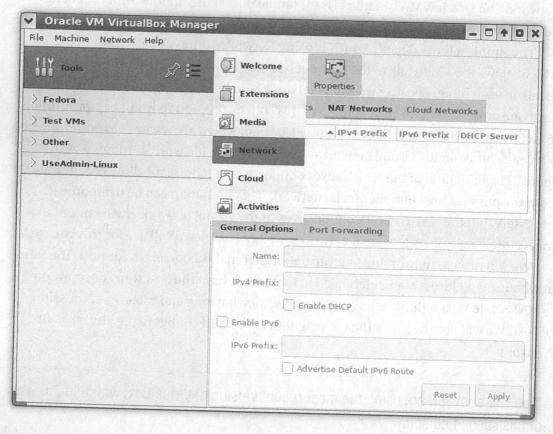

Figure 4-7. *Select the Network folder to add a NAT Network*

4. Be sure the **NAT Networks** tab is selected. Then click the **Create** icon to add a new NAT Network. The network is added and configured automatically.

5. In the General Options of the network dialog box, change the network name to StudentNetwork as in Figure 4-8.

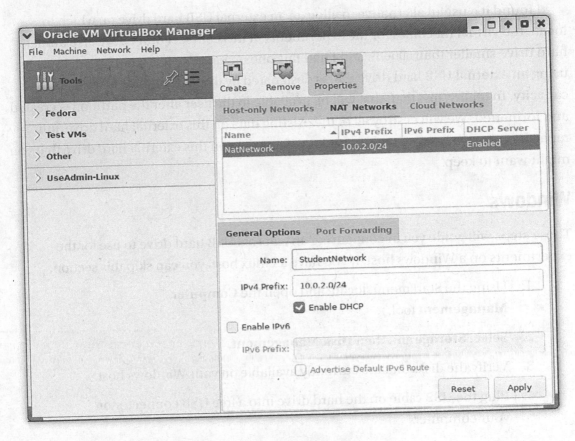

Figure 4-8. *Change the network name to StudentNetwork*

6. Do not change anything else on this dialog.

7. Click the *Apply* button to complete the name change.

The virtual network configuration is complete.

Preparing Disk Space

In order to have space for the virtual machines that we will be using in this course, it may be necessary to clear some space on a hard drive. You should make backups of your system before taking this step. If you have a host with about 300GB of free hard drive space already available for your home directory, you can skip this section. If you have less than that amount of space available, you will need to allocate some disk space for storing the virtual storage devices and other files required for the virtual machines.

I found it a useful alternative to allocate an external USB hard drive on which to locate the virtual machines for the experiments in this course. I don't have an external hard drive smaller than 500GB, and I had this one on hand, so it is what I used. I suggest using an external USB hard drive that is designated by the vendor to be at least 300GB capacity. In reality, less than that will be available to the user after the partition is created and formatted. We will destroy all of the existing data on this external hard drive and repartition it, so be sure to make a backup of any data on this external hard drive that you might want to keep.

Windows

These steps will guide you in configuring an external USB hard drive to use for the experiments on a Windows host. If you have a Linux host, you can skip this section.

1. Using the Start menu, locate and open the **Computer Management** tool.

2. Select **Storage** and then **Disk Management**.

3. Verify the disks that are currently available on your Windows host.

4. Plug the USB cable on the hard drive into a free USB connector on your computer.

5. After a moment or two, the disk management tool will display the new disk drive, as shown in Figure 4-9. On my Windows VM, this new disk is Disk 1, and the space is shown as unallocated because I previously deleted the existing partition. This may be a different disk for you.

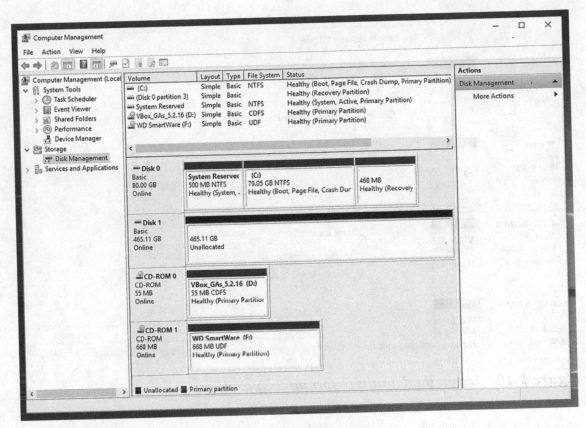

Figure 4-9. *Disk 1 is the new external USB hard drive*

6. Right-click Disk 1 and choose **New Simple Volume** to begin preparing the drive. The New Simple Volume Wizard welcome dialog is displayed.

7. Click **Next** to continue.

8. Do not make any changes to the Specify Volume Size dialog. This will assign the entire physical drive to this partition. Click **Next** to continue.

9. Accept the suggested drive letter on the Assign Drive Letter or Path dialog. On my Windows VM, this is E:. This drive assignment will most likely be different on your host. Be sure to make a note of this drive letter because you will need it soon. Click the **Next** button to continue.

10. Take the defaults on the Format Partition dialog as you can see in Figure 4-10. Click **Next** to continue.

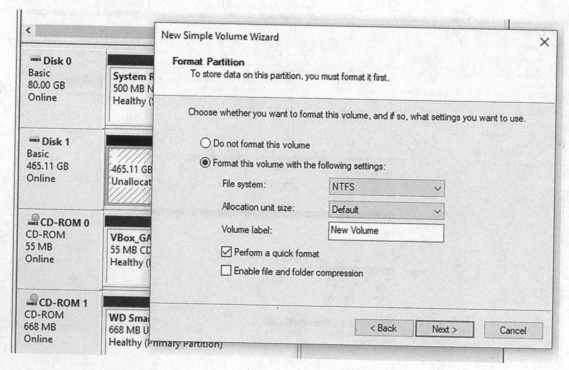

Figure 4-10. *Accept the defaults to format the partition*

11. Click the Finish button on the Completing the New Simple
    Volume Wizard dialog to start the format process. Figure 4-11
    shows the final result.

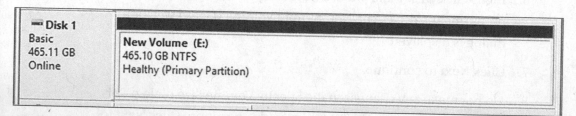

Figure 4-11. *The completed disk partition*

Note that the final formatted disk provides less than the 500GB specified by the
drive vendor. This is normal and is due to the reserve of spare sectors to be used in case
regular data sectors grow defects and the overhead incurred by the filesystem metadata.

Linux

Skip this section if your host computer is running Windows.

This section will guide you through adding an external USB hard drive to your Linux host. This hard drive will be the storage location for the virtual hard drive and other files required for the virtual machines used for the experiments in the rest of this course.

There is a GUI desktop tool for Linux that works very similarly to the disk management tool for Windows. Just so you see we could do that, I have included a screenshot of the disk tool in Figure 4-12.

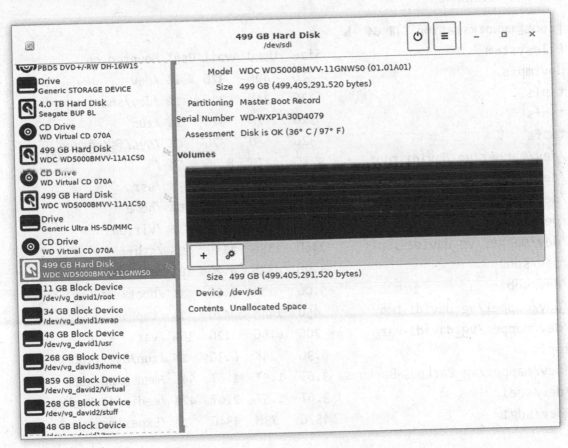

Figure 4-12. *The Linux GUI disk management tools provide functionality similar to that of the Windows Disk Manager tools. We are not going to use them*

We are not going to use this gnome-disks GUI tool shown in Figure 4-12. Instead we are going to use the command-line interface (CLI) because there is no time like the present to start learning the command-line tools. This is so that you will become familiar with the tools themselves as well as some of the other concepts such as device identification. We will go into great detail about many of the things you will encounter here as we proceed through the course.

Your entries are shown in **bold**. Press the Enter key when you see **<Enter>**. You must be root to perform all of the following tasks.

1. You should already have a terminal open and be logged in as root. Run the following command, like I did on my physical workstation, to determine whether you have enough space available:

```
[root@myworkstation /]# df -h
Filesystem                       Size  Used  Avail Use% Mounted on
devtmpfs                         32G   40K   32G   1%  /dev
tmpfs                            32G   24M   32G   1%  /dev/shm
tmpfs                            32G   2.2M  32G   1%  /run
tmpfs                            32G   0     32G   0%  /sys/fs/cgroup
/dev/mapper/vg_david1-root       9.8G  437M  8.9G  5%  /
/dev/mapper/vg_david1-usr        45G   9.6G  33G   23% /usr
/dev/mapper/vg_david3-home       246G  46G   190G  20% /home
/dev/mapper/vg_david2-Virtual    787G  425G  323G  57% /Virtual
/dev/mapper/vg_david2-stuff      246G  115G  119G  50% /stuff
/dev/sdb2                        4.9G  433M  4.2G  10% /boot
/dev/sdb1                        5.0G  18M   5.0G  1%  /boot/efi
/dev/mapper/vg_david1-tmp        45G   144M  42G   1%  /tmp
/dev/mapper/vg_david1-var        20G   6.6G  12G   36% /var
tmpfs                            6.3G  24K   6.3G  1%  /run/user/1000
/dev/mapper/vg_Backups-Backups   3.6T  1.9T  1.6T  54% /media/Backups
/dev/sde1                        3.6T  1.5T  2.0T  42% /media/4T-Backup
/dev/sdg1                        457G  73M   434G  1%  /Experiments
```

This is the output of the df command on my workstation. It shows the space available on each disk volume of my workstation. The output from this command on your physical host will be different from this. I have a couple places that conform to the LFHS[4] on which I could locate the virtual machines' data on my filesystems, but I choose to use the /Experiments filesystem and directory rather than mix this data in with other data, even that of my other virtual machines. You will now configure your external USB hard drive like I did /Experiments.

2. Plug in the external USB hard drive. It will take a few moments for it to spin up and be initialized at the hardware level.

3. Run the following command to determine the drive ID assigned to the new device:

```
[root@myworkstation /]# dmesg
<SNIP>
[72781.328503] usb 1-14.3: new high-speed USB device number 11 using xhci_hcd
[72781.419360] usb 1-14.3: New USB device found, idVendor=1058, idProduct=070a, bcdDevice=10.32
[72781.419372] usb 1-14.3: New USB device strings: Mfr=1, Product=2, SerialNumber=3
[72781.419375] usb 1-14.3: Product: My Passport 070A
[72781.419378] usb 1-14.3: Manufacturer: Western Digital
[72781.419381] usb 1-14.3: SerialNumber: 575838314132305832363135
[72781.421007] usb-storage 1-14.3:1.0: USB Mass Storage device detected
[72781.422540] usb-storage 1-14.3:1.0: Quirks match for vid 1058 pid 070a: 200000
[72781.423506] scsi host9: usb-storage 1-14.3:1.0
[72782.432258] scsi 9:0:0:0: Direct-Access  WD    My Passport 070A 1032 PQ: 0 ANSI: 4
[72782.432897] scsi 9:0:0:1: CD-ROM         WD    Virtual CD 070A  1032 PQ: 0 ANSI: 4
[72782.439756] scsi 9:0:0:2: Enclosure      WD    SES Device       1032 PQ: 0 ANSI: 4
[72782.446248] sd 9:0:0:0: Attached scsi generic sg9 type 0
[72782.446537] sd 9:0:0:0: [sdg] 975400960 512-byte logical blocks: (499 GB/465 GiB)
[72782.448186] sr 9:0:0:1: [sr2] scsi3-mmc drive: 51x/51x caddy
```

---

[4] We will discuss the Linux Hierarchical Filesystem Standard (LHFS) in Chapter 19. The LHFS defines the approved directory structure of the Linux filesystem and provides direction on what types of files are to be located in which directories.

101

```
[72782.449626] sd 9:0:0:0: [sdg] Write Protect is off
[72782.449631] sd 9:0:0:0: [sdg] Mode Sense: 23 00 10 00
[72782.453926] sr 9:0:0:1: Attached scsi CD-ROM sr2
[72782.454026] sr 9:0:0:1: Attached scsi generic sg10 type 5
[72782.454278] ses 9:0:0:2: Attached Enclosure device
[72782.454365] ses 9:0:0:2: Attached scsi generic sg11 type 13
[72782.454760] sd 9:0:0:0: [sdg] No Caching mode page found
[72782.454765] sd 9:0:0:0: [sdg] Assuming drive cache: write back
[72782.472017] sd 9:0:0:0: [sdg] Attached SCSI disk
```

The data from the preceding **dmesg** command is displayed at the end of a long list of kernel messages. The **dmesg** command is used to display the kernel messages because they can be used in situations like this, as well as providing information that can be used in debugging problems. The numbers inside the square brackets, such as [72782.472017], are the time in seconds down to the nanosecond since the computer was booted up.

You could also use the **lsblk** command, which generates a list of block devices.[5] All HDD, SSD, and USB storage devices are block devices:

```
[root@david ~]# lsblk
NAME                 MAJ:MIN  RM     SIZE RO  TYPE MOUNTPOINTS
sda                      8:0   0   931.5G  0  disk
└─vg03-Virtual         253:7   0   931.5G  0  lvm  /Virtual
sdb                     8:16   0     2.7T  0  disk
└─sdb1                  8:17   0     2.7T  0  part
  ├─vg04-stuff         253:8   0     250G  0  lvm  /stuff
  └─vg04-VMArchives    253:9   0     800G  0  lvm  /VMArchives
sdc                     8:32   0     3.6T  0  disk
└─sdc1                  8:33   0     3.6T  0  part
  └─vg_Backups-Backups 253:10  0     3.6T  0  lvm  /media/Backups
```

---

[5] A block device is one that transfers data in blocks of 512 bytes or some even multiple of that.

sdd	8:48	0	3.6T	0	disk	
└─sdd1	8:49	0	3.6T	0	part	/media/EXT-Backup
sde	8:64	1	0B	0	disk	
sdf	8:80	0	465.1G	0	disk	
└─sdf1	8:81	0	465.1G	0	part	/run/media/dboth/USB-X47GF
sdg	8:96	0	465.1G	0	disk	
└─sdg1	8:81	0	465.1G	0	part	
sr0	11:0	1	1024M	0	rom	
sr1	11:1	1	668M	0	rom	
sr2	11:2	1	668M	0	rom	
zram0	252:0	0	8G	0	disk	[SWAP]
nvme1n1	259:0	0	476.9G	0	disk	
└─vg02-home	253:3	0	250G	0	lvm	/home
nvme0n1	259:1	0	476.9G	0	disk	
├─nvme0n1p1	259:2	0	5G	0	part	/boot/efi
├─nvme0n1p2	259:3	0	5G	0	part	/boot
└─nvme0n1p3	259:4	0	466.9G	0	part	
vg01-root	253:0	0	10G	0	lvm	/
├─vg01-swap	253:1	0	10G	0	lvm	
├─vg01-usr	253:2	0	50G	0	lvm	/usr
├─vg01-var	253:4	0	50G	0	lvm	/var
├─vg01-tmp	253:5	0	45G	0	lvm	/tmp
└─vg01-ansible	253:6	0	15G	0	lvm	/root/ansible

```
[root@david ~]#
```

We are looking for the drive device identifier so that we can use it in the next few commands; in this case, the device identifier for the entire hard drive is **sdg**. The **sdg1** device is the first and only partition on this drive. We are going to delete the existing partition in order to start from the very beginning because that is what I would do with any new storage device. On your Linux host, the drive identifier is more likely to be /dev/sdb or /dev/sdc.

Warning! Be sure you use the correct device identifier for the USB hard drive in the next step, or you might wipe out your main hard drive and all of its data.

---

4.   Start fdisk and then see if there are any existing partitions and how many:

```
[root@myworkstation /]# fdisk /dev/sdg

Welcome to fdisk (util-linux 2.32.1).
Changes will remain in memory only, until you decide to write them.
Be careful before using the write command.

        Command (m for help): p
        Disk /dev/sdg: 465.1 GiB, 499405291520 bytes, 975400960 sectors
        Units: sectors of 1 * 512 = 512 bytes
        Sector size (logical/physical): 512 bytes / 512 bytes
        I/O size (minimum/optimal): 512 bytes / 512 bytes
        Disklabel type: dos
        Disk identifier: 0x00021968

        Device     Boot Start      End        Sectors    Size   Id Type
        /dev/sdg1       2048   975400959  975398912  465.1G  83 Linux
```

5.   If there are no partitions on the hard drive, skip this step.

Delete the existing partitions and then create a new one with fdisk. Be sure to use /dev/sdg and not /dev/sdg1 because we are working on the disk and not the partition. The **d** sub-command deletes the existing partition:

```
Command (m for help): d
Selected partition 1
Partition 1 has been deleted.
```

If there are more partitions on the hard drive, delete those, too, also using **d**.

6.   Now let's create the new partition and write the results to the partition table on the USB drive. We use the n sub-command to create a new partition and then mostly just hit the Enter key to take the defaults. This would be a bit more complex if we were

going to create multiple partitions on this hard drive, and we will
do that later in this course. Your entries are shown in **bold**. Press
the Enter key when you see **<Enter>** to take the defaults:

```
Command (m for help): n
Partition type
   p   primary (0 primary, 0 extended, 4 free)
   e   extended (container for logical partitions)
Select (default p): <Enter>

Using default response p.
Partition number (1-4, default 1): <Enter>
First sector (2048-975400959, default 2048): <Enter>
Last sector, +sectors or +size{K,M,G,T,P} (2048-975400959, default
975400959): <Enter>

Created a new partition 1 of type 'Linux' and of size 465.1 GiB.
```

7. If you do not get the following message, skip this step. You must
    respond with **y** to remove the previous partition signature:

```
Partition #1 contains a ext4 signature.

Do you want to remove the signature? [Y]es/[N]o: y

The signature will be removed by a write command.
```

8. The following **p** sub-command prints the current partition table
    and disk information to the terminal:

```
Command (m for help): p
Disk /dev/sdg: 465.1 GiB, 499405291520 bytes, 975400960 sectors
Units: sectors of 1 * 512 = 512 bytes
Sector size (logical/physical): 512 bytes / 512 bytes
I/O size (minimum/optimal): 512 bytes / 512 bytes
Disklabel type: dos
Disk identifier: 0x00021968
```

```
Device      Boot Start      End      Sectors   Size   Id Type
/dev/sdg1        2048 975400959   975398912   465.1G  83 Linux
```

Filesystem/RAID signature on partition 1 will be wiped.

Command (m for help):

9.   If your operating system automatically mounted the new
     partition when you created it, be sure to unmount (eject) it. Now
     write the revised partition table to the disk and exit back to the
     command line:

```
Command (m for help): w
The partition table has been altered.
Calling ioctl() to re-read partition table.
Syncing disks.

[root@myworkstation /]#
```

10. Create an EXT4 filesystem on the partition. Be careful to specify
     the correct device identifier so that the correct partition is
     formatted. I use the device ID of sdx1 in the following command,
     but you should be sure to use the device ID for the specific disk
     you are preparing:

```
[root@myworkstation /]# mkfs -t ext4 /dev/sdx1
mke2fs 1.44.2 (14-May-2018)
Creating filesystem with 121924864 4k blocks and 30482432 inodes
Filesystem UUID: 1f9938a0-82cd-40fb-8069-57be0acd13fd
Superblock backups stored on blocks:
        32768, 98304, 163840, 229376, 294912, 819200, 884736, 1605632, 2654208,
        4096000, 7962624, 11239424, 20480000, 23887872, 71663616, 78675968,
        102400000

Allocating group tables: done
Writing inode tables: done
Creating journal (262144 blocks): done
Writing superblocks and filesystem accounting information: done

[root@myworkstation /]#
```

11. Now let's add a label to the partition. This label makes it easy for us humans to identify a disk device. It also allows us to use the label so that the computer can identify and mount the device in the correct location on the filesystem directory structure. We will get to that in a few steps:

```
[root@myworkstation /]# e2label /dev/sdg1 Experiments
```

This invocation of the e2label command lists the current label for that partition:

```
[root@myworkstation /]# e2label /dev/sdg1
Experiments
[root@myworkstation /]#
```

12. Create the Experiments directory. This will be the directory on which we mount the filesystem that we are creating on the USB drive. Create this in the root (/) directory:

```
[root@myworkstation ~]# mkdir /Experiments
```

13. At this point we could mount the filesystem on the USB drive onto the /Experiments directory, but let's make it a bit easier by adding a line to the /etc/fstab (filesystem table) file. This will reduce the amount of typing we need to do in the long run. The easy way to do this, since we have not discussed the use of editors, yet, is to use the following simple command to append the line we need to the end of the existing fstab file. Be sure to enter the entire command on a single line:

```
[root@myworkstation ~]# echo "LABEL=Experiments /Experiments ext4
user,owner,noauto,defaults  0 0" >> /etc/fstab
```

If the command wraps around on your terminal, that is okay. Just do not hit the **Enter** key until you have typed the entire line. Be sure to use the double >>, or you will overwrite the entire fstab file. That would not be a good thing. We will talk about backups and other options for editing files later, but for now just be careful.

14. Mount the new drive and verify that it is present:

```
[root@myworkstation ~]# mount /Experiments ; df -h
Filesystem                        Size  Used Avail Use% Mounted on
devtmpfs                          32G   40K   32G   1% /dev
tmpfs                             32G   34M   32G   1% /dev/shm
tmpfs                             32G  2.2M   32G   1% /run
tmpfs                             32G     0   32G   0% /sys/fs/cgroup
/dev/mapper/vg_david1-root        9.8G  437M  8.9G   5% /
/dev/mapper/vg_david1-usr         45G  9.6G   33G  23% /usr
/dev/mapper/vg_david3-home        246G   46G  190G  20% /home
/dev/mapper/vg_david2-Virtual     787G  425G  323G  57% /Virtual
/dev/mapper/vg_david2-stuff       246G  115G  119G  50% /stuff
/dev/sdb2                         4.9G  433M  4.2G  10% /boot
/dev/sdb1                         5.0G   18M  5.0G   1% /boot/efi
/dev/mapper/vg_david1-tmp         45G  144M   42G   1% /tmp
/dev/mapper/vg_david1-var         20G  6.8G   12G  37% /var
tmpfs                             6.3G   28K  6.3G   1% /run/user/1000
/dev/mapper/vg_Backups-Backups    3.6T  1.9T  1.6T  56% /media/Backups
/dev/sde1                         3.6T  1.5T  2.0T  43% /media/4T-Backup
/dev/sdh1                         458G  164G  272G  38% /run/media/dboth/USB-
X47GF
/dev/sdg1                         457G   73M  434G   1% /Experiments
```

15. I have highlighted the line for our new device in bold at the bottom of the output. This tells us that the new filesystem has been properly mounted on the root filesystem. It also tells us how much space is used and how much is available. The -h

option tells the **df** command to display the numeric results in human-readable format instead of bytes. Go ahead and run the **df** command without any options and see the difference. Which is easier to read and interpret?

16. Now look at the contents of our new directory:

```
[root@myworkstation ~]# ll -a /Experiments/
total 24
drwxr-xr-x   3 root root  4096 Aug  8 09:34 .
dr-xr-xr-x. 24 root root  4096 Aug  8 11:18 ..
drwx------   2 root root 16384 Aug  8 09:34 lost+found
```

If you see the lost+found directory, then everything is working as it should.

17. We still have a bit more to do to prepare this directory. First, we need to change the Group ownership and permissions of this directory so that VirtualBox users can have access to it. First, let's look at its current state. Piping the output of the grep[6] command allows us to see only the Experiments directory for clarity:

```
[root@myworkstation ~]# cd / ; ll | grep Exp
drwxr-xr-x   3 root root  4096 Aug  8 09:34 Experiments
```

18. This way we can verify the changes actually happen.

19. Make the changes. First, we change the PWD (present working directory) to the root directory (/). Then we will make the changes and finally verify them:

```
[root@myworkstation /]# cd /
[root@myworkstation /]# chgrp vboxusers /Experiments
[root@myworkstation /]# chmod g+w /Experiments
[root@myworkstation /]# ll | grep Exp
drwxrwxr-x   3 root root  4096 Aug  8 09:34 Experiments
[root@myworkstation /]#
```

---

[6] grep, the Global Regular Expression Print command, was written by Ken Thompson in 1974. We will explore grep in detail in multiple parts of this course.

20. Some things you might notice here – or possibly even before this. Now is a good time to explain. The **chgrp** (change group) and **chmod** (change file mode, that is, the access permissions) commands were quiet. They did not announce their success. This is one of the Linux Philosophy tenets – that "silence is golden." Also, the **ll** command is an alias that expands into **ls -l** to give a long listing of the current directory. We will go into much more detail about things like this as we get further into the course.

21. Now we need to add our own non-root user account to the vboxusers group in the /etc/group file. I use my own personal user ID in this case, but you should use the non-root account you are logged into and will use to create and use the virtual machine.

```
[root@myworkstation /]# cd /etc
[root@myworkstation etc]# grep vboxusers group
vboxusers:x:973:
[root@myworkstation etc]# usermod -G vboxusers dboth
[root@myworkstation etc]# grep vboxusers group
vboxusers:x:973:dboth
[root@myworkstation /]#
```

You have completed preparation of the hard drive. Regardless of whether you prepared this USB hard drive on a Windows or Linux host, you are already doing the work of a SysAdmin. These are exactly the types of tasks required of SysAdmins on a regular basis.

Download the ISO Image File

Now is a good time to download the Fedora[7] ISO live image file. This is just a file that is an image we can copy to a CD or USB thumb drive. You can insert the CD or thumb drive into a computer and boot from it to run Linux in a test drive environment. Booting this live image device on your computer will not make any changes to the hard drive of the computer until you install Linux.

---

[7] Fedora Project, *Fedora's Mission and Foundations*, https://docs.fedoraproject.org/en-US/project/

For our purposes we will not need to create a hardware device; all we need to do is download the image, so this will be very easy. The VM we create will boot directly from the live image file when we are ready to install Linux – no external physical media will be needed.

We will use the Fedora 37 image for Xfce,[8] which is one of the alternate desktops. We could use KDE or GNOME, but for this course we will use Xfce, which is much smaller and uses far less system resources. It is also fast and has all of the features we need in a desktop for this course without a lot of extra features that cause code bloat and reduced performance. The Xfce desktop is also very stable so does not change much between Fedora releases, which occur every six months or so.[9]

For Fedora 37, which is the current release as of this second edition, the file Fedora-Xfce-Live-x86_64-33-1.2.iso is about 1.5G in size. Be sure to use the Fedora Xfce release that is most current at the time you take this course.

1. Use your favorite browser and navigate to the URL https://spins.fedoraproject.org/xfce/download/index.html.

2. Click the button with the **Download** label.

3. For students with a Linux host, select the /tmp directory in which to store the download and click the **Save** button. If you have a Windows host or a browser that does not allow you to select a download directory, the default download directory is fine.

4. If the downloaded file is not in the /tmp directory, move or copy it from the ~/Downloads directory to /tmp:

```
[dboth@myworkstation ~]$ cd Downloads/ ; ll Fedora*
-rw-rw-r-- 1 dboth dboth 1517289472 Dec 20 12:56  Fedora-Xfce-Live-x86_64-
33-1.2.iso
[dboth@myworkstation Downloads]$ mv Fedora* /tmp
[dboth@myworkstation Downloads]$
```

We will use this file when we install Fedora Linux on the VM, but we need to create the virtual machine first.

---

[8] Fedora Project, *Xfce*, https://spins.fedoraproject.org/xfce/
[9] For us, this Xfce stability means that the desktop images in this book will be correct through several releases of Fedora.

Creating the VM

To create the VM we will use in the rest of this course, we need to first create it and then make some configuration changes.

1. Switch back to the VirtualBox Manager to perform these steps.

2. Click the **Tools** icon. This shows the list of current virtual machines and the configuration details of one that is selected. I already have several VMs in five groups. Don't worry about creating or using groups of VMs in VirtualBox. That is not necessary to the function or success of these experiments.

3. Click the **New** icon to start the process of creating the new VM.

4. Figure 4-13 shows the first section of the **Create Virtual Machine** dialog, **Name and Operating System**. Each section can be opened by clicking it. Only one section can be open at a time.

5. Set Name to **StudentVM1**.

6. Set Folder to **/Experiments**.

7. Set ISO Image to the directory and name of the ISO image, that is, the full pathname. In my case that is **/home/dboth/Downloads/ Fedora-Xfce-Live-x86_64-37-1.7.iso**.

8. Enter **Linux** for Type.

9. Set Version to **Fedora (64-bit)**.

Tip   The Type and Version fields should be automatically filled when you select the correct ISO image.

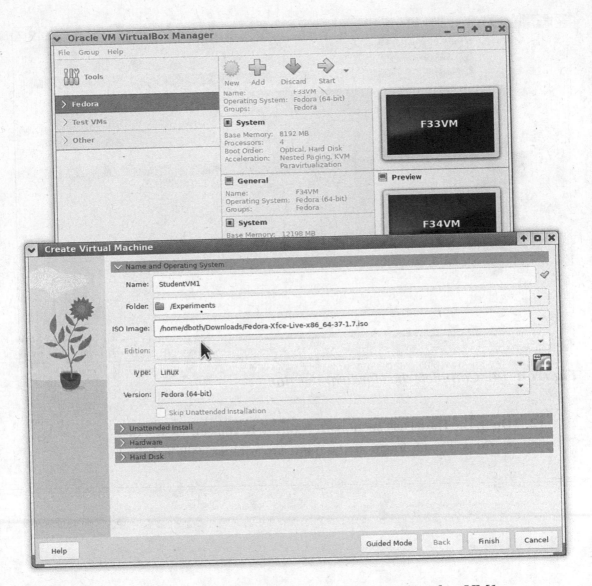

Figure 4-13. Creating the virtual machine with the name StudentVM1

10. We will skip the Unattended Install section and go directly to the Hardware section. So click the **Hardware** section to open it.

11. Set the Base Memory size (RAM) to **4096MB** and the number of CPUs to **2**, and check **Enable EFI** as in Figure 4-14. These can be changed at any time later so long as the VM is powered off. For now this should be more than enough RAM.

113

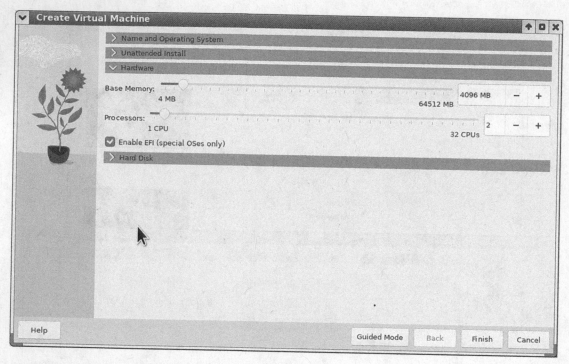

Figure 4-14. *Complete the Hardware section*

12. Open the Hard Disk section. In Figure 4-15 you can see the disk settings. The file location and name are automatically supplied.

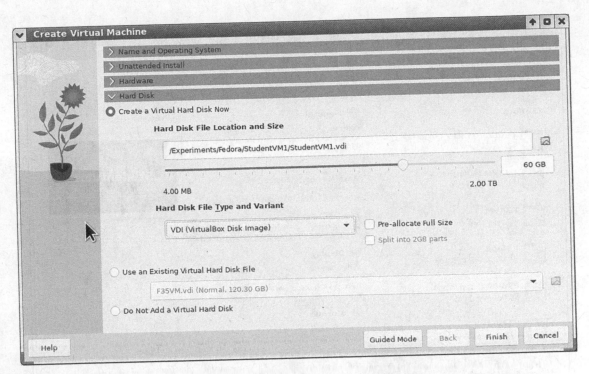

Figure 4-15. Configure the Hard Disk section

The .vdi extension is the VirtualBox Disk Image file format. You could select other formats, but this VDI format will be perfect for our needs. Use the slider or the text box to set 60GB for the size of the virtual hard drive file. Be sure to use the default dynamic allocation of disk space. This ensures that the disk will take up no more space on the hard drive than is actually needed. For example, even though we specified this disk size as 60GB, if we only use 24GB, the space required on the physical hard drive will be about 24GB. This space allocation will expand as needed but only up to the maximum of 60GB.

13. Click the **Finish** button to create the virtual machine. At this point the basic virtual machine has been created, but we need to make a few changes to some of the configuration.

14. Click the entry for the new VM. If the VM details are not shown on the right side of the VirtualBox Manager as it is in Figure 4-16, click the **Details** button using the menu icon on the right side of the StudentVM1 entry in the VM list.

Figure 4-16. *The details for the StudentVM1 virtual machine we just created*

15. Click the **Settings** icon to open the Settings dialog in Figure 4-17
     and then select the **System** page in the list on the left.

16. On the **Motherboard** tab, deselect the **Floppy** disk icon, if it is selected, and then use the down arrow button to move it down the **Boot Order** to below **Hard Disk**. This is so the VM will first attempt to boot from the CD/DVD optical drive and then from the hard disk if no optical disk is present.

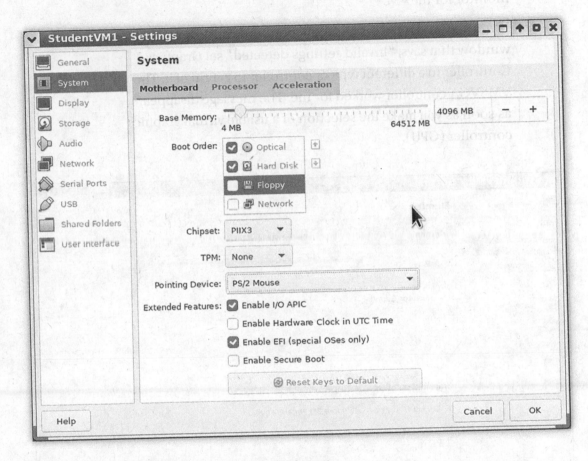

Figure 4-17. *The modified motherboard settings*

17. Set **Pointing Device** to **PS/2 Mouse**.

18. Remove the check from **Enable Hardware Clock in UTC Time**. The VM should use local time.

19.   If your physical host has 8G of RAM or more, click the Display page and increase the amount of video memory to 128MB as shown in Figure 4-18. It is neither necessary nor recommended that you enable 2D or 3D video acceleration because it is not needed for this course. Neither should you use more than one monitor for the VM.

If you see an error message at the bottom of this display settings window that says, "Invalid settings detected," set Graphics Controller to a different type of controller to get rid of it. The VMSVGA controller worked for me. The message disappears as soon as you make the selection of a usable virtual graphics controller (GPU).

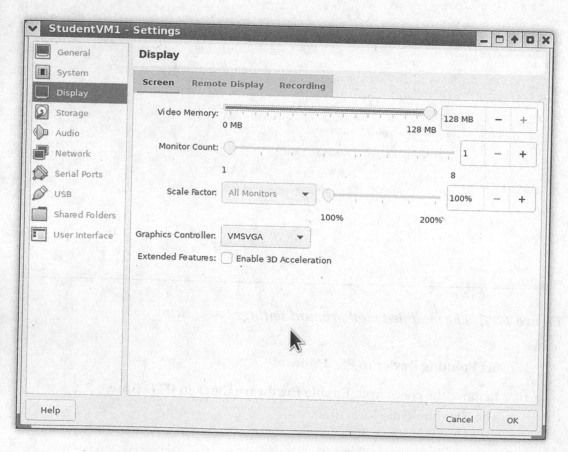

Figure 4-18. *With sufficient RAM in the physical host, you can increase the amount of video memory assigned to the virtual machine*

20. Click the Storage page as shown in Figure 4-19. The port count for the VM must be at least five in order to add new disk devices in later chapters. Previous versions of VirtualBox defaulted to two ports, while VB 6.0 defaults to only one, which means we need to add more ports to the existing SATA controller (but not add a new controller) in order to accommodate additional SATA storage devices in later chapters. Increase the port count to five or more. We will need some of these additional drive ports in Chapter 19 in this volume and Chapter 20 in Volume 2.

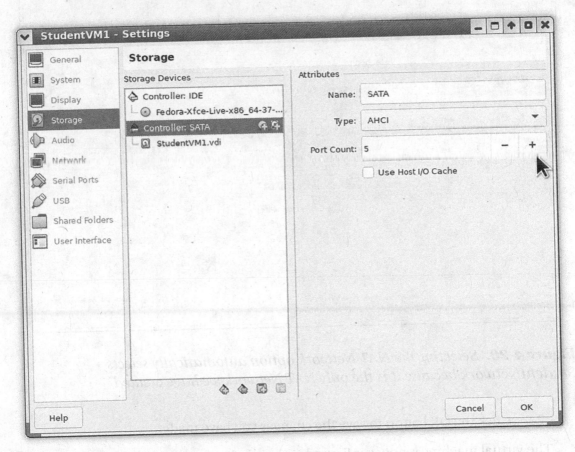

Figure 4-19. Set the number of SATA ports to 5

21. Select the **Network** page and, on the **Adapter 1** tab, select **NAT Network** in the **Attached to:** field, as seen in Figure 4-20. Because we have created only one NAT Network, the StudentNetwork, that network will be automatically selected for us. Click the little blue triangle next to Advanced to view the rest of the configuration for this device. Do not change anything else on this page.

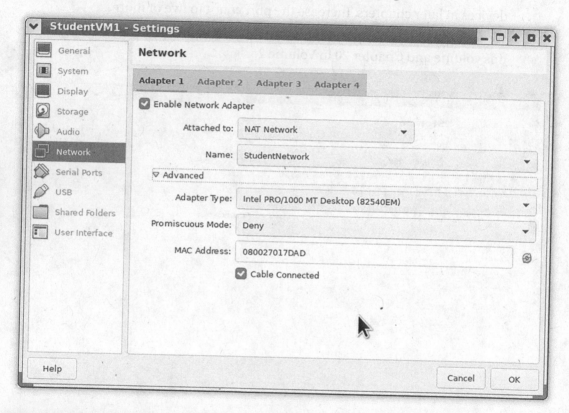

Figure 4-20. *Selecting the NAT Network option automatically selects StudentNetwork because it is the only NAT Network we have created*

22. Click the OK button to save the changes you have made.

The virtual machine is now configured and ready for you to install Linux.

Chapter Summary

You have finished preparations for installing Fedora and performing the experiments in the rest of this course. You prepared an external USB disk drive to hold the virtual machine we will use in this course, and you have created that VM. You have also made some modifications to the VM that could not be made during its initial creation, such as the network adapter settings and the number of processors allocated to the VM.

We will install the latest release of Fedora in Chapter 5.

Note that you will be required to create another virtual machine and install Linux on it in Volume 3 of this course. The steps in creating the VM and installing Linux on it will be nearly the same. The only differences will be that the second VM will need a different name, MAC address, and IP address.

Exercises

Do the following exercises to complete this chapter:

1. Define "virtual machine."

2. What command used in this chapter might be used to discover information about the hardware components of a computer system?

3. How does "NAT Network" differ from "NAT" as a network type when using VirtualBox?

4. Why might you want more than a single network adapter on a VM?

CHAPTER 5

Installing Linux

Objectives

In this chapter you will learn to

- Install the latest version of Fedora on your VM.

- Partition a hard drive using recommended standards.

- Create snapshots of your VM.

- Reboot the VM and complete the installation.

Overview

In this chapter you begin to do the work of the SysAdmin. One of the many tasks that SysAdmins do is install Linux, and that is what you will do in this chapter. I will try to explain as much as I can as we go through this chapter, but there are probably some things you won't yet understand. Don't worry – we will get to them.

Note This second edition of *Using and Administering Linux: Zero to SysAdmin* has been revised where necessary to show the use of Fedora 37. Later releases of Fedora will also work but may look different from the graphics in this course.

Just as a reminder, this course has been updated to use Fedora 37 with the Xfce desktop for the experiments that we will be doing. You should be sure to use the most current version of Fedora Xfce for this course. Both the Xfce desktop and the Linux tools we will be using are stable and should not change appreciably over the next several releases of Fedora.

© David Both 2023
D. Both, *Using and Administering Linux: Volume 1*, https://doi.org/10.1007/978-1-4842-9618-9_5

Please install the most recent version of Fedora as the Linux distribution for this course. This will make it much easier for you because you won't have to make allowances for the differences that exist between Fedora and some other distributions. Even other Red Hat–based distributions such as RHEL and CentOS differ from Fedora. You will find, however, that after finishing this course, the knowledge you gain from it will transfer easily to other distributions.

Insert the Fedora Live Image

If this were a physical host, you would create a physical USB thumb drive with the ISO image on it and plug it into a USB slot on your host. In order to boot the live ISO image in our VM, it needs to be "inserted" into a logical device. You already did this in Chapter 4 when you created the VM.

However, in case you did not do that or you ever need to do it again, here are the steps needed to insert the ISO image into a VM:

1. Ensure that the VM is turned off and not running.

2. Open **Settings** for the StudentVM1 VM.

3. Select the **Storage** page.

4. Click the **Empty** disk icon on the **IDE** controller. If you do not have an IDE (integrated development environment) controller on your VM – which is possible but very unlikely – you can right-click in the white space in the Storage Devices panel and choose to add a new IDE controller. Only one IDE controller can be added.

5. Click the **CD** icon to the right of the **Optical Drive** field of the IDE controller. As you can see in Figure 5-1, this opens a selection list that enables us to select which ISO image to mount[1] on this device.

---

[1] We will discuss the term "mount" and all it means in Chapter 19. For now, if you want more information, see Wikipedia, `https://en.wikipedia.org/wiki/Mount_(computing)`

6. Unlike my workstation, your computer will probably have no images in this list. Select the **Choose/Create a Virtual Optical Disk...** item.

Note   Notice in Figure 5-1 that the name of the optical drive is "IDE Secondary Device 0." This terminology replaces the old, racist terms master and slave. These older terms are still in use in many places, but most modern companies and open source organizations are working to replace them as quickly as possible. The old terms were still in place for the VirtualBox software when I wrote the first edition of this course.

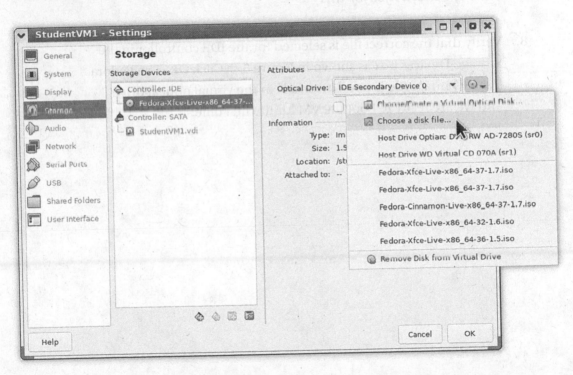

Figure 5-1. *Select **Choose a disk file...** to locate and mount the ISO image*

7. Navigate to the location in which you stored the file when you downloaded it and click the file and then click ***Select*** to set the mount. In Figure 5-2 we see the ISO image file, which is located in my Downloads directory.

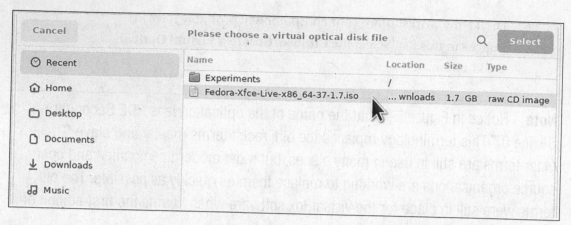

Figure 5-2. *Select the ISO image file and then click **Select**. Be sure to use the most recent version of Fedora Xfce for this*

8. Verify that the correct file is selected for the IDE controller in the Storage Devices box as shown in Figure 5-3. Click OK. The Fedora live ISO image file is now "inserted" in the virtual optical drive, and we are ready to boot the VM for the first time.

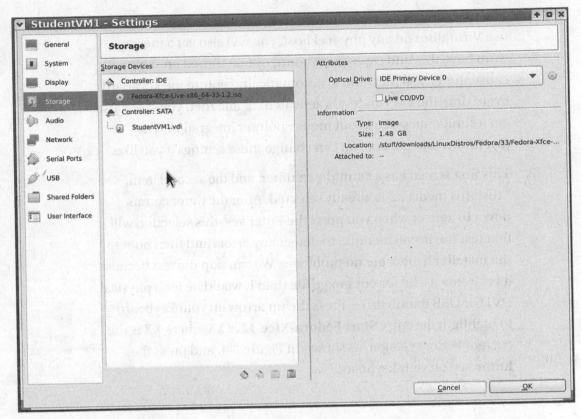

Figure 5-3. *The Fedora live image ISO file is now "inserted" in the virtual optical drive*

9. Although the USB device is a live image, do not place a check in the "Live CD/DVD" box.

The VM is now ready to boot.

Boot the Live Image

Regardless of whether the ISO image was inserted during creation of the VM or after, using the preceding procedure, booting the live image is the same.

1. To boot the VM, be sure that the **StudentVM1** virtual machine is selected and click the green **Start** arrow in the icon bar of the VirtualBox Manager. This launches the VM, which opens a window in which the VM will run and boot to the image file.

The first screen you see is shown in Figure 5-4. The first time you use VirtualBox on any physical host, you will also get a message, "You have the Auto capture keyboard option turned on. This will cause the Virtual Machine to automatically capture the keyboard every time the VM window is activated...," and then you'll see also get a similar message about mouse pointer integration. They're just informational, but you can change these settings if you like.

2. This first screen has a countdown timer, and the second item, "Test this media...," is already selected. After the timer counts down to zero or when you press the Enter key, this selection will first test the install medium to detect any errors and then boot to the installer if there are no problems. We can skip the test because it is far less useful for our image file than it would be for a physical DVD or USB thumb drive. Press the up arrow on your keyboard to highlight the entry **Start Fedora-Xfce-Live XX** where XX is the current Fedora version, as shown in Figure 5-4, and press the **Enter** key on your keyboard.

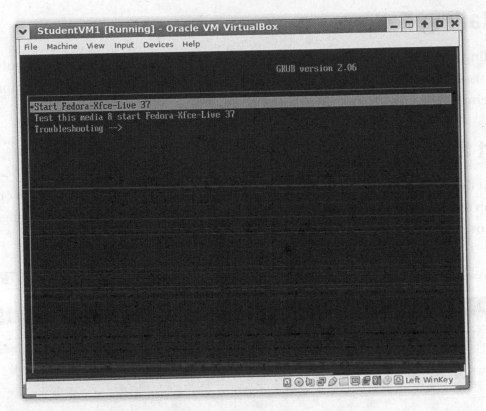

Figure 5-4. *Select the* **Start Fedora-Xfce-Live** *XX menu item and press* **Enter**

Tip   If you do not see the GRUB (GRand Unified Bootloader) menu in Figure 5-4 and you get an "Aborted" message, you may need to go to the System page of the Settings menu and remove the check from the "Enable EFI..." option. I have seen the occasional inconsistency with this on my VMs. It does not seem to occur with real hardware.

Your VM is now booted to the live image, and you could spend some time exploring Linux without installing it. In fact, if I go shopping at my local computer store – I stay away from the big-box stores because they never have what I want – I take my trusty live Linux thumb drive and try out the various systems that my local computer store has on display. This lets me test Linux on them and not disturb the Windows installations that are already there.

We do not need to do any exploration right now, although you can if you like. We will do plenty of exploration after the installation. So let's get right to the installation.

Installing Fedora

Installing Fedora from the live image is easy, especially when using all of the defaults. We won't use the defaults because we are going to make a few changes, the most complex one being to the virtual hard drive partitioning.

Start the Installation

To start the Fedora Linux installation, double-click the **Install to Hard Drive** icon on the desktop as shown in Figure 5-5. As on any physical or virtual machine, the live image does not touch the hard drive until we tell it to install Linux.

Figure 5-5. *Double-click the* **Install to Hard Drive** *icon to start the Fedora installation*

A double-click on **Install to Hard Drive** launches the Linux installer, which is named "Anaconda." The first screen displayed by Anaconda is the welcome screen where you can choose the language that will be used during the installation process. If your preferred language is not English, select the correct language for you on this screen. Then click the **Continue** button.

Set the Host Name

Click the **Network & Host Name** option on the **Installation Summary** dialog as shown in Figure 5-6. This host name is the one that the computer will be known to itself as. It is the host name that you will see on the command prompt line.

The external world, that is, any node on the network to which this host is connected, sees a computer as the host name set up in whichever name service you are using. So it is possible that you might ping or ssh to a computer using one name and that it will have a different name once you are logged into it.

By convention, computer host names are usually in lowercase. Note that the name of the VM is in mixed case, StudentVM1, but that is not the host name and has no functional usage.

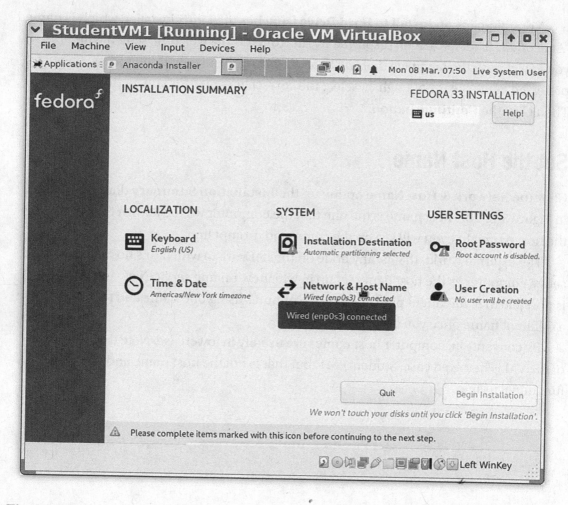

Figure 5-6. *Select **Network & Host Name** to set the host name for the VM*

In the **Host Name** field, type the host name **studentvm1** in all lowercase letters and then click **Apply**. That is all we need to do on this dialog, so click the blue **Done** button on the upper left. This will take you back to the Installation Summary dialog.

There are no options for selecting any additional software packages to install in any of the live images. If you want to install additional software, you must do it after the basic installation has completed.

User Accounts

Click the **Root Password** menu item in Figure 5-6 to configure the root account. The root user is the administrative account for Linux. We discuss the root account in detail in Chapter 11 of this volume.

Click the **Enable root account** radio button. Choose a secure password but one that can be easily remembered. Type the password in the **Root Password** field shown in Figure 5-7 and again in the **Confirm** field. Do not make any other changes on this menu.

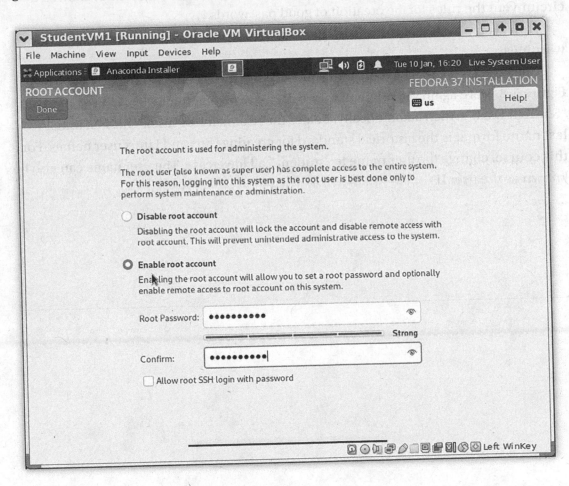

Figure 5-7. Configuring the root account

As root you can choose a weak password. If you do, a warning will be displayed at the bottom of the **Root Account** screen. You can choose to keep the weak password, but even in a training environment, I recommend against that. Click the blue Done button twice if you kept the weak password to return to the main installation screen.

If, as root, you set a weak password for root or a non-privileged user from the command line, you would receive a similar message, but you could continue anyway. This is because root can do anything, even set weak passwords for themselves or non-root users. The non-privileged users must set a good password and are not allowed to circumvent the rules for the creation of good passwords.

However, you should enter a stronger password – one which does not generate any warnings.

Click the User Creation icon, and you will enter the Create User dialog shown in Figure 5-8. Here again you might use a weak password but don't. Full Name should be "Student User," which automatically creates the user name of suser. This first initial + last name format is the historical standard for creating Unix and Linux user names. For this course, change the user name to "student," all lowercase. The user name can also be known as the user ID.

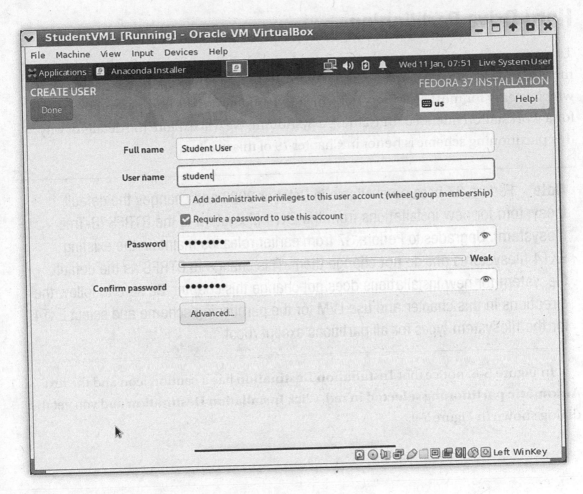

Figure 5-8. Create the student user

Uncheck the box "**Add administrative privileges…**" to prevent this user from being an administrator. We will revisit this later in the course. Do not change any of the other fields on this dialog. Click the blue **Done** button.

Hard Drive Partitioning

The next and most important thing we need to change is to partition the hard drive in a more standard, recommended manner. We do this rather than taking the default way, which is easy for most beginners but which is definitely not the best partitioning setup for a workstation intended for training a SysAdmin. We will explore the details of why this partitioning scheme is better in Chapter 19 of this volume.

Note   Fedora 37 became available in October 2020 and changes the default filesystem for new installations from the EXT4 filesystem to the BTRFS (B-Tree filesystem). Upgrades to Fedora 37 from earlier releases maintain the existing EXT4 filesystems and do not change them. This change to BTRFS as the default filesystem for new installations does not change this chapter. Be sure to follow the directions in this chapter and use LVM for the partitioning scheme and select EXT4 for the filesystem types for all partitions except /boot.[2]

In Figure 5-6, notice that **Installation Destination** has a caution icon and the text **Automatic partitioning selected** in red. Click **Installation Destination** and you get the dialog shown in Figure 5-9.

---

[2] The article "Choose between Btrfs and LVM-ext4" at *Fedora Magazine* has a short but good explanation of the similarities and differences between the two filesystems.

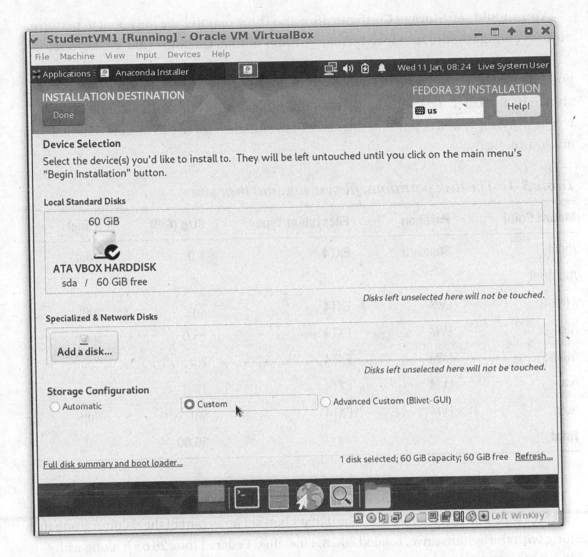

Figure 5-9. *Select **Custom** for **Storage Configuration**, and then click **Done***

We only have a single virtual disk drive in this VM, but if we had multiple storage devices, they could be selected here as part of the installation target.

The size of the VM display window at this point may be too small to contain the entire dialog box. It is hard to see, but there is a scroll bar on the right side of this dialog. Scroll down using the scroll bar or the scroll wheel on your mouse until you get to the bottom. You should also be able to resize the window in which the VM is running to make it big enough to see the entire dialog box.

You should see **Storage Configuration** and three options. We are going to perform a custom configuration, so select the middle radio button, **Custom**. Then click **Done**.

The next dialog, which you can see in Figure 5-10, is the one where we will do a good deal of work. What we need to do is create a partitioning scheme like the one shown in Table 5-1. The partition sizes in this table are not appropriate for most real-world working systems, but they are more than sufficient for use in this educational environment.

Table 5-1. *The disk partitions, filesystems, and their sizes*

Mount Point	Partition	Filesystem Type	Size (GiB)	Label
/boot	Standard	EXT4	1.0	boot
/boot/efi				
/ (root)	LVM	EXT4	2.0	root
/usr	LVM	EXT4	15.0	usr
/home	LVM	EXT4	2.0	home
/var	LVM	EXT4	10.0	var
/tmp	LVM	EXT4	5.0	tmp
Total			**35.00**	

However, with that said, I used to have an old ASUS Eee PC netbook with a built-in 4GB SSD and a 32GB removable SD card that I had set up as part of the volume group that, along with the system drive, totaled 36GB. I installed Fedora Linux 28 on it along with LibreOffice. Until the hardware died, I used this little system for presentations, note-taking in some meetings, and other projects. There was still over 17GB of "disk" space available. So it is possible and not unreasonable to install a working Fedora system with a GUI desktop in about 20GB. Of course it would be somewhat limited, but it would be usable.

Warning   Be sure to set the device type to LVM as shown in Figure 5-10 before continuing with disk partitioning.

Notice that the device type is BTRFS for B-Tree File System. Be sure to set the device type to LVM before continuing. BTRFS became the default filesystem starting with Fedora 37. We will use LVM for this training course.

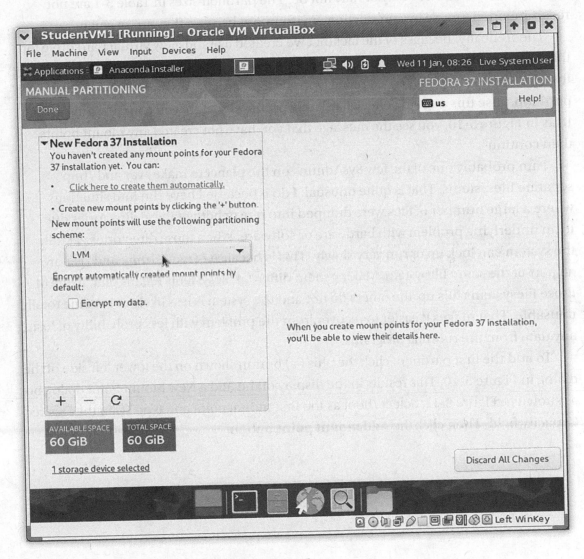

Figure 5-10. *The Manual Partitioning dialog*

In Table 5-1 you can see what are usually considered the standard filesystems that many books and SysAdmins – well at least I – recommend. Note that for Red Hat–based distributions including Fedora, the directory structure is always created, but separate filesystems – partitions – may or may not be. The partition sizes in Table 5-1 are not recommended for use in a production environment because they are so small.

Theoretically, because of the fact that we created a brand-new virtual hard drive for this VM, there should be no existing partitions on this hard drive. If you are not following these instructions exactly or are using a physical or virtual hard drive with existing partitions, use this page to delete all existing partitions before you continue any further. If, as in Figure 5-10, you see the message that you have not created any mount points, then continue.

I am probably one of the few SysAdmins on the planet to make /var and /tmp separate filesystems. That is quite unusual. I do it because I have run into situations where a large number of files were dumped into one or both of these directories due to an underlying problem with hardware or software. When those directories get full, the system can lock up or run very slowly. This is because / (root), /tmp, and /var are all part of the same filesystem. Making them different filesystems means that, if one of those filesystems fills up, the others do not and the system is less likely to become totally unusable. That makes it easier to recover from the problem with less probability of losing any data from the running programs.

To add the first partition, click the plus (+) button shown on the lower left side of the dialog in Figure 5-10. This results in the display of the Add a New Mount Point dialog box as shown in Figure 5-11. Select /boot as the first mount point and type 1G in the Desired Capacity field. Then click the **Add mount point** button.

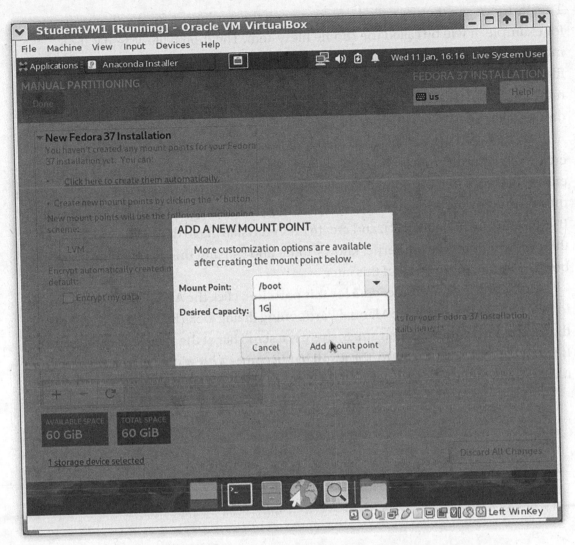

Figure 5-11. *Set the mount point and size desired for the /boot partition*

Although we will go into more detail in later chapters, let's take a moment to talk about partitions, filesystems, and mount points. Hopefully this will temporarily answer questions you might have about the apparently conflicting and definitely confusing terminology.

First, the entire Linux directory structure starting at the top with the root (/) directory can be called the **Linux filesystem**. A raw partition on a hard drive or a logical volume can be formatted with an EXT3, EXT4, BTRFS, XFS, or another filesystem meta-structure.

The partition can then be called a filesystem. If the partition is for the /home directory, for example, it will be called the /home filesystem. The /home filesystem is then mounted on the /home mount point, which is simply the /home directory on the root filesystem, and then it becomes a logical and functional part of the root filesystem. Just remember that not all root-level directories can be separate filesystems and others just don't make sense to make separate.

So after all of the partitions are defined, Anaconda, the installation program, will create the volume group, the logical volumes, any raw partitions such as /boot, and the entire directory tree including the mount points (directories) on the / filesystem; format the volumes or partitions with the selected filesystem type (EXT4 for the most part or BTRFS starting in Fedora 37); and create the /etc/fstab file to define the mounts and their mount points so the kernel knows about and can find them every time the system is booted. Again, more on all of this later.

After entering the correct data for this partition, click the **Add mount point** button to proceed. At this point the Manual Partitioning dialog looks like Figure 5-12. Notice that, if the VM window is a bit small, there is a scroll bar at the right side of the screen. If you hover your mouse there, the scroll bar becomes a bit wider so is easier to see and manipulate. You can also resize the VM window if you have not already.

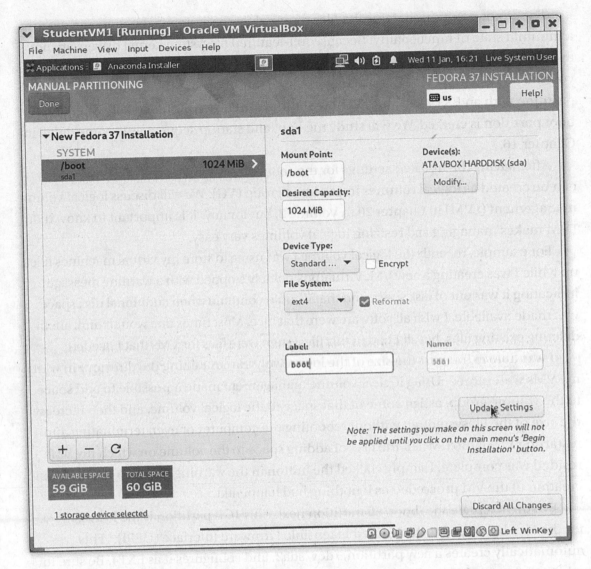

Figure 5-12. *Creating the /boot partition*

If necessary, scroll down so that you can see the Label field. Enter the label for this partition as "boot" without the quotes. As mentioned before, I find that labels make working with various components of the filesystem much easier than would be possible without them.

After typing in the label, click the **Update Settings** button to save the changes you made.

The /boot partition contains the files required for the system to boot up and get to a minimal state of functionality. Because full-featured filesystem kernel drivers are not available at the beginning of this process, drivers that would allow the use of logical volume management (LVM), the /boot partition must be a standard, non-LVM[3] Linux partition with an EXT4 filesystem. These settings are chosen automatically when the /boot partition is created. We will study the boot and startup sequences in some detail in Chapter 16.

After saving the updated settings for the /boot filesystem, the rest of the partitions can be created as logical volumes in a volume group (VG). We will discuss logical volume management (LVM) in Chapter 20 in Volume 2, but for now it is important to know that LVM makes managing and resizing logical volumes very easy.

For example, recently the logical volume I was using to store my virtual machines filled up while I was creating a new VM. VirtualBox politely stopped with a warning message indicating it was out of disk space and that it could continue when additional disk space was made available. I wish all software were that nice. Most times one would think about deleting existing files, but all I had in this filesystem were files for VMs that I needed.

I was able to increase the size of the logical volume containing the directory in which my VMs were stored. Using logical volume management made it possible to add space to the volume group, assign some of that space to the logical volume, and then increase the size of the filesystem, all without rebooting the computer or even terminating and restarting VirtualBox. When the task of adding space to the volume on which my VMs resided was complete, I simply clicked the button in the warning dialog to continue, and creation of the VM proceeded as if nothing had happened.

Be sure to create the /boot/efi partition next. This 1GB partition is the location for the files belonging to the Unified Extensible Firmware Interface (UEFI).[4] This automatically creates a new partition, /dev/sda2, and configures it as EXT4. Be sure to add the label for this partition as "efi."

Let's continue creating mount points. Once again, start by clicking the + button. Select / (the root filesystem) and type 2G for the size as shown in Figure 5-13. Click **Add mount point** to continue.

The root filesystem is the top level of the Linux directory tree on any Linux host. All other filesystems will be mounted at various mount points on the root filesystem.

---

[3] Logical volume manager.

[4] Wikipedia, *UEFI*, https://en.wikipedia.org/wiki/UEFI

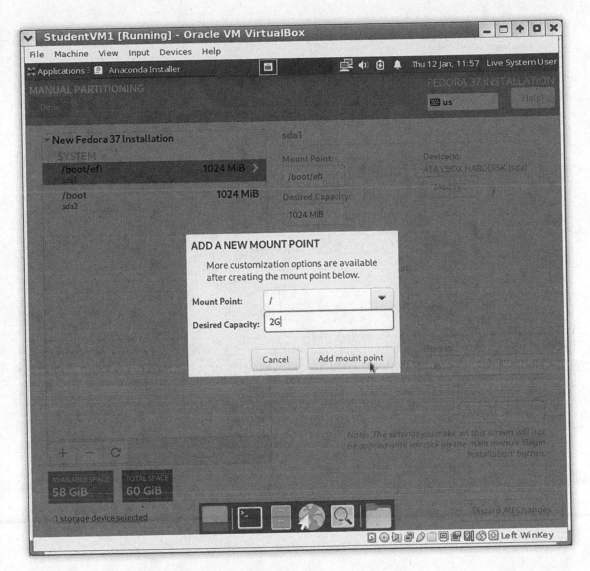

Figure 5-13. *Adding the root filesystem*

Add the label "root" as shown in Figure 5-14.

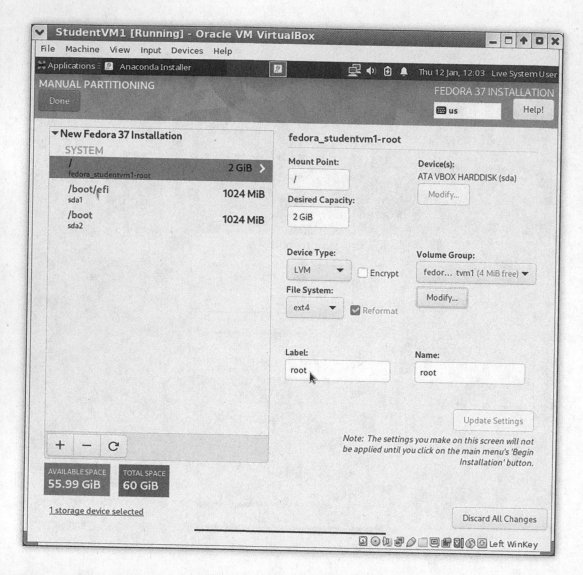

Figure 5-14. *After entering the "root" label, click* **Modify** *to make changes to the volume group*

We are not yet done because we want to do one more thing before proceeding. If we do nothing else to define the size of the volume group that will be created when the hard drive is formatted, the volume group will take only the 35G or so, as we specify our filesystems in Table 5-1, and it will leave the rest of the disk empty and inaccessible. We could fix that later and the result would work, but it would be less than elegant.

In order to include all of the remaining space available on our virtual disk in the volume group (VG), we need to modify the VG specification. Click the **Modify** button under **Volume Group**.

We will not need to modify the volume group size more than once. After making the change to the volume group while creating this logical volume (LV), the VG size is set, and we don't need to do this on following LVs. The only change we need to make on the rest of the logical volumes is to set the label.

The Configure Volume Group dialog would also allow us to change other things like the name of the volume group, but unless there is some imperative to do so, we should leave the rest of these configuration items alone. Nothing that we will do in this course requires any further changes to the volume group configuration.

Under the **Size policy** selection box in the **Configure Volume Group** dialog box, click **As large as possible** as shown in Figure 5-15. This will cause the volume group to expand to include all of the remaining free space on the hard drive. Then click **Save**. Add the label "root" and click the Update Settings button.

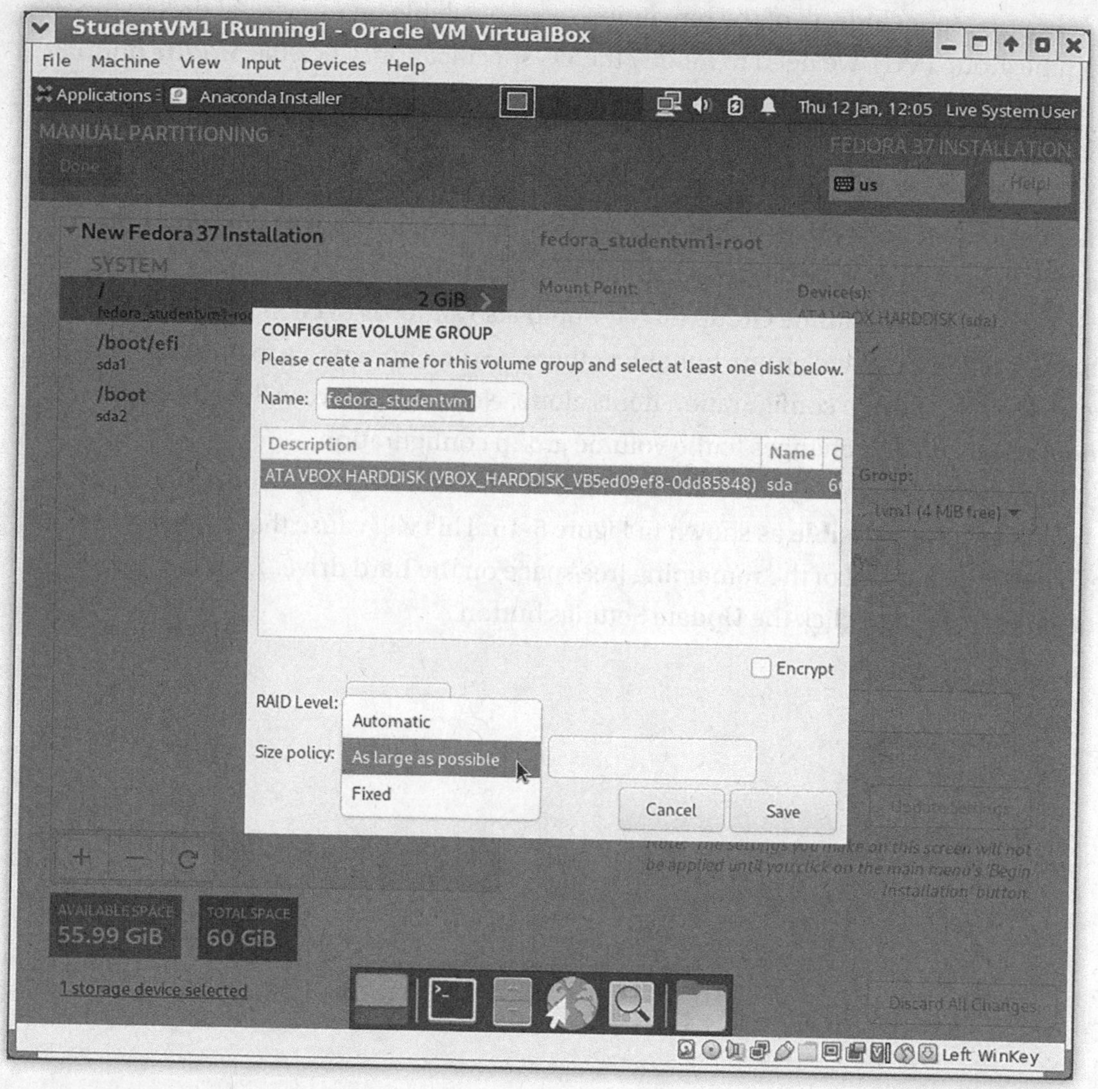

Figure 5-15. *Configuring the volume group to use all available disk space*

I usually like to change the name of the volume group to something simple like "vg-01," but the default of "fedora_studentvm1" is fine for this course. This name is generated automatically by the Anaconda installation software.

Go ahead and add the other partitions, except for the swap partition, as shown in Table 5-1. You will notice that the /usr and /tmp partitions are not in the list of mount points. For these partitions just type in the partition names, being sure to use the leading slash (/), and then proceed as you would with any other partition.

About Swap Space

Swap space is a common and important aspect of computing today regardless of operating system. Linux uses swap space to substitute for RAM when it becomes too full to effectively support additional programs or data. It is a way to temporarily enable the system to keep running albeit at the cost of reduced performance.

SysAdmins have differing ideas about swap space – in particular how much is the right amount.[5]

Although there are no definitive answers for all situations, Chapter 24 in Volume 2 provides some explanations and guidelines about swap space, how much is needed, and a new approach to swap space. This new approach is the use of a Zram virtual disk to provide in-memory compressed swap space. Although this seems counterintuitive, it provides a fast alternative to storage-based swap space.

For now just go with the fact that despite not having configured any storage-based swap space, your Linux VM has 8GB of Zram allocated for swap.

Finish Partitioning

When you have created all of the partitions listed in Table 5-1, click the blue **Done** button. You will then see a dialog entitled **Summary of Changes**. Click **Accept Changes** to return to the **Installation Summary** dialog.

Tip   When you click Done, you may see a message indicating you need to add a 1MB partition named biosboot. If you do see that message, go ahead and create that partition and then click **Done** again.

Begin the Installation

We have now completed all of the configuration items needed for our VM. To start the installation procedure, click the blue **Begin Installation** button.

---

[5] Both, David, Opensource.com, *What's the right amount of swap space for a modern Linux system?*, https://opensource.com/article/19/2/swap-space-poll

Finish the Installation

When completed, the Anaconda installer dialog will indicate "Complete!" on the progress bar, and the success message at the bottom right in Figure 5-16 will be displayed along with the blue **Finish Installation** button.

Click **Finish Installation** to quit the Anaconda installer, which is an application running on the live image desktop. The hard drive has been partitioned and formatted, and Fedora has been installed. In earlier Fedora releases, this button was labeled Quit.

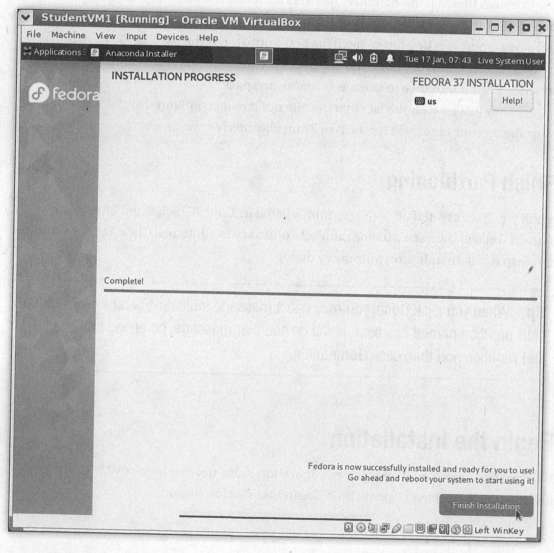

Figure 5-16. *The installation is complete. Click Finish Installation to exit the Anaconda installer*

Shut Down the Live System

Before we do anything else, look at the Live system Xfce desktop. It looks and works the same as the Xfce desktop you will use when we reboot the VM using its own virtual disk instead of the Live system. The only difference will be that some of the Live filesystem icons will no longer be present. So using this desktop will be the same as using the Xfce desktop on any installed system.

Figure 5-17 shows how to shut down the Live system. The Xfce panel across the top of the screen starts with the Applications launcher on the left and has space for the icons of running applications, a clock, the system tray containing icons of various functions and notifications, and the User button on the far right, which always displays the name of the current logged-in user.

Figure 5-17. *Shut down the VM after the installation is complete*

Click the **Live System User** button and then click the **Shut Down** action button. A dialog with a 30-second countdown will display. This dialog will allow you to shut down immediately or cancel the shutdown. If you do nothing, the system will shut down when the 30-second timer counts down to zero.

This shutdown will power off the virtual machine, and the VM window will close.

Reconfigure the VM

Before rebooting the VM, we need to reconfigure it a little by removing the Fedora ISO image file from the virtual optical drive. If we were to leave the ISO image inserted in the virtual drive, the VM would boot from the image.

1. Open **Settings** for StudentVM1.

2. Click **Storage**.

3. Select the Fedora Live CD, which is under the IDE controller in the **Storage Devices** panel.

4. Click the little **CD** icon on the Optical Drive line in the Attributes panel.

5. At the bottom of the list, choose the menu option **Remove Disk from Virtual Drive**. The entry under the IDE controller should now be empty.

6. Click the **OK** button of the Settings dialog.

The StudentVM1 virtual machine is now ready to run the experiments you will encounter in the rest of this course.

Create a Snapshot

Before we boot the VM, we want to create a snapshot that you can return to in case the VM gets borked up so badly that you cannot recover without starting over. The snapshot will make it easy to recover to a pristine system without having to perform a complete reinstallation.

Figure 5-18 shows the Snapshots view for the StudentVM1 virtual machine, which we just created. To get to this view in the VirtualBox Manager, select the **StudentVM1** VM and then click the menu icon on the right side of the StudentVM1 selection bar. This pops up a short menu with Snapshots in it. Click **Snapshots** in the menu. The Current State entry is the only one shown, so there are no snapshots.

You can take many snapshots of the same virtual machine as you progress through this course, which will make it easy to back up to a recent snapshot instead of going back all the way to the first one, which we will create here. I suggest creating a snapshot at the end of each chapter if you have enough room on the hard drive where the virtual machine files are stored.

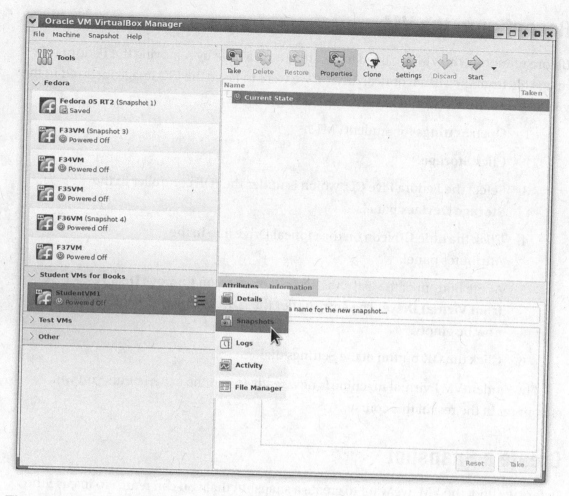

Figure 5-18. *The Snapshots view of StudentVM1 before taking a snapshot*

To create a snapshot, simply click the **Take** button – the one with the green + sign. This opens the **Take Snapshot of Virtual Machine** dialog where you can change the default name to something else. There is also a Description field where you can enter any type of notes or identifying data that you want. I kept the name and just entered "Before first boot" in the Description field. Enter whatever you want in the Description field, but I suggest keeping the default snapshot names. The Snapshots view looks like Figure 5-19 after taking your first snapshot.

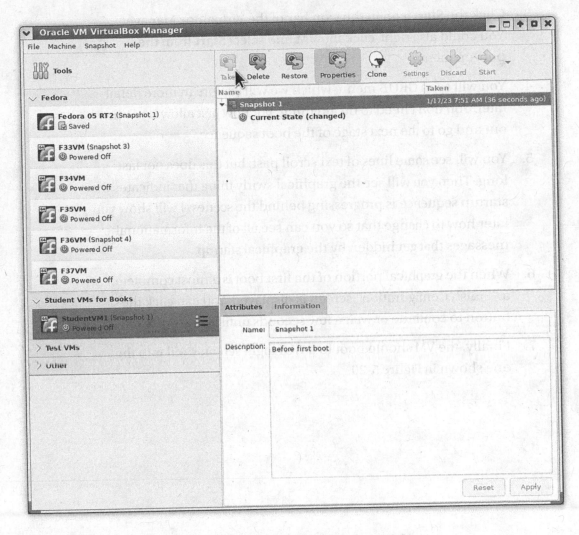

Figure 5-19. *After taking the first snapshot of StudentVM1*

First Boot

It is now time to boot up the VM.

1. Select the StudentVM1 virtual machine.

2. Be sure that the **Current State** of the VM is selected in the Snapshots dialog.

155

3. Click the **Start** icon in the icon bar of the VirtualBox Manager.
    You could also right-click the VM and select **Start** from the
    pop-up menu.

4. You will see a GRUB menu, which we will explore in more detail
    later. You don't need to do anything. For now just allow it to time
    out and go to the next stage of the boot sequence.

5. You will see some lines of text scroll past, but this does not last
    long. Then you will see the graphical swirly thing that indicates the
    startup sequence is progressing behind the scenes. I will show you
    later how to change that so you can see all of the informational
    messages that get hidden by the graphical startup.

6. When the graphical portion of the first boot is almost complete,
    a "Finish Configuration" screen is displayed. You can click the
    button to continue or wait a few seconds until it also times out.

7. Finally, the VM should boot to a GUI login screen similar to the
    one shown in Figure 5-20.

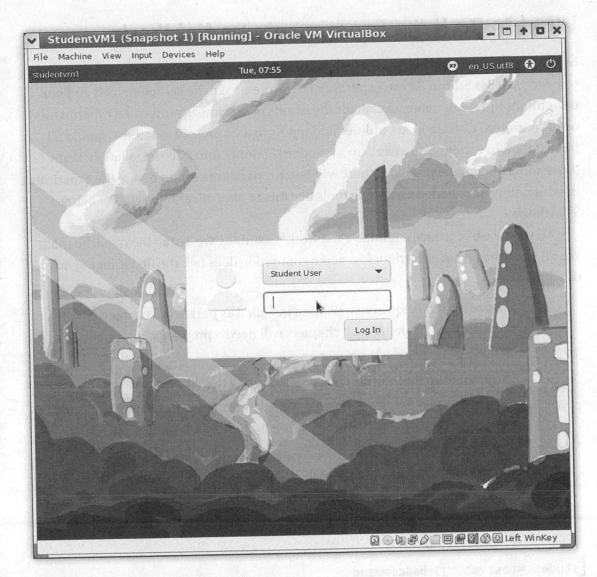

Figure 5-20. The Fedora GUI login screen

But don't log in just yet. We will get to that in Chapter 6 where we will explore this login screen and some other things a bit before we actually log in and explore the Xfce desktop.

If you are not ready to continue to the next chapter, you can leave the VM running in this state or shut it down from the login screen. In the upper-right corner of the VM login screen is a universal on/off symbol. Click that and select **Shut Down...** to power off the VM.

What to Do If the Experiments Do Not Work

Starting in the next chapter, you will have experiments to perform as part of learning to become a SysAdmin. These experiments are intended to be self-contained and not dependent upon any setup, except for the results of previously performed experiments or preparation. Certain Linux utilities and tools must be present, but these should all be installed or available to install on a standard Fedora Linux Xfce installation. If any of these tools need to be installed, there will be a preparation section before the experiment in which they are needed. Installing tools like this is, after all, another part of being a SysAdmin.

All of these experiments should "just work" assuming we install the requisite tools. We all know how that goes, right? So when something does fail, the first things to do are the obvious.

1. Ensure that the required tools were installed as part of the chapter preparation section. Not all chapters will need a preparation section.

2. Verify that the commands were entered correctly. This is the most common problem I encounter for myself; it sometimes seems as if my fingers are not typing the things my brain sends to them.

3. You may see an error message indicating that the command was not found. The bash shell shows the bad command; in this case I made up badcommand. It then gives a brief description of the problem. This error message is displayed for both missing and misspelled commands:

```
[student@testvm1 ~]$ badcommand
bash: badcommand: command not found...
```

Check the command spelling and syntax multiple times to verify that it is correct.

4. Use the man command to view the manual pages (man pages) in order to verify the correct syntax and spelling of commands.

5. Ensure that the required commands are, in fact, installed. Install them if they are not already installed.

6. For experiments that require you to be logged in as root, ensure that you have done so. Many of the experiments in this course require that you be logged in as root – performing them as a non-root user will not work, and the tools will throw errors.

7. For the experiments that require being performed as a non-root user, be sure that you are using the student account.

There is not much else that should go wrong – but if you encounter a problem that you cannot make work using these tips, contact me at LinuxGeek46@both.org, and I will do my best to help figure out the problem.

Chapter Summary

1. You have now installed the latest release of the Xfce spin of Fedora Linux on the virtual machine you created in the previous chapter.

2. You used the Anaconda Installer to create the directory structure that is typically recommended for mounting as separate filesystems using logical volume management. You created a non-root user and set passwords for that user and for root. You also set the system's hostname.

3. After the installation you created a snapshot of the VM in case you run into problems and need to roll back to the beginning.

4. Finally, you rebooted the system and got to the login screen.

Exercises

Perform the following exercises to complete this chapter:

1. Can the name of the volume group created by the Anaconda installer be changed during the installation?

2. How much swap space is recommended in the Fedora documentation for a host with 10GB of RAM that does not require hibernation?

3. How much total space was used by the installation?

4. What is the purpose of snapshots?

5. Is it possible to take a snapshot while the VM is up and running?

CHAPTER 6

Using the Xfce Desktop

Objectives

In this chapter you will learn

- Why Xfce is a good desktop to use for this course as well as for regular use
- The basic usage and navigation of the Xfce desktop
- How to launch programs
- Basic usage of the Xfce4 terminal emulator
- How to install all current updates as well as some new software
- How to use the Settings Manager
- How to add program launchers to the bottom panel
- How to configure the Xfce desktop

Why Xfce

Xfce seems like an unusual choice for the desktop to use in a Linux course rather than the more common GNOME or KDE desktop. I started using Xfce a few years ago, and I find that I like it a lot and am enjoying its speed and lightness. The Xfce desktop is thin and fast with an overall elegance that makes it easy to figure out how to do things. Its lightweight design conserves both memory and CPU cycles. This makes it ideal for older hosts with few resources to spare for a desktop and resource-constrained virtual machines. However, Xfce is flexible and powerful enough to satisfy my needs as a power user.

161

The Desktop

Xfce is a lightweight desktop that has a very small memory footprint and CPU usage compared with some of the other desktops such as KDE and GNOME. On my system the programs that make up the Xfce desktop take a tiny amount of memory for such a powerful desktop. Very low CPU usage is also a hallmark of the Xfce desktop. With such a small memory footprint, I am not especially surprised that Xfce is also very sparing of CPU cycles.

Note   The Xfce desktop is very stable. It has changed very little since the first edition of this course, which was based on Fedora 29. It is still almost the same in Fedora 37 except for different background wallpaper images and some differences in the icons. Although I have updated the graphic figures in this chapter, they still look very similar to those of previous releases of Xfce on Fedora. I expect that they will not change much in the future, either.

The Xfce desktop, as seen in Figure 6-1, is simple and uncluttered with fluff. The basic desktop has two panels and a vertical line of icons down the left side.

Panel 1 is at the top and has an Applications launcher as well as a "Workspace Switcher" that allows the user to switch between multiple workspaces. A workspace is an organizational entity like a desktop, and having multiple workspaces is like having multiple desktops, which you can use to work with a different project on each.

Panel 2 is at the bottom and consists of some basic application launchers, as well as the "Applications" icon which provides access to all of the applications on the system. The panels can be modified with additional items such as new launchers or altering their height and width.

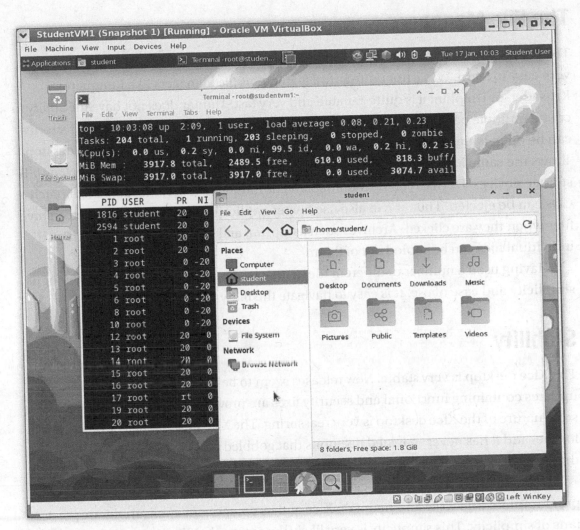

Figure 6-1. *The Xfce desktop with the Thunar file manager and the Xfce4 terminal open.*

The icons down the left side of the desktop consist of the home directory and Trash icons. It can also display icons for the complete filesystem directory tree and any connected pluggable USB storage devices. These icons can be used to mount and unmount the device, as well as to open the default file manager. They can also be hidden, if you prefer, with the filesystem, Trash, and home directory icons being separately controllable. The removable drives can be hidden or displayed as a group.

The File Manager

Thunar is the default file manager for Xfce. It is simple, easy to use and configure, and very easy to learn. While not quite as full featured as file managers like Konqueror, Krusader, or Dolphin, it is quite capable and very fast. Thunar does not have the ability to create multiple panes in its window, but it does provide tabs so that multiple directories can be open at the same time. Thunar also has a very nice sidebar that, like the desktop, shows the same icons for the complete filesystem directory tree and any connected USB storage devices. Devices can be mounted and unmounted, and removable media such as CDs can be ejected. Thunar can also use helper applications such as ark to open archive files when they are clicked. Archives such as zip, tar, and rpm files can be viewed, and individual files can be copied out of them.

Having used a number of different file managers, I must say that I like Thunar for its simplicity and ease of use. It is easy to navigate the filesystem using the sidebar.

Stability

The Xfce desktop is very stable. New releases seem to be on a three-year cycle although updates containing functional and security fixes are provided as necessary. The rock-solid nature of the Xfce desktop is very reassuring. The Xfce desktop has never crashed for me, and it has never spawned daemons that gobbled up system resources. It just sits there and works, which is what I want.

Xfce is simply elegant. Simplicity is one of the hallmarks of elegance. Clearly the programmers who write and maintain Xfce and its component applications are great fans of simplicity. This simplicity is very likely the reason that Xfce is so stable, but it also results in a clean look, a responsive interface, an easily navigable structure that feels natural, and an overall elegance that makes it a pleasure to use.

Xfce4 Terminal Emulator

The Xfce4 terminal emulator is a powerful emulator that uses tabs to allow multiple terminals in a single window, like many other terminal emulators. This terminal emulator is simple compared with other emulators like Tilix, Terminator, and Konsole, but it does get the job done. The tab names can be changed, and the tabs can be rearranged by drag and drop, by using the arrow icons on the toolbar, or by the options on the menu bar. One thing I especially like about the tabs on the Xfce terminal emulator is that they display the name of the host to which they are connected regardless of how many other hosts are connected through to make that connection, that is, host1 ➤ host2 ➤ host3 ➤ host4 properly shows host4 on the tab. Other emulators show host2 at best.

Many aspects of its function and appearance can be easily configured to suit your needs. Like other Xfce components, this terminal emulator uses very little in the way of system resources.

Configurability

Within its limits, Xfce is very configurable. While not offering as much configurability as a desktop like KDE, it is far more configurable and more easily so than GNOME, for example. I found that the Settings Manager is the doorway to everything that is needed to configure Xfce. The individual configuration apps are separately available, but the Settings Manager collects them all into one dialog for ease of access. All of the important aspects of the desktop can be configured to meet my own personal needs and preferences.

Getting Started

Before we log in for the first time, let's take a quick look at the GUI login screen shown in Figure 6-2. There are some interesting things to explore here. The login screen, that is, the greeter, is displayed and controlled by the display manager (dm), lightdm,[1] which is only one of several graphical login managers called display managers.[2] Each display manager also has one or more greeters – graphical interfaces – that can be changed by the user.

Note   Most of the illustrations in this chapter are from Fedora 37. If you are using later releases of Fedora, such as Fedora 38, the background and other cosmetic elements may be different from Fedora 37. However, the technical and functional characteristics remain the same. Even earlier releases such as Fedora 29, which was originally used for this course, look nearly identical except for the background wallpaper image.

---

[1] Wikipedia, *LightDM*, https://en.wikipedia.org/wiki/LightDM
[2] Wikipedia, *Display Manager*, https://en.wikipedia.org/wiki/X_display_manager_(program_type)

In the center of the screen is the login dialog. The student user is already selected because there are no other users who can log in at the GUI. The root user is not allowed to log in using the GUI. Like everything else in Linux, this behavior is configurable, but I recommend against changing that. If there were other users created for this host, they would be selectable using the selection bar.

The panel across the top of the login screen contains information and controls. Starting from the left, we see first the name of the host. Many of the display managers I have used – and there are several – do not display the host name.

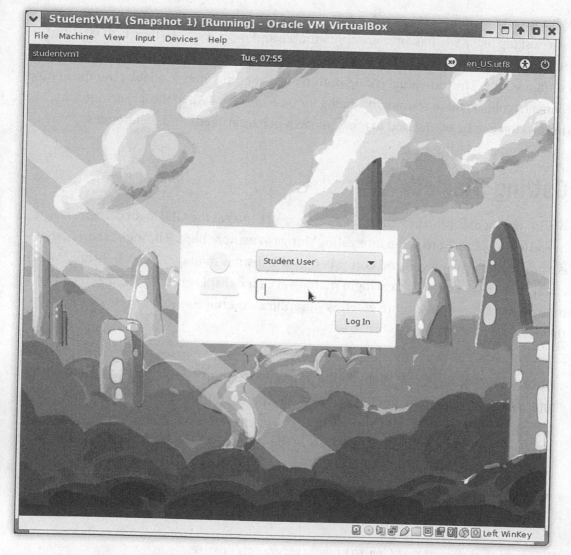

Figure 6-2. *Type in the password and click the **Log In** button*

Next, we have a clock, then a human person with arms and legs spread wide that represents accessibility choices for large font and high contrast color selections for the desktop. Next there is a keyboard icon that shows the current keyboard layout selection and then a clock. Last and furthest to the right is the universal icon of a power button. Click this to get a sub-menu that allows you to suspend, hibernate, or quit. Selecting the Quit option shows additional options to restart (reboot) and shut down (power off) the system.

Login

Before we can use the Xfce desktop, we need to log in. The StudentVM1 virtual machine should already be up and running and waiting for you to log in as shown in Figure 6-2; however, if you closed it at the end of the previous chapter, start it now.

On the right side of the login dialog, we find a circle that contains xf", which stands for Xfce. This control allows you to select any one of multiple desktops if you have more than one Xfce installed. Linux has many desktops available, such as KDE, GNOME, Xfce, LXDE, Mate, and many more. You can install any or all of these and switch between them whenever you log in. You would need to select the desired desktop before you log in.

Click the VM screen, then type in the password you chose for the student user, and click the **Log In** button.

First Look

The Xfce desktop has a panel at the top and one at the bottom as shown in Figure 6-3. The top panel contains several components that provide access and control over some important functions.

On the far left of the top panel is the **Applications** menu. Click this to see a menu and several sub-menus that allow you to select and launch programs and utilities. Just click the desired application to launch it.

Next is some currently empty space where the icons for running applications will be displayed. Then we have four squares, one of which is dark gray, and the other three are lighter gray. This is the desktop selector, and the darker one is the currently selected desktop. The purpose of having more than one desktop is to enable placing windows for different projects on different desktops to help keep things organized. Application windows and icons are displayed in the desktop selector if any are running. Just click the desired desktop to switch to it. Running applications can be moved from one desktop to another. Drag the application from one desktop in the switcher to another, or right-click the application title bar to raise a menu that provides a desktop switching option.

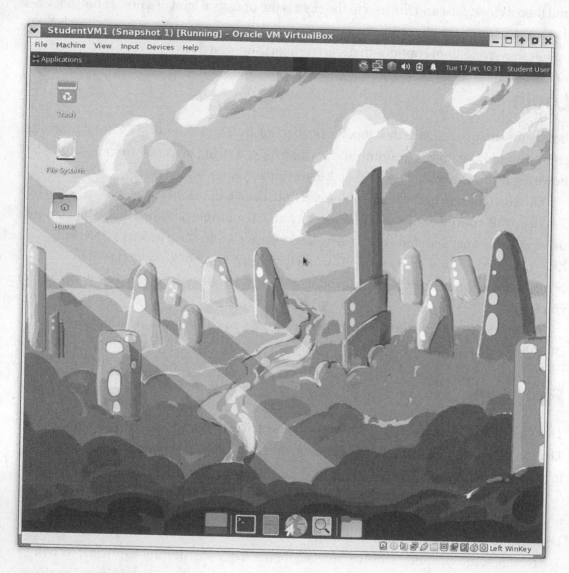

Figure 6-3. *The Xfce desktop*

To the immediate right of the desktop switcher is the system tray which contains icons that provide system notifications and allow some interaction such as to start and stop the network or to choose a wireless network. Next is the clock. You can right-click the clock to configure it to display the date as well as the time in different formats. Next is the system tray, which contains icons to install software updates; connect, disconnect, and check the status of the network; and check the battery status. The network is connected by default at boot time, but you can also find information about the current connection. On a laptop you would also have wireless information.

Soon after you log in, and at regular intervals thereafter, the dnfdragora program – the orange and blue icon that is hard to see – will check for updates and notify you if there are any. There will very likely be a large number after the installation and first boot. For now just ignore this. Do not try to install updates now; we will do that from the command line later in this chapter.

The bottom panel contains launchers for some basic applications. Be sure to note the second icon from the left, which will launch the Xfce4 terminal emulator. We will look at the rest of these launchers in more detail soon.

Exploring the Xfce Desktop

Let's spend some time exploring the Xfce desktop itself. This includes reducing the annoyance level of the screensaver, doing some configuration to set default applications, adding launchers to panel 2 – the bottom panel – to make them more easily accessible, and using multiple desktops.

As we proceed through this exploration of the Xfce desktop, you should take time to do a bit of exploration on your own. I find that is the way I learn best. I like to fiddle with things to try to get them the way I want them – or until they break – whichever comes first. When they break, I get to figure out what went wrong and fix them.

Screensaver

Like all decent desktops, Xfce has a screensaver that also locks the screen. This can get annoying – as it has for me while I write this – so we are going to reconfigure the screensaver first. Figure 6-4 shows us how to get started.

EXPERIMENT 6-1: TURN OFF THE SCREENSAVER

Do this experiment as the student user. In this experiment we explore the screensaver and then turn it off so it won't interfere with our work.

1. To launch the screensaver application, use panel 1 (the top one) and select **Applications ➤ Settings ➤ Screensaver**.

Figure 6-4. *Launching the screensaver configuration application*

2. Figure 6-5 shows the **Screensaver Preferences** dialog. Click the Enable Screensaver slide switch to disable the screensaver.

3. Then click the Lock Screen tab and disable all of the options except for Enable Lock Screen. This prevents the lock screen from automatically locking the screen, but it still allows you to manually lock the screen from the Student User drop-down menu on the top panel.

Figure 6-5. *Disable the screensaver application*

4.   Close the Screensaver Preferences dialog.

For my physical hosts, I usually select the blank screen for my screensaver and set the time long enough that it won't blank while I am still working at my desk but not touching the mouse or keyboard. I set the screen to lock a few minutes after that. My tolerance levels change over time, so I do reset these occasionally. You should set them to your own needs.

Settings Manager

Let's look at how we can access the various desktop settings for Xfce. There are two ways to do so, and one is to use the Applications button on panel 1, select Settings, and then select the specific setting item you want to view or change. The other option is to open the Settings Manager at the top of the Settings menu. The Settings Manager has all of the other settings in one window for easy access. Figure 6-6 shows both options. On the left you can see the Applications menu selection, and on the right is the Settings Manager.

Figure 6-6. *There are two ways of accessing the various Xfce desktop settings. Notice that I have resized the window of the StudentVM1 virtual machine so that there would be enough vertical space to show all of the settings in the Settings Manager*

Adding Launchers to Panel 2

I prefer to use the Settings Manager for making changes as it aggregates most of the settings tools in one window. I also like to make it easier for myself to access the Settings Manager itself. Three clicks to go through the menu tree every time I want to access a settings tool is hard, but one click is always better than three. This is part of being the lazy SysAdmin; less typing and fewer mouse clicks are always more efficient. So let's take a side trip to add the Settings Manager icon to panel 2, the bottom panel, as a launcher.

EXPERIMENT 6-2: ADD A SETTINGS MANAGER LAUNCHER

In this experiment we will add the Settings Manager to panel 2 on the Xfce desktop.

1. Open the Applications menu as shown in Figure 6-7, and locate the Settings Manager at the top of the Settings menu.

2. Click the **Settings Manager** as if you were going to open it, but hold the mouse button down and drag it to the left side of panel 2 like I have in Figure 6-7. Hover over the small space between the leftmost icon and the vertical separator on the panel until the vertical red bar appears. This bar shows where the new launcher will be added.

Figure 6-7. *Adding the Settings Manager to panel 2*

Tip   New launchers can only be added to the panel at either end or just next to one of the spacers.

3. When the red bar is in the desired location on the panel, release the mouse button to drop it there.

4. An interrogatory dialog will open that asks if you want to "Create new launcher from 1 desktop file." Click the **Create Launcher** button. The new launcher now appears on panel 2 as shown in Figure 6-8.

Figure 6-8.   *The Settings Manager launcher added to panel 2*

You can now launch the Settings Manager from the panel. You could have placed the launcher anywhere on the panel or on the desktop.

Note that only one click is required to launch applications from the panel. I add all of my most used applications to panel 2, which prevents me from having to search for them in the menus every time I want to use one of them. As we work our way through this course, you can add more launchers to the panel to enhance your own efficiency.

Default Applications

We can now return to setting our default applications. Default applications are choices like which terminal emulator or web browser that you want all other applications to launch when one of those is needed. For example, you might want your word processor to launch Chrome when you click a URL embedded in the text. Xfce calls these default applications.

The preferred terminal emulator is already configured as the xfce4-terminal, which you have had an opportunity to use. We will go into much more detail about the Xfce4 terminal in Chapter 7.

The icons at the bottom of the Xfce desktop, on panel 2, include a couple for which we should choose default applications, the web browser and the file manager. If you were to click the web browser icon, the Earth with a mouse pointer on it, you would be given a choice of which of the installed web browsers you want to use as the default. At the moment, only the Firefox web browser is installed, so there aren't any real choices available.

There is also a better way, and that is to make all of the preferred application selections at one time.

EXPERIMENT 6-3: DEFAULT APPLICATIONS

In this experiment we will set the default applications for the student user.

1. If the **Settings Manager** is not already open, open it now.

2. Locate the **Default Applications** icon in the Settings dialog and click it once to open it. This dialog opens to its Internet tab, which allows selection of the browser and email application. Neither has a preferred application at this time, so we need to set one for the browser.

3. Firefox has been preselected as the default browser. The only option at this time is Firefox, but you can install other browsers later and select one of those as the new default.

4. Switch to the Utilities tab of the Default Applications dialog shown in Figure 6-9. Notice that both items here already have selections made.

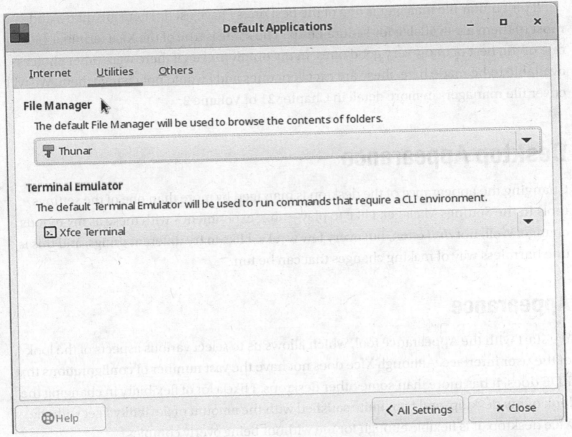

Figure 6-9. *The Utilities tab of the Default Applications dialog allows selection of the default GUI file manager and the default terminal emulator*

Thunar is the only option available as the file manager, and the Xfce terminal is the only option for the terminal emulator.

The fact that there are no other options available for any of these applications is due to the basic installation that is performed by the desktop installer.

1. You can look at the **Others** tab, but there is nothing that needs changing there. Making any changes there would also require significant knowledge of the various file types and the applications that can be used for each.

2. Click the All Settings button shown in Figure 6-9 to return to the main Settings Manager.

The Thunar file manager is one of the best ones I have used. There are many, and most of them are available for Fedora Linux. The same is true of the Xfce terminal – it is one of the best of many very good ones. In my opinion, even if there were other choices available to be made here, these are excellent ones and I would not change them. We will cover file managers in more detail in Chapter 21 of Volume 2.

Desktop Appearance

Changing the appearance of the desktop is managed by more than one of the settings tools in the Settings Manager. I like to play – uh… experiment – with these as my moods change. Well, not *that* often, but every few weeks. I like to try different things, and this is one harmless way of making changes that can be fun.

Appearance

We start with the Appearance tool, which allows us to select various aspects of the look of the user interface. Although Xfce does not have the vast number of configurations that KDE does, it has more than some other desktops. I like a lot of flexibility in changing the look of my desktop, and I am quite satisfied with the amount of flexibility I get with the Xfce desktop. It is flexible enough for me without being overly complex.

The Appearance tool has four tabs that provide controls to adjust different parts of the Xfce desktop. The Appearance dialog opens to the Style tab. This tab is mostly about color schemes, but it also has some effect on the rendering of buttons and sliders. For example, controls may have a flat or 3D appearance in different styles.

The second tab, Icons, allows selection of an icon theme from among several available ones. Others can be downloaded and installed as well.

The third tab, Fonts, allows the user to select a font theme for the desktop. A default variable-width font can be selected as well as a default monospace font.

The fourth tab, Settings, allows selection of whether the icons have text or not and where it is located. It also provides the ability to determine whether some buttons and menu items have images on them. You can also turn sounds for events on or off on this tab.

EXPERIMENT 6-4: CHANGE THE DESKTOP LOOK AND FEEL

This experiment will provide you with an opportunity to try making changes to the look and feel of your desktop. Experimenting with these changes can suck up a lot of time, so try not to get too distracted by it. The main idea here is to allow you to familiarize yourself with changing the appearance of the Xfce desktop.

To begin, open the Settings Manager using the icon you added to panel 2 in Experiment 6-2. Then click the Appearance icon, which is in the upper left of the Settings Manager window. Figure 6-10 shows the Style tab. This tab allows you to choose the basic color scheme and some of the visual aspects of the Xfce desktop.

Click some of the different schemes to see how they look in your VM. I have noticed (at the time of this writing) that the Xfce selections look good with respect to the colors, but that the menu bars, on windows that have them, seem to jam the menu items together so they become difficult to read. For your new style, you should consider one of the others. I like the Greybird-dark style.

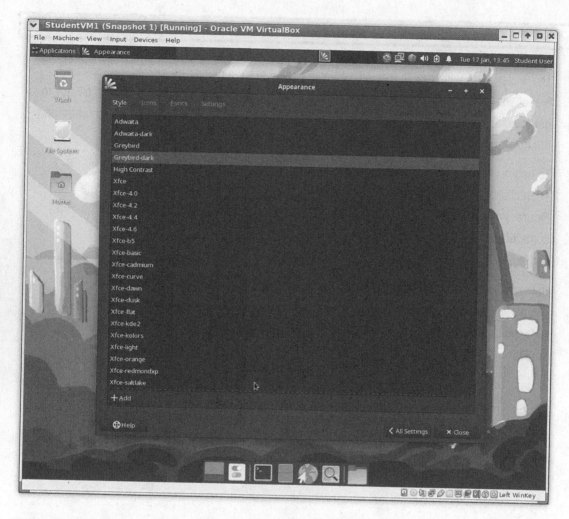

Figure 6-10. *Setting the style elements of the Xfce desktop*

Now go to the Icons tab and select some different icon schemes to see how they look. This is not the mouse pointer icon, but the application icons. I like the Fedora icon set.

Notice that all changes take place almost as soon as you select them.

When you have finished setting the appearance of your desktop, click the All Settings button to return to the main Settings dialog. Then click Window Manager. These settings enable you to change the look of the window decorations – things like the title bar, the icons on the title bar, and the size and look of the window borders. In Figure 6-11 I have chosen the B6 window decorations. Try some of the other themes in this menu.

Tip   Be sure to open another window such as Thunar to see the changes. The Settings Manager cannot be changed. This is different from the past when it would change along with the other windows.

The Keyboard tab allows you to change some of the keyboard shortcuts, but I seldom make any changes here. The Focus tab gives you the ability to determine when a window gets the focus so that it is the active window. The Advanced tab determines whether windows snap to invisible grid lines when moved and the granularity of the grid. It also allows you to configure how windows dragged to the edge of the screen act.

Leave the Settings Manager open for now.

Figure 6-11. *The Window Manager settings allow you to change the look of the window decorations*

You should also take a little time to explore the other dialogs found in the Settings Manager.

Don't forget that you can return to the Settings Manager at any time to change the appearance of your desktop. So if you don't like tomorrow what you selected today, you can choose another look and feel for your desktop.

Configuring the look and feel of the desktop may seem a bit frivolous, but I find that having a desktop that looks good to me and that has launchers for the applications I use most frequently and that can be easily modified goes a long way to making my work pleasant and easy. Besides, it is fun to play with these settings, and SysAdmins just want to have fun.

Multiple Desktops

Another feature of the Xfce desktop, and all except the simplest of the others I have used, is the ability to use multiple desktops, or workspaces as they are called in Xfce. I use this feature often, and many people find it useful to organize their work by placing the windows belonging to each project on which they are working on different desktops.

For example, I have four workspaces on my Xfce desktop. I have my email, an instance of the Chromium web browser, and a terminal session on my main workspace. I have VirtualBox and all of my running VMs on a second workspace along with another terminal session. I have my writing tools on a third workspace, including various documents that are open in LibreOffice, another instance of Chromium for research, a file manager to open and manage the documents that comprise this book, and another terminal emulator session with multiple tabs, each of which is logged in via SSH to one of the VMs I have running.

EXPERIMENT 6-5: WORKING WITH MULTIPLE DESKTOPS

This experiment is designed to give you practice with using multiple desktops. Your desktop should look very similar to that in Figure 6-12, with the Settings Manager and Thunar file manager open.

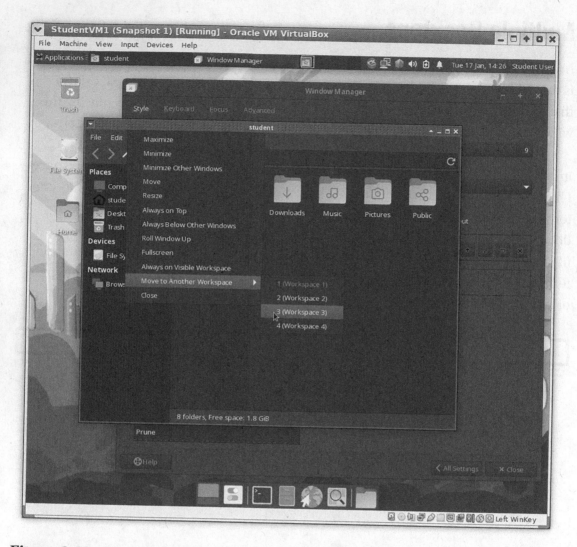

Figure 6-12. *Move the Thunar file manager to another workspace using the System menu*

To start, click the filing cabinet icon in the center of panel 2 (the bottom panel). If you hover the mouse pointer over this icon, the tooltip will pop up showing the title "File Manager." The default file manager is Thunar, and it can be used to explore the files and directories in your home directory as well as other system directories to which you have access, such as /tmp.

But we want to move this file manager to a different desktop. There are two different ways to do this. First, right-click anywhere on the file manager's title bar at the top of the window. Then select **Move to Another Workspace** as in Figure 6-12, and then click **Workspace 3**. You could also access the same menu with a right click on the button for the running application on the top panel, panel 1.

The Workspace Switcher now shows the window for the file manager on workspace 3 while the Settings Manager is still on workspace 1, as shown in Figure 6-13. You can click any workspace in the switcher to go immediately to that workspace. So click workspace 3 to go there.

Figure 6-13. *The Workspace Switcher shows windows on workspaces 1 and 3*

Notice that the windows in the switcher are a reasonable approximation of their relative size on the workspaces that the switcher represents. The windows in the switcher also have icons that represent the application running in the window. This makes it fairly easy for us to use the switcher to move windows from one workplace to another.

However, if the panel size is too small, the windows may not be replicated in the desktop switcher, or just the outline of the window will be present without an icon. If there are no windows in the desktop switcher, you should skip the next paragraph.

Drag the file manager icon from workspace 3 to workspace 4 and drop it there. The file manager window disappears from the workspace and the icon for the file manager is now on workspace 4. Click workspace 4 to go there.

As with all things Linux, there are multiple ways to manage these workspaces and the application windows in each. I find that there are times when placing windows that belong to a specific project on a workspace by themselves is a good way to simplify the clutter on my primary workspace.

Installing Updates

It is important to ensure that the Linux operating system and software are always up to date. Although it is possible to install updates using the dnfdragora software management tool that is found in the system tray on the desktop, SysAdmins are more likely to perform updates from the command line.

Software updates are installed to fix problems with existing versions or to add some new function. Updates do not install a complete new release version of Fedora. The last experiment in this chapter will explore using a terminal session on the desktop as root to install software updates.

EXPERIMENT 6-6: INSTALLING UPDATES

On the bottom panel, panel 2, click once the terminal emulator icon, the third from the left in Figure 6-14. You can hover the mouse pointer over the icon to view a terse description of the program represented by the icon.

Figure 6-14. *Use panel 2 to open a terminal session*

Updates can only be installed by root. Even if we used the graphical dnfdragora software management tool on the desktop, we would need to use the root password. We need to switch user to root in the terminal session:

```
[student@studentvm1 ~]$ su -
Password: <Enter the root password>
[root@studentvm1 ~]#
```

Notice that we always add a hyphen after the **su** command, like so: **su -**. We will go into more detail about this in a later chapter, but for now it is sufficient to say that the hyphen ensures that root is working in the correct environment. The root user has its own home directory and environment variables like the path ($PATH), and some command-line tools are a bit different for root than for other users.

Now we install all of the available updates. This is very important because it is always a best practice to ensure that things are working as they should by having the latest updates installed. The latest updates will contain the most recent security patches as well as functional fixes.

This is easy, but it will require waiting while the process completes. The nice thing is that Linux updates, even when they do require a reboot, don't reboot automatically and you can continue working until you are ready to do the reboot.

Enter the following command:

```
[root@studentvm1 ~]# dnf -y update
```

On my VM this installed over 400 updates. This number will vary greatly depending upon how recent the ISO image you installed Linux from is and how many updates there are. I have not shown the lengthy output produced from this command, but you should pay some attention to it as the **dnf** command does its work. This will give you an idea of what to expect when you do updates later.

The installation of some updates, especially some kernel packages, may appear to stop for a period of time or be hung. Don't worry; this is normal.

Because the kernel was updated, we will do a reboot so that the new kernel is loaded. There are some ways to do this on the GUI, but I prefer rebooting from the command line. After the updates have been installed and the message "**Complete!**" is displayed, we will do the reboot – but not before:

```
[root@studentvm1 ~]# reboot
```

During the reboot, be sure to look at the GRUB menu. Note that there are multiple kernels shown, two, for now. You can use the up and down arrow keys on your keyboard to select a different kernel than the default, which is always the most recent. We will talk more about this later, but having multiple kernels from which to boot can be very helpful at times. Don't change this for now.

Log into the desktop and open a terminal session. There is something else that needs to be done after an update to ensure that the man(ual) pages – the help facility – are up to date. I have had times when the database was not properly updated and the man command did not display the man page for a command. This command ensures that all of the man pages are up to date:

```
[root@studentvm1 ~]# mandb
<snip>
Purging old database entries in /usr/share/man/ko...
Processing manual pages under /usr/share/man/ko...
Purging old database entries in /usr/local/share/man...
Processing manual pages under /usr/local/share/man...
0 man subdirectories contained newer manual pages.
0 manual pages were added.
0 stray cats were added.
2 old database entries were purged.
```

Not very much resulted from this on my system, but two old manual database items were purged.

Chapter Summary

You have logged in using the GUI greeter for the Xfce desktop and familiarized yourself with the desktop. You launched and learned very basic usage of the Xfce4 terminal emulator. You installed all current updates.

You have explored the Xfce desktop and learned a number of ways to configure it to create a different look and feel. You have also explored some ways to make the desktop work a bit more efficiently for you, such as adding launchers to the panel and using multiple desktops.

I did an online search to try to discover what Xfce means, and there is a historical reference to XForms Common Environment, but Xfce no longer uses the Xforms tools. Some years ago I found a reference to "Xtra fine computing environment," and I like that a lot and will use that despite not being able to find the page reference again.

Exercises

Perform the following exercises to complete this chapter:

1. What does the term "lightweight" mean when applied to the Xfce desktop?

2. Do you think that using multiple workspaces will be beneficial to you and the way you like to work?

3. How many options are there for the terminal emulator in the Default Applications configuration dialog?

4. Can you change the number of available workspaces?

5. What would you use multiple desktops for?

6. What is the name of the default file manager for the Xfce desktop? How does this file manager compare with others you have used?

7. How is it possible to obtain a terminal login as root?

CHAPTER 7

Using the Linux Command Line

Objectives

In this chapter you will learn

- Command-line terminology and the differences between the terms *terminal, console, shell, command line,* and *session*
- Three different methods for gaining access to the Linux command-line interface (CLI)
- To use the bash shell
- About some other, alternative shells
- Why it can be useful to have multiple command-line sessions open simultaneously
- At least three different ways to deal with multiple command-line interfaces
- Some basic but important Linux commands

Introduction

The Linux command line is "Linux Command Central" to a SysAdmin. The Linux CLI is a nonrestrictive interface because it places no limits on how you use it.

© David Both 2023
D. Both, *Using and Administering Linux: Volume 1*, https://doi.org/10.1007/978-1-4842-9618-9_7

A graphical user interface (GUI) is by definition a very restrictive interface. You can only perform the tasks you are allowed in a prescribed manner, and all of that is chosen by the programmer. You cannot go beyond the limits of the imagination of the programmer who wrote the code or – more likely – the restrictions placed on the programmer by the pointy-haired bosses.

In my opinion, the greatest drawback of any graphical interface is that it suppresses any possibility for automation. No GUI offers any capability to truly automate tasks. Instead there are only repetitive mouse clicks to perform the same or similar operations multiple times on slightly different data. Simple "search and replace" operations are about the best it gets with most GUI programs.

The CLI, on the other hand, allows for great flexibility in performing tasks. The reason for this is that each Linux command, not just the GNU core utilities but also the vast majority of the Linux commands, was written using tenets of the Linux Philosophy such as "Everything is a file," "Always use STDIO," "Each program should do one thing well," "Avoid captive user interfaces," and so on. You get the idea. Even though we discussed each of these tenets and some of their implications in Chapter 3 of this book, don't worry too much if you don't yet fully understand what they mean. I will point out some of their practical applications throughout this course.

The bottom line for the SysAdmin is that when developers follow the tenets, the power of the command line can be fully exploited. The vast power of the Linux CLI lies in its complete lack of restrictions. In this chapter we will begin to explore the command line in ways that will illuminate the power that it literally places at your fingertips.

There are many options for accessing the command line such as virtual consoles, many different terminal emulators, and other related software that can enhance your flexibility and productivity. All of those possibilities will be covered in this chapter as well as some specific examples of how the command line can perform seemingly impossible tasks – or just satisfy the pointy-haired boss.

Preparation

Before we get any further into our discussion about the command line, there is a little preparation we need to take care of.

The default Linux shell is bash, which just happens to be the one I prefer. Like many other things, there are many shells from which you can choose. Many of these shells are available for both Linux and *nix systems including Apple's macOS. You will install a few of them here so you can try them out, along with a couple other interesting programs that we will explore later.

PREPARATION: USING THE COMMAND LINE

Not all distributions install several of the software packages we will use during this chapter, so we will install them now. These packages are primarily shells.

If one or more of these packages are already installed, a message will be displayed to indicate that, but the rest of the packages will still install correctly. Some additional packages will be installed to meet the prerequisites of the ones we are installing.

Do this as root:

```
[root@studentvm1 ~]# dnf -y install tilix screen ksh tcsh zsh
sysstat
```

On my VM, the command installed the packages listed and some additional packages to meet dependencies.

Defining the Command Line

The command line is a tool that provides a text-mode interface between the user and the operating system. The command line allows the user to type commands into the computer for processing and to see the results.

The Linux command-line interface is implemented with shells such as bash (Bourne again shell), csh (C shell), ksh (Korn shell), and zsh (Z shell) to name just a few of the many that are available. The function of any shell is to interpret commands typed by the user and pass the results to the operating system, which executes the commands and returns the results to the shell. We will look at the Z shell and the Korn shell very briefly later in this chapter just so you can see what other shells look like and how to launch and exit from them. However, the bash shell is the default shell for Fedora and most other Linux distributions, so the rest of the time during this entire course when I say "shell," I mean the bash shell. All experiments and discussion will be about the bash shell.

Access to the command line is through a terminal interface of some type. There are three primary types of terminal interface that are common in modern Linux computers, but the terminology can be confusing. So indulge me while I define those terms as well as some other terms that relate to the command line – in some detail.

CLI Terminology

There are several terms relating to the command line that are often used interchangeably. This indiscriminate usage of the terms caused me a good bit of confusion when I first started working with Unix and Linux. I think it is important for SysAdmins to understand the differences between the terms *console, virtual console, terminal, terminal emulator, terminal session*, and *shell*.

Of course you can use whatever terminology works for you so long as you get your point across. Within the pages of this book, I will try to be as precise as possible because the reality is that there are significant differences in the meanings of these terms and it sometimes matters.

Command Prompt

The command prompt is a string of characters like this one that sits there with a cursor, which may be flashing and waiting – prompting – for you to enter a command:

```
[student@studentvm1 ~]$ ▮
```

The typical command prompt in a modern Linux installation consists of the user name, the host name, and the present working directory (PWD), also known as the "current" directory, all enclosed in square braces. The tilde (~) character indicates the home directory.

Command Line

The command line is the line on the terminal that contains the command prompts and any command you enter.

All of the modern mainstream Linux distributions provide at least three ways to access the command line. If you use a graphical desktop, most distributions come with multiple terminal emulators from which to choose. The graphical terminal emulators run in a window on the GUI desktop, and more than one terminal emulator can be open at a time.

Linux also provides the capability for multiple virtual consoles to allow for multiple logins from a single keyboard and monitor (KVM). Virtual consoles can be used on systems that don't have a GUI desktop, but they can be used even on systems that do have a GUI.

194

The last method to access the command line on a Linux computer is via a remote login. Telnet was a common tool for remote access for many years, but because of greatly increased security concerns, it has largely been replaced by Secure Shell (SSH).

Command-Line Interface

The command-line interface (CLI) is any text-mode user interface to the Linux operating system that allows the user to type commands and see the results as text output.

Command

Commands are what you type on the command line in order to tell Linux what you want it to do for you. Commands have a general syntax that is easy to understand. The basic command syntax for most shells is

```
command [-o(ptions)] [arg1] [arg2] ... [argX]
```

Options may also be called switches. They are usually a single character and are binary in meaning, that is, to turn on a feature of the command, such as using the -l option in **ls -l** to show a long listing of the directory contents. Arguments are usually text or numerical data that the command needs to have in order to function or produce the desired results. For example, the name of a file, directory, user name, and so on would be an argument. Many of the commands that you will discover in this course use one or more options and sometimes an argument.

If you run a command that simply returns to the CLI command prompt without printing any additional data to the terminal, don't worry; that is what is supposed to happen with most commands. If a Linux command works as it is supposed to without any errors, most of the time it will not display any result at all. Only if there is an error will any message display. This is in line with that part of the Linux Philosophy – and there is a significant discussion about that, which I won't cover here – that says, "Silence is golden."

Command names are also usually very short. This is called the "lazy admin" part of the Linux Philosophy; less typing is better. The command names also usually have some literal relation to their function. Thus, the "**ls**" command means "list" the directory contents, "**cd**" means change directory, and so on.

Note that Linux is case sensitive. Commands will not work if entered in uppercase. **ls** will work but LS will not. File and directory names are also case sensitive.

Terminal

The original meaning of the word "terminal" in the context of computers is an old bit of hardware that provides a means of interacting with a mainframe or Unix computer host. In this book the term will refer to terminal emulator software that performs the same function.

The terminal is not the computer; the terminals merely connect to mainframes and Unix systems. Terminals – the hardware kind – are usually connected to their host computer through a long serial cable. Terminals such as the DEC VT100 shown in Figure 7-1 are usually called "dumb terminals" to differentiate them from a PC or another small computer that may act as a terminal when connecting to a mainframe or Unix host. Dumb terminals have just enough logic in them to display data from the host and to transfer keystrokes back to the host. All of the processing and computing is performed on the host to which the terminal is connected.

Figure 7-1. *A DEC VT100 dumb terminal*

This file is licensed under the Creative Commons Attribution 2.0 Generic license. Author: Jason Scott

Terminals that are even older, such as mechanical teletype (TTY) machines, predate the common use of CRT displays. They used rolls of newsprint-quality paper to provide a record of both the input and results of commands. The first college course I took on computer programming used these TTY devices, which were connected by telephone line at 300 bits per second to a GE (yes, General Electric) time-sharing computer a couple hundred miles away. Our university could not afford a computer of their own at that time.

Much of the terminology pertaining to the command line is rooted by historical usage in these dumb terminals of both types. For example, the term *TTY* is still in common use, but I have not seen an actual TTY device in many years. Look again in the /dev directory of your Linux or Unix computer, and you will find a large number of TTY device files.

Terminals were designed with the singular purpose of allowing users to interact with the computer to which they were attached by typing commands and viewing the results on the roll of paper or the screen. The term "terminal" tends to imply a hardware device that is separate from the computer while being used to communicate and interact with it.

Console

A console is a special terminal because it is the primary terminal connected to a host. It is the terminal at which the system operator would sit to enter commands and perform tasks that were not allowed at other terminals connected to the host. The console is also the only terminal on which the host would display system-level error messages when problems occurred.

Figure 7-2 shows Unix developers Ken Thompson and Dennis Ritchie at a DEC computer running Unix. Thompson is sitting at a teletype terminal used as a console to interface with the computer.

Figure 7-2. *Unix developers Ken Thompson and Dennis Ritchie. Thompson is sitting at a teletype terminal used as a console to interface with a DEC computer running Unix*

Peter Hamer – uploaded by Magnus Manske

There can be many terminals connected to mainframes and Unix hosts, but only one can act as a console. On most mainframes and Unix hosts, the console was connected through a dedicated connection that was designated specifically for the console. Like Unix, Linux has runlevels, and some of the runlevels such as runlevel 1, single-user mode, and recovery mode are used only for maintenance. In these runlevels only the console is functional to allow the SysAdmin to interact with the system and perform maintenance.

Note   KVM stands for Keyboard, Video, and Mouse, the three devices that most people use to interact with their computers.

On a PC the physical console is usually the keyboard, monitor (video), and sometimes mouse (KVM) that are directly attached to the computer. These are the physical devices used to interact with BIOS during the BIOS boot sequence and can be used during the early stages of the Linux boot process to interact with GRUB and choose a different kernel to boot or modify the boot command to boot into a different runlevel.

Because of the close physical connection to the computer of the KVM devices, the SysAdmin must be physically present at this console during the boot process in order to interact with the computer. Remote access is not available to the SysAdmin during the boot process and only becomes available when the SSHD service is up and running.

Virtual Consoles

Modern personal computers and servers that run Linux do not usually have dumb terminals that can be used as a console. Linux typically provides the capability for multiple virtual consoles to allow for multiple logins from a single, standard PC keyboard and monitor. Red Hat Enterprise Linux, CentOS, and Fedora Linux usually provide for six or seven virtual consoles for text-mode logins. If a graphical interface is used, the first virtual console, vc1, becomes the first graphical (GUI) session after the X Window System (X) starts, and vc7 becomes the second GUI session.

Each virtual console is assigned to a function key corresponding to the console number. So vc1 would be assigned to function key F1 and so on. It is easy to switch to and from these sessions. On a physical computer, you can hold down the **Ctrl-Alt** keys and press **F2** to switch to vc2. Then hold down the **Ctrl-Alt** keys and press **F1** to switch to vc1 and what is usually the graphical desktop interface. We will cover how to do this on a VM in Experiment 7-1. If there is no GUI running, vc1 will be simply another text console.

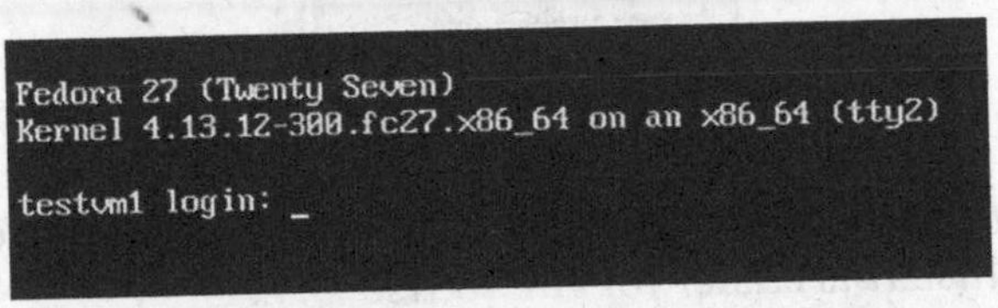

```
Fedora 27 (Twenty Seven)
Kernel 4.13.12-300.fc27.x86_64 on an x86_64 (tty2)

testvm1 login: _
```

Figure 7-3. *Login prompt for virtual console 2*

Virtual consoles provide a means to access multiple consoles using a single physical system console, the keyboard, video display, and mouse (KVM). This gives administrators more flexibility to perform system maintenance and problem solving. There are some other means for additional flexibility, but virtual consoles are always available if you have physical access to the system or a KVM device is directly attached or some logical KVM extension such as Integrated Lights-Out (ILO). Other means such as the screen command might not be available in some environments, and a GUI desktop will probably not be available on most servers.

Using Virtual Consoles

EXPERIMENT 7-1: USING VIRTUAL CONSOLES

For this experiment you will use one of the virtual consoles to log into the command line as root. The command line is where you will do most of your work as a system administrator. You will have an opportunity to use a terminal session on the GUI desktop later, but this is what your system will look like if you do not have a GUI.

If you were on a physical host, you would press Ctrl-Alt-F2 to access virtual console 2. Because we are on virtual machines, however, pressing that key combination would not take us to virtual console 2 for the physical host. We need to do something a bit different for the virtual machine.

Click the VM to give it the focus. There is a key called the Host Key that we will use to simulate the Ctrl-Alt key combination. The current Host Key is indicated in the lower-right corner of the VM window as you can see in Figure 7-4. As you can see there, I have changed the default Host Key on my VirtualBox installation to be the Left WinKey because I find it easier to use than the right Ctrl key.[1] The WinKeys are the keys on your physical keyboard that usually have the Windows icon on them.

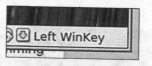

Figure 7-4. *The Right WinKey is the default Host Key, but I have changed mine to the Left WinKey because it is easier for me to use*

To change to virtual console 2 (vc2) now that the VM has the focus, press and hold the Host Key for your VM, and then press the F2 key (**HostKey-F2**) on your keyboard. Your VM window should now look like that in Figure 7-5. Note that I have resized the VM window so that the entire window can be easily shown here.

---

[1] Use the **File ➤ Preferences** menu on the VM window's menu bar and then choose **Input** to change the Host Key and other key combinations.

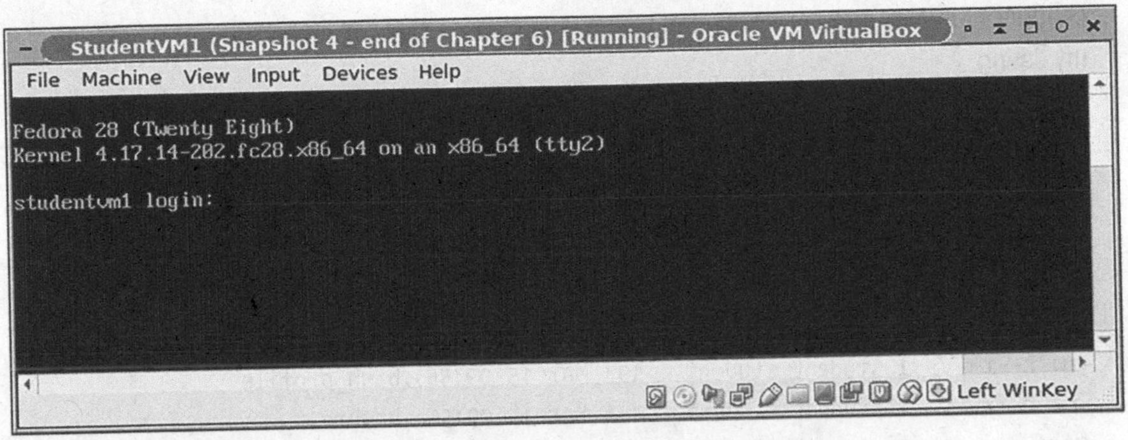

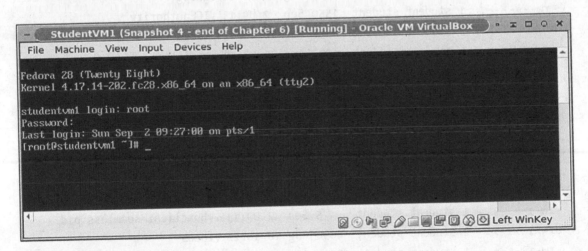

Figure 7-5. The VM window showing the virtual console 2 login

If you are not already logged in, and you probably are not, log into virtual console session 2 as root. Type **root** on the login line and press the **Enter** key as shown in Figure 7-6. Type in your root password and press **Enter** again. You should now be logged in and at the command prompt.

Figure 7-6. vc2 after logging in as root

The # prompt shows that this is a root login.

Use **HostKey-F3** to change to virtual console session 3 (vc3). Log in on this console as student. Note that any user can be logged in multiple times using any combination of the virtual consoles and GUI terminal emulators. Note the $ prompt, which denotes the prompt for a non-root (non-privileged) user. On vc3, run the **ls -la** command. Notice the bash and other configuration files, most of which start with a dot (.). Your listing will probably be different from my listing:

```
[student@studentvm1 ~]$ ls -la
total 160
drwx------.  15 student student  4096 Sep  2 09:14 .
drwxr-xr-x.  5 root    root      4096 Aug 19 08:52 ..
-rw-------.   1 student student    19 Aug 29 13:04 .bash_history
-rw-r--r--.   1 student student    18 Mar 15 09:56 .bash_logout
-rw-r--r--.   1 student student   193 Mar 15 09:56 .bash_profile
-rw-r--r--.   1 student student   231 Mar 15 09:56 .bashrc
drwx------.   9 student student  4096 Sep  2 09:15 .cache
drwx------.   8 student student  4096 Aug 19 15:35 .config
drwxr-xr-x.   2 student student  4096 Aug 18 17:10 Desktop
drwxr-xr-x.   2 student student  4096 Aug 18 10:21 Documents
drwxr-xr-x.   2 student student  4096 Aug 18 10:21 Downloads
-rw-------.   1 student student    16 Aug 18 10:21 .esd_auth
drwx------.   3 student student  4096 Aug 18 10:21 .gnupg
-rw-------.   1 student student  1550 Sep  2 09:13 .ICEauthority
drwxr-xr-x.   3 student student  4096 Aug 18 10:21 .local
drwxr-xr-x.   4 student student  4096 Apr 25 02:19 .mozilla
drwxr-xr-x.   2 student student  4096 Aug 18 10:21 Music
drwxr-xr-x.   2 student student  4096 Aug 18 10:21 Pictures
drwxr-xr-x.   2 student student  4096 Aug 18 10:21 Public
drwxr-xr-x.   2 student student  4096 Aug 18 10:21 Templates
-rw-r-----.   1 student student     5 Sep  2 09:13 .vboxclient-clipboard.pid
-rw-r-----.   1 student student     5 Sep  2 09:13 .vboxclient-display.pid
-rw-r-----.   1 student student     5 Sep  2 09:13 .vboxclient-draganddrop.pid
-rw-r-----.   1 student student     5 Sep  2 09:13 .vboxclient-seamless.pid
drwxr-xr-x.   2 student student  4096 Aug 18 10:21 Videos
-rw-rw-r--.   1 student student 18745 Sep  2 09:24 .xfce4-session.verbose-log
-rw-rw-r--.   1 student student 20026 Sep  2 09:12 .xfce4-session.verbose-
log.last
-rw-rw-r--.   1 student student  8724 Aug 18 21:45 .xscreensaver
-rw-------.   1 student student  1419 Sep  2 09:13 .xsession-errors
-rw-------.   1 student student  1748 Sep  2 09:12 .xsession-errors.old
[student@studentvm1 ~]$
```

Use the clear command to clear the console screen:

```
[student@studentvm1 ~]$ clear
```

The **reset** command resets all terminal settings. This is useful if the terminal becomes unusable or unreadable, such as after **cat**'ing a binary file. Even if you cannot read the **reset** command as you input it, it will still work. I have on occasion had to use the **reset** command twice in a row.

If you are not currently logged into a terminal emulator session on the GUI, do so now. Use **HostKey-F1** to return to the GUI and open the terminal emulator. Because you are already logged into the GUI desktop, it is unnecessary to log into the terminal emulator session.

Open a terminal window if you do not already have one open and type **w** to list currently logged-in users and uptime. You should see at least three logins; one for root on tty2 and one for student on tty3 and one for student on tty1, which is the GUI console session:

```
[student@studentvm1 ~]$ w
 16:48:31 up 2 days,  7:35,  5 users,  load average: 0.05, 0.03, 0.01
USER     TTY         LOGIN@   IDLE   JCPU   PCPU WHAT
student  tty1        Sun09    2days 10.41s  0.05s /bin/sh
/etc/xdg/xfce4/xinitrc -- vt
student  pts/1       Sun09    18:57m 0.15s  0.05s sshd: student [priv]
root     tty2        13:07    3:41m  0.02s  0.02s -bash
student  pts/3       13:17    4.00s  0.05s  0.03s w
student  tty3        13:21    3:24m  0.03s  0.03s -bash
[student@studentvm1 ~]$
```

I have more logins listed than you will because I also have logged in "remotely" from the physical host workstation using SSH. This makes it a bit easier for me to copy and paste the results of the commands. Due to the setup of the virtual network, you will not be able to SSH into the virtual machine from a different host until Chapter 42 in Volume 3 of this course.

Notice the first line of data that shows student logged in on tty1. tty1 is the GUI desktop. You will also see the logins for tty2 and tty3 as well as two logins using pseudo-terminals (pts) pts/1 and pts/3. These are my remote SSH login sessions.

Enter the **who** command. It provides similar, slightly different information than **w**:

```
[student@studentvm1 ~]$ who
student  tty1         2018-09-02 09:13 (:0)
student  pts/1        2018-09-02 09:26 (192.168.0.1)
root     tty2         2018-09-04 13:07
student  pts/3        2018-09-04 13:17 (192.168.0.1)
student  tty3         2018-09-04 13:21
[student@studentvm1 ~]$
```

In the results of the who command, you can also see the IP address from which I logged in using SSH. The **(:0)** string is not an emoji; it is an indicator that tty1 is attached to display :0 – the first display.

Type whoami to display your current login name:

```
[student@studentvm1 ~]$ whoami
student
[student@studentvm1 ~]$
```

Of course your login name is also displayed in the text of the command prompt. However, you may not always be who you think you are.

Type the **id** command to display your real and effective ID and GID. The **id** command also shows a list of the groups to which your user ID belongs:

```
[student@studentvm1 ~]$ id
uid=1000(student) gid=1000(student) groups=1000(student)
context=unconfined_u:unconfined_r:unconfined_t:s0-s0:c0.c1023
[student@studentvm1 ~]$
```

We will discuss user IDs, groups, and group IDs in detail later.

The part of the output from the id command that starts with "context" is split onto a second line here, but it is probably displayed on a single line in your terminal. However, the split here is a convenient way to see the SELinux information. SELinux is Secure Linux, and the code was written by the CIA to ensure that even if a hacker gains access to a host protected by SELinux, the potential damage is extremely limited. We will cover SELinux in a little more detail in Volume 3, Chapter 52.

Switch back to console session 2. Use the **whoami**, **who**, and **id** commands the same as in the other console session. Let's also use the **who am i** command:

```
[student@studentvm1 ~]$ whoami
student
[student@studentvm1 ~]$ who
root      pts/1        2019-01-13 14:13 (192.168.0.1:S.0)
root      pts/2        2019-01-14 12:09 (192.168.0.1:S.1)
student   pts/3        2019-01-15 16:15 (192.168.0.1)
student   tty1         2019-01-15 21:53 (:0)
student   pts/5        2019-01-15 22:04 (:pts/4:S.0)
student   pts/6        2019-01-15 22:04 (:pts/4:S.1)
student   tty2         2019-01-15 22:05
student   tty3         2019-01-15 22:06
student   pts/8        2019-01-15 22:19
[student@studentvm1 ~]$ id
uid=1000(student) gid=1000(student) groups=1000(student)
context=unconfined_u:unconfined_r:unconfined_t:s0-s0:c0.c1023
[student@studentvm1 ~]$ who am i
student   pts/8        2019-01-15 22:19
```

Log out of all the virtual console sessions.

Use Ctrl-Alt-F1 (HostKey-F1) to return to the GUI desktop.

The virtual consoles are assigned to device files such as /dev/tty2 for virtual console 2 as in Figure 7-3. We will go into much more detail on device files throughout this course and especially in Chapter 3 of Volume 2. The Linux Console[2] is the terminal emulator for the Linux virtual consoles.

---

[2]Wikipedia, *Linux Console*, https://en.wikipedia.org/wiki/Linux_console

Terminal Emulator

Let's continue with our terminology. A terminal emulator is a software program that emulates a hardware terminal. Most of the current graphical terminal emulators, like the Xfce4 terminal emulator seen in Figure 7-7, can emulate several different types of hardware terminals. Most terminal emulators are graphical programs that run on any Linux graphical desktop environment like Xfce, KDE, Cinnamon, LXDE, GNOME, and others.

You can see in Figure 7-7 that a right click in the Xfce4 terminal emulator window brings up a menu that allows opening another tab or another emulator window. This figure also shows that there are currently two tabs open. You can see them just under the menu bar.

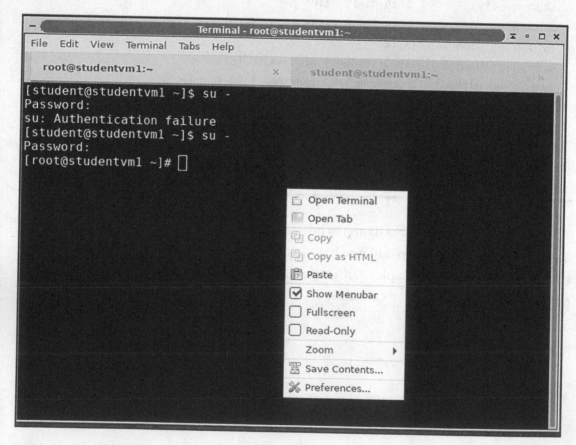

Figure 7-7. *The Xfce4 terminal emulator with two tabs open*

The first terminal emulator was Xterm,[3] which was originally developed in 1984 by Thomas Dickey.[4] The original Xterm is still maintained and is packaged as part of many modern Linux distributions. Other terminal emulators include xfce4-terminal,[5] GNOME terminal,[6] Tilix,[7] rxvt-unicode,[8] Terminator,[9] Konsole,[10] and many more. Each of these terminal emulators has a set of interesting features that appeal to specific groups of users. Some have the capability to open multiple tabs or terminals in a single window. Others provide just the minimum set of features required to perform their function and are typically used when small size and efficiency are called for.

My favorite terminal emulators are xfce4-terminal, Konsole, and Tilix because they offer the ability to have many terminal emulator sessions in a single window. The Xfce4 and Konsole terminals do this using multiple tabs that I can switch between. Tilix offers the ability to tile multiple emulator sessions in a window session, as well as providing multiple sessions. My current terminal emulator of choice is Xfce4, primarily because it offers a good feature set that is as good as terminal, yet is also very lightweight and uses far fewer system resources. Other terminal emulator software provides many of these features but not as adroitly and seamlessly as Xfce4, terminal, and Tilix.

For this course we will use the Xfce4 terminal because it is the default for the Xfce desktop, it is very sparing of system resources, and it has all of the features we need. We will install and explore other terminal emulators in Chapter 14.

Pseudo-terminal

A pseudo-terminal is a Linux device file to which a terminal emulator is attached in order to interface with the operating system. The device files for pseudo-terminals are located in the /dev/pts directory and are created only when a new terminal emulator

---

[3] Wikipedia, *Xterm*, https://en.wikipedia.org/wiki/Xterm

[4] Wikipedia, *Thomas Dickey*, https://en.wikipedia.org/wiki/Thomas_Dickey

[5] Xfce Documentation, *xcfe4-terminal*, https://docs.xfce.org/apps/terminal/introduction

[6] Wikipedia, *GNOME terminal*, https://en.wikipedia.org/wiki/GNOME_Terminal

[7] Fedora Magazine, *Tilix*, https://fedoramagazine.org/try-tilix-new-terminal-emulator-fedora/

[8] Wikipedia, *Rxvt*, https://en.wikipedia.org/wiki/Rxvt

[9] Wikipedia, *Terminator*, https://en.wikipedia.org/wiki/Terminator_(terminal_emulator)

[10] KDE, *Konsole terminal emulator*, https://konsole.kde.org/

session is launched. That can be a new terminal emulator window or a new tab or panel in an existing window of one of the terminal emulators, such as terminal, that supports multiple sessions in a single window.

The device files in /dev/pts are simply a number for each emulator session that is opened. The first emulator would be /dev/pts/1, for example.

Device Special Files

Let's take a brief side trip. Linux handles almost everything as a file. This has some interesting and amazing implications. This concept makes it possible to copy an entire hard drive, boot record included, because the entire hard drive is a file, just as are the individual partitions. "Everything is a file" is possible because all devices are implemented by Linux as these things called device files. Device files are not device drivers; rather, they are gateways to devices that are exposed to the user.

Device files are more accurately known as device special files.[11] Device files are employed to provide the operating system and, even more importantly in an open operating system, the users an interface to the devices that they represent. All Linux device files are located in the /dev directory, which is an integral part of the root (/) filesystem because they must be available to the operating system during early stages of the boot process – before other filesystems are mounted.

We will encounter device special files throughout this course, and you will have an opportunity to experiment extensively with device special files in Chapter 22 of Volume 2. For now, just having a bit of information about device special files will suffice.

Session

Session is another of those terms that can apply to different things while retaining essentially the same meaning. The most basic application of the term is to a terminal session. That is a single terminal emulator connected to a single user login and shell. So in its most basic sense, a session is a single window or virtual console logged into a local or remote host with a command-line shell running in it. The Xfce4 terminal emulator supports multiple sessions by placing each session on a separate tab.

---

[11] Wikipedia, *Device File*, https://en.wikipedia.org/wiki/Device_file

Shell

A shell is the command interpreter for the operating system. Each of the many shells available for Linux interprets the commands typed by the user or SysAdmin into a form usable by the operating system. When the results are returned to the shell program, it displays them on the terminal.

The default shell for most Linux distributions is the bash shell. Bash stands for Bourne again shell because the bash shell is based upon the older Bourne shell, which was written by Steven Bourne in 1977. Many other shells are available. The four I list here are the ones I encounter most frequently, but many others exist[12]:

- **csh**: The C shell for programmers who like the syntax of the C language

- **ksh**: The Korn shell, written by David Korn and popular with Unix users

- **tcsh**: A version of csh with more ease-of-use features

- **zsh**: Which combines many features of other popular shells

All shells have some built-in commands that supplement or replace the commands provided by the core utilities. Open the man page for bash and find the "BUILT-INS" section to see the list of commands provided by the shell itself.

I have used the C shell, the Korn shell, and the Z shell. I still like the bash shell better than any of the others I have tried. Each shell has its own personality and syntax. Some will work better for you and others not so well. Use the one that works best for you, but that might require that you at least try some of the others. You can change shells quite easily.

Using Different Shells

So far we have been using the bash shell, so you have a brief experience with it. There are some other shells that might be better suited for your needs. We will look at three others in this experiment.

---

[12]Wikipedia, *Comparison of command shells*, https://en.wikipedia.org/wiki/Comparison_of_command_shells

EXPERIMENT 7-2: USING DIFFERENT SHELLS

Because most Linux distributions use the bash shell as the default, I will assume that is the one you have been using and that it is your default shell. In our preparation for this chapter, we installed three other shells, ksh, tcsh, and zsh.

Do this experiment as the user student. First, look at your command prompt, which should look like this:

```
[student@studentvm1 ~]$
```

This is the standard bash prompt for a non-root user. Now let's change this to ksh. Just enter the name of the shell:

```
[student@studentvm1 ~]$ ksh
$
```

You can tell by the difference in the prompt that this is a different shell. There is also a fun trick you can use if you need to know exactly which shell you're using:

```
$ echo $0
ksh
```

Run a couple simple commands such as ls and free just to see that there is no difference in how the commands work. This is because most of the commands are separate from the shell, except for the built-ins. Try the ll command:

```
$ ll
ksh: ll: not found [No such file or directory]
$
```

That fails because Korn shell aliases are different from bash aliases. Try scrolling up to get a command history like bash. It does not work.

```
$ zsh
This is the Z Shell configuration function for new users,
zsh-newuser-install.
You are seeing this message because you have no zsh startup files
(the files .zshenv, .zprofile, .zshrc, .zlogin in the directory
~).  This function can help you with a few settings that should
make your use of the shell easier.
```

You can:

(q) Quit and do nothing. The function will be run again next time.

(0) Exit, creating the file ~/.zshrc containing just a comment.
     That will prevent this function being run again.

(1) Continue to the main menu.

--- Type one of the keys in parentheses ---

If you continue by entering a "1", you will be taken through a series of menus that will help you configure the Z shell to suit your needs – as best you might know them at this stage. I chose "Q" to just go on to the prompt, which looks like just a bit different from the bash prompt:

```
[student@studentvm1]~%
```

Run a few simple commands while you are in the Z shell. Then type exit twice to get back to the original, top-level bash shell:

```
[student@studentvm1]~% w
 14:30:25 up 3 days,  6:12,  3 users,  load average: 0.00, 0.00, 0.02
USER     TTY          LOGIN@   IDLE   JCPU   PCPU WHAT
student  pts/0        Tue08    0.00s  0.07s  0.00s w
root     pts/1        Wed06    18:48  0.26s  0.26s -bash
student  pts/2        08:14    6:16m  0.03s  0.03s -bash
[student@studentvm1]~% exit
$ exit
[student@studentvm1 ~]$
```

What do you think might happen if you start a bash shell while you are already in a bash shell?

```
[student@studentvm1 ~]$ bash
[student@studentvm1 ~]$ ls
Desktop Documents Downloads Music Pictures Public Templates Videos
[student@studentvm1 ~]$ exit
exit
[student@studentvm1 ~]$
```

You just get into another bash shell is what.

This illustrates more than it might appear superficially. First, there is the fact that each shell is a layer. Starting a new shell does not terminate the previous one. When you started zsh from bash, the bash shell remained in the background, and when you exited from zsh, you were returned to the waiting bash shell.

It turns out that this is exactly what happens when running any command or process from a shell. The command runs in its own session, and the parent shell – process – waits until that sub-command – child process – ends and control is returned to it before being able to continue processing further commands.

So if you have a script that runs other commands – which is the purpose of a script – the script runs each command, waiting for it to finish before moving on to run the next command.

That behavior can be modified by appending an ampersand (&) to the end of a command, which places the called command in the background and allows the user to continue to interact with the shell or for the script to continue processing more commands. You would only want to do this with commands that do not require further human interaction or output to STDOUT. You would also not want to run a command in the background when the results of that command are needed by other commands that will be run later, but perhaps before the background task has finished.

Because of the many options available to SysAdmins and users in Linux, there is little need for moving programs to the background. Just open another terminal emulator on the desktop, start another terminal emulator in a screen session, or switch to an available virtual console. This capability might be more useful in scripts to launch programs that will run while your script continues to process other commands.

You can change your shell with the **chsh** command so that it will be persistent every time you log in and start a new terminal session. We will explore terminal emulators and shells in more detail in Chapter 14.

Secure Shell (SSH)

SSH is not really a shell. The **ssh** command starts a secure communication link between itself as the client and another host with the SSHD server running on it. The actual command shell used at the server end is whatever the default shell set for that account on the server side, such as bash, Korn or csh. SSH is simply a protocol that creates a secure communications tunnel between two Linux hosts.

Screen

You might at first think of "screen" as the device on which your Linux desktop is displayed. That is one meaning.

For SysAdmins like us, screen is a program, a screen manager, that enhances the power of the command line. The screen utility allows launching multiple shells in a single terminal session and provides means to navigate between the running shells.

I have many times had a remote session running a program when the communications link failed. When that happened the running program was terminated as well, and I had to restart it from the beginning. It could get very frustrating. The screen program can prevent that. A screen session will continue to run even if the connectivity to the remote host is broken because the network connection fails. It also allows the intentional disconnection of the screen session from the terminal session and reconnecting later from the same or a different computer. All of the CLI programs running in the screen terminal sessions will continue to run on the remote host. This means that once communications is re-established, one can log back into the remote host and use the **screen -r** command at the remote command line to reattach the screen session to the terminal.

So I can start up a bunch of terminal sessions in screen, use **Ctrl-a + d** to disconnect from screen, and log out. Then I can go to another location, log into a different host, SSH to the host running my programs in screen, log in, and use the **screen -r** command to reconnect to the screen session, and all of the terminal sessions and their respective programs will still be running.

The screen command can be useful in some environments where physical access to a hardware console is not available to provide access to the virtual consoles but the flexibility of multiple shells is needed. You will probably find it convenient to use the screen program, and in some cases it will be necessary to do so in order to work quickly and efficiently.

EXPERIMENT 7-3: USING SCREEN

In this experiment we explore the use of the screen program. Perform this experiment in a terminal session as the student user. Before we begin, let's discuss how to send commands to the screen program itself in order to do things like open a new terminal and switch between running terminal sessions.

In this experiment I provide instructions such as "press **Ctrl-A + C**" to open a new terminal. That means that you should hold down the Ctrl key while you press the "A" key; at this point you can release the Ctrl and "A" keys because you have alerted the screen program that the next keystroke is intended for it. Now press the "C" key. This sequence of keystrokes seems a bit complicated, but I soon learned it as muscle memory, and it is quite natural by now.

For the **Ctrl-A + "** (double quote) sequence, which shows a list of all open terminals in that screen session, do **Ctrl-A**, release those keys, and then press **Shift + "**.

Use the **Ctrl-A + Ctrl-A** sequence that toggles between the most recent two terminal sessions. You must continue to hold down the Ctrl key and press the "A" key twice.

1. Enter the **screen** command, which will clear the display and leave you at a command prompt. You are now in the screen display manager with a single terminal session open and displayed in the window.

2. Type any command such as **ls** to have something displayed in the terminal session besides the command prompt.

3. Press **Ctrl-A + C** to open a new shell within the screen session.

4. Enter a different command, such as **df –h**, in this new terminal.

5. Type **Ctrl-a + a** to switch between the terminals.

6. Enter **Ctrl-a + c** to open a third terminal.

7. Type **Ctrl-a + "** to list the open terminals. Choose any one except the last one by using the up/down arrow key and hit the **Enter** key to switch to that terminal.

8. To close the selected terminal, type **exit** and press the **Enter** key.

9. Type the command **Ctrl-a + "** to verify that the terminal is gone. Notice that the terminal with the number you have chosen to close is no longer there and that the other terminals have not been renumbered.

10. To reopen a fresh terminal, use **Ctrl-a + c**.

11. Type **Ctrl-a + "** to verify that the new terminal has been created. Notice that it has been opened in the place of the terminal that was previously closed.

12. To disconnect from the screen session and all open terminals, press **Ctrl-A + D**. Note that this leaves all of the terminals and the programs in them intact and still running.

13. Enter the **screen -list** command on the command line to list all of the current screen sessions. The **screen -ls** command does the same thing and is a bit shorter. Either way, this can be useful to ensure that you reconnect to the correct screen session if there are multiple ones.

14. Use the command **screen –r** to reconnect to the active screen session. If multiple active screen sessions are open, then a list of them will be displayed, and you can choose the one to which you wish to connect; you will have to enter the name of the screen session to which you want to connect.

I recommend that you not open a new screen session inside of an existing screen session. It can be difficult to switch between the terminals because the screen program does not always understand which of the embedded sessions to which to send the command.

I use the screen program all the time. It is a powerful tool that provides me with extreme flexibility for working on the command line.

The GUI and the CLI

You may like and use any of the many graphical user interfaces, that is, desktops, that are available with almost all Linux distributions; you may even switch between them because you find one particular desktop such as KDE more usable for certain tasks and another like GNOME better suited for other tasks. But you will also find that most of the graphical tools required to manage a Linux computer are simply wrappers around the underlying CLI commands that actually perform those functions.

A graphical interface cannot approach the power of the CLI because the GUI is inherently limited to those functions the programmers have decided you should have access to. This is how Windows and other restrictive operating systems work. They only allow you to have access to the functions and power that they determine you should have. This might be because the developers think you really do want to be shielded from the full power of your computer, or it might be due to the fact that they don't think you are capable of dealing with that level of power, or it might be that writing a GUI to do everything a CLI can do is time consuming and a low priority for the developer.

Just because the GUI is limited in some ways does not mean that good SysAdmins cannot leverage it to make their jobs easier. I do find that I can leverage the GUI with more flexibility for my command-line tasks. By allowing multiple terminal windows on the desktop or by using advanced terminal emulation programs such as Xfce, Tilix, and terminal that are designed for a GUI environment, I can improve my productivity. Having multiple terminals open on the desktop gives me the capability of being logged into multiple computers simultaneously. I can also be logged into any one computer multiple times. I can open multiple terminal sessions using my own user ID and more terminal sessions as root.

For me, having multiple terminal sessions available at all times, in multiple ways, is what the GUI is all about. A GUI can also provide me with access to programs like LibreOffice, which I am using to write this book, graphical email and web browsing applications, and much more. But the real power for SysAdmins is in the command line.

Linux uses the GNU core utilities, which were originally written by Richard M. Stallman,[13] a.k.a. RMS, as the open source utilities required by any free version of Unix or Unix-like operating systems. The GNU core utilities are the basic file, shell, and text manipulation utilities of any GNU Operating System such as GNU/Linux and can be counted upon by any SysAdmin to be present on every version of Linux. In addition, every Linux distribution has an extended set of utilities that provide even more functions.

You can enter the command **info coreutils** to view a list of the GNU core utilities and select individual commands for more information. You can also use the **man <command>** to view the man page for each of these commands and all of the many hundreds of other Linux commands that are also standard with every distribution.

Some Important Linux Commands

The most basic Linux commands are those that allow you to determine and change your current location in the directory structure; create, manage, and look at files; view various aspects of system status; and more. These next experiments will introduce you to some basic commands that enable you to do all of these things. It also covers some advanced commands that are frequently used during the process of problem determination.

---

[13] Wikipedia, *Richard M. Stallman*, https://en.wikipedia.org/wiki/Richard_Stallman

Most of the commands covered in these experiments have many options, some of which can be quite esoteric. These experiments are neither meant to cover all of the Linux commands available (there are several hundred), nor are they intended to cover all of the options on any of these commands. This is meant only as an introduction to these commands and their uses.

The PWD

The term "PWD" refers to present working directory, which you might know as the "current directory." The PWD is important because all command actions take place in the PWD unless another location is explicitly specified in the command. The **pwd** command means "print working directory," that is, print the name of the current directory on the shell output. Notice that the pwd command is all lowercase.

Directory Path Notation Styles

A path is a notational method for referring to directories in the Linux directory tree. This gives us a method for expressing the path to a directory or a file that is not in the PWD. Linux uses paths extensively for easy location of and access to executable files, making it unnecessary to type the entire path to the executable.

For example, it is easier to type "ls" than it is to type "/usr/bin/ls" to run the ls command. The shell uses the PATH variable where it finds a list of directories in which to search for the executable by the name "ls".

EXPERIMENT 7-4: PATH NOTATION STYLES

This simple experiment simply displays the content of the PATH environment variable for the student user:

```
[student@studentvm1 ~]$ echo $PATH
/usr/local/bin:/usr/bin:/usr/local/sbin:/usr/sbin:/home/student/.local/bin:/
home/student/bin
[student@studentvm1 ~]$
```

The various paths – directories – that the shell will search are listed in the output from the preceding command. Each path is separated by a colon (:).

There are two types of notation we can use to express a path – absolute and relative. An absolute path is specified completely starting with the root directory. So if the PWD is the Downloads directory of my home directory, I would specify the absolute path as /home/student/Downloads. With that as my PWD, I need to specify the absolute path to my Documents/Work directory as /home/student/Documents/Work. I could also specify that path in relative notation from my current PWD, as ../Documents/Work. I could also use the notation ~/Documents/Work because the tilde (~) is a shorthand notation for my home directory.

Moving Around the Directory Tree

Let's start by looking at how to move around the Linux filesystem directory tree at the command line. Many times working on or in a directory is easier if it is the PWD. Moving around the filesystem is a very important capability, and there are a number of shortcuts that can help as well.

EXPERIMENT 7-5: MOVING AROUND THE DIRECTORY TREE

Perform this experiment as the student user. You should already be logged into the Xfce desktop with an Xfce terminal session open as the student user. If not, do that now.

Moving around the Linux filesystem directory tree is important for many reasons. You will use these skills throughout this course and in real life as a SysAdmin.

Start in the terminal session as the user student. Check the present working directory:

```
[student@studentvm1 tmp]$ pwd
/tmp
[student@studentvm1 tmp]$ cd
[student@studentvm1 ~]$ pwd
/home/student
[student@studentvm1 ~]$
```

The first time I checked, the PWD was the /tmp directory because I had been working there. Your PWD will probably be your home directory, (~). Using the cd command with no options always makes your home directory the PWD. Notice in the command prompt that the tilde (~) is a shorthand indicator for your home directory.

Now just do a simple command, long list, to view the content of your home directory. These directories are created when a new user logs into the account using the GUI for the first time:

```
[student@studentvm1 ~]$ ll
total 212
drwxr-xr-x. 2 student student  4096 Aug 18 17:10 Desktop
drwxr-xr-x. 2 student student  4096 Aug 18 10:21 Documents
drwxr-xr-x. 2 student student  4096 Aug 18 10:21 Downloads
drwxr-xr-x. 2 student student  4096 Aug 18 10:21 Music
drwxr-xr-x. 2 student student  4096 Aug 18 10:21 Pictures
drwxr-xr-x. 2 student student  4096 Aug 18 10:21 Public
drwxr-xr-x. 2 student student  4096 Aug 18 10:21 Templates
drwxr-xr-x. 2 student student  4096 Aug 18 10:21 Videos
[student@studentvm1 ~]$
```

This command does not show the so-called hidden files in your home directory, which makes it easier to scan the rest of the contents.

Let's create a few files to work with since there are none other than the hidden configuration files created by default. The following command-line program will create a few files so that we have more than just directories to look at. We will look at command-line programming in some detail as we proceed through the course. Enter the program all on one line. It is okay if the line wraps on your screen; just do not press Enter until you have completed the entire command:

```
[student@studentvm1 ~]$ for X in dmesg.txt dmesg1.txt dmesg2.txt dmesg3.txt
dmesg4.txt ; do dmesg > $X ; done
[student@studentvm1 ~]$ ll
total 252
drwxr-xr-x. 2 student student  4096 Sep 29 15:31 Desktop
-rw-rw-r--. 1 student student 41604 Sep 30 16:13 dmesg1.txt
-rw-rw-r--. 1 student student 41604 Sep 30 16:13 dmesg2.txt
-rw-rw-r--. 1 student student 41604 Sep 30 16:13 dmesg3.txt
-rw-rw-r--. 1 student student 41604 Sep 30 16:13 dmesg4.txt
-rw-rw-r--. 1 student student 41604 Sep 30 16:13 dmesg.txt
drwxr-xr-x. 2 student student  4096 Sep 29 15:31 Documents
drwxr-xr-x. 2 student student  4096 Sep 29 15:31 Downloads
drwxr-xr-x. 2 student student  4096 Sep 29 15:31 Music
drwxr-xr-x. 2 student student  4096 Sep 29 15:31 Pictures
drwxr-xr-x. 2 student student  4096 Sep 29 15:31 Public
```

```
drwxr-xr-x. 2 student student  4096 Sep 29 15:31 Templates
drwxr-xr-x. 2 student student  4096 Sep 29 15:31 Videos
[student@studentvm1 ~]$
```

This long listing shows the ownership and file permissions for each file and directory. The data drwxr-xr-x shows first that this is a directory with the leading "d", while a file has a hyphen (-) in that position. The file permissions are three triplets of (R)ead, (W)rite, and e(X)ecute. Each triplet represents User, the owner of the file; Group, the group that owns the file; and Other, for all other users. These permissions represent something a bit different on a directory. We will explore file and directory ownership and permissions in more detail in Chapter 18.

Make /var/log the PWD and list the contents:

```
[student@studentvm1 ~]# cd /var/log ; ll
total 18148
drwxrwxr-x. 2 root    root        4096 Aug 13 16:24 anaconda
drwx------. 2 root    root        4096 Jul 18 13:27 audit
drwxr-xr-x. 2 root    root        4096 Feb  9  2018 blivet-gui
-rw-------. 1 root    root       74912 Sep  2 09:13 boot.log
-rw-rw----. 1 root    utmp         768 Sep  2 09:26 btmp
-rw-rw----. 1 root    utmp         384 Aug 18 10:21 btmp-20180901
<snip>
drwxr-xr-x. 2 lightdm lightdm     4096 Sep  2 09:13 lightdm
-rw-------. 1 root    root           0 Sep  2 03:45 maillog
-rw-------. 1 root    root           0 Apr 25 02:21 maillog-20180819
-rw-------. 1 root    root           0 Aug 19 03:51 maillog-20180831
-rw-------. 1 root    root           0 Aug 31 14:47 maillog-20180902
-rw-------. 1 root    root     2360540 Sep  6 13:03 messages
-rw-------. 1 root    root     1539520 Aug 19 03:48 messages-20180819
-rw-------. 1 root    root     1420556 Aug 31 14:44 messages-20180831
-rw-------. 1 root    root      741931 Sep  2 03:44 messages-20180902
drwx------. 3 root    root        4096 Jul  8 22:49 pluto
-rw-r--r--. 1 root    root        1040 Jul 18 07:39 README
<snip>
-rw-r--r--. 1 root    root       29936 Sep  4 16:48 Xorg.0.log
-rw-r--r--. 1 root    root       28667 Sep  2 09:12 Xorg.0.log.old
-rw-r--r--. 1 root    root       23533 Aug 18 10:16 Xorg.9.log
[root@studentvm1 log]#
```

Can you determine which are files and which are directories? Try to display the content of the messages file:

```
[student@studentvm1 log]$ cat messages
cat: messages: Permission denied
[student@studentvm1 log]$
```

If you are using Fedora as recommended, there should be a README file in /var/log. Use the **cat** command to view the contents:

```
[student@studentvm1 log]$ cat README
```

Why can you view the contents of this file? Let's change the PWD to /etc:

```
[student@studentvm1 log]$ cd /etc ; pwd
/etc
[student@studentvm1 etc]$
```

Now change to the Documents subdirectory of your home directory (~):

```
[student@studentvm1 etc]$ cd ~/Documents/ ; ll
total 0
[student@studentvm1 Documents]$
```

Notice that I used the tilde (~) to represent the home directory, which would otherwise have to be typed out as /home/student/Documents.

When I want to return to the /etc directory, I can save a bit of typing using this next shortcut:

```
[student@studentvm1 Documents]$ cd -
/etc
[student@studentvm1 etc]$
```

The hyphen (-), a.k.a. the minus sign, will always return you to the previous PWD. How? Look a bit at the environment that defines many environment variables including $PWD and $OLDPWD. The **env** command prints all of the current environment variables, and the **grep** command extracts and sends to STDOUT only those lines that contain "PWD":

```
[student@studentvm1 etc]$ env | grep -i PWD
PWD=/etc
OLDPWD=/home/student/Documents
[student@studentvm1 etc]$
```

The hyphen (-), when used as an option to the **cd** command, is a shorthand notation for the $OLDPWD variable. The command could also be issued in the following manner:

```
[student@studentvm1 Documents]$ cd $OLDPWD
[student@studentvm1 etc]$
```

Return to the home directory and create a new directory that is a few layers deep. The **mkdir** command can do that when used with the -p option. You can also create other directories in the PWD at the same time. Enter the following command all on one line:

```
[student@studentvm1 etc]$ cd ; mkdir -p
./testdir1/testdir2/testdir3/testdir4/testdir5 testdir6 testdir7
[student@studentvm1 ~]$ tree
.
├── Desktop
├── dmesg1.txt
├── dmesg2.txt
├── dmesg3.txt
├── dmesg.txt
├── Documents
├── Downloads
├── Music
├── newfile.txt
├── Pictures
├── Public
├── Templates
├── testdir1
│   └── testdir2
│       └── testdir3
│           └── testdir4
│               └── testdir5
├── testdir6
├── testdir7
└── Videos
```

The first string was a directory with a number of parents. This command also added two more directories to be created in the current directory. The **mkdir** utility, like so many others, accepts a list of arguments, not just a single one. In this case the list was of new directories to create.

There is also a shorthand notation for the PWD that we can use in commands. The variable $PWD would work, but the dot (.) is much faster. So for some commands that need a source and a target directory, we can use the . for either. Note that in the previous step, the top of the tree command output starts with a dot, which indicates the current directory.

```
[student@studentvm1 ~]$ mv ./dmesg2.txt /tmp
[student@studentvm1 ~]$ cp /tmp/dmesg2.txt .
[student@studentvm1 ~]$ cp /tmp/dmesg2.txt ./dmesg4.txt
```

In this experiment we have looked at how to navigate the directory tree and how to create new directories. We have also practiced using some of the many notational shortcuts available to us.

Tab Completion Facility

Bash provides a facility for completing partially typed program and host names, file names, and directory names. Type the partial command or a file name as an argument to a command and press the **Tab** key. If the host, file, directory, or program exists and the remainder of the name is unique, bash will complete entry of the name. Because the Tab key is used to initiate the completion, this feature is sometimes referred to as "Tab completion."

Tab completion is programmable and can be configured to meet many different needs. However, unless you have specific needs that are not met by the standard configurations provided by Linux, the core utilities, and other CLI applications, there should never be a reason to change the defaults.

Note   The bash man page has a detailed and mostly unintelligible explanation of "programmable completion." The book *Beginning the Linux Command Line* has a short and more readable description,[14] and Wikipedia[15] has more information, examples, and an animated GIF to aid in understanding this feature.

---

[14] van Vugt, Sander, *Beginning the Linux Command Line*, Apress, 2015, 22
[15] Wikipedia, *Command-Line Completion*, https://en.wikipedia.org/wiki/Command-line_completion

Experiment 7-6 provides a very short introduction to command completion.

EXPERIMENT 7-6: TAB COMPLETION

Perform this experiment as the student user. Your home directory should have a subdirectory named Documents for this experiment. Most Linux distributions create a Documents subdirectory for each user.

Be sure that your home directory is the PWD. We will use completion to change into the ~/ Documents directory. Type the following partial command into the terminal:

```
[student@studentvm1 ~]$ cd D<Tab>
```

<Tab> means to press the Tab key once. Nothing happens because there are three directories that start with "D". You can see that by pressing the Tab key twice in rapid succession, which lists all of the directories that match what you have already typed:

```
[student@studentvm1 ~]$ cd D<tab><Tab>
Desktop/    Documents/ Downloads/
[student@studentvm1 ~]$ cd D
```

Now add the "o" to the command and press Tab twice more:

```
[student@studentvm1 ~]$ cd Do<tab><Tab>
Documents/ Downloads/
[student@studentvm1 ~]$ cd Do
```

You should see a list of both directories that start with "Do". Now add the "c" to the command and press the Tab key once:

```
[student@studentvm1 ~]$ cd Doc<Tab>
[student@studentvm1 ~]$ cd Documents/
```

So if you type cd Doc<Tab>, the rest of the directory name is completed in the command. Press **Enter** to change to the new directory.

Now make your home directory the PWD.

Let's take a quick look at completion for commands. In this case the command is relatively short, but most are. Assume we want to determine the current uptime for the host:

```
[student@studentvm1 ~]$ up<Tab><Tab>
update-alternatives    updatedb                        update-mime-database       upower
update-ca-trust              update-desktop-database  update-pciids              uptime
update-crypto-policies   update-gtk-immodules     update-smart-drivedb
[student@studentvm1 ~]$ up
```

We can see several commands that begin with "up", and we can also see that typing one
more letter, "t", will complete enough of the uptime command that the rest will be unique.

```
[student@studentvm1 ~]$ upt<Tab>ime
 07:55:05 up 1 day, 10:01,  7 users,  load average: 0.00, 0.00, 0.00
```

The completion facility only completes the command, directory, or file name when the
remaining text string needed is unequivocally unique.

Tab completion works for commands, some sub-commands, as well as file names
and directory names. I find that completion is most useful for completing the directory
and file names, which tend to be longer, and a few of the longer commands and some
sub-commands.

Many Linux commands are so short already that using the completion facility can
actually be less efficient than typing the command. The short Linux command names
are quite in keeping with being a lazy SysAdmin. So it just depends on whether you find
it more efficient or consistent for you to use completion on short commands. Once you
learn which commands are worthwhile for Tab completion and how much you need to
type, you can use those that you find helpful.

Exploring Files

The commands we will be exploring in this next experiment are all related to creating
and manipulating files as objects.

EXPERIMENT 7-7: EXPLORING FILES

Perform this experiment as the student user. You should already be logged into your Linux
computer as the user student on the GUI and have an Xcfe4 terminal session open.

Open a new tab by selecting **File** from the terminal menu bar and selecting **Open Tab** from
the drop-down menu. The new tab will become the active one, and it is already logged in as

the user student. An alternate and easy way to open a new tab in a terminal is to right-click anywhere in the terminal window and select **Open Tab** from the pop-up menu.

Enter the pwd command to determine the present working directory (PWD). It should be **/home/student** as shown here:

```
[student@studentvm1 ~]$ pwd
/home/student
[student@studentvm1 ~]$
```

If the PWD is not your home directory, change to your home directory using the **cd** command without any options or arguments.

Let's create some new files like you did as root in an earlier project. The **cp** command is used to copy files. Use the following commands to create and copy some files:

```
[student@studentvm1 ~]$ touch newfile.txt
[student@fstudentvm1 ~]$ df -h > diskusage.txt
```

Use the command **ls -lah** to display a long list of all files in your home directory and display their sizes in human-readable format. Note that the time displayed on each file is the mtime, which is the time the file or directory was last modified. There are a number of "hidden" files that have a dot (.) as the first character of their names. Use **ls -lh** if you don't need to see all of the hidden files.

The **touch dmesg2.txt** changes all of the times for that file:

```
[student@studentvm1 ~]$ touch dmesg2.txt
[student@studentvm1 ~]$ ls -lh
total 212K
drwxr-xr-x. 2 student student 4.0K Aug 18 17:10 Desktop
-rw-rw-r--. 1 student student 1.8K Sep  6 09:08 diskusage.txt
-rw-rw-r--. 1 student student  44K Sep  6 10:52 dmesg1.txt
-rw-rw-r--. 1 student student  44K Sep  6 10:54 dmesg2.txt
-rw-rw-r--. 1 student student  44K Sep  6 10:52 dmesg3.txt
-rw-rw-r--. 1 student student  44K Sep  6 10:52 dmesg.txt
drwxr-xr-x. 2 student student 4.0K Aug 18 10:21 Documents
drwxr-xr-x. 2 student student 4.0K Aug 18 10:21 Downloads
drwxr-xr-x. 2 student student 4.0K Aug 18 10:21 Music
-rw-rw-r--. 1 student student    0 Sep  6 10:52 newfile.txt
drwxr-xr-x. 2 student student 4.0K Aug 18 10:21 Pictures
```

```
drwxr-xr-x. 2 student student 4.0K Aug 18 10:21 Public
drwxr-xr-x. 2 student student 4.0K Aug 18 10:21 Templates
drwxr-xr-x. 2 student student 4.0K Aug 18 10:21 Videos
[student@studentvm1 ~]$
```

Enter the commands **ls -lc** and **ls -lu** to view the ctime (time the inode (index-node) last changed) and atime (time the file was last accessed or used or the contents viewed), respectively.

Enter the command **cat dmesg1.txt**, but don't worry about the fact that the data spews off the screen. Now use the commands **ls -l**, **ls -lc**, and **ls -lu** to again view the dates and times of the files and notice that the file dmesg1.txt has had its atime changed. The atime of a file is the time that it was last accessed for read by some program. Note that the ctime has also changed. Why? If you don't figure this out now, it will be covered later, so no worries.

Enter **stat dmesg1.txt** to display a complete set of information about this file, including its [acm]times, its size, permissions, the number of storage data blocks assigned to it, its ownership, and even its inode number. We will cover inodes in detail in a later session:

```
[student@studentvm1 ~]$ stat dmesg1.txt
  File: dmesg1.txt
  Size: 44297        Blocks: 88         IO Block: 4096   regular file
Device: fd07h/64775d    Inode: 213          Links: 1
Access: (0664/-rw-rw-r--)  Uid: ( 1000/ student)   Gid: ( 1000/ student)
Context: unconfined_u:object_r:user_home_t:s0
Access: 2018-09-06 10:58:48.725941316 -0400
Modify: 2018-09-06 10:52:51.428402753 -0400
Change: 2018-09-06 10:52:51.428402753 -0400
 Birth: -
[student@studentvm1 ~]$
```

Notice that the **stat** command displays the files' timestamps in microseconds. The reason for this granularity is to deal with high-speed, high-volume transaction-based environments in which transaction timing sequence is important.

Tip   The /tmp directory is readable and writable by all users. This makes it a good place to share files temporarily. But that can also make it a security issue.

Perhaps you were curious – that is a good thing – and repeated the last part of this experiment multiple times, in which case you would have noticed that the atime did not change after the first **cat** command to access the file content. This is because the file content is now in cache and does not need to be accessed again to read the content. Use the following commands to change the content and then stat it to view the results:

```
[student@studentvm1 ~]$ echo "hello world" >> dmesg1.txt ;
cat dmesg1.txt ; stat dmesg1.txt
```

Move the file dmesg3.txt to the /tmp directory with the **mv dmesg3.txt /tmp** command. Use the **ls** command in both the current directory and the /tmp directory to verify that the file has been moved.

Enter the command **rm /tmp/dmesg3.txt** to delete the file and verify that it has been deleted.

This experiment has explored creating, copying, and moving files. It also provided some tools that allow you to expose metadata about files.

More Commands

There are some additional commands that you will find useful.

EXPERIMENT 7-8: MORE COMMANDS

Perform this experiment as the student user.

Start by looking at what happens when too much data is displayed by a command and it scrolls off the top of the screen.

The dmesg command displays the messages generated by Linux during the initial boot process. Enter the command **dmesg** and watch the output quickly scroll off the screen. There are lots of data there that could be missed.

Enter the **dmesg | less** command. You should see the top of the output from the dmesg command. At the bottom of the terminal, you should see a colon and the cursor as in the following example.

: █

To see a single new line at the bottom of the screen, press the **Enter** key.

Press the **space bar** to see a whole new page of output from the command.

You can also use the **up** and **down** arrow keys to move one line at a time in the respective direction. The **Page Up** and **Page Down** keys can be used to move up or down a page at a time. Use these four keys to navigate the output stream. You will see (END) at the bottom left of the screen when the end of the data stream has been reached.

You can also specify a line number and use the **G** key to "Goto" the specified line number. The following entry will go to line 256, which will display at the top of the terminal:

256G

Capital G without a line number takes you to the end of the data stream:

G

Lowercase g takes you to the beginning of the data stream:

g

Press the **Q** key to quit and return to the command line.

The movement commands in `less` are very similar to those of `vim`, so this should be familiar.

Time and date are important, and the Linux **date** and **cal** commands provide some interesting capabilities.

Enter the date command to display today's date:

```
[student@studentvm1 ~]$ date
Thu Jan 19 11:15:46 AM EST 2023
[student@studentvm1 ~]$
```

Enter the **cal** command to display a calendar for the current month:

```
[student@studentvm1 ~]$ cal
    January 2023
Su Mo Tu We Th Fr Sa
 1  2  3  4  5  6  7
 8  9 10 11 12 13 14
15 16 17 18 19 20 21
22 23 24 25 26 27 28
29 30 31
```

```
[student@studentvm1 ~]$
```

Enter the following command to display a calendar for the entire year of 1949:

```
[student@studentvm1 ~]$ cal 1949
```

Use the command **cat /etc/passwd | less** to display the contents of the password file. Hint: It does not actually contain any passwords. After browsing around a bit, quit from less.

Enter the following command to generate a data stream and pipe the results through the wc (word count) command to count the words, lines, and characters in the data stream:

```
[student@studentvm1 ~]$ cat /etc/services | wc
  11473    63130  692241
[student@studentvm1 ~]$
```

This shows that the **wc** command counted 11,473 lines, 63,130 words, and 692,241 characters in the data stream. The numbers in your result should be the same or very close. The **services** file is a list of the standard assigned and recognized ports used by various network services to communicate between computers.

The wc command can be used on its own. Use **wc -l /etc/services** to count the lines in that file. That is -L in lowercase for "line."

Command Recall and Editing

Lazy admins don't like typing. We especially don't like repetitive typing, so we look for ways to save time and typing. Using the bash shell history can help do that. The history command displays the last 1000 commands issued from the command line. You can use the up/down arrow key to scroll through that history on the command line and then execute the same or modified commands with no or minimal retyping.

Command-line editing can make entering lots of similar commands easier. Previous commands can be located by using the **up arrow** key to scroll back through the command history. Then some simple editing can be performed to make modifications to the original command. The **left arrow** and **right arrow** keys are used to move through the command being edited. The **Backspace** key is used to delete characters, and simply typing can complete the revised command.

EXPERIMENT 7-9: COMMAND RECALL AND EDITING

Start this experiment as the student user. We will switch to root partway through. In this experiment we look at using the bash history, command-line recall, and editing the recalled command line.

Enter the history command to view the current command history:

```
[student@studentvm1 ~]$ history
    1  su -
    2  poweroff
    3  su -
    4  ls -la
    5  clear
    6  w
    7  who
    8  whoami
    9  id
   10  ksh
   11  exit
   12  infor core-utils
   13  info core-utils
   14  info coreutils
   15  info utils-linux
   16  info utilslinux
   17  info utils
   18  info coreutils
   19  ls -la
   20  tty
<snip>
  257  dnf list installed
  258  dnf list installed | wc
  259  dnf list available | wc
  260  dnf list available
  261  dnf info zorba
  262  dnf info zipper
  263  history
[student@studentvm1 ~]$
```

Use the up arrow key to scroll through the history. When you find a nondestructive command, like one of the many ls commands that should be in the history, just hit the Enter key to issue that command again.

Use the history command to view the history again. Pick a command you want to execute again and enter the following command, where XXX is the number of the command you want to run. Then press the **Enter** key:

```
[student@studentvm1 ~]$ !XXX
```

Switch to a root terminal session to perform the rest of this experiment.

Change the PWD to /var/log/ and do a listing of the files there. You will see, among others, a file named boot.log. We will use this file for some of the next tasks.

Use the **cat** command to print the contents of the boot.log file to the screen:

```
[root@studentvm1 log]# cat boot.log
```

Count the lines in the boot.log file. Use the **up** arrow key to return to the previous line. The changes to the command are added to the end, so just type until the command looks like this:

```
[root@studentvm1 log]# cat boot.log | wc
```

Now view the lines that have the word "kernel" in them. Return to the previous command using the **up** arrow key. Backspace to remove "wc" but leave the pipe (|). Add the grep command, which we will cover in more detail in Chapter 9, to show only those lines containing the term "kernel":

```
[root@studentvm1 log]# cat boot.log | grep kernel
```

But what if some lines contain "Kernel" with an uppercase K? Return to the last command and use the left arrow key to move the cursor to the space between "grep" and "kernel" then add -i (ignore case) so the command looks like this:

```
[root@studentvm1 log]# cat boot.log | grep -i kernel
```

Edit that last command to add | wc to the end to count the total lines with the word "kernel" in both upper- and lowercases.

Although using the CLI history as in these examples seems a bit trivial, if you have to repeat some very long and complex commands, it can really save a lot of typing, and perhaps mistyping, which can be even more frustrating.

Chapter Summary

You can see from these simple examples just a little of the vast power available to the SysAdmin when using the command line.

In this chapter you have discovered that Linux provides a large number of methods to access the command line and perform your work as a SysAdmin. You can use the virtual consoles and any of a number of different terminal emulators and shells. You can combine those with the screen program in order to further enhance the flexibility you have at the command line.

We have also explored a number of important Linux commands and learned how to recall and edit commands from the bash history.

The examples in this chapter are informative in themselves, but they also are just the beginning. As we proceed through this course, you will encounter many ways in which the power and flexibility of the command line will be enhanced by combining the many options discussed in this chapter.

Exercises

Complete the following exercises to finish this chapter:

1. Why does the bash shell use different characters to denote root and non-root sessions, that is, $ and #?

2. Why do you think that there are so many different shells available for Linux?

3. If you already have a favorite terminal emulator, how does it compare to the Xfce terminal emulator, and which features of each do you prefer?

4. What is the function of any terminal emulator?

5. What command would you use to temporarily switch to the tcsh shell?

6. How does SSH differ from virtual consoles and terminal emulators?

7. Can an unprivileged user such as student display the contents
    of the /var/log/messages file? Why or why not – from a technical
    perspective rather than an architectural design decision one?

8. What command would you use to return the PWD to the
    previous PWD?

9. What do the last two entries of the student user's PATH tell you?

10. Can the cat command be used to list the contents of more than
    one file at a time?

11. If you want to repeat the previous command, how would you do
    that if you don't want to type it in again?

12. How can you list all of the commands previously issued at the
    command line?

CHAPTER 8

Core Utilities

Objectives

In this chapter you will learn

- Some history of the GNU core utilities
- Some history of the util-linux utilities
- How to use some of the basic core utilities

I frequently do research for articles and books I am writing – yes, this one among others – and the GNU core utilities show up quite frequently. All SysAdmins use these utilities regularly pretty much without thinking about them. There is also another set of basic utilities, util-linux, that we should also look at because they also are important Linux utilities.

Together these two sets of utilities comprise many of the most basic tools the Linux system administrator uses to complete everyday tasks. These tasks include management and manipulation of text files, directories, data streams, various types of storage media, process controls, filesystems, and much more. The primary functions of these tools are the ones that allow SysAdmins to perform many of the basic tasks required to administer a Linux computer. These tools are indispensable because without them it is not possible to accomplish any useful work on a Unix or Linux computer.

GNU Coreutils

To understand the origins of the GNU core utilities, we need to take a short trip in the Wayback machine to the early days of Unix at Bell Labs. Unix was originally written so that Ken Thompson, Dennis Ritchie, Doug McIlroy, and Joe Ossanna could continue with something they had started while working on a large multitasking and multiuser

235

© David Both 2023
D. Both, *Using and Administering Linux: Volume 1*, https://doi.org/10.1007/978-1-4842-9618-9_8

computer project called Multics. That little something was a game called *Space Travel*. As is true today, it always seems to be the gamers that drive forward the technology of computing. This new operating system was much more limited than Multics as only two users could log in at a time, so it was called UNICS. This name was later changed to Unix.

Over time, Unix turned out to be such a success that Bell Labs began essentially giving it away to universities, and later to companies, for the cost of the media and shipping. Back in those days, system-level software was shared between organizations and programmers as they worked to achieve common goals within the context of system administration.

Eventually the PHBs at AT&T decided that they should start making money on Unix and started using more restrictive – and expensive – licensing. This was taking place at a time when software in general was becoming more proprietary, restricted, and closed. It was becoming impossible to share software with other users and organizations.[1]

Some people did not like this and fought it with free software. Richard M. Stallman, a.k.a. RMS, led a group of rebels who were trying to write an open and freely available operating system that they call the "GNU Operating System." This group created what would become the GNU core utilities[2] but did not as yet produce a viable kernel.

When Linus Torvalds first began working on and compiled the Linux kernel, he needed a set of very basic system utilities to even begin to perform marginally useful work. The kernel does not provide commands themselves or any type of command shell such as bash. It is useless by itself. So Linus used the freely available GNU core utilities and recompiled them for Linux. This gave him a complete operating system even though it was quite basic.

These commands were originally three separate collections, fileutils, shellutils, and textutils, which were combined into the Linux core utilities in 2002.

EXPERIMENT 8-1: INTRODUCING THE GNU CORE UTILITIES

Before performing this experiment, you need to install the info package. The info command contains information about the coreutils and other tools that is not available anywhere else. Install the info package:

```
[root@studentvm1 ~]# dnf -y install info
```

---

[1] Wikipedia, *History of Unix*, https://en.wikipedia.org/wiki/History_of_Unix
[2] GNU Operating System, *Core utilities*, www.gnu.org/software/coreutils/coreutils.html

The rest of this experiment can be performed as the student user.

You can learn about all of the individual programs that comprise the GNU Utilities with the **info** command. If you do not already have a terminal emulator open on the Xfce desktop, please open one now:

```
[student@studentvm1 ~]$ info coreutils
Next: Introduction,  Up: (dir)

GNU Coreutils
*************

This manual documents version 8.29 of the GNU core utilities, including
the standard programs for text and file manipulation.

   Copyright © 1994-2017 Free Software Foundation, Inc.

     Permission is granted to copy, distribute and/or modify this
     document under the terms of the GNU Free Documentation License,
     Version 1.3 or any later version published by the Free Software
     Foundation; with no Invariant Sections, with no Front-Cover Texts,
     and with no Back-Cover Texts.  A copy of the license is included in
     the section entitled "GNU Free Documentation License".

* Menu:

* Introduction::                 Caveats, overview, and authors
* Common options::               Common options
* Output of entire files::       cat tac nl od base32 base64
* Formatting file contents::     fmt pr fold
<SNIP>
* Numeric operations::           factor numfmt seq
* File permissions::             Access modes
* File timestamps::              File timestamp issues
* Date input formats::           Specifying date strings
* Opening the software toolbox:: The software tools philosophy
* GNU Free Documentation License:: Copying and sharing this manual
* Concept index::                General index

   -  The Detailed Node Listing  -
-----Info: (coreutils)Top, 344 lines --
Top---------------------------------
```

The utilities are grouped by function to make specific ones easier to find. This page is interactive. Use the arrow keys on the keyboard to highlight the group you want more information on and press the **Enter** key.

Scroll down the list so that the block cursor is on the line "Working context::" and press **Enter**. The following page is displayed:

```
Next: User information,  Prev: File name manipulation,  Up: Top

19 Working context
*******************
```

```
This section describes commands that display or alter the context in
which you are working: the current directory, the terminal settings, and
so forth.  See also the user-related commands in the next section.
```

```
* Menu:

* pwd invocation::              Print working directory.
* stty invocation::             Print or change terminal characteristics.
* printenv invocation::         Print environment variables.
* tty invocation::              Print file name of terminal on standard input.
```

Now highlight the bottom line of the listed utilities and press **Enter**.

```
Prev: printenv invocation,  Up: Working context

19.4 'tty': Print file name of terminal on standard input
=========================================================
```

```
'tty' prints the file name of the terminal connected to its standard
input.  It prints 'not a tty' if standard input is not a terminal.
Synopsis:

     tty [OPTION]...

   The program accepts the following option.  Also see *note Common
options::.

'-s'
'--silent'
'--quiet'
     Print nothing; only return an exit status.
```

```
Exit status:

    0 if standard input is a terminal
    1 if standard input is a non-terminal file
    2 if given incorrect arguments
    3 if a write error occurs
```

You can read the information about this utility. So now let's use it. If you don't already have a second terminal emulator open and ready, open a new one now – you might want to open a second tab in the existing Xfce4 terminal emulator. This way you can see or easily switch between the info page and the command line on which you will be working. Enter the following command in the second terminal:

```
[student@studentvm1 ~]$ tty
/dev/pts/52
[student@studentvm1 ~]$
```

You can see we are getting essentially the same information as we did from the **w** and **who** commands, but this is in a format that shows the complete path to the device special file. This would be useful when you need that information for a script because it is easier than writing code to extract the date needed from either of those other two commands.

To do some basic maneuvering in info, use the following keys. A node is a page about a specific command or group of commands:

- **p**: Previous info node in the menu sequence.

- **n**: Next info node in the menu sequence.

- **u**: Up one menu layer.

- **l (lowercase L)**: Last visited node in history.

- **q**: Quit the info facility.

- **H**: Help/exit help.

Take some time to use the info facility to look at a few of the core utilities.

You have learned a bit about the GNU Utilities in this experiment. You have also received a quick tutorial in using the **info** utility for locating information about Linux commands. To learn more about using the info facility, use the command **info info**. And – of course – all of these utilities can be found in the man pages, but the documentation in the info facility is more complete.

There are 102 utilities in the GNU core utilities. They cover many of the basic functions necessary to perform some basic tasks on a Unix or Linux host. However, many basic utilities are still missing. For example, the mount and umount commands are not in this group of utilities. Those and many of the other commands that are not in the GNU Coreutils can be found in the util-linux collection.

util-linux

The util-linux[3] package of utilities contains many of the other common commands that SysAdmins use. These utilities are distributed by the Linux Kernel Organization. As you can see from the following list, they cover many aspects of Linux system administration:

agetty	fsck.minix	mkfs.bfs	setpriv
blkdiscard	fsfreeze	mkfs.cramfs	setsid
blkid	fstab	mkfs.minix	setterm
blockdev	fstrim	mkswap	sfdisk
cal	getopt	more	su
cfdisk	hexdump	mount	sulogin
chcpu	hwclock	mountpoint	swaplabel
chfn	ionice	namei	swapoff
chrt	ipcmk	newgrp	swapon
chsh	ipcrm	nologin	switch_root
colcrt	ipcs	nsenter	tailf
col	isosize	partx	taskset
colrm	kill	pg	tunelp
column	last	pivot_root	ul
ctrlaltdel	ldattach	prlimit	umount
ddpart	line	raw	unshare
delpart	logger	readprofile	utmpdump
dmesg	login	rename	uuidd
eject	look	renice	uuidgen
fallocate	losetup	reset	vipw
fdformat	lsblk	resizepart	wall

---

[3]Wikipedia, *util-linux*, https://en.wikipedia.org/wiki/Util-linux

fdisk	lscpu	rev	wdctl
findfs	lslocks	rtcwake	whereis
findmnt	lslogins	runuser	wipefs
flock	mcookie	script	write
fsck	mesg	scriptreplay	zramctl
fsck.cramfs	mkfs	setarch	

Note that some of these utilities have been deprecated and will likely fall out of the collection at some point in the future. You should check the Wikipedia reference for util-linux for some information on many of the utilities. The man pages can be used to learn the details of these commands, but there are no corresponding info pages for these utilities. Notice that **mount** and **umount** are a part of this group of commands.

Let's look at a couple of these utilities just to see what they are about.

EXPERIMENT 8-2: INTRODUCING THE UTIL-LINUX UTILITIES

Do this experiment as the student user.

Let's start with the cal command, which generates a calendar. Without any options, it shows the current month with today's date highlighted:

```
[student@studentvm1 ~]$ cal
    September 2018
Su Mo Tu We Th Fr Sa
                   1
 2  3  4  5  6  7  8
 9 10 11 12 13 14 15
16 17 18 19 20 21 22
23 24 25 26 27 28 29
30
[student@studentvm1 ~]$
```

Using the -3 option prints three months with the current month in the middle:

```
[student@studentvm1 ~]$ cal -3
      August 2018           September 2018          October 2018
Su Mo Tu We Th Fr Sa    Su Mo Tu We Th Fr Sa    Su Mo Tu We Th Fr Sa
          1  2  3  4                        1     1  2  3  4  5  6
 5  6  7  8  9 10 11     2  3  4  5  6  7  8     7  8  9 10 11 12 13
```

```
12 13 14 15 16 17 18    9 10 11 12 13 14 15   14 15 16 17 18 19 20
19 20 21 22 23 24 25   16 17 18 19 20 21 22   21 22 23 24 25 26 27
26 27 28 29 30 31      23 24 25 26 27 28 29   28 29 30 31
                       30
[student@studentvm1 ~]$
```

Using a year as an argument displays a calendar of that entire year:

```
[student@studentvm1 ~]$ cal 1948
                            1948

         January                February                 March
 Su Mo Tu We Th Fr Sa   Su Mo Tu We Th Fr Sa   Su Mo Tu We Th Fr Sa
             1  2  3     1  2  3  4  5  6  7       1  2  3  4  5  6
  4  5  6  7  8  9 10    8  9 10 11 12 13 14    7  8  9 10 11 12 13
 11 12 13 14 15 16 17   15 16 17 18 19 20 21   14 15 16 17 18 19 20
 18 19 20 21 22 23 24   22 23 24 25 26 27 28   21 22 23 24 25 26 27
 25 26 27 28 29 30 31   29                     28 29 30 31

<SNIP>

         October                November                December
 Su Mo Tu We Th Fr Sa   Su Mo Tu We Th Fr Sa   Su Mo Tu We Th Fr Sa
                1  2        1  2  3  4  5  6             1  2  3  4
  3  4  5  6  7  8  9    7  8  9 10 11 12 13    5  6  7  8  9 10 11
 10 11 12 13 14 15 16   14 15 16 17 18 19 20   12 13 14 15 16 17 18
 17 18 19 20 21 22 23   21 22 23 24 25 26 27   19 20 21 22 23 24 25
 24 25 26 27 28 29 30   28 29 30               26 27 28 29 30 31
 31
[student@studentvm1 ~]$
```

Use the command **man cal** to find additional information about the **cal** command. I do use the cal command, so you might find it useful too.

I use some commands to find information about the hardware – real or virtual – to which I am logged in. For example, it can be useful for a SysAdmin to know about the CPU:

```
[student@studentvm1 ~]$ lscpu
Architecture:          x86_64
CPU op-mode(s):        32-bit, 64-bit
```

```
Byte Order:            Little Endian
CPU(s):                2
On-line CPU(s) list:   0,1
Thread(s) per core:    1
Core(s) per socket:    2
Socket(s):             1
NUMA node(s):          1
Vendor ID:             GenuineIntel
CPU family:            6
Model:                 85
Model name:            Intel(R) Core(TM) i9-7960X CPU @ 2.80GHz
Stepping:              4
CPU MHz:               2807.986
BogoMIPS:              5615.97
Hypervisor vendor:     KVM
Virtualization type:   full
L1d cache:             32K
L1i cache:             32K
L2 cache:              1024K
L3 cache:              22528K
NUMA node0 CPU(s):     0,1
Flags:                 fpu vme de pse tsc msr pae mce cx8 apic sep mtrr pge mca
cmov pat pse36 clflush mmx fxsr sse sse2 ht syscall nx rdtscp lm constant_tsc
rep_good nopl xtopology nonstop_tsc cpuid pni pclmulqdq ssse3 cx16 pcid
sse4_1 sse4_2 x2apic movbe popcnt aes xsave avx rdrand hypervisor lahf_lm abm
3dnowprefetch invpcid_single pti fsgsbase avx2 invpcid rdseed clflushopt
```

The **lscpu** command provides a great deal of information about the installed CPU(s). Some of this information is very useful when writing scripts that may have need to know it. Note that VirtualBox sees most hardware and passes on the virtualized version just the same as the physical.

The lsblk command – list block devices that are usually disk drives – is very useful in helping me understand the structure of the partitions, volume groups, and physical and logical volumes of disks using logical volume management (LVM):

```
[student@studentvm1 ~]$ lsblk
NAME                    MAJ:MIN RM  SIZE RO TYPE MOUNTPOINTS
sda                       8:0    0   60G  0 disk
```

```
├─sda1                              8:1    0    1M  0 part
├─sda2                              8:2    0    1G  0 part /boot
├─sda3                              8:3    0    1G  0 part /boot/efi
└─sda4                              8:4    0   58G  0 part
  ├─fedora_studentvm1-root 253:0    0    2G  0 lvm  /
  ├─fedora_studentvm1-usr  253:1    0   15G  0 lvm  /usr
  ├─fedora_studentvm1-tmp  253:2    0    5G  0 lvm  /tmp
  ├─fedora_studentvm1-var  253:3    0   10G  0 lvm  /var
  └─fedora_studentvm1-home 253:4    0    2G  0 lvm  /home
sr0                              11:0    1 1024M  0 rom
zram0                           252:0    0  3.8G  0 disk [SWAP]
[student@studentvm1 ~]$
```

I used the -i option to produce the results in ASCII format because it transfers better to a document like this. You can use -i, but you should also try the command without any options to get a version that looks a little nicer on the display.

The **df** command (from the original GNU core utilities) shows similar data but with somewhat different detail:

```
[student@studentvm1 ~]$ df -h
Filesystem                            Size  Used Avail Use% Mounted on
devtmpfs                              2.0G     0  2.0G   0% /dev
tmpfs                                 2.0G     0  2.0G   0% /dev/shm
tmpfs                                 2.0G  1.2M  2.0G   1% /run
tmpfs                                 2.0G     0  2.0G   0% /sys/fs/cgroup
/dev/mapper/fedora_studentvm1-root    2.0G   49M  1.8G   3% /
/dev/mapper/fedora_studentvm1-usr      15G  3.8G   11G  27% /usr
/dev/sda1                             976M  185M  724M  21% /boot
/dev/mapper/fedora_studentvm1-tmp     4.9G   21M  4.6G   1% /tmp
/dev/mapper/fedora_studentvm1-var     9.8G  494M  8.8G   6% /var
/dev/mapper/fedora_studentvm1-home    2.0G  7.3M  1.8G   1% /home
tmpfs                                 395M  8.0K  395M   1% /run/user/1000
tmpfs                                 395M     0  395M   0% /run/user/0
```

I used the -h option to show the disk space in easily human-readable numbers like GB and MB. Note that the names of commands that list things tend to start with "ls", which in Linux-speak usually means "list."

There are several temporary filesystems shown in the output of both the **df** and **lsblk** commands. We will talk about some temporary filesystems later in this course. We will also explore the logical volume manager (LVM) that creates the entries like /dev/mapper/fedora_studentvm1-tmp.

Chapter Summary

These two collections of basic Linux utilities, the GNU core utilities and util-linux, together provide the basic utilities required to administer a basic Linux system. As I researched this chapter, I found several interesting utilities in this list that I never knew about. Many of these commands are seldom needed. But when you do, they are indispensable.

Between these two collections, there are over 200 Linux utilities. The typical Linux distribution has many more commands, but these are the ones that are needed to manage the most basic functions of the typical Linux host.

We explored a couple commands from each of these utility packages, but we will definitely encounter more as we proceed through this course. It makes much more sense to only cover the utilities that we will encounter and use the most rather than try to learn all of these commands.

Just a note about terminology so that we are working with the same understanding: From this point on in this course, when I say core utilities, I mean both sets of these utilities. If I intend to refer to either set individually, I will name them explicitly.

Exercises

Complete these exercises to finish this chapter:

1. What is the overall purpose of these two groups of core utilities?

2. Why were the GNU core utilities important to Linus Torvalds?

3. Which core utility would you use to determine how much space is left in each filesystem?

4. What is the model name of the CPU in your VM?

5. How many CPUs does your physical host have and how many are allocated to the VM?

6. Does allocating a CPU to the VM make it unavailable to the host machine?

CHAPTER 9

Data Streams

Objectives

In this chapter you will learn

- How text data streams form the architectural basis for the extreme flexibility of the Linux command line

- How to generate streams of text data

- How to create a new logical volume (LV) for use in the experiments in this chapter

- How to use pipes, STDIO, and many of the core utilities to manipulate text data streams

- How to redirect data streams to and from files

- Basic usage of some of the special device files in the /dev directory

Data Streams as Raw Materials

Everything in Linux revolves around streams of data – particularly text streams.

Data streams are the raw materials upon which the core utilities and many other CLI tools perform their work. As its name implies, a data stream is a stream of data – text data – being passed from one file, device, or program to another using Standard Input/Output (STDIO). This chapter introduces the use of pipes to connect streams of data from one filter program to another using STDIO. You will learn that the function of these programs is to transform the data in some manner. You will also learn about the use of redirection to redirect the data to a file. A filter is defined as

247

A program that processes an input data stream into an output data stream in some well-defined way, and does no I/O to anywhere else except possibly on error conditions; one designed to be used as a stage in a pipeline.

—The Free On-line Dictionary of Computing (FOLDOC)

Data streams can be manipulated by inserting one or more filter programs into the stream using pipes. Each filter is used by the SysAdmin to perform some operation on the data in the stream, thus changing its contents in some well-defined manner. Redirection can then be used at the end of the pipeline to direct the data stream to a file. As has already been mentioned, that file could be an actual data file on the hard drive or a device file such as a drive partition, a printer, a terminal, a pseudo-terminal, or any other device[1] connected to a computer.

The ability to manipulate these data streams using these small yet powerful filters is central to the power of the Linux command-line interface. Many of the core utilities are filter programs and use STDIO.

I recently Googled "data stream," and most of the top hits are concerned with processing huge amounts of streaming data in single entities such as streaming video and audio or financial institutions processing streams consisting of huge numbers of individual transactions. This is not what we are talking about here although the concept is the same, and a case could be made that current applications use the stream processing functions of Linux as the model for processing many types of data.

In the Linux world, a stream is a flow of text data that originates at some source; the stream may flow to one or more programs that transform it in some way, and then it may be stored in a file or displayed in a terminal session. As a SysAdmin your job is intimately associated with manipulating the creation and flow of these data streams. In this chapter we will explore data streams – what they are, how to create them, and a little bit about how to use them.

---

[1] In Linux systems all hardware devices are treated as files. More about this in Chapter 22, Volume 2.

Text Streams: A Universal Interface

The use of Standard Input/Output (STDIO) for program input and output is a key foundation of the Linux way of doing things. STDIO was first developed for Unix and has found its way into most other operating systems since then, including DOS, Windows, and Linux.

> *This is the Unix philosophy: Write programs that do one thing and do it well. Write programs to work together. Write programs to handle text streams, because that is a universal interface.*
>
> —Doug McIlroy, Basics of the Unix Philosophy[2,3]

STDIO was developed by Ken Thompson[4] as a part of the infrastructure required to implement pipes on early versions of Unix. Programs that implement STDIO use standardized file handles for input and output rather than files that are stored on a disk or other recording media. STDIO is best described as a buffered data stream, and its primary function is to stream data from the output of one program, file, or device to the input of another program, file, or device.

STDIO File Handles

There are three STDIO data streams, each of which is automatically opened as a file at the startup of a program – well, those programs that use STDIO. Each STDIO data stream is associated with a file handle, which is just a set of metadata that describes the attributes of the file. File handles 0, 1, and 2 are explicitly defined by convention and long practice as STDIN, STDOUT, and STDERR, respectively.

STDIN, file handle 0, is standard input, which is usually input from the keyboard. STDIN can be redirected from any file including device files instead of the keyboard. It is not common to need to redirect STDIN, but it can be done.

---

[2] Raymond, Eric S., *The Art of Unix Programming*, www.catb.org/esr/writings/taoup/html/ch01s06.html

[3] Linuxtopia, *Basics of the Unix Philosophy*, www.linuxtopia.org/online_books/programming_books/art_of_unix_programming/ch01s06.html

[4] Wikipedia, *Ken Thompson*, https://en.wikipedia.org/wiki/Ken_Thompson

STDOUT, file handle 1, is standard output, which sends the data stream to the terminal by default. It is common to redirect STDOUT to a file or to pipe it to another program for further processing.

STDERR is associated with file handle 2. The data stream for STDERR is also usually sent to the terminal.

If STDOUT is redirected to a file, STDERR continues to be displayed on the screen. This ensures that when the data stream itself is not displayed on the terminal, that STDERR is, thus, ensuring that the user will see any errors resulting from execution of the program. STDERR can also be redirected to the same or passed on to the next filter program in a pipeline.

STDIO is implemented in a standard C library header file, stdio.h, which can be included in the source code of programs so that it can be compiled into the resulting executable.

Preparing a Logical Volume for Testing

Many of the experiments in this chapter can be dangerous when performed on the logical volumes that have already been created during the installation. Therefore, you will create a new LV (logical volume) for use in testing. You can perform the following experiments safely with a test volume that is not being used for anything else.

Performing this and other tasks on logical volumes and volume groups is a very typical task for SysAdmins. I do things like this quite frequently. We will explore logical volume management in detail in Volume 2, Chapter 20.

Storage Device Logical Structure

Let's take a little side trip so you can get a better understanding of what you will be doing in this section. Look again at the storage devices on your VM. We are especially interested in the tree belonging to the /dev/sda device:

```
[root@studentvm1 ~]# lsblk
NAME              MAJ:MIN RM   SIZE RO TYPE MOUNTPOINTS
sda                 8:0    0    60G  0 disk
└─sda1              8:1    0     1M  0 part
```

```
├─sda2                         8:2    0    1G   0 part /boot
├─sda3                         8:3    0    1G   0 part /boot/efi
└─sda4                         8:4    0   58G   0 part
  ├─fedora_studentvm1-root  253:0    0    2G   0 lvm  /
  ├─fedora_studentvm1-usr   253:1    0   15G   0 lvm  /usr
  ├─fedora_studentvm1-tmp   253:2    0    5G   0 lvm  /tmp
  ├─fedora_studentvm1-var   253:3    0   10G   0 lvm  /var
  └─fedora_studentvm1-home  253:4    0    2G   0 lvm  /home
  sr0                         11:0    1 50.5M   0 rom
zram0                        252:0    0    8G   0 disk [SWAP]
```

This tree illustrates the logical meta-structure created on the storage device during the installation of Fedora. This structure was created from the partitioning and LVM specifications you entered on the Manual Partitioning page of the Anaconda installer.

The Type column shows the kind of meta-structure for each of the devices in the tree. The sda device is the ID for the disk device as a whole. sda1 through sda3 are partitions created for files related to bootup. The sda1 partition is the BIOS boot partition. The other two boot partitions are obvious.

All these partitions are standard Linux Type 83 partitions.[5] The sda4 partition has then been configured as a physical volume (PV) for logical volume management (LVM).[6] The entire PV was then configured as a volume group (VG) that was named fedora_studentvm1 by the installer. The various logical volumes (LV) were created in the VG.

The sr0 partition is the (virtual) DVD device, and zram0 is used as swap space.

Creating the New Volume

In this section you will create a new LV in the existing VG, fedora_studentvm1. This is a rather long procedure. If you get interrupted, it is okay to come back to it later. Just be sure to mark which step will be next.

---

[5] Type 83 is a standard Linux partition. Linux supports many different partitions. Filesystems and types are covered in Chapter 19 of this volume.

[6] LVM is covered in Volume 2, Chapter 20.

PREPARATION 9: PREPARE A TEST VOLUME

Prepare a new LV for use with these experiments. Start by looking at the current LV configuration. The **lvs** command lists the logical volumes:

```
[root@studentvm1 ~]# lvs
  LV    VG              Attr        LSize ...
  home  fedora_studentvm1 -wi-ao----  2.00g
  root  fedora_studentvm1 -wi-ao----  2.00g
  tmp   fedora_studentvm1 -wi-ao----  5.00g
  usr   fedora_studentvm1 -wi-ao---- 15.00g
  var   fedora_studentvm1 -wi-ao---- 10.00g
[root@studentvm1 ~]#
```

And the **vg** command lists the volume group(s) (VG(s)) and some of their statistics. This can show the amount of space left in the VG that is not already assigned to an LV:

```
[root@studentvm1 ~]# vgs
  VG                #PV #LV #SN Attr   VSize   VFree
  fedora_studentvm1   1   5   0 wz--n- <58.00g <24.00g
[root@studentvm1 ~]#
```

From this you can see that there is about 24GB of space left on the VG that has not yet been allocated to an LV. For these experiments we only need a small amount of space, so we will use 500MB for our test volume. Create the new volume and verify that it has been created properly:

```
[root@studentvm1 ~]# lvcreate -L 500M -n test fedora_studentvm1
  Logical volume "test" created.
[root@studentvm1 ~]# lvs
  LV    VG              Attr        LSize   ...
  home  fedora_studentvm1 -wi-ao----    2.00g
  root  fedora_studentvm1 -wi-ao----    2.00g
  test  fedora_studentvm1 -wi-a-----  500.00m
  tmp   fedora_studentvm1 -wi-ao----    5.00g
  usr   fedora_studentvm1 -wi-ao----   15.00g
  var   fedora_studentvm1 -wi-ao----   10.00g
[root@studentvm1 ~]#
```

In the preceding command, -L defines this as a linear volume, 500M is the size, -n test is the name of the new volume, and fedora_studentvm1 is the name of the existing volume group.

The second step in this process is to create an EXT4 filesystem on the new volume. In the following mkfs (make filesystem) command, -t ext4 creates an EXT4 filesystem, and the path is for the device file for this volume. The "mapper" portion of the path is a special location in the device tree that is where LVM devices are managed:

```
[root@studentvm1 ~]# mkfs -t ext4 /dev/mapper/fedora_studentvm1-test
mke2fs 1.46.5 (30-Dec-2021)
Creating filesystem with 512000 1k blocks and 128016 inodes
Filesystem UUID: 8dfb1594-5d7a-4deb-8cf8-2dd0af0e2a0d
Superblock backups stored on blocks:
        8193, 24577, 40961, 57345, 73729, 204801, 221185, 401409

Allocating group tables: done
Writing inode tables: done
Creating journal (8192 blocks): done
Writing superblocks and filesystem accounting information: done

[root@studentvm1 ~]#
```

You can use the following command to verify that the LV has been properly created:

```
[root@studentvm1 ~]# lsblk
NAME                          MAJ:MIN RM  SIZE RO TYPE MOUNTPOINTS
sda                             8:0    0   60G  0 disk
|-sda1                          8:1    0    1M  0 part
|-sda2                          8:2    0    1G  0 part /boot
|-sda3                          8:3    0    1G  0 part /boot/efi
`-sda4                          8:4    0   58G  0 part
  |-fedora_studentvm1-root    253:0    0    2G  0 lvm  /
  |-fedora_studentvm1-usr     253:1    0   15G  0 lvm  /usr
  |-fedora_studentvm1-tmp     253:2    0    5G  0 lvm  /tmp
  |-fedora_studentvm1-var     253:3    0   10G  0 lvm  /var
  |-fedora_studentvm1-home    253:4    0    2G  0 lvm  /home
  `-fedora_studentvm1-test    253:5    0  500M  0 lvm  /test
sro                            11:0    1 50.5M  0 rom
zram0                         252:0    0    8G  0 disk [SWAP]
[root@studentvm1 ~]#
```

253

```
[root@studentvm1 ~]# mount /dev/sdb1 /test
[root@studentvm1 ~]#
```

You will recall that we added a label to each volume we created during the installation. For the sake of consistency, let's do that now for this new volume. The volume does not need to be mounted for this. First, verify that there is no label, then add the label, and verify that it has been added:

```
[root@studentvm1 ~]# e2label /dev/mapper/fedora_studentvm1-test

[root@studentvm1 ~]# e2label /dev/mapper/fedora_studentvm1-test test
[root@studentvm1 ~]# e2label /dev/mapper/fedora_studentvm1-test
test
[root@studentvm1 ~]#
```

The new volume needs a directory where it can be mounted on the filesystem directory tree. This is called a mount point and is nothing more than a regular directory. Create the /test directory:

```
[root@studentvm1 ~]# mkdir /test
```

You could mount the new test volume manually after every reboot, but that is not the way of the lazy SysAdmin. We can easily add a line to the /etc/fstab (filesystem table)[7] file even without using an editor.[8] The following command-line program appends the required line to /etc/fstab:

```
[root@studentvm1 ~]# echo "/dev/mapper/fedora_studentvm1-test /test
ext4  defaults 1 2" >> /etc/fstab
```

Now verify that the new line has been added to the bottom of the file:

```
[root@studentvm1 ~]# cat /etc/fstab
```

The next command tells the system to re-read the fstab file:

```
[root@studentvm1 ~]# systemctl daemon-reload
```

The last step is to mount the new filesystem:

---

[7] The /etc/fstab file is explored in detail in Chapter 19 in this volume.

[8] Editors are coming up in the next chapter.

```
[root@studentvm1 ~]# mount /test ; lsblk
NAME                         MAJ:MIN RM   SIZE RO TYPE MOUNTPOINTS
sda                            8:0    0    60G  0 disk
|-sda1                         8:1    0     1M  0 part
|-sda2                         8:2    0     1G  0 part /boot
|-sda3                         8:3    0     1G  0 part /boot/efi
`-sda4                         8:4    0    58G  0 part
  |-fedora_studentvm1-root   253:0    0     2G  0 lvm  /
  |-fedora_studentvm1-usr    253:1    0    15G  0 lvm  /usr
  |-fedora_studentvm1-tmp    253:2    0     5G  0 lvm  /tmp
  |-fedora_studentvm1-var    253:3    0    10G  0 lvm  /var
  |-fedora_studentvm1-home   253:4    0     2G  0 lvm  /home
  `-fedora_studentvm1-test   253:5    0   500M  0 lvm  /test
sr0                           11:0    1  50.5M  0 rom
zram0                        252:0    0     8G  0 disk [SWAP]
[root@studentvm1 ~]#
```

Enter and run the following command-line program to create some files with content on the drive. We use the dmesg command simply to provide data for the files to contain. The contents don't matter so much as just the fact that each file has some content:

```
[root@studentvm1 ~]# cd /test
[root@studentvm1 test]# for I in 0 1 2 3 4 5 6 7 8 9 ; do dmesg >
file$I.txt ; done
```

Verify that there are now at least ten files on the drive with the names file0.txt through file9.txt:

```
[root@studentvm1 test]# ll
total 702
-rw-r--r--. 1 root root 69827 Jan 21 16:13 file0.txt
-rw-r--r--. 1 root root 69827 Jan 21 16:13 file1.txt
-rw-r--r--. 1 root root 69827 Jan 21 16:13 file2.txt
-rw-r--r--. 1 root root 69827 Jan 21 16:13 file3.txt
-rw-r--r--. 1 root root 69827 Jan 21 16:13 file4.txt
-rw-r--r--. 1 root root 69827 Jan 21 16:13 file5.txt
-rw-r--r--. 1 root root 69827 Jan 21 16:13 file6.txt
-rw-r--r--. 1 root root 69827 Jan 21 16:13 file7.txt
-rw-r--r--. 1 root root 69827 Jan 21 16:13 file8.txt
-rw-r--r--. 1 root root 69827 Jan 21 16:13 file9.txt
```

```
drwx------. 2 root root 12288 Jan 21 10:16 lost+found
[root@studentvm1 test]#
```

The new volume is ready for the experiments in this chapter.

Do not unmount the USB device or detach it from the VM. The test volume is now ready for use in some of the experiments in this chapter.

Generating Data Streams

Most of the core utilities use STDIO as their output stream, and those that generate data streams, rather than acting to transform the data stream in some way, can be used to create the data streams that we will use for our experiments. Data streams can be as short as one line or even a single character and as long as needed.[9]

Let's try our first experiment and create a short data stream.

EXPERIMENT 9-1: GENERATE A SIMPLE DATA STREAM

If you have not done so already, log into the host you are using for these experiments as the user "student." If you have logged into a GUI desktop session, start your favorite terminal emulator; if you have logged into one of the virtual consoles or a terminal emulator, you are ready to go.

Use the command shown in the following to generate a stream of data:

```
[student@studentvm1 test]$ ls -la
total 465229
-rw-r--r--. 1 root root     69827 Jan 21 16:53 file0.txt
-rw-r--r--. 1 root root     69827 Jan 21 16:53 file1.txt
-rw-r--r--. 1 root root     69827 Jan 21 16:53 file2.txt
-rw-r--r--. 1 root root     69827 Jan 21 16:53 file3.txt
-rw-r--r--. 1 root root     69827 Jan 21 16:53 file4.txt
-rw-r--r--. 1 root root     69827 Jan 21 16:53 file5.txt
-rw-r--r--. 1 root root     69827 Jan 21 16:53 file6.txt
```

---

[9] A data stream taken from special device files random, urandom, and zero, for example, can continue forever without some form of external termination such as the user entering Ctrl-c, a limiting argument to the command, or a system failure.

```
-rw-r--r--. 1 root root      69827 Jan 21 16:53 file7.txt
-rw-r--r--. 1 root root      69827 Jan 21 16:53 file8.txt
-rw-r--r--. 1 root root      69827 Jan 21 16:53 file9.txt
drwx------. 2 root root      12288 Jan 21 10:16 lost+found
-rw-r--r--. 1 root root 475674443 Jan 21 17:11 testfile.txt
[root@studentvm1 test]#
```

The output from this command is a short data stream that is displayed on STDOUT, the console or terminal session that you are logged into.

Some GNU core utilities are designed specifically to produce streams of data. Let's take a look at some of these utilities.

EXPERIMENT 9-2: THE YES COMMAND

The **yes** command produces a continuous data stream that consists of repetitions of the data string provided as the argument. The generated data stream will continue until it is interrupted with a Ctrl-C, which is displayed on the screen as ^C.

Enter the command as shown and let it run for a few seconds. Press Ctrl-C when you get tired of watching the same string of data scroll by:

```
[student@studentvm1 test]$ yes 123465789-abcdefg
123465789-abcdefg
123465789-abcdefg
123465789-abcdefg
123465789-abcdefg
123465789-abcdefg
123465789-abcdefg
123465789-abcdefg
1234^C
```

Now just enter the yes command with no options:

```
[student@studentvm1 test]$ yes
y
y
y
y
```

257

```
y
y^C
```

The primary function of the **yes** command is to produce a stream of data.

"What does this prove?" you ask. Just that there are many ways to create a data stream that might be useful. When run as root, the **rm** ***** command will erase every file in the present working directory (PWD) – but it asks you to enter "y" for each file to verify that you actually want to delete that file.[10] This means more typing.

EXPERIMENT 9-3: USING YES AS INPUT TO COMMANDS

Perform this experiment as the root user in using /test as the PWD.

I haven't talked about pipes yet, but as a SysAdmin, or someone who wants to become one, you should know how to use them. The following CLI program will supply the response of "y" to each request by the rm command and will delete all of the files in the PWD.

Start by trying to delete all of the files in the /test directory. Ensure that /test is the PWD:

```
[root@studentvm1 test]# rm file*txt
rm: remove regular file 'file0.txt'?
```

Press Ctrl-C[11] to exit this command, which will ask for a separate permission to delete each file. This can be a bit time consuming for you when there are very large numbers of files.

The following command-line program provides the necessary input to the **rm** command, so no further intervention is required by you:

```
[root@studentvm1 test]# yes | rm file*txt ; ll
rm: remove regular file 'file0.txt'? rm: remove regular file 'file1.txt'? rm:
remove regular file 'file2.txt'? rm: remove regular file 'file3.txt'? rm:
remove regular file 'file4.txt'? rm: remove regular file 'file5.txt'? rm:
remove regular file 'file6.txt'? rm: remove regular file 'file7.txt'? rm:
remove regular file 'file8.txt'? rm: remove regular file 'file9.txt'? total 0
```

---

[10] The -f option to the **rm** command forces the **rm** command to delete all files without asking the user. But this experiment is a good illustration of the use of the yes command.

[11] The Ctrl-C key combination kills the process. Press and hold the Ctrl key and then press the C key.

```
[root@studentvm1 test]# ll
total 12
drwx------. 2 root root 12288 Jan 21 10:16 lost+found
[root@studentvm1 test]#
```

Warning!   Do not run this command anywhere but the /test location as specified in this experiment because it will delete all of the files in the PWD.

Now recreate the files we just deleted using the seq (sequence) command to generate the file numbers instead of providing them as a list as we did previously. Then verify that the files have been recreated:

```
[root@studentvm1 test]# for I in `seq 0 9` ; do dmesg > file$I.txt ;
done ; ll
```

You can also use **rm -f f*t**, which would also forcibly delete all of the files in the PWD. The -f means "force" the deletions. Be sure you are in the /test directory where the USB device is mounted. Then run the following commands to delete all the files we just created, and verify they are gone:

```
rm -f f*t ; ll
```

This is something you should not do without ensuring that the files really should be deleted.

Once more, recreate the test files in /test. Note that you can save some time using command-line recall. Simply press the up arrow key to scroll back through the previous commands until you get to the one you want. Then press the Enter key.

Do not unmount the USB device.

Test a Theory with Yes

Another option for using the yes command is to fill a directory with a file containing some arbitrary and irrelevant data in order to – well – fill up the directory. I have used this technique to test what happens to a Linux host when a particular directory becomes full. In the specific instance where I used this technique, I was testing a theory because a customer was having problems and could not log into their computer.

EXPERIMENT 9-4: TESTING WITH YES

This experiment should be performed as root.

In order to prevent filling the root filesystem, this experiment will use the test volume that you should have prepared in advance in the "Preparing a Logical Volume for Testing" section of this chapter. This experiment will not affect the existing files on that volume.

Make sure that /test is the PWD.

Let's take the time to learn two more tools, the **watch** utility, which works nicely to make a static command such as **df** into one that continuously updates. The **df** utility displays the filesystems, their sizes, free space, and mount points. Just run the **df** command first to see what that looks like:

```
[root@studentvm1 test]# df
Filesystem                        1K-blocks     Used  Available Use% Mounted on
devtmpfs                               4096        0       4096   0% /dev
tmpfs                               8190156       12    8190144   1% /dev/shm
tmpfs                               3276064     1192    3274872   1% /run
/dev/mapper/fedora_studentvm1-root  1992552    39600    1831712   3% /
/dev/mapper/fedora_studentvm1-usr  15375304  4817352    9755136  34% /usr
/dev/sda2                            996780   233516     694452  26% /boot
/dev/sda3                           1046508    17804    1028704   2% /boot/efi
/dev/mapper/fedora_studentvm1-tmp   5074592      392    4795672   1% /tmp
/dev/mapper/fedora_studentvm1-home  1992552    29716    1841596   2% /home
/dev/mapper/fedora_studentvm1-var  10218772   404012    9274088   5% /var
tmpfs                               1638028       88    1637940   1% /run/user/1000
tmpfs                               1638028       64    1637964   1% /run/user/0
/dev/mapper/fedora_studentvm1-test   469328      704     438928   1% /test
[root@studentvm1 test]#
```

The -h option presents the numbers in (h)uman-readable format:

```
[root@studentvm1 test]# df -h
Filesystem                              Size  Used  Avail Use% Mounted on
devtmpfs                                4.0M     0  4.0M   0% /dev
tmpfs                                   7.9G   12K  7.9G   1% /dev/shm
tmpfs                                   3.2G  1.2M  3.2G   1% /run
/dev/mapper/fedora_studentvm1-root      2.0G   39M  1.8G   3% /
/dev/mapper/fedora_studentvm1-usr        15G  4.6G  9.4G  34% /usr
/dev/sda2                               974M  229M  679M  26% /boot
/dev/sda3                              1022M   18M 1005M   2% /boot/efi
/dev/mapper/fedora_studentvm1-tmp       4.9G  392K  4.6G   1% /tmp
/dev/mapper/fedora_studentvm1-home      2.0G   30M  1.8G   2% /home
/dev/mapper/fedora_studentvm1-var       9.8G  395M  8.9G   5% /var
tmpfs                                   1.6G   88K  1.6G   1% /run/user/1000
tmpfs                                   1.6G   64K  1.6G   1% /run/user/0
/dev/mapper/fedora_studentvm1-test      459M  704K  429M   1% /test
[root@studentvm1 test]#
```

Note that the default units for the df command are 1K blocks. In one root terminal session, start the watch command and use the df command as its argument. This constantly updates the disk usage information and allows us to watch as the USB device fills up. The -n option on the watch command tells it to run the df command every one second instead of the default two seconds. That looks like this:

```
[root@studentvm1 ~]# watch -n 1 df
Every 1.0s: df                                              studentvm1: Fri Jan 20 16:06:11 2023

Filesystem                           1K-blocks      Used Available Use% Mounted on
devtmpfs                                  4096         0      4096   0% /dev
tmpfs                                  2006112         0   2006112   0% /dev/shm
tmpfs                                   802448      1244    801204   1% /run
/dev/mapper/fedora_studentvm1-root     1992552     25932   1845380   2% /
/dev/mapper/fedora_studentvm1-usr     15375304   4819656   9752832  34% /usr
/dev/mapper/fedora_studentvm1-home     1992552     29168   1842144   2% /home
/dev/mapper/fedora_studentvm1-tmp      5074592       228   4795836   1% /tmp
/dev/mapper/fedora_studentvm1-var     10218772    341856   9336244   4% /var
/dev/sda2                               996780    233516    694452  26% /boot
```

```
/dev/sda3                                       1046508     17804    1028704     2% /boot/efi
tmpfs                                            401220        88     401132     1% /run/user/1000
tmpfs                                            401220        64     401156     1% /run/user/0
/dev/sdb1                                       7812864        16    7812848     1% /test
```

The data will update every second.

Place this terminal session somewhere on your desktop so that you can see it; then, as root open another terminal session and run the command shown in the following. Depending upon the size of your USB filesystem, the time to fill it may vary, but it should be quite fast on a small-capacity test volume. The first time I tested this, it took 18 minutes and 55 seconds on my system with a 4GB USB device.

Note that we are redirecting a long data stream. Watch the /dev/sdb1 filesystem on /test as it fills up:

```
[root@studentvm1 test]# yes 123456789-abcdefgh >> /test/testfile.txt
yes: standard output: No space left on device
[root@studentvm1 test]#
```

When the filesystem fills up, the error is displayed and the program terminates. The **df** command output should look like this:

```
Filesystem                         1K-blocks    Used Available Use% Mounted on
devtmpfs                                4096       0      4096   0% /dev
tmpfs                                8190156      12   8190144   1% /dev/shm
tmpfs                                3276064    1200   3274864   1% /run
/dev/mapper/fedora_studentvm1-root   1992552   39600   1831712   3% /
/dev/mapper/fedora_studentvm1-usr   15375304 4817352   9755136  34% /usr
/dev/sda2                             996780  233516    694452  26% /boot
/dev/sda3                            1046508   17804   1028704   2% /boot/efi
/dev/mapper/fedora_studentvm1-tmp    5074592     392   4795672   1% /tmp
/dev/mapper/fedora_studentvm1-home   1992552   29716   1841596   2% /home
/dev/mapper/fedora_studentvm1-var   10218772  404024   9274076   5% /var
tmpfs                                1638028      88   1637940   1% /run/user/1000
tmpfs                                1638028      64   1637964   1% /run/user/0
/dev/mapper/fedora_studentvm1-test    469328  465231         0 100% /test

[root@studentvm1 test]# ll
total 465229
-rw-r--r--. 1 root root   69827 Jan 21 16:53 file0.txt
-rw-r--r--. 1 root root   69827 Jan 21 16:53 file1.txt
-rw-r--r--. 1 root root   69827 Jan 21 16:53 file2.txt
```

```
-rw-r--r--. 1 root root     69827 Jan 21 16:53 file3.txt
-rw-r--r--. 1 root root     69827 Jan 21 16:53 file4.txt
-rw-r--r--. 1 root root     69827 Jan 21 16:53 file5.txt
-rw-r--r--. 1 root root     69827 Jan 21 16:53 file6.txt
-rw-r--r--. 1 root root     69827 Jan 21 16:53 file7.txt
-rw-r--r--. 1 root root     69827 Jan 21 16:53 file8.txt
-rw-r--r--. 1 root root     69827 Jan 21 16:53 file9.txt
drwx------. 2 root root     12288 Jan 21 10:16 lost+found
-rw-r--r--. 1 root root 475674443 Jan 21 17:11 testfile.txt
[root@studentvm1 test]#
```

Your results should look similar to mine. Be sure to look at the line from the **df** output that refers to the /test volume. This shows that 100% of the space on that filesystem is used.

Now delete testfile.txt from /test:

```
[root@studentvm1 ~]# rm -f /test/testfile.txt
```

I used the simple test in Experiment 9-4 on the /tmp directory of one of my own computers as part of my testing to assist me in determining my customer's problem. After /tmp filled up, users were no longer able to log into a GUI desktop, but they could still log in using the consoles. That is because logging into a GUI desktop creates new files in the /tmp directory, and there was no room left so the login failed. The console login does not create new files in /tmp, so they succeeded. My customer had not tried logging into the console because they were not familiar with the CLI.

After testing this on my own system as verification, I used the console to log into the customer host and found a number of large files taking up all of the space in the /tmp directory. I deleted those and helped the customer determine how the files were being created, and we were able to put a stop to that.

The Boot Record

It is now time to do a little exploring, and to be as safe as possible, you will – mostly – use the test volume that you have already been experimenting with. In this experiment we will look at some of the filesystem structures.

Let's start with something simple, the **dd** command. Officially known as "disk dump," many SysAdmins call it "disk destroyer" for good reason. Many of us have inadvertently destroyed the contents of an entire hard drive or partition using the **dd** command. That is why we will use the test volume to perform some of these experiments.

Despite its reputation, **dd** can be quite useful in exploring various types of storage media, storage devices, and partitions. We will also use it as a tool to explore other aspects of Linux.

EXPERIMENT 9-5: EXPLORING THE BOOT RECORD

This experiment must be performed as root. Log into a terminal session as root if you are not already.

The boot record is a single block of data located at the beginning of every storage device. Having installed Linux on the only HDD on the VM, /dev/sda, the boot record is the first sector of that device. The boot record is not located in any partition or logical volume.

As root in a terminal session, look at the block (HDD or SSD) devices on the VM:

```
[root@studentvm1 test]# lsblk
NAME                        MAJ:MIN RM  SIZE RO TYPE MOUNTPOINTS
sda                             8:0  0   60G  0 disk
|-sda1                          8:1  0    1M  0 part
|-sda2                          8:2  0    1G  0 part /boot
|-sda3                          8:3  0    1G  0 part /boot/efi
`-sda4                          8:4  0   58G  0 part
  |-fedora_studentvm1-root    253:0  0    2G  0 lvm  /
  |-fedora_studentvm1-usr     253:1  0   15G  0 lvm  /usr
  |-fedora_studentvm1-tmp     253:2  0    5G  0 lvm  /tmp
  |-fedora_studentvm1-var     253:3  0   10G  0 lvm  /var
  |-fedora_studentvm1-home    253:4  0    2G  0 lvm  /home
  `-fedora_studentvm1-test    253:5  0  500M  0 lvm  /test
```

```
sr0                          11:0    1 50.5M  0 rom
zram0                       252:0    0    8G  0 disk [SWAP]
```

Use the dd command to view the boot record of the virtual hard drive, /dev/sda. The bs=
argument is not what you might think; it simply specifies the block size. And the count=
argument specifies the number of blocks to dump to STDIO. The if= (input file) argument
specifies the source of the data stream, in this case the test volume:

```
[root@studentvm1 test]# dd if=/dev/sda bs=1024 count=1
�c�������t��pt���y|1��⌐ʍ ��d|<�t��R��}��|
�A��U�ZRr=��U�u7��t21��D@�D���D�f�\|f�f�`|f�\
Z������}��f�cd�@�D�����������@�������`|f       �uNf�\|
f1�f�4��1�f�t;}7�����0������Z�2p��1ʌ�r��`���1������
�a�&Z|��}���}�4��}�.�▓▓��GRUB GeomHard DiskRead Error
����<u�����������U�EFI PART\(`*��"���    @�T
F����1>���~J�
1+0 records in
1+0 records out
1024 bytes (1.0 kB, 1.0 KiB) copied, 0.00160644 s, 637 kB/s
[root@studentvm1 test]#
```

This prints the text of the boot record, which is the first block on the storage device – any HDD
or SSD. In this case, there is information about the filesystem and, although it is unreadable
because it is stored in binary format, the partition table. Since this is a bootable device, stage
1 of GRUB or some other boot loader is located in this sector. The last three lines contain data
about the number of records and bytes processed.

Now do the same experiment, but on the first record of the first partition.

EXPERIMENT 9-6: LOOKING AT A PARTITION RECORD

Run the following command as root. This looks at the first record in the first partition of the /
dev/sda device, /dev/sda1:

```
[root@studentvm1 test]# dd if=/dev/sda1 bs=1024 count=1
RV���9^��f�-����|�tF��Mf1�9�)f�U��Df�f�L�DpP�D�B����p�ff�Ef
���f�f1�f�4�T
f1�f�t�T
    �D;}y�*D
```

```
���Lf�U�T
�ьlZR�t
        P�p��1ʳ�rF�ÎE
��E
`����1�1����#��Wa��$�����%��BZ����6��-��.�2���loading.
^
Б��d��$�����ċ�f� �_����i�
����"�f�{�f1�_�����f�U��W��V1�S�É1�x+���t������d��čš��$1�
1���~���H��[��^_]Ä�t ��t������������1��U��WVS��1+0 records in
1+0 records out
1024 bytes (1.0 kB, 1.0 KiB) copied, 0.66347 s, 1.5 kB/s
[root@studentvm1 test]#
```

This experiment shows the that there are differences between a boot record and the first record of a partition. It also shows that the **dd** command can be used to view data in the partitions as well as for the disk itself.

What else is out there on the test volume? Depending upon the specifics of the USB device you are using for these experiments, you may have somewhat different results from mine. I will show you what I did, and you can modify that if necessary to achieve the desired result.

What we are attempting to do is use the **dd** command to locate the directory entries for the files we created on the test volume and then some of the data. If we had enough knowledge of the metadata structures, we could interpret them directly to find the locations of this data on the drive, but we don't so we will have to do this the hard way – print out data until we find what we want.

So let's start with what we do know and proceed with a little finesse. We know that the data files we created during the LV preparation were in the first partition on the device. Therefore, we don't need to search the space between the boot record and the first partition, which contains lots of emptiness. At least that is what it should contain.

Starting with the beginning of /dev/sda1, let's look at a few blocks of data at a time to find what we want. The command in Experiment 9-7 is similar to the previous one except that we specify a few more blocks of data to view. You may have to specify fewer blocks if your terminal is not large enough to display all of the data at one time, or you can pipe the data through the less utility and use that to page through the data. Either way works. Remember we are doing all of this as root user because non-root users do not have the required permissions.

Digging Deeper

There is far more to storage devices than only the boot record. So let's look further into the partitions on the storage device sda.

EXPERIMENT 9-7: DISPLAY MANY RECORDS OF A PARTITION

Enter the same command as you did in the previous experiment, but this time use /dev/sda4 and increase the block count to be displayed to 2000 as shown in the following in order to show more data.

Note that "^@^@^@^@^@" is essentially null data. There can be a lot of it between the first record of the partition and the beginning of the data area:

```
[root@studentvm1 ~]# dd if=/dev/sda4 bs=512 count=2000 | less
```

Page down until you see something like this:

```
^@^@^@^@^@^@^@^@^@^@^@^@^@^@^@^@^@^@^@^@^@^@^@^@^@^@^@^@^@^@^@^@^@^@^@^@^@^@^@^@^@^
@^@^@^@^@^@^@^@^@^@^@^^@^@^@^@^@^@^@^@^@^@^@^@^@^@^@^@^@^@^@^@^@^@^@^@^@^@^@^@^@^@^
@^@^@^@^@^@^@^@^@^@^@^@^@^@^@^@^@^@^@^^@^@^@^@^@^@^@^@^@^@^@^@^@^@^@^@^@^@^@^@^@^@^
@^@^@^@^@^@^@^@^@^@^@^@^@^@^@^@^@^@^@^@^@^@^@^@^@^@^@^@^@^^@^@^@^@^@^@^@^@^@^@^@^@^
@^@^@^@^@^@^@^@^@^@^@^@^@^@^@^@^@^@^@^@^@^@^@^@^@^@^@^@^@fedora_studentvm1 {
id = "KUZ1r9-FGf5-QXR1-xvx9-8gff-N85k-sicFij"
seqno = 1
format = "lvm2"
status = ["RESIZEABLE", "READ", "WRITE"]
flags = []
extent_size = 8192
max_lv = 0
max_pv = 0
metadata_copies = 0

physical_volumes {

pv0 {
id = "czfgYd-e5tH-b4PK-2PXd-74Tx-9vkC-SWduDi"
device = "/dev/sda4"
```

```
status = ["ALLOCATABLE"]
flags = []
dev_size = 121628672
pe_start = 2048
pe_count = 14847
}
```

This data is part of the metadata for the volume group. There is quite a bit of LVM metadata so it will take a while to scroll through it. Scroll down some more until you see something like this. This is the LVM metadata for the /home volume. All of the volume definitions are located in this area of the sda4 device:

```
home {
id = "sfKPPQ-7kAx-fIdF-S74h-St3W-Ppw3-HfNhlZ"
status = ["READ", "WRITE", "VISIBLE"]
flags = []
creation_time = 1673958577
creation_host = "localhost-live"
segment_count = 1

segment1 {
start_extent = 0
extent_count = 512

type = "striped"
stripe_count = 1

stripes = [
"pv0", 3840
]
}
}
```

It can take a long time to scroll through this data, but we do have another option.

Let's look at a new option for the dd command, one which gives us a little more flexibility.

EXPERIMENT 9-8: STARTING AT OTHER THAN THE FIRST RECORD

We now want to display 100 blocks of data at a time, but we don't want to start at the beginning of the partition, we want to skip the blocks we have already looked at.

Enter the following command and add the `skip` argument, which skips the first 2000 blocks of data and displays the next 100:

```
[root@studentvm1 test]# dd if=/dev/sda4 bs=512 count=100 skip=2000
10+0 records in
10+0 records out
5120 bytes (5.1 kB, 5.0 KiB) copied, 0.01786 s, 287 kB/s
```

This set of parameters may not display the file data for you if your test volume is a different size or is formatted differently, but it should be a good place to start. You can continue iterating until you find the data. You should definitely take some time on your own to explore the contents of the other partitions. You might be surprised at what you find.

Randomness

It turns out that randomness is a desirable thing in computers. Who knew. There are a number of reasons that SysAdmins might want to generate a stream of random data. A stream of random data is sometimes useful to overwrite the contents of a complete partition, such as /dev/sda1, or even the entire hard drive as in /dev/sda.

Although deleting files may seem permanent, it is not. Many forensic tools are available and can be used by trained specialists to easily recover files that have supposedly been deleted. It is much more difficult to recover files that have been overwritten by random data. I have frequently needed not just to delete all of the data on a hard drive but to overwrite it so it cannot be recovered. I do this for customers and friends who have "gifted" me with their old computers for reuse or recycling.

Regardless of what ultimately happens to the computers, I promise the people who donate the computers that I will scrub all of the data from the hard drive. I remove the drives from the computer, put them in my plugin hard drive docking station, and use a command similar to the one in Experiment 9-9 to overwrite all of the data, but instead of just spewing the random data to STDOUT as in this experiment, I redirect it to the device file for the hard drive that needs to be overwritten – but don't do that.

EXPERIMENT 9-9: GENERATING RANDOMNESS

Perform this experiment as the student user. Enter this command to print an unending stream of random data to STDIO:

```
[student@studentvm1 test]$ cat /dev/urandom
```

Use **Ctrl-C** to break out and stop the stream of data. You may need to use **Ctrl-C** multiple times.

If you are extremely paranoid, the **shred** command can be used to overwrite individual files as well as partitions and complete drives. It can write over the device as many times as needed for you to feel secure, with multiple passes using both random data and specifically sequenced patterns of data designed to prevent even the most sensitive equipment from recovering any data from the hard drive. As with other utilities that use random data, the random stream is supplied by the /dev/urandom device.

Random data is also used as the input seed to programs that generate random passwords and random data and numbers for use in scientific and statistical calculations. We will cover randomness and other interesting data sources in a bit more detail in Volume 2, Chapter 22.

Pipe Dreams

Pipes are critical to our ability to do the amazing things on the command line, so much so that I think it is important to recognize that they were invented by Douglas McIlroy[12] during the early days of Unix. Thanks, Doug! The Princeton University website has a fragment of an interview[13] with McIlroy in which he discusses the creation of the pipe and the beginnings of the Unix Philosophy.

---

[12] Wikipedia, *Biography of Douglas McIlroy*, www.cs.dartmouth.edu/~doug/biography
[13] Princeton University, *Interview with Douglas McIlroy*, www.princeton.edu/~hos/frs122/precis/mcilroy.htm

Notice the use of pipes in the simple command-line program shown in Experiment 9-10 that lists each logged-in user a single time no matter how many logins they have active.

EXPERIMENT 9-10: INTRODUCING PIPES

Perform this experiment as the student user. Enter the command shown in the following:

```
[student@studentvm1 test]$ w | tail -n +3 | awk '{print $1}' | sort |
uniq
root
student
[student@studentvm1 test]$
```

The results from this command produce two lines of data that show that the users root and student are both logged in. It does not show how many times each user is logged in.

Pipes – represented by the vertical bar (|) – are the syntactical glue, the operator, that connects these command-line utilities together. Pipes allow the standard output from one command to be "piped," that is, streamed from the standard output of one command to the standard input of the next command.

The |& operator can be used to pipe STDERR along with STDOUT to STDIN of the next command. This is not always desirable, but it does offer flexibility in the ability to record the STDERR data stream for the purposes of problem determination.

A string of programs connected with pipes is called a pipeline.

Think about how this program would have to work if we could not pipe the data stream from one command to the next. The first command would perform its task on the data, and then the output from that command would have to be saved in a file. The next command would have to read the stream of data from the intermediate file and perform its modification of the data stream, sending its own output to a new, temporary data file. The third command would have to take its data from the second temporary data file and perform its own manipulation of the data stream and then store the resulting data stream in yet another temporary file. At each step the data file names would have to be transferred from one command to the next in some way.

I cannot even stand to think about that because it is so complex. Remember that simplicity rocks!

Building Pipelines

When I am doing something new, solving a new problem, I usually do not just type in a complete bash command pipeline from scratch, as in Experiment 9-10 off the top of my head. I usually start with just one or two commands in the pipeline and build from there by adding more commands to further process the data stream. This allows me to view the state of the data stream after each of the commands in the pipeline and make corrections as they are needed.

In Experiment 9-11 you should enter the command shown on each line and run it as shown to see the results. This will give you a feel for how you can build up complex pipelines in stages.

EXPERIMENT 9-11: BUILDING A PIPELINE

Enter the commands as shown on each line. Observe the changes in the data stream as each new filter utility is inserted to the data stream using the pipe.

Log in as root to two of the Linux virtual consoles and as the student user to two additional virtual consoles, and open several terminal sessions on the desktop. This should give plenty of data for this experiment:

```
[student@studentvm1 test]$ w
[student@studentvm1 test]$ w | tail -n +3
[student@studentvm1 test]$ w | tail -n +3 | awk '{print $1}'
[student@studentvm1 test]$ w | tail -n +3 | awk '{print $1}' | sort
[student@studentvm1 test]$ w | tail -n +3 | awk '{print $1}' | sort |
uniq
```

The results of this experiment illustrate the changes to the data stream performed by each of the filter utility programs in the pipeline.

It is possible to build up very complex pipelines that can transform the data stream using many different utilities that work with STDIO.

Redirection

Redirection is the capability to redirect the STDOUT data stream of a program to a file instead of to the default target of the display. The "greater than" (>) character, a.k.a. "gt", is the syntactical symbol for redirection. Experiment 9-12 shows how to redirect the output data stream of the df -h command to the file diskusage.txt.

EXPERIMENT 9-12: REDIRECTING STDOUT

Redirecting the STDOUT of a command can be used to create a file containing the results from that command:

```
[student@studentvm1 test]$ df -h > diskusage.txt
```

There is no output to the terminal from this command unless there is an error. This is because the STDOUT data stream is redirected to the file and STDERR is still directed to the STDOUT device, which is the display. You can view the contents of the file you just created using this next command:

```
[student@studentvm1 test]$ cat diskusage.txt
Filesystem                          Size  Used Avail Use% Mounted on
devtmpfs                            2.0G     0  2.0G   0% /dev
tmpfs                               2.0G     0  2.0G   0% /dev/shm
tmpfs                               2.0G  1.2M  2.0G   1% /run
tmpfs                               2.0G     0  2.0G   0% /sys/fs/cgroup
/dev/mapper/fedora_studentvm1-root  2.0G   49M  1.8G   3% /
/dev/mapper/fedora_studentvm1-usr    15G  3.8G   11G  27% /usr
/dev/sda1                           976M  185M  724M  21% /boot
/dev/mapper/fedora_studentvm1-tmp   4.9G   21M  4.6G   1% /tmp
/dev/mapper/fedora_studentvm1-var   9.8G  504M  8.8G   6% /var
/dev/mapper/fedora_studentvm1-home  2.0G  7.3M  1.8G   1% /home
tmpfs                               395M  8.0K  395M   1% /run/user/1000
tmpfs                               395M     0  395M   0% /run/user/0
/dev/sdb1                            60M  440K   59M   1% /test
[student@studentvm1 test]$
```

When using the > symbol for redirection, the specified file is created if it does not already exist. If it already does exist, the contents are overwritten by the data stream from the command. You can use double greater than symbols, >>, to append the new data stream to any existing content in the file as illustrated in Experiment 9-13.

EXPERIMENT 9-13: APPENDING REDIRECTED DATA STREAMS

This command appends the new data stream to the end of the existing file:

```
[student@studentvm1 test]$ df -h >> diskusage.txt
```

You can use cat and/or less to view the diskusage.txt file in order to verify that the new data was appended to the end of the file.

The < (less than) symbol redirects data to the STDIN of the program. You might want to use this method to input data from a file to STDIN of a command that does not take a file name as an argument but that does use STDIN. Although input sources can be redirected to STDIN, such as a file that is used as input to **grep**, it is generally not necessary as **grep** also takes a file name as an argument to specify the input source. Most other commands also take a file name as an argument for their input source.

One example of using redirection to STDIN is with the **od** command as shown in Experiment 9-14. The -N 50 option prevents the output from continuing forever. You could use Ctrl-C to terminate the output data stream if you don't use the -N option to limit it.

EXPERIMENT 9-14: REDIRECTING STDIN

This experiment illustrates the use of redirection as input to STDIN:

```
[student@studentvm1 test]$ od -c -N 50 < /dev/urandom
0000000 331 203   _ 307   ]   { 335 337   6 257 347       $   J   Z   U
0000020 245  \0   `  \b   8 307 261 207   K   :   }   S   \ 276 344   ;
0000040 336 256 221 317 314 241 352   ` 253 333 367 003 374 264 335   4
0000060   U  \n 347   (   h 263 354 251   u   H   ] 315 376   W 205  \0
```

```
0000100   323  263  024    %  355  003  214  354  343    \    a  254    #    `    {    _
0000120     b  201  222    2  265    [  372  215  334  253  273  250    L    c  241  233
<snip>
```

It is much easier to understand the nature of the results when formatted using **od** (Octal Display), which formats the data stream in a way that is a bit more intelligible. Read the man page for **od** for more information.

Redirection can be the source or the termination of a pipeline. Because it is so seldom needed as input, redirection is usually used as termination of a pipeline.

EXPERIMENT 9-15: USING ECHO TO GENERATE TEXT STREAMS

Perform this experiment as the student user. This activity provides examples of some aspects of redirection not yet covered. The **echo** command is used to print text strings to STDOUT.

Make your home directory the PWD and create a small text file:

```
[student@studentvm1 test]$ echo "Hello world" > hello.txt
```

Read the contents of the file by redirecting it to STDIN:

```
[student@studentvm1 test]$ cat < hello.txt
Hello world
[student@studentvm1 test]$
```

Add another line of text to the existing file:

```
[student@studentvm1 test]$ echo "How are you?" >> hello.txt
```

View the contents:

```
[student@studentvm1 test]$ cat hello.txt
Hello world
How are you?
[student@studentvm1 test]$
```

Delete (remove) the file and list the contents of your home directory to verify that the file has been erased:

```
[student@studentvm1 test]$ rm hello.txt ; ls -l
```

Create the file again:

```
[student@studentvm1 test]$ echo "Hello world" >> hello.txt ; ll
```

Verify that the file was recreated using the ls and cat commands:

Note that in this last case, the >> operator created the file because it did not exist. If it has already existed, the line would have been added at the end of the existing file as it was in step 4. Also notice the quotes are standard ASCII quotes, the same before and after the quoted string, and not extended ASCII, which are different before and after.

Just grepping Around

The **grep** command is used to select lines that match a specified pattern from a stream of data. **grep** is one of the most commonly used filter utilities and can be used in some very creative and interesting ways. The **grep** command is one of the few that can correctly be called a filter because it does filter out all the lines of the data stream that you do not want; it leaves only the lines that you do want in the remaining data stream.

According to Klaatu, my reviewer for Volume 3 of this course, "One of the classic Unix commands, developed way back in 1974 by Ken Thompson, is the Global Regular Expression Print (grep) command. It's so ubiquitous in computing that it's frequently used as a verb ('grepping through a file') and, depending on how geeky your audience, it fits nicely into real-world scenarios, too. (For example, 'I'll have to grep my memory banks to recall that information.') In short, grep is a way to search through a file for a specific pattern of characters. If that sounds like the modern Find function available in any word processor or text editor, then you've already experienced grep's effects on the computing industry."[14]

EXPERIMENT 9-16: INTRODUCING GREP

We need to create a file with some random data in it. We can use a tool that generates random passwords, but we first need to install it as root:

```
dnf -y install pwgen
```

---

[14] Kenlon, Seth, a.k.a. Klaatu, Opensource.com, *Practice using the Linux grep command*, March 18, 2021

Now as the student user, let's generate some random data and create a file with it. If the PWD is not /test, make it so. The following command creates a stream of 5000 lines of random data that are each 75 characters long and stores them in the random.txt file:

```
pwgen 75 5000 > random.txt
```

Considering that there are so many passwords, it is very likely that some character strings in them are the same. Use the grep command to locate some short, randomly selected strings from the last ten passwords on the screen. I saw the words "see" and "loop" in one of those ten passwords, so my command looked like this:

```
grep see random.txt
```

You can try that, but you should also pick some strings of your own to check. Short strings of two to four characters work best.

Use the grep filter to locate all of the lines in the output from dmesg with CPU in them:

```
dmesg | grep cpu
```

List all of the directories in your home directory with the command

```
ls -la | grep ^d
```

This works because each directory has a "d" as the first character in a long listing. The caret (^) is used by grep and other tools to anchor the text being searched to the beginning of the line.

To list all of the files that are not directories, reverse the meaning of the previous grep command with the -v option:

```
ls -la | grep -v ^d
```

Chapter Summary

You probably noticed that this chapter was not just about creating random data streams. You created meaningful data streams and then manipulated them to view or use specific data. Much of that data relates to storage because you need an LV for more experiments in later chapters, and this is a good opportunity to explore both data streams and disk and LVM structure.

It is only with the use of pipes, pagers, and redirection that many of the amazing and powerful tasks that can be performed on the Linux command line are possible. It is the pipes that transport STDIO data streams from one program or file to another. In this chapter you have learned that piping streams of data through one or more filter programs supports powerful and flexible manipulation of data in those streams.

Each of the programs in the pipelines demonstrated in the experiments is small, and each does one thing well. They are also filters, that is, they take the standard input, process it in some way, and then send the result to the standard output. Implementation of these programs as filters to send processed data streams from their own standard output to the standard input of the other programs is complementary to and necessary for the implementation of pipes as a Linux tool.

You also learned that STDIO is nothing more than streams of data. This data can be almost anything from the output of a command to list the files in a directory to an unending stream of data from a special device like /dev/urandom or even a stream that contains all of the raw data from a hard drive, an LV, or a partition. You learned some different and interesting methods to generate different types of data streams and how to use the **dd** command to explore the contents of a hard drive.

Any device on a Linux computer can be treated like a data stream. You can use ordinary tools like **dd** and **cat** to dump data from a device into a STDIO data stream that can be processed using other ordinary Linux tools.

Exercises

Do the following exercises to complete this chapter:

1. What is the function of the greater than symbol (>)?

2. Is it possible to append the content of a data stream to an existing file?

3. Design a short command-line program to display the line containing the CPU model name and nothing else.

4. Create a file in the /test directory that consists of ten lines of random data.

CHAPTER 10

Text Editors

Objectives

In this chapter you will learn

- Why text editors are needed
- About several text editors, some intended for use in a terminal session and others for the GUI desktop
- How to use the nano text editor
- How to use the vim text editor
- Why you should use the text editor of your choice

Why We Need Text Editors

Before there were word processing programs, there were text editors. The initial use for early text editors was for the creation and maintenance of text files such as shell scripts, programs written in C and other programming languages, and system configuration files.

Soon after, document preparation software such as LaTeX[1] was developed to automate the process of typesetting various types of documents, particularly technical documents and journals. This is not word processing but rather typesetting. LaTeX, which is still in heavy use and is quite popular, is about the content of a document and not about the formatting and look. The text files created for input to LaTeX are ASCII plain text files created by text editors such as vim.

---

[1] The LaTeX project, www.latex-project.org

279

D. Both, *Using and Administering Linux: Volume 1*, https://doi.org/10.1007/978-1-4842-9618-9_10

Text editors were developed for an environment where the text characters and strings were the only important aspect of the resulting file. Editors create text files that are free from the extraneous markup characters used by word processing programs to denote fonts, styles, various heading levels, fancy tables, and graphical illustrations. The entire point of an editor is to create a file containing text only. For the Intel PC and related processors, this means ASCII[2] text.

It is true that LibreOffice Writer and other word processing programs can save files as ASCII text. But it takes a few extra steps to do that, and the results are still not true ASCII. For example, I tried to create a small ASCII text file as an executable program. Very simple. I created the following text in a LibreOffice Writer document and saved it as a "text" document.

CODE SAMPLE 10-1: ASCII – NOT!

```
#!/usr/bin/bash
# This is an ASCII text file.
echo "This is a BASH program created by LibreOffice"
exit
```

Can you see the problem here?

Look at the double quotes in the echo statement. These are not true ASCII; they are extended ASCII, which has left and right quotes. These extended ASCII quotes are not interpreted properly by the bash shell or any other. This program will run, but the result is that the entire string including the quotes is printed. The intent of this type of code is to print the string within the quotes and not the quotes themselves. Only the standard ASCII double quote character (Hex 22) or the ASCII single quote (Hex 27) works correctly.

There are ways to convince LibreOffice to use the standard ASCII double quote, but it can be a pain when switching from documents that use standard ASCII and those that use anything else.

---

[2] Wikipedia, *ASCII*, https://en.wikipedia.org/wiki/ASCII

There is also the fact that you cannot use a GUI program of any kind when logged into a host that does not have a GUI desktop installed, such as most servers. What is available – always, on any Linux distribution – is Vim or vim.[3] No other editor can be expected to be available on any distribution at any target runlevel.

Vim

The vim editor is an enhanced version of the vi text editor that is distributed with many versions of Unix. There are a few instances when the vi editor is available and vim is not. This may be the case with older distributions when the system is booted to recovery mode or single-user mode. Current Fedora distributions use vim in rescue mode.

Although vim may appear at first glance to be a very simple text editor, it is, in fact, quite powerful. Vim can be configured extensively, and many plugins are available for it. When used with a terminal and shell that support color, various predefined color schemes can be used. When color is available, vim can highlight the syntactical and logical structures of various programming and scripting languages to enhance the programmer's ability to visualize the code's structure and functionality.

Vim has a powerful search and replace capability that surpasses that of any word processor. Using regular expressions (regex), vim can locate and modify text strings in ways that my favorite word processor, LibreOffice Writer, cannot possibly equal. Vim calls this substitution. Vim also has its own scripting language, Vim Script.

The bash shell that is the default for most Linux distributions has a lot of very powerful built-in commands, and many more tools are available as part of the Linux core utilities. All of these are available directly from inside the vim editor.

This is a great example of a number of tenets of the Linux Philosophy; among them, every program should do one thing and do it very well. One particular example of this is the sort core utility. The sort utility is a small program that is very good at sorting. It only sorts. When the vim developers decided that it would be a good idea to perform some tasks like sorting that were already available as core utilities, they made the decision to simply use those utilities that were already available. Why reinvent the wheel and make vim more complex. Using the external sort command – and any and all other external commands – means that adding those and any future features was simple; merely add the capability to use those commands that already exist outside of vim.

---

[3] Vim website, *Vim*, www.vim.org/

Vim can work in a split-screen mode to edit two files in the same screen or even different files in one screen. It also has a built-in help feature that is displayed in split screen along with the file being edited.

To make things even better for vim users, it is available as gVim for GUI desktop environments. Vim can also be configured to work as a simpler version of itself, evim, or easy vim. There is also an option to use vim mode for command-line editing in the bash shell. The vim editor, vim in Fedora and other Red Hat–based distributions, is one of the most powerful tools a system administrator can have in their toolbox.

I suggest learning Vim or vim because it is always present in all releases and distributions of Linux down to the very most minimal installation. It is also the most readily available editor in other Unixes as well. No other editor is so ubiquitous. Because of this wide availability of vim, that is what we will use in this course.

Other Editors

There are many other editors available to Linux SysAdmins, so let's look at a very few to give you an idea of what is out there.

A Google search using "Linux open source text editors" as the search phrase results in many hits. Many of these results are articles with titles like "X Best Text Editors …," so there are lots of options here. There are so many editors that there is no way to include them all. All of these editors are perfectly good, and each has its own strengths and weaknesses. I have tried some of these other editors but always return to vim. Therefore, I am not very knowledgeable about them, so I will only include the ones I have tried here.

Nano

The nano editor is very popular and is now the default editor for many Linux distributions including Fedora. Nano is designed to be more user-friendly than other editors. It opens files in editing mode, which vim does not, and has a display of the most commonly used keystrokes at the bottom of the screen.

I do like the relative simplicity of nano, and I think it is a better choice for anyone new to Linux and text editing. I have added a short section on getting started with nano to this second edition and suggest that you use it as your default editor for this course.

Both vim and nano are installed by default in the Fedora Xfce versions.

Tip   Even though I recommend using nano as your editor for this course, there may still be some remaining references to using vim to edit files. You can use either nano or vim, whichever you like best.

Emacs

GNU Emacs[4] is arguably the other favorite and most used open source editor. With a very extensible architecture and a large number of plugins, Emacs is very powerful. It is a text-mode editor but, like vim, there is also a GUI version.

Emacs does syntax highlighting for many programming and scripting languages. It has a scripting language, Emacs Lisp, and extensive built-in documentation. Some people have called Emacs an operating system itself because it is possible to write many types of programs with Emacs, including games, that run in an Emacs session.

Emacs mode is also the default editing mode for the bash shell. If you like Emacs, then the default bash command-line editing will be second nature for you.

gnome-text-editor

GNOME text editor is a simple editor for the desktop. It was designed explicitly for GNOME but will also work on other desktops. It quite basically has few features, but the one I especially like is that you can open multiple documents, each on its own tab.

gedit

The gedit text editor is a GUI program that provides syntax highlighting, plugins, built-in spell-checking, and a side pane that can show a list of open text documents. It was developed to be simple and easy to use, but it still boasts a powerful feature set.

---

[4] GNU Emacs website, www.gnu.org/software/emacs/

gedit is still available but is not installed by default as it has been replaced by gnome-text-editor.

Leafpad

Leafpad is another GUI text editor I have tried. It is very simple with only a couple features. You can turn on word wrap, auto-indent, and line numbering. If you want the simplest GUI editor of all, this is definitely in the running.

Kate

Kate is an advanced GUI desktop text editor designed for the KDE environment, but it works on other desktops as well. It has syntax highlighting, multiple panes like split screen, a side panel for a document overview, line numbering, and more. Kate also supports plugins, and it has a vi mode for those of us with deeply ingrained vim muscle memory.

Unlike many other KDE-related tools, Kate does not have a large number of KDE package requirements. When I installed it, only one additional dependency was installed.

Kate has many features that are designed for use in a programming environment. If you are a developer and work on a GUI desktop, Kate is an editor you should consider.

xfw

The xfw editor is also known as X File Write. It is a very basic GUI text editor that provides few features beyond basic search and replace. It has only a few configuration options. If you like very simple and clean, xfw is a good choice.

xed

xed is another simple GUI editor. It does have spell-check and syntax highlighting, so it might be a better choice for some users who do coding or long text documents.

Learning Nano

Many Linux distributions bundle vim as their default text editor. This appeals to many longtime Linux users, and those who don't like it can change it promptly after install anyway. Vim is a funny editor, though, as it's one of the few that opens to a mode that doesn't permit text entry. That's a puzzling choice for any user, and it's confusing for a new one.

Thanks to GNU nano, there's a common alternative to vim for a lightweight terminal-based text editor, and it's so easy to use – it has its most important commands listed at the bottom of its window. Nano seems to be overtaking vim as the default editor in many Linux distributions, and Fedora is no exception.

EXPERIMENT 10-1: INTRODUCING NANO

On Linux and macOS, you probably already have GNU nano installed. You can verify as the student user with the `which` command:

```
$ which nano
```

```
/bin/nano
```

If you don't have it installed, you can install it from the Fedora repository. Do this as root:

```
# dnf -y install nano
```

Launch nano from the terminal, either alone…

```
$ nano
```

… or you can open a specific file by following your command with a path to a file. If the file you name doesn't already exist, it's created:

```
$ nano example.txt
```

Nano is, with just a little reading, pretty self-explanatory. When you launch it, nano opens to either an empty buffer or the file you opened. At the bottom of the screen, there's a list of functions and their corresponding keyboard shortcuts. More functions are available by pressing **Ctrl-G** for Get Help.

Here are the most important application commands:

- **Ctrl-S** saves your work to the existing file.
- **Ctrl-W** allows you to save the file to a new file name.

- **Ctrl-R** loads a file. Like the "Read" (r) command in vim, it reads the contents of a file into the cursor position in the document currently being edited.

- **Ctrl-X** quits or exits. This also asks if you want to save your work if it has not been saved since the last change.

- **Ctrl-G** is for Get Help with a short description and a list of the most common commands.

Here are the most common editing commands:

- **Alt-A** selects ("marks") a region.

- **Ctrl-K** cuts the marked text.

- **Ctrl-U** pastes ("uncuts").

- **Alt-F** is to undo the latest action.

- **Alt-E** is to redo the latest action.

The It's FOSS website has a good introduction to using nano.[5] Check it out now and then do the following.

As the student user, ensure that your home directory is the PWD. Create a new file with nano and type several paragraphs of text into it. Move some sentences around. Delete some text, undo the delete, and then redo it.

Spend some time to get a little familiarity with nano so you can compare it with vim. Then you can choose which editor you prefer for use through the rest of this course.

Nano isn't as extensible as Emacs or vim, but you can do some significant customization in a file called ~/.nanorc. In this file, you can set global preferences, including word wrap settings, color schemes, line numbering, and more. You can also create your own key bindings, so if you want to use **Ctrl-V** to paste instead of nano's default **Ctrl-U**, you can change the binding assigned to the **paste** function:

```
bind ^V paste all
```

---

[5] It's FOSS, *Getting Started With Nano Text Editor [Beginner's Guide]*, https://itsfoss.com/nano-editor-guide/

You can get a list of all available functions in the GNU nano documentation.[6]

GNU nano is a no-nonsense, straightforward text editor. It's easy to use and provides all the functionality you expect from a text editor. Try it out and see if you enjoy the simplicity of intuitive editing.

Learning Vim

Learning any editor can be challenging. Learning the vim editor can be very beneficial for all SysAdmins because vim or vi will always be available. Fortunately, vim has an excellent tutorial, vimtutor. Install and start the tutorial using the directions in Experiment 10-2.

EXPERIMENT 10-2: A VIM TUTORIAL

The vimtutor tutorial may already be installed, but let's make sure that it is. Vimtutor is located in the vim-enhanced package.

In a terminal session as root, install the vim-enhanced package:

```
[root@studentvm1 ~]# dnf -y install vim-enhanced
```

In a terminal session as the student user, type the command vimtutor to start the tutorial:

```
[student@studentvm1 ~]$ vimtutor
```

Read the file that vimtutor loads and follow the directions it gives. All of the information you need to complete the tutorial is in the vimtutor file.

There are many jokes in the SysAdmin community about new users' inability to exit vim. That is covered in vimtutor lesson 1.2, so be sure to pay attention to that. It is not hard, but if you don't know how to do it, you would get very frustrated.

The vimtutor tutorial provides you with a basic set of skills that will enable you to perform the editing required. However, vimtutor barely scratches the surface of vim's capabilities. You will encounter situations in this course as well as out in the real world

---

[6] *Gnu nano documentation*, www.nano-editor.org/dist/latest/nanorc.5.html

where you will wish that vim had a particular capability. It is highly likely that it does have whatever you were thinking about. Use the help facility to see if you can locate the feature or capability that you need.

I can also recommend the book *Pro Vim*,[7] which provides an excellent way to learn vim from the ground up.

Setting SELinux to Permissive

Now it's time to put one of these editors to work.

SELinux is a security protocol originally created by the NSA to prevent crackers from making changes to a Linux computer even if they have gained access. It is a good security measure, and it is open source so that many developers outside the NSA have had a chance to inspect it to verify that there are no backdoors. Due to potential problems that SELinux may cause with some future experiments, you must change SELinux to "permissive."

EXPERIMENT 10-3: SET SELINUX TO PERMISSIVE

First, check the current status of SELinux:

```
[root@studentvm1 ~]# getenforce
Enforcing
[root@studentvm1 ~]#
```

As root, use your preferred editor to set SELinux to "permissive" in the /etc/selinux/config file. In the example I show how to launch vim with the SELinux config file:

```
[root@studentvm1 ~]# vim /etc/selinux/config
```

Change the SELINUX line from

```
SELINUX=enforcing
```

to

```
SELINUX=permissive
```

---

[7] McDonnell, Mark, *Pro Vim*, Apress, 2014

The file should look like the following one when you have finished editing it. I have highlighted the changed line, showing what it should be:

```
# This file controls the state of SELinux on the system.
# SELINUX= can take one of these three values:
#     enforcing - SELinux security policy is enforced.
#     permissive - SELinux prints warnings instead of enforcing.
#     disabled - No SELinux policy is loaded.
SELINUX=permissive
# SELINUXTYPE= can take one of these three values:
#     targeted - Targeted processes are protected,
#     minimum - Modification of targeted policy. Only selected processes are protected.
#     mls - Multi Level Security protection.
SELINUXTYPE=targeted
```

Save the file, exit from the editor, and reboot the virtual machine. After rebooting, run the following command as root to verify the current state of SELinux:

```
[root@studentvm1 ~]# getenforce
permissive
[root@studentvm1 ~]#
```

This is one of the very few times that a reboot is required to effect the desired changes to the Linux configuration. It may take a few minutes during the reboot while SELinux relabels the targeted files and directories. Labeling is the process of assigning a security context to a process or a file. The system will reboot again at end of the relabel process.

We will cover SELinux in more detail in Chapter 46 of Volume 3.

Use Your Favorite Text Editor

"Use your favorite text editor" is a tenet of *the Linux Philosophy for system administrators*.[8] I think it is important because arguing about editors can be the cause of a great deal of wasted energy. Everyone has their favorite editor, and it might not be the same as mine. So what?

---

[8] Both, David, *The Linux Philosophy for SysAdmins*, Apress, 2018, 371–379

I use vim as my editor. I have used it for years and like it very much. I am used to it. It meets my needs more than any other editor I have tried. If you can say that about your editor – whichever one that might be – then you are in editor nirvana.

I started using vim when I began learning Solaris over 20 years ago. My mentor suggested that I start learning to edit with vim because it would always be present on every system. That has proven to be true whether the operating system is Solaris or Linux. The vim editor is always there so I can count on it. For me, this works.

The vim editor can also be used as the editor for bash command-line editing. Although the default for command editing is Emacs, I use the vim option because I already know the vim keystrokes. The option to use vim-style editing in bash can be set by adding the line "set -o vi" to the ~/.bashrc file for just your own use. For setting the vim option globally, a configuration file in /etc/profile.d/ is used, so that all users, root and non-privileged, have that as part of their bash configuration.

Other tools that use vim editing are the crontab and visudo commands; both of these are wrappers around vi. Lazy SysAdmins use code that already exists, especially when it is open source. Using the vim editor for these tools is an excellent example of that.

There are many other editors available that are also great and powerful and fantastic. I still prefer vim. You should use what you want, and don't worry about what everyone else is using. Just because I use vim does not mean you have to use it. Using the best editor for you is important for your productivity. Once you have learned the keystroke combinations and commands that you use most frequently in an editor, you can be very efficient in editing files of all types.

Chapter Summary

This chapter is mostly about introducing you to the nano and vim editors. This is partly because one or both will always be present in any Linux distribution. It is also because they both have amazing power. It is possible to learn only the basics of either and be very productive. Learning their more advanced features can enhance their power and allow you to become even more productive.

As noted in this chapter, there are also many other open source text editors available. Some are extremely popular with large numbers of developers and users and others not so much. But all have features to recommend them.

You may find one of these other editors more conducive to your own style, and if you do you should certainly use it. But your knowledge of vim and nano will always be useful too.

Exercises

Complete the following exercises to finish this chapter:

1. How do text editors differ from word processors?

2. What vim command would you use to delete five words?

3. What two modes of operation does vim use?

4. How would you navigate the cursor to a specific line number – assuming you already know the line number?

5. Use nano to create a file named fruit.txt in the student user's home directory that contains a list of at least ten fruits, one on each line. Save the file and then use the **cat** utility to display the contents of the file.

6. Use vim to edit the fruit.txt file and sort the names of the fruits into alphabetical order. Save the file and again display its contents with **cat**.

7. Do nano and vim have a spell-check feature? How did you determine that?

CHAPTER 11

Working as Root

Objectives

In this chapter you will learn

- The functional difference between root and non-root users
- The advantages of having root access
- The disadvantages of having root access
- To raise the privilege level of a non-root user to enable access to privileged tasks
- The correct usage of sudo
- How to assign a non-root user root privileges to run a single program

Why Root?

All Linux computer systems need an administrator. The system administrator – SysAdmin – is the user with assigned authority to perform any necessary administrative task on a computer. For Unix and Linux, that administrator is called root. A commonly used synonym for root is superuser.

The root user can do anything and perform any task on a Linux computer regardless of which user owns the file, directory, or process. Root can delete undeletable files and add and delete users. Root can change the priority (via the "nice" number) of any running program and kill or suspend execution of any running program. Root can explore all of the deep and fascinating corners of the filesystem directory tree as well as the structure of the filesystems themselves.

293

Non-root users, that is, users without the raised privilege level assigned to the root user, do not have the authority to perform root-level tasks on a Linux computer. For example, non-privileged users may not enter the home directory or any directories belonging to other users, and they may not delete files belonging to other users unless root or that other non-root user that owns the files has explicitly set permissions on the files that will allow other non-root users to do so. That is because Linux protects files and processes of one user from being deleted or changed by other users. This is necessary in a multiuser operating system like Linux.

What non-root, non-privileged users can do is manage their own files and directories and access those shared ones to which they have been allowed access. They can also manage programs they have launched to perform some work for them.

Although it is possible for the user of a non-root account to have root privileges, it is not a best practice to do so. Best practice is to have a designated, knowledgeable person with access to the root account. If one or more non-privileged, non-root users need access to one or two commands that require root privilege, the appropriate practice is to use the sudo facility to allow them access to those few commands. We will cover the use of sudo in more detail later in this chapter.

More About the su Command

The su (switch user, also called substitute user) command gives us a powerful tool that allows us to work on the command line as a different user from the one we logged in as. We have already used this command at the command line to switch from the student user to the root user, but it requires more attention.

This command is necessary in today's Linux environment because users are discouraged from logging in as root directly to the graphical desktop. This restriction is usually implemented by the display manager as the requirement to type the user name root while all other valid user names are displayed for selection. This can be circumvented, but it is used to discourage the SysAdmin from doing everything as root, which could cause security problems. Each SysAdmin should have a non-root login and then switch to the root user only when necessary to perform some action that requires root privileges.

About that hyphen (-). If a non-root user, student, for example, were to use the command su without the hyphen to obtain root privilege, the environment, $PATH, and other environment variables, for example, would remain those of the student user, and the PWD would remain the same; this behavior is for historical backward compatibility. Adding the hyphen to the command tells the su command to start up as a login shell, which sets the root environment and makes /root, root's home directory, the PWD. If root is using su to switch to a non-root user, the hyphen causes the environment to be set to that of the target user. Let's explore this.

The path as defined in the $PATH environment variable tells Linux where to find executable files for the current user whether root or a non-root user. The path is sequence sensitive, so the first executable located in the $PATH series of locations is the executable file used for the command. If the $PATH environment variable were null – that is, empty – you would need to type the fully qualified directory name (FQDN) to tell Linux where to find the executable file.

EXPERIMENT 11-1: THE SU ENVIRONMENT

Start this experiment as the student user. Open a terminal session if necessary. Switch to the root user using the su command without the hyphen:

```
[student@studentvm1 ~]$ su
Password: <Enter the root password>
[root@studentvm1 student]# echo $PATH
/root/.local/bin:/root/bin:/home/student/.local/bin:/home/student/
bin:/usr/local/bin:/usr/bin:/usr/local/sbin:/usr/sbin
```

The exit command exits from the sub-shell created by the su command and returns us to the original bash shell:

```
[root@studentvm1 student]# exit
[student@studentvm1 ~]$ su -
Password: <Enter the root password>
[root@studentvm1 ~]# echo $PATH
/root/.local/bin:/root/bin:/usr/local/sbin:/usr/local/bin:/usr/sbin:/
usr/bin
[root@studentvm1 ~]# exit
[student@studentvm1 ~]$
```

Notice the difference in the PWD and the significant difference in the $PATH environment variable. Because of these and other differences in the shell environment, the results of some commands may not be correct and might provide misleading results.

The results of Experiment 11-1 inform us that it is important to always use the hyphen when switching users to root and, by extension, any other user.

Root can use the su - command to switch to any other user without the need for a password. This makes it possible for the root user to switch to any other user to perform tasks as that user. This is usually to assist in problem determination by trying the same commands the regular user is having problems with. We look at this aspect of the su command near the end of this chapter.

Read the man page for su for more information.

Another option for performing tasks that require root access is the sudo (switch user and do) command. The sudo command has its uses, and we will discuss its relative advantages and disadvantages later in this chapter.

Getting to Know the Root Account

The root account has some unique attributes that identify it to the operating system. Each Linux user account has attributes that provide the operating system with information about how to handle the account, files that belong to the account, and any commands entered at the command line or issued by programs and utilities on behalf of the account. Two of these are the user ID (UID) and group ID (GID). Let's start by looking at the user and group information for root.

EXPERIMENT 11-2: GETTING STARTED WITH ROOT

This simple experiment should be performed as root. The information we need to find the UID and GID for the root user can be extracted from the /etc/passwd file with the id command along with some information about the security context of the user.

On the VM you are using for this course, if a terminal emulator logged into root is not already open, do so and **su** - to root:

```
[student@studentvm1 ~]$ su -
Password: <Enter root password here>
[root@studentvm1 ~]#
```

In Chapter 7 we used the **id** command to look at the account information for the student user. Let's now use that command for root:

```
[root@studentvm1 ~]# id
uid=0(root) gid=0(root) groups=0(root)
[root@studentvm1 ~]#
```

This shows that the UID and GID for root are both 0 (zero) and that the root user is a member of the root group with a GID of 0. If SELinux were set to "enforcing," this command would display additional information about the SELinux context.

Now let's look at the files in root's home directory. The -n option in the second ll command displays the ownership as the numeric UID of the User and Group ownership rather than as the user and group names:

```
[root@studentvm1 ~]# ll
total 12
-rw-------. 1 root root 1354 Aug 13 16:24 anaconda-ks.cfg
-rw-r--r--. 1 root root 1371 Aug 18 10:16 initial-setup-ks.cfg
[root@studentvm1 ~]# ll -n
total 12
-rw-------. 1 0 0 1354 Aug 13 16:24 anaconda-ks.cfg
-rw-r--r--. 1 0 0 1371 Aug 18 10:16 initial-setup-ks.cfg
[root@studentvm1 ~]#
```

You can see that the User and Group ownership is UID and GID of zero, which is root.

The UID and GID of 0, as shown in Experiment 11-2, are recognized by Linux as belonging to root and are handled differently than any other user. We will explore user management and the files that contain user and group information in detail in Chapter 38 of Volume 2. For now we need only know that the root account is different and can do anything and perform any task in a Linux system and that all other accounts are limited in specific ways that ensure one user can't impinge upon the resources of another or those of the system itself.

You have already done some work as root while setting up VirtualBox and installing the Linux virtual machine. You have also installed some new software packages and performed some experiments as root. None of those tasks that you were instructed to perform as root during that setup and preparation could have been accomplished by a non-root user.

In order to more fully understand the capabilities of the root user, we will start with an exploration of the limits of non-root users.

EXPERIMENT 11-3: NON-ROOT USER LIMITS

Let's start with a simple illustration of creating a directory. As the user student, use the commands shown in the following examples to try to create a new directory, testdir, in various locations in the filesystem directory tree:

```
[student@studentvm1 ~]$ mkdir /testdir
mkdir: cannot create directory '/testdir': Permission denied
[student@studentvm1 ~]$ mkdir /etc/testdir
mkdir: cannot create directory '/etc/testdir': Permission denied
[student@studentvm1 ~]$ mkdir /var/testdir
mkdir: cannot create directory '/var/testdir': Permission denied
[student@studentvm1 ~]$ mkdir /media/testdir
mkdir: cannot create directory '/media/testdir': Permission denied
[student@studentvm1 ~]$ mkdir /mnt/testdir
mkdir: cannot create directory '/mnt/testdir': Permission denied
[student@studentvm1 ~]$ mkdir testdir
[student@studentvm1 ~]$
```

The student user cannot create a new directory in most parts of the directory tree. The attempts result in a "Permission denied" error message. The only location that the student user could create a new directory was in its own home directory.

There is one directory in which non-root users such as student can create a new directory. Can you think of where that might be?

Try the following:

```
[student@studentvm1 ~]$ mkdir /tmp/testdir
[student@studentvm1 ~]$ ll /tmp
total 264
-rw-r--r--. 1 root     root     1654 Jan 17 07:54 anaconda.log
<SNIP>
drwxr-xr-x  2 student student 4096 Jan 22 17:13 testdir
-rw-r--r--  1 student student 2353 Jan 22 14:32 tmp1_0161i5.png
<SNIP>
[student@studentvm1 ~]$
```

In this instance there is no error, and we can confirm that the /tmp/testdir directory was created. Why does this work?

To explain why non-root users cannot create new directories – or files as well – we need to look at the ownership and permissions set on these directories.

EXPERIMENT 11-4: A QUICK LOOK AT PERMISSIONS

Take a look at the ownership and permissions for two of the directories in which the student user tried to create a new directory:

```
[student@studentvm1 ~]$ ls -la /
total 76
dr-xr-xr-x.  18 root root   4096 Apr 25 02:19 .
dr-xr-xr-x.  18 root root   4096 Apr 25 02:19 ..
<SNIP>
dr-xr-xr-x.  13 root root      0 Sep 12 17:18 sys
drwxrwxrwxt. 10 root root   4096 Sep 13 16:45 tmp
drwxr-xr-x.  13 root root   4096 Apr 25 02:19 usr
drwxr-xr-x.  22 root root   4096 Apr 25 02:23 var
[student@studentvm1 ~]$
```

This information tells us what we need to know. I have highlighted two entries in this list of directories that illustrate this.

In the two highlighted directories shown in Experiment 11-4, you can see there is a difference in the permissions. Notice also that both directories are owned by root and the Group ownership is also root. Let's look at what those permissions mean when applied to directories. We will cover file and directory permissions in detail in Chapter 18.

Figure 11-1 shows a breakdown of the Linux permissions structure for files and directories.

User	Group	Other
rwx	rwx	rwx

Figure 11-1. *Linux permissions as applied to directories*

File and directory permissions and ownership are one aspect of security provided by Linux as they are related to user accounts. Each file and directory on a Linux system has a user that owns it, a group to which it belongs, and a set of access permissions. It is important to understand a bit about file ownership and permissions in the context of user accounts and their ability to work with files and directories. The permissions settings of a file or directory are also known as the file mode. Look at the entry for the /usr directory:

```
drwxr-xr-x.  13 root root  4096 Apr 25 02:19 usr
```

The first character, "d" in this case, tells us that this is a directory. An "l" would indicate that the entry is a link; we will look at links in detail in Chapter 18. A hyphen (-) in the first position indicates no character, and by default this represents a file – any type of file as can be seen in root's home directory:

```
-rw-------. 1 root root 2118 Dec 22 11:07 anaconda-ks.cfg
-rw-r--r--. 1 root root 2196 Dec 22 12:47 initial-setup-ks.cfg
```

Then there are three categories of permissions, each category providing (R)ead, (W)rite, and e(X)ecute access to the file. The permissions categories are (U)ser, (G)roup, and (O)ther.

The User is the owner of the file or directory. The permissions for the (U)ser are rwx, which means that user root can list the contents (read) and create new files (write) in this directory. The (G)roup and (O)ther permissions are r-x, which means that any user that is a member of the group root – and there should not be any – can enter this directory (x) and read (r) the files in it. The "Other" category access permissions may allow all other users – those that are not root and that are not members of the group root that owns the file – to enter the directory and read contents but not create files or directories inside this directory.

The result of this is that the student user can make /usr the PWD and can list the files and other directories there. In all cases access to read and write the individual files in the directory is managed by the mode of each file.

EXPERIMENT 11-5: CHANGING PERMISSIONS

Perform this experiment as root. First, create a directory in /test:

```
[root@studentvm1 ~]# mkdir /test/testdir1 ; cd /test
[root@studentvm1 test]# ll
total 1076
```

```
-rw-r--r--. 1 root root  69827 Jan 22 10:09 file0.txt
<SNIP>
-rw-r--r--. 1 root root     25 Jan 22 11:06 hello.txt
drwx------  2 root root  12288 Jan 21 10:16 lost+found
-rw-r--r--. 1 root root 380000 Jan 22 11:37 random.txt
drwxr-xr-x  2 root root   1024 Jan 23 08:35 testdir1
```

Now change the permissions on the directory using the chmod (change mode) command. The easy way to do this is with octal numeric permissions. Permissions of 000 mean that no one has access to the directory – even root:

```
[root@studentvm1 test]# chmod 000 testdir1 ; ll
total 1076
-rw-r--r--. 1 root root  69827 Jan 22 10:09 file0.txt
<SNIP>
-rw-r--r--. 1 root root     25 Jan 22 11:06 hello.txt
drwx------  2 root root  12288 Jan 21 10:16 lost+found
-rw-r--r--. 1 root root 380000 Jan 22 11:37 random.txt
d---------  2 root root   1024 Jan 23 08:35 testdir1
```

At this point – theoretically – even the user (owner) of the /tmp/testdir1 directory should not be able to enter it or create a file in it. And yet we get the following results when we try that as root:

```
[root@studentvm1 test]# cd testdir1 ; pwd
/test/testdir1
[root@studentvm1 testdir1]# cd testdir1 ; echo "This is a new file" >
testfile.txt ; ll
total 1
-rw-r--r-- 1 root root 19 Jan 23 08:41 testfile.txt
[root@studentvm1 testdir1]#
```

You should cat testfile.txt to verify its actual content, but we can see from the listing that it contains 19 bytes of data.

We will explore file modes with non-root users later, but for now you can assume the fact that this will not work for users other than root. Other users will not be able to create files in directories that belong to them when the permissions are 000.

Return to root's home directory as the PWD.

So you can now see that actions taken by root override the permissions set on the directory and the root user is able to enter and create a file containing data in a directory that has no permissions at all. The key point here is that *root can do anything*. Despite the fact that there are a couple intentional ways to limit root, it is quite easy for the root user to overcome those relatively minor limitations.

Disadvantages of Root

Because root can do anything on a Linux system, there is great danger. Any error made by root has the potential to cause catastrophic harm to a Linux host. I used the following quote back in Chapter 1 to help illustrate the vast power of Linux.

> *Unix was not designed to stop its users from doing stupid things, as that would also stop them from doing clever things.*

—Doug Gwyn

This quote is absolutely true, especially for the root user. Although there are a few limits on the powers of root just to assist in preventing a few easily made mistakes, those can all be circumvented just as easily. The problem is that many times when I am working as root, I do things automatically – muscle memory is powerful. It is easy to make a mistake that can wipe out a file or a whole directory structure. It is also easy to power off or reboot the wrong machine when working as root remotely via SSH connections to multiple hosts.

It is incumbent upon us as SysAdmins to be very careful when we work as root. The power of the root user is complete, and it is easy to cause damage that may not be completely recoverable. At the very least, it may take hours to recover from the unintentional slip of the fingers.

Escalating User Privilege

It is possible to raise the privilege level of non-root users in order to enable them to perform tasks that only root can usually do. The reasons for doing this are usually to enable non-root users to perform some tasks for which only the root user has permissions. This is a common requirement and can easily be done safely.

The Bad Ways

I have, however, seen many instances where SysAdmins simply give the user the root password. This is dangerous and can lead to problems caused by an inexperienced user. This is a horrible way to assist users in doing their legitimate jobs while offloading some repetitive tasks from the root user. This is definitely not a safe way in which to allow unprivileged users access to commands that require root privileges.

There is another horrible way of providing complete privilege escalation. You should know what they are because you should be able to identify them so you can disable them. Change the UID and GID of the user to zero. You can edit the passwd, group, and shadow files to do this. We will explore those files in Volume 2, Chapter 38. Approaches like this may be leftovers from previous administrators who were improperly trained – if at all – or who just did not understand how insecure these methods are. They may also be due to a PHB who, out of ignorance, demands one of these approaches.

There is a better way.

Using sudo

Using the sudo facility to provide legitimate access to specific privileged commands by non-root users can reduce the system administrator's workload while maintaining security and providing a log of the users' actions by ID and command. The sudo facility can be used to allow unprivileged users some escalation of privileges for one command or a group of related commands.

EXPERIMENT 11-6: INTRODUCING SUDO

In a terminal session as root, enter the following command, which will display information about the Internet connections on your test VM. The nmcli command (NetworkManager Command Line Interface) is the most recent tool for use in managing network interfaces. The NMCLI tool is covered in Chapter 33 of Volume 2:

```
[root@studentvm1 ~]# nmcli
enp0s3: connected to Wired connection 1
        "Intel 82540EM"
        ethernet (e1000), 08:00:27:01:7D:AD, hw, mtu 1500
        ip4 default
```

```
        inet4 10.0.2.22/24
        route4 10.0.2.0/24 metric 100
        route4 default via 10.0.2.1 metric 100
        inet6 fe80::b36b:f81c:21ea:75c0/64
        route6 fe80::/64 metric 1024

enp0s9: connected to Wired connection 2
        "Intel 82540EM"
        ethernet (e1000), 08:00:27:FF:C6:4F, hw, mtu 1500
        inet4 192.168.0.181/24
        route4 192.168.0.0/24 metric 101
        route4 default via 192.168.0.254 metric 101
        inet6 fe80::6ce0:897c:5b7f:7c62/64
        route6 fe80::/64 metric 1024

lo: unmanaged
        "lo"
        loopback (unknown), 00:00:00:00:00:00, sw, mtu 65536

DNS configuration:
        servers: 192.168.0.52 8.8.8.8 8.8.4.4
        domains: both.org
        interface: enp0s3

        servers: 192.168.0.52 8.8.8.8 8.8.4.4
        domains: both.org
        interface: enp0s9

Use "nmcli device show" to get complete information about known devices
and "nmcli connection show" to get an overview on active connection
profiles.

Consult nmcli(1) and nmcli-examples(7) manual pages for complete usage
details.
[root@studentvm1 ~]#
```

Look at the first entry (highlighted in the preceding code), which contains the name of the NIC that is configured on this VM. It should probably be enp0s3 and the IP address should be 10.0.2.22/24 or at least in that IP range as it is on my VM, but check to be sure. If it is not the same as mine, be sure to use the NIC[1] name that matches the one on your VM.

---

[1] Network interface card.

Just so you know, I have a second NIC, enpOs9, on my VM. I have configured this NIC so that I can directly log into the VM from a terminal session on my primary workstation. This makes copy and paste easier while writing these books. You will get to set up a second NIC in Volume 3. Unless it serves to illustrate a point, I will probably delete most further references to it.

Enter the next command as the student user to attempt to view the details of the NIC:

```
[student@studentvm1 ~]$ mii-tool -v enpOs3
SIOCGMIIPHY on 'enpOs3' failed: Operation not permitted
[student@studentvm1 ~]$
```

This fails because the student user does not have the privileges required to run this command.

Give the user student sudo access to this single command. Working in a terminal session as root, use the visudo command:

```
[root@studentvm1 ~]# visudo
```

Add the following line to the bottom of the /etc/sudoers file. This line gives the student user access to use only this one privileged command:

```
student ALL=/usr/sbin/mii-tool
```

If you don't yet feel comfortable editing configuration files with vim or another editor, you could also enter the following command on a single line, which appends a single line to the bottom of /etc/sudoers:

```
[root@studentvm1 ~]# echo "student ALL=/usr/sbin/mii-tool" >>
/etc/sudoers
```

I was frankly surprised that this command works because using visudo to edit the sudoers file is recommended.

Run the following command to test the ability of the user student to execute the mii-tool command:

```
[student@studentvm1 ~]$ sudo mii-tool -v enpOs3
```

We trust you have received the usual lecture from the local System Administrator. It usually boils down to these three things:

```
#1) Respect the privacy of others.
#2) Think before you type.
#3) With great power comes great responsibility.
```

```
[sudo] password for student: <Enter student password>
enpOs3: no autonegotiation, 1000baseT-FD flow-control, link ok
  product info: Yukon 88E1011 rev 4
  basic mode:    autonegotiation enabled
  basic status: autonegotiation complete, link ok
  capabilities: 1000baseT-FD 100baseTx-FD 100baseTx-HD 10baseT-FD
10baseT-HD
  advertising:   1000baseT-FD 100baseTx-FD 100baseTx-HD 10baseT-FD
10baseT-HD flow-control
  link partner: 1000baseT-HD 1000baseT-FD 100baseTx-FD 100baseTx-HD
10baseT-FD 10baseT-HD
[student@studentvm1 ~]$
```

Note that the first time a user uses sudo, they get a little on-screen lecture. The SysAdmin should always give a stern lecture to users with sudo privileges. ☺

The user must enter their own password, and the command is then executed. Notice that if you execute the same command or any other allowed command within 5 minutes, it is not necessary to re-enter your password. This expiration time is configurable.

Now try another privileged command as the student user. The vgs command lists the volume groups currently available in the host whether active or not:

```
[student@studentvm1 ~]$ vgs
  WARNING: Running as a non-root user. Functionality may be unavailable.
  /run/lock/lvm/P_global:aux: open failed: Permission denied
```

This command fails because the user student has only been given privileges to a single command.

Do Do That sudo That You Do So Well

Let's look at the sudoers file in a bit more detail. I recently wrote a short bash program to copy some MP3 files from a USB thumb drive on one network host to another network host. The files are copied from a workstation to a specific directory on a server from where they can be downloaded and played.

This program does a few other things, like changing the name of the files before they are copied so that they are automatically sorted by date on the web page. It also deletes all of the files on the USB drive after verifying that the transfer has taken place correctly.

This nice little program has a few options such as -h to display help, -t for test mode, and a couple others.

My program, wonderful as it is, needs to run as root in order to perform its primary functions. Unfortunately, this organization has only a couple people besides myself who have any interest in administering our audio and computer systems, which puts me in the position of finding semi-technical people to train to log into the computer we use to perform the transfer and run this little program.

It is not that I cannot run the program myself, but I am not always there for various reasons such as travel or illness. Even when I am present, as the "lazy SysAdmin," I like to delegate tasks to others so that they have learning opportunities. So I wrote scripts to automate those tasks and used sudo to anoint a couple users to run the scripts.

Many Linux administrative commands require the user to be root in order to run. The sudo program is a handy tool that allows me as a SysAdmin with root access to delegate responsibility for all or a few administrative tasks to other users of the computer as I see fit. It allows me to perform that delegation without compromising the root password and thus maintain a high level of security on the host.

Let's assume, for example, that I have given a regular user, "ruser," access to my bash program, "myprog," which must be run as root in order to perform part of its functions. First, the user logs in as ruser with their own password. The user then uses the following command to run myprog:

```
sudo myprog
```

The sudo program checks the /etc/sudoers file and verifies that ruser is permitted to run myprog. If so, sudo requests that the user enter their own password – not the root password. After ruser enters their own password, the program is run. The sudo program also logs the facts of the access to myprog with the date and time the program was run, the complete command, and the user who ran it. This data is logged in /var/log/secure.

I have done this to delegate authority to run a single program to myself and a couple other users. However, sudo can be used to do so much more. It can allow the SysAdmin to delegate authority for managing network functions or specific services to a single person or to a group of trusted users. It allows these functions to be delegated while protecting the security of the root password.

The sudoers File

As a SysAdmin I can use the /etc/sudoers file to allow users or groups of users access to a single command, defined groups of commands, or all commands. This flexibility is key to both the power and the simplicity of using sudo for delegation. I have not reproduced the sudoers file here in order to save space. You can view the sudoers file using the less command.

EXPERIMENT 11-7: A LOOK AT THE SUDOERS FILE

Perform this experiment as root. Enter the following command to view the sudoers file:

```
[root@studentvm1 ~]# less /etc/sudoers
```

You can use the Page Up and Page Down keys to scroll through the file a page at a time and the up arrow and down arrow keys to scroll one line at a time. When you are done viewing the sudoers file, just press "Q" – the Q key – to quit and return to a command prompt.

I found the sudoers file very confusing the first time I encountered it. Hopefully it won't be quite so obscure for you by the time we get through this explanation. I do like that Red Hat–based distributions tend to have default configuration files with lots of comments and examples to provide guidance. This does make things easier because much less Internet searching is necessary.

Normally we edit the sudoers file rather than just appending new lines to the end. Do not use your standard editor to modify the sudoers file. Use the **visudo** command because it is designed to enable any changes as soon as the file is saved and you exit from the editor. The **visudo** command is a wrapper around the vi editor. It is possible to use editors besides **vi** in the same way as **visudo**.

Let's start analyzing this file at the beginning with a couple types of aliases. Scroll through the sudoers file as we examine each section.

Host Aliases

The Host Aliases section is used to create groups of hosts on which commands or command aliases can be used to provide access. The basic idea is that this single file will be maintained for all hosts in an organization and copied to /etc of each host. Some hosts, such as servers, can thus be configured as a group to allow some users access to specific commands such as the ability to start and stop services like HTTPD, DNS, and networking, the ability to mount filesystems, and so on. IP addresses can be used instead of host names in the host aliases.

User Aliases

The next set of configuration samples is user aliases. This allows root to sort users into aliased groups so that an entire group can be provided access to certain root capabilities. You can create your own aliases in this section.

For the little program I wrote, I added the following alias to this section:

```
User_Alias AUDIO = dboth, ruser
```

It is possible, as stated in the sudoers file, to simply use groups defined in the /etc/group file instead of aliases. If you already have a group defined there that meets your needs, such as "audio", use that group name preceded by a % sign like so, %group, when assigning commands available to groups later in the sudoers file.

Command Aliases

Further down the sudoers file is a section with command aliases. These aliases are lists of related commands such as networking commands or commands required to install updates or new RPM packages. These aliases allow the SysAdmin to easily allow access to groups of commands. There are a number of aliases already set up in this section that make it easy to delegate access to specific types of commands.

Environment Defaults

The next section sets up some default environment variables. The item that is most interesting in this section is the !visiblepw line, which prevents sudo from running if the user environment is set to show the password. This is a security precaution that should not be overridden.

Command Section

This section is the main part of the sudoers file. Everything necessary can be done without all of the aliases by adding enough entries here. The aliases just make it a whole lot easier.

This section uses the aliases already defined to tell sudo who can do what on which hosts. The examples are self-explanatory once you understand the syntax in this section. Here we have a sample entry for our user account, ruser:

```
ruser    ALL=(ALL) ALL
```

The first "ALL" in the preceding line indicates that this rule applies on all hosts. The second ALL allows ruser to run commands as any other user. By default commands are run as root user, but ruser can specify on the sudo command line that a program be run as any other user. The last ALL means that ruser can run all commands without restriction. This entry would give ruser full root capabilities. I did not use a line like this to solve my problem because that would give too much power to users who did not need it.

Note that there is an entry for root. This entry allows root to have all-encompassing access to all commands on all hosts.

The following entry is the one I added to control access to myprog. It specifies that users who are listed in the AUDIO group, as defined near the top of the sudoers file, have access to only the one program, myprog, on one host, guest1:

```
AUDIO    guest1=/usr/local/bin/myprog
```

Note that the syntax of the AUDIO group command specifies only the host on which this access is to be allowed and the program. It does not specify that the user may run the program as any other user.

Bypassing Passwords

It is possible to use NOPASSWORD to allow the users specified in the group AUDIO to run myprog without the need for entering their passwords. The revised entry in the command section would look like this:

```
AUDIO    guest1=NOPASSWORD : /usr/local/bin/myprog
```

I did not do this for my program because I believe that relatively inexperienced users with sudo access must stop and think about what they are doing, and this may help a bit with that. I just used the entry for my little program as an example.

wheel

The wheel specification in the command section of the sudoers file as shown in the following allows all users in the "wheel" group to run all commands on any host. The wheel group is defined in the /etc/group file, and users must be added to the group there for this to work. The % sign preceding the group name means that sudo should look for that group in the /etc/group file:

```
%wheel   ALL = (ALL) ALL
```

This is a good way to delegate full root access to multiple users without providing the root password. Just adding a user to the wheel group gives them access to full root powers. It also provides a means to monitor their activities via the log entries created by sudo. Some distributions such as Ubuntu add users' IDs to the wheel group in /etc/group, which allows them to use the sudo command to use all privileged commands.

I have used sudo in this case for a very limited objective – providing one or two users with access to a single command. I accomplished this with two lines. Delegating the authority to perform certain tasks to users who do not have root access is simple and can save you as a SysAdmin a good deal of time. It also generates log entries that can help detect problems.

The sudoers file offers a plethora of capabilities and options for configuration. Check the man pages for the sudo command and the sudoers file for the down-and-dirty details.

Real SysAdmins Don't sudo

I recently read a very interesting article that contained some good information about a Linux feature that I want to learn about. I won't tell you the name of the article, what it was about, or even the website on which I read it, but the article itself made me shudder.

The reason I found this article so cringe-worthy is that it prefaced every command with the sudo command. The issue I have with this is that the article is allegedly for SysAdmins, and real SysAdmins don't use sudo in front of every command they issue. This is a misuse of the sudo command.

sudo or Not sudo

I think that part of being a system administrator and using your favorite tools is to use the tools we have correctly and to have them available without any restrictions. In this case I find that the sudo command is used in a manner for which it was never intended.

[SysAdmins] don't use sudo.

—Paul Venezia

Venezia explains in his InfoWorld[2] article that sudo is used as a crutch for SysAdmins. He does not spend a lot of time defending this position or explaining it. He just states this as a fact. And I agree with him – for SysAdmins.

So let's be clear about this – I recommend that you use the su - command whenever you are performing an administrative task requiring more than one use of root privileges – multiple commands – just as you have been throughout this course so far. Use sudo when you only need to use one or two commands that require root privilege in fairly rapid sequence.

If it is necessary to meet your organizational security and operational procedures, there is another option for using sudo. You can use the sudo command to launch a new instance of the bash (or another) shell. This effectively eliminates both the timeout and detailed logging of the user's activities while providing a brief record indicating that the user may have performed some privileged tasks.

EXPERIMENT 11-8: ADVANCED USERS AND SUDO

In this experiment you will use the sudo command to launch a new instance of the bash shell.

First, you need to configure the sudoers file so that the advanced user has access to the bash shell. Edit the /etc/sudoers file with your preferred text editor and add the following lines for the student user. It's okay to add them to the end of the file:

```
# Allow the student user to sudo to Bash
student ALL=/usr/bin/bash
```

---

[2]Venizia, Paul, InfoWorld, *Nine traits of the veteran Unix admin,* www.infoworld.com/article/2623488/unix/nine-traits-of-the-veteran-unix-admin.html

Now you can sudo to bash. Explore this environment just a bit:

```
[student@studentvm1 ~]$ sudo bash
[root@studentvm1 student]# echo $PATH
/root/.local/bin:/root/bin:/usr/local/sbin:/usr/local/bin:/usr/sbin:/usr/
bin:/sbin:/bin:/var/lib/snapd/snap/bin
[root@studentvm1 student]# pwd
/home/student
[root@studentvm1 student]#
```

You can see that the $PATH is correct for the root user but that the PWD is still the student user's home directory, which was the PWD when the sudo command was executed. At this point any and all commands are available to you with root privilege.

I recommend that only advanced users who can be trusted implicitly be provided with this type of access.

Valid Uses for sudo

The sudo facility does have its uses. The real intent of sudo is to enable the root user to delegate to one or two non-root users access to one or two specific privileged commands that they need on a regular basis. The reasoning behind this is that of the lazy SysAdmin; allowing the users access to a command or two that require elevated privileges and that they use constantly, many times per day, saves the SysAdmin a lot of requests from the users and eliminates the wait time that the users would otherwise experience. But most non-root users should never have full root access, just to the few commands that they need.

I sometimes need non-root users to run programs that require root privileges. In cases like this, I set up one or two non-root users and authorize them to run that single command. The sudo facility also keeps a log of the user ID of each user that uses it. This might enable me to track down who made an error. That's all it does; it is not a magical protector.

The sudo facility was never intended to be used as a gateway for commands issued by a SysAdmin. It cannot check the validity of the command. It does not check to see if the user is doing something stupid. It does not make the system safe from users who have access to all of the commands on the system even if it is through a gateway that forces them to say "please" – that was never its intended purpose.

Unix never says please.

—Rob Pike

This quote about Unix is just as true about Linux as it is about Unix. We SysAdmins log in as root when we need to do work as root, and we log out of our root sessions when we are done. Some days we stay logged in as root all day long, but we always work as root when we need to. We never use sudo because it forces us to type more than necessary in order to run the commands we need to do our jobs. Neither Unix nor Linux asks us if we really want to do something, that is, it does not say, "Please verify that you want to do this."

Yes, I dislike the way some distros use the sudo command.

Using su as Root

So far we have looked at using the su and sudo commands to elevate our privilege level from that of a regular user to that of root, the superuser. There are times when it becomes necessary to switch to another user.

For example, I may be working as a non-root user like student, and another user, say student1, borks[3] up their account so that weird things are happening and they can't fix it or explain it. Believe me, it happens. So as the SysAdmin my job is to figure this out. And being the lazy SysAdmin that I am, I have no desire to walk to wherever it is that student1 is located, if in walking distance at all, just to look at their screen so I can observe the symptoms.

I can simply use su - student1 in one of my terminal sessions to switch to student1. All I need is student1's password – except that I don't have it – and if I were to ask student1 for their password and get a positive response, they would have broken one of the most basic security rules: never, ever share your password, even with root.

But root can do anything even if not quite directly. I can su - from student to root and then use the command su - student1 to complete the two-step switch. At this point I can see what is going on and resolve the problem. The root user does not require a non-root user's password in order to switch to that user.

---

[3] To break in almost any way possible, usually the manner in which the most damage is done.

Chapter Summary

In this chapter we have looked at the root user and explored a few of root's capabilities. The bottom line is that root can do anything. In Linux the root user is all-powerful even to the extent that it can perform tasks that are completely self-destructive with complete impunity. The power we have as SysAdmins when working as root is limitless as far as the Linux host is concerned.

Non-root users do have some limitations that are intended only to prevent them from interfering with or damaging the work of others. Using sudo enables the SysAdmin to assign certain limited additional privileges to regular users to enable them to perform specific tasks that require root privilege.

SysAdmins should never use sudo themselves and should bypass it if working on a Linux distribution that implements that as a requirement. You configured the sudoers file so that non-privileged users may utilize sudo to obtain limited access to one or a very few commands that they might need when a SysAdmin is not available.

Exercises

Complete the following exercises to finish this chapter:

1. What is the function of the root account?

2. In Experiment 11-1, we explored switching users from student to root using the su command. What happens when root uses su to switch to a non-privileged user with and without the hyphen?

3. Why should SysAdmins use su - for their own work?

4. What advantage is there to the SysAdmin that might make it useful to use sudo to provide administrative access for a non-privileged user to one or a few programs?

5. Experiment 11-5 shows that root can create files in a directory with all permissions set to off (000). The directory used in that experiment was owned by root. In an earlier chapter, the student user created a directory in /tmp also. Can root still create files in a directory owned by another user with all permissions set to 000? Prove your answer.

6. Are there any limitations to what the root account can do in a
    Linux host?

7. Why does the use of sudo in Experiment 11-8 eliminate the usual
    timeout after a privileged command?

8. Edit the sudoers file to allow the student user to use the vgs
    command – and only the vgs command – and test the result.

CHAPTER 12

Installing and Updating Software

Objectives

In this chapter you will learn

- Why the RPM Package Manager (RPM) was created

- The deficiencies of the Red Hat Package Manager in today's Internet-connected world

- The advantages of the DNF package manager

- How to use DNF to install, update, and manage software packages

- How the RPM tool can still be used productively

The purpose of package management and tools like RPM and DNF is to provide for easy installation and management of software on Linux hosts. DNF is a wrapper around RPM and was developed to compensate for the deficiencies of RPM. In this chapter we will explore the use and deficiencies of RPM and the use of DNF for installing and updating software.

Dependency Hell

I think it important to understand the full impact of dependency hell – at least as much as possible without actually having been there. Dependency hell is the difficult process of resolving multiple layers of complex dependencies, a common problem before the development of modern package management tools.

317

© David Both 2023
D. Both, *Using and Administering Linux: Volume 1*, https://doi.org/10.1007/978-1-4842-9618-9_12

One time during my very early experiences with Linux, the original Red Hat Linux, before Red Hat Enterprise Linux (RHEL), CentOS, and Fedora, I installed Linux on one of my computers. Not knowing what software I might need eventually, I just installed a few basic things. After I got the system up and running, I decided I wanted to install some additional software, so I tried to install a word processor; I don't even remember which one, but it was not LibreOffice or even one of its predecessors. All of the software I needed was on the distribution CD, so it should have been easy. Hah!

I first tried to install the word processor itself. I received a very long list of package dependencies, which I would need to install first. So I started working my way down the list. The first dependency was a package of library files. I tried to install that and received another list of dependencies, which had not been previously listed and which were required before the library package could be installed. So I started down that list. After installing several dependencies, I managed to get the libraries installed. So I started on the second dependency in the original list only to get another list of dependencies that needed to be fulfilled.

I had discovered dependency hell. It took me a full day to get all of the package dependencies installed before I could actually install the word processor. This was a bad situation and was probably one of the reasons that Linux was considered to be very hard to use in those early days. Something else was needed.

You have already used DNF to install updates and some new software. Now let's look at package management and DNF specifically in more detail. Both RPM and DNF can do more than just software installations and updates.

RPM

RPM[1] is the RPM Package Manager. It is both a system and a program that provides the capability to install, remove, upgrade, and manage RPM packages. RPM is the name of the Red Hat Package Management system. It is also the name of the program, rpm, used to install and manage RPM packages, and .rpm is the file extension for RPM packages.

The rpm program has some drawbacks such as its inability to deal with dependencies in RPMs being installed or removed. This means that you might try to install a new software package that you want to use only to receive an error message indicating that there is a missing dependency – or a long list of them.

---

[1] Wikipedia, *RPM*, https://en.wikipedia.org/wiki/Rpm_(software)

The RPM program can only operate on RPM packages that have been already downloaded to the local host. It has no capability to access remote repositories, that is, repos.

Despite all of its drawbacks, RPM was a major step forward in making Linux available to more users than ever before. By replacing the need to download and compile every software package using the so-called five-step process, RPM simplified and standardized software installation for Linux. The old and cumbersome five-step process took time and patience. The following list of steps assumes that the compiler and make programs are installed and that you know how to use them. It also assumes that there is an easily accessible site on the Internet from which the sources can be downloaded:

1. Download the source code. These are usually distributed as tarballs.[2]

2. Untar the tarball in the desired development location in your directory tree.

3. Run the **make configure** command to configure the procedure for the specific host machine on which these steps are being performed.

4. Run the **make** command to perform the actual compilation of the source code into executable files.

5. Run **make install** to install the executable binary file, any libraries created by the compile process, and any documentation including man pages into the correct locations in the filesystem directory structure.

The RPM package management system was the first available for any distribution, and it made installing and maintaining Linux hosts far easier than it had been previously. It also provides security in the form of signing keys. A packager can use the RPM program to sign an RPM package with a GPG[3] signing key, and then the key can be used to verify the authenticity of the RPM when it is downloaded. The signing key is used

---

[2] Similar in function to zip files, tarballs are created with the tar command and have the .tar filename extension.
[3] GNU Privacy Guard.

by package management systems like DNF to ensure that any packages downloaded from a package repository such as the Fedora repositories are safe and have not been tampered with.

Despite its shortcomings and more capable wrappers like DNF, the rpm program is powerful and still useful. Because dnf is a program wrapper around the rpm program, understanding how RPM works is an important part of understanding advanced package management with DNF. You will also find many reasons to use RPM itself.

Let's start exploring RPM by attempting to install a simple RPM package. The wget command you will encounter in Experiment 12-1 can be used to download files directly from the Internet so long as you know the complete URL. This means not having to open a web browser and navigating to the correct URL, which can be time consuming.

EXPERIMENT 12-1: USING RPM

Perform this experiment as root. This experiment is intended to illustrate the issues of the rpm program. We will attempt to install an RPM package that I created for this experiment, utils-1.0.0-1.noarch.rpm.

Make /tmp the PWD. Download the RPM file to be used in this experiment into the /tmp directory:

```
[root@studentvm1 tmp]# wget https://github.com/Apress/using-and-
administering-linux-volume-1/raw/master/utils-1.0.0-1.noarch.rpm
```

Use the following command to install the downloaded RPM. The options are (i)nstall, (v)erbose, and (h)ash (to display a progress bar):

```
[root@studentvm1 tmp]# rpm -ivf utils-1.0.0-1.noarch.rpm
error: Failed dependencies:
        mc is needed by utils-1.0.0-1.noarch
[root@studentvm1 tmp]#
```

This error is caused by the fact that the mc (Midnight Commander) package is not already installed.

The rpm program cannot resolve this dependency, so it simply throws an error and quits. At least it tells us what is wrong.

The rpm program by itself cannot resolve the dependency encountered in Experiment 12-1. It would be necessary to download the Midnight Commander package from the repo and then use rpm to install that before attempting again to install the **utils** package. Of course that assumes that Midnight Commander does not have any unfulfilled dependencies.

Before we look at the solutions to those problems, let's look at some of the things that RPM *can* do.

EXPERIMENT 12-2: EXPLORE AN RPM PACKAGE

This experiment must be performed as root. We will use RPM to explore the utils package and find out more about it.

Let's look at the utils-1.0.0-1.noarch.rpm file and find all of the dependencies that it has. The -q option is a query, and the R option is the type of query, in this case Requires, which means the dependencies or requirements. The -q option must always precede any other query option:

```
[root@studentvm1 tmp]# rpm -qR utils-1.0.0-1.noarch.rpm
/bin/bash
/bin/sh
/bin/sh
/bin/sh
/bin/sh
bash
dmidecode
mc
rpmlib(CompressedFileNames) <= 3.0.4-1
rpmlib(FileDigests) <= 4.6.0-1
rpmlib(PayloadFilesHavePrefix) <= 4.0-1
rpmlib(PayloadIsXz) <= 5.2-1
screen
[root@studentvm1 tmp]#
```

We may also want to know what files are going to be installed by this RPM package. The l (lowercase L) lists the files that will be installed. These are primarily little scripts I have written and the GPL license information:

```
[root@studentvm1 tmp]# rpm -ql utils-1.0.0-1.noarch.rpm
/usr/local/bin/create_motd
```

321

```
/usr/local/bin/die
/usr/local/bin/mymotd
/usr/local/bin/sysdata
/usr/local/share/utils/Copyright.and.GPL.Notice.txt
/usr/local/share/utils/GPL_LICENSE.txt
/usr/local/share/utils/utils.spec
[root@studentvm1 tmp]#
```

Note that this list of files shows the complete absolute path into which the files will be installed.

The -i option displays the package detailed information as seen in the following:

```
[root@studentvm1 tmp]# rpm -qi utils-1.0.0-1.noarch.rpm
Name         : utils
Version      : 1.0.0
Release      : 1
Architecture: noarch
Install Date: (not installed)
Group        : System
Size         : 71985
License      : GPL
Signature    : (none)
Source RPM   : utils-1.0.0-1.src.rpm
Build Date   : Thu 30 Aug 2018 10:16:42 AM EDT
Build Host   : testvm1.both.org
Relocations  : (not relocatable)
Packager     : David Both
URL          : http://www.both.org
Summary      : Utility scripts for testing RPM creation
Description  :
A collection of utility scripts for testing RPM creation.
```

Sometimes the RPM database becomes corrupted. You will know when this happens because the rpm command will throw an error indicating that the database is corrupt. It can be rebuilt with the following command:

```
[root@studentvm1 tmp]# rpm --rebuilddb
[root@studentvm1 tmp]#
```

This rebuilds the database of *installed* packages. RPM has no means of knowing what packages are available but not installed.

Read the man page for rpm to learn more of the capabilities of RPM:

```
[root@studentvm1 tmp]# man rpm
```

RPM can be used to delete (erase) installed packages. Simply use the -e option and the name of the RPM. RPM won't erase packages that are needed as dependencies by other packages. It will just quit with an error message.

YUM

The YUM[4] (Yellow Dog Updater Modified) program was an early – but not the first – attempt to resolve the problem of dependency hell as well as to make Red Hat Linux RPM packages available from repositories on the Internet. This eliminated the need to insert the CD in the system every time you needed to install new software. It also made it possible to install updates easily over the Internet.

YUM was written by Seth Vidal and Michael Stenner at Duke University Department of Physics to do for Red Hat and RPM packages what the original, YUP, did for an early Linux distribution called Yellow Dog. YUM was very successful, but as it aged several problems were uncovered. It was slow and used a great deal of memory, and much of its code needed to be rewritten.

There is little point in discussing YUM any further. As a drop-in replacement, the syntax for DNF is identical except for the command name itself. Prior to RHEL 8 YUM is still used by RHEL and CentOS as the package manager, but whatever you learn for DNF will also apply to YUM. Both the yum and dnf commands for current releases of Fedora and RHEL 8 are simply links to the dnf-3 command. We will explore links in Chapter 18 of this volume, but for now, it is sufficient to say that a link is a pointer to a file and multiple links are allowed.

[4]Wikipedia, *YUM*, https://en.wikipedia.org/wiki/Yum_(software)

EXPERIMENT 12-3: YUM

Perform this experiment as root. Let's look at the links for the **yum** and **dnf** utilities:

```
[root@studentvm1 ~]# for I in `which yum dnf` ; do ll $I ; done
lrwxrwxrwx. 1 root root 5 Dec 13 05:33 /usr/bin/yum -> dnf-3
lrwxrwxrwx. 1 root root 5 Dec 13 05:33 /usr/bin/dnf -> dnf-3
```

The **which** utility locates the executables for both **yum** and **dnf** . The for loop uses that result to perform a long listing of the files it finds.

You might try **which yum dnf** by itself.

DNF

The DNF[5] facility replaced YUM as the default package manager in Fedora 22. It is a wrapper around the RPM program. It provides for installation of RPM packages from local or remote repositories and deals with dependencies as required. DNF's handling of dependencies includes the ability to recursively determine all dependencies that might prevent the target package from being installed and to fulfill them. This means that if the target package has 25 dependent packages, it will identify them all, determine whether they are already installed, and mark them for installation if they are not. It then checks those dependencies for further dependencies and marks them for installation; it continues to recurse through all newly marked packages until no further dependencies are found. It then downloads all of the marked packages and installs them.

DNF stands for "DaNdiFied YUM." The syntax of DNF commands is identical to that of YUM, making the switch from YUM to DNF easy. DNF can install and remove packages. It can also install updates and provide us with information about installed packages and packages that are available in the repositories and that have not been installed. DNF allows packages that have been signed to be automatically checked to prevent counterfeit packages from installing malware on your Fedora system.

DNF can automatically download GPG signing keys[6] and check RPM packages for authenticity after they are downloaded and before they are installed.

---

[5] Wikipedia, *DNF*, https://en.wikipedia.org/wiki/DNF_(software)

[6] Gnu Privacy Guard – used to ensure that downloaded packages are from the correct source and have not been altered.

Installing Packages

Installing new software is the first thing most of us do after installing Linux on a new system. Because of the lack of options when doing an installation from the Fedora live USB sticks, most software needs to be installed after the initial installation of the operating system.

EXPERIMENT 12-4: INSTALLING RPMS WITH DNF

This experiment must be performed as root. The RPM and DNF tools can only perform much of their work when run as the root user.

Let's now try to install the utils package that we attempted earlier. The utils-1.0.0-1.noarch. rpm package should be in the /tmp directory, so make /tmp the PWD.

Install this package using dnf:

```
[root@studentvm1 tmp]# dnf -y install ./utils-1.0.0-1.noarch.rpm
Last metadata expiration check: 3:58:01 ago on Tue 24 Jan 2023 04:15:51 AM EST.
Dependencies resolved.
=============================================================================
 Package          Architecture    Version          Repository     Size
=============================================================================
Installing:
 utils            noarch          1.0.0-1          @commandline   24 k
Installing dependencies:
 mc               x86_64          1:4.8.28-3.fc37  fedora         1.9 M

Transaction Summary
=============================================================================
Install  2 Packages

Total size: 1.9 M
Total download size: 1.9 M
Installed size: 7.0 M
Downloading Packages:
mc-4.8.28-3.fc37.x86_64.rpm                          1.5 MB/s | 1.9 MB   00:01
-----------------------------------------------------------------------
```

```
Total                                          1.3 MB/s | 1.9 MB    00:01
Running transaction check
Transaction check succeeded.
Running transaction test
Transaction test succeeded.
Running transaction
  Preparing        :                                                    1/1
  Installing       : mc-1:4.8.28-3.fc37.x86_64                          1/2
  Running scriptlet: utils-1.0.0-1.noarch                               2/2
  Installing       : utils-1.0.0-1.noarch                               2/2
  Running scriptlet: utils-1.0.0-1.noarch                               2/2
  Verifying        : mc-1:4.8.28-3.fc37.x86_64                          1/2
  Verifying        : utils-1.0.0-1.noarch                               2/2

Installed:
  mc-1:4.8.28-3.fc37.x86_64                      utils-1.0.0-1.noarch

Complete!
```

How amazing is that! Not only did DNF determine which packages were needed to fulfill the dependencies of the package that you installed; it also downloaded them and installed them for you. No more dependency hell.

If you remember back in Experiment 12-2, we looked at the dependencies specified in the utils package, and libssh2 was not among them. It is likely that this is a dependency for the mc (Midnight Commander) package. We can check that as follows:

```
[root@studentvm1 tmp]# dnf repoquery --deplist mc
Last metadata expiration check: 0:22:27 ago on Sun 23 Sep 2018 09:11:46 PM
EDT.
package: mc-1:4.8.19-7.fc27.x86_64
  dependency: /bin/sh
   provider: bash-4.4.23-1.fc28.x86_64
  dependency: /usr/bin/perl
   provider: perl-interpreter-4:5.26.2-413.fc28.x86_64
  dependency: /usr/bin/python
   provider: python2-2.7.15-2.fc28.i686
   provider: python2-2.7.15-2.fc28.x86_64
  dependency: libc.so.6(GLIBC_2.15)(64bit)
   provider: glibc-2.27-32.fc28.x86_64
```

```
dependency: libglib-2.0.so.0()(64bit)
 provider: glib2-2.56.1-4.fc28.x86_64
dependency: libgmodule-2.0.so.0()(64bit)
 provider: glib2-2.56.1-4.fc28.x86_64
dependency: libgpm.so.2()(64bit)
 provider: gpm-libs-1.20.7-15.fc28.x86_64
dependency: libpthread.so.0()(64bit)
 provider: glibc-2.27-32.fc28.x86_64
dependency: libpthread.so.0(GLIBC_2.2.5)(64bit)
 provider: glibc-2.27-32.fc28.x86_64
dependency: libslang.so.2()(64bit)
 provider: slang-2.3.2-2.fc28.x86_64
dependency: libslang.so.2(SLANG2)(64bit)
 provider: slang-2.3.2-2.fc28.x86_64
dependency: libssh2.so.1()(64bit)
 provider: libssh2-1.8.0-7.fc28.x86_64
dependency: perl(File::Basename)
 provider: perl-interpreter-4:5.26.2-413.fc28.x86_64
dependency: perl(File::Temp)
 provider: perl-File-Temp-0.230.600-1.fc28.noarch
dependency: perl(POSIX)
 provider: perl-interpreter-4:5.26.2-413.fc28.x86_64
dependency: perl(bytes)
 provider: perl-interpreter-4:5.26.2-413.fc28.x86_64
dependency: perl(strict)
 provider: perl-libs-4:5.26.2-413.fc28.i686
 provider: perl-libs-4:5.26.2-413.fc28.x86_64
dependency: rtld(GNU_HASH)
 provider: glibc-2.27-32.fc28.i686
 provider: glibc-2.27-32.fc28.x86_64
[root@studentvm1 tmp]#
```

You will see libssh.so.2 as one of the result lines from this query.

Installing Updates

DNF, like most package managers, can install updates to software that is already installed. This usually consists of one or more – usually lots more – updated RPM packages that contain bug fixes, documentation updates, and sometimes software version updates. This procedure does not install a complete upgrade from one release of Fedora to another, such as from Fedora 37 to Fedora 29.

EXPERIMENT 12-5: INSTALLING UPDATES

This experiment must be performed as root. We start by using DNF to ascertain whether updates are available and then proceed to install the updates.

DNF also allows us to check for a list of updates that need to be installed on our system:

```
[root@studentvm1 tmp]# dnf check-update
```

You may want to pipe the resulting data stream through the less utility to enable you to page through the results.

When you finish viewing the list of packages that need to be updated, let's go ahead and perform the updates. The tee utility duplicates the data stream that is sent to STDOUT to the specified file for later viewing. There are other DNF log files, but this saves what we would have seen on the display screen to the /tmp/update.log file as a record for us to view later:

```
[root@studentvm1 tmp]# dnf -y update | tee /tmp/update.log
```

I won't include the output data stream for this command because it is very long. Observe the update process. Notice that there will be a large number of packages to update. It will take some time to perform this task, which takes place in phases.

1. Determine which installed packages have updates available.

2. Check for and add dependencies.

3. Download the required packages or deltas.

4. Verify the integrity of the downloaded RPM files.

5. Rebuild RPMs using deltas.

6. Install the updates.

I was lucky as I reverified this experiment for this second edition. An error occurred during the download, and one of the files did not match the GPG security signature. This is indicated by the "md5 mismatch" phrase in the output data stream. The DNF tool is smart enough to detect this and download that file again:

```
/var/cache/dnf/updates-fd4d3d0d1c34d49a/packages/kernel-modules-6.1.6-
200.fc37_6.1.7-200.fc37.x86_64.drpm: md5 mismatch of result
```

After the update has completed, use the **less** utility to view the results stored in /etc/update. log that we created with the **tee** command.

DNF creates log files of its own. Let's take a look:

```
[root@studentvm1 tmp]# cd /var/log
[root@studentvm1 log]# ll dnf*
-rw-------  1 root root 1606065 Sep 24 11:48 dnf.librepo.log
-rw-------. 1 root root 1202827 Sep  2 03:35 dnf.librepo.log-20180902
-rw-------. 1 root root 4944897 Sep 12 17:29 dnf.librepo.log-20180912
-rw-------. 1 root root 2603370 Sep 16 02:57 dnf.librepo.log-20180916
-rw-------  1 root root 6019320 Sep 23 02:57 dnf.librepo.log-20180923
-rw-------  1 root root  178075 Sep 24 11:48 dnf.log
-rw-------. 1 root root   46411 Sep  2 03:35 dnf.log-20180902
-rw-------. 1 root root  271613 Sep 12 17:29 dnf.log-20180912
-rw-------. 1 root root   98175 Sep 16 02:57 dnf.log-20180916
-rw-------  1 root root  313358 Sep 23 02:57 dnf.log-20180923
-rw-------  1 root root   27576 Sep 24 11:48 dnf.rpm.log
-rw-------. 1 root root    1998 Sep  2 03:35 dnf.rpm.log-20180902
-rw-------. 1 root root    9175 Sep 12 17:28 dnf.rpm.log-20180912
-rw-------. 1 root root    4482 Sep 16 02:57 dnf.rpm.log-20180916
-rw-------  1 root root   10839 Sep 23 02:57 dnf.rpm.log-20180923
[root@studentvm1 log]#
```

Using the * (asterisk/star/splat) symbol allows us to specify all files that begin with "dnf" and have zero or more additional characters following that and that only those files that match this specification will be displayed. This is called file globbing, and * is one of the globbing characters that are available. More on file globbing in Chapter 15.

Note that the files with dates in their names are older log files. Linux rotates log files regularly so that no one file grows too large.

Make /var/log the PWD. Then use `less` to view dnf.log. You should be able to locate the log data for your installation of the utils package. The less utility allows you to search the content of the viewed file. Just type a forward slash and then the string for which you want to search. Use /util, which should easily locate the first entry. Each entry is preceded with the date and time that it occurred in Zulu, which is what the Z stands for. Zulu is the military way of saying GMT:

```
2018-09-24T01:04:09Z DDEBUG Command: dnf -y install utils-1.0.0-1.noarch.rpm
```

Press the "N" key to find the next instance of the string. You should find the entire transaction that installs the utils package and its dependencies.

Scroll through the dnf.log file to explore its content. You should be able to find the entries for the system update we did in step 5 of this experiment. Exit from `less` when you have finished your exploration.

Use `less` to explore the dnf.librepo.log and dnf.rpm.log files.

The dnf command has some options that make it easy to get information from its log files. This first command lists the most recently installed packages:

```
[root@studentvm1 ~]# dnf list recent
```

This one lists all of the installed packages – every one of them:

```
[root@studentvm1 ~]$ dnf list installed | wc -l
```

And this one lists all packages that are available from the repositories and that have not been installed:

```
[root@studentvm1 ~]$ dnf list available | wc -l
```

Pipe the data stream from the `dnf` command through the wc (word count) command to determine how many packages are installed and how many are available. I have 1503 packages installed on my student virtual machine, but it is fine if your number is a bit different.

The only time it is necessary to reboot a Linux computer is after a new kernel or glibc package has been installed; this is the only way to load the new kernel. It is also a good idea to reboot after glibc has been updated. It is highly likely that the kernel or glibc packages were updated. Check the log to verify that a new kernel has been installed and reboot if so.

After the system has started the reboot process, you will see the GRUB menu screen that lists multiple kernels.

Before this screen passes, be sure to press the Escape key. The default timeout is five seconds, so you will need to be ready. Pressing the space bar or Escape key stops the countdown and lets you view the options. You could select any of the available kernels using the arrow keys and select any of the listed kernels to boot. Check out this menu because we will come back to it later.

Boot from the top – default – kernel by pressing the **Enter** key to continue.

GRUB – actually GRUB2 – is the GRand Unified Bootloader and is responsible for the initial stages of the Linux boot process. We will discuss GRUB, kernels, and booting in detail in Chapter 16.

Post-update Tasks

There is usually at least one additional step to take after performing an update, especially when many RPM packages have been updated. It is always a good idea to update the man(ual) page database to include new and revised pages as well as to delete obsolete ones.

EXPERIMENT 12-6: UPDATING THE MAN DATABASE

This experiment must be performed as the root user. Update the man page database:

```
[root@studentvm1 ~]# mandb
Purging old database entries in /usr/share/man...
Processing manual pages under /usr/share/man...
Purging old database entries in /usr/share/man/ru...
Processing manual pages under /usr/share/man/ru...
Purging old database entries in /usr/share/man/zh_CN...
Processing manual pages under /usr/share/man/zh_CN...
Purging old database entries in /usr/share/man/cs...
<snip>
Purging old database entries in /usr/local/share/man...
Processing manual pages under /usr/local/share/man...
3 man subdirectories contained newer manual pages.
27 manual pages were added.
```

```
0 stray cats were added.
5 old database entries were purged.
[root@studentvm1 ~]#
```

Now you will have the most recent man pages available when you need them.

I am not sure why the man database is not being updated automatically at this time.

Removing Packages

DNF can also remove packages (**dnf remove**), and it will also remove the dependencies that were installed with a package. So removing the utils package would also remove the libssh2 and mc packages.

EXPERIMENT 12-7: REMOVING PACKAGES

Perform this experiment as root. In this experiment we remove the utils package using the following command. Do not use the -y option so that DNF will ask whether we want to proceed or not. I use this as a safety device when attempting to remove packages that I thought were orphans or unused; it has saved me from removing hundreds of files that were still needed:

```
[root@studentvm1 log]# dnf remove utils
Dependencies resolved.
==============================================================================
 Package          Arch         Version          Repository        Size
==============================================================================
Removing:
 utils            noarch       1.0.0-1          @@commandline     70 k
Removing dependent packages:
 mc               x86_64       1:4.8.19-7.fc27  @fedora           6.7 M
Removing unused dependencies:
 libssh2          x86_64       1.8.0-7.fc28     @fedora           197 k

Transaction Summary
==============================================================================
Remove  3 Packages

Freed space: 7.0 M
```

This command will remove the three listed packages. There is a problem with this. The removal of the utils package also causes the removal of the mc (Midnight Commander) package. Midnight Commander is not truly a dependency of the utils package. In another root session, use the following command to query the repository database and list the dependencies – requirements – for mc:

```
[root@studentvm1 log]# dnf repoquery --requires mc
```

Why do you think DNF tries to remove mc as a dependency? Return to the terminal session with the deletion waiting and enter y to continue the removal:

```
Is this ok [y/N]: y
Running transaction check
Transaction check succeeded.
Running transaction test
Transaction test succeeded.
Running transaction
  Preparing        :                                              1/1
  Erasing          : utils-1.0.0-1.noarch                         1/3
  Running scriptlet: utils-1.0.0-1.noarch                         1/3
  Erasing          : mc-1:4.8.19-7.fc27.x86_64                    2/3
  Erasing          : libssh2-1.8.0-7.fc28.x86_64                  3/3
  Running scriptlet: libssh2-1.8.0-7.fc28.x86_64                  3/3
  Verifying        : utils-1.0.0-1.noarch                         1/3
  Verifying        : libssh2-1.8.0-7.fc28.x86_64                  2/3
  Verifying        : mc-1:4.8.19-7.fc27.x86_64                    3/3

Removed:
  utils.noarch 1.0.0-1   mc.x86_64 1:4.8.19-7.fc27      libssh2.x86_64
1.8.0-7.fc28

Complete!
[root@studentvm1 tmp]#
```

Although DNF already seems like a major improvement over the stand-alone RPM system of package management, there is another capability it has that can make our work as SysAdmins much easier – groups.

Groups

There are many complex software systems that require many packages – sometimes hundreds – to be fully complete. Think about GUI desktops or an integrated development environment (IDE) such as Eclipse or a set of development tools. All of these require many separate packages to be fully functional.

DNF has a "group" capability that allows packagers to define all of the individual packages that are required to create a fully functional system such as a desktop, educational software, electronic lab, Python classroom, and more.

EXPERIMENT 12-8: INSTALLING GROUPS – LIBREOFFICE

This experiment must be performed as root.

We start by listing all groups:

```
[root@studentvm1 tmp]# dnf grouplist
```

The groups in the resulting list are separated into categories. The groups listed in the *Available Environment Groups* category tend to be desktop environments. The *Installed Groups* category is obvious. There should be only one group listed in this category. The *Available Groups* category consists of groups that have not been installed and that are not desktops.

Look at the information about one of the groups. Notice the use of quotes around group names that have spaces in them is required for all DNF group commands:

```
[root@studentvm1 ~]# dnf groupinfo "Audio Production" | less
```

You should see a long list of packages that will be installed with this group.

Now let's install a group that might be useful for you in real life. I use the LibreOffice suite to write my books – like this one – and to create spreadsheets and presentations. LibreOffice uses the widely accepted Open Document Format (ODF) for its documents, and it can also create and use Microsoft Office documents, spreadsheets, presentations, and more.

First, use DNF to view the group information for LibreOffice and then install the LibreOffice group. Do not use the -y option so that you can see the list of dependencies that need to be installed:

```
[root@studentvm1 ~]# dnf group install LibreOffice
```

Depending upon the speed of your Internet connection, that should have only taken a couple minutes to download and install a complete office suite.

Many packages do not belong to any group. Groups are a means to manage complex software systems that require many packages. It is also true that packages that are members of one or more groups may be installed without installing the entire group.

Adding Repositories

Not all of the software you might need when using Fedora is located in the standard Fedora repositories. Adding other repos, particularly a trusted repo like RPMFusion, can make adding new software that is not part of the Fedora distribution much easier and faster.

The RPMFusion repositories contain many packages that are not provided with the Fedora distributions. The RPMFusion repos and the packages in them are well maintained and signed and can be trusted. If you wish, use your browser to explore the RPMFusion website at www.rpmfusion.org. Installation of the two RPMFusion repos is straightforward.

For CentOS and RHEL, you must first install the EPEL (Extra Programs for Enterprise Linux) repository, but that will not be necessary for us because we are using Fedora.

EXPERIMENT 12-9: ADDING A REPOSITORY

This experiment must be performed as root. We will download the RPMs for the RPMFusion free and non-free repositories and install them.

Make /tmp the PWD:

```
[root@studentvm1 ~]# cd /tmp
```

Use wget to download the RPMFusion RPMs into /tmp. Enter each of the following two commands. Each command should be on a single line. They are split here due to space issues.

Tip   Although there are "stable" releases of these two repositories, as of this writing, they have not been updated to install under Fedora 37. For this reason we need to download and install the RPM package for the specific Fedora release installed on the host being used to perform these experiments. I am using Fedora 37, but you may be using a different, later, release. This problem may be fixed by the time you perform this experiment, but if the RPMFusion stable RPMs fail to install, then be sure to use the installed release. Once the RPMFusion repositories are installed, it is not necessary to reinstall them. This is strictly an installation problem with the stable packages. Once installed, the repo files that are located in /etc/yum.repo.d are identical.

Be sure to use the correct release number for your Fedora system. We use 37 here because that is what is installed on the host I'm using to perform this experiment.

There are two methods to use to download and install RPMs like this.

The Two-Step Method

This two-step method uses separate download and install commands. The wget command is used to easily download files from known locations on the Internet. Then they can be installed locally using the dnf command:

```
[root@studentvm1 tmp]# wget
http://download1.rpmfusion.org/free/fedora/rpmfusion-free-release-37.noarch.rpm
--2023-01-24 09:29:09--  http://download1.rpmfusion.org/free/fedora/rpmfusion-free-
release-37.noarch.rpm
Resolving download1.rpmfusion.org (download1.rpmfusion.org)... 193.28.235.6,
2001:67c:1740:800d::65
Connecting to download1.rpmfusion.org (download1.rpmfusion.org)|193.28.235.6|:80...
connected.
HTTP request sent, awaiting response... 200 OK
Length: 11374 (11K) [application/x-rpm]
Saving to: 'rpmfusion-free-release-37.noarch.rpm'

rpmfusion-free-release-37 100%[====================================>]  11.11K  --.-
KB/s    in 0s

2023-01-24 09:29:09 (78.3 MB/s) - 'rpmfusion-free-release-37.noarch.rpm' saved
[11374/11374]
[root@studentvm1 tmp]# wget
http://download1.rpmfusion.org/nonfree/fedora/rpmfusion-nonfree-release-37.noarch.rpm
--2023-01-24 09:29:30--  http://download1.rpmfusion.org/nonfree/fedora/rpmfusion-
nonfree-release-37.noarch.rpm
Resolving download1.rpmfusion.org (download1.rpmfusion.org)... 193.28.235.6,
2001:67c:1740:800d::65
```

```
Connecting to download1.rpmfusion.org (download1.rpmfusion.org)
|193.28.235.6|:80... connected.
HTTP request sent, awaiting response... 200 OK
Length: 11431 (11K) [application/x-rpm]
Saving to: 'rpmfusion-nonfree-release-37.noarch.rpm'

rpmfusion-nonfree-release 100%[=======================================>]
11.16K  --.-KB/s    in 0s

2023-01-24 09:29:31 (83.4 MB/s) - 'rpmfusion-nonfree-release-37.noarch.rpm' saved
[11431/11431]

[root@studentvm1 tmp]#
```

Install both RPMs locally with the following command.

```
[root@studentvm1 tmp]# dnf -y install ./rpmfusion*
```

The One-Step Method

The one-step method uses the dnf command to download and install each RPM with a single command:

```
# dnf install http://download1.rpmfusion.org/free/fedora/rpmfusion-free-release-37.noarch.rpm
# dnf install http://download1.rpmfusion.org/nonfree/fedora/rpmfusion-nonfree-release-37.noarch.rpm
```

After these RPMs have been installed, change the PWD to the /etc/yum.repos.d directory and list the files there. You should see several RPMFusion repositories. You should also see the default fedora and fedora-updates repository configuration files.

Look at the contents of some of these files. Notice that the testing and rawhide repositories have enabled=0, which means that they are disabled. These are repositories used for testing and should never be enabled unless you are a programming expert and like a bit of self-flagellation.

We can now easily install RPM packages from the RPMFusion repositories.

Some repositories simply have you download the repo file and place it in /etc/yum.repos.d instead of packaging them in an RPM.

Other Software

My yoga teacher, Cyndi, with whom I co-authored the book *Linux for Small Business Owners*,[7] was forced by COVID to change her business model from the old normal of in-person classes. She now uses Zoom on Fedora to run many of her yoga classes and has found that it works very well for her and integrates into the technology of her workflow. Although Zoom can be used with a browser, some of the features that Cyndi needs as the meeting host are only available in the client software available from Zoom.

Zoom is not included in any of the Fedora repositories, so she and I have had to download it from the Zoom download website in order to install it using the command line. It is actually quite easy. Sometimes it is necessary to install software from sources other than the Fedora repositories, so let's do that now with Zoom.

Installing Zoom

This procedure can be used with software downloaded from other sources – so long as they can be trusted and are RPM packages.

Tip   This procedure which we are using to install the Zoom client is essentially the same as it would be for any other software that is not contained in the Fedora repositories.

```
EXPERIMENT 12-10: INSTALLING OTHER SOFTWARE
```

Go to the Zoom download center for Linux at
`https://zoom.us/download#client_4meeting` and select Fedora in the **Linux Type** drop-down. When the Linux download file manager appears, select the temporary directory /tmp in which to store the file. The file name for Zoom is always zoom_x86_64.rpm, which makes it hard to know which version is contained in the RPM file.

---

[7] Both, David, and Bulka, Cyndi, *Linux for Small Business Owners*, Apress, 2022, `www.both.org/?page_id=2024`

Then if Zoom is already running, exit out of it. Open a terminal session and switch to the root user. You will need the root password for this. Although I use the **su** command, you could also use **sudo** to escalate your privileges:

```
$ su -
Password: <Enter the root password>
#
```

Be sure to use the trailing dash (-) or it won't work properly. Change the working directory to /tmp:

```
# cd /tmp
```

Run the next command to do the installation. The -i option means install and y means to automatically answer "yes" to any questions asked by the DNF install procedure:

```
# dnf install -y zoom_x86_64.rpm
```

The installation should only take a few moments, and you should be ready for your Zoom meeting.

Updating Zoom

After using the Zoom client for a few months, Cyndi started getting messages indicating she'd need to update to the newest version or her Zoom client would no longer work. Installing an update to an existing Zoom installation is just as easy. The steps are almost the same as earlier for installation. Only the final step differs.

EXPERIMENT 12-11: UPDATING OTHER SOFTWARE

You probably won't be able to perform this experiment until an update to Zoom is released. But as you can see, the process is almost identical.

Download the latest Zoom package from the Zoom website and store it in /tmp. Open a terminal session and switch user to root. Make /tmp the present working directory (PWD) and issue the following command:

```
# dnf update -y zoom_x86_64.rpm
```

Like the installation, the update should only take a few moments.

Tip   Any files stored in the /tmp directory will be automatically deleted upon Linux startup whenever the system is rebooted or when the files are ten days old. If you want to save the Zoom package file for a longer time, you should copy it to a different directory. I use /root for some of the files I intend to keep for a few weeks, for example. I have a completely separate directory that I use for files I expect to keep for several months or longer.

About the Kernel

You should have noticed during the DNF update of installed packages that the new kernel was not "updated"; it was installed. This is because DNF provides an option to keep multiple old kernels installed in case a new kernel causes a problem with the system. Such problems may be that some programs no longer work, especially those that depend upon certain kernels such as the VMWare virtualization software. I have also had other software that fails to work or works incorrectly after a kernel update. It does not happen frequently but it does happen. Keeping older kernels has allowed me to boot to one of them in case there is a problem with the newest one. Figure 12-1 shows the GRUB menu on StudentVM1 with three kernels. The default kernel is always the top one.

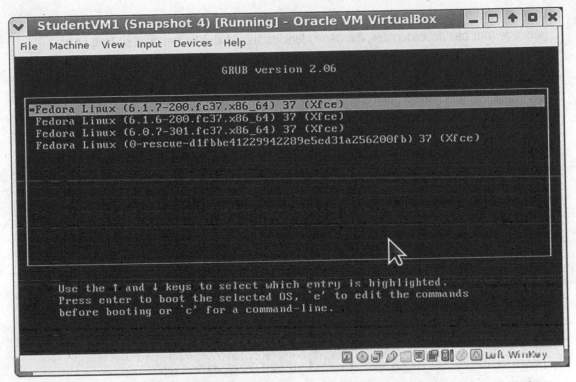

Figure 12-1. *After updating the system a couple times, the GRUB menu shows three regular kernels and one rescue option. The most recent kernel is at the top, but you can use the arrow keys to select an older kernel to boot to*

EXPERIMENT 12-12: KEEPING OLD KERNELS

Perform this experiment as root. Let's look at the configuration items that enable us to maintain multiple kernels from which we can choose to boot. We will also change the number of older kernels to retain.

Use vim to edit the /etc/dnf/dnf.conf configuration file. Change the line

installonly_limit=3

to

installonly_limit=5

in order to increase the total number of kernels to keep to 5.

Look at the line clean_requirements_on_remove=True. This means that, when removing a package that has dependencies, the dependencies should also be removed so long as no other installed packages depend upon them. Do not change this because it does help keep our Linux hosts free of unneeded and unused RPMs. Old unneeded stuff, whether RPMs, other old programs, old and unused code within a program, and unused files of any kind, are all referred to as cruft.

The **gpgcheck=1** line means that downloaded RPMs will be checked against the GPG signing key to ensure that they are valid and have not been altered.

Save the file and exit from it.

Now let's look at the repo files in the /etc/yum.repo.d directory. Make /etc/yum.repo.d the PWD and list the contents of the directory:

```
[root@studentvm1 yum.repos.d]# ls
fedora-cisco-openh264.repo      rpmfusion-free-updates.repo
fedora.repo                     rpmfusion-free-updates-testing.repo
fedora-updates.repo             rpmfusion-nonfree.repo
fedora-updates-testing.repo     rpmfusion-nonfree-updates.repo
rpmfusion-free.repo             rpmfusion-nonfree-updates-testing.repo
[root@studentvm1 yum.repos.d]#
```

Your list of repos should look similar to this.

Use the **cat** command to view at least the contents of the fedora repository configuration files. Notice that the fedora.repo file has multiple sections. The first section **[fedora]** is enabled. The other two sections, **[fedora-debuginfo]** and **[fedora-source]**, are disabled. You would only enable these sections if you were using debug code to try to solve a problem or if you were installing source code RPMs (.src.rpm) to modify and recompile one or more packages. Most of us never need to enable either of these sections.

Any and all repositories can be disabled using the configuration files in /etc/yum.repo.d. Also, repos can be enabled or disabled temporarily for a single DNF command at a time using the **disablerepo=<reponame>** or **enablerepo=<reponame>** option. Be sure to read the DNF man page.

Chapter Summary

Updating software and installing new software are easy with tools like DNF, the DaNdiFied YUM package manager. DNF is a wrapper around the powerful RPM Package Manager, but DNF offers advanced features such as the ability to provide automated handling of dependencies; it will determine the dependencies, download them from the repository on the Internet, and install them.

DNF uses the concept of groups to enable installation and removal of large numbers of related packages such as would be used by complex software systems. Using groups to define things like desktops, development environments, office suites, and scientific and related technology packages makes it easy to install complete systems with a single command.

DNF and RPM both provide tools that enable exploring the content of RPM packages. It is possible to list the files that will be installed by an RPM package and the other packages upon which it is dependent.

We installed some additional repositories beyond the default repos provided by Fedora. These additional repos make it easier to install software that is not part of the distribution.

We also downloaded Zoom from the Zoom website and installed the downloaded package from the /tmp directory using the command line.

Exercises

Perform the following exercises to complete this chapter:

1. In Experiment 12-7 you removed the utils package, and the mc (Midnight Commander) package was also removed. Provide a detailed explanation for why DNF removed mc too.

2. Did you know that you can browse the Internet, receive and send email, download files from remote servers, and more, all in a terminal command-line text-based environment? Identify all of the packages required to perform these tasks and install them.

3. Reboot your student VM and select one of the older kernels but not the recovery option. Use a few of the tools you have already learned to explore and determine that everything seems to be working fine.

4. On occasion the DNF database and cache may become corrupted or at least out of sync with the system. How would you correct that situation?

## CHAPTER 13

Tools for Problem Solving

Objectives

In this chapter you will learn

- A procedure to use for solving problems
- To install some useful problem solving tools that are not always installed by default
- To select and use the correct tools to investigate the status of various Linux system resources such as CPU, memory, and disk
- To create command-line programs that simulate certain problems
- To use available tools to locate and resolve the simulated problems
- To create a FIFO (First In First Out) named pipe to illustrate the function of buffers

This chapter introduces a few powerful and important tools that can be used for locating and solving problems. This is a very long chapter because there is so much to know about these tools. I have intentionally grouped these tools into this one chapter because they are all closely related in at least two ways. First, they are some of the most basic and commonly used tools used for problem determination. Second, these tools offer significant overlap in the data that they provide, so your choice of which tool to use for a particular purpose can be rather flexible.

All of these tools are powerful and flexible and offer many options for how the data they can access is displayed. Rather than cover every possible option, I will try to provide you with enough information about these tools to pique your curiosity and encourage your own explorations into their depths. "Follow your curiosity" is one of the tenets of *The Linux Philosophy for SysAdmins.*[1]

---

[1] Both, David, *The Linux Philosophy for SysAdmins*, Apress, 2018, Chapter 22

© David Both 2023
D. Both, *Using and Administering Linux: Volume 1*, https://doi.org/10.1007/978-1-4842-9618-9_13

The Art of Problem Solving

One of the best things that my mentors helped me with was the formulation of a defined process that I could always use for solving problems of nearly any type. This process is very closely related to the scientific method.

I find this short article entitled "How the Scientific Method Works"[2] to be very helpful. It describes the scientific method using a diagram very much like the one I have created for my Five Steps of Problem Solving. So I pass this on as a mentor, and it is my contribution to all of you young SysAdmins. I hope that you find it as useful as I have.

Solving problems of any kind is art, science, and – some would say – perhaps a bit of magic too. Solving technical problems, such as those that occur with computers, requires a good deal of specialized knowledge as well. Any approach to solving problems of any nature – including problems with Linux – must include more than just a list of symptoms and the steps necessary to fix or circumvent the problems that caused the symptoms. This so-called "symptom-fix" approach looks good on paper to the managers – the pointy-haired bosses, the PHBs – but it really sucks in practice. The best way to approach problem solving is with a large base of knowledge of the subject and a strong methodology.

The Five Steps of Problem Solving

There are five basic steps that are involved in the problem solving process as shown in Figure 13-1. This algorithm is very similar to that of the scientific method referred to in footnote 2 but is specifically intended for solving technical problems.

You probably already follow these steps when you troubleshoot a problem but do not even realize it. These steps are universal and apply to solving almost any type of problem, not just problems with computers or Linux. I used these steps for years in various types of problems without realizing it. Having them codified for me made me much more effective at solving problems because when I became stuck, I could review the steps I had taken, verify where I was in the process, and restart at any appropriate step.

---

[2] Harris, William, *How the Scientific Method Works*, https://science.howstuffworks.com/innovation/scientific-experiments/scientific-method6.htm

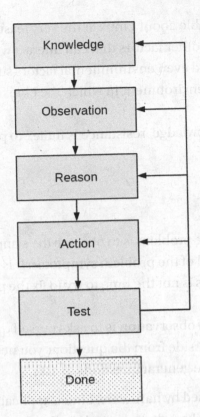

Figure 13-1. The algorithm I use for troubleshooting

You may have heard a couple other terms applied to problem solving in the past. The first three steps of this process are also known as problem determination, that is, finding the root cause of the problem. The last two steps are problem resolution, which is actually fixing the problem. The next sections cover each of these five steps in more detail.

Knowledge

Knowledge of the subject in which you are attempting to solve a problem is the first step. All of the articles I have seen about the scientific method seem to assume this as a prerequisite. However, the acquisition of knowledge is an ongoing process, driven by curiosity and augmented by the knowledge gained from using the scientific method to explore and extend your existing knowledge through experimentation. This is one of the reasons I use the term "experiment" in this course rather than something like "lab project."

You must be knowledgeable about Linux at the very least, and even more, you must be knowledgeable about the other factors that can interact with and affect Linux, such as hardware, the network, and even environmental factors such as how temperature, humidity, and the electrical environment in which the Linux system operates can affect it.

Remember, "Without knowledge, resistance is futile," to paraphrase the Borg. Knowledge is power.

Observation

The second step in solving the problem is to observe the symptoms of the problem. It is important to take note of all of the problem symptoms. It is also important to observe what is working properly. This is not the time to try to fix the problem; it is merely to observe.

Another important part of observation is to ask yourself questions about what you see and what you do not see. Aside from the questions you need to ask that are specific to the problem, there are some general questions to ask:

- Is this problem caused by hardware, Linux, application software, or perhaps lack of user knowledge or training?

- Is this problem similar to others I have seen?

- Is there an error message?

- Are there any log entries pertaining to the problem?

- What was taking place on the computer just before the error occurred?

- What did I expect to happen if the error had not occurred?

- Has anything about the system hardware or software changed recently?

As you gather data, never assume that the information obtained from someone else is correct. Observe everything yourself. The best problem solvers are those who never take anything for granted. They never assume that the information they have is 100% accurate or complete. When the information you have seems to contradict itself or the symptoms, start over from the beginning as if you had no information at all.

In one very strange incident, I fixed a large computer by sitting on it. That is a long story and amounts to the fact that I observed a very brief symptom that was caused by sitting on the workspace that was the top of a very large printer control unit. The complete story can be found in my book *The Linux Philosophy for SysAdmins*.[3]

Reasoning

Use reasoning skills to take the information from your observations of the symptoms, your knowledge to determine a probable cause for the problem. The process of reasoning through your observations of the problem, your knowledge, and your past experience is where art and science combine to produce inspiration, intuition, or some other mystical mental process that provides some insight to the root cause of the problem.

It helps remember that the symptom is not the problem. The problem causes the symptom. You want to fix the true problem, not just the symptom.

Action

Now is the time to perform the appropriate repair action. This is usually the simple part. The hard part is what came before – figuring out what to do. After you know the cause of the problem, it is usually easy to determine the correct repair action to take.

The specific action you take will depend upon the cause(s) of the problem. Remember, we are fixing the root cause, not just trying to get rid of or cover up the symptom.

Make only one change at a time. If there are several actions that can be taken that might correct the cause of a problem, only make the one change or take the one action that is most likely to resolve the root cause. The selection of the corrective action with the highest probability of fixing the problem is what you are trying to do here. Whether it is your own experience telling you which action to take or the experiences of others, move down the list from highest to lowest priority, one action at a time. Test the results after each action.

---

[3] Both, David, *The Linux Philosophy for SysAdmins*, Apress, 2018, 471–472

Test

After taking some overt repair action, the repair should be tested. This usually means performing the task that failed in the first place, but it could also be a single, simple command that illustrates the problem.

Make a single change, one potential corrective action, and then test the results of that action. This is the only way in which we can be certain which corrective action fixed the problem. If we were to make several corrective actions and then test one time, there would be no way to know which action was responsible for fixing the problem. This is especially important if we want to walk back those ineffective changes we made after finding the solution.

Be sure to check the original observed symptoms when testing. It is possible that they have changed due to the action you have taken, and you need to be aware of this in order to make informed decisions during the next iteration of the process. Even if the problem has not been resolved, the altered symptom could be very valuable in determining how to proceed.

As you work through a problem, it will be necessary to iterate through at least some of the steps. Figure 13-1 shows that you may need to iterate to any previous step in order to continue.

Be flexible. Don't hesitate to step back and start over if nothing else produces some forward progress.

System Performance and Problem Solving

Now let's explore some commands that enable you to observe various configuration and performance aspects of your Linux system. Be sure to use the man pages for each command if you have questions about the syntax or interpreting the data displayed.

There are a large number of Linux commands that are used in the process of analyzing system performance and problem determination. Most of these commands obtain their information from various files in the /proc filesystem, which we will explore later. You may wish to use multiple terminal sessions side by side in order to make some of the comparisons between commands and their output.

I use top, htop, and atop as my primary tools when starting the process of problem determination. These three tools all display much of the same information, but each does it in its own way and with different emphasis. All three of these tools display system data in near real time. The `top` and `htop` utilities are also interactive and allow the SysAdmin to renice and kill processes by sending them signals. The `atop` tool can kill processes, but it cannot renice them.

Note   The `nice` command can be used change the nice number (renice) of a process in order to modify its priority level and so how much CPU time it might be allocated by the Linux scheduler. We will explore nice numbers, priority, and scheduling as we proceed through this chapter and also in Volume 2, Chapter 23.

Let's look at each of these three tools in some detail.

top

The `top` command is my go-to tool when I am solving problems that involve any type of performance issues. I like it because it has been around since forever and is always available while the other tools may not be installed. The `top` utility is always installed by Fedora and all of the other distributions I have worked with.

The `top` program is a very important and powerful tool to observe memory and CPU usage as well as load averages in a dynamic setting. The information provided by `top` can be instrumental in helping diagnose an extant problem; it is usually the first tool I use when troubleshooting a new problem.

Understanding the information that `top` is presenting is key to using it to greatest effect. Let's look at some of the data that can alert us to performance problems and explore their meanings in more depth. Much of this information also pertains to the other system monitors we will study, which also display some of this same information.

The `top` utility displays system information in near real time, updating (by default) every three seconds. Fractional seconds are allowed, although very small values can place a significant load on the system. It is also interactive, and the data columns to be displayed and the sort column can be modified.

EXPERIMENT 13-1: TOP

Perform this experiment as root on StudentVM1. Start top:

[root@StudentVM1 ~]# **top**

The results are displayed full screen and are live, updating every three seconds. top is an interactive tool that allows changes to things like which programs are displayed and how the displayed results are sorted. It also allows some interaction with programs such as renicing them to change their priority and to kill them:

```
top - 12:19:00 up  2:16,  2 users,  load average: 0.08, 0.04, 0.01
Tasks: 158 total,   1 running, 157 sleeping,   0 stopped,   0 zombie
%Cpu(s):  0.0 us,  0.2 sy,  0.0 ni, 97.6 id,  0.0 wa,  0.9 hi,  1.3 si,  0.0 st
MiB Mem :  15996.4 total,  15065.5 free,    289.7 used,    641.2 buff/cache
MiB Swap:   8192.0 total,   8192.0 free,      0.0 used.  15434.7 avail Mem
```

PID	USER	PR	NI	VIRT	RES	SHR	S	%CPU	%MEM	TIME+	COMMAND
808	systemd+	20	0	16428	6332	5460	S	0.2	0.0	0:08.35	systemd-oomd
1009	root	20	0	473224	19968	17112	S	0.2	0.1	0:00.37	NetworkManager
1317	root	20	0	16128	6632	4852	S	0.2	0.0	0:00.16	sshd
1586	root	20	0	0	0	0	I	0.2	0.0	0:00.10	kworker/0:3-events
1	root	20	0	103172	13812	9816	S	0.0	0.1	0:02.47	systemd
2	root	20	0	0	0	0	S	0.0	0.0	0:00.00	kthreadd
3	root	0	-20	0	0	0	I	0.0	0.0	0:00.00	rcu_gp
4	root	0	-20	0	0	0	I	0.0	0.0	0:00.00	rcu_par_gp
5	root	0	-20	0	0	0	I	0.0	0.0	0:00.00	slub_flushwq
6	root	0	-20	0	0	0	I	0.0	0.0	0:00.00	netns
8	root	0	-20	0	0	0	I	0.0	0.0	0:00.00	kworker/0:0H-events_h+
10	root	0	-20	0	0	0	I	0.0	0.0	0:00.00	mm_percpu_wq
12	root	20	0	0	0	0	I	0.0	0.0	0:00.00	rcu_tasks_kthread
13	root	20	0	0	0	0	I	0.0	0.0	0:00.00	rcu_tasks_rude_kthread
14	root	20	0	0	0	0	I	0.0	0.0	0:00.00	rcu_tasks_trace_kthre+
15	root	20	0	0	0	0	S	0.0	0.0	0:00.07	ksoftirqd/0
16	root	20	0	0	0	0	I	0.0	0.0	0:00.07	rcu_preempt
17	root	rt	0	0	0	0	S	0.0	0.0	0:00.00	migration/0
19	root	20	0	0	0	0	S	0.0	0.0	0:00.00	cpuhp/0
20	root	20	0	0	0	0	S	0.0	0.0	0:00.00	kdevtmpfs
21	root	0	-20	0	0	0	I	0.0	0.0	0:00.00	inet_frag_wq

```
<SNIP>
```

Let that run as you study it. Then press the **s** (lowercase) key. The `top` utility displays **Change delay from 3.0 to**, and you type **1** and press the **Enter** key. This sets the display update to one second. I find this to be a bit more responsive and is more to my liking than the default three seconds.

Now press the **1** key to display both CPUs in this VM to show the statistics for each CPU on a separate line in the header section. Pressing **1** again returns to display of the aggregate CPU data. Do that a couple times to compare the data, but leave it so that top displays both CPUs separately when you are finished.

After making these changes, we want to make them permanent. The `top` utility does not automatically save these changes, so we must press **W** (uppercase) to write the modified configuration to the ~/.toprc file.

Let `top` run while you read about the various sections in the display.

The top display is divided into two sections. The "Summary" section is the topmost section of the output, and the "Process" section is the lower portion of the output; I will use this terminology for `top`, `atop`, and `htop` in the interest of consistency.

The top program has a number of useful interactive commands you can use to manage the display of data and to manipulate individual processes. Use the **h** command to view a brief help page for the various interactive commands. Be sure to press **H** twice to see both pages of help. Use the **Q** key to quit from help and return to the active display.

Summary Section

The `top` Summary section contains information that provides an excellent overview of the current system status. This section can inform you of the basic facts of overall CPU and memory usage as well as CPU load trends.

The first line shows the system uptime and the 1-, 5-, and 15-minute load averages. In Experiment 13-1 the load averages are all nearly zero because the host is doing very little. Figure 13-2 shows load averages on a system that has some work going on. The second line shows the number of processes currently active and the status of each.

The lines containing CPU statistics are shown next. There can be a single line that combines the statistics for all CPUs present in the system or, as in Figure 13-2, one line for each CPU, in this case a single quad-core CPU. Press the **1** key to toggle between the consolidated display of CPU usage and the display of the individual CPUs. The data in these lines is displayed as percentages of the total CPU time available.

The last two lines in the Summary section are memory usage. They show the physical memory usage including both RAM and swap space.

Many of the other tools we will look at present some or all of this same information. The next few sections explore this displayed information in detail, and this will also apply to the same information when it is displayed in all of those other tools.

Load Averages

The first line of the output from top contains the current load averages. Load averages represent the 1-, 5-, and 15-minute load averages for a system. In Figure 13-2, which was taken from a host with four CPUs, the load averages are 2.49, 1.37, and 0.60, respectively.

```
top - 12:21:44 up 1 day,  3:25,  7 users,  load average: 2.49, 1.37, 0.60
Tasks: 257 total,   5 running, 252 sleeping,   0 stopped,   0 zombie
Cpu0 : 33.2%us, 32.3%sy,  0.0%ni, 34.5%id,  0.0%wa,  0.0%hi,  0.0%si,  0.0%st
Cpu1 : 51.7%us, 24.0%sy,  0.0%ni, 24.2%id,  0.0%wa,  0.0%hi,  0.0%si,  0.0%st
Cpu2 : 24.6%us, 48.5%sy,  0.0%ni, 27.0%id,  0.0%wa,  0.0%hi,  0.0%si,  0.0%st
Cpu3 : 67.1%us, 21.6%sy,  0.0%ni, 11.3%id,  0.0%wa,  0.0%hi,  0.0%si,  0.0%st
Mem:   6122964k total, 3582032k used,  2540932k free,   358752k buffers
Swap:  8191996k total,       0k used,  8191996k free,  2596520k cached
```

Figure 13-2. *The load averages in this* top *sample indicate a recent increase in CPU usage*

But what does this really mean when I say that the 1-minute (or 5- or 10-minute) load average is 2.49? Load average can be considered a measure of demand for the CPU; it is a number that represents the average number of instructions waiting for CPU time. Thus, in a single-processor system, a fully utilized CPU would have a load average of 1. This means that the CPU is keeping up exactly with the demand; in other words it has perfect utilization. A load average of less than 1 means that the CPU is underutilized, and a load average of greater than 1 means that the CPU is overutilized and that there is pent-up, unsatisfied demand. For example, a load average of 1.5 in a single-CPU system indicates that some instructions are forced to wait to be executed until the one preceding them has completed.

This is also true for multiple processors. If a four-CPU system has a load average of 4, then it has perfect utilization. If it has a load average of 3.24, for example, then three of its processors are fully utilized, and one is underutilized by about 76%. In the preceding example, a four-CPU system has a 1-minute load average of 2.49, meaning that there is still significant capacity available among the four CPUs. A perfectly utilized four-CPU system would show a load average of 4.00.

The optimum condition for load average in idealistic server environments is for it to equal the total number of CPUs in a system. That would mean that every CPU is fully utilized and yet no instructions must be forced to wait.

Also note that the longer-term load averages provide indication of the overall utilization trend. It appears in the preceding example that the short-term load average is indicative of a short-term peak in utilization but that there is still plenty of capacity available.

Linux Journal has an excellent article describing load averages, the theory and the math behind them, and how to interpret them in the December 1, 2006, issue.[4]

CPU Usage

CPU usage is a fairly simple measure of how much CPU time is being used by executing instructions. These numbers are displayed as percentages and represent the amount of time that a CPU is being used during the defined time period. CPU and memory usage are shown in Figure 13-3.

The default update time interval is usually three seconds although this can be changed using the "**s**" key, and I normally use one second. Fractional seconds are also accepted down to .01 seconds. I do not recommend very short intervals, that is, less than one second, as this adds load to the system and makes it difficult to read the data. However, as with everything Linux and its flexibility, it may occasionally be useful to set the interval to less than one second.

```
top - 09:47:38 up 13 days, 24 min,  6 users,  load average: 0.13, 0.04, 0.01
Tasks: 180 total,   1 running, 179 sleeping,   0 stopped,   0 zombie
Cpu0 :  0.0%us,  0.0%sy,  0.0%ni,100.0%id,  0.0%wa,  0.0%hi,  0.0%si,  0.0%st
Cpu1 :  0.9%us,  0.9%sy,  0.0%ni, 98.1%id,  0.0%wa,  0.0%hi,  0.0%si,  0.0%st
Cpu2 :  0.0%us,  0.0%sy,  0.0%ni,100.0%id,  0.0%wa,  0.0%hi,  0.0%si,  0.0%st
Cpu3 :  1.0%us,  0.0%sy,  0.0%ni, 99.0%id,  0.0%wa,  0.0%hi,  0.0%si,  0.0%st
Mem:   2056456k total,   797768k used,  1258688k free,    92028k buffers
Swap:  4095992k total,       88k used,  4095904k free,   336252k cached
```

Figure 13-3. *The Summary section of* ***top*** *contains a comprehensive overview of CPU and memory usage data*

---

[4]Walker, Ray, Linux Journal, *Examining Load Average*, December 1, 2006, www.linuxjournal.com/article/9001?page=0,0

There are eight fields that describe CPU usage in more detail. The **us**, **sy**, **ni**, **id**, **wa, hi**, **si**, and **st** fields subdivide the CPU usage into categories that can provide more insight into what is using CPU time in the system:

- **us**: User space is CPU time spent performing tasks in user space as opposed to system or kernel space. This is where user-level programs run.

- **sy**: System is CPU time spent performing system tasks. These are mostly kernel tasks such as memory management, task dispatching, and all the other tasks performed by the kernel.

- **ni**: This is "nice" time, CPU time spent on tasks that have a positive nice number. A positive nice number makes a task nicer, that is, it is less demanding of CPU time, and other tasks may get priority over it.

- **id**: Idle time is any time that the CPU is free and is not performing any processing or waiting for I/O to occur.

- **wa**: I/O wait time is the amount of time that a CPU is waiting on some I/O such as a disk read or write to occur. The program running on that CPU is waiting for the result of that I/O operation before it can continue and is blocked until then.

- **hi**: The percentage of CPU time waiting for hardware interrupts in the time interval. A high number here, especially when I/O wait is also high, can be indicative that hardware speed is too slow for the existing load.

- **si**: The number of software interrupts during the time interval. A high number here, especially when I/O wait is also high, can be indicative that some software application(s) may be in some sort of tight loop or a race condition.

- **st**: This is time stolen from "this" VM because it can run but another VM is running and the VM hypervisor cannot allocate time to "this" VM. This should always be zero for a non-virtual host. In a virtual host, a number significantly greater than zero might mean that more physical CPU power is required for the given real and virtual system load.

These times should usually add up to 100% for each CPU give or take a bit of rounding error.

Process Section

The Process section of the output from top is a listing of the running processes in the system – at least for the number of processes for which there is room on the terminal display. The default columns displayed by top are described in the following. Several other columns are available, and each can usually be added with a single keystroke; refer to the top man page for details:

- **PID**: The process ID.

- **USER**: The user name of the process owner.

- **PR**: The priority of the process.

- **NI**: The nice number of the process.

- **VIRT**: The total amount of virtual memory allocated to the process.

- **RES**: Resident size (in kb unless otherwise noted) of non-swapped physical RAM consumed by a process.

- **SHR**: The amount of shared memory in kb used by the process.

- **S**: The status of the process. This can be R for running, I for idle time, S for sleeping, and Z for zombie. Less frequently seen statuses can be T for traced or stopped, I for idle, and D for deep, uninterruptible sleep.

- **%CPU**: The percentage of CPU cycles used by this process during the last measured time period.

- **%MEM**: The percentage of physical system memory used by the process.

- **TIME+**: The cumulative CPU time to 100ths of a second consumed by the process since the process was started.

- **COMMAND**: This is the command that was used to launch the process.

Use the **Page Up** and **Page Down** keys to scroll through the list of running processes. You can use the < and > keys to sequence the sort column to the left or right.

The **k** key can be used to kill a process or the **r** key to renice it. You have to know the process ID (PID) of the process you want to kill or renice, and that information is displayed in the Process section of the top display. When killing a process, top asks first for the PID and then for the signal number to use in killing the process. Type them in and press the Enter key after each. Start with signal 15, SIGTERM, and if that does not kill the process, use 9, SIGKILL.

Things to Look for with CPU Usage

You should check a couple things with CPU usage when you are troubleshooting a problem. Look for one or more CPUs that have 0% idle time for extended periods. You may especially have a problem if all CPUs have zero or very low idle time. You should then look to the Task area of the display to determine which process is using the CPU time.

Be careful to understand whether the high CPU usage might be normal for a particular environment or program, so you will know whether you might be seeing normal or transient behavior. The load averages can be used to help with determination of whether the system is overloaded or just very busy.

Let's explore the use of top to observe CPU usage when we have programs that suck it up.

EXPERIMENT 13-2: FINDING A CPU HOG

Start a second terminal session as user student and position it near the root terminal session that is already running top so that they can both be seen simultaneously.

As the user student, create a file named cpuHog in your home directory and make it executable with the permissions rwxr_xr_x:

```
[student@studentvm1 ~]$ touch cpuHog
[student@studentvm1 ~]$ chmod 755 cpuHog
```

Use the vim editor to add the following content to the file:

```
#!/bin/bash
# This little program is a cpu hog
X=0;while [ 1 ];do echo $X;X=$((X+1));done
```

Save this bash shell script, close vim, and run the cpuHog program with the following command:

```
[student@studentvm1 ~]$ ./cpuHog
```

The preceding program simply prints the current value of X to STDOUT and counts up by one. And it sucks up CPU cycles to do this. Observe the effect this has on system performance in top. CPU usage should immediately go up, and the load averages should also start to increase over time.

What is the priority of the cpuHog program?

Now open another terminal session as the student user and run the same program in it. You should now have two instances of this program running. Notice in top that the two processes tend to get about the same amount of CPU time on average. Sometimes one gets more than the other, and sometimes they get about the same amount.

Figure 13-4 shows the results in top when two of these CPU hogs are running. Note that I have logged in remotely using SSH and am using the screen program to perform these experiments on the VM, so both of those tools show up with HIGH CPU usage In Figure 13-4. You should not have those two entries in your top output. The results you see are essentially the same.

```
top - 11:46:13 up 20:55,  6 users,  load average: 3.64, 2.46, 1.14
Tasks: 161 total,   5 running,  97 sleeping,   0 stopped,   0 zombie
%Cpu0  :  3.0 us, 73.7 sy,  0.0 ni,  0.0 id,  0.0 wa, 12.1 hi, 11.1 si,  0.0 st
%Cpu1  : 11.2 us, 85.7 sy,  0.0 ni,  0.0 id,  0.0 wa,  3.1 hi,  0.0 si,  0.0 st
KiB Mem :  4038488 total,  3015548 free,   240244 used,   782696 buff/cache
KiB Swap: 10485756 total, 10485756 free,        0 used.  3543352 avail Mem

  PID USER      PR  NI    VIRT    RES    SHR S  %CPU %MEM     TIME+ COMMAND
 1893 student   20   0  214388   1180   1036 R  52.0  0.0   0:19.30 cpuHog
 1919 student   20   0  214388   1184   1040 R  33.3  0.0   4:07.18 cpuHog
15017 root      20   0       0      0      0 I  13.7  0.0   0:27.36 kworker/u4:2-ev
15158 root      20   0       0      0      0 I  13.7  0.0   0:22.97 kworker/u4:0-ev
  814 root      20   0   98212   6704   5792 S   1.0  0.2   0:02.01 rngd
13103 root      20   0  257244   4384   3628 R   1.0  0.1   1:16.87 top
    1 root      20   0  171068   9488   6880 S   0.0  0.2   0:04.82 systemd
    2 root      20   0       0      0      0 S   0.0  0.0   0:00.02 kthreadd
    3 root       0 -20       0      0      0 I   0.0  0.0   0:00.00 rcu_gp
<SNIP>
```

Figure 13-4. *The top command showing what happens when two CPU hog programs are running*

Notice on your VM, as is illustrated on my VM in Figure 13-4, that the load averages will rise over time until they eventually stabilize. You can also see that one or both CPUs will start to show waits for both hardware and software interrupts.

As the root user, use top to set the nice number for one of these CPU hogs first to +19 and then to -20 and observe the results of each setting for a short time. We will discuss the details of renicing and priorities in Volume 2, Chapter 23, but for now it is sufficient to know that a higher number means more nice and a lower, even negative number means less nice. A nicer program has a higher number for its priority and will receive fewer CPU cycles than an identical program that has a lower number. If this seems counterintuitive, it is. This is a case of RPL – reverse programmer logic – at least at first glance.

Tip   Press the **r** (lowercase) key for renice, and follow the directions on the screen just below the "Swap" line.

To change the nice number for a running program using top, simply type **r**. When top asks for the PID to renice, enter the PID (process ID) number as shown in Figure 13-5. The PIDs of your running processes will be different from mine. The top utility will then ask what value. Enter **19** and press **Enter**. I suggest choosing the PID of the cpuHog program that has the most accumulated time – TIME+ – to watch the other cpuHog catch up over time. I have highlighted the relevant data lines in bold.

```
top - 11:46:13 up 20:55,  6 users,  load average: 3.64, 2.46, 1.14
Tasks: 160 total,   5 running,  97 sleeping,   0 stopped,   0 zombie
%Cpu0  :  2.0 us, 64.6 sy,  0.0 ni,  0.0 id,  0.0 wa, 15.2 hi, 18.2 si,  0.0 st
%Cpu1  :  6.1 us, 91.9 sy,  0.0 ni,  0.0 id,  0.0 wa,  2.0 hi,  0.0 si,  0.0 st
KiB Mem :  4038488 total,  3015028 free,   240208 used,   783252 buff/cache
KiB Swap: 10485756 total, 10485756 free,        0 used.  3543356 avail Mem
PID to renice [default pid = 15217] 1893
  PID USER      PR  NI    VIRT    RES    SHR S  %CPU %MEM     TIME+ COMMAND
 1893 student   20   0  214388   1184   1040 R  34.7  0.0  10:06.25 cpuHog
 1919 student   20   0  214388   1180   1036 R  33.7  0.0   7:01.68 cpuHog
15158 root      20   0       0      0      0 I  13.9  0.0   1:21.88 kworker/u4:0-ev
    9 root      20   0       0      0      0 R   2.0  0.0   0:12.88 ksoftirqd/0
15505 root      20   0  257244   4256   3504 R   1.0  0.1   0:06.23 top
<SNIP>
```

Figure 13-5. *Renicing one of the cpuHog programs*

You will experience very little change in overall system performance and responsiveness despite having these two cpuHogs running because there are no other programs seriously competing for resources. However, the CPU hog with the highest priority (most negative number) will consistently get the most CPU time even if by just a little bit. You should notice the nice number and the actual priority as displayed by top. Figure 13-6 shows the results after several hours of runtime with PID 1893 at a nice number of +19. Notice that, while PID 1893 had the most cumulative time in Figure 13-5, it now has the least of the two CPU hogs.

```
top - 21:11:30 up  8:36,  6 users,  load average: 3.98, 3.79, 3.88
Tasks: 177 total,   5 running, 172 sleeping,   0 stopped,   0 zombie
%Cpu0  : 20.1 us, 33.8 sy, 17.7 ni,  0.0 id,  0.0 wa, 15.7 hi, 12.7 si,  0.0 st
%Cpu1  :  6.1 us, 60.8 sy,  8.5 ni, 13.8 id,  0.0 wa,  9.2 hi,  1.7 si,  0.0 st
MiB Mem :  15996.1 total,  15015.0 free,    326.1 used,    655.1 buff/cache
MiB Swap:   8192.0 total,   8192.0 free,      0.0 used.  15397.8 avail Mem

  PID USER      PR  NI    VIRT    RES    SHR S  %CPU  %MEM     TIME+ COMMAND
 1919 student   20   0  222940   1424   1268 R  42.0   0.0 116:07.21 cpuHog
 1893 student   39  19  222940   1332   1172 R  41.8   0.0 105:06.44 cpuHog
 2319 root      20   0       0      0      0 I   0.0   0.0   0:59.25 kworker/u4:3-
 1789 root      20   0  224736   3512   2936 R   0.2   0.0   0:46.40 top
 2331 root      20   0       0      0      0 I   4.3   0.0   0:39.97 kworker/u4:0-
<SNIP>
```

Figure 13-6. *After running for almost three hours with a nice number of +19, cpuHog PID 1893 has fallen behind cpuHog PID 1919 in cumulative CPU time*

Now set the nice number for the process with the higher nice number from +19 to -20. We are changing the PID of cpuHog 1893 from +19 to -20 and will leave the nice number of the other cpuHog at 0 (zero). Figure 13-7 shows the results of that change after several more hours of runtime.

```
top - 07:48:17 up 19:13,  6 users,  load average: 3.64, 3.75, 3.89
Tasks: 179 total,   3 running, 176 sleeping,   0 stopped,   0 zombie
%Cpu0  : 21.6 us, 41.5 sy,  0.0 ni,  3.7 id,  0.0 wa, 20.2 hi, 13.1 si,  0.0 st
%Cpu1  : 30.1 us, 61.9 sy,  0.0 ni,  1.0 id,  0.0 wa,  5.6 hi,  1.5 si,  0.0 st
MiB Mem : 15996.1 total, 15005.3 free,    335.6 used,    655.2 buff/cache
MiB Swap:  8192.0 total,  8192.0 free,      0.0 used.  15388.3 avail Mem

  PID USER      PR  NI    VIRT    RES    SHR S  %CPU  %MEM     TIME+ COMMAND
 1893 student    0 -20  222940   1332   1172 R  36.2   0.0 391:58.50 cpuHog
 1919 student   20   0  222940   1424   1268 R  46.6   0.0 377:44.29 cpuHog
 1869 student   20   0  224080   2544   1628 S  33.0   0.0  92:11.01 screen
 1822 student   20   0   16236   6820   5040 S  23.1   0.0  69:57.38 sshd
```

Figure 13-7. *After changing the nice number of PID 1893 from +19 to -20. Task 1893 has now accumulated more CPU time*

Eventually cpuHog 1893 accumulates more time than cpuHog 1919 because of its higher priority. Leave top and the two cpuHog instances running for now. Notice also that the load averages have continued to converge.

Be aware that the nice number is only a single factor used by the kernel scheduler, a "suggestion" as the info page puts it. Thus, a very negative nice number may not result in a process that receives more CPU time. It all depends upon the overall load, and many other data points are used in calculating which process gets CPU time and when. But our cpuHogs help us understand that just a bit.

Memory Statistics

Performance problems can also be caused by lack of memory. Without sufficient memory in which to run all the active programs, the kernel memory management subsystems will spend time moving the contents of memory between swap space on the disk and RAM in order to keep all processes running. This swapping takes CPU time and I/O bandwidth, so it slows down the progress of productive work. Ultimately a state known as "thrashing" can occur in which the majority of the computer's time is spent on moving memory contents between disk and RAM and little or no time is available to spend on productive work. In Figure 13-8 we can see that there is plenty of free RAM left and that no swap space has been used.

```
top - 07:50:07 up 19:14,   6 users,   load average: 3.74, 3.76, 3.88
Tasks: 177 total,    3 running, 174 sleeping,    0 stopped,    0 zombie
%Cpu0  : 20.6 us, 45.0 sy,  0.0 ni,  0.3 id,  0.0 wa, 20.2 hi, 13.9 si,  0.0 st
%Cpu1  : 23.1 us, 69.9 sy,  0.0 ni,  0.1 id,  0.0 wa,  5.8 hi,  1.1 si,  0.0 st
MiB Mem :  15996.1 total,  14876.5 free,     365.9 used,     753.7 buff/cache
MiB Swap:   8192.0 total,   8192.0 free,       0.0 used.  15345.6 avail Mem

    PID USER      PR  NI    VIRT    RES    SHR S  %CPU  %MEM     TIME+ COMMAND
   1893 student    0 -20  222940   1332   1172 R  42.4   0.0 392:48.38 cpuHog
   1919 student   20   0  222940   1424   1268 R  42.0   0.0 378:28.64 cpuHog
     15 root      20   0       0      0      0 S   0.2   0.0   7:49.21 ksoftirqd/0
   1789 root      20   0  224736   3512   2936 R   0.0   0.0   4:18.78 top
<SNIP>
```

Figure 13-8. *The top memory statistics show that we have plenty of virtual and real memory available*

The memory total, free, and used amounts for both RAM and swap space are obvious. The number that is not quite so obvious is the buff/cache one. Buff/cache is RAM, but not swap space, that is used for temporary storage.

Buffers are typically a designated area of memory where the operating system will store data that is being transmitted over the network, a serial communications line, or another program, for example, for a short period of time until the program or utility that is using that data can catch up and process it. Data in the buffer is not altered before it is removed and used. Buffers enable processes that may work at differing speeds to communicate without loss of data due to that speed mismatch.

Linux provides a tool called a named pipe that works as a storage buffer between two (or more) programs. A user – any user – can create a named pipe, which appears as a file in the directory in which it is created. The named pipe is a FIFO (First In First Out) buffer because the data comes out in the same order in which it went in. Named pipes can be used for any number of purposes. They can provide interprocess communication between scripts and other executable programs, as well as a place to store output data for later use by other programs.

EXPERIMENT 13-3. NAMED PIPES

This experiment should be performed as the student user. In this experiment we will look at one type of buffer called a named pipe. Because it is easily created and used by any user, it allows us to illustrate the function of a buffer.

You will need two open terminal sessions as the student user for this experiment. In one terminal, create a named pipe called mypipe in your home directory, and then do a long listing of the contents of your home directory and look at the entry for mypipe. It should have a "p" as the file type in the first column to indicate that it is a pipe:

```
[student@studentvm1 ~]$ mkfifo mypipe
[student@studentvm1 ~]$ ll
total 158964
-rwxr-xr-x  1 student student        91 Jan 24 16:40 cpuHog
<SNIP>
prw-r--r--  1 student student         0 Jan 25 08:02 mypipe
<SNIP>
[student@studentvm1 ~]$
```

Now let's put some data into the pipe. We could use any command that creates a data stream, but for this experiment let's use the **lsblk** command to list the block devices – essentially the disk drives – on the system and redirect the output to the named pipe. Run the following command in one of the terminal sessions:

```
[student@studentvm1 ~]$ lsblk -i > mypipe
```

Notice that you do not get returned to the command prompt; you are left with a blank line. Do not press Ctrl-C to return to the command prompt.

In the other terminal session, use the cat command to read the data from the named pipe. This simple, standard, core command retrieves the data from the pipe and sends it to STDOUT. At that point we could do anything we want with it:

```
[student@studentvm1 ~]$ cat mypipe
NAME              MAJ:MIN RM  SIZE RO TYPE MOUNTPOINT
sda                 8:0   0   60G  0 disk
|-sda1              8:1   0    1M  0 part
|-sda2              8:2   0    1G  0 part /boot
```

```
|-sda3                            8:3    0     1G    0 part /boot/efi
`-sda4                            8:4    0    58G    0 part
  |-fedora_studentvm1-root  253:0    0     2G    0 lvm  /
  |-fedora_studentvm1-usr   253:1    0    15G    0 lvm  /usr
  |-fedora_studentvm1-tmp   253:2    0     5G    0 lvm  /tmp
  |-fedora_studentvm1-var   253:3    0    10G    0 lvm  /var
  |-fedora_studentvm1-home  253:4    0     2G    0 lvm  /home
  `-fedora_studentvm1-test  253:5    0   500M    0 lvm  /test
sr0                             11:0    1  50.5M    0 rom
zram0                          252:0    0     8G    0 disk [SWAP]
[student@studentvm1 ~]$
```

Note that all of the data in the pipe is sent to STDOUT. Return to the terminal session in which you added data to the pipe. Notice that it has been returned to the command prompt.

Add more data to the pipe using some different commands and then read it again.

Cache is RAM memory that is allocated especially to data that may be changing and that may be used at some time in the near future or that may be discarded if it is not required.

Hardware cache is also common in processors. A CPU cache is different from the RAM cache monitored by top. This is a separate memory space located on the processor chip itself and that is used to cache – store – data that has been transferred from RAM until it is needed by the CPU. Not all of the data in a CPU cache will necessarily be used, and some may just be discarded to make room for data from RAM that has a higher probability of being used by the CPU. Cache in the CPU is faster than normal system RAM, so getting data into cache that has a high probability of being used by the CPU can improve overall processing speeds. This is definitely not the type of cache that is monitored by the top program.

Buffers and cache space are very similar in that they are both allocated in RAM to be used for temporary storage. The difference is in the manner in which they are used.

The Task List

The top task list provides a view of the tasks consuming the most of a particular resource. The task list can be sorted by any of the displayed columns including CPU and memory usage. By default top is sorted by CPU usage from high to low. This provides a quick way to view the processes consuming the most CPU cycles. If there is one that stands out such as sucking up 90% or more of the available CPU cycles, this could be indicative

365

of a problem. That is not always the case; some applications just gobble huge amounts of CPU time. The task list also presents us with other data, which, if not immediately obvious, can be obtained from the help option or the top man page.

Again, it is imperative that you observe a correctly running system to understand what is normal so you will know when you see abnormal. I spend a great deal of time using top and these other tools just observing the activities of my hosts when there are no extant problems. This enables me to understand what is "normal" for these hosts and gives me the knowledge I need to understand when they are not running normally.

Signals

The top, atop, and htop utilities allow you to send signals to running processes. Each of these signals has a specific function though some of them can be defined by the receiving program using signal handlers.

The kill command, which is separate from top, can also be used to send signals to processes outside of the monitors. The kill -1 can be used to list all possible signals that can be sent. The use of the kill command to send signals can be confusing if you do not actually intend to kill the process. The thing to remember is that the kill command is used to send signals to processes and that at least three of those signals can be used to terminate the process with varying degrees of prejudice:

- **SIGTERM (15)**: Signal 15, SIGTERM is the default signal sent by top and the other monitor programs when the "k" key is pressed. It may also be the least effective because the program must have a signal handler built into it. The program's signal handler must intercept incoming signals and act accordingly. So for scripts, most of which do not have signal handlers, SIGTERM is ignored. The idea behind SIGTERM is that by simply telling the program that you want it to terminate itself, it will take advantage of that and clean up things like open files and then terminate itself in a controlled manner.

- **SIGKILL (9)**: Signal 9, SIGKILL provides a means of killing even the most recalcitrant programs, including scripts and other programs that have no signal handlers. For scripts and other programs with no signal handler, however, it not only kills the running script but it also kills the shell session in which the script is running; this may not be the behavior that you want. If you want to kill a process and you don't care about being nice, this is the signal you want. This signal cannot be intercepted by a signal handler in the program code.

- **SIGINT (2)**: Signal 2, SIGINT can be used when SIGTERM does not work and you want the program to die a little more nicely, for example, without killing the shell session in which it is running. SIGINT sends an interrupt to the session in which the program is running. This is equivalent to terminating a running program, particularly a script, with the Ctrl-C key combination.

There are many other signals, but these are the ones I have found that pertain to terminating a program. They are actually the only ones I use as a SysAdmin.

Consistency

One more thing about top and many of its relatives: It does not need to run continuously in order to display the correct and consistent current statistics. For example, data such as TIME+ is cumulative starting with the time that the system booted or that the process was launched. Starting top or restarting it does not alter the accuracy of the data. This is not due to any intrinsic capabilities of top; rather, it is the fact that top and other programs like it obtain their information from the /proc virtual filesystem.

Other top-Like Tools

Like all things Linux, there are other programs that work in a top-like manner and that can be used if you prefer them. In this section we will look at three of these alternatives, htop, atop, and iotop. None of these tools are likely to be installed on your Fedora VM, so let's do that now.

PREPARATION 13-1: INSTALLING HTOP, ATOP, AND IOTOP

Perform this preparation step as root. Install the tools we will need for this chapter:

```
[root@studentvm1 ~]# dnf -y install htop atop iotop
```

Note that the package name for atop might show up as being packaged for an earlier version. This is uncommon, but it can happen if a tool has not yet been repackaged for the most current version of Fedora. Jason, my technical reviewer, and I both noted this. It is not a problem. If it were a problem, the older package would not appear in the repository for the current Fedora release.

---

htop

The htop utility is very much like top but offers a bit different capability to interact with the running processes. htop allows selection of multiple processes so that they can be acted upon simultaneously. It allows you to kill and renice the selected processes and to send signals simultaneously to one or more processes.

EXPERIMENT 13-4: USING HTOP

Leave top and the two CPU hog programs running. In another terminal session as the root user, start htop:

```
[root@studentvm1 ~]# htop
```

Notice the bar graphs and load average data at the top of the screen in Figure 13-9. I have removed some lines of data to reduce the page space required, but you can still see that the data displayed is very similar to top. The function key menu at the bottom of the screen provides easy access to many functions:

```
0[||||||||||||||||||||||||||||||||||||100.0%] Tasks: 75, 57 thr, 107 kthr; 2 running
1[||||||||||||||||||||||||||||||||||||100.0%] Load average: 3.08 3.34 3.42
Mem[||||||                     353M/15.6G] Uptime: 20:02:01
Swp[                             0K/8.00G]


[Main] [I/O]
  PID USER        PRI  NI  VIRT   RES   SHR S  CPU%▽MEM%   TIME+  Command
 1893 student       0 -20  217M  1332  1172 R  69.4  0.0 6h59:14 /bin/bash ./cpuHog
 1919 student      20   0  217M  1424  1268 R  61.1  0.0 6h44:09 /bin/bash ./cpuHog
 1869 student      20   0  219M  3056  1628 S  35.2  0.0 5h15:18 SCREEN
 3697 root         20   0  218M  4784  3520 R   2.1  0.0 0:04.63 htop
  857 dbus         20   0  6056  3996  2580 S   1.0  0.0 0:01.27 dbus-broker --log 4
    1 root         20   0  166M 15404  9756 S   0.0  0.1 0:03.90 /usr/lib/systemd/sys
  664 root         20   0 49060 20592 19320 S   0.0  0.1 0:00.90 /usr/lib/systemd/sys
  676 root         20   0 32176 10212  7480 S   0.0  0.1 0:00.24 /usr/lib/systemd/sys
  826 systemd-oo   20   0 16428  6392  5528 S   0.0  0.0 0:57.43 /usr/lib/systemd/sys
  827 systemd-re   20   0 20796 12944 10720 S   0.0  0.1 0:00.29 /usr/lib/systemd/sys
  828 root         16  -4 91616  2440  1700 S   0.0  0.0 0:00.06 /sbin/auditd
  829 root         16  -4 91616  2440  1700 S   0.0  0.0 0:00.00 /sbin/auditd
  830 root         20   0 15860  6908  6036 S   0.0  0.0 0:00.39 /usr/lib/systemd/sys
  831 root         16  -4  6068  2588  2320 S   0.0  0.0 0:00.00 /usr/sbin/sedispatch
  832 root         16  -4 91616  2440  1700 S   0.0  0.0 0:00.00 /sbin/auditd
```

Figure 13-9. htop shows data similar to that of top but provides different configuration options and a bit different presentation of the data

Press **H** to read the short help page. You should also take a bit of time to read the man page for htop.

Press **F2** to display the "Setup" menu. In this menu you can modify the layout of the header information and choose some alternative ways to display the data. Press the **Esc** key to return to the main display. We will see in Chapter 14 why the F1 and F10 keys don't work as you would expect in this situation and how to fix that problem.

Use the **F6** key to display the "Sort By" menu and select CPU%. Observe the CPU usage data for the two CPU hogs for a few moments.

Use the up/down arrow key to highlight one of the CPU hogs, and then use the **F7** and **F8** keys to first decrement the nice number to -20 and then increment it to +19, observing both states for a few moments. Watch how the priority of the process changes as the nice number changes.

Highlight first one cpuHog and press the space bar to select it, and then do the same for the second cpuHog. It is okay for the highlight bar to rest on another process while performing this task because only the selected processes are affected. Use the **F7** and **F8** keys to adjust the nice number for these two processes. Assuming that the cpuHogs started with different nice numbers, what happens when one process reaches the upper or lower limit?

A process can be deselected. Highlight it and then press the space bar again. Deselect the cpuHog that has the highest amount of cumulative CPU time (TIME+), and then set the nice number of the other cpuHog process, which should still be selected, to be a more negative number than the deselected process.

Use the **F5** key to display the process tree view. I like this view because it shows the parent/child hierarchy of the running programs. Scroll down the list of processes until you find the CPU hogs.

There is much more to **htop** than we have explored here. I recommend that you spend some time exploring it and learning its powerful capabilities. Do not terminate the **htop** tool.

atop

The **atop** utility provides much of the same data as **top** and **htop**. Figure 13-10 illustrates that as well as the significantly different organization of the data.

EXPERIMENT 13-5: USING ATOP

Start the atop program in another root terminal session:

```
[root@studentvm1 ~]# atop
```

You should now have top, htop, and atop running along with the two CPU hogs. I have reduced the font size on the output shown in the following in order to have room for more data. You can see in the following the additional information displayed by atop. The atop utility provides detailed information on I/O usage including aggregated, per-device, and per-process data. It should be easy to pick that data out of the following information as well as on your student VM.

```
ATOP - studentvm1          2023/01/25  10:44:03    -----X-----------          10s elapsed

PRC |  sys   12.76s  |  user    5.88s  |  #proc    179  |  #zombie   0  |  #exit     0  |
CPU |  sys    124%   |  user     61%   |  irq      15%  |  idle      0% |  wait      0%  |
cpu |  sys     55%   |  user     41%   |  irq       4%  |  idle      0% |  cpu000 w  0%  |
cpu |  sys     69%   |  user     20%   |  irq      11%  |  idle      0% |  cpu001 w  0%  |
CPL |  numcpu    2   |  avg1    3.64   |  avg5    3.73  |  csw  2724942 |  intr  572365  |
MEM |  tot    15.6G  |  free   14.3G   |  cache 858.3M  |  buff  105.6M |  slab  127.3M  |
MEM |  numnode   1   |  shmem   8.1M   |  shrss   6.7M  |  tcpsk   0.0M |  udpsk   0.0M  |
SWP |  tot     8.0G  |  free    8.0G   |  swcac   0.0M  |  vmcom 810.2M |  vmlim  15.8G  |
PSI |  cpusome  37%  |  memsome   0%   |  memfull   0%  |  iosome    0% |  iofull    0%  |
NET |  transport     |  tcpi      18   |  tcpo      17  |  udpi      0  |  udpo      0   |
NET |  network       |  ipi       18   |  ipo       17  |  ipfrw     0  |  deliv     18  |
NET |  enp0s9    0%  |  pcki      18   |  pcko      17  |  si    1 Kbps |  so    2 Kbps  |
No colors will be used...
  PID SYSCPU USRCPU RDELAY BDELAY  VGROW  RGROW   RDDSK   WRDSK CPUNR  CPU CMD           1/2
 1893  2.97s  3.89s  3.10s  0.00s     0B     0B      0B      0B     0  74% cpuHog
 1919  5.05s  0.91s  3.98s  0.00s     0B     0B      0B      0B     1  65% cpuHog
 1869  2.03s  1.05s  0.08s  0.00s     0B     0B      0B      0B     1  33% screen
 3929  1.34s  0.00s  0.21s  0.00s     0B     0B      0B      0B     0  15% kworker/u4:3-e
 3949  1.34s  0.00s  0.21s  0.00s     0B     0B      0B      0B     0  15% kworker/u4:0-e
 3945  0.02s  0.01s  0.03s  0.00s     0B     0B      0B      0B     0   0% atop
 1270  0.00s  0.01s  0.00s  0.00s     0B     0B      0B    4.0K     0   0% lightdm-gtk-gr
  826  0.01s  0.00s  0.00s  0.00s     0B     0B      0B      0B     0   0% systemd-oomd
  857  0.00s  0.01s  0.00s  0.00s     0B     0B      0B      0B     1   0% dbus-broker
 1249  0.00s  0.00s  0.00s  0.00s     0B     0B      0B      0B     1   0% Xorg
 1030  0.00s  0.00s  0.00s  0.00s     0B     0B      0B      0B     0   0% NetworkManager
  866  0.00s  0.00s  0.00s  0.00s     0B     0B      0B      0B     0   0% rsyslogd
  868  0.00s  0.00s  0.00s  0.00s     0B     0B      0B      0B     1   0% accounts-daemo
 3943  0.00s  0.00s  0.00s  0.00s     0B     0B      0B      0B     0   0% systemd-userwo
 3944  0.00s  0.00s  0.00s  0.00s     0B     0B      0B      0B     1   0% systemd-userwo
 1333  0.00s  0.00s  0.00s  0.00s     0B     0B      0B      0B     1   0% sshd
 1164  0.00s  0.00s  0.00s  0.00s     0B     0B      0B      0B     1   0% crond
  883  0.00s  0.00s  0.00s  0.00s     0B     0B      0B      0B     1   0% VBoxService
 1359  0.00s  0.00s  0.00s  0.00s     0B     0B      0B      0B     1   0% screen
 1360  0.00s  0.00s  0.00s  0.00s     0B     0B      0B      0B     1   0% screen
  867  0.00s  0.00s  0.00s  0.00s     0B     0B      0B      0B     1   0% rtkit-daemon
   22  0.00s  0.00s  0.00s  0.00s     0B     0B      0B      0B     1   0% ksoftirqd/1
   31  0.00s  0.00s  0.00s  0.00s     0B     0B      0B      0B     0   0% kcompactd0
<SNIP>
```

Figure 13-10. *atop presents a different look at system resource utilization including network statistics*

The atop program provides some network utilization data as well as combined and individual detailed CPU usage data. By default it shows only the processes that actually receive CPU time during the collection interval. Press the **A** key to display all processes. atop also shows data in the header space if there is some activity. You will see this as you watch the output for a time. It can kill a process but it cannot renice one.

The atop program starts with an interval of ten seconds. To set the interval to one second, first type **i** and then **1**.

To access the help facility, type **h**. Scan this help to learn about the many capabilities of this tool. Enter **q** to exit help.

atop provides insight into a great deal of information, and I find it to be very helpful. It has an option to create a log file, so it can be used to monitor long-term system performance, which can be reviewed at a later time. Press **Q** to exit from atop.

These three tools are the ones I start with when looking for problems. Between them they can tell me almost everything I need to know about my running system. I find that atop has the most complex interface, and on a terminal that does not have enough width (columns), the output may be misaligned and distorted.

More Tools

There are many more tools available to us as SysAdmins. Most of these concentrate on a single aspect of system operation such as memory or CPU usage. Let's look briefly at a few of them by type.

Memory Tools

The free and vmstat utilities look at memory usage. The vmstat tool also provides data about the CPU usage breakdown such as user, system, and idle time. These tools are both static – they take a snapshot of memory state at a moment in time. They do not offer any interactive functions.

EXPERIMENT 13-6: USING THE FREE COMMAND

You should perform this experiment as root, but these commands can be used with identical results as any non-privileged user as well.

Use the free command to display the system memory information:

```
[root@studentvm1 ~]# free
              total        used         free      shared   buff/cache    available
Mem:       16380056      331504     14964008        8252      1084544     15747756
Swap:       8388604           0      8388604
```

Does it agree fairly closely with the output from top? It should because they both get their data from the /proc filesystem.

The vmstat command shows the virtual memory statistics including some of the data shown in top and other utilities. The data output form this command may need more explanation than some of the others, so use the man page to interpret it if you need to:

```
[root@studentvm1 ~]# vmstat
procs -----------memory---------- ---swap-- -----io---- -system-- ------cpu-----
 r  b   swpd   free    buff  cache   si   so    bi    bo    in   cs us sy id wa st
 4  0      0 14963768 109336 975284   0    0     6     3   106   65 20 60 19  0  0
```

Neither of these commands is interactive; that is, they display data one time and exit. The watch command can help us turn them into repeating tools. Enter the command shown in the following and watch it for a while. The output actually appears at the top of the terminal:

```
[root@studentvm1 ~]# watch free

Every 2.0s: free                          studentvm1: Sat Oct 27 10:24:26 2018

              total        used         free      shared   buff/cache    available
Mem:        4038488      255932      2864320        6092       918236      3516804
Swap:      10485756           0     10485756
```

The data on the screen will update at the default two-second interval. That interval can be changed, and the differences between refresh instances can be highlighted. Of course the watch command also works with other tools as well. The watch command has a number of interesting capabilities that you can explore using the man page. When finished, you can use **Ctrl-C** to exit from the watch program.

Tools That Display Disk I/O Statistics

Although top and atop both provide some insight into I/O usage, this data is limited to I/O waits in top. The atop utility provides a significant amount of I/O information including disk reads and writes. The iostat program provides, like the free command, a point-in-time view of disk I/O statistics, while iotop provides a top-like view of disk I/O statistics.

EXPERIMENT 13-7: I/O TOOLS

Perform this experiment as root. Look first at the results of the **iostat** tool. Figure 13-11 shows the results on my personal workstation. Your VM will have fewer devices shown.

```
[root@myworkstation ~]# iostat
Linux 5.10.10-200.fc33.x86_64 (david.both.org)        02/18/2021        _x86_64_  (32 CPU)

avg-cpu:  %user   %nice %system %iowait  %steal   %idle
           0.49   84.45   15.03    0.00    0.00    0.03

Device            tps    kB_read/s    kB_wrtn/s    kB_dscd/s    kB_read     kB_wrtn    kB_dscd
dm-0             0.05         0.69         0.23         5.69    1146291      377237    9388240
dm-1             0.00         0.00         0.00         0.00       2216           0          0
dm-10            2.60       379.55         2.18       106.94  626576552     3596334  176547684
dm-2             0.37         4.73         0.39        23.59    7814765      636041   38943708
dm-3            17.31        16.55      2034.99        73.82   27316881  3359484897  121870348
dm-4             0.07         0.01        11.00        32.09      13165    18160709   52974036
dm-5             0.05         0.41         0.13         9.03     683809      211397   14911968
dm-6             2.50        25.29        33.25       135.83   41749049    54887481  224238188
dm-7             7.26       250.71       291.42         0.00  413893089   481097720          0
dm-8             0.03         4.27         0.03         0.00    7053716       54448          0
dm-9             0.00         0.00         0.00         0.00       2997          33          0
nvme0n1         24.49        22.43      2046.05       156.37   37022567  3377740936  258148924
nvme1n1          1.55        25.30        32.89       135.83   41762393    54299845  224238188
sda              3.05       250.73       291.42         0.00  413912958   481089656          0
sdb              0.04         4.29         0.03         0.00    7076582       54373          0
sdc              2.58       379.56         2.16       106.94  626594231     3570658  176547684
sdd              3.74       373.61       351.48         0.00  616770824   580251344          0
sdf              0.49        20.45        17.72         0.00   33752429    29247408          0
scd0             0.00         0.00         0.00         0.00          1           0          0
scd1             0.00         0.00         0.00         0.00       1148           0          0
zram0            0.18         0.21         0.52         0.00     341248      863640          0
```

Figure 13-11. *The iostat command displays statistics for storage devices such as HDDs and SSDs*

The iostat utility in Figure 13-12 provides point-in-time data about storage device reads and writes per second as well as cumulative read and write data. The sda device is the entire hard drive, so the data in that row is an aggregate for all filesystems on that entire device. The dm devices are the individual filesystems on the /dev/sda device. You can use the following command to view the filesystem names.

```
[root@studentvm1 tmp]# iostat -j ID
Linux 4.18.9-200.fc28.x86_64 (studentvm1)          10/28/2018       _x86_64_          (2-CPU)

avg-cpu:  %user   %nice %system %iowait  %steal   %idle
          8.56    11.10   42.79    0.54    0.00   37.01

       tps    kB_read/s    kB_wrtn/s    kB_read    kB_wrtn Device
      2.09         2.57        15.57     670835    4059184 ata-VBOX_HARDDISK_VBb426cd38-
22c9b6be
      0.00         0.00         0.00        280         44 dm-0
      0.01         0.08         0.02      20917       5640 dm-1
      0.01         0.08         0.02      20853       5640 dm-2
      0.01         0.14         0.02      37397       6028 dm-name-fedora_studentvm1-root
      0.00         0.01         0.00       3320          0 dm-name-fedora_studentvm1-swap
      0.15         1.41         0.13     368072      34580 dm-name-fedora_studentvm1-usr
      0.00         0.01         0.00       2916        412 -dm-name-fedora_studentvm1-home
      2.28         1.00        11.59     261985    3021780 dm-name-fedora_studentvm1-var
      0.01         0.02         4.09       6252    1065412 dm-name-fedora_studentvm1-tmp
<SNIP>
```

Figure 13-12. *The iostat command showing filesystems*

The iostat program has many options that can be used to provide a more dynamic view of this data as well as to create log files for later perusal.

The iotop utility consists of a two-line header that displays the total and actual disk reads and writes for the current interval, which is one second by default. First, we start the iotop program in one terminal as the user root:

```
[root@studentvm1 tmp]# iotop
```

At first the full-screen output will look like this sample with not much going on. This output includes all of the processes that will fit in the terminal window regardless of whether any of them are actually performing I/O or not:

```
Total DISK READ :        0.00 B/s | Total DISK WRITE :        0.00 B/s
Actual DISK READ:        0.00 B/s | Actual DISK WRITE:        0.00 B/s
   TID  PRIO  USER     DISK READ  DISK WRITE  SWAPIN      IO>    COMMAND
     1 be/4 root        0.00 B/s    0.00 B/s  0.00 %  0.00 % systemd --
switched-root~system --deserialize 32
     2 be/4 root        0.00 B/s    0.00 B/s  0.00 %  0.00 % [kthreadd]
     3 be/0 root        0.00 B/s    0.00 B/s  0.00 %  0.00 % [rcu_gp]
     4 be/0 root        0.00 B/s    0.00 B/s  0.00 %  0.00 % [rcu_par_gp]
<snip>
```

Although the cpuHog programs should still be running, they do not perform any disk I/O, so we need a little program to do that for us. Keep the iotop utility running in this terminal window.

Open another terminal as the student user such that the running iotop program can be seen in the previous terminal window. Run the following short command-line program shown in the following. This dd command makes an image backup of the /.home filesystem and stores the result in /tmp. If you created the filesystems according to the filesystem sizes I provided in Table 5-1, this should not fill up the 5GB /tmp filesystem with the content of the 2.0 GB /home filesystem:

```
[root@studentvm1 tmp]# time dd if=/dev/mapper/fedora_studentvm1-home
of=/tmp/home.bak
4194304+0 records in
4194304+0 records out
2147483648 bytes (2.1 GB, 2.0 GiB) copied, 96.1923 s, 22.3 MB/s

real    1m36.194s
user    0m0.968s
sys     0m14.808s
[root@studentvm1 ~]#
```

I used the time utility to get an idea of how long the dd program would run. On my VM it ran for a little over a minute and a half of real time, but this will vary depending on the specifications of the underlying physical host and its other loads.

The output of the iotop command should change to look somewhat like that in the following. Your results will depend upon the details of your system, but you should at least see some disk activity:

```
Total DISK READ:        53.88 M/s | Total DISK WRITE:       53.93 M/s
Current DISK READ:      53.88 M/s | Current DISK WRITE:      0.00 B/s
    TID PRIO USER      DISK READ DISK WRITE>     COMMAND
   4185 be/4 root       53.88 M/s   53.93 M/s dd
if=/dev/mapper/fedora_st~ntvm1-home of=/tmp/home.bak
      1 be/4 root        0.00 B/s    0.00 B/s systemd rhgb --switched-
root --system --deserialize 35
      2 be/4 root        0.00 B/s    0.00 B/s [kthreadd]
```

If the backup completes before you are able to observe it in iotop, run it again.

I leave it as an exercise for you to determine the option that can be used with iotop to show only processes that are actually performing I/O. Perform the last part of this experiment with that option set.

The /proc Filesystem

All of the data displayed by the commands in this chapter, and many other tools that let us look into the current status of the running Linux system, are stored by the kernel in the /proc filesystem. Because the kernel already stores this data in an easily accessible location and in ASCII text format for the most part, it is possible for other programs to access it with no impact upon the performance of the kernel.

There are two important points to understand about the /proc filesystem. First, it is a virtual filesystem, and it does not exist on any physical hard drive – it exists only in RAM. Second, the /proc filesystem is a direct interface between the internal conditions and configuration settings of the kernel itself and the rest of the operating system. Simple Linux commands enable us humans to view the current state of the kernel and its configuration parameters. It is also possible to alter many kernel configuration items instantly without a reboot. More on that in Volume 2, Chapter 24.

EXPERIMENT 13-8: EXPLORING /PROC

This experiment should be performed as root. First, make /proc the PWD and do a short list of the directory contents:

```
[root@studentvm1 proc]# ls
1      1321  2     4127  52   736  858       crypto         misc
10     1324  20    4155  521  74   86        devices        modules
100    1325  21    4157  530  75   860       diskstats      mounts
1000   1333  22    4158  548  756  862       dma            mtrr
1002   1334  24    4184  549  788  863       driver         net
101    1359  25    42    58   789  866       dynamic_debug  pagetypeinfo
1030   1360  250   4209  588  79   867       execdomains    partitions
1043   1361  26    4212  589  792  868       fb             pressure
1046   14    27    4217  59   793  875       filesystems    schedstat
1157   15    29    4220  6    797  876       fs             scsi
1164   16    3     4221  60   798  877       interrupts     self
12     1652  30    4222  61   799  879       iomem          slabinfo
1225   17    31    4223  62   8    883       ioports        softirqs
1249   1771  32    4225  63   80   884       irq            stat
1256   1790  33    4228  64   800  905       kallsyms       swaps
1261   1809  34    44    65   803  934       kcore          sys
1262   1812  35    45    66   804  979       keys           sysrq-trigger
1270   1814  3582  461   664  81   980       key-users      sysvipc
1272   1822  36    462   67   826  981       kmsg           thread-self
1273   1823  37    466   676  827  acpi      kpagecgroup    timer_list
1274   1868  38    470   68   828  bootconfig kpagecount    tty
1279   1869  39    472   69   830  buddyinfo kpageflags     uptime
1280   1870  4     473   72   831  bus       latency_stats  version
1282   1893  40    475   73   835  cgroups   loadavg        vmallocinfo
13     1894  41    476   732  836  cmdline   locks          vmstat
1312   19    4120  479   733  856  consoles  mdstat         zoneinfo
1314   1919  4125  5     734  857  cpuinfo   meminfo
[root@studentvm1 proc]# ll
```

First, notice the directories with numerical names. Each directory name is the PID (process ID) of a running process. The data contained inside these directories exposes all of the pertinent information about each process. Let's take a look at one to see what that means.

Use htop to find the PID of one of the cpuHogs. These are 1919 and 1893 on my VM, but your PIDs probably will be different. Select one of those PIDs and then make it the PWD. I used PID 1919, so my current PWD is /proc/1919.

Now cat the loginuid file. Notice that most of the data in these files – at least the last item – may not have an ending line feed character. This means that sometimes the new command prompt is printed on the same line as the data. That is what is happening here:

```
[root@studentvm1 1919]# cat loginuid
1000[root@studentvm1 1919]#
```

The UID of the user who started this process is 1000. Now go to a terminal that is logged in as the student user and enter this command:

```
[student@studentvm1 ~]$ id
uid=1000(student) gid=1000(student) groups=1000(student)
[student@studentvm1 ~]$
```

Thus, we see that the user ID (UID) of the student user is 1000 so that the user student started the process with PID 1919. Now let's watch the scheduling data for this process. I won't reproduce my results here, but you should be able to see the changes in this live data as they occur. In a root terminal session, run the following command:

```
[root@studentvm1 1919]# watch cat sched
```

Now return to /proc as the PWD. Enter the following commands to view some of the raw data from the /proc filesystem:

```
[root@studentvm1 proc]# cat /proc/meminfo
[root@studentvm1 proc]# cat /proc/cpuinfo
[root@studentvm1 proc]# cat /proc/loadavg
```

These are just a few of the files in /proc that contain incredibly useful information. Spend some time exploring more of the data in /proc. Some of the data is in formats that require a bit of manipulation in order to make sense to us humans, and much of it would only be useful to kernel or system developers.

We have just touched upon a very tiny bit of the /proc filesystem. Having all of this data exposed and available to us as SysAdmins, not to mention the system developers, makes it easy to obtain information about the kernel, hardware, and running programs. This means that it is not necessary to write code that needs to access the kernel or its data structures in order to discover all of the knowable aspects of a Linux system.

The CentOS/RHEL 7.2 documentation has a list of many of the more useful files in the /proc filesystem.[5] Some older Fedora documentation also contains this information. The Linux Documentation Project has a brief description of some of the data files in /proc.[6]

Exploring Hardware

Sometimes – frequently, actually – I find it is nice to know very specific information about the hardware installed in a host, and we have some tools to assist with this. Two that I like are the lshw (list hardware) and dmidecode (Desktop Management Interface[7] decode) commands, which both display as much hardware information as is available in SMBIOS.[8] The man page for dmidecode states, "SMBIOS stands for System Management BIOS, while DMI stands for Desktop Management Interface. Both standards are tightly related and developed by the DMTF (14.4Desktop Management Task Force)."

These utility tools use data stored in SMBIOS, which is a data storage area on system motherboards that allows the BIOS boot process to store data about the system hardware. Because the task of collecting hardware data is performed at BIOS boot time, the operating system does not need to probe the hardware directly in order to collect

---

[5] *Red Hat Linux 7.2: The Official Red Hat Linux Reference Guide*, Chapter 4, The /proc Filesystem, www.centos.org/docs//2/rhl-rg-en-7.2/ch-proc.html

[6] Linux Documentation Project, *The Linux System Administrator's Guide*, 3.7, The /proc filesystem, www.tldp.org/LDP/sag/html/proc-fs.html

[7] Wikipedia, *Desktop Management Interface*, https://en.wikipedia.org/wiki/Desktop_Management_Interface

[8] Wikipedia, *System Management BIOS*, https://en.wikipedia.org/wiki/System_Management_BIOS

information that can be used to perform tasks such as determination of which hardware-related kernel modules to load during the Linux kernel portion of the boot and startup process. We will discuss the boot and startup sequence of a Linux computer in some detail in Chapter 16.

The data collected into SMBIOS can be easily accessed by tools such as lshw and dmidecode for use by SysAdmins. I use this data when planning upgrades, for example. The last time I needed to install more RAM in a system, I used the dmidecode utility to determine the total amount of memory capacity available on the motherboard, the current memory type such as DD4, and whether any memory slots were still open. Many times the motherboard vendor, model, and serial number are also available. This makes it easy to obtain the information needed to locate documentation on the Internet.

Other tools, such as lsusb (list USB) and lspci (list PCI), do not use the DMI information; they use data from the special filesystems /proc and /sys, which are generated during Linux boot. We will explore these special filesystems in Volume 2, Chapter 24.

Because these are command-line tools, we have access to the hardware details of systems that are local or halfway around the planet. The value of being able to determine detailed hardware information about systems without having to dismantle them to do so is incalculable.

EXPERIMENT 13-9: EXPLORING HARDWARE

Perform this experiment as root to install the lshw (list hardware) package:

```
[root@studentvm1 ~]# dnf install -y lshw
```

This program lists data about the motherboard, CPU, and other installed hardware. Run the following command to list the hardware on your host. It may take a few moments to extract and display the data, so be patient. Look through the data to see all of the (virtual) hardware in your VM:

```
[root@studentvm1 ~]# lshw | less
```

Now run dmidecode and do the same:

```
[root@studentvm1 ~]# dmidecode | less
```

It is also possible to list hardware information by DMI type. For example, the motherboard is DMI type 2, so you can use the following command to list the hardware information for just the motherboard:

```
[root@studentvm1 ~]# dmidecode -t 2
```

You can find the type codes for different types of hardware in the dmidecode man page.

There are two commands available to list USB and PCI devices. Both should be installed already. Run the following commands and take some time to review the output. The -v option means verbose:

```
[root@studentvm1 ~]# lsusb -v | less
[root@studentvm1 ~]# lspci -v | less
```

Caution   The results for the dmidecode and lshw tools can be questionable. According to both of their man pages, "More often than not, information contained in the DMI tables is inaccurate, incomplete or simply wrong."

In large part this information deficiency is because hardware vendors do not always cooperate by storing data about their hardware in a way that is useful – when they provide any data at all.

Monitoring Hardware Temperatures

Keeping computers cool is essential for helping ensure that they have a long life. Large data centers spend a great deal of energy to keep the computers in them cool. Without going into the details, designers need to ensure that the flow of cool air is directed into the data center and specifically into the racks of computers to keep them cool. It is even better if they can be kept at a fairly constant temperature.

Proper cooling is essential even in a home or office environment. In fact, it is even more essential in those environments because the ambient temperature is usually higher than a computer center as it is primarily for the comfort of the humans. One can measure the temperature of many different points in a data center as well as within individual racks. But how can the temperature of the internals of a computer be measured?

Fortunately, modern computers have many sensors built into various components to enable monitoring of temperatures, fan speeds, and voltages. If you have ever looked at some of the data available when a computer is in BIOS configuration mode, you can see many of these values. But this cannot show what is happening inside the computer when it is in a real-world situation under loads of various types.

Linux has some software tools available to allow system administrators to monitor those internal sensors. Those tools are all based on the lm_sensors, SMART, and hddtemp library modules, which are available on all Red Hat–based distributions such as Fedora and CentOS and most others as well.

The simplest tool is the `sensors` command. Before the sensors command is run, the `sensors-detect` command is used to detect as many of the sensors installed on the host system as possible. The `sensors` command then produces output including motherboard and CPU temperatures, voltages at various points on the motherboard, and fan speeds. The sensors command also displays the range temperatures considered to be normal, high, and critical.

The `hddtemp` command displays temperatures for a specified hard drive. The `smartctl` command shows the current temperature of the hard drive, various measurements that indicate the potential for hard drive failure, and, in some cases, an ASCII text history graph of the hard drive temperatures. This last output can be especially helpful in some types of problems.

There are also a number of good graphical monitoring tools that can be used to monitor the thermal status of your computers. I like GKrellM for my desktop, and there are plenty of others available for you to choose from.

I suggest installing these tools and monitoring the outputs on every newly installed system. That way you can learn what temperatures are normal for your computers. Using tools like these allows you to monitor the temperatures in real time and understand how added loads of various types affect those temperatures.

EXPERIMENT 13-10: EXPLORING TEMPERATURES

As root, install the lm_sensors and hddtemp packages. If the physical host for your virtual machine is a Linux system, you may perform these experiments on that system if you have root access:

```
[root@studentvm1 proc]# dnf -y install lm_sensors hddtemp
```

It is necessary to configure the lm_sensors package before useful data can be obtained. Unfortunately this is a highly interactive process, but you can usually just press the **Enter** key to take all of the defaults, some of which are "no," or pipe **yes** to answer yes to all options:

```
[root@studentvm1 proc]# yes | sensors-detect
```

Because these utilities require real hardware, they do not produce any results on a virtual machine. So I will illustrate the results with data from one of my own hosts, my primary workstation:

```
[root@myworkstation proc]# sensors
coretemp-isa-0000
Adapter: ISA adapter
Package id 0:   +54.0°C  (high = +86.0°C, crit = +96.0°C)
Core 0:         +44.0°C  (high = +86.0°C, crit = +96.0°C)
Core 1:         +51.0°C  (high = +86.0°C, crit = +96.0°C)
Core 2:         +49.0°C  (high = +86.0°C, crit = +96.0°C)
Core 3:         +51.0°C  (high = +86.0°C, crit = +96.0°C)
Core 4:         +51.0°C  (high = +86.0°C, crit = +96.0°C)
Core 5:         +50.0°C  (high = +86.0°C, crit = +96.0°C)
Core 6:         +47.0°C  (high = +86.0°C, crit = +96.0°C)
Core 7:         +51.0°C  (high = +86.0°C, crit = +96.0°C)
Core 8:         +48.0°C  (high = +86.0°C, crit = +96.0°C)
Core 9:         +51.0°C  (high = +86.0°C, crit = +96.0°C)
Core 10:        +53.0°C  (high = +86.0°C, crit = +96.0°C)
Core 11:        +47.0°C  (high = +86.0°C, crit = +96.0°C)
Core 12:        +52.0°C  (high = +86.0°C, crit = +96.0°C)
Core 13:        +52.0°C  (high = +86.0°C, crit = +96.0°C)
Core 14:        +54.0°C  (high = +86.0°C, crit = +96.0°C)
Core 15:        +52.0°C  (high = +86.0°C, crit = +96.0°C)
```

```
radeon-pci-6500
Adapter: PCI adapter
temp1:          +40.5°C  (crit = +120.0°C, hyst = +90.0°C)

asus-isa-0000
Adapter: ISA adapter
cpu_fan:          0 RPM

[root@myworkstation proc]# hddtemp
/dev/sda: TOSHIBA HDWE140: 38°C
/dev/sdb: ST320DM000-1BD14C: 33°C
/dev/sdc: ST3000DM001-1CH166: 31°C
/dev/sdd: ST1000DM003-1CH162: 32°C
/dev/sdg: WD My Passport 070A:  drive supported, but it doesn't have a
temperature sensor.
[root@myworkstation proc]#
```

Monitoring Storage Drives

Storage devices are one of the most common failure points in computers, right after
fans. They have moving parts, and those are always more prone to failure than electronic
integrated circuit chips. Knowing in advance that a hard drive is likely to fail soon
can save much time and aggravation. The Self-Monitoring, Analysis, and Reporting
Technology[9] (SMART) capabilities built into modern storage drives enable SysAdmins
like us to identify drives that are likely to fail soon and replace them during a scheduled
maintenance.

Although they do not have moving parts, SSD storage devices that use SATA
connections to the host also support SMART capabilities, as do some external USB
storage devices.

The **smartctl** command is used to access the data and statistics available from
SMART-enabled storage drives. Most storage devices are SMART-enabled these days, but
not all, especially very old storage devices and some external USB storage drives.

---

[9] Wikipedia, *S.M.A.R.T.*, https://en.wikipedia.org/wiki/S.M.A.R.T.

EXPERIMENT 13-11: MONITORING STORAGE DRIVES

Tip   This experiment does not work in a VM. I have used one of my physical hosts for this so that you can see what it will look like. If you have root access to an appropriate physical host, you can safely perform this experiment on that.

Perform this experiment as root.

This experiment does not work in a VM. So I have used one of my physical hosts for this so that you can see what it will look like.

You might need to install the smartmontools package on your host:

```
[root@myworkstation ~]# dnf -y install smartmontools
```

Verify the device name of your hard drive. There should only be one hard drive, sda, on your VM because that is the way we created it. But it never hurts to verify the device on which you are working.

Use the following command to print all SMART data and pipe it through the less filter. This assumes that your hard drive is /dev/sda:

```
[root@myworkstation ~]# smartctl -x /dev/sda
```

These are the results from one of the storage devices on my primary workstation. This is quite a long data stream, but I have not shortened it because it is important for you to see what all of the data you can find with a physical host and hard drive:

```
[root@myworkstation ~]# smartctl -x /dev/sda
smartctl 6.6 2017-11-05 r4594 [x86_64-linux-4.18.16-200.fc28.x86_64]
(local build)
Copyright (C) 2002-17, Bruce Allen, Christian Franke,
www.smartmontools.org

=== START OF INFORMATION SECTION ===
Model Family:     Toshiba X300
Device Model:     TOSHIBA HDWE140
Serial Number:    46P2K0DZF58D
LU WWN Device Id: 5 000039 6fb783fa0
```

Firmware Version: FP2A
User Capacity: 4,000,787,030,016 bytes [4.00 TB]
Sector Sizes: 512 bytes logical, 4096 bytes physical
Rotation Rate: 7200 rpm
Form Factor: 3.5 inches
Device is: In smartctl database [for details use: -P show]
ATA Version is: ATA8-ACS (minor revision not indicated)
SATA Version is: SATA 3.0, 6.0 Gb/s (current: 6.0 Gb/s)
Local Time is: Wed Oct 31 08:59:01 2018 EDT
SMART support is: Available - device has SMART capability.
SMART support is: Enabled
AAM feature is: Unavailable
APM level is: 128 (minimum power consumption without standby)
Rd look-ahead is: Enabled
Write cache is: Enabled
DSN feature is: Unavailable
ATA Security is: Disabled, frozen [SEC2]
Wt Cache Reorder: Enabled

=== START OF READ SMART DATA SECTION ===
SMART overall-health self-assessment test result: PASSED

General SMART Values:
Offline data collection status: (0x82)   Offline data collection
                                          activity
                                 was completed without error.
                                 Auto Offline Data Collection: Enabled.
Self-test execution status: (0)   The previous self-test routine
                                          completed
                                 without error or no self-test has ever
                                 been run.
Total time to complete Offline
data collection: (120) seconds.
Offline data collection
capabilities: (0x5b) SMART execute Offline
                                         immediate.

387

Auto Offline data collection on/off support.
Suspend Offline collection upon new command.
Offline surface scan supported.
Self-test supported.
No Conveyance Self-test supported.
Selective Self-test supported.

SMART capabilities: (0x0003)   Saves SMART data before entering
power-saving mode.
Supports SMART auto save timer.

Error logging capability: (0x01)   Error logging supported.
General Purpose Logging supported.

Short self-test routine
recommended polling time: (2) minutes.
Extended self-test routine
recommended polling time: (469) minutes.
SCT capabilities: (0x003d)   SCT Status supported.
SCT Error Recovery Control supported.
SCT Feature Control supported.
SCT Data Table supported.

SMART Attributes Data Structure revision number: 16
Vendor Specific SMART Attributes with Thresholds:

ID#	ATTRIBUTE_NAME	FLAGS	VALUE	WORST	THRESH	FAIL	RAW_VALUE
1	Raw_Read_Error_Rate	PO-R--	100	100	050	-	0
2	Throughput_Performance	P-S---	100	100	050	-	0
3	Spin_Up_Time	POS--K	100	100	001	-	4146
4	Start_Stop_Count	-O--CK	100	100	000	-	132
5	Reallocated_Sector_Ct	PO--CK	100	100	050	-	0
7	Seek_Error_Rate	PO-R--	100	100	050	-	0
8	Seek_Time_Performance	P-S---	100	100	050	-	0
9	Power_On_Hours	-O--CK	051	051	000	-	19898
10	Spin_Retry_Count	PO--CK	102	100	030	-	0
12	Power_Cycle_Count	-O--CK	100	100	000	-	132

```
191 G-Sense_Error_Rate        -O--CK   100   100   000   -   63
192 Power-Off_Retract_Count   -O--CK   100   100   000   -   82
193 Load_Cycle_Count          -O--CK   100   100   000   -   162
194 Temperature_Celsius       -O---K   100   100   000   -   36 (Min/
Max 24/45)
196 Reallocated_Event_Count   -O--CK   100   100   000   -   0
197 Current_Pending_Sector    -O--CK   100   100   000   -   0
198 Offline_Uncorrectable     ----CK   100   100   000   -   0
199 UDMA_CRC_Error_Count      -O--CK   200   253   000   -   0
220 Disk_Shift                -O----   100   100   000   -   0
222 Loaded_Hours              -O--CK   051   051   000   -   19891
223 Load_Retry_Count          -O--CK   100   100   000   -   0
224 Load_Friction             -O---K   100   100   000   -   0
226 Load-in_Time              -OS--K   100   100   000   -   210
240 Head_Flying_Hours         P-----   100   100   001   -   0
                             |||||||_ K auto-keep
                             ||||||__ C event count
                             |||||___ R error rate
                             ||||____ S speed/performance
                             ||_____ O updated online
                             |_____ P prefailure warning
```

General Purpose Log Directory Version 1
SMART   Log Directory Version 1 [multi-sector log support]

Address	Access	R/W	Size	Description
0x00	GPL,SL	R/O	1	Log Directory
0x01	SL	R/O	1	Summary SMART error log
0x02	SL	R/O	51	Comprehensive SMART error log
0x03	GPL	R/O	64	Ext. Comprehensive SMART error log
0x04	GPL,SL	R/O	8	Device Statistics log
0x06	SL	R/O	1	SMART self-test log
0x07	GPL	R/O	1	Extended self-test log
0x08	GPL	R/O	2	Power Conditions log
0x09	SL	R/W	1	Selective self-test log
0x10	GPL	R/O	1	NCQ Command Error log

```
0x11        GPL      R/O       1  SATA Phy Event Counters log
0x24        GPL      R/O   12288  Current Device Internal Status Data log
0x30        GPL,SL   R/O       9  IDENTIFY DEVICE data log
0x80-0x9f   GPL,SL   R/W      16  Host vendor specific log
0xa7        GPL      VS        8  Device vendor specific log
0xe0        GPL,SL   R/W       1  SCT Command/Status
0xe1        GPL,SL   R/W       1  SCT Data Transfer
```

SMART Extended Comprehensive Error Log Version: 1 (64 sectors)
No Errors Logged

SMART Extended Self-test Log Version: 1 (1 sectors)
No self-tests have been logged. [To run self-tests, use: smartctl -t]

SMART Selective self-test log data structure revision number 1
```
 SPAN  MIN_LBA  MAX_LBA  CURRENT_TEST_STATUS
   1        0        0  Not_testing
   2        0        0  Not_testing
   3        0        0  Not_testing
   4        0        0  Not_testing
   5        0        0  Not_testing
```
Selective self-test flags (0x0):
  After scanning selected spans, do NOT read-scan remainder of disk.
If Selective self-test is pending on power-up, resume after 0
minute delay.

```
SCT Status Version:                       3
SCT Version (vendor specific):            1 (0x0001)
SCT Support Level:                        1
Device State:                             Active (0)
Current Temperature:                       36 Celsius
Power Cycle Min/Max Temperature:          34/45 Celsius
Lifetime    Min/Max Temperature:          24/45 Celsius
Under/Over Temperature Limit Count:        0/0

SCT Temperature History Version:          2
Temperature Sampling Period:              1 minute
Temperature Logging Interval:             1 minute
```

```
Min/Max recommended Temperature:      5/55 Celsius
Min/Max Temperature Limit:            5/55 Celsius
Temperature History Size (Index):     478 (197)

Index    Estimated Time     Temperature Celsius
 198    2018-10-31 01:02       37   *****************
 ...    ..( 12 skipped).       ..   *****************
 211    2018-10-31 01:15       37   *****************
 212    2018-10-31 01:16       36   ****************
 ...    ..(137 skipped).       ..   ****************
<snip>
  16    2018-10-31 05:58       35   ***************
  17    2018-10-31 05:59       36   ****************
 ...    ..(179 skipped).       ..   ****************
 197    2018-10-31 08:59       36   ****************

SCT Error Recovery Control:
         Read: Disabled
        Write: Disabled
```

```
Device Statistics (GP Log 0x04)
Page  Offset Size          Value Flags Description
0x01  =====  =                 =  ===  == General Statistics (rev 2) ==
0x01  0x008  4               132  ---  Lifetime Power-On Resets
0x01  0x010  4             19898  ---  Power-on Hours
0x01  0x018  6       37056039193  ---  Logical Sectors Written
0x01  0x020  6          31778305  ---  Number of Write Commands
0x01  0x028  6       46110927573  ---  Logical Sectors Read
0x01  0x030  6         256272184  ---  Number of Read Commands
0x02  =====  =                 =  ===  == Free-Fall Statistics (rev 1) ==
0x02  0x010  4                63  ---  Overlimit Shock Events
0x03  =====  =                 =  ===  == Rotating Media Statistics
                                             (rev 1) ==
0x03  0x008  4             19897  ---  Spindle Motor Power-on Hours
0x03  0x010  4             19891  ---  Head Flying Hours
0x03  0x018  4               162  ---  Head Load Events
```

```
0x03   0x020   4            0   ---   Number of Reallocated
Logical Sectors
0x03   0x028   4            0   ---   Read Recovery Attempts
0x03   0x030   4            0   ---   Number of Mechanical Start Failures
0x04   =====   =            =   ===   == General Errors Statistics
                                          (rev 1) ==
0x04   0x008   4            0   ---   Number of Reported
Uncorrectable Errors
0x04   0x010   4            1   ---   Resets Between Cmd Acceptance and
Completion
0x05   =====   =            =   ===   == Temperature Statistics
                                          (rev 1) ==
0x05   0x008   1           36   ---   Current Temperature
0x05   0x010   1           37   N--   Average Short Term Temperature
0x05   0x018   1           38   N--   Average Long Term Temperature
0x05   0x020   1           45   ---   Highest Temperature
0x05   0x028   1           24   ---   Lowest Temperature
0x05   0x030   1           41   N--   Highest Average Short Term
                                      Temperature
0x05   0x038   1           30   N--   Lowest Average Short Term
                                      Temperature
0x05   0x040   1           39   N--   Highest Average Long Term
                                      Temperature
0x05   0x048   1           32   N--   Lowest Average Long Term
                                      Temperature
0x05   0x050   4            0   ---   Time in Over-Temperature
0x05   0x058   1           55   ---   Specified Maximum Operating
                                      Temperature
0x05   0x060   4            0   ---   Time in Under-Temperature
0x05   0x068   1            5   ---   Specified Minimum Operating
                                      Temperature
0x06   =====   =            =   ===   == Transport Statistics (rev 1) ==
0x06   0x008   4         1674   ---   Number of Hardware Resets
0x06   0x018   4            0   ---   Number of Interface CRC Errors
```

```
0x07  =====  =                   =  ===  == Solid State Device Statistics
                                             (rev 1) ==
                                 |||_ C monitored condition met
                                 ||__ D supports DSN
                                 |___ N normalized value

Pending Defects log (GP Log 0x0c) not supported

SATA Phy Event Counters (GP Log 0x11)
ID      Size    Value  Description
0x0001  4          0   Command failed due to ICRC error
0x0002  4          0   R_ERR response for data FIS
0x0003  4          0   R_ERR response for device-to-host data FIS
0x0004  4          0   R_ERR response for host-to-device data FIS
0x0005  4          0   R_ERR response for non-data FIS
0x0006  4          0   R_ERR response for device-to-host non-data FIS
0x0007  4          0   R_ERR response for host-to-device non-data FIS
0x0008  4          0   Device-to-host non-data FIS retries
0x0009  4         15   Transition from drive PhyRdy to drive PhyNRdy
0x000a  4         16   Device-to-host register FISes sent due to a
                       COMRESET
0x000b  4          0   CRC errors within host-to-device FIS
0x000d  4          0   Non-CRC errors within host-to-device FIS
0x000f  4          0   R_ERR response for host-to-device data FIS, CRC
0x0010  4          0   R_ERR response for host-to-device data
                       FIS, non-CRC
0x0012  4          0   R_ERR response for host-to-device non-data
                       FIS, CRC
0x0013  4          0   R_ERR response for host-to-device non-data
                       FIS, non-CRC

[root@myworkstation ~]#
```

One easy-to-understand part of this long and complex result is the START OF READ SMART DATA SECTION. The result shown earlier is

SMART overall-health self-assessment test result: PASSED

The specific data shown for a particular hard drive will vary depending upon the device vendor and model. More recent versions of the software can take advantage of additional information stored by newer storage devices. SSDs will have some different information than HHDs because they are of such a different technology.

The SMART[10] reports contain a great deal of information, which can be useful if it can be understood. At first glance the data can be very confusing, but a little knowledge can be very helpful. Contributing to the confusion is the fact that there are no standards for the information being displayed and different vendors implement SMART in different ways.

One large cloud storage company has been keeping records of close to 40,000 storage devices over the last few years and posting their data on the Web. According to an article[11] on the Computerworld website, the company identified the following five data points that can predict hard drive (not SSD) failures:

- **SMART 5**: Reallocated_Sector_Count

- **SMART 187**: Reported_Uncorrectable_Errors

- **SMART 188**: Command_Timeout

- **SMART 197**: Current_Pending_Sector_Count

- **SMART 198**: Offline_Uncorrectable

Each of these attributes is listed in the SMART Attributes section of the output, and low numbers are good. If any one or especially more than one of these attributes have high numbers, then it would be a good idea to replace the hard drive before a full-on failure occurs.

---

[10] Wikipedia, *S.M.A.R.T.*, https://en.wikipedia.org/wiki/S.M.A.R.T.

[11] Mearian, Lucas, Computerworld, *The 5 SMART stats that actually predict hard drive failure*, www.computerworld.com/article/2846009/the-5-smart-stats-that-actually-predict-hard-drive-failure.html

System Statistics with SAR

The sar command is one of my favorite tools when it comes to resolving problems. SAR stands for System Activity Reporter. Its primary function is to collect system performance data for each day and store it in log files for later display. Data is collected as ten-minute averages, but more granular collection can also be configured. Data is retained for one month.

The only time I have made any changes to the SAR configuration is when I needed to collect data every minute instead of every ten minutes in order to get a better handle on the exact time a particular problem was occurring. The SAR data is stored in two files per day in the /var/log/sa directory. Collecting data more frequently than every ten minutes can cause these files to grow very large.

In one place I worked, we had a problem that would start and escalate so quickly that the default ten-minute interval was not very helpful in determining which occurred first, CPU load, high disk activity, or something else. Using a one-minute interval, we determined that not only was CPU activity high, but that it was preceded by a short interval of high network activity as well as high disk activity. It was ultimately determined that this was an unintentional denial of service (DOS) attack on the web server that was complicated by the fact that there was too little RAM installed in the computer to handle the temporary overload. Adding 2GB of RAM to the existing 2GB resolved the problem, and further DOS attacks did not cause problems.

Installation and Configuration

SAR is installed as part of the sysstat package in Red Hat–based distributions; however, it is not installed by default in at least some of the current Fedora distributions. We installed it in Chapter 7. By now the SAR data collection has been running long enough to accumulate a significant amount of data for us to explore.

After installing SAR as part of the sysstat package, there is normally nothing that needs to be done to alter its configuration or to start it collecting data. Data is collected on every ten-minute mark of each hour.

Examining Collected Data

The output from the sar command can be very detailed. A full day of data on my primary workstation, the one with 16 Intel cores and 32 CPUs, produced 14,921 lines of data. You can deal with this in multiple ways. You can choose to limit the data displayed by specifying only certain subsets of data, you can grep out the data you want, or you can pipe it through the less tool and page through the data using less's built-in search feature.

EXPERIMENT 13-12: SAR

Perform this experiment as the student user. The root privileges are not required to run the sar command. Because of the very large amount of data that can be emitted by SAR, I will not reproduce it all here except for headers and a few lines of data to illustrate the results.

Note   Some options for the **sar** command are in uppercase as shown. Using lowercase will result in an error or incorrect data being displayed.

First, just enter the sar command with no options, which displays only aggregate CPU performance data. The sar command uses the current day by default, starting at midnight or the time in the current day when the system was booted. If the host was rebooted during the current day, there will be a notification in the results. Note that some of the output of the SAR command can be very wide:

```
[student@studentvm1 ~]$ sar
Linux 4.18.9-200.fc28.x86_64 (studentvm1)    11/01/2018 _x86_64_   (2-CPU)

08:44:38      LINUX RESTART      (2-CPU)

08:50:01 AM    CPU     %user    %nice    %system    %iowait    %steal    %idle
09:00:05 AM    all      0.01     0.03       0.13       1.54      0.00     98.28
09:10:05 AM    all      0.01     0.00       0.09       0.95      0.00     98.95
09:20:05 AM    all      0.01     0.00       0.08       1.14      0.00     98.77
09:30:02 AM    all      0.02     0.00       0.09       1.17      0.00     98.72
09:40:05 AM    all      0.01     0.00       0.08       0.95      0.00     98.96
09:50:02 AM    all      0.01     0.00       0.09       1.04      0.00     98.86
```

		%user	%nice	%system	%iowait	%steal	%idle
10:00:01 AM	all	0.01	0.01	0.09	1.29	0.00	98.61
10:10:01 AM	all	0.01	0.00	0.08	0.93	0.00	98.98
10:20:05 AM	all	6.26	3.91	82.39	0.18	0.00	7.26
Average:	all	0.68	0.42	8.89	1.02	0.00	88.98

11:10:03 AM	LINUX RESTART	(2-CPU)					
11:20:31 AM	CPU	%user	%nice	%system	%iowait	%steal	%idle
11:30:31 AM	all	18.41	10.15	71.34	0.00	0.00	0.10
11:40:07 AM	all	20.07	10.93	68.83	0.00	0.00	0.17
11:50:18 AM	all	18.68	10.32	70.88	0.00	0.00	0.13
12:00:31 PM	all	17.83	10.09	71.98	0.00	0.00	0.09
12:10:31 PM	all	17.87	10.95	71.07	0.00	0.00	0.11
Average:	all	18.55	10.48	70.84	0.00	0.00	0.12

```
[student@studentvm1 ~]$
```

All of this data is an aggregate for all CPUs, in this case two, for each ten-minute time period. It also is the same data you would see in top, htop, and atop for CPU usage. Use the next command to view details for each individual CPU:

```
[student@studentvm1 ~]$ sar -P ALL
Linux 4.18.9-200.fc28.x86_64 (studentvm1)    11/01/2018  _x86_64_   (2-CPU)
```

08:44:38	LINUX RESTART	(2-CPU)					
08:50:01 AM	CPU	%user	%nice	%system	%iowait	%steal	%idle
09:00:05 AM	all	0.01	0.03	0.13	1.54	0.00	98.28
09:00:05 AM	0	0.02	0.00	0.12	0.24	0.00	99.61
09:00:05 AM	1	0.01	0.05	0.14	2.85	0.00	96.95
09:00:05 AM	CPU	%user	%nice	%system	%iowait	%steal	%idle
09:10:05 AM	all	0.01	0.00	0.09	0.95	0.00	98.95
09:10:05 AM	0	0.02	0.00	0.08	0.10	0.00	99.80
09:10:05 AM	1	0.01	0.00	0.10	1.80	0.00	98.09
`<snip>`							
12:20:31 PM	CPU	%user	%nice	%system	%iowait	%steal	%idle
12:30:31 PM	all	15.4%	13.6%	70.8%	0.0%	0.0%	0.2%
12:30:31 PM	0	16.9%	15.3%	67.7%	0.0%	0.0%	0.1%
12:30:31 PM	1	13.9%	11.8%	73.9%	0.0%	0.0%	0.4%

Average:	CPU	%user	%nice	%system	%iowait	%steal	%idle
Average:	all	18.3%	10.7%	70.9%	0.0%	0.0%	0.1%
Average:	0	18.8%	15.6%	65.6%	0.0%	0.0%	0.0%
Average:	1	17.8%	5.9%	76.1%	0.0%	0.0%	0.2%

Now use the following command to view disk statistics. The -h option makes the data more easily readable by humans and, for block devices (disks), also shows the name of the device. The -d option specifies that SAR is to display disk activity:

```
[student@studentvm1 ~]$ sar -dh
Linux 4.18.9-200.fc28.x86_64 (studentvm1)    11/01/2018    _x86_64_    (2-CPU)

08:44:38    LINUX RESTART    (2-CPU)
```

08:50:01 AM DEV	tps	rkB/s	wkB/s	areq-sz	aqu-sz	await	svctm	%util
09:00:05 AM sda	8.12	168.8k	13.5k	22.5k	0.07	7.88	4.49	3.6%
09:00:05 AM fedora_studentvm1-pool00_tmeta	0.00	0.0k	0.0k	0.0k	0.00	0.00	0.00	0.0%
09:00:05 AM fedora_studentvm1-pool00_tdata	0.09	0.5k	0.1k	7.1k	0.00	15.53	9.13	0.1%
09:00:05 AM fedora_studentvm1-pool00-tpool	0.09	0.5k	0.1k	7.1k	0.00	15.53	9.13	0.1%
09:00:05 AM fedora_studentvm1-root	0.09	0.7k	0.2k	9.5k	0.00	15.53	9.13	0.1%
09:00:05 AM fedora_studentvm1-swap	0.00	0.0k	0.0k	0.0k	0.00	0.00	0.00	0.0%
09:00:05 AM fedora_studentvm1-usr	0.86	14.3k	1.1k	18.1k	0.01	10.25	4.41	0.4%
09:00:05 AM fedora_studentvm1-home	0.00	0.0k	0.0k	0.0k	0.00	0.00	0.00	0.0%
09:00:05 AM fedora_studentvm1-var	7.71	154.0k	12.3k	21.6k	0.06	8.39	4.21	3.2%
09:00:05 AM fedora_studentvm1-tmp	0.06	0.0k	0.2k	4.0k	0.00	27.37	23.71	0.1%
09:10:05 AM sda	1.74	0.4k	8.3k	5.0k	0.10	55.05	14.06	2.4%
09:10:05 AM fedora_studentvm1-pool00_tmeta	0.00	0.0k	0.0k	0.0k	0.00	0.00	0.00	0.0%

```
09:10:05 AM   0.02      0.0k      0.1k      3.7k      0.00    34.25    34.25    0.1%
fedora_studentvm1-pool00_tdata
09:10:05 AM   0.02      0.0k      0.1k      3.7k      0.00    34.25    34.25    0.1%
fedora_studentvm1-pool00-tpool
<snip>
```

Try the preceding command without the -h option.

Run the following command to view all of the output for the current day or at least since the host was booted for the first time during the current day:

```
[student@studentvm1 ~]$ sar -A | less
```

Use the man page for the sar command to interpret the results and to get an idea of the many options available. Many of those options allow you to view specific data such as network and disk performance.

I typically use the **sar -A** command because many of the types of data available are interrelated and sometimes I find something that gives me a clue to a performance problem in a section of the output that I might not have looked at otherwise.

You can limit the total amount of data to just the total CPU activity. Try that and notice that you only get the composite CPU data, not the data for the individual CPUs. Also try the -r option for memory and -S for swap space. It is also possible to combine these options, so the following command will display CPU, memory, and swap space:

```
[student@studentvm1 ~]$ sar -urS
```

If you want only data between certain times, you can use -s and -e to define the start and end times, respectively. The following command displays all CPU data, both individual and aggregate, for the time period between 7:50 a.m. and 8:11 a.m. today:

```
[student@studentvm1 ~]$ sar -P ALL -s 07:50:00 -e 08:11:00
```

Note that all times must be specified in 24-hour format. If you have multiple CPUs, each CPU is detailed individually, and the average for all CPUs is also given.

The next command uses the -n option to display network statistics for all interfaces:

```
[student@studentvm1 ~]$ sar -n ALL | less
```

Data collected for previous days can also be examined by specifying the desired log file. Assume that you want to see the data for the second day of the month. The following command displays all collected data for that day. The last two digits of each file name are the day of the month on which the data was collected.

I used the file sa02 in the following example, but you should list the contents of the /var/log/sa directory and choose a file that exists there for your host:

```
[student@studentvm1 ~]$ sar -A -f /var/log/sa/sa02 | less
```

You can also use SAR to display (nearly) real-time data. The following command displays memory usage in five-second intervals for ten iterations:

```
[student@studentvm1 ~]$ sar -r 5 10
```

This is an interesting option for sar as it can provide a series of data points for a defined period of time that can be examined in detail and compared.

The SAR utility is very powerful and has many options. We have merely touched on a few of them, and all are listed in the man page. I suggest you familiarize yourself with SAR because it is very useful for locating those performance problems that occur when no one is around to see them.

If you are not very familiar with Intel and related hardware, some of the output from the sar command may not be particularly meaningful to you. Over time SysAdmins are pretty much bound to learn a great deal about hardware, and you will too. The best way I can suggest to do this in a relatively safe manner is to use the tools you are learning in this course to explore all of the VMs and physical hosts you have available to you.

Cleanup

A little cleanup may be required at this point. We want to kill the cpuHogs, and you may also want to close many but not all of the terminal sessions you opened during the course of the experiments in this chapter.

Use **top** to kill one of the CPU hog processes using signal 2. Now use **htop** to kill the other CPU hog process with signal 15. Quit the **top**, **htop**, and **atop** programs and close all but one or two of the terminal sessions.

Chapter Summary

This chapter has introduced you to some of the most common tools that SysAdmins use for determining the source of many types of performance problems. Each tool that we explored provides useful information that can help locate the source of a problem. Although I start with **top**, I also depend upon all of the other tools as well because they are useful and valuable. Each one has enabled me to resolve a problem when the others could not.

There are many other tools available, and a good number of them are tools that can be used on a GUI desktop to display pretty graphs of many types. We have looked at these specific tools because they are the ones that are most likely to be available or easily installed on almost any Linux host. As you progress in your experience as a SysAdmin, you will find other tools that will be useful to you.

In no way should you try to memorize every option of every tool. Just knowing that these tools are there and that they each have useful and interesting capabilities gives you a place to start when trying to solve problems. You can explore more as time permits, and having a specific task, such as fixing a broken system, can focus your efforts on the specifics needed for that problem.

In my opinion it is completely unnecessary to purchase expensive tools that merely repackage the content of the /proc filesystem – because that is exactly what they do. Nothing can give you any more information than what is already available to you using standard Linux tools. Linux even has many GUI tools from which to choose than can display graphs of all of the data we have looked at here and more and can do it with both local and remote hosts.

And finally, by now you should be used to viewing the man and info pages as well as the available help options on most commands we are using to learn more about them. So I suspect you are as tired of reading those suggestions as I am of writing them. Let's just stipulate that one thing you should always do when you read about a new command is to use those tools to assist you in learning more.

Exercises

Perform the following exercises to complete this chapter:

1. Can you set the refresh delay for the top command to sub-second, such as 0.2 or 0.5 seconds?

2. Define the three load average numbers.

3. Using top, how much memory and swap space are free on the StudentVM1 virtual host?

4. List at least three other tools that you can find the memory usage information.

5. What does the TIME+ value in the top display tell you?

6. How much memory and swap space are free on this VM?

7. What is the default sort column for top?

8. Change the top sort column first to PID and then to TIME+. What is the PID of the process with the most CPU time?

9. What is the original source of data for top and every other tool we have explored in this chapter?

10. Is it possible to buffer data from more than one program in the same named pipe before reading any data from it?

11. Which of the tools discussed in this chapter provides network I/O information?

12. Which of the tools discussed in this chapter allows operations such as renicing to be performed simultaneously on multiple processes?

13. Using htop, on which column would you sort to determine which processes have accumulated the most total CPU time?

14. What is the difference between total and actual disk reads and writes as displayed by iotop?

15. Use the setup feature of htop to add the host name and the time-of-day clock to the top of the right-hand header column.

16. What command would you use to obtain a time-domain graph of the internal temperatures of a hard drive?

17. Use SAR to view the network statistics for the current day.

18. View all of the recorded system activity for yesterday as of this reading and if your VM was running at that time. If not, choose another day in the SAR data collection.

19. What type of CPU is installed in your VM? Make: _____
Model: _____ Speed: _____ GHz

CHAPTER 14

Terminal Emulator Mania

Objectives

In this chapter you will learn

- To use multiple different terminal emulators
- To use advanced features of these terminal emulators to work more efficiently
- To use advanced bash shell tools like wildcards, sets, brace expansion, meta-characters, and more to easily locate and act upon single or multiple files

The function of any terminal emulator is to provide us with a window on the GUI desktop that allows us to access the Linux command line where we can have unfettered access to the full power of Linux. In this chapter we will explore several terminal emulators in some detail as a means to better understand how these terminal emulators can make our use of the CLI more productive.

About Terminals

A terminal emulator is a software program that emulates a hardware terminal. Most terminal emulators are graphical programs that run on any Linux graphical desktop environment like Xfce, KDE, Cinnamon, LXDE, GNOME, and others.

In Chapter 7 we explored the command-line interface (CLI) and the concept of the terminal emulator[1] in some detail. We specifically looked at the xfce4-terminal to get us started on the command line, but we did not explore it in much depth. We will look at its features more closely along with several other terminal emulators.

---

[1] Wikipedia, *Terminal Emulator*, https://en.wikipedia.org/wiki/Terminal_emulator

405

© David Both 2023
D. Both, *Using and Administering Linux: Volume 1*, https://doi.org/10.1007/978-1-4842-9618-9_14

```
┌─────────────────────────────────────────────────────────────────┐
│        PREPARATION 14-1: INSTALL TERMINAL EMULATORS             │
└─────────────────────────────────────────────────────────────────┘
```

Fedora doesn't install all of the terminal emulators we will use during this chapter, so we will install them now. Do this as root. Enter the following command to install the terminal emulators we will be exploring:

```
# dnf -y install tilix lxterminal konsole5 rxvt-unicode terminator
```

You will notice that there were lots of dependencies installed in addition to the emulators themselves.

All of these terminal emulators should now appear in the Accessories or System sub-menu of the Applications launcher on the Xfce desktop panel.

My Requirements

As a Linux SysAdmin with many systems to manage in multiple locations, my life is all about simplification and making access to and monitoring of those systems easy and flexible. I have used many different terminal emulators in the past, all the way from the venerable Xterm to Terminator and Konsole.

With as many as 25 or 30 terminal sessions open simultaneously much of the time, having only one or two windows in which to manage those sessions prevents having large numbers of windows open on my desktop. As a person who generally keeps a messy physical desktop – they do say that is the sign of high intelligence, *cough, cough* – and lots of open windows on my Linux desktop, wrangling all of my terminal sessions into a couple windows is a great step forward in terms of decluttering.

Figure 14-1 shows the desktop of my own primary workstation as I write this chapter. I have three different emulators open. I understand that it is impossible to discern any details in Figure 14-1, but it does give you a good image of the flexibility provided by having multiple terminal emulators open on a single GUI desktop.

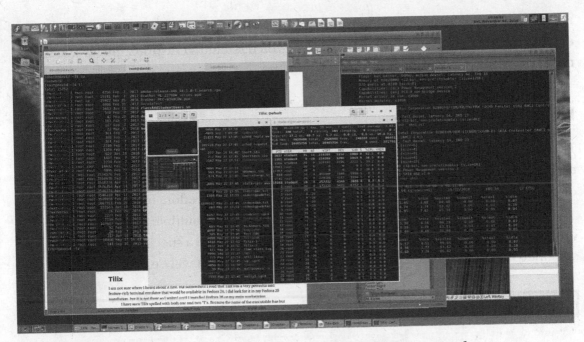

Figure 14-1. *My main workstation desktop with multiple terminal emulators open*

There are many terminal emulators available for Linux. Their different approaches to this task were defined by the needs, likes, dislikes, and philosophies of the developers who created them. One website has an article entitled "35 Best Linux Terminal Emulators for 2018"[2] that should give you an idea of how many options there are. Unfortunately there are too many for us to examine all of them here.

The Terminal Emulators

The emulators we explore in this section have features that enable us to massively leverage the power of the command line to become more efficient and effective in performing our jobs. I have used all of these terminal emulators at one time or another, and they all provide powerful features to do that. Sometimes I use more than one terminal emulator at the same time because each may fit the way I work better for a specific task. So while my – current – favorite terminal emulator happens to be Konsole

---

[2] *35 Best Linux Terminal Emulators for 2018*, www.slant.co/topics/794/~best-linux-terminal-emulators

and I have multiple instances of that open, I may also have instances of other terminal emulators open, too, such as xfce4-terminal, which is another favorite. But let's do look more closely at a few of these terminal emulators.

rxvt

There are some very minimalistic terminals out there. The rxvt terminal emulator is one of these. We installed the rxvt-unicode package earlier, which is a unicode upgrade to the original rxvt package, which was used in earlier releases of Fedora including Fedora 29.

The rxvt terminal emulator has no features like tabs or multiple panes that can be opened in a single window. Its font support is primitive, and a specific font must be specified on the command line or the very basic default font will be used.

EXPERIMENT 14-1: RXVT

Open an rxvt instance on the desktop of your VM. The rxvt window has no menu or icon bars. A right click in the window does nothing. But you can use it as a basic terminal emulator.

Experiment with rxvt for a few minutes just to get a feel for a truly old-style but functional terminal emulator.

The reason I included this terminal emulator in our exploration is to give you a baseline for comparing the advanced features of some of the other terminal emulators. Also, you may prefer this type of terminal emulator. There are people who do, and that is your choice and perfectly fine.

The rxvt terminal executable is 197,472 bytes in size, and it uses 226MB of virtual memory when running. This is the smallest memory footprint of any terminal emulators I looked at for this chapter. But it is also a minimalist project. It has no features of any kind other than the fact that it works as a terminal emulator. It does have some options that can be used as part of the command line used to launch it, but these, too, are very minimal.

xfce4-terminal

The xfce4-terminal is a powerful emulator that uses tabs to allow multiple terminals in a single window. It is flexible and easy to use. This terminal emulator is simple compared with emulators like Tilix, Terminator, and Konsole, but it gets the job done. And, yes, xfce4-terminal is the name of the executable for this emulator.

One of my favorite features of the xfce4-terminal are the tabs. You can open many tabs in a single window. Think of each tab as a separate terminal session. This provides a huge amount of flexibility to run multiple terminal sessions while maintaining a single window on the desktop.

I like the tabs on the xfce4-terminal emulator because they display the name of the host to which they are connected regardless of how many other hosts are connected through to make that connection, for example, host1 ==> host2 ==> host3 ==> host4 properly shows host4 on the tab. Other emulators show host2 at best. Like other components of the Xfce desktop, this terminal emulator uses very little in the way of system resources. You can also use the mouse to drag the tabs and change their order; a tab can also be dragged completely out of the window and onto the desktop, which places it in a window of its own where you can then add more tabs if you like.

Let's try it now. Because we are using the Xfce desktop, you should have already been using the xfce4-terminal up to this point. You should, therefore, already be somewhat familiar with it.

EXPERIMENT 14-2: XFCE4

Perform this experiment as the student user. If you do not already have an available instance of the xfce4-terminal open on your desktop, open one now. This launcher is located third from left on the bottom panel. Another launcher is located in the main Applications pull-down menu.

Figure 14-2 shows an xfce4-terminal window with three tabs open. There should still be only a single tab open in your instance. Perform a simple task just to have some content in this first terminal session, such as the **ll** command.

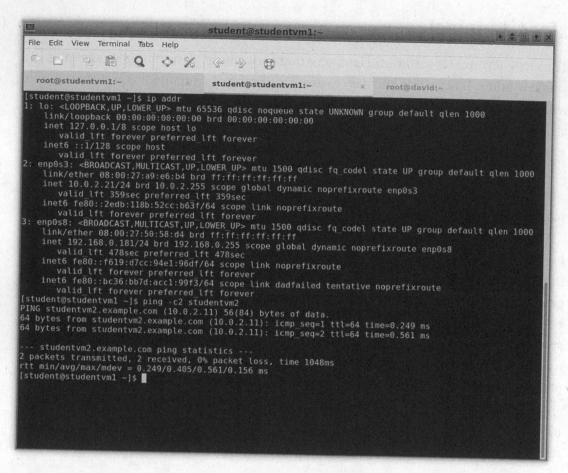

Figure 14-2. *The xfce4-terminal emulator sports an easy-to-use interface that includes tabs for switching between emulator sessions. Each tab may be logged in as a different user to a different host or any combination*

In addition to the standard menu bar, the xfce4-terminal emulator also has an icon bar, which can be used to open another tab or another emulator window. We need to turn on the icon bar in order to see it. On the menu bar, select **View ➤ Show Toolbar**. Hover the mouse pointer over the leftmost icon on the icon bar. The tooltip indicates that this icon will launch another tab in the current window. Click the tab icon. The new tab is inserted in the rightmost position of the tab bar, which is created if there was only one terminal session open previously. Open a couple more tabs and **su -** to root in one of them.

The tab names can be changed, and the tabs can be rearranged by drag and drop or by selecting the options on the menu bar. Double-click one of the tabs to open a small dialog that allows you to specify a new static name for the tab. Type in the name "My Tab". Drag "My Tab" to a new location on the tab bar. Now drag one tab completely away from the xfce4-terminal window and drop it somewhere else on the desktop. This creates a new window that contains only that tab. The new window now acts just the same as the original, and you can open new tabs in it as well.

Many aspects of function and appearance can be easily configured to suit your needs. Opening the Terminal Preferences configuration menu shown in Figure 14-3 gives access to five tabs that enable you to configure various aspects of the xfce4-terminal's look and feel. Open the terminal **Edit ➤ Preferences** dialog and select the **Appearance** tab. Choose different fonts and font sizes to view the differences. The htop utility uses bold text for some types of data, so remove the check mark from the **Allow bold text** item to see how that looks.

I sometimes fuss with the options on the Colors tab to enable some colors to be more readable. The Colors tab also has some presets from where you can start your modifications. I usually start with green or white on black and modify some of the individual colors to improve readability. Select the **Colors** tab. Load a couple of the different presets to view the differences. Feel free to experiment with this tab.

Select the tab with htop running on it. Press the **F1** key to see the htop help.

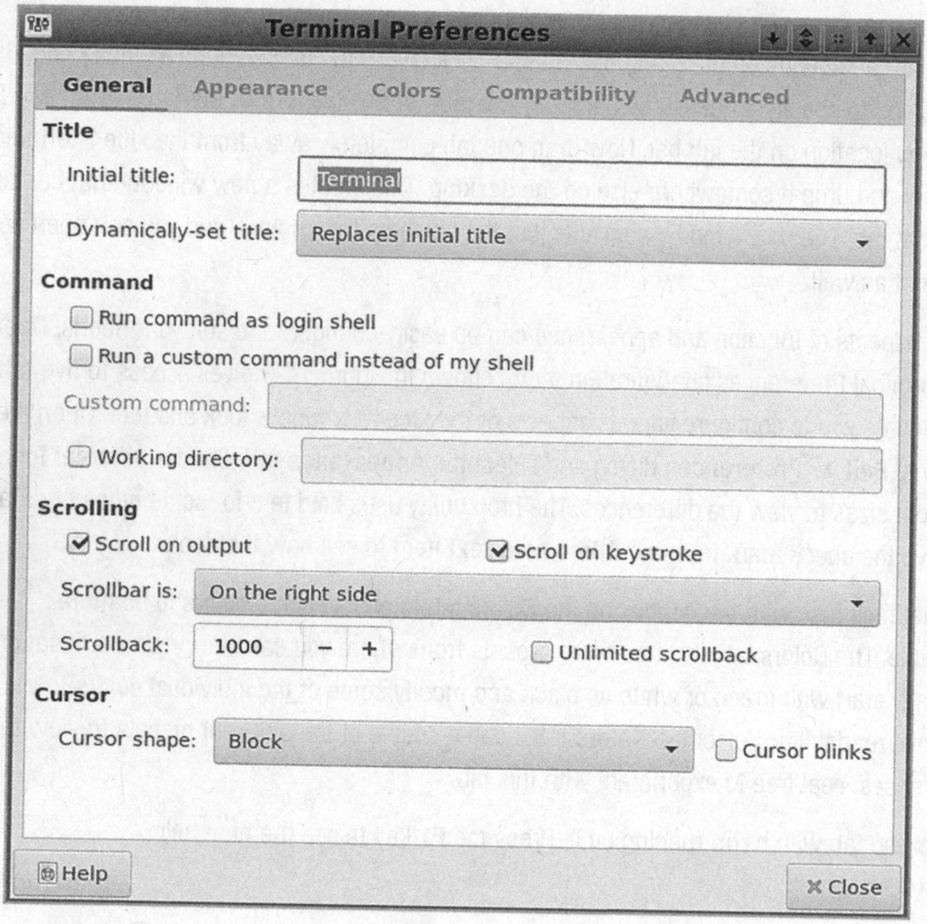

Figure 14-3. *The xfce4-terminal Terminal Preferences dialog allows configuration of many aspects of its look and feel*

Press **F1** again to close the htop help page. Close all of the open xfce4-terminal windows.

In my opinion, the xfce4-terminal emulator is one of the three best overall terminal emulators I have used. It just works and it has the features that work for me. So long as there is horizontal space available in the emulator window, the tabs are wide enough to show the entire host and directory name or certainly enough to figure out the rest. Other terminal emulators with tabs usually have fixed-size tabs that restrict the view of the available information on the tab.

The xfce4-terminal executable is just a little over 255KB in size. This emulator uses 576MB of virtual memory when running, which is the second lowest of the advanced emulators I tested.

LXTerminal

The LXTerminal emulator uses the least amount of RAM and has the smallest executable file of any of the other terminal emulators I have used. It has few extraneous features, but it does have tabs to enable multiple sessions in a single emulator window.

The LXTerminal window has no icon bar; it uses only a menu bar and pop-up menus and dialog boxes when you right-click in the window.

EXPERIMENT 14-3: LXTERMINAL

Open an instance of LXTerminal as the student user. Run a short command such as **ll** to show some content in the first session. No tabs are displayed yet.

Right-click in the existing session to display a pop-up menu and select **New tab** to open a second tab. Two tabs should now be visible at the top of the terminal emulator window. Now open the **File** menu from the menu bar and open a new tab. There should now be three open tabs as you can see in Figure 14-4.

Use the menu bar and open **Edit ➤ Preferences** to display the minimalistic configuration options. You can change the terminal font and adjust the colors and cursor style on the **Style** tab. I sometimes adjust one or more of these colors to make certain colorized text a bit more readable. Choose a couple of the color palettes to see what is available, and then modify by using that as a starting point.

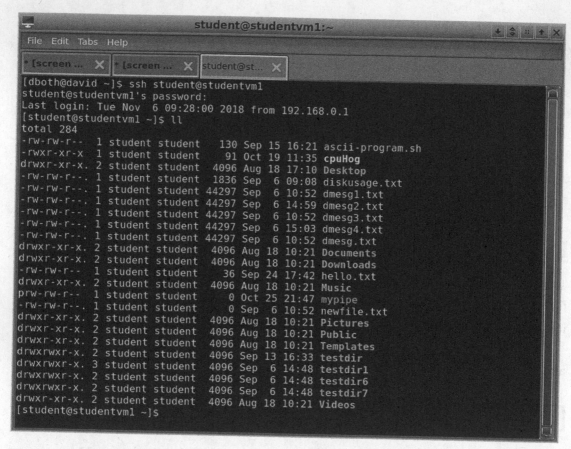

Figure 14-4. *The LXTerminal window with three tabs open*

Notice that no preference changes take effect until you click the **OK** button, which also closes the Preferences dialog. This is one thing I dislike. Save your current changes to see how that looks.

Open **Preferences** again and select the **Display** tab. I like having the tabs at the top, but you may prefer to have them at the bottom of the window. Select **Bottom** and save the change. The Display tab also allows changing the number of scrollback lines, which I usually do not change, and the default window size when a new LXTerminal window is opened. I currently have this adjusted to 130 columns by 65 lines. I have a lot of screen real estate, so that is fine on my wide screen. Play around with the window size and start a new session of LXTerminal to see how that works for you.

Other options on this tab enable you to hide various tools like the scroll bar and the menu bar. Play around with this to see how you might work in an environment without those tools. I never hide any of them.

Switch to the **Advanced** tab. The only thing I ever do on this tab is disable the F10 menu shortcut key. The **Shortcuts** tab provides the ability to change that key to something else, but I never change the defaults there, either.

Spend some time exploring LXTerminal on your own so you can get a better feel for how it works for you. When finished, close all instances of LXTerminal.

LXTerminal is a very lightweight terminal emulator, which is reflected in its small size and relatively few configuration options. The important thing with this terminal emulator is that it has all of the things we need as SysAdmins to do our jobs quickly and easily. These two facts make LXTerminal perfect for small systems such as smaller and older laptops with low amounts of RAM but also powerful enough to be just as perfect in big systems like my primary workstation.

The LXTerminal executable is 98,592 bytes in size, and it consumes 457MB of virtual memory when running. Both of these numbers are the smallest of any of the more advanced emulators that I have tested.

Tilix

Tilix helps me organize at least a bit by allowing me to keep all – or at least a large number – of my terminal sessions in one very flexible window. I can organize my terminal sessions in many different ways due to the extreme power and flexibility of Tilix. Figure 14-5 shows a typical – at least for me – Tilix window with one of the two active sessions that contains three terminals. Each terminal in this session – session 2 of 2 – is connected to a different host using SSH. Note that the title bar in each terminal displays the user, host name, and current directory for that terminal.

The Tilix instance in Figure 14-5 is running on my personal workstation. I have used SSH to log into three different hosts in the student virtual network. The left half of the screen is a host that I use for testing, testvm1. The top-right terminal is logged into a VM server, studentvm2, that I have installed on my virtual test network.[3] The terminal at the

---

[3] The referenced server is created in Volume 3.

bottom right is logged into studentvm1. This can make it easy for me to monitor all three hosts in my virtual network. Some of the details may be difficult to see in Figure 14-5, but you can see how this ability to have multiple terminals open in a single emulator window can allow easy comparison of multiple systems or multiple utilities on a single host and can be very useful.

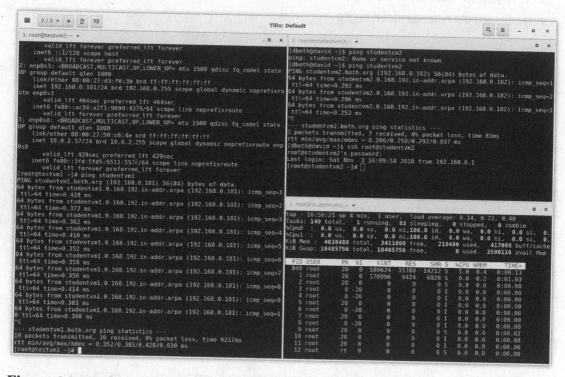

Figure 14-5. *This Tilix instance has two open sessions with two tabs active in the visible session with two terminals open on the tab on the right*

Let's ensure that we keep our terminology straight because it can be confusing. In Tilix, a "session" is a page in a Tilix window that contains one or more terminals. Opening a new session opens a new page with a single terminal emulation session. Tilix sessions can be created or subdivided horizontally and vertically, and general configuration can be performed using the tools on the Tilix title bar. Placing the window and session controls on the window title bar saves the space usually used for separate menu and icon bars.

EXPERIMENT 14-4: TILIX

As the student user, start by opening an instance of Tilix on your VM desktop. Like the other terminal emulators that provide for multiple terminal sessions in a single window, only one session is opened when the emulator is launched.

Figure 14-6 shows the top portion of the Tilix window with only one emulator session open. You can open another terminal in a new session, as defined previously, or in this session. For this instance, let's open a new terminal in this session vertically next to the existing terminal.

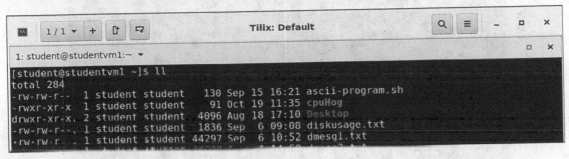

Figure 14-6. *The title bar of the Tilix window contains a non-standard set of icons that are used to help manage the terminal sessions*

On the left side of the title bar are the icons that let us open new terminals in various ways. The two icons in Figure 14-7 open a new terminal in the current session.

Figure 14-7. *These two icons allow you to open a new terminal either to the right of or under an active existing one*

Click the left icon of this pair to open a terminal to the right of the existing one. The session window will be split down the middle and will now contain two terminals, one on the left and one on the right. The result looks like that in Figure 14-8. These two side-by-side terminals allow you to do things like use top to watch the effects of commands executed in one terminal on system resources in the other.

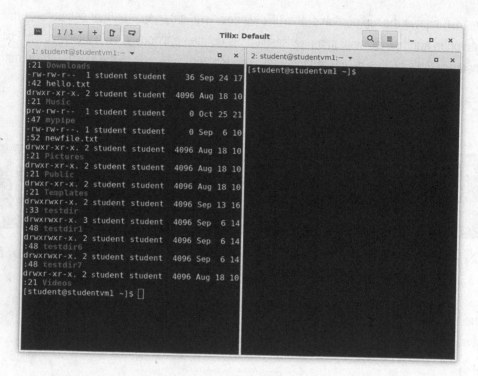

Figure 14-8. *The Tilix session after creation of a second terminal*

Now select the terminal on the left and click the button on the right of Figure 14-7. This opens a new terminal such that terminal 1 is on the top and terminal 3 is on the bottom, with terminal 2 still taking the entire right side of the session. Figure 14-9 shows how this looks.

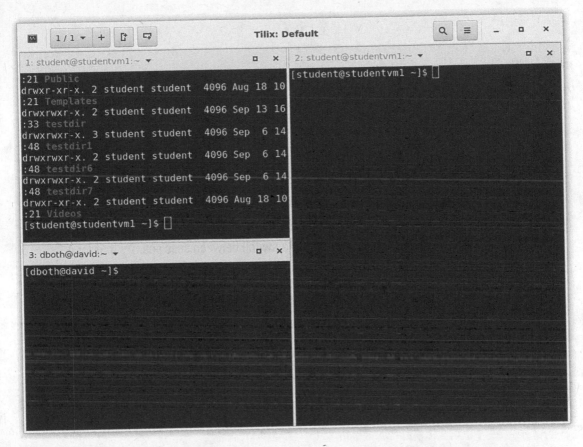

Figure 14-9. *The Tilix window now has three terminals in this one session*

You can move the splitters between the terminals to adjust their relative size. Adjust both the horizontal and vertical splitters to see how they work.

So far we have worked with only a single session. To create a second session in this Tilix window, click the plus sign (+) icon shown in Figure 14-10. The new session is created and is now the focus. The first session with its three terminals is now hidden. The count in the icon now shows "2/2" because we are in the second session. Click anywhere in the left part of this icon to show the sidebar. Displayed on the left of the Tilix window, the sidebar displays smaller images of the open sessions. Click the desired session to switch to it.

419

1 / 1 ▾ | +

Figure 14-10. *These icons allow you to create new sessions and navigate between them*

The icon on the far left of the title bar looks like a terminal screen, and we would normally expect that to be the standard System menu. For Tilix windows that would be incorrect. Tilix places its own menu in that icon. One of the choices in that menu is **Preferences**. Open the **Preferences** dialog.

I will let you find your own way through this Preferences dialog. I do suggest that you try switching from use of the sidebar to using tabs to switch between sessions. Try that for a while and see which you like better.

There is one default profile for configuring the look and feel of Tilix, and other profiles can be added as needed. Each profile sets alternate values for the functions and appearance of Tilix. Existing profiles can be cloned to provide a starting place for new ones.

To select from a list of profiles for an already open window, click the name of the terminal window and select **Profiles** and then the profile you want to change to. You can also select one profile to be the one used when a new Tilix session or terminal is launched.

For me, using a terminal emulator on a GUI desktop adds the power of a GUI to that of the command line. When using a terminal emulator like Tilix, Terminator, or Konsole that allows multiple pages and split screens, my ability to work efficiently is increased exponentially. Although there are other powerful terminal emulators out there that allow multiple terminal sessions in a single window, I have found that Tilix meets my need for this feature better than any I have tried so far.

Tilix offers me most standard features that xfce4-terminal, LXTerminal, Konsole, Terminator, and other terminal emulation software does while providing me some that they do not. It implements those features in a classy interface that is easy to learn, configure, and navigate, and it maximizes the use of on-screen real estate. I find that Tilix fits my desktop working style very nicely, and that is what it is all about, isn't it? The Tilix executable is 2.9MB in size, and it consumes 675MB of virtual memory when running.

There are other options for managing multiple terminal emulator sessions in a single window. We have already explored one of those, the GNU screen utility, and tmux (Terminal Multiplexer) is another. Both of these tools can be run in any terminal session using a single window, virtual console, or remote connection to provide creation of and access to multiple terminal emulator sessions in that one window. These two command-line tools are completely navigable by simple – or at least moderately simple – keystrokes. They do not require a GUI of any kind to run.

The terminal emulators we are discussing in this chapter, as well as many we are not, are GUI tools that use multiple tabs or the ability to split an emulator window into multiple panes, each with a terminal emulator session. Some of these GUI terminal emulators, like Tilix, can divide the screen into multiple panes and use tabs too. One of the advantages of having multiple panes is that it is easy to place sessions we want to compare or to observe together in a single window. It is easy, however, to split the screen into so many panes that there is not enough space in them to really see what is happening.

So we can use the fancy multi-paned, tabbed terminal emulators and then run screen or tmux in one or more of those emulator sessions. The only disadvantage I find to any of this is that I sometimes lose track of the existing sessions that are open and so forget that I already have one open already for a task I need to do. The combinations can get to be very complex.

All of these interesting features make it possible to manage a large number of terminal sessions in a few windows, which keeps my desktop less cluttered. Finding a particular session might be a bit problematic, though. It can also be easy to type a command into the wrong terminal session, which could create chaos.

Konsole

Konsole is the default terminal emulator for the KDE desktop environment. It can be installed and used with any desktop, but it does install a large number of KDE libraries and packages that are not needed by other terminal emulators. Konsole is my current favorite terminal emulator.

EXPERIMENT 14-5: KONSOLE

Open a Konsole terminal emulator instance. Let's make one configuration change before we go any further. Open **Settings ➤ Configure Konsole** and choose the **Tab Bar** tab. Change **Tab Bar Visibility** to **Always Show Tab Bar** and place a check mark in **Show 'New Tab'** and **'Close Tab' buttons**. Click the **OK** button to make these changes take effect. Konsole does not need to be restarted.

Now you can see that Konsole provides icons to open and close the tabs on either side of the tab bar, and it allows us to simply double-click in the empty space on the tab bar to open a new tab. New tabs can also be opened in the **File** menu.

Open a second tab using one of the methods just mentioned. Your Konsole window should now look like Figure 14-11.

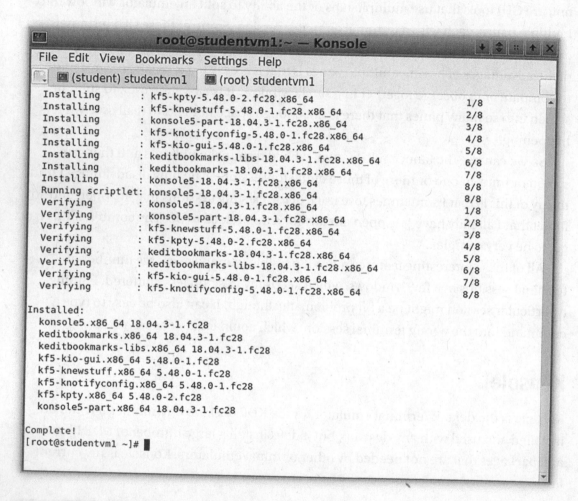

Figure 14-11. *The Konsole terminal emulator with two tabs open. A double-click in the empty space on the tab bar opens a new tab*

Konsole has a very flexible profiles capability, which can be accessed through **Settings ➤ Manage Profiles...**, which opens the **Configure** dialog. Select the **Profiles** tab and click **New Profile...** to create a new profile using this tab and configure it in different ways to explore the options here. Be sure to place a check mark in the **Show** column of the Profiles list to enable the new profile(s). Click **OK** to save the changes. Now open **Settings ➤ Switch Profile** and click the name of your new profile.

There are many other aspects of Konsole that you can explore. Take some additional time and let your curiosity take you to some of those interesting places.

I like Konsole very much because it provides tabs for multiple terminal sessions while maintaining a clean and simple user interface. I do have a concern about the KDE Plasma workspace because it seems to be expanding and becoming bloated and slow in general. I have experienced performance issues and crashes with the KDE Plasma desktop, but I have not had any performance problems with Konsole.

An instance of Konsole uses 859MB of virtual memory.

Terminator

Terminators is another powerful and feature-rich terminal emulator. Although it is based upon the GNOME terminal, its objective is to provide a tool for SysAdmins that can be used in many simultaneous terminals in tabs and grids within each tab.

EXPERIMENT 14-6: TERMINATOR

As the student user, open an instance of Terminator. Now right-click in the window to open the menu as seen in Figure 14-12. Choose **Split Vertically** to split the window in half and open a new terminal in the right half.

You may want to resize the Terminator window to make it larger as you proceed through the rest of this experiment.

Start the **top** program in the right terminal session. Open the man page for Terminator in the left terminal.

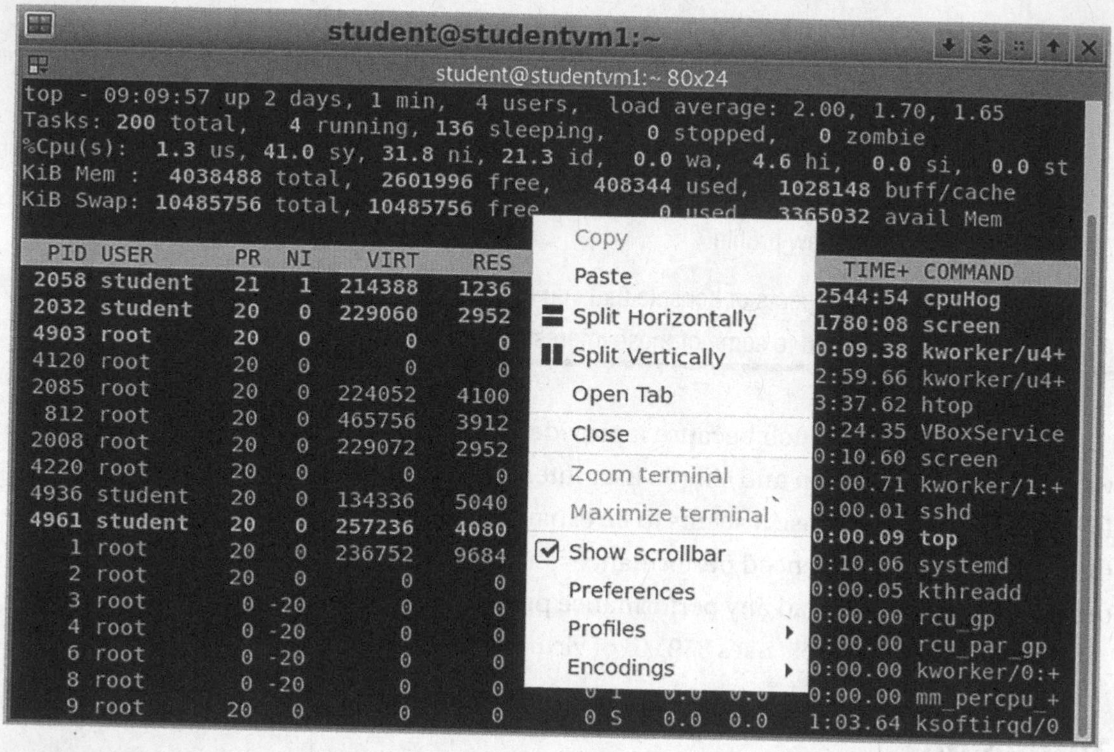

Figure 14-12. *All interaction with the Terminator features is through the pop-up menu*

Split the right-side terminal horizontally. The terminal with `top` running should be the upper one, and the new terminal should be on the bottom. Run a simple program like `ll` in the bottom-right terminal. Split the bottom-right terminal vertically.

It may help to adjust the relative sizes of the terminal sessions to make some larger in order to see better. The terminal sessions are delineated by drag bars. Move the mouse pointer over the vertical drag bar between the left and right sides. Then drag the bar to the left to make more room for the terminal sessions on the right.

Note   The double-arrow icons are used unlike any other application. When the pointer encounters a vertical drag bar, the up/down double-arrow icon is displayed. All other terminal emulators use the right/left arrow to indicate the direction in which movement is possible.

Your Terminator instance should look similar to Figure 14-13. Now open a second tab and split that tab into at least three terminal sessions.

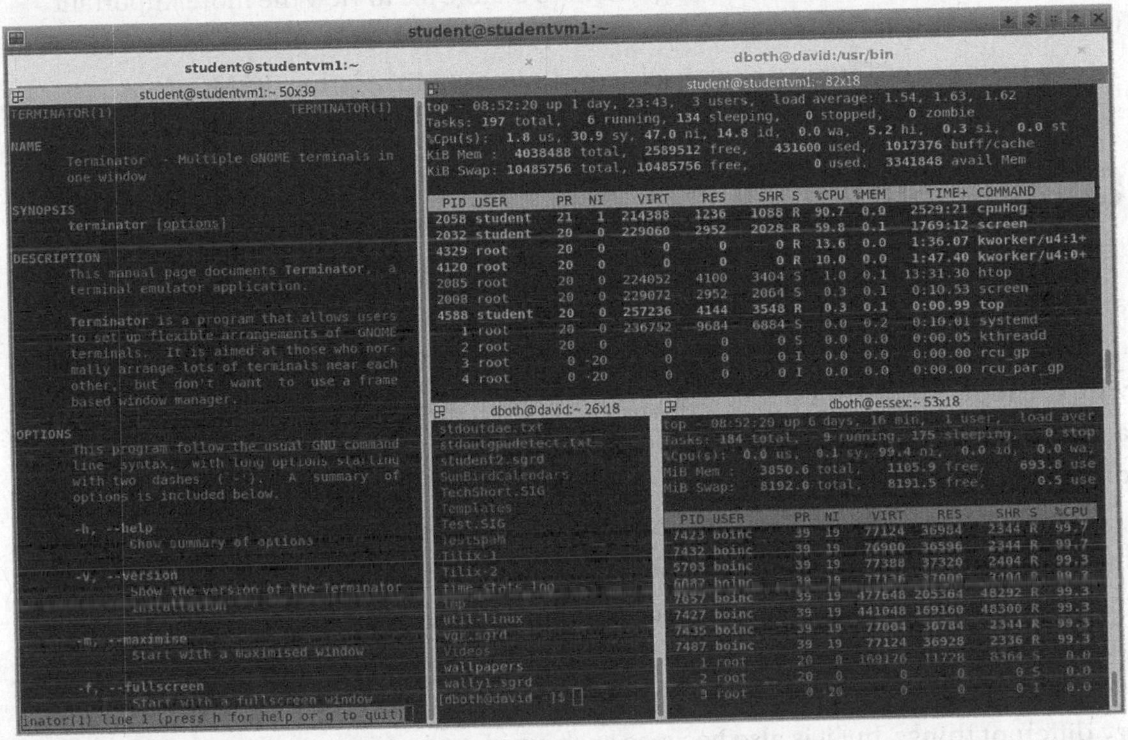

Figure 14-13. *A Terminator instance with two tabs open and four sessions in the visible tab*

Terminal sessions can be rearranged in the window using drag and drop. Select the title bar for one of the windows in the first tab. Drag that terminal session to another location in the window. Move the terminals around in the window to get a feel for how this feature works. Terminal sessions cannot be dragged to the desktop to open another Terminator window; they can be only dragged to other locations within the window in which they already exist.

Right-click to open the Terminator menu and choose **Preferences**. Here is where you can make configuration changes and create new profiles. Try creating a new profile using a green on black color scheme and a slightly larger font. Create a third profile using a color scheme of your own choosing. Switch between profiles. Each open terminal must be switched individually to the new scheme.

Spend some time exploring Terminator on your own, especially the various preferences.

I find it very useful when I need to have many terminal sessions open and to have several of them visible at the same time. I do find that I sometimes end up with many small windows, so I need to rearrange them to enable me to view the more important terminals.

An instance of Terminator typically consumes 753MB of virtual RAM.

Chapter Summary

As with almost every other aspect of Linux, there are many choices available to users and SysAdmins with respect to terminal emulators. I have tried many, but the ones I discussed in this chapter are generally those I have used the most and that provide me with the tools to work most efficiently. If you already have a favorite terminal emulator and I have not included it here, I apologize – there are just too many to include all of them.

I keep using each of these repeatedly because I like them, even if for different features. I also keep searching for other terminal emulators that I have not previously encountered because it is always good to learn about new things, and one of them might be the terminal emulator that I could use to the exclusion of all others.

My favorite terminal emulators change over time. I think that is because I do like to try different things, but it is also because each emulator has features that work better for different projects that I have going at any point in time.

You should spend some time using each of these terminal emulators outside the bounds of the experiments. Use different terminal emulators for the experiments in the rest of this course. That way you will have an opportunity to understand better how they can help leverage your use of the command line. Do not think that you must use any of these terminal emulators if they do not meet your needs. By all means try others you find and use the ones you like best. You may find that, like me, your favorites change over time.

Exercises

Perform the following exercises to complete this chapter:

1. Why are there so many choices for terminal emulators?

2. Add a profile to Tilix that configures it so that it meets your needs and wants better than the default. You might want to change colors, fonts, and the default terminal size.

3. Use DNF and the Internet to find new terminal emulators that were not explored in this chapter. Install at least two of them and explore their capabilities.

4. Of the terminal emulator features we have explored in this chapter, which ones are most important to you at this time?

5. Choose an appropriate terminal emulator and open terminal sessions in it so that you can start and view the following programs all at the same time – top, iotop, and sar to view network statistics in real time.

6. Have you developed a preference for a particular terminal emulator yet? If so, which one? Why?

CHAPTER 15

Advanced Shell Topics

Objectives

In this chapter you will learn

- Advanced usage of the bash shell

- The use of shell options

- The difference between internal and external commands

- How to plan for when commands fail

- How to determine whether an internal command or an external command will be used

- How to specify that the external command be used

- The use of globbing to match multiple file names to be acted upon by commands

- How the PATH variable affects which commands can be used

- Where to place shell scripts for use by one user or all users

- The use of command-line programs

- The use of basic flow control in simple command-line programs

- To use grep advanced pattern matching to extract lines from a data stream

- How to use find to locate files based on simple or complex criteria

© David Both 2023
D. Both, *Using and Administering Linux: Volume 1*, https://doi.org/10.1007/978-1-4842-9618-9_15

In Chapter 7 we looked briefly at the use of the bash shell and defined some terms to ensure that we have the same understanding of what a terminal emulator is vs. a shell vs. the command line and many more potentially confusing terms. In Chapter 9 we looked at some basic Linux commands and the use of some simple pipelines and redirection.

In this chapter we look more closely at the bash shell. We will explore in some detail the bash internal commands and the environment and the variables contained there. We explore the effect of the environment on the execution of shell commands. We will also make a start with command-line programming by exploring the capabilities of command-line programs and then moving on to some advanced tools, grep and find.

The Bash Shell

We have already been using the bash shell, and it should now seem at least a little familiar in the sense that we know a bit about how it works. A shell – any shell – is a command-line interpreter. The function of a shell is to take commands entered on the command line; expand any file globs, that is wildcard characters * and ? and sets, into complete file or directory names; convert the result into tokens for use by the kernel; and then pass the resulting command to the kernel for execution. The shell then sends any resulting output from execution of the command to STDOUT.

Bash is both a command interpreter and a programming language. It can be used to create large and complex programs that use all of the common programming language structures such as flow control and procedures. The bash shell is like any other command-line program. It can be called using command-line options and arguments. It also has an extensive man page to describe those and other aspects including its internal commands.

Shell Options

Bash shell options can be set when the bash executable is launched, but we as users do not usually have access to the command that launches the shell. So the creators of bash have provided us with the shopt (SHell OPTions) command that lets us view and alter many of the options that define the details of the shell's behavior while the shell is running.

The shopt command allows the user access to a superset of the options available with the bash set command. I have not found it necessary to change any of the options accessible to the shopt command, but I do use the set command to set command-line editing to vi mode.

The shopt command can be used without options to list the current state of the bash options that have been explicitly set to enabled or disabled. It does not list all of the options available. The bash man page has details of both set and shopt including all of the options they can be used to set.

EXPERIMENT 15-1: SHELL OPTIONS

Perform this experiment as the student user. We will just take a quick look at the shell options but won't change any of them. List the shell options by using the shopt command without any options or arguments:

```
[student@studentvm1 ~]$ shopt
autocd                  off
cdable_vars             off
cdspell                 off
checkhash               off
checkjobs               off
checkwinsize            on
cmdhist                 on
compat31                off
<snip>
nullglob                off
progcomp                on
promptvars              on
restricted_shell        off
shift_verbose           off
sourcepath              on
xpg_echo                off
```

I have pruned the preceding list, so you should see more output than shown here. As I mentioned, I have never had the need to change any of these shell options.

Shell Variables

We will explore environment and shell variables in more detail in Chapter 17, but let's take a quick look now.

A variable is a named entity that represents a location in memory that contains a value. The value of a variable is not fixed and can be changed as a result of various numeric or string operations. Bash shell variables are not typed; that is, they can be manipulated as a number or a string.

EXPERIMENT 15-2: SHELL VARIABLES

Perform this experiment as the student user. First, let's print the value of the $HOSTNAME variable in the shell because it already exists. Any time we wish to access the value of a variable in a script or from a CLI command, we use the $ sign to refer to it. The $ sign indicates to the bash shell that the name that follows (with no empty spaces) is the name of a variable:

```
[student@studentvm1 ~]$ echo $HOSTNAME
studentvm1
```

Now let's look at another variable – one that does not already exist that we will name MYVAR:

```
[student@studentvm1 ~]$ echo $MYVAR

[student@studentvm1 ~]$
```

Because this variable does not yet exist, it is null, so the shell prints a null line. Let's assign a value to this variable and then print the variable again:

```
[student@studentvm1 ~]$ MYVAR="Hello World!"
[student@studentvm1 ~]$ echo $MYVAR
Hello World!
[student@studentvm1 ~]$
```

So you can see that we use the variable name without the preceding $ sign to set a value into the variable. In this case the bash shell can infer from the context that the name followed by the equal sign is a variable name.

Tip   The bash shell syntax is very strict and sometimes requires spaces or requires no spaces. In the case of a variable assignment, there must be no spaces on either side of the equal sign.

I sometimes use "PATH" or "path" as a reference to the path as a general concept, but when I use $PATH it will always refer to the variable or its value.

Commands

The purpose of the shell is to make human interaction with the computer easy and efficient. Shells take the commands we type, modify them so the kernel will understand them, and pass them to the operating system, which then executes them. Shells provide the tools to enable this interaction.

Commands fall into two categories. There are internal commands that are an integral part of the shell program and external commands that are those with separate existence, that have their own executable files, such as the GNU and Linux core utilities. Other external commands are tools provided separately or by various Linux components such as logical volume management (LVM).

This distinction is important because shell internal commands are executed before an external command with the same name. For example, there is a bash internal echo command and the external echo command. Unless you specify the path to the external command as part of the command line, the bash internal echo command will be used. This may be a problem if the commands work a bit differently.

Let's get very specific about how the bash shell works when a command is entered:

1.   Type in the command and press Enter.

2.   Bash parses the command to see if there is a path prepended to the command name. If there is, skip to step 4.

3.   Bash checks to see if the command is internal. If it is, the bash shell forks a new sub-process and runs the command immediately. This forking takes time as well as system resources such as CPU, I/O, and RAM.

4. If a path is used as part of the command, Bash forks a new sub-process in which to execute the command and then runs the command. This forking takes time as well as system resources such as CPU, I/O, and RAM.

5. If no path to the command is specified and this is not an internal command, bash searches the list of aliases and shell functions – system and user-created procedures. If one is found, it forks a new shell sub-process and executes the function or alias. Again this all takes time although very small amounts.

6. If no alias or function is located, bash then searches the list of directories specified in the $PATH shell variable to locate the command. When the command is located, bash forks a new sub-shell to execute the command. More time is consumed.

7. If a command is run in a sub-shell, the sub-shell terminates, and execution returns to the parent shell.

The PATH

The $PATH is an important environment variable for the shell. It defines a colon-separated list of directories in which the system and the shell look for executable files. The shell looks in each directory listed in $PATH for executable files when a non-internal command is entered.

The $PATH environment variable can be altered for the current shell or for all shell instances for a specific user or even for all users. This is usually neither necessary nor desirable because the default $PATH takes into consideration the need of individual users to maintain executable files like shell scripts on their own home directory tree as we will see.

EXPERIMENT 15-3: EXPLORING $PATH

Perform this experiment as the student user. Let's start by discovering the default value of $PATH:

```
[student@studentvm1 ~]$ echo $PATH
/usr/local/bin:/usr/bin:/usr/local/sbin:/usr/sbin:/home/student/.local/bin:/
home/student/bin
```

Consider the elements of this PATH. The first is /usr/local/bin, which is a specifically defined location for storing locally created executable files such as shell scripts for SysAdmins or for use by all users. The /usr/local/etc directory is used for storing configuration files for the executables in /usr/local/bin.

The second element is /usr/bin. This is for most user executable binary files and is intended for use by all users. The third is /usr/local/sbin, which is for standard but non-essential system binaries for use by the SysAdmin.

The last two directory specifiers are in the user's directory tree. So if a user had some private executables, again such as personal shell scripts, those would usually be stored in ~/bin where the kernel will search for them because they are in the user's $PATH.

The $PATH saves a good bit of typing. Remember how we were required to start the cpuHog program?

```
./cpuHog
```

The reason we had to precede the command with ./ (dot-slash) is that the cpuHog executable shell script is in the student user's home directory, /home/student/, which is not part of $PATH.

Try it with the student user's home directory as the PWD and without specifying the home directory in some manner:

```
[student@studentvm1 ~]$ cpuHog
Bash: /home/student/bin/cpuHog: No such file or directory
```

We receive an error, so we need to specify the path using, in this case, the relative path of the current directory. The dot (.) notation is a shortcut for the current directory. We could have issued this command in the following ways:

- ./cpuHog

- ~/cpuHog

- /home/cpuHog

Terminate any currently running instances of the cpuHog. Ensure that the PWD for the student user is the home directory (~). Then let's try the two methods we have not yet used.

Method #1 assumes that the cpuHog script is in the PWD. Method #2 makes no assumptions about the current PWD and uses the ~ (tilde) shortcut for the user's home directory. Switch to a different directory and start the cpuHog using method #2:

```
[student@studentvm1 ~]$ cd /tmp ; ~/cpuHog
```

Use Ctrl-C to terminate this instance of the cpuHog. Remain in the /tmp/ directory and use method #3:

```
[student@studentvm1 tmp]$ /home/student/cpuHog
```

This method also works but it does require much more typing. All of these methods require more typing than simply placing the cpuHog file in the user's private executable file directory, ~/bin. Don't forget that the lazy SysAdmin does everything possible to type as few keystrokes as necessary.

Change the PWD to the home directory and find ~/bin. It is not there so we have to create it. We can do that, move the cpuHog into it, and launch the program – all in a single command-line program:

```
[student@studentvm1 ~]$ cd ; mkdir ~/bin ; mv cpuHog ./bin ; cpuHog
```

The function of the $PATH is to provide defined locations in which executable files can be stored so that it is not necessary to type out the path to them.

We will talk more about command-line programs later in this chapter.

Internal Commands

Linux shells have a large number of internal, built-in, commands of their own. The bash shell is no exception. The man and info pages provide a list of these commands, but which ones are the internal commands can be a bit difficult to dig out of all the other information.

These internal commands are part of the shell itself and do not have an existence outside the bash shell. This is why they are defined as "internal."

EXPERIMENT 15-4: INTERNAL COMMANDS

Perform this experiment as the student user. The **help** command is the easiest way to list the internal bash commands:

```
[student@studentvm1 ~]$ help
GNU bash, version 5.2.15(1)-release (x86_64-redhat-linux-gnu)
These shell commands are defined internally.  Type `help' to see this list.
Type `help name' to find out more about the function `name'.
Use `info bash' to find out more about the shell in general.
Use `man -k' or `info' to find out more about commands not in this list.

A star (*) next to a name means that the command is disabled.

 job_spec [&]                              history [-c] [-d offset] [n] or history -a>
 (( expression ))                          if COMMANDS; then COMMANDS; [ elif COMMAND>
 . filename [arguments]                    jobs [-lnprs] [jobspec ...] or jobs -x com>
 :                                         kill [-s sigspec | -n signum | -sigspec] p>
 [ arg... ]                                let arg [arg ...]
 [[ expression ]]                          local [option] name[=value] ...
 alias [-p] [name[=value] ... ]           logout [n]
 bg [job_spec ...]                         mapfile [-d delim] [-n count] [-O origin] >
 bind [-lpsvPSVX] [-m keymap] [-f filename] >  popd [-n] [+N | -N]
 break [n]                                 printf [-v var] format [arguments]
 builtin [shell-builtin [arg ...]]         pushd [-n] [+N | -N | dir]
 caller [expr]                             pwd [-LP]
 case WORD in [PATTERN [| PATTERN]...) COMMA>  read [-ers] [-a array] [-d delim] [-i text>
 cd [-L|[-P [-e]] [-@]] [dir]              readarray [-d delim] [-n count] [-O origin>
 command [-pVv] command [arg ...]          readonly [-aAf] [name[=value] ...] or read>
 compgen [-abcdefgjksuv] [-o option] [-A act>  return [n]
 complete [-abcdefgjksuv] [-pr] [-DEI] [-o o>  select NAME [in WORDS ... ;] do COMMANDS; >
```

```
compopt [-o|+o option] [-DEI] [name ...]        set [-abefhkmnptuvxBCEHPT] [-o option-name>
continue [n]                                    shift [n]
coproc [NAME] command [redirections]            shopt [-pqsu] [-o] [optname ...]
declare [-aAfFgiIlnrtux] [name[=value] ...]>    source filename [arguments]
dirs [-clpv] [+N] [-N]                          suspend [-f]
<SNIP>
```

Note   The greater than character, gt (>), at the ends of some lines in each column of the help output indicates that the line was truncated in the terminal for lack of space.

For details on each command, use the man page for bash or just type help with the name of the internal command, for example:

```
[student@studentvm1 ~]$ help echo
echo: echo [-neE] [arg ...]
    Write arguments to the standard output.

    Display the ARGs, separated by a single space character and followed by a
    newline, on the standard output.
<snip>
```

The man pages provide information for external commands only. The information for the internal commands is only located in the man and info pages for bash itself:

```
[student@studentvm1 ~]$ man bash
```

To find the shell internal commands, search /^SHELL BUILTIN. Yes, in all caps.

The forward slash (/) starts the search. The caret (^) is an anchor character that indicates that the search should only find this string if it starts at the beginning of the line. This string does appear in many places, but those all refer to the single location where it starts the section at the beginning of the line, saying, "see SHELL BUILTIN COMMANDS below."

Each internal command is listed in the SHELL BUILTIN COMMANDS section along with its syntax and possible options and arguments. Many of the bash internal commands, such as for, continue, break, declare, getopts, and others, are for use in scripts or command-line programs rather than as stand-alone commands on the command line. We will look at some of these later in this chapter. Scroll through the SHELL BUILTIN COMMANDS section of the bash man page.

Let's take three of these commands and use the type utility to identify them:

```
[student@studentvm1 ~]$ type echo getopts egrep
echo is a shell builtin
getopts is a shell builtin
egrep is aliased to `egrep --color=auto'
```

The type command enables us to easily identify those commands that are shell internals. Like many Linux commands, it can take a list of arguments.

External Commands

External commands are those that exist as executable files and that are not part of the shell. These are executable files stored in locations like /bin, /usr/bin, /sbin, and so on.

EXPERIMENT 15-5: EXTERNAL COMMANDS

First, make /bin the PWD and do a long list of the files there.

```
[student@studentvm1 bin]$ ll | less
```

Scroll through the list and locate some familiar commands. You will also find both echo and getopts in these external commands. Why did the type command not show us this? It can if we use the -a option, which locates commands in any form, even aliases:

```
[student@studentvm1 bin]$ type -a echo getopts egrep
echo is a shell builtin
echo is /usr/bin/echo
getopts is a shell builtin
getopts is /usr/bin/getopts
egrep is aliased to `egrep --color=auto'
egrep is /usr/bin/egrep
[student@studentvm1 bin]$
```

The **type** command searches for executables in the same sequence as the shell would search if it were going to execute the command. Without the -a option, **type** stops at the first instance, thus showing the executable that would run if the command were to be executed. The -a option tells it to display all instances.

What about our **cpuHog** shell script? What does **type** tell us about that? Try it and find out.

Forcing the Use of External Commands

As we have seen, it is possible for both internal and external versions of some commands to be present at the same time. When this occurs one command may work a bit differently from the other – despite having the same name – and we need to be aware of that possibility in order to use the command that provides the desired result.

If it becomes necessary to ensure that the external command runs and that the internal command with the same name does not, simply add the path to the command name as in /usr/bin/echo. This is where an understanding of how the bash shell searches for and executes commands is helpful.

Command-Line Programs

We have already used some very simple command-line programs. The simplest form of command-line programs is just stringing several commands together in a sequence on the command line; such commands are separated by a semicolon, which defines the end of a command.

You can build up command-line programs in the same way as you built complex pipelines of commands. To create a simple series of commands on a single line, simply separate each command using a semicolon, like this:

```
command1 ; command2 ; command3 ; command4 ; … etc. ;
```

No final semicolon is required because pressing the Enter key implies the end of the final command. Adding that last semicolon for consistency is fine. This list of several commands might be something like we did at the end of Experiment 15-3 in which we created a new directory, moved the cpuHog file into that directory, and then executed the cpuHog. In such a case, the functioning of later commands does depend upon the correct result of the preceding commands:

```
cd ; mkdir ~/bin ; mv cpuHog ./bin ; cpuHog
```

Those commands will all run without a problem so long as no errors occur. But what happens when an error occurs? We can anticipate and allow for errors using the **&&** and **||** built-in bash control operators. These two control operators provide us with some flow control and enable us to alter the sequence of code execution. The semicolon is also considered to be a bash control operator as is the newline character.

The && operator simply says that if command1 is successful, then run command2. If command1 fails for any reason, then command2 is skipped. That syntax looks like this:

```
command1 && command2
```

This works because every command sends a return code (RC) to the shell that indicates whether it completed successfully or there was some type of failure during execution. By convention a return code of zero (0) indicates success, while any positive number indicates some type of failure. Some of the tools we use as SysAdmins return only a one (1) to indicate a failure, but many can return other codes as well to further define the type of failure that occurred.

The bash shell has a variable, $?, that can be checked very easily by a script, the next command in a list of commands, or even us SysAdmins.

EXPERIMENT 15-6: COMMAND-LINE PROGRAMS

First, look at return codes. Run a simple command and then immediately check the return code. The return code will always be for the last command that was run prior to viewing $?:

```
[student@studentvm1 ~]$ ll ; echo "RC = $?"
total 284
-rw-rw-r--  1 student student   130 Sep 15 16:21 ascii-program.sh
drwxrwxr-x  2 student student  4096 Nov 10 11:09 bin
drwxr-xr-x. 2 student student  4096 Aug 18 17:10 Desktop
-rw-rw-r--. 1 student student  1836 Sep  6 09:08 diskusage.txt
-rw-rw-r--. 1 student student 44297 Sep  6 10:52 dmesg1.txt
<snip>
drwxrwxr-x. 2 student student  4096 Sep  6 14:48 testdir7
drwxr-xr-x. 2 student student  4096 Aug 18 10:21 Videos
RC = 0
[student@studentvm1 ~]$
```

The return code (RC) is zero (0), which means the command completed successfully. Now try the same command on a directory for which we do not have permissions:

```
[student@studentvm1 ~]$ ll /root ; echo "RC = $?"
ls: cannot open directory '/root': Permission denied
RC = 2
[student@studentvm1 ~]$
```

441

Where can you find the meaning of this return code? Yes, I mean for you to find it.

Try the && control operator as it might be used in a command-line program. We start with something simple. Our objective is to create a new directory and create a new file in it. We only want to do this if the directory can be created successfully.

We can use ~/testdir, which was created in a previous chapter for this experiment. The following command is intended to create a new directory in ~/testdir, which should currently be empty. The -p option means create any necessary parent directories, so this command will also create the ~/testdir if it does not already exist. You can run the tree -d command to see the current directory structure before we create the new ones:

```
[student@studentvm1 ~]$ tree
.
├── cpuHog
├── Desktop
├── diskusage.txt
├── dmesg1.txt
├── dmesg2.txt
├── dmesg3.txt
├── dmesg4.txt
├── Documents
├── Downloads
├── Music
├── mypipe
├── newfile.txt
├── Pictures
├── Public
├── Templates
├── testdir
├── testdir1
│   └── testdir2
│       └── testdir3
│           └── testdir4
│               └── testdir5
├── testdir6
├── testdir7
├── Videos
└── zoom_x86_64.rpm
```

```
17 directories, 9 files
[student@studentvm1 ~]$ mkdir -p ~/testdir/testdir8 && touch ~/testdir/
testdir8/testfile1
[student@studentvm1 ~]$ tree
.
├── cpuHog
<SNIP>
├── Templates
├── testdir
│   └── testdir8
│       └── testfile1
├── testdir1
│   └── testdir2
│       └── testdir3
│           └── testdir4
│               └── testdir5
├── testdir6
├── testdir7
├── Videos
└── zoom_x86_64.rpm

18 directories, 10 files
[student@studentvm1 ~]$
```

Everything worked as it should because the testdir directory is accessible and writable.

Change the permissions on testdir so it is no longer accessible to the student user. We will explore file ownership and permissions in Chapter 18 of this volume:

```
[student@studentvm1 ~]$ chmod 076 testdir ; ll | grep testdir ; tree
d---rwxrw-  2 student student      4096 Jan 27 08:05 testdir
drwxr-xr-x. 3 student student      4096 Jan 21 16:36 testdir1
drwxr-xr-x. 2 student student      4096 Jan 21 16:36 testdir6
drwxr-xr-x. 2 student student      4096 Jan 21 16:36 testdir7
.
├── cpuHog
<SNIP>
├── Templates
├── testdir  [error opening dir]
```

443

```
├── testdir1
│       └── testdir2
│               └── testdir3
│                       └── testdir4
<SNIP>
├── Videos
└── zoom_x86_64.rpm

17 directories, 9 files
[student@studentvm1 ~]$
```

Using the grep command after the long list (**ll**) shows us the listing for all directories with testdir in their names. You can see that the user student no longer has any access to the testdir directory.[1] Now let's run almost the same commands as before but with a different directory name to create in testdir:

```
[student@studentvm1 ~]$ mkdir ~/testdir/testdir9 && touch ~/testdir/testdir9/
testfile1
mkdir: cannot create directory '/home/student/testdir/testdir9':
Permission denied
[student@studentvm1 ~]$
```

Using the && control operator prevents the touch command from running because there was an error in creating testdir9. This type of command-line program flow control can prevent errors from compounding and making a real mess of things. But let's get a little more complicated.

The || control operator allows us to add another program statement that executes when the initial program statement returns a code larger than zero. The basic syntax looks like this:

```
command1 || command2
```

This syntax reads: if command1 fails, execute command2. That implies that if command1 succeeds, command2 is skipped. Let's try this with our attempt to create a new directory:

```
[student@testvm1 ~]$ mkdir ~/testdir/testdir9 || echo "testdir9 was not created."
mkdir: cannot create directory '/home/student/testdir/testdir9':
Permission denied
testdir9 was not created.
[student@testvm1 ~]$
```

---

[1] We will explore file and directory permissions in detail in Chapter 18.

This is exactly what we expected. Because the new directory could not be created, the first command failed, which resulted in execution of the second command.

Combining these two operators gives us the best of both:

```
[student@studentvm1 ~]$ mkdir ~/testdir/testdir9 && touch ~/testdir/testdir9/
testfile1 || echo "."
mkdir: cannot create directory '/home/student/testdir/testdir9':
Permission denied

[student@studentvm1 ~]$
```

Now reset the permissions on ~/testdir to 775 and try this last command again.

Our command-line programs' syntax using some flow control now takes this general form when we use both of the && and || control operators:

```
preceding commands ; command1 && command2 || command3 ; following commands
```

This syntax can be stated like so: if command1 exits with a return code of 0, then execute command2; otherwise, execute command3. The command-line programs using the control operators may be preceded and followed by other commands that can be related to the ones in the flow control section but that are unaffected by the flow control. All of the preceding and following commands will execute without regard to anything that takes place inside the flow control command-line programs.

Time-Saving Tools

There are some additional tools that we have available both as SysAdmins and non-privileged users that give us a lot of flexibility when performing a wide range of tasks. The use of globbing and sets enables us to match character strings in file names and data streams in order to perform further transformations or actions on them. Brace expansion lets us expand strings that have some commonalities into multiple but different strings. We have already seen several of the meta-characters available in bash; they provide programming capabilities that greatly enhance the functionality of the shell.

Brace Expansion

Let's start with brace expansion because we will use this tool to create a large number of files to use in experiments with special pattern characters. Brace expansion can be used to generate lists of arbitrary strings and insert them into a specific location within an enclosing static string or at either end of a static string. This may be hard to visualize, so let's just do it.

EXPERIMENT 15-7: BRACE EXPANSION

First, let's just see what a basic brace expansion does:

```
[student@studentvm1 ~]$ echo {string1,string2,string3}
string1 string2 string3
```

Well, that is not very helpful, is it? But look what happens when we use it just a bit differently:

```
[student@studentvm1 ~]$ echo "Hello "{David,Jen,Rikki,Jason}.
Hello David. Hello Jen. Hello Rikki. Hello Jason.
```

That looks like something we might be able to use because it can save a good deal of typing. Now try this:

```
[student@studentvm1 ~]$ echo b{ed,olt,ar}s
beds bolts bars
```

Here is how we can generate file names for testing:

```
[student@studentvm1 ~]$ echo testfile{0,1,2,3,4,5,6,7,8,9}.txt
testfile0.txt testfile1.txt testfile2.txt testfile3.txt testfile4.txt
testfile5.txt testfile6.txt testfile7.txt testfile8.txt testfile9.txt
```

And here is an even better method for creating sequentially numbered files:

```
[student@studentvm1 ~]$ echo test{0..9}.file
test0.file test1.file test2.file test3.file test4.file test5.file test6.file
test7.file test8.file test9.file
```

The {x..y} syntax, where x and y are integers, expands to be all integers between and including x and y. The following is a little more illustrative of that:

```
[student@studentvm1 ~]$ echo test{20..54}.file
test20.file test21.file test22.file test23.file test24.file test25.file
test26.file test27.file test28.file test29.file test30.file test31.file
test32.file test33.file test34.file test35.file test36.file test37.file
test38.file test39.file test40.file test41.file test42.file test43.file
test44.file test45.file test46.file test47.file test48.file test49.file
test50.file test51.file test52.file test53.file test54.file
```

Now try this one:

```
[student@studentvm1 ~]$ echo test{0..9}.file{1..4}
```

And this one:

```
[student@studentvm1 ~]$ echo test{0..20}{a..f}.file
```

And this one, which prepends leading zeros to keep the length of the numbers and thus the length of the file names equal. This makes for easy searching and sorting:

```
[student@studentvm1 ~]$ echo test{000..200}{a..f}.file
```

So far all we have done is to create long lists of strings. Before we do something more or less productive, let's move into a directory in which we can play around… I mean experiment with creating and working with files. If you have not already done so, make the directory ~/testdir7 the PWD. Verify that there are no other files in this directory and delete them if there are.

Now let's change the format just a bit and then actually create files using the results as file names:

```
[student@studentvm1 testdir7]$ touch {my,your,our}.test.file.{000..200}
{a..f}.{txt,asc,file,text}
```

That was fast. I want to know just how fast, so let's delete the files we just created and use the time command to, well, time how long it takes:

```
[student@studentvm1 testdir7]$ rm ~/testdir7/* ; time touch {my,your,our}.
test.file.{000..200}{a..f}.{txt,asc,file,text}
```

```
real    0m0.385s
user    0m0.056s
sys  -  0m0.321s
[student@studentvm1 testdir7]$
```

447

It took .385 seconds of real time to create 14,472 empty files. Verify that using the **wc** command. If you get 14,473 as the result, why? Can you find a simple way to obtain the correct result?

You will use these files in some of the following experiments. Do not delete them.

Special Pattern Characters

Although most SysAdmins talk about file globbing,[2] we really mean special pattern characters that allow us significant flexibility in matching file names and other strings when performing various actions. These special pattern characters allow matching single, multiple, or specific characters in a string.

- ?: Matches only one of any character in the specified location within the string.

- *: Zero or more of any character in the specified location within the string.

In all likelihood you have used these before. Let's experiment with some ways we can use these effectively.

EXPERIMENT 15-8: SPECIAL PATTERN CHARACTERS

You might have used file globbing to answer the question I posed in Experiment 15-7:

```
[student@studentvm1 testdir7]$ ls *test* | wc
   14472    14472   340092
[student@studentvm1 testdir7]$
```

In order to achieve this result, we must understand the structure of the file names we created. They all contain the string "test", so we can use that. The command uses the shell's built-in file globbing to match all files that contain the string "test" anywhere in their names and that can have any number of any character both before and after that one specific string. Let's just see what that looks like without counting the number of lines in the output:

```
[student@studentvm1 testdir7]$ ls *test*
```

---

[2]Wikipedia, *Glob*, https://en.wikipedia.org/wiki/Glob_(programming)

I am sure that "you" don't want any of "my" files in your home directory. First, see how many of "my" files there are and then delete them all and verify that there are none left:

```
[student@studentvm1 testdir7]$ ls my* | wc ; rm -v my* ; ls my*
```

The -v option of the **rm** command lists every file as it deletes it. This information could be redirected to a log file for keeping a record of what was done. This file glob enables the ls command to list every file that starts with "my" and perform actions on them.

Find all of "our" files that have txt as the ending extension:

```
[student@studentvm1 testdir7]$ ls our*txt | wc
```

Locate all files that contain 6 in the tens position of the three-digit number embedded in the file names and that end with asc:

```
[student@studentvm1 testdir7]$ ls *e.?6?*.asc
```

We must do this with a little extra work to ensure that we specify the positioning of the "6" carefully to prevent listing all of the files that only contain a 6 in the hundreds or ones position but not in the tens position of the three-digit number. We know that none of the file names contains 6 in the hundreds position, but this makes our glob a bit more general so that it would work in both of those cases.

We do not care whether the file name starts with our or your, but we use the final "e." of "file." – with the dot – to anchor the next three characters. After "e." in the file name, all of the files have three digits. We do not care about the first and third digits, just the second one. So we use the ? to explicitly define that we have one and only one character before and after the 6. We then use the * to specify that we don't care how many or which characters we have after that but that we do want to list files that end with "asc".

We want to add some content to some of the files. The file pattern specification we have now is almost where we want it. Let's add content to all files that have a 6 in the middle position of the three-digit number, but which also have an "a" after the number, as in x6xa. We want all files that match this pattern regardless of the trailing extension, asc, txt, text, or file.

First, let's make certain that our pattern works correctly:

```
[student@studentvm1 testdir7]$ ls *e.?6?a.*
our.test.file.060a.asc    our.test.file.163a.text    your.test.file.067a.asc
our.test.file.060a.file   our.test.file.163a.txt     your.test.file.067a.file
our.test.file.060a.text   our.test.file.164a.asc     your.test.file.067a.text
```

```
our.test.file.060a.txt    our.test.file.164a.file    your.test.file.067a.txt
our.test.file.061a.asc    our.test.file.164a.text    your.test.file.068a.asc
our.test.file.061a.file   our.test.file.164a.txt     your.test.file.068a.file
our.test.file.061a.text   our.test.file.165a.asc     your.test.file.068a.text
<snip>
our.test.file.162a.file   your.test.file.065a.txt    your.test.file.169a.file
our.test.file.162a.text   your.test.file.066a.asc    your.test.file.169a.text
our.test.file.162a.txt    your.test.file.066a.file   your.test.file.169a.txt
our.test.file.163a.asc    your.test.file.066a.text
our.test.file.163a.file   your.test.file.066a.txt
```

That looks like what we want. The full list is 160 files. We want to store some arbitrary data in these files, so we need to install a little program to generate random passwords, pwgen. Normally this tool would be used to generate decent passwords, but we can just as easily use this random data for other things too. It might already be installed but let's make sure:

```
[root@studentvm1 ~]# dnf -y install pwgen
```

Test the pwgen tool. The following CLI command generates 50 lines of 80 random characters each:

```
[root@studentvm1 ~]# pwgen 80 50
```

Now we will build a short command-line program to place a little random data into each existing file that matches the pattern:

```
[student@studentvm1 testdir7]$ for File in `ls *e.?6?a.*` ; do pwgen 80 50 >
$File ; done
```

To verify that these files contain some data, we check the file sizes:

```
[student@studentvm1 testdir7]$ ll *e.?6?a.*
```

Use cat to view the content of a few of the files.

File globbing – the use of special pattern characters to select file names from a list – is a powerful tool. However, there is an extension of these special patterns that gives us more flexibility and that makes things we could do with complex patterns much easier. This tool is the set.

Sets

Sets are a form of special pattern characters. They provide a means to specify that a particular one-character location in a string contains any character from the list inside the square braces []. Sets can be used alone or in conjunction with other special pattern characters.

A set can consist of one or more characters that will be compared against the characters in a specific, single position in the string for a match. The following list shows some typical example sets and the string characters they match:

[0-9]: Any numerical character

[a-z]: Lowercase alpha

[A-Z]: Uppercase alpha

[a-zA-Z]: Any uppercase or lowercase alpha

[abc]: The three lowercase alpha characters, a, b, and c

[!a-z]: No lowercase alpha

[!5-7]: No numbers 5, 6, or 7

[a-gxz]: Lowercase a through g, x, and z

[A-F0-9]: Uppercase A through F or any numeric

Once again, this will be easier to explain if we just go right to the experiment.

EXPERIMENT 15-9: SETS

Perform this experiment as the student user. The PWD should still be ~/testdir7. Start by finding the files that contain a 6 in the center of the three-digit number in the file name:

```
[student@studentvm1 testdir7]$ ls *[0-9]6[0-9]*
```

We could use this alternate pattern because we know that the leftmost digit must be 0 or 1. Count the number of file names returned for both cases to verify this:

```
[student@studentvm1 testdir7]$ ls *[01]6[0-9]*
```

Now let's look for the file names that contain a 6 in only the center position, but not in either of the other two digits:

```
[student@studentvm1 testdir7]$ ls *[!6]6[!6]*
```

Find the files that match the pattern we have so far but which also end in t:

```
[student@studentvm1 testdir7]$ ls *[!6]6[!6]*t
```

Now find all of the files that match the preceding pattern but which also have "a" or "e" immediately following the number:

```
[student@studentvm1 testdir7]$ ls *[!6]6[!6][ae]*t
```

These are just a few examples of using sets. Continue to experiment with them to enhance your understanding.

Sets provide a powerful extension to pattern matching that gives us even more flexibility in searching for files. It is important to remember, however, that the primary use of these tools is not merely to "find" these files so we can look at their names. It is to locate files that match a pattern so that we can perform some operation on them, such as deleting, moving, adding text to them, searching their contents for specific character strings, and more.

Meta-characters

Meta-characters are ones that have special meaning to the shell. The bash shell has defined a number of these meta-characters, many of which we have already encountered in our explorations:

$	Shell variable
~	Home directory variable
&	Run command in background
;	Command termination/separation
>, >>, <	I/O redirection

|	Command pipe
; " \	Meta quotes
$()	Command substitution – preferred POSIX standard method
`...`	Command substitution
(), {}	Command grouping
&&, ||	Shell control operators; conditional command execution

As we progress further through this course, we will explore the meta-characters we already know in more detail, and we will learn about the few we do not already know.

Using grep

Using file globbing patterns can be very powerful, as we have seen. We have been able to perform many tasks on large numbers of files very efficiently. As its name implies, however, file globbing is intended for use on file names, so it does not work on the content of those files. It is also somewhat limited in its capabilities.

There is a tool, grep, that can be used to extract and print to STDOUT all of the lines from a data stream based on matching patterns. Those patterns can range from simple text patterns to very complex regular expressions (regex). Written by Ken Thompson[3] and first released in 1974, the grep utility is provided by the GNU Project[4] and is installed by default on every version of Unix and Linux distribution I have ever used.

In terms of globbing characters, which grep does not understand, the default search pattern for the grep command is *PATTERN*. There is an implicit wildcard match before and after the search pattern. Thus, you can assume that any pattern you specify will be found no matter where it exists in the lines being scanned. It could be at the beginning, anywhere in the middle, or at the end. Thus, it is not necessary to explicitly state that there are characters in the string before and/or after the string for which we are searching.

---

[3] Wikipedia, *Ken Thompson*, https://en.wikipedia.org/wiki/Ken_Thompson
[4] The GNU Project, www.gnu.org

EXPERIMENT 15-10: USING GREP

Perform this experiment as root. Although non-privileged users have access to some of the data we will be searching, only root has access to all of it.

One of the most common tasks I do that requires the use of the grep utility is scanning through log files to find information pertaining to specific things. For example, I may need to determine information about how the operating system sees the network interface cards (NICs) starting with their BIOS names,[5] ethX. Information about the NICs installed in the host can be found using the dmesg command as well as in the messages log files in /var/log.

We'll start by looking at the output from dmesg. First, just pipe the output through less and use the search facility built into less:

```
[root@studentvm1 ~]# dmesg | less
```

You can page through the screens generated by less and use the Mark I Eyeball[6] to locate the "eth" string, or you can use the search. Initiate the search facility by typing the slash (/) character and then the string for which you are searching: /eth. The search will highlight the string, and you can use the "n" key to find the next instance of the string and the "b" key to search backward for the previous instance.

Searching through pages of data, even with a good search facility, is easier than eyeballing it, but not as easy as using grep. The -i option tells grep to ignore case and display the "eth" string regardless of the case of its letters. It will find the strings eth, ETH, Eth, eTh, and so on, which are all different in Linux:

```
[root@studentvm1 ~]# dmesg | grep -i eth
[    1.861192] e1000 0000:00:03.0 eth0: (PCI:33MHz:32-bit) 08:00:27:a9:e6:b4
[    1.861199] e1000 0000:00:03.0 eth0: Intel(R) PRO/1000 Network Connection
[    2.202563] e1000 0000:00:08.0 eth1: (PCI:33MHz:32-bit) 08:00:27:50:58:d4
[    2.202568] e1000 0000:00:08.0 eth1: Intel(R) PRO/1000 Network Connection
[    2.205334] e1000 0000:00:03.0 enp0s3: renamed from eth0
[    2.209591] e1000 0000:00:08.0 enp0s8: renamed from eth1
[root@studentvm1 ~]#
```

---

[5] Most modern Linux distributions rename the NICs from the old BIOS names, ethX, to something like enp0s3. That is a discussion we will encounter in Chapters 36 and 38 of Volume 2.

[6] Wikipedia, *Visual Inspection*, https://en.wikipedia.org/wiki/Visual_inspection

These results show data about the BIOS names, the PCI bus on which they are located, the MAC addresses, and the new names that Linux has given them. Now look for instances of the string that begins the new NIC names, "enp". Did you find any?

Note   The numbers enclosed in square braces, [2.205334], are timestamps that indicate the log entry was made that number of seconds after the kernel took over control of the computer.

In this first example of usage, grep takes the incoming data stream using STDIN and then sends the output to STDOUT. The grep utility can also use a file as the source of the data stream. We can see that in this next example in which we grep through the messages log files for information about our NICs:

```
[root@studentvm1 ~]$ cd /var/log ; grep -i eth messages*
<snip>
messages-20181111:Nov  6 09:27:36 studentvm1 dbus-daemon[830]: [system]
Rejected send message, 2 matched rules; type="method_call", sender=":1.89"
(uid=1000 pid=1738 comm="/usr/bin/pulseaudio --daemonize=no ")
interface="org.freedesktop.DBus.ObjectManager" member="GetManagedObjects"
error name="(unset)" requested_reply="0" destination="org.bluez" (bus)
messages-20181111:Nov  6 09:27:36 studentvm1 pulseaudio[1738]: E:
[pulseaudio] bluez5-util.c: GetManagedObjects() failed: org.freedesktop.
DBus.Error.AccessDenied: Rejected send message, 2 matched rules;
type="method_call", sender=":1.89" (uid=1000 pid=1738 comm="/usr/bin/
pulseaudio --daemonize=no ") interface="org.freedesktop.DBus.ObjectManager"
member="GetManagedObjects" error name="(unset)" requested_reply="0"
destination="org.bluez" (bus)
messages-20181118:Nov 16 07:41:00 studentvm1 kernel: e1000 0000:00:03.0 eth0:
(PCI:33MHz:32-bit) 08:00:27:a9:e6:b4
messages-20181118:Nov 16 07:41:00 studentvm1 kernel: e1000 0000:00:03.0 eth0:
Intel(R) PRO/1000 Network Connection
messages-20181118:Nov 16 07:41:00 studentvm1 kernel: e1000 0000:00:08.0 eth1:
(PCI:33MHz:32-bit) 08:00:27:50:58:d4
messages-20181118:Nov 16 07:41:00 studentvm1 kernel: e1000 0000:00:08.0 eth1:
Intel(R) PRO/1000 Network Connection
<SNIP>
```

The first part of each line in our output data stream is the name of the file in which the matched lines were found. If you do a little exploration of the current messages file, which is named just that with no appended date, you may or may not find any lines matching our search pattern. I did not with my VM, so using the file glob to create the pattern "messages*" searches all of the files starting with messages. This file glob matching is performed by the shell and not by the grep tool.

You will notice also that, on this first try, we found more than we wanted. Some lines have the "eth" string in them that was found as part of the word "method." So let's be a little more explicit and use a set as part of our search pattern:

```
[root@studentvm1 log]# grep -i eth[0-9] messages*
```

This is better, but we also want the lines that pertain to our NICs after they were renamed. So we now know the names that our old NIC names were changed to, so we can also search for those. Fortunately for us, grep provides some interesting options such as using -e to specify multiple search expressions. Each search expression must be specified using a separate instance of the -e option:

Tip   Each expression is additive. That is, the eth[0-9] expression finds all messages that contain that phrase, and the enp0 expression finds all messages that contain that one. So lines containing either one or the other or both expressions are displayed. Therefore, this next command will produce a long data stream.

```
[root@studentvm1 log]# grep -i -e eth[0-9] -e enp0 messages*
```

That does work, but there is also an extension that allows us to search using extended regular expressions.[7] The **grep** patterns we have been using so far are basic regular expressions (BRE). To get more complex, we can use extended regular expressions (ERE). To do this we can use egrep:

```
[root@studentvm1 log]# egrep "eth[0-9] | enp0" messages*
```

---

[7] Chapter 25 in Volume 2 explores the subject of Regular Expressions in detail.

You may wish to use the wc (word count) command to verify that both of the last two commands produce the same number of lines for their results.

Note that the extended regular expression is enclosed in double quotes.

Now make /etc the PWD. Sometimes I have previously needed to list all of the configuration files in the /etc directory. These files typically end with a .conf or .cnf extension or with rc. To do this we need an anchor to specify that the search string is at the end of the string being searched. We use the dollar sign ($) for that. The syntax of the search string in the following command finds all the configuration files with the listed endings. The -R option for the **ll** or **ls** command causes the command to recurse into all of the subdirectories:

```
[root@studentvm1 etc]# ls -aR | grep -E "conf$|cnf$|rc$"
```

Use word count to display the number of files selected and then use the equivalent egrep command and see that it selects the same number of files.

We can also use the caret (^) to anchor the beginning of the string. Suppose that we want to locate all files in /etc that begin with kde because they are used in the configuration of the KDE desktop:

```
[root@studentvm1 etc]# ls -R | grep -E "^kde"
kde
kde4rc
kderc
kde.csh
kde.sh
kdebugrc
```

One of the advanced features of **grep** is the ability to read the search patterns from a file containing one or more patterns. This is very useful if the same complex searches must be performed on a regular basis.

The **grep** tool is powerful and complex. The man page offers a good amount of information, and the GNU Project provides a free 36-page manual[8] to assist with learning and using **grep**. That document is available in HTML so it can be read online with a web browser, as ASCII text, as an info document, as a downloadable PDF file, and more.

---

[8]GNU Project, *GNU grep*, `www.gnu.org/software/grep/manual/`

Finding Files

The ls command and its aliases such as ll are designed to list all of the files in a directory. Special pattern characters and the grep command can be used to narrow down the list of files sent to STDOUT. But there is still something missing. There is a bit of a problem with the command ls -R | grep -E "^kde" that we used in Experiment 15-10. Some of the files it found were in subdirectories of /etc/, but the ls command does not display the names of the subdirectories in which those files are stored.

Fortunately the find command is designed explicitly to search for files in a directory tree using patterns and to either list the files and their directories or to perform some operation on them. The find command can also use attributes such as the date and time a file was created or accessed, files that were created or modified before or after a date and time, its size, permissions, user ID, group ID, and much more. These attributes can be combined to become very explicit, such as all files that are larger than 12M in size, that were created more than 5 years ago, that have not been accessed in more than a year, that belong to the user with UID XXXX, and that are regular files (in other words, not directories, symbolic links, sockets, named pipes, and more) – and more.

Once these files are found, the find command has the built-in options to perform actions such as to list, delete, print, or even execute system commands using the file name as an option, such as to move or copy them. This is a very powerful and flexible command.

EXPERIMENT 15-11: FINDING FILES

Perform this experiment as the root user. The following command finds all files in /etc and its subdirectories that start with "kde", and, because it uses -iname instead of -name, the search is not case sensitive:

```
[root@studentvm1 etc]# find /etc -iname "kde*"
/etc/xdg/kdebugrc
/etc/profile.d/kde.csh
/etc/profile.d/kde.sh
/etc/kde4rc
/etc/kderc
```

```
/etc/kde
[root@studentvm1 ~]#
```

Perform the rest of these commands as the student user. Make the student user's home directory (~) the PWD.

Suppose you want to find all of the empty (zero-length) files that were created in your home directory as part of our earlier experiments. The next command does this. It starts looking at the home (~) directory for files (type f) that are empty and that contain in the file names the string "test.file":

```
[student@studentvm1 ~]$ find . -type f -empty -name "*test.file*" | wc -l
    9488
[student@studentvm1 ~]$
```

I have 9,488 empty files from previous experiments in my home directory, but your number may be different. This large number is to be expected since we created a very large number of files that are empty for some earlier experiments. Run this same command except do not run the data stream through the wc command. Just list the names. Notice that the file names are not sorted.

But let's also see if there are any of these files that are not part of our previous experiments, so we want to look for empty files whose file names do not contain the string "test.file". The "bang" (!) character inverts the meaning of the -name option so that only files that do not match the string we supply for the file name are displayed:

```
[student@studentvm1 ~]$ find . -type f -empty ! -name "*test.file*"
./link3
./.local/share/ranger/tagged
./.local/share/vifm/Trash/000_file02
./.local/share/vifm/Trash/000_file03
./.local/share/orage/orage_persistent_alarms.txt
./.local/share/mc/filepos
./.local/share/user-places.xbel.tbcache
./.cache/abrt/applet_dirlist
./file005
./newfile.txt
```

```
./testdir/file006
./testdir/file077
./testdir/link2
./testdir/file008
./testdir/file055
./testdir/file007
<snip>
```

Let's also find the files that are not empty:

```
[student@studentvm1 ~]$ find . -type f ! -empty -name "*test.file*" | wc -l
160
[student@studentvm1 ~]$
```

We now know that 160 files that contain the string "test.file" in their names are not empty. Now we know that performing an action on the files we found in the previous command such as deleting them will not affect any other important files. So let's delete all of the empty files with the string "test.file" in their names. Then verify that none of these empty files remain and that the non-empty files are still there:

```
[student@studentvm1 ~]$ find . -type f -empty -name "*test.file*" -delete
[student@studentvm1 ~]$ find . -type f -empty -name "*test.file*"
[student@studentvm1 ~]$ find . -type f ! -empty -name "*test.file*" | wc -l
   160
```

Here are a couple more interesting things to try. First, create a file that is quite large for our next example, so create a file that is over 1GB in size and that contains random data. It took about 26 minutes to generate this file on my VM, so be patient:

```
[student@studentvm1 ~]$ pwgen -s 80 14000000 > testdir7/bigtestfile.txt
```

Use the -ls option to provide a sorted listing of the files found and provide information like the ls -dils command. Note that the inode[9] number will be the leftmost column, which means that the data is sorted by inode number:

```
[student@studentvm1 ~]$ find . -type f ! -empty -name "*test.file*" -ls
```

---

[9]inodes will be covered in Chapter 18.

We must do something a bit different to sort the results by size. This next command finds all files larger than 3K in size, generates a listing of them, and then pipes that data stream through the sort command, which uses options -n for numeric sort and -k 7 to sort on the seventh field of the output lines, which is the file size in bytes. White space is the default field separator:

```
[student@studentvm1 ~]$ find -type f -size +3k -ls | sort -nk 7
```

We will see more of the **find** command later.

I use the find command frequently because of its ability to locate files based on very exacting criteria. This gives me very exacting yet flexible control over the files. I can use automation to choose on which to perform some SysAdmin tasks.

Chapter Summary

This chapter has provided an exploration of the bash shell and using shell tools such as file globbing, brace expansion, control operators, and sets. It has also introduced us to some important and frequently used command-line tools.

We have looked at many aspects of using the bash shell and understanding how to perform some powerful and amazing things. For even more detail on the bash shell, gnu. org has the complete GNU Bash Manual[10] available in several formats including PDF and HTML.

This is most certainly not a complete exploration of bash and some of the advanced command-line tools available to us as SysAdmins. It should be enough to get you started and to interest you in learning more.

---

[10] Free Software Foundation, *GNU Bash Manual*, www.gnu.org/software/Bash/manual/

Exercises

Perform the following exercises to complete this chapter:

1. In Chapter 7 we installed some additional shells. Choose one of those and spend a little time performing simple tasks with it to gain a little knowledge of the grammar and syntax. Read the man page for the shell you chose to determine which commands are internal.

2. Do bash and the shell you chose in Exercise 1 have some of the same internal commands?

3. What does the type command do if the cpuHog shell script is located in your home directory rather than ~/bin?

4. What is the function of the $PATH environment variable?

5. Why might you want to use an external command instead of a shell internal command that performs the same function and that has the same name?

6. Locate all of the configuration files in your home directory and all of its subdirectories.

7. What is the largest file in the /etc directory?

8. What is the largest file in the entire filesystem (/)?

CHAPTER 16

Linux Boot and Startup

Objectives

In this chapter you will learn

- The difference between Linux boot and startup

- What happens during the hardware boot sequence

- The functions of and differences between the MBR and GPT

- What happens during the Linux boot sequence

- What happens during the Linux startup sequence

- How to manage and modify the Linux boot and startup sequences

- The function of the display and window managers

- How the login process works for both virtual consoles and a GUI

- What happens when a user logs off

This chapter presents and explores the hardware boot sequence, the bootup sequence using the GRUB2 bootloader, and the startup sequence as performed by the systemd initialization system. It covers in detail the sequence of events required to change the state of the computer from off to fully up and running with a user logged in.

This chapter is about modern Linux distributions like Fedora and other Red Hat–based distributions that use systemd for startup, shutdown, and system management. systemd is the modern replacement for init and SystemV init scripts.

© David Both 2023
D. Both, *Using and Administering Linux: Volume 1*, https://doi.org/10.1007/978-1-4842-9618-9_16

Overview

The complete process that takes a Linux host from an off state to a running state is complex, but it is open and knowable. Before we get into the details, a quick overview of the time the host hardware is turned on until the system is ready for a user to log in will help orient us. Most of the time we hear about "the boot process" as a single entity, but it is not. There are, in fact, three parts to the complete boot and startup process:

- Hardware boot, which initializes the system hardware

- Linux boot in which the GRUB2 bootloader loads the Linux kernel and systemd from a storage drive

- Linux startup in which systemd makes the host ready for productive work

It is important to separate the hardware boot from the Linux boot process from the Linux startup and to explicitly define the demarcation points between them. Understanding these differences and what part each plays in getting a Linux system to a state where it can be productive makes it possible to manage these processes and to better determine the portion in which a problem is occurring during what most people refer to as "boot."

Hardware Boot

The first step of the Linux boot process really has nothing whatever to do with Linux. This is the hardware portion of the boot process and is the same for any Intel-based operating system.

When power is first applied to the computer, or the VM we have created for this course, it runs the Power-On Self-Test (POST),[1] which is part of BIOS[2] or the much newer Unified Extensible Firmware Interface[3] (UEFI). BIOS stands for Basic I/O System, and POST stands for Power-On Self-Test. When IBM designed the first PC back in 1981, BIOS was designed to initialize the hardware components. POST is the part of BIOS whose task

---

[1] Wikipedia, *Power-On Self-Test*, http://en.wikipedia.org/wiki/Power-on_self-test

[2] Wikipedia, *BIOS*, http://en.wikipedia.org/wiki/BIOS

[3] Wikipedia, *Unified Extensible Firmware Interface*, https://en.wikipedia.org/wiki/Unified_Extensible_Firmware_Interface

is to ensure that the computer hardware functions correctly. If POST fails, the computer may not be usable, and so the boot process does not continue.

Most modern motherboards provide the newer UEFI as a replacement for BIOS. Many motherboards also provide legacy BIOS support. Both BIOS and UEFI perform the same functions – hardware verification and initialization and loading the boot loader.

BIOS/UEFI POST checks basic operability of the hardware. Then it locates the boot sectors on all attached bootable devices including rotating or SSD storage devices, DVD or CD ROM, or bootable USB memory sticks like the live USB device we used to install the StudentVM1 virtual machine. The first boot sector it finds that contains a valid Master Boot Record (MBR)[4] is loaded into RAM, and control is then transferred to the RAM copy of the boot sector.

The BIOS/UEFI user interface can be used to configure the system hardware for things like overclocking, specifying CPU cores as active or inactive, specific devices from which the system might boot, and the sequence in which those devices are to be searched for a bootable boot sector. I do not create or boot from bootable CD or DVD devices any more. I only use bootable USB thumb drives to boot from external, removable devices.

Because I sometimes do boot from an external USB drive – or in the case of a VM, a bootable ISO image like that of the live USB device – I always configure my systems to boot first from the external USB device and then from the appropriate internal disk drive. This is not considered secure in most commercial environments, but I do a lot of boots to external USB drives. If they steal the whole computer or if it is destroyed in a natural disaster, I can revert to backups[5] I keep in my safe deposit box.

In most environments you will want to be more secure and set the host to boot from the internal boot device only. Use a BIOS password to prevent unauthorized users from accessing BIOS to change the default boot sequence.

Hardware boot ends when the boot sector assumes control of the system.

The Boot Sector

The boot sector is always located in the first sector of the storage device whether HDD or SSD, and it contains the partition table as part of the Master Boot Record (MBR). This MBR partitioning methodology dates back to 1983 and imposes limits on modern storage hardware to less than its full capabilities.

---

[4] Wikipedia, *Master Boot Record*, https://en.wikipedia.org/wiki/Master_boot_record
[5] Backups are discussed in Chapter 40 of Volume 2.

Modern partitioning schemes use the GUID Partition Table[6] (GPT) to overcome those limitations.

In this section we look very briefly at both MBR and GPT.

The MBR

The MBR[7] is very small – only 512 bytes. Therefore, the space is very limited and must contain both a tiny bit of code, GRUB stage 1, and the partition table for the drive. The partition table defines the partitions that subdivide the space on the storage drive.

The MBR is capable of supporting four primary partitions although one partition could be created as a so-called extended partition, which supports additional logical partitions so that the space on the drive could be further subdivided. The total disk size supported by the MBR methodology is approximately 2.2TB (2.2×10^{12}), which is smaller than many storage devices currently available.

The GPT

The GPT is a new, modern standard for disk partition tables. Designed both for much greater disk sizes and systemic redundancy, it is larger than the MBR, so it supports much larger storage devices – up to 9.44 zetabytes, 9.44×10^{21}.

GPT uses an MBR in the first sector of the disk although it is used as a protective structure to provide an identifier so that system tools don't see the drive as an empty storage device.

Impact

Most of the time the difference between MBR and GPT is not relevant to the operation of Linux hosts or the task of problem solving. The function of both is to partition storage devices into usable chunks and to provide a tiny bit of code to provide a transition between BIOS/UEFI hardware boot and the main portion of the GRUB bootloader.

---

[6] Wikipedia, *GUID Partition Table*, https://en.wikipedia.org/wiki/GUID_Partition_Table. This entry contains an excellent description of the MBR, its problems, and the function and structure of the GPT.

[7] Wikipedia, *Disk Partitioning – Partition Table*, https://en.wikipedia.org/wiki/Disk_partitioning#Partition_table

Using different disk partitioning strategies during the Fedora installation can make a difference between whether the Anaconda installer installs an MBR or GPT. Either works with the Linux filesystems typically used today, EXT4, BTRFS, ZFS, and others. The only functional difference is that GPT supports extremely large-capacity storage devices, the kinds of devices that – for now – would certainly not be found outside the data center even in large businesses, let alone homes and small to medium businesses.

Linux Boot

The boot sector that is loaded by BIOS is stage 1 of the GRUB[8] boot loader. The Linux boot process itself is composed of multiple stages of GRUB. We consider each stage in this section.

GRUB

The primary function of GRUB is to get the Linux kernel loaded into memory and running. The use of GRUB2 commands within the pre-OS environment is outside the scope of this chapter. Although GRUB does not officially use the "stage" terminology for its three stages, it is convenient to refer to them in that way. GRUB2 is the newest version of the GRUB bootloader[9] and is used much more frequently these days. We will not cover GRUB1 or LILO in this course because they are much older than GRUB2.

Because it is easier to write and say GRUB than GRUB2, I will use the term GRUB in this course, but I will be referring to GRUB2 unless specified otherwise. GRUB2 stands for "GRand Unified Bootloader, version 2," and it is now the standard bootloader for many current Linux distributions. GRUB is the program that makes the computer just smart enough to find the operating system kernel and load it into memory, but it takes three stages of GRUB to do this. Wikipedia has an excellent article on GNU GRUB.[10]

GRUB has been designed to be compatible with the multiboot specification, which allows GRUB to boot many versions of Linux and other free operating systems. It can also chain load the boot record of proprietary operating systems like Windows. GRUB can allow the user to choose to boot from among several different kernels for your Linux

---

[8] GNU, *GRUB*, www.gnu.org/software/grub/manual/grub

[9] Wikipedia, *GNU GRUB*, https://en.wikipedia.org/wiki/GNU_GRUB

[10] GNU, *GNU GRUB*, www.gnu.org/software/grub/grub-documentation.html

distribution if there are more than one present due to system updates. This affords the ability to boot to a previous kernel version if an updated one fails somehow or is incompatible with an important piece of software. GRUB is configured using the /boot/grub/grub.conf file.

Red Hat–based distros upgraded to GRUB2 around Fedora 15 and CentOS/RHEL 7. GRUB2 provides the same boot functionality as GRUB1, but GRUB2 also provides a mainframe-like command-based pre-OS environment and allows more flexibility during the pre-boot phase.

GRUB Stage 1

As mentioned in the "Hardware Boot" section, at the end of POST, BIOS/UEFI searches the attached disks for a boot record, which is located in the Master Boot Record (MBR), loads the first one it finds into memory, and then starts execution of the boot record. The bootstrap code, that is, GRUB stage 1, is very small because it must fit into the first 512-byte sector on the hard drive along with the partition table.[11] The total amount of space allocated for the actual bootstrap code in a classic, generic MBR is 446 bytes. The 446-byte file for stage 1 is named boot.img and does not contain the partition table. The partition table is created when the device is partitioned and is overlaid onto the boot record starting at byte 447.

In UEFI systems the partition table has been moved out of the MBR and into the space immediately following the MBR. This provides more space for defining partitions, so it allows a larger number of partitions to be created.

Because the boot record must be so small, it is not very smart and does not understand filesystem structures such as EXT4. Therefore, the sole purpose of stage 1 is to load GRUB stage 1.5, which can access filesystems. In order to accomplish this, stage 1.5 of GRUB must be located in the space between the boot record and the UEFI partition data and the first partition on the drive. After loading GRUB stage 1.5 into RAM, stage 1 turns control over to stage 1.5.

---

[11] Wikipedia, *GUID Partition Table*, https://en.wikipedia.org/wiki/GUID_Partition_Table

EXPERIMENT 16-1: THE BOOT RECORD

Log into a terminal session as root if there is not one already available. As root in a terminal session, run the following command to verify the identity of the boot drive on your VM. It should be the same drive as the boot partition:

```
[root@studentvm1 ~]# lsblk -i
NAME                          MAJ:MIN RM  SIZE RO TYPE MOUNTPOINT
sda                            8:0     0   60G  0 disk
|-sda1                         8:1     0    1G  0 part /boot
`-sda2                         8:2     0   59G  0 part
  |-fedora_studentvm1-root 253:0      0    2G  0 lvm  /
  |-fedora_studentvm1-swap 253:1      0    6G  0 lvm  [SWAP]
  |-fedora_studentvm1-usr  253:2      0   15G  0 lvm  /usr
  |-fedora_studentvm1-home 253:3      0    4G  0 lvm  /home
  |-fedora_studentvm1-var  253:4      0   10G  0 lvm  /var
  `-fedora_studentvm1-tmp  253:5      0    5G  0 lvm  /tmp
[root@studentvm1 ~]#
```

Use the **dd** command to view the boot record of the boot drive. For this experiment I assume it is assigned to the /dev/sda device. The bs= argument in the command specifies the block size, and the count= argument specifies the number of blocks to dump to STDIO. The if= argument (InFile) specifies the source of the data stream, in this case the USB device:

```
[root@studentvm1 ~]# dd if=/dev/sda bs=512 count=1
�c��M��?~��|����!��8u
                     �����u����|���t�L��|
������t��pt���y|1�~м �d|<�t��R�|1�D@�D��D�f�\|
f�f�`|f�\
�Dp�B�r�p��K`���1������a`���f��u����f1�f�TCPAf�f
�a�&Z|�}��.}�4�3}�.���GRUB GeomHard DiskRead Error
����<u�� .~���� ������ �_U�1+0 records in
1+0 records out
512 bytes copied, 9.9294e-05 s, 5.2 MB/s
[root@studentvm1 ~]#
```

This prints the text of the boot record, which is the first block on the disk — any disk. In this case, there is information about the filesystem and, although it is unreadable because it is stored in binary format, the partition table. Stage 1 of GRUB or some other boot loader is located in this sector, but that, too, is mostly unreadable by us mere humans. We can see a couple messages in ASCII text that are stored in the boot record. It might be easier to read these messages if we do this a bit differently. The od command (Octal Display) displays the data stream piped to it in octal format in a nice matrix that makes the content a bit easier to read. The -a option tells the command to convert into readable ASCII format characters where possible. The last - at the end of the command tells od to take input from the STDIN stream rather than a file:

```
[root@studentvm1 ~]# dd if=/dev/sda bs=512 count=1 | od -a -
1+0 records in
1+0 records out
0000000   k   c dle dle  so   P   <  nul   O   8 nul nul  so   X  so   @
0000020   {   > nul   |   ? nul ack   9 nul stx   s   $   j   ! ack nul
0000040 nul   >   > bel   8 eot   u  vt etx   F dle soh   ~   ~ bel   u
0000060   s   k syn   4 stx   O soh   ; nul   |   2 nul  nl   t soh  vt
0000100   L stx   M dc3   j nul   | nul nul   k   ~ nul nul nul nul nul
0000120 nul nul nul nul nul nul nul nul nul nul nul nul soh nul nul nul
0000140 nul nul nul nul del   z dle dle   v   B nul   t enq   v   B   p
0000160   t stx   2 nul   j   y   | nul nul   1   @  so   X  so   P   <
0000200 nul  sp   {  sp   d   |   < del   t stx  bs   B   R   > enq   |
0000220   1   @  ht   D eot   @  bs   D del  ht   D stx   G eot dle nul
0000240   f  vt  rs   \   |   f  ht   \  bs   f  vt  rs   `   |   f  ht
0000260   \  ff   G   D ack nul   p   4   B   M dc3   r enq   ; nul   p
0000300   k stx   k   K   `  rs   9 nul soh  so   [   1   v   ? nul nul
0000320  so   F   |   s   %  us   a   `   8 nul   ;   M sub   f enq   @
0000340   u  gs   8 bel   ;   ? nul nul   f   1   v   f   ;   T   C   P
0000360   A   f   9 nul stx nul nul   f   : bs nul nul nul   M sub   a
0000400 del   &   Z   |   >  us   }   k etx   >   .   }   h   4 nul   >
0000420   3   }   h   . nul   M can   k   ~   G   R   U   B  sp nul   G
0000440   e   o   m nul   H   a   r   d  sp   D   i   s   k nul   R   e
0000460   a   d nul  sp   E   r   r   o   r  cr  nl nul   ; soh nul   4
0000500  so   M dle   ,   < nul   u   t   C nul nul nul nul nul nul nul
0000520 nul nul nul nul nul nul nul nul nul nul nul nul nul nul nul nul
*
0000660 nul nul nul nul nul nul nul nul   \   ;   ^   . nul nul nul eot
0000700 soh eot etx   ~   B del nul  bs nul nul nul nul  sp nul nul   ~
0000720   B del  so   ~   B del nul  bs  sp nul nul   x   _ bel nul nul
```

```
0000740 nul nul nul nul nul nul nul nul nul nul nul nul nul nul nul nul
0000760 nul nul nul nul nul nul nul nul nul nul nul nul nul nul   U   *
0001000
```

Note the star (*) (splat/asterisk) between addresses 0000520 and 0000660. This indicates that all of the data in that range is the same as the last line before it, 0000520, which is all null characters. This saves space in the output stream. The addresses are in octal, which is base 8.

A generic boot record that does not contain a partition table is located in the /boot/grub2/i386-pc directory. Let's look at the content of that file. It is not necessary to specify the block size and the count if we use dd because we are looking at a file that already has a limited length. We can also use od directly and specify the file name rather than using the dd command, although we could do that too:

```
[root@studentvm1 ~]# od -a /usr/lib/grub/i386-pc/boot.img
0000000   k   c dle nul nul nul nul nul nul nul nul nul nul nul nul nul
0000020 nul nul nul nul nul nul nul nul nul nul nul nul nul nul nul nul
*
0000120 nul nul nul nul nul nul nul nul nul nul nul nul soh nul nul nul
0000140 nul nul nul nul del   z   k enq   v   B nul   t enq   v   B   p
0000160   t stx   2 nul   j   y   | nul nul   1   @  so   X  so   P   <
0000200 nul  sp   {  sp   d   |   < del   t stx  bs   B   R   > enq   |
0000220   1   @  ht   D eot   @  bs   D del  ht   D stx   G eot dle nul
0000240   f  vt  rs   \   |   f  ht   \  bs   f  vt  rs   `   |   f  ht
0000260   \  ff   G   D ack nul   p   4   B   M dc3   r enq   ; nul   p
0000300   k stx   k   K   `  rs   9 nul soh  so   [   1   v   ? nul nul
0000320  so   F   |   s   % us   a   `   8 nul   ;   M sub   f enq   @
0000340   u  gs   8 bel   ;   ? nul nul   f   1   v   f   ;   T   C   P
0000360   A   f   9 nul stx nul nul   f   :  bs nul nul nul   M sub   a
0000400 del   &   Z   |   > us   }   k etx   >   .   }   h   4 nul   >
0000420   3   }   h   . nul   M can   k   ~   G   R   U   B  sp nul   G
0000440   e   o   m nul   H   a   r   d  sp   D   i   s   k nul   R   e
0000460   a   d nul  sp   E   r   r   o   r  cr  nl nul   ; soh nul   4
0000500  so   M dle   ,   < nul   u   t   C nul nul nul nul nul nul nul
0000520 nul nul nul nul nul nul nul nul nul nul nul nul nul nul nul nul
*
0000760 nul nul nul nul nul nul nul nul nul nul nul nul nul nul   U   *
0001000
```

471

There is a second area of duplicated data in this output, between addresses 0000020 and 0000120. Because that area is different from the actual boot record and it is all null in this file, we can infer that this is where the partition table is located in the actual boot record. There is also an interesting utility that enables us to just look at the ASCII text strings contained in a file:

```
[root@studentvm1 ~]# strings /boot/grub2/i386-pc/boot.img
ZRr=
`|f
\|f1
GRUB
Geom
Hard Disk
Read
 Error
Floppy
```

This tool is easier to use to locate actual text strings than sorting through many lines of the occasional random ASCII characters to find meaningful strings. But note that, like the first line of the preceding output, not all text strings have meaning to humans.

The point here is that the GRUB boot record is installed in the first sector of the hard drive or other bootable media, using the boot.img file as the source. The partition table is then superimposed on the boot record in its specified location.

GRUB Stage 1.5

Stage 1.5 of GRUB must be located in the space between the boot record and the UEFI partition data and the first partition on the disk drive. This space was left unused historically for technical and compatibility reasons and is sometimes called the "boot track" or the "MBR gap." The first partition on the hard drive begins at sector 63, and with the MBR in sector 0, that leaves 62 512-byte sectors – 31,744 bytes – in which to store stage 1.5 of GRUB, which is distributed as the core.img file. The core.img file is 28,535 bytes as of this writing, so there is plenty of space available between the MBR and the first disk partition in which to store it.

EXPERIMENT 16-2: GRUB STAGE 1.5

The file containing stage 1.5 of GRUB is stored as /boot/grub2/i386-pc/core.img. You can
verify this as we did previously with stage 1 by comparing the code in the file to that stored in
the MBR gap of the boot drive:

```
[root@studentvm1 ~]# dd if=/dev/sda bs=512 count=1 skip=1 | od -a -
1+0 records in
1+0 records out
512 bytes copied, 0.000132697 s, 3.9 MB/s
0000000   E   F   I  sp   P   A   R   T nul nul soh nul   \ nul nul nul
0000020   (   `   *  so nul nul nul nul soh nul nul nul nul nul nul nul
0000040 del del del bel nul nul nul nul   " nul nul nul nul nul nul nul
0000060   ^ del del bel nul nul nul nul   | ht   @ ack   _  sp nl   F
0000100 dc1 ff   c   ?   1   > so etx stx nul nul nul nul nul nul nul
0000120 nul nul nul nul nul nul nul nul ack   ~   ]   $ nul nul nul nul
0000140 nul nul nul nul nul nul nul nul nul nul nul nul nul nul nul nul
*
0001000
```

```
    [root@studentvm1 ~]# dd if=/boot/grub2/i386-pc/core.img bs=512 count=1
| od -a -
1+0 records in
1+0 records out
512 bytes copied, 5.1455e-05 s, 10.0 MB/s
0000000   R   V   > esc soh   h   9 soh   ^   ?   t soh   f  vt   - etx
0000020   } bs nul  si eot   b nul nul   | del nul   t   F   f  vt gs
0000040   f  vt   M eot   f   1   @   0 del   9   E bs del etx  vt   E
0000060  bs   )   E bs   f soh enq   f etx   U eot nul   G eot dle nul
0000100  ht   D stx   f  ht   \ bs   f  ht   L ff   G   D ack nul   p
0000120   P   G   D eot nul nul   4   B   M dc3  si stx   / nul   ; nul
0000140   p   k   f   f  vt   E eot   f  ht   @ si enq etb nul   f  vt
0000160 enq   f   1   R   f   w   4 bs   T nl   f   1   R   f   w   t
0000200 eot bs   T  vt  ht   D ff   ;   D bs   }   y  vt eot   *   D
0000220  nl   9   E bs del etx  vt   E bs   )   E bs   f soh enq   f
0000240 etx   U eot nul  nl   T  cr   @   b ack  nl   L  nl   ~   A bs
0000260   Q  nl   l ff   Z   R  nl   t  vt   P   ; nul   p  so   C   1
0000300   [   4 stx   M dc3   r   F ff   C  so   E  nl   X   A   ` enq
```

```
0000320 soh   E  nl   `   rs   A    `  etx  ht   A   1 del   1   v  so   [
0000340  |    s  %  us   >   #  soh  h   W  nul   a etx   }  bs nul  si
0000360 enq   $ del etx  o  ff   i  syn del   >   % soh   h   B nul   Z
0000400  j  nul stx nul nul   >   (  soh  h   6 nul  k ack   >   - soh
0000420  h   . nul   >   2 soh   h   (  nul  k   ~   l   o   a   d   i
0000440  n   g nul   . nul  cr  nl nul   G   e   o  m nul   R   e   a
0000460  d nul  sp   E   r   r   o   r nul   ; soh nul   4  so   M dle
0000500  F  nl eot   < nul   u   r   C nul nul nul nul nul nul nul nul
0000520 nul nul nul nul nul nul nul nul nul nul nul nul nul nul nul nul
*
0000760 nul nul nul nul stx nul nul nul nul nul nul nul   ? nul  sp  bs
0001000
[root@studentvm1 ~]#
```

The first sector of each will do for verification, but you should feel free to explore more of the code if you like. There are tools that we could use to compare the file with the data in GRUB stage 1.5 on the hard drive, but it is obvious that these two sectors of data are identical.

At this point we know the files that contain stages 1 and 1.5 of the GRUB bootloader and where they are located on the hard drive in order to perform their function as the Linux bootloader.

Because of the larger amount of code that can be accommodated for stage 1.5 than for stage 1, it can have enough code to contain a few common filesystem drivers, such as the standard EXT, XFS, and other non-Linux filesystems like FAT and NTFS. The GRUB2 core.img is much more complex and capable than the older GRUB1 stage 1.5. This means that stage 2 of GRUB2 can be located on a standard EXT filesystem, but it cannot be located on a logical volume because it needs to be read from a specific location on the bootable volume before the filesystem drivers have been loaded.

Note that the /boot directory must be located on a filesystem that is supported by GRUB such as EXT4. Not all filesystems are. The function of stage 1.5 is to begin execution with the filesystem drivers necessary to locate the stage 2 files in the /boot filesystem and load the needed drivers.

GRUB Stage 2

All of the files for GRUB stage 2 are located in the /boot/grub2 directory and its subdirectories. GRUB2 does not have an image file like stages 1 and 2. Instead, it consists of those files and runtime kernel modules that are loaded as needed from the /boot/grub2 directory and its subdirectories. Some Linux distributions may store these files in the /boot/grub directory.

The function of GRUB stage 2 is to locate and load a Linux kernel into RAM and turn control of the computer over to the kernel. The kernel and its associated files are located in the /boot directory. The kernel files are identifiable as they are all named starting with vmlinuz. You can list the contents of the /boot directory to see the currently installed kernels on your system.

EXPERIMENT 16-3: LINUX KERNELS

Your list of Linux kernels should look similar to the ones on my VM, but the kernel versions and the releases will be different. You should be using the most recent release of Fedora on your VM, so it should be release 39 or even higher by the time you installed your VMs. That should make no difference to these experiments:

```
[root@studentvm1 ~]# ll /boot
total 275508
-rw-r--r--. 1 root root    251528 Nov  4 14:55 config-6.0.7-301.fc37.x86_64
-rw-r--r--. 1 root root    253534 Jan 14 12:12 config-6.1.6-200.fc37.x86_64
-rw-r--r--  1 root root    253512 Jan 18 12:29 config-6.1.7-200.fc37.x86_64
drwx------  4 root root      4096 Dec 31  1969 efi
drwx------. 5 root root      4096 Jan 29 08:28 grub2
-rw-------. 1 root root 105160151 Jan 17 07:39 initramfs-0-rescue-
d1fbbe41229942289e5ed31a256200fb.img
-rw-------. 1 root root  36685746 Jan 17 07:40 initramfs-6.0.7-301.fc37.x86_64.img
-rw-------. 1 root root  34616617 Jan 17 21:33 initramfs-6.1.6-200.fc37.x86_64.img
-rw-------  1 root root  34617482 Jan 24 08:29 initramfs-6.1.7-200.fc37.x86_64.img
drwxr-xr-x. 3 root root      4096 Jan 17 07:36 loader
drwx------. 2 root root     16384 Jan 17 07:29 lost+found
lrwxrwxrwx. 1 root root        45 Jan 17 07:36 symvers-6.0.7-301.fc37.x86_64.
gz -> /lib/modules/6.0.7-301.fc37.x86_64/symvers.gz
```

```
lrwxrwxrwx. 1 root root          45 Jan 17 21:32 symvers-6.1.6-200.fc37.x86_64.
gz -> /lib/modules/6.1.6-200.fc37.x86_64/symvers.gz
lrwxrwxrwx  1 root root          45 Jan 24 08:28 symvers-6.1.7-200.fc37.x86_64.
gz -> /lib/modules/6.1.7-200.fc37.x86_64/symvers.gz
-rw-------. 1 root root     7252122 Nov  4 14:55 System.map-6.0.7-301.fc37.x86_64
-rw-------. 1 root root     5984440 Jan 14 12:12 System.map-6.1.6-200.fc37.x86_64
-rw------- 1 root root      5988800 Jan 18 12:29 System.map-6.1.7-200.fc37.x86_64
-rwxr-xr-x. 1 root root    12727016 Jan 17 07:37 vmlinuz-0-rescue-
d1fbbe41229942289e5ed31a256200fb
-rwxr-xr-x. 1 root root    12727016 Nov  4 14:55 vmlinuz-6.0.7-301.fc37.x86_64
-rwxr-xr-x. 1 root root    12761928 Jan 14 12:12 vmlinuz-6.1.6-200.fc37.x86_64
-rwxr-xr-x  1 root root    12781480 Jan 18 12:29 vmlinuz-6.1.7-200.fc37.x86_64
```

You can see that there are four kernels at the bottom of this list. The kernel files start with "vmlinuz", but that "vm" in the name has nothing to do with "virtual machine."

Their supporting files are also in this list including the rescue kernel. The System.map files are symbol tables that map the physical addresses of the symbols such as variables and functions. The initramfs files are used early in the Linux boot process before the kernel and filesystem drivers have been loaded and the filesystems mounted.

GRUB supports booting from one of a selection of installed Linux kernels. The Red Hat Package Manager, DNF, supports keeping multiple versions of the kernel so that if a problem occurs with the newest one, an older version of the kernel can be booted. As shown in Figure 16-1, GRUB provides a pre-boot menu of the installed kernels, including a rescue option and, if configured, a recovery option for each kernel.

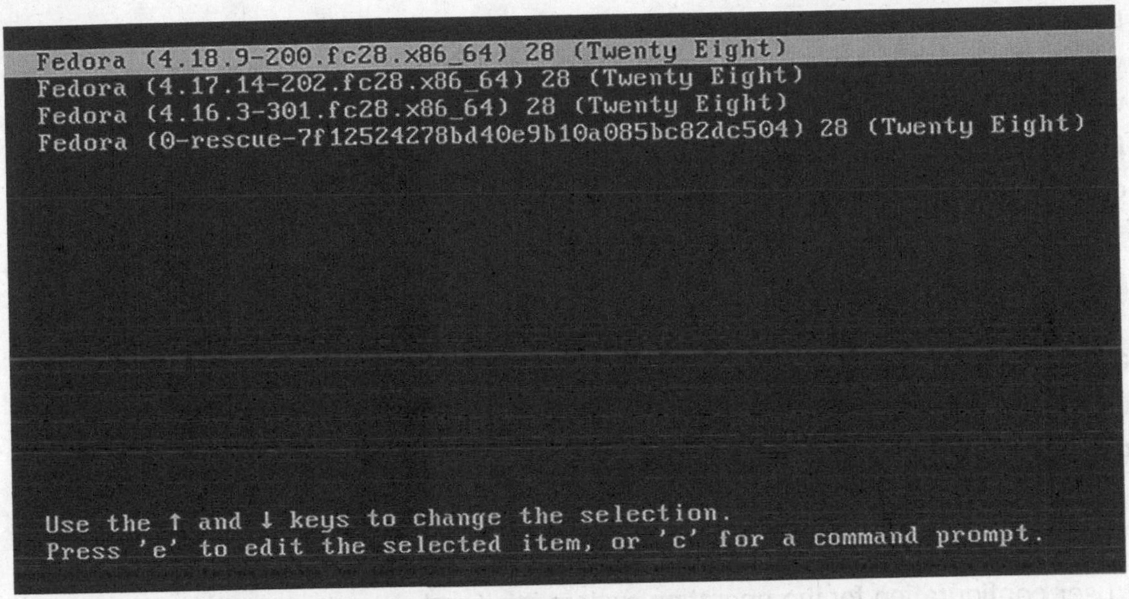

```
Fedora (4.18.9-200.fc28.x86_64) 28 (Twenty Eight)
Fedora (4.17.14-202.fc28.x86_64) 28 (Twenty Eight)
Fedora (4.16.3-301.fc28.x86_64) 28 (Twenty Eight)
Fedora (0-rescue-7f12524278bd40e9b10a085bc82dc504) 28 (Twenty Eight)
```

```
Use the ↑ and ↓ keys to change the selection.
Press 'e' to edit the selected item, or 'c' for a command prompt.
```

Figure 16-1. *The GRUB boot menu allows selection of a different kernel. This image is from Fedora 28, but what you see on later releases will be the same except for the release and version numbers. It also works the same, which is the really important part*

The default kernel is always the most recent one that has been installed during updates, and it will boot automatically after a short timeout of five seconds. If the up and down arrows are pressed, the countdown stops, and the highlight bar moves to another kernel. Press **Enter** to boot the selected kernel.

If almost any key other than the up and down arrow keys or the "**E**" or "**C**" key is pressed, the countdown stops and waits for more input. Now you can take your time to use the arrow keys to select a kernel to boot and then press the **Enter** key to boot from it. Stage 2 of GRUB loads the selected kernel into memory and turns control of the computer over to the kernel.

The rescue boot option is intended as a last resort when attempting to resolve boot problems – ones that prevent the Linux system from completing the boot process. When some types of errors occur during boot, GRUB will automatically fall back to boot from the rescue image.

The GRUB menu entries for installed kernels have been useful to me. Before I became aware of VirtualBox, I used to use some commercial virtualization software that sometimes experienced problems when Linux was updated. Although the company tried to keep up with kernel variations, they eventually stopped updating their software to run with every kernel version. Whenever they did not support a kernel version to which I had updated, I used the GRUB menu to select an older kernel that I knew would work. I discovered that maintaining only three older kernels was not always enough, so I configured the DNF package manager to save up to ten kernels. DNF package manager configuration is covered in this volume, Chapter 12.

Configuring GRUB

GRUB is configured with /boot/grub2/grub.cfg, but we do not change that file because it can get overwritten when the kernel is updated to a new version. Instead, we make modifications to the /etc/default/grub file.

Tip   This is the first instance you will encounter of the Linux way of allowing user configuration for the operating system itself and many tools and applications. There is a default configuration file and a second file that allows adding entries that modify the defaults. Thus, if we make really bad errors in the secondary configuration file, all we need to do is delete, move, or rename the secondary file while we figure out what we did wrong. We can then make the corrections or start over. So we never need to or should make changes to the primary configuration file and can always return to a functional configuration.

EXPERIMENT 16-4: CONFIGURING GRUB

Let's start by looking at the unmodified version of the /etc/default/grub file:

```
[root@studentvm1 ~]# cd /etc/default ; cat grub
GRUB_TIMEOUT=5
GRUB_DISTRIBUTOR="$(sed 's, release .*$,,g' /etc/system-release)"
GRUB_DEFAULT=saved
GRUB_DISABLE_SUBMENU=true
GRUB_TERMINAL_OUTPUT="console"
GRUB_CMDLINE_LINUX="resume=/dev/mapper/fedora_studentvm1-swap rd.lvm.
lv=fedora_studentvm1/root rd.lvm.lv=fedora_studentvm1/swap rd.lvm.lv=fedora_
studentvm1/usr rhgb quiet"
```

```
GRUB_DISABLE_RECOVERY="true"
[root@studentvm1 default]#
```

Chapter 6 of the GRUB documentation referenced in footnote 6 contains a complete listing of all the possible entries in the /etc/default/grub file, but there are three that we should look at here.

I always change GRUB_TIMEOUT, the number of seconds for the GRUB menu countdown, from 5 to 10, which gives a bit more time to respond to the GRUB menu before the countdown hits zero.

I used to change GRUB_DISABLE_RECOVERY from "true" to "false", which is a bit of reverse programmer logic. This is supposed to create a rescue boot option for each installed kernel. Since Fedora 30 it no longer does.

Note   Changing GRUB_DISABLE_RECOVERY in the GRUB default configuration no longer works starting in Fedora 30. The other changes, GRUB_TIMEOUT and removing "rhgb quiet" from the GRUB_CMDLINE_LINUX variable, still work.

The GRUB_CMDLINE_LINUX line can be changed too. This line lists the command-line parameters that are passed to the kernel at boot time. I usually delete the last two parameters on this line. The "rhgb" parameter stands for Red Hat Graphical Boot, and it causes the little graphical animation of the Fedora icon to display during the kernel initialization instead of showing startup-time messages. The "quiet" parameter prevents the display of the startup messages that document the progress of the startup and any errors that might occur. Delete both of these entries because SysAdmins need to be able to see these messages. If something goes wrong during boot, the messages displayed on the screen can point us to the cause of the problem.

Change these two lines as described so that your grub file looks like this:

```
[root@studentvm1 default]# cat grub
GRUB_TIMEOUT=10
GRUB_DISTRIBUTOR="$(sed 's, release .*$,,g' /etc/system-release)"
GRUB_DEFAULT=saved
GRUB_DISABLE_SUBMENU=true
GRUB_TERMINAL_OUTPUT="console"
```

```
GRUB_CMDLINE_LINUX="resume=/dev/mapper/fedora_studentvm1-swap rd.lvm.lv=
fedora_studentvm1/root rd.lvm.lv=fedora_studentvm1/swap rd.lvm.lv=fedora_
studentvm1/usr"
GRUB_DISABLE_RECOVERY="true"
[root@studentvm1 default]#
```

Check the current timestamp of the /boot/grub2/grub.cfg file. Check the contents of the file for those specific variables.

Run the following command to update the /boot/grub2/grub.cfg configuration file:

```
[root@studentvm1 default]# grub2-mkconfig > /boot/grub2/grub.cfg
Generating grub configuration file ...
Adding boot menu entry for UEFI Firmware Settings ...
done
[root@studentvm1 default]#
```

Recheck the timestamp and content of /boot/grub2/grub.cfg, which should reflect the changes. You can grep for the specific lines we changed to verify that the changes occurred.

We could also use an alternative form of this command with -o (oh not zero) to specify the output file:

```
grub2-mkconfig -o /boot/grub2/grub.cfg
```

Either form works and the results are the same.

Finishing GRUB Boot

After loading GRUB stage 2, the GRUB menu displays, giving the user an opportunity to choose an optional kernel that is not the default. The user can also allow the timeout to expire or press the Enter key on the default selection. Either of these last two options boots the default kernel.

GRUB stage 2 locates and loads the selected kernel and turns control over to it.

The Linux Kernel

All Linux kernels are in a self-extracting, compressed format to save space. The kernels are located in the /boot directory, along with an initial RAM disk image and symbol maps. After the selected kernel is loaded into memory by GRUB and begins executing, it must first extract itself from the compressed version of the file before it can perform any useful work. The kernel has extracted itself, loads systemd, and turns control over to it.

This is the end of the boot process. At this point, the Linux kernel and systemd are running but unable to perform any productive tasks for the end user because nothing else is running, no shell to provide a command line, no background processes to manage the network or other communication links, nothing that enables the computer to perform any productive function.

Linux Startup

The startup process follows the boot process and brings the Linux computer up to an operational state in which it is usable for productive work. The startup process begins when the kernel takes control of the system.

Text-Mode Startup

Text-mode startup displays much more information than the default GUI startup mode. This additional information allows the SysAdmin better opportunity to locate the source of the problem. However, viewing the data stream on a working host can help your understanding of what a startup should look like when everything is working properly. Both text and GUI startup end up at the same place, the default.target. More on that later in this chapter.

EXPERIMENT 16-5: EXPLORING TEXT-MODE STARTUP

Because of the speed with which Linux boots and the large number of informational messages it emits into the data stream, it is not possible for us mere "humons[12]"[sic] to follow most of it. However, the Linux kernel developers have provided us with an excellent alternative in the dmesg command.

---

[12] Refer to *Start Trek DS9.*

The dmesg command lists all of the startup messages that were displayed on the screen and lets us explore what happens during startup. This includes all kernel messages such as locating memory and devices, as well as the startup of system services performed by systemd.

Perform this experiment as the root user:

```
[root@studentvm1 ~]# dmesg | less
[    0.000000] Linux version 6.1.7-200.fc37.x86_64 (mockbuild@bkernel01.
iad2.fedoraproject.org) (gcc (GCC) 12.2.1 20221121 (Red Hat 12.2.1-4), GNU ld
version 2.38-25.fc37) #1 SMP PREEMPT_DYNAMIC Wed Jan 18 17:11:49 UTC 2023
[    0.000000] Command line: BOOT_IMAGE=(hd0,gpt2)/vmlinuz-6.1.7-200.
fc37.x86_64 root=/dev/mapper/fedora_studentvm1-root ro rd.lvm.lv=fedora_
studentvm1/root rd.lvm.lv=fedora_studentvm1/usr
[    0.000000] x86/fpu: Supporting XSAVE feature 0x001: 'x87 floating point
registers'
[    0.000000] x86/fpu: Supporting XSAVE feature 0x002: 'SSE registers'
[    0.000000] x86/fpu: Supporting XSAVE feature 0x004: 'AVX registers'
[    0.000000] x86/fpu: xstate_offset[2]:  576, xstate_sizes[2]:  256
[    0.000000] x86/fpu: Enabled xstate features 0x7, context size is 832
bytes, using 'standard' format.
[    0.000000] signal: max sigframe size: 1776
[    0.000000] BIOS-provided physical RAM map:
[    0.000000] BIOS-e820: [mem 0x0000000000000000-0x000000000009fbff] usable
[    0.000000] BIOS-e820: [mem 0x000000000009fc00-0x000000000009ffff] reserved
[    0.000000] BIOS-e820: [mem 0x00000000000f0000-0x00000000000fffff] reserved
[    0.000000] BIOS-e820: [mem 0x0000000000100000-0x00000000dffeffff] usable
[    0.000000] BIOS-e820: [mem 0x00000000dfff0000-0x00000000dfffffff] ACPI data
[    0.000000] BIOS-e820: [mem 0x00000000fec00000-0x00000000fec00fff] reserved
[    0.000000] BIOS-e820: [mem 0x00000000fee00000-0x00000000fee00fff] reserved
[    0.000000] BIOS-e820: [mem 0x00000000fffc0000-0x00000000ffffffff] reserved
[    0.000000] BIOS-e820: [mem 0x0000000100000000-0x000000041fffffff] usable
[    0.000000] NX (Execute Disable) protection: active
[    0.000000] SMBIOS 2.5 present.
[    0.000000] DMI: innotek GmbH VirtualBox/VirtualBox, BIOS VirtualBox 12/01/2006
[    0.000000] Hypervisor detected: KVM
[    0.000000] kvm-clock: Using msrs 4b564d01 and 4b564d00
<SNIP>
[    3.749441] Run /init as init process
[    3.749793]   with arguments:
```

```
[    3.749795]    /init
[    3.749797]   with environment:
[    3.749798]    HOME=/
[    3.749799]    TERM=linux
[    3.749800]    BOOT_IMAGE=(hd0,gpt2)/vmlinuz-6.1.7-200.fc37.x86_64
[    3.760797] systemd[1]: systemd 251.10-588.fc37 running in system mode
(+PAM +AUDIT +SELINUX -APPARMOR +IMA +SMACK +SECCOMP -GCRYPT +GNUTLS +OPENSSL
+ACL +BLKID +CURL +ELFUTILS +FIDO2 +IDN2 -IDN -IPTC +KMOD +LIBCRYPTSETUP
+LIBFDISK +PCRE2 +PWQUALITY +P11KIT +QRENCODE +TPM2 +BZIP2 +LZ4 +XZ +ZLIB
+ZSTD +BPF_FRAMEWORK +XKBCOMMON +UTMP +SYSVINIT default-hierarchy=unified)
[    3.763176] systemd[1]: Detected virtualization oracle.
[    3.765139] systemd[1]: Detected architecture x86-64.
[    3.765569] systemd[1]: Running in initial RAM disk.
[    3.767893] systemd[1]: Hostname set to <studentvm1>.
[    5.208337] systemd[1]: bpf-lsm: LSM BPF program attached
[    5.309583] systemd[1]: Queued start job for default target initrd.target.
[    5.310415] systemd[1]: Reached target initrd-usr-fs.target - Initrd /usr
File System.
[    5.315207] systemd[1]: Reached target local-fs.target - Local File Systems.
[    5.316402] systemd[1]: Reached target slices.target - Slice Units.
[    5.317445] systemd[1]: Reached target swap.target - Swaps.
[    5.318450] systemd[1]: Reached target timers.target - Timer Units.
[    5.319616] systemd[1]: Listening on dbus.socket - D-Bus System Message
Bus Socket.
[    5.321141] systemd[1]: Listening on systemd-journald-audit.socket -
Journal Audit Socket.
[    5.322570] systemd[1]: Listening on systemd-journald-dev-log.socket -
    Journal Socket (/dev/log).
[    5.324061] systemd[1]: Listening on systemd-journald.socket -
    Journal Socket.
```

The numbers like [5.321141] are the time in nanoseconds (millionths) since the kernel started running.

Page through the data and look for events such as filesystem mounts and network interface card (NIC) configurations.

---

systemd

systemd[13,14] is the mother of all processes. Its process ID (PID) is always 1. It is responsible for bringing the Linux host up to a state in which productive work can be done. Some of its functions, which are far more extensive than the old SystemV[15] init program, are to manage many aspects of a running Linux host, including mounting filesystems and starting and managing system services required to have a productive Linux host. Any of systemd's tasks that are not related to the startup sequence are outside the scope of this chapter, but we will explore them in Volume 2, Chapter 35.

systemd mounts the filesystems as defined by the /etc/fstab (filesystem table) file, including any swap files or partitions. At this point it can access the configuration files located in /etc, including its own. It uses its configuration link, /etc/systemd/system/default.target, to determine which state or target into which it should boot the host. The default.target file is a symbolic link[16] – a pointer – to the true target file. For a desktop workstation, this is typically going to be the graphical.target, which is equivalent to runlevel 5 in SystemV. For a server, the default is more likely to be the multi-user.target, which is like runlevel 3 in SystemV. The emergency.target is similar to single-user mode. Targets and services are systemd units.

Figure 16-2 is a comparison of the systemd targets with the old SystemV startup runlevels. The systemd target aliases are provided by systemd for backward compatibility. The target aliases allow scripts – and many SysAdmins like myself – to use SystemV commands like init 3 to change runlevels. Of course the SystemV commands are forwarded to systemd for interpretation and execution.

---

[13] Wikipedia, *systemd*, https://en.wikipedia.org/wiki/Systemd

[14] Yes, systemd should always be spelled like this without any uppercase even at the beginning of a sentence. The documentation for systemd is very clear about this.

[15] Wikipedia, *Runlevel*, https://en.wikipedia.org/wiki/Runlevel

[16] Links are covered in Chapter 18 of this volume.

Systemd Targets	SystemV Runlevel	Target Aliases	Description
default.target			This target is always aliased with a symbolic link to either multi-user.target or graphical.target. systemd always uses the default.target to start the system. The default.target should never be aliased to halt.target, poweroff.target, or reboot.target.
graphical.target	5	runlevel5.target	Multi-user.target with a GUI.
	4	runlevel4.target	Unused. Runlevel 4 was identical to runlevel 3 in the SystemV world. This target could be created and customized to start local services without changing the default multi-user.target.
multi-user.target	3	runlevel3.target	Multiuser with all services running but command-line interface (CLI) only.
	2	runlevel2.target	Multiuser, without NFS but all other non-GUI services running.
rescue.target	1	runlevel1.target	A basic system including mounting the filesystems with only the most basic services running and a rescue shell on the main console.
emergency.target	S		No services are running; filesystems are not mounted. This is the most basic level of operation with only an emergency shell running on the main console for the user to interact with the system. Single user mode in SystemV.
halt.target			Halts the system without powering it down.
reboot.target	6	runlevel6.target	Reboot
poweroff.target	0	runlevel0.target	Halts the system and turns the power off.

Figure 16-2. *Comparison of SystemV runlevels with systemd targets and some target aliases*

Each target has a set of dependencies described in its configuration file. systemd starts the required dependencies. These dependencies are the services required to run the Linux host at a specific level of functionality. When all of the dependencies listed in the target configuration file are loaded and running, the system is running at that target level.

systemd also looks at the legacy SystemV init directories to see if any startup files exist there. If so, systemd uses those as configuration files to start the services described by the files. The deprecated network service is a good example of one of those that still use SystemV startup files in Fedora.

Figure 16-3 is copied directly from the bootup man page.[17] It shows a map of the general sequence of events during systemd startup and the basic ordering requirements to ensure a successful startup.

The sysinit.target and basic.target targets can be considered as checkpoints in the startup process. Although systemd has as one of its design goals to start system services in parallel, there are still certain services and functional targets that must be started before other services and targets can be started. These checkpoints cannot be passed until all of the services and targets required by that checkpoint are fulfilled.

The sysinit.target is reached when all of the units on which it depends are completed. All of those units, mounting filesystems, setting up swap files, starting udev, setting the random generator seed, initiating low-level services, and setting up cryptographic services if one or more filesystems are encrypted, must be completed, but within the sysinit.target those tasks can be performed in parallel.

The sysinit.target starts up all of the low-level services and units required for the system to be marginally functional and that are required to enable moving on to the basic.target.

After the sysinit.target is fulfilled, systemd next starts the basic.target, starting all of the units required to fulfill it. The basic target provides some additional functionality by starting units that are required for all of the next targets. These include setting up things like paths to various executable directories, communication sockets, and timers.

---

[17] Use the command **man bootup**.

Finally, the user-level targets, multi-user.target or graphical.target, are initialized. The multi-user.target must be reached before the graphical target dependencies can be met. The underlined targets in Figure 16-3 are the usual startup targets. When one of these targets is reached, then startup has completed. If the multi-user.target is the default, then you should see a text-mode login on the console. If graphical.target is the default, then you should see a graphical login; the specific GUI login screen you see will depend upon the default display manager.

The bootup man page also describes and provides maps of the boot into the initial RAM disk and the systemd shutdown process.

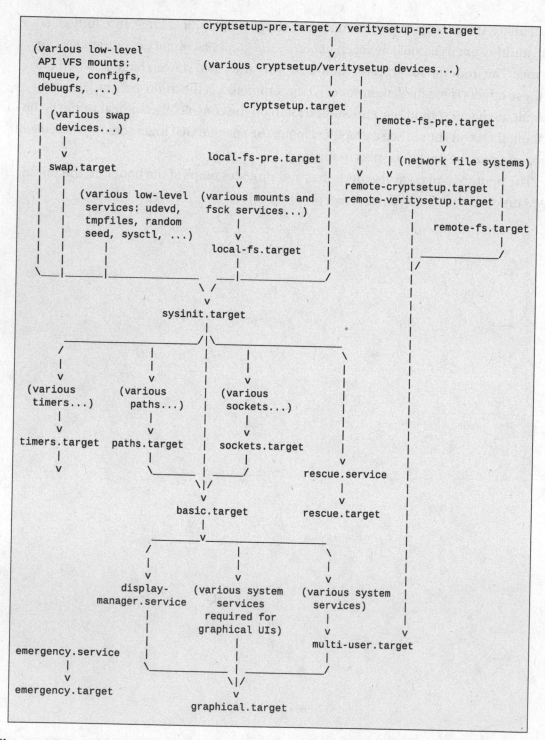

Figure 16-3. *The systemd startup map from the bootup man page*

EXPERIMENT 16-6: CHANGING THE DEFAULT TARGET

So far we have only booted to the graphical.target, so let's change the default target to multi-user.target to boot into a console interface rather than a GUI.

As the root user on StudentVM1, change to the directory in which systemd configuration is maintained and do a long listing:

```
[root@studentvm1 ~]# cd /etc/systemd/system/ ; ll
total 56
drwxr-xr-x. 2 root root 4096 Nov  5 04:17  basic.target.wants
drwxr-xr-x. 2 root root 4096 Nov  5 04:17  bluetooth.target.wants
lrwxrwxrwx. 1 root root   37 Nov  5 04:17  ctrl-alt-del.target -> /usr/lib/
systemd/system/reboot.target
<SNIP>
lrwxrwxrwx. 1 root root   40 Jan 17 07:39  default.target -> /usr/lib/
systemd/system/graphical.target
drwxr-xr-x. 2 root root 4096 Nov  5 04:18  'dev-virtio\x2dports-org.qemu.
guest_agent.0.device.wants'
lrwxrwxrwx  1 root root   39 Feb  7 16:18  display-manager.service -> /usr/
lib/systemd/system/lightdm.service
drwxr-xr-x. 2 root root 4096 Nov  5 04:17  getty.target.wants
drwxr-xr-x. 2 root root 4096 Jan 17 07:54  graphical.target.wants
drwxr-xr-x. 2 root root 4096 Nov  5 04:18  local-fs.target.wants
drwxr-xr-x. 2 root root 4096 Jan 25 13:52  multi-user.target.wants
drwxr-xr-x. 2 root root 4096 Nov  5 04:17  network-online.target.wants
drwxr-xr-x. 2 root root 4096 Nov  5 04:18  remote-fs.target.wants
drwxr-xr-x. 2 root root 4096 Nov  5 04:18  sockets.target.wants
drwxr-xr-x. 2 root root 4096 Jan 17 02:53  sysinit.target.wants
drwxr-xr-x. 2 root root 4096 Jan 20 11:28  sysstat.service.wants
drwxr-xr-x. 2 root root 4096 Nov  5 04:18  timers.target.wants
drwxr-xr-x. 2 root root 4096 Nov  5 04:18  vmtoolsd.service.requires
```

The default.target entry is a symbolic link to the directory /lib/systemd/system/graphical.target. List that directory to see what else is there:

```
[root@studentvm1 system]# ll /lib/systemd/system/ | less
```

You should see files, directories, and more links in this listing, but look for multi-user.target and graphical.target. Now display the contents of default.target, which is a link to the file /lib/systemd/system/graphical.target. The cat command shows the content of the linked file. You can see that this link provides access to a file that is actually located in a different directory from the PWD – just as if it were in the PWD:

```
[root@studentvm1 system]# cat default.target
#  SPDX-License-Identifier: LGPL-2.1+
#
#  This file is part of systemd.
#
#  systemd is free software; you can redistribute it and/or modify it
#  under the terms of the GNU Lesser General Public License as published by
#  the Free Software Foundation; either version 2.1 of the License, or
#  (at your option) any later version.

[Unit]
Description=Graphical Interface
Documentation=man:systemd.special(7)
Requires=multi-user.target
Wants=display-manager.service
Conflicts=rescue.service rescue.target
After=multi-user.target rescue.service rescue.target display-manager.service
AllowIsolate=yes
[root@studentvm1 system]#
```

This link to the graphical.target file now describes all of the prerequisites and needs that the graphical user interface requires. To enable the host to boot to multi-user mode, we need to delete the existing link and then create a new one that points to the correct target. Make /etc/systemd/system the PWD if it is not already:

```
# rm -f default.target
# ln -s /lib/systemd/system/multi-user.target default.target
```

List the default.target link to verify that it links to the correct file:

```
# ll default.target
lrwxrwxrwx 1 root root 37 Nov 28 16:08 default.target -> /lib/systemd/system/
multi-user.target
[root@studentvm1 system]#
```

If your link does not look exactly like that, delete it and try again. List the content of the default.target link:

```
[root@studentvm1 system]# cat default.target
# SPDX-License-Identifier: LGPL-2.1+
#
# This file is part of systemd.
#
# systemd is free software; you can redistribute it and/or modify it
# under the terms of the GNU Lesser General Public License as published by
# the Free Software Foundation; either version 2.1 of the License, or
# (at your option) any later version.

[Unit]
Description=Multi-User System
Documentation=man:systemd.special(7)
Requires=basic.target
Conflicts=rescue.service rescue.target
After=basic.target rescue.service rescue.target
AllowIsolate=yes
[root@studentvm1 system]#
```

The default.target has different requirements in the [Unit] section. It does not require the graphical display manager.

Reboot. Your VM should boot to the console login for virtual console 1, which is identified on the display as tty1. Now that you know what is necessary to change the default target, change it back to the graphical.target using a command designed for the purpose. Let's first check the current default target:

```
# systemctl get-default
multi-user.target
```

Now change the default target with the command used explicitly for that purpose:

```
# systemctl set-default graphical.target
Removed /etc/systemd/system/default.target.
Created symlink /etc/systemd/system/default.target →
/usr/lib/systemd/system/graphical.target.
[root@studentvm1 ~]#
```

Having changed the default target using both methods, you now understand the details of what is happening when using the systemctl command. Understanding these details can help you when trying to locate the true source of a problem.

Type the following command to go directly to the display manager login page without having to reboot:

```
# systemctl isolate default.target
```

I am unsure why the term "isolate" was chosen for this sub-command by the developers of systemd. However, its effect is to switch targets from one target to another, in this case from the emergency target to the graphical target. The preceding command is equivalent to the old **init 5** command in the days of SystemV start scripts and the init program.

Log into the GUI desktop.

We will explore systemd in more detail in Chapters 35 through 37 of Volume 2.

GRUB and the systemd init system are key components in the boot and startup phases of most modern Linux distributions. These two components work together smoothly to first load the kernel and then to start up all of the system services required to produce a functional GNU/Linux system.

Although I do find both GRUB and systemd more complex than their predecessors, they are also just as easy to learn and manage. The man pages have a great deal of information about systemd, and freedesktop.org has a website that describes the complete startup process[18] and a complete set of systemd man pages[19] online.

Graphical Login Screen

There are still two components that figure into the very end of the boot and startup process for the graphical.target, the display manager (dm) and the window manager (wm). These two programs, regardless of which ones you use on your Linux GUI desktop system, always work closely together to make your GUI login experience smooth and seamless before you even get to your desktop.

---

[18] Freedesktop.org, *systemd bootup process*, www.freedesktop.org/software/systemd/man/bootup.html

[19] Freedesktop.org, *systemd index of man pages*, www.freedesktop.org/software/systemd/man/index.html

Display Manager

The display manager[20] is a program with the sole function of providing the GUI login screen for Linux. After login to a GUI desktop, the display manager turns control over to the window manager. When you log out of the desktop, the display manager is given control again to display the login screen and wait for another login.

There are several display managers; some are provided with their respective desktops. For example, the kdm display manager is provided with the KDE desktop. Many display managers are not directly associated with a specific desktop. Any of the display managers can be used for your login screen regardless of which desktop you are using. And not all desktops have their own display managers. Such is the flexibility of Linux and well-written, modular code.

The typical desktops and display managers are shown in Figure 16-4. The display manager for the first desktop that is installed, that is, GNOME, KDE, etc., becomes the default one. For Fedora, this is usually gdm, which is the GNOME display manager. If GNOME is not installed, then the display manager for the installed desktop is the default. If the desktop selected during installation does not have a default display manager, then gdm is installed and used. If you use KDE as your desktop, the new sddm[21] will be the default display manager.

---

[20] Wikipedia, *X Display Manager*, https://en.wikipedia.org/wiki/X_display_manager_ (program_type)

[21] Wikipedia, *Simple Desktop Display Manager*, https://en.wikipedia.org/wiki/ Simple_Desktop_Display_Manager

Desktop	Display Manager	Comments
GNOME	gdm	GNOME display manager
KDE	kdm	KDE display manager (up through Fedora 20)
	lightdm	Lightweight Display Manager
LXDE	lxdm	LXDE display manager
KDE	sddm	Simple Desktop Display Manager (Fedora 21 and above)
	xdm	Default X Window System display manager

Figure 16-4. *A short list of display managers*

Regardless of which display manager is configured as the default at installation time, later installation of additional desktops does not automatically change the display manager used. If you want to change the display manager, you must do it yourself from the command line. Any display manager can be used, regardless of which window manager and desktop are used.

Window Manager

The function of a window manager[22] is to manage the creation, movement, and destruction of windows on a GUI desktop including the GUI login screen. The window manager works with the X Window[23] System or the newer Wayland[24] to perform these tasks. The X Window System provides all of the graphical primitives and functions to generate the graphics for a Linux or Unix graphical user interface.

---

[22] Wikipewdia, *X Window Manager*, https://en.wikipedia.org/wiki/X_window_manager
[23] Wikipedia, *X Window System*, https://en.wikipedia.org/wiki/X_Window_System
[24] Wikipedia, *Wayland*, https://en.wikipedia.org/wiki/Wayland_(display_server_protocol)

494

The window manager also controls the appearance of the windows it generates. This includes the functional and decorative aspects of the windows, such as the look of buttons, sliders, window frames, pop-up menus, and more.

As with almost every other component of Linux, there are many different window managers from which to choose. The list in Figure 16-5 represents only a sample of the available window managers. Some of these window managers are stand-alone, that is, they are not associated with a desktop and can be used to provide a simple graphical user interface without the more complex, feature-rich, and more resource-intensive overhead of a full desktop environment. Stand-alone window managers should not be used with any of the desktop environments.

Desktop	Window Manager	Comments
Unity	Compiz	
	Fluxbox	
	FVWM	
	IceWM	
KDE	Kwin	Starting with KDE Plasma 4 in 2008
GNOME	Metacity	Default for GNOME 2
GNOME	Mutter	Default starting with GNOME 3
LXDE	Openbox	
	twm	A very old and simple tiling window manager. Some distros use it as a fallback in case no other window manager or desktop is available.
Xfce	xfwm4	

Figure 16-5. *A short list of window managers*

495

Most window managers are not directly associated with any specific desktop. In fact some window managers can be used without any type of desktop software, such as KDE or GNOME, to provide a very minimalist GUI experience for users. Many desktop environments support the use of more than one window manager.

How Do I Deal with All These Choices?

In most modern distributions, the choices are made for you at installation time and are based on your selection of desktops and the preferences of the packagers of your distribution. The desktop, window manager, and display manager can be easily changed.

Now that systemd has become the standard startup system in many distributions, you can set the preferred display manager in /etc/systemd/system, which is where the basic system startup configuration is located. There is a symbolic link (symlink) named display-manager.service that points to one of the display manager service units in /usr/lib/systemd/system. Each installed display manager has a service unit located there. To change the active display manager, remove the existing display-manager.service link and replace it with the one you want to use.

EXPERIMENT 16-7: DISPLAY AND WINDOW MANAGERS

Perform this experiment as root. We will install additional display managers and stand-alone window managers and then switch between them.

Check and see which window managers are already installed. The RPMs in which the window managers are packaged have inconsistent naming, so it is difficult to locate them using a simple DNF search unless you already know their RPM package names, which, after a bit of research, I do:

```
# dnf list compiz fluxbox fvwm icewm xorg-x11-twm xfwm4
Last metadata expiration check: 0:19:40 ago on Sun 05 Feb 2023
01:37:32 PM EST.
Installed Packages
xfwm4.x86_64                    4.16.1-6.fc37                    @anaconda
Available Packages
compiz.i686                     1:0.8.18-6.fc37                  fedora
compiz.x86_64                   1:0.8.18-6.fc37                  fedora
```

fluxbox.x86_64	1.3.7-20.fc37	fedora
fvwm.x86_64	2.6.9-8.fc37	fedora
icewm.x86_64	3.3.1-1.fc37	updates

Now let's look at some of the display managers:

```
# dnf list gdm kdm lightdm lxdm sddm xfdm xorg-x11-xdm
Last metadata expiration check: 0:20:23 ago on Sun 05 Feb 2023
01:37:32 PM EST.
Installed Packages
lightdm.x86_64          1.32.0-2.fc37                              @anaconda
Available Packages
gdm.i686                1:43.0-3.fc37                              fedora
gdm.x86_64              1:43.0-3.fc37                              fedora
kdm.x86_64              1:4.11.22-36.fc37                          fedora
lightdm.i686            1.32.0-2.fc37                              fedora
lxdm.x86_64             0.5.3-22.D20220831git2d4ba970.fc37         fedora
sddm.i686               0.19.0^git20221025.fc24321-1.fc37          fedora
sddm.x86_64             0.19.0^git20221025.fc24321-1.fc37          fedora
```

Each display manager is started as a systemd service, so another way to determine which ones are installed is to check the /usr/lib/systemd/system/ directory. The lightdm display manager shows up twice as installed and available because there was an update for it at the time this task was performed:

```
# cd /usr/lib/systemd/system/ ; ll *dm.service
-rw-r--r--. 1 root root 1081 Jul 21  2022 lightdm.service
[root@studentvm1 system]#
```

Like my VM, yours should have only a single dm, the lightdm. Let's install lxdm as the additional display manager, with FVWM, Fluxbox, and IceWM for window managers:

```
# dnf install -y lxdm compiz fvwm fluxbox icewm
```

Now we must restart the display manager service to display the newly installed window managers in the display manager selection tool. The simplest way is to log out of the desktop and restart the dm from a virtual console session:

```
# systemctl restart display-manager.service
```

Or we could do this by switching to the multi-user target and then back to the graphical target. Do this, too, just to see what switching between these targets looks like:

```
# systemctl isolate multi-user.target
# systemctl isolate graphical.target
```

But this second method is a lot more typing. Log out, if necessary, to switch back to the lightdm login on vc1 and look in the upper-right corner of the lightdm login screen. The leftmost icon, which on my VM looks like a sheet of paper with a wrench,[25] allows us to choose the desktop or window manager we want to use before we log in. Click this icon and choose FVWM from the menu in Figure 16-6, and then log in.

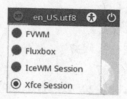

Figure 16-6.   *The lightdm display manager menu now shows the newly installed window managers*

Explore this window manager by using a left click in the desktop, open an Xterm instance, and locate the menu option that gives access to application programs. Figure 16-7 shows the FVWM desktop (this is not a desktop environment like KDE or GNOME) with an open Xterm instance and a menu tree that is opened with a left click in the display. A different menu is opened with a right click.

FVWM is a very basic but usable window manager. Like most window managers, it provides menus to access various functions and a graphical display that supports simple windowing functionality. FVWM also provides multiple windows in which to run programs for some task management capabilities.

Notice that the XDGMenu in Figure 16-7 also contains Xfce applications. The Start Here menu item leads to the FVWM menus that include all of the standard Linux applications that are installed on the host.

---

[25] The icon on your version of lightdm might be different. This icon is used to show the currently selected DM so will change when you select a different one.

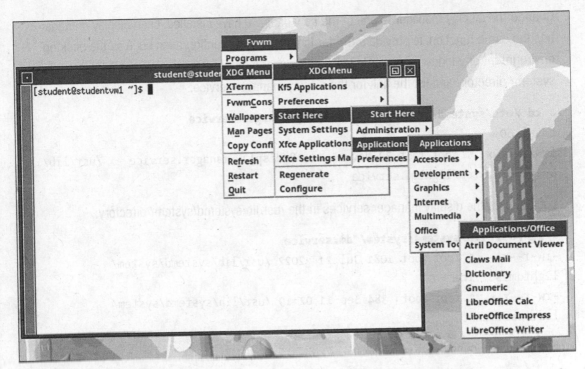

Figure 16-7. *The FVWM window manager with an Xterm instance and some of the available menus*

After spending a bit of time exploring the FVWM interface, log out. Can't find the way to do that? Neither could I as it is very nonintuitive. Left click in the desktop and open the FvwmConsole. Then type in the command **Quit** – yes, with the uppercase Q – and press **Enter**. We could also open an Xterm session and use the following command, which kills all instances of the FVWM window manager belonging to the student user:

```
# killall fvwm
```

Try each of the other window managers, exploring the basic functions of launching applications and a terminal session. When you have finished that, exit whichever window manager you are in and log in again using the Xfce desktop environment.

Change the display manager to one of the new ones we have installed. Each display manager has the same function, to provide a GUI for login and some configuration such as the desktop environment or window manager to start as the user interface. Change into the /etc/systemd/system/ directory and list the link for the display manager service:

```
# cd /etc/systemd/system/ ; ll display-manager.service
total 60
lrwxrwxrwx. 1 root root 39 Nov  5 04:18 display-manager.service -> /usr/lib/
systemd/system/lightdm.service
```

Locate all of the display manager services in the /usr/lib/systemd/system/ directory:

```
# ll /usr/lib/systemd/system/*dm.service
-rw-r--r--. 1 root root 1081 Jul 21  2022 /usr/lib/systemd/system/
lightdm.service
-rw-r--r--  1 root root  384 Sep 11 02:19 /usr/lib/systemd/system/
lxdm.service
```

And make the change:

```
# rm -f display-manager.service
# ln -s /usr/lib/systemd/system/lxdm.service display-manager.service
# ll display-manager.service
lrwxrwxrwx 1 root root 36 Feb  5 16:08 display-manager.service -> /usr/lib/
systemd/system/lxdm.service
```

As far as I can tell at this point, rebooting the host is the only way to reliably activate the new dm. Go ahead and reboot your VM now to do that. Figure 16-8 shows what the lxdm display manager looks like.

Figure 16-8. *The lxdm display manager looks a bit different from lightdm but performs the same function to allow you to select a window manager and to log in*

Log in using lxdm. Then log out and switch back to the lightdm.

Different distributions and desktops have various means of changing the window manager but, in general, changing the desktop environment also changes the window manager to the default one for that desktop. For current releases of Fedora Linux, the desktop environment can be changed on the display manager login screen. If stand-alone window managers are also installed, they also appear in the list with the desktop environments.

There are many different choices for display and window managers available. When you install most modern distributions with any kind of desktop, the choices of which ones to install and activate are usually made by the installation program. For most users, there should never be any need to change these choices. For others who have different needs or for those who are simply more adventurous, there are many options and combinations from which to choose. With a little research, you can make some interesting changes.

Recovery Mode

There are three different terms that are typically applied to recovery mode: *recovery*, *rescue*, and *maintenance*. These are all functionally the same. Maintenance mode is typically used when the Linux host fails to boot to its default target due to some error that occurs during the boot and startup.

The function of recovery mode is to allow the SysAdmin to access the system when it is running at a low level with no system services running and no users except root can be logged in. This can prevent users from losing data, but it also prevents unauthorized remote access, such as through SSH, which would enable the remote user to install malware or to steal data. The root user has the freedom to work in recovery mode without having to worry about the effect on other users.

Many maintenance tasks cannot be performed when running in the graphical.target or the multi-user.target. So those tasks must be performed in maintenance mode.

EXPERIMENT 16-8: RECOVERY MODE

Reboot the StudentVM1 virtual machine. Press the **Esc** key when the GRUB menu is displayed.
After checking out this menu, select the recovery mode as shown in Figure 16-9 and
press **Enter**.

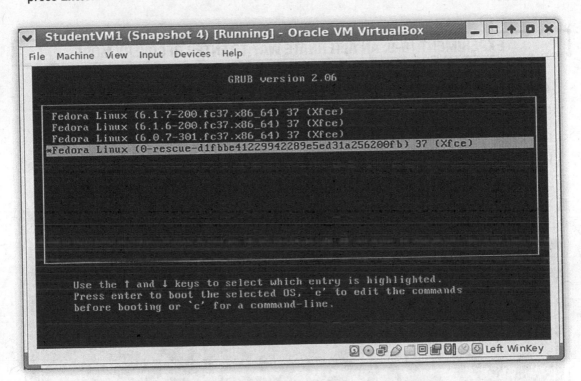

Figure 16-9. *Select the recovery kernel*

I found that this did not work and the computer ended up running the graphical.target. Rescue
mode has not worked correctly for some time. However, it may be fixed in the future, so you
should know this method for entering it.

When Booting to Rescue Mode Fails

The probability is very high that the entry into rescue mode has failed for you. This section will show you a consistent method for entering rescue mode in order to perform system maintenance. It is just a bit more work, but it is easy and you end up in the same place.

EXPERIMENT 16-9: AN ALTERNATE WAY TO ENTER RECOVERY MODE

This experiment shows you an alternate way to enter recovery mode. Despite the fact that you need to modify the kernel command line – and that sounds scary – it is quite easy.

Reboot the VM and when you get to the GRUB menu, as shown in Figure 16-10, press the **E** key to edit the Linux kernel command line. Do not press the Shift key when you press **E**.

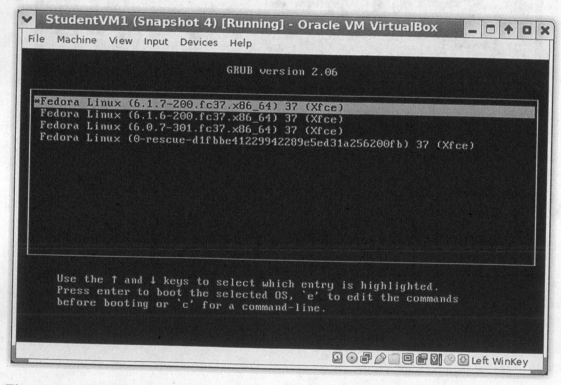

Figure 16-10. Press the E key to edit the kernel command line

At this point you will be immediately taken to a simple editor that will allow you to modify the kernel command line as shown in Figure 16-11. Use the down arrow key to move the cursor down to the line that starts "linux". Then press the **End** key on the keyboard to go to the end of that line. Type **1** to add it to the end of the line. The large arrow in Figure 16-11 shows where the 1 will end up.

Figure 16-11 also shows the basic editing instructions at the bottom of the screen. Read those instructions, but be sure you understand that using Ctrl-C or F2 to get to a command line means a GRUB command line and not the bash command line. There is a big difference.

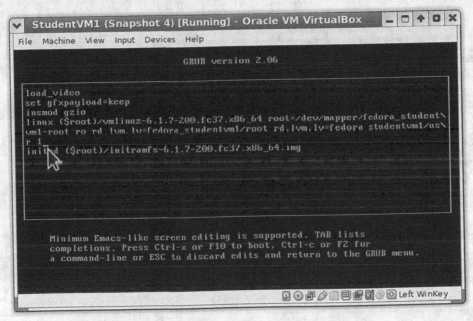

Figure 16-11. *Add a "1" to the end of the kernel command line and press the "F10" key to boot into rescue mode*

After adding a 1 to the end of the kernel command line, press the **F10** key to boot into rescue mode.

Working in Rescue Mode

Now that you are in rescue mode, you can perform a simple experiment in which you will learn about the use of this mode.

EXPERIMENT 16-10: EXPLORING RESCUE MODE

When the system reaches the maintenance login shown in Figure 16-12, enter the root password and press Enter.

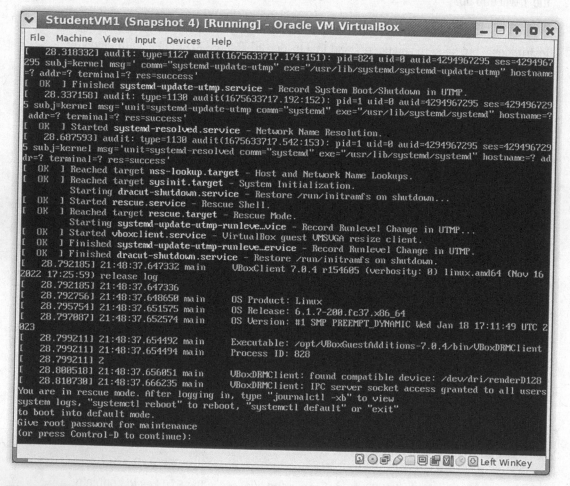

Figure 16-12. *After booting to a recovery-mode kernel, you use the root password to enter maintenance (recovery) mode*

While in recovery mode, explore the system while it is in the equivalent of what used to be called single-user mode.

The lsblk utility will show that all of the filesystems are mounted in their correct locations, and the nmcli command will show that networking has not been started. The computer is up and running, but it is in a very minimal mode of operation. Only the most essential services are available to enable problem solving. The runlevel command will show that the host is in the equivalent of the old SystemV runlevel 1.

Figure 16-13 shows the results of these commands.

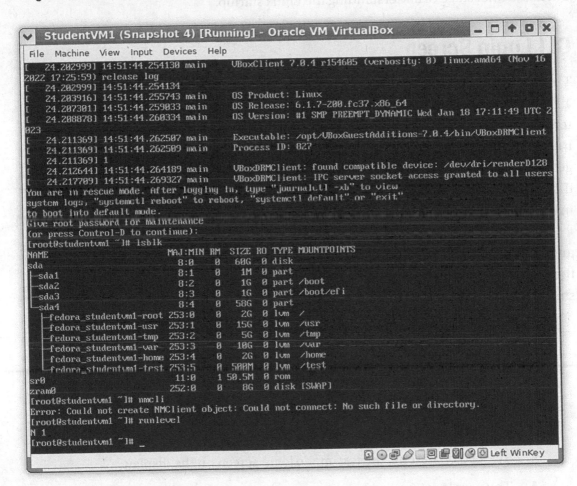

Figure 16-13. *Working in rescue mode*

Take a few minutes to explore rescue mode.

About the Login

After a Linux host is turned on, it boots and goes through the startup process. When the startup process is completed, we are presented with a graphical or command-line login screen. Without a login prompt, it is impossible to log in to a Linux host.

How the login prompt is displayed and how a new one is displayed after a user logs out is the final stage of understanding the Linux startup.

CLI Login Screen

The CLI login screen is initiated by a program called a getty, which stands for GEt TTY. The historical function of a getty was to wait for a connection from a remote dumb terminal to come in on a serial communications line. The getty program would spawn the login screen and wait for a login to occur. When the remote user would login, the getty would terminate, and the default shell for the user account would launch and allow the user to interact with the host on the command line. When the user logged out, the init program would spawn a new getty to listen for the next connection.

Today's process is much the same with a few updates. We now use an agetty, which is an advanced form of getty, in combination with the systemd service manager to handle the Linux virtual consoles as well as the increasingly rare incoming modem lines. The steps listed in the following shows the sequence of events in a modern Linux computer:

1. systemd starts the systemd-getty-generator daemon.

2. The systemd-getty-generator spawns an agetty on each of the virtual consoles using the serial-getty@.service.

3. The agettys wait for virtual console connection, that is, the user switching to one of the VCs.

4. The agetty presents the text-mode login screen on the display.

5. The user logs in.

6. The shell specified in /etc/passwd is started.

7. Shell configuration scripts run.

8. The user works in the shell session.

9. The user logs off.

10. The systemd-getty-generator spawns an agetty on the logged-out
     virtual console.

11. Go to step 3.

Starting with step 3 this is a circular process that repeats as long as the host is up and running. New login screens are displayed on a virtual console immediately after the user logs out of the old session.

GUI Login Screen

The GUI login screen as displayed by the display manager is handled in much the same way as the systemd-getty-generator handles the text-mode login:

1. The specified display manager (dm) is launched by systemd at the
    end of the startup sequence.

2. The display manager displays graphical login screen, usually on
    virtual console 1.

3. The dm waits for a login.

4. The user logs in.

5. The specified window manager is started.

6. The specified desktop GUI, if any, is started.

7. The user performs work in the window manager/desktop.

8. The user logs out.

9. systemd respawns the display manager.

10. Go to step 2.

The steps are almost the same, and the display manager functions as a graphical version of the agetty.

Chapter Summary

We have explored the Linux boot and startup processes in some detail. This chapter explored reconfiguration of the GRUB bootloader to display the kernel boot and startup messages as well as to create recovery-mode entries, ones that actually work, for the GRUB menu. Because there is a bug when attempting to boot to the rescue-mode kernel, we discussed our responsibility as SysAdmins to report bugs through the appropriate channels.

We installed and explored some different window managers as an alternative to more complex desktop environments. The desktop environments do depend upon at least one of the window managers for their low-level graphical functions while providing useful, needed, and sometimes fun features. We also discovered how to change the default display manager to provide a different GUI login screen as well as how the GUI and command-line logins work.

This chapter has also been about learning the tools like **dd** that we used to extract the data from files and from specific locations on the hard drive. Understanding those tools and how they can be used to locate and trace data and files provides SysAdmins with skills that can be applied to exploring other aspects of Linux.

Exercises

1. Describe the Linux boot process.

2. Describe the Linux startup process.

3. What does GRUB do?

4. Where is stage 1 of GRUB located on the hard drive?

5. What is the function of systemd during startup?

6. Where are the systemd startup target files and links located?

7. Configure the StudentVM1 host so that the default.target is reboot. target and reboot the system. After watching the VM reboot a couple times, reconfigure the default.target to point to the graphical.target again and reboot.

8. Can the root (/) partition be unmounted when in rescue mode?

9. What is the function of an agetty?

10. Describe the function of a display manager.

11. What Linux component attaches to a virtual console and displays the text-mode login screen?

12. List and describe the Linux components involved and the sequence of events that take place when a user logs into a virtual console until they log out.

13. What happens when the display manager service is restarted from a root terminal session on the desktop using the command **systemctl restart display-manager.service**?

CHAPTER 17

Shell Configuration

Objectives

In this chapter you will learn

- How the bash shell is configured
- How to modify the configuration of the bash shell so that your changes won't be overwritten during updates
- The names and locations of the files used to configure Linux shells at both global and user levels
- Which shell configuration files should not be changed
- How to set shell options
- The locations in which to place or find supplementary configuration files
- How to set environment variables from the command line
- How to set environment variables using shell configuration files
- The function of aliases and how to set them

In this chapter we will learn to configure the bash shell because it is the default shell for almost every Linux distribution. Other shells have very similar configuration files, and many of them coexist with the bash configuration files in both the /etc directory for global configuration and the users' home directories for local configuration.

We will explore environment variables and shell variables and how they contribute to the behavior of the shell itself and the programs that run in a shell. We will discover the files that can be used to configure the bash shell globally and for individual users.

513

© David Both 2023
D. Both, *Using and Administering Linux: Volume 1*, https://doi.org/10.1007/978-1-4842-9618-9_17

This chapter is not about learning every possible environment variable. It is more about learning where the files used to configure the bash shell are located and how to manage them.

We have looked at the $PATH and $? environment variables, but there are many more variables than just those. The $EDITOR variable, for example, defines the name of the default text-mode editor to be used when programs call for an editor, and, as we have already seen, the $PATH environment variable defines a list of directories in which the shell will look for commands.

Most of these variables are used to help define how the shell and the programs running in the shell behave. Running programs, whether command line or GUI, can extract the values of one or more environment variables in order to determine specific behaviors.

Starting the Shell

The sequence of events that takes place when we start a shell provides us with the information we need to understand its configuration. This sequence begins with global configuration files and then proceeds to local configuration files, which allow users to override global configuration settings. All of the files we encounter in this section are ASCII text files, so they are open and knowable. Some of these files should not be changed, but their content can be overridden in local configuration files.

Before we can explore any further, we need to define a couple terms. There are multiple ways that one can start a shell, and this results in multiple sets of circumstances under which the shell might be started. There are two circumstances that we are concerned about here, and they do result in different environments and a different sequence in which the shell initialization is performed:

- **Login shell**: A login shell is one where you need to use a user ID and password to gain access. This is the case with a virtual console or when you log in remotely using SSH. The GUI desktop[1] also constitutes a login shell.

- **Non-login shell**: A non-login shell is one that is spawned or launched from within another, already running shell. This parent shell can be a login shell or another non-login shell. Non-login shells can be

---

[1] In many ways a GUI desktop can be considered a shell, and its login sequence is very similar to that of a login to a virtual console.

514

launched from within a GUI desktop, by the **screen** command, or
from within a terminal emulator where multiple tabs or windows can
each contain a shell instance.

There are five main files and one directory containing system-level configuration
files that are used to configure the bash environment. We will look at each of these in a
bit more detail, but they are listed here along with their main functions:

- **/etc/profile**: System-wide environment and startup programs.

- **/etc/bashrc**: System-wide functions and aliases.

- **~/.bash_profile**: User-specific environment and startup programs.

- **~/.bashrc**: User-specific aliases and functions.

- **~/.bash_logout**: User-specific commands to execute when the user
  logs out.

- **/etc/profile.d/**: This directory contains system-wide scripts for
  configuring various CLI tools such as vim and mc. The SysAdmin can
  also place custom configuration scripts in this directory.

All user shell configuration files that are located in the /etc/skel directory, such as
~/.bash_profile and ~/.bashrc, are copied into the new account home directory when
each new user account is created. We will explore managing users and the creation of
new accounts in Volume 2, Chapter 35.

The sequence of execution for all of the bash configuration files is shown in
Figure 17-1. It can seem convoluted and it is. But once we unravel it, you will understand
how bash is configured. You will know where you can make changes that can override
the defaults, add to the $PATH, and prevent future updates from overwriting the
changes you have made. Note that the global configuration files are located in /etc or a
subdirectory and the local bash configuration files are located in the login user's home
directory (~).

Let's walk through the sequence using the flowchart in Figure 17-1 and then do
a couple experiments that will enable you to understand how to follow the sequence
yourself if that should ever be necessary. Note that the dashed lines in Figure 17-1
indicate that the script calls an external script and then control returns to the calling
script. So /etc/profile and /etc/bashrc both call the scripts located in /etc/profile.d, and
~/.bash_profile calls ~/.bashrc, and, when those scripts have completed, control returns
to the script that called them.

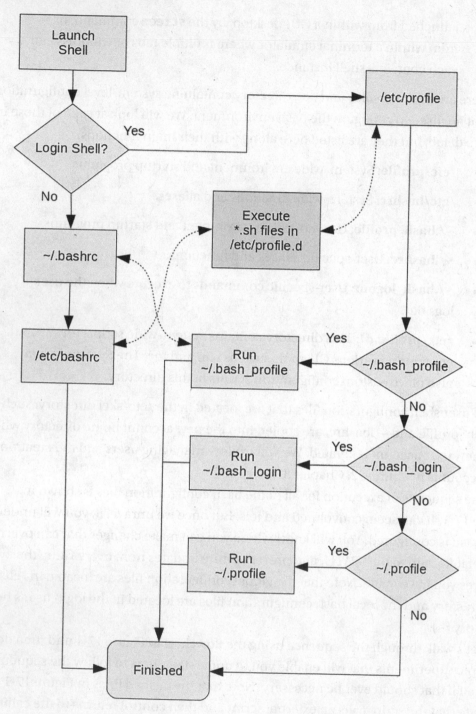

Figure 17-1. *The bash shell configuration sequence of shell programs*

Non-login Shell Startup

We start with the non-login shell because it is a bit simpler. Starting in the upper left-hand corner of Figure 17-1, we launch the shell. A determination is made that it is a non-login shell, so we take the **No** path out of the decision diamond. This is the case because we are already logged into the desktop.

This path leads us through execution of ~/.bashrc, which calls /etc/bashrc. The /etc/bashrc program contains code that calls each of the files ending with *.sh and the file sh.local that are located in /etc/profile.d. These are not the only files in that directory, as other shells also store configuration files there. After all of the bash configuration files in /etc/profile.d complete their execution, control returns to /etc/bashrc, which performs a bit of cleanup and then exits. At this point the bash shell is fully configured.

Login Shell Startup

The startup and configuration sequence through these shell scripts is more complex for a login shell than it is for a non-login shell. Yet most of the same configuration takes place.

This time we take the **Yes** path out of the first decision point in the upper-left corner of Figure 17-1. This causes the /etc/profile script to execute. The /etc/profile script contains some of its own code that executes all of the files ending with *.sh and the file sh.local that are located in /etc/profile.d. After these files have finished running, control returns to /etc/profile, which finishes its own execution.

The shell looks now for three files in sequence, ~/.bash_profile, ~/.bash_login, and ~/.profile. It runs the first one it finds and ignores the others. Fedora home directories typically contain the ~/.bash_profile file, so that is the one that is executed. The other two files do not exist because there is no point to that. These two files, ~/.bash_login and ~/.profile, are considered by some to be possible alternate files that might exist in some old legacy hosts, so the shell continues to look for them so as to maintain backward compatibility. Some software such as the Torch machine learning framework stores its environment variables in ~/.profile, and other software might also use these legacy files.

The ~/.bash_profile configuration file also calls the ~/.bashrc file, which is also executed, and then control returns to ~.bash_profile. When ~.bash_profile finishes execution, the shell configuration is complete.

Exploring the Global Configuration Scripts

The scripts in /etc, /etc/profile, and /etc/bashrc, as well as all of the *.sh scripts in /etc/profile.d, are the global configuration scripts for the bash shell. Global configuration is inherited by all users. A little knowledge of the content of these scripts helps us better understand how it all fits together.

EXPERIMENT 17-1: GLOBAL CONFIGURATION SCRIPTS

Perform this experiment as the student user. Set /etc as the PWD, and then look at the permissions of /etc/profile:

```
# cd /etc ; ll profile
-rw-r--r--. 1 root root 2078 Apr 17  2018 profile
```

It is readable by all but can only be modified by root. Note that its eXecute permission is not set. In fact, none of these configuration files are marked as executable despite the fact that the commands in them must be executed in order to set up the environment. That is because the shell "sources" /etc/profile, which then sources other setup files. After sourcing the file, which can be done with the **source** command or the much shorter alternative, dot (.), the instructions in the file are executed.

Use **less** to look at the content of /etc/profile to see what it does. It is not necessary to analyze this entire file in detail. But you should be able to see where some of the environment variables are set programmatically. Search for instances of PATH to see how the $PATH is set. The first thing you see after the comments describing the file is a procedure named "pathmunge", which is called by code further down when the initial path needs to be modified:

```
pathmunge () {
    case ":${PATH}:" in
        *:"$1":*)
            ;;
        *)
            if [ "$2" = "after" ] ; then
                PATH=$PATH:$1
            else
                PATH=$1:$PATH
```

```
            fi
    esac
}
```

After this there is some code that determines the effective user ID, $EUID, of the user launching the shell. Then here is the code that sets the first elements of the $PATH environment variable based on whether the $EUID is root with a value of zero (0) or another non-root, non-zero user:

```
# Path manipulation
if [ "$EUID" = "0" ]; then
    pathmunge /usr/sbin
    pathmunge /usr/local/sbin
else
    pathmunge /usr/local/sbin after
    pathmunge /usr/sbin after
fi
```

The path is different for root than it is for other users, and this is the bash shell code that makes that happen. Now let's look at some code down near the bottom of this file. The next bit of code is the part that locates and executes the bash configuration scripts in /etc/profile.d:

```
for i in /etc/profile.d/*.sh /etc/profile.d/sh.local ; do
    if [ -r "$i" ]; then
        if [ "${-#*i}" != "$-" ]; then
            . "$i"
        else
            . "$i" >/dev/null
        fi
    fi
done
```

List the files in the /etc/profile.d directory:

```
$ ll /etc/profile.d/*.sh
-rw-r--r--. 1 root root  664 Jun 18 06:41 /etc/profile.d/Bash_completion.sh
-rw-r--r--. 1 root root  201 Feb  7  2018 /etc/profile.d/colorgrep.sh
-rw-r--r--. 1 root root 1706 May 29 12:30 /etc/profile.d/colorls.sh
-rw-r--r--. 1 root root   56 Apr 19  2018 /etc/profile.d/colorsysstat.sh
-rw-r--r--. 1 root root  183 May  9  2018 /etc/profile.d/colorxzgrep.sh
```

```
-rw-r--r--. 1 root root  220 Feb  9  2018 /etc/profile.d/colorzgrep.sh
-rw-r--r--. 1 root root  757 Dec 14  2017 /etc/profile.d/gawk.sh
-rw-r--r--  1 root root   70 Aug 31 08:25 /etc/profile.d/gnome-ssh-askpass.sh
-rw-r--r--  1 root root  288 Mar 12  2018 /etc/profile.d/kde.sh
-rw-r--r--. 1 root root 2703 May 25 07:04 /etc/profile.d/lang.sh
-rw-r--r--. 1 root root  253 Feb 17  2018 /etc/profile.d/less.sh
-rwxr-xr-x 1 root root  153 Aug  3  2017 /etc/profile.d/mc.sh
-rw-r--r--  1 root root  488 Oct  3 13:49 /etc/profile.d/myBashConfig.sh
-rw-r--r--. 1 root root  248 Sep 19 04:31 /etc/profile.d/vim.sh
-rw-r--r--. 1 root root 2092 May 21  2018 /etc/profile.d/vte.sh
-rw-r--r--. 1 root root  310 Feb 17  2018 /etc/profile.d/which2.sh
```

Can you see the file I added? It is the myBashConfig.sh file, which does not exist on your VM but does on my primary workstation. Here is the content of myBashConfig.sh. I have set some aliases, set vi editing mode for my bash shell command line, and set a couple environment variables:

```
################################################################
# The following global changes to Bash configuration added by me
################################################################
alias lsn='ls --color=no'
alias vim='vim -c "colorscheme desert" '
alias glances='glances -t1'
# Set vi for Bash editing mode
set -o vi
# Set vi as the default editor for all apps that check this
# Set some shell variables
EDITOR=vi
TERM=xterm
```

Look at the content of some of the other bash configuration files in /etc/profile.d to see what they do.

This last bit of code in /etc/profile is to source and run the /etc/bashrc file if it exists and to see if the $BASH_VERSION- variable is not null:

```
if [ -n "${BASH_VERSION-}" ] ; then
     if [ -f /etc/bashrc ] ; then
             # Bash login shells run only /etc/profile
             # Bash non-login shells run only /etc/bashrc
```

```
# Check for double sourcing is done in /etc/bashrc.
. /etc/bashrc
```
```
    fi
fi
```

So now look at the content of /etc/bashrc. As the first comment in this file states, its function is to set system-wide functions and aliases. This includes setting the terminal emulator type, the command prompt string, the umask that defines the default permissions of new files when they are created, and – very importantly – the $SHELL variable, which defines the fully qualified path and name of the bash shell executable. We will explore umask in Chapter 18 in this volume.

None of the default files used for global configuration of the bash shell should be modified. To modify or add to the global configuration, you should add a custom file to the /etc/profile.d directory that contains the configuration mods you wish to make. The name of the file is unimportant other than it must end in ".sh", but I suggest naming it something noticeable.

Exploring the Local Configuration Scripts

The local bash configuration files are located in each user's home directory. Each user can modify these files in order to configure the shell environment to their own preferences. The local configuration files, .bashrc and .bash_profile, contain some very basic configuration items.

EXPERIMENT 17-2: LOCAL CONFIGURATION SCRIPTS

When a login shell is started, bash first runs /etc/profile, and when that finishes, the shell runs ~/.bash_profile. View the ~/.bash_profile file. The local files we are viewing in this experiment are small enough to reproduce here in their entirety:

```
$ cat .bash_profile
# .bash_profile

# Get the aliases and functions
if [ -f ~/.bashrc ]; then
        . ~/.bashrc
fi
```

```
# User specific environment and startup programs

PATH=$PATH:$HOME/.local/bin:$HOME/bin

export PATH
```

First, ~/.bash_profile runs ~/.bashrc to set the aliases and functions into the environment. It then sets the path and exports it. That means that the path is then available to all future non-login shells.

The ~/.bashrc config file is called by ~/.bash_profile. This file, as shown in the following, calls /etc/bashrc:

```
$ cat .bashrc
# .bashrc

# Source global definitions
if [ -f /etc/bashrc ]; then
        . /etc/bashrc
fi

# Uncomment the following line if you don't like systemctl's auto-paging
feature:
# export SYSTEMD_PAGER=

# User specific aliases and functions
[student@studentvm1 ~]$
```

The comments in these files inform the users where they can insert any local configuration such as environment variables or aliases.

Testing It

That explanation is all nice and everything, but what does it really mean? There is one way to find out, and this is a technique I use frequently to test for the sequence of execution of a complex and interrelated system of shell programs or of procedures within shell programs. I just add an echo statement at the beginning of each of the programs in question stating which shell program is running.

EXPERIMENT 17-3: TRACING CONFIG SCRIPT EXECUTION

Edit each of the following shell programs and add one line to the beginning of the program. I have highlighted the lines to be added in bold so you know where to place them. For this experiment, it is safe to ignore the warning comments embedded in each program against changing them.

These first three programs need to be modified by root.

Edit the /etc/profile configuration file:

```
# /etc/profile

# System wide environment and startup programs, for login setup
# Functions and aliases go in /etc/bashrc

# It's NOT a good idea to change this file unless you know what you
# are doing. It's much better to create a custom.sh shell script in
# /etc/profile.d/ to make custom changes to your environment, as this
# will prevent the need for merging in future updates.

pathmunge () {
    case ":${PATH}:" in
        *:"$1":*)
            ;;
        *)
            if [ "$2" = "after" ] ; then
                PATH=$PATH:$1
            else
                PATH=$1:$PATH
            fi
    esac
}

echo "Running /etc/profile"

if [ -x /usr/bin/id ]; then
    if [ -z "$EUID" ]; then
        # ksh workaround
        EUID=`id -u`
        UID=`id -ru`
```

523

```
        fi
        USER="`id -un`"
        LOGNAME=$USER
        MAIL="/var/spool/mail/$USER"
fi
```

Note that in the case of /etc/profile, we add our bit of code after the pathmunge procedure. This is because all procedures must appear before any in-line code.[2]

Edit the /etc/bashrc file:

```
# /etc/bashrc

# System wide functions and aliases
# Environment stuff goes in /etc/profile

# It's NOT a good idea to change this file unless you know what you
# are doing. It's much better to create a custom.sh shell script in
# /etc/profile.d/ to make custom changes to your environment, as this
# will prevent the need for merging in future updates.

echo "Running /etc/bashrc"

# Prevent doublesourcing
if [ -z ".bashrcSOURCED" ]; then
  .bashrcSOURCED="Y"
```

Add a new bash shell program, /etc/profile.d/myBashConfig.sh, and add the following two lines to it. It does not need to be made executable:

```
# /etc/profile.d/myBashConfig.sh
echo "Running /etc/profile.d/myBashConfig.sh"
```

The files .bash_profile and .bashrc should be altered by the student user for the student user's account.

Edit ~/.bash_profile:

```
# .bash_profile
echo "Running ~/.bash_profile"
```

---

[2] We will discuss bash coding, procedures, and program structure in Volume 2, Chapter 10.

```
# Get the aliases and functions
if [ -f ~/.bashrc ]; then
    . ~/.bashrc
fi

# User specific environment and startup programs

PATH=$PATH:$HOME/.local/bin:$HOME/bin

export PATH
```

Edit the ~/.bashrc file:

```
# .bashrc
echo "Running ~/.bashrc"

# Source global definitions
if [ -f /etc/bashrc ]; then
    . /etc/bashrc
fi

# Uncomment the following line if you don't like systemctl's auto-paging
feature:
# export SYSTEMD_PAGER=

# User specific aliases and functions
```

After all of the files have been modified as shown previously, open a new terminal session on the desktop. Each file that executes should print its name on the terminal. That should look like this:

```
Running ~/.bashrc
Running /etc/bashrc
Running /etc/profile.d/myBashConfig.sh
[student@studentvm1 ~]$
```

So you can see by the sequence of shell config scripts that were run that this is a non-login shell as shown in Figure 17-1. Switch to virtual console 2 and log in as the student user. You should see the following data:

```
Last login: Sat Nov 24 11:20:41 2018 from 192.178.0.1
Running /etc/profile
Running /etc/profile.d/myBashConfig.sh
Running /etc/bashrc
Running ~/.bash_profile
```

```
Running ~/.bashrc
Running /etc/bashrc
[student@studentvm1 ~]$
```

This experiment shows exactly which files are run and in what sequence. It verifies most of what I have read in other documents and my analysis of the code in each of these files. However, I have intentionally left one error in my analysis and the diagram in Figure 17-1. Can you figure out what the difference is and why?[3]

Exploring the Environment

We have already looked at some environment variables and learned that they affect how the shell behaves under certain circumstances. Environment variables are just like any other variable, a variable name and a value. The shell or programs running under the shell check the content of certain variables and use the values of those variables to determine how they respond to specific input, data values, or other triggering factors. A typical variable looks like this:

```
VARIABLE_NAME=value
```

The environment variables and their values can be explored and manipulated with simple tools. Permanent changes need to be made in the configuration files, but temporary changes can be made with basic commands from the command line.

EXPERIMENT 17-4: INTRODUCING THE ENVIRONMENT

Perform this experiment in a terminal session as the student user. Close all currently open terminal sessions and then open a new terminal session. View the current environment variables using the **printenv** command:

```
$ printenv | less
```

Some environment variables such as LS_COLORS and TERMCAP contain very long strings of text. The LS_COLORS string defines the colors used for display of specific text when various commands are run if the terminal is capable of displaying color. The TERMCAP (TERMinal CAPabilities) variable defines the capabilities of the terminal emulator.

---

[3] Hint: Look for duplicates.

Look at some individual values. What is the value of HOME?

```
$ echo $HOME
/home/student
```

Do you think that this might be how the shell knows which directory to make the PWD using the command **cd** ~? What are the values of LOGNAME, HOSTNAME, pwd, OLDPWD, and USER?

Why is OLDPWD empty, that is, null? Make /tmp the PWD and recheck the values of pwd and OLDPWD. What are they now?

User Shell Variables

Shell variables are part of the local environment. That is, they are accessible to programs, scripts, and user commands. Users can create environment variables within a shell, which then become part of the environment for that one shell. No other shells have access to these local user variables.

If a change is made to a user shell variable or a new one created, it must be explicitly "exported" in order for any sub-processes forked after the new variable is created and exported to see the change. Recall that shell variables are local to the shell in which they were defined. A modified or added shell variable is only available in the current shell. To make a shell variable available as an environment variable for shells launched after the change, use the **export** **VARNAME** command without the dollar $ sign.

Note   By convention, environment variable names are all uppercase, but they can be mixed or all lowercase if that works for you. Just remember that Linux is case sensitive, so Var1 is not the same as VAR1 or var1.

Let's now look at setting new user shell variables.

EXPERIMENT 17-5: ENVIRONMENT VARIABLES

In the existing terminal session as the student user, start by ensuring that a new environment variable named MyVar does not exist and set it. Then verify that it now exists and contains the correct value. The blank line immediately following the command indicates that there is no such variable. Remember "Silence is golden"?

527

```
[student@studentvm1 ~]$ echo $MyVar ; MyVar="MyVariable" ; echo $MyVar
MyVariable
[student@studentvm1 ~]$
```

Open another bash terminal session as the student user and verify that the new variable you created does not exist in this shell:

```
[student@studentvm1 ~]$ echo $MyVar

[student@studentvm1 ~]$
```

Exit from this second shell. In the first terminal session, the one in which the $MyVar variable exists, verify that it still exists and start a screen session:

```
[student@studentvm1 ~]$ echo $MyVar
MyVariable
[student@studentvm1 ~]$ screen
```

Now check for $MyVar:

```
[student@studentvm1 ~]$ echo $MyVar

[student@studentvm1 ~]$
```

Note that $MyVar does not exist in this screen instance of the bash shell. Enter the **exit** command once to exit from the screen session.

Now run the export command and then start another screen session:

```
[student@studentvm1 ~]$ export MyVar="MyVariable" ; echo $MyVar
MyVariable
[student@studentvm1 ~]$ screen
```

Now check for $MyVar again while in the screen session:

```
[student@studentvm1 ~]$ echo $MyVar
MyVariable
[student@studentvm1 ~]$
```

Exit from the screen session again and unset MyVar:

```
[student@studentvm1 ~]$ exit
[screen is terminating]
[student@studentvm1 ~]$ unset MyVar
[student@studentvm1 ~]$ echo $MyVar
```

```
[student@studentvm1 ~]$
```

Let's try one last thing. The **env** utility allows us to set an environment variable temporarily for a program or in this case a sub-shell. The **Bash** command must be an argument of the **env** command in order for this to work:

```
[student@studentvm1 ~]$ env MyVar=MyVariable Bash
[student@studentvm1 ~]$ echo $MyVar
MyVariable
[student@studentvm1 ~]$ exit
exit
[student@studentvm1 ~]$
```

This last tool can be useful when testing scripts or other tools that require an environment a bit different from the one in which you normally work.

Perform a little cleanup – exit from all terminal sessions.

We have now discovered empirically that when local variables are set, they become part of the environment for that shell only. Even after exporting the variable, it only becomes part of the environment of a new shell if that is launched via the screen command.

I have very seldom had any reason to temporarily create a local user environment variable. I usually add my variable creation statements to the ~/.bashrc file if it is for my login account only, or I add it to a custom shell configuration script in /etc/profile.d if it is intended for all users of the system.

Aliases

I dislike typing. I grew up and went to school in a time when boys did not learn typing, so I have really horrible typing skills. Therefore, I prefer to type as little as possible. Of course lazy SysAdmins like to minimize typing just to save time regardless of the state of their typing skills.

Aliases are a good way to reduce typing, which will, therefore, reduce errors. They are a method for substituting a long command for a shorter one that is easier to type because it has fewer characters. Aliases are a common way to reduce typing by making it unnecessary to type in long options that we might use constantly by including them in the alias.

```
EXPERIMENT 17-6: ALIASES
```

As the student user, enter the **alias** command to view the current list of aliases. I did not know until I looked at these aliases that the ls command was already aliased. So when I enter **ls** on the command line, the shell expands that to **ls --color=auto**, which would be a lot of extra typing if I had to do it myself:

```
[student@testvm1 ~]$ alias
alias egrep='egrep --color=auto'
alias fgrep='fgrep --color=auto'
alias glances='glances -t1'
alias grep='grep --color=auto'
alias l.='ls -d .* --color=auto'
alias ll='ls -l --color=auto'
alias ls='ls --color=auto'
alias lsn='ls --color=no'
alias mc='. /usr/libexec/mc/mc-wrapper.sh'
alias vi='vim'
alias vim='vim -c "colorscheme desert" '
alias which='(alias; declare -f) | /usr/bin/which --tty-only --read-
alias --read-functions --show-tilde --show-dot'
alias xzegrep='xzegrep --color=auto'
alias xzfgrep='xzfgrep --color=auto'
alias xzgrep='xzgrep --color=auto'
alias zegrep='zegrep --color=auto'
alias zfgrep='zfgrep --color=auto'
alias zgrep='zgrep --color=auto'
```

Your results should look similar to mine, but I have added some additional aliases. One is for the glances utility, which is not a part of most distributions.

Since vi has been replaced by vim and a lot of SysAdmins like myself have legacy muscle memory and continue to type **vi**, **vi** is aliased to **vim**. Another alias is for **vim** to use the "desert" color scheme. So when I type **vi** on the command line and press the Enter key, the bash shell first expands **vi** to **vim**, and then it expands **vim** to **vim -c "colorscheme desert"** and then executes that command.

Note   For the root user in Fedora, vi is not automatically aliased to vim.

Although these aliases are almost all added to the global environment by the shell configuration files in /etc/profile.d, you can add your own using your local configuration files as well as by adding them at the command line. The command-line syntax is identical to that shown previously.

The aliases shown in Experiment 17-6 are primarily intended to set up default behavior such as color and some standard options. I particularly like the ll alias because I like the long listing of directory contents and instead of typing ls -l I can just type ll. I use the ll command a lot, and it saves typing three characters every time I use it. For slow typists like me that can amount to a lot of time. Aliases also enable me to use complex commands without the need to learn and remember a long and complex command with lots of options and arguments.

I strongly recommend that you do not use aliases to alias Linux commands to those you used in another operating system like some people have done. You will never learn Linux that way.

In Experiment 17-6 the alias for the vim editor sets a color scheme that is not the default. I happen to like the desert color scheme better than the default, so aliasing the vim command to the longer command that also specifies my favorite color scheme is one way to get what I want with less typing.

You can use the alias command to add your own new aliases to the ~/.bashrc file to make them permanent between reboots and logout/login. To make the aliases available to all users on a host, add them to a customization file in /etc/profile.d as discussed earlier. The syntax in either case is the same as from the command line.

Chapter Summary

Does shell startup and configuration seem arcane and confusing to you? I would not be surprised because I was – and sometimes still am – confused. I learned and relearned a lot during my research for this chapter.

The primary thing to remember is that there are specific files used for permanent configuration and that they are executed in different sequences depending upon whether a login or non-login shell is launched. We have explored the shell startup sequence, and we have looked at the content of the bash configuration files and at the proper methods for changing the environment.

We have also learned to use aliases to reduce the amount of typing we need to do.

Exercises

Perform the following exercises to complete this chapter:

1. What is the difference between shell and environment variables? Why is this distinction important?

2. When starting a non-login bash shell, which configuration file is run first?

3. Can a non-privileged user set or change their own shell variables?

4. Which configuration file is the first one to be executed by a newly launched shell on the desktop?

5. What is the value of the COLUMNS variable in each of the open terminal sessions on your current desktop? If you don't see a difference, resize one or more terminal windows and recheck the values. What might this variable be used for?

6. What is the sequence of shell configuration files run when you log in using a virtual console?

7. Why is it important to understand the sequence in which bash configuration files are executed?

8. Add an alias that launches vim with a different color scheme and that is used only for the student user. The color schemes and an informative README.txt file are located in the directory /usr/share/vim/vim81/colors. Try a couple different color schemes and test them by opening one of the bash configuration files.

9. Where did you add the alias in question 8?

10. What sequence of bash configuration files is run when you use the su command to switch to the root user?

11. What sequence of bash configuration files is run when you use the sudo command?

12. You have an environment variable to add so that it becomes part of the environment for all users. In what file do you add it?

13. Which shell configuration files are executed when the system is booted into recovery mode?

CHAPTER 18

Files, Directories, and Links

Objectives

In this chapter you will learn

- To define the term "file"
- To describe the purpose of files
- To read and describe file permissions
- How the umask command and settings affect the creation of files by users
- To set file permissions
- The structure of the metadata for files including the directory entry and the inode
- To describe the three types of Linux file timestamps
- To find, use, and set the three timestamps of a Linux file
- The easy way to identify what type a file is, binary or text
- To obtain the metadata for a file
- To define hard and soft links
- How to use and manage links

535

© David Both 2023
D. Both, *Using and Administering Linux: Volume 1*, https://doi.org/10.1007/978-1-4842-9618-9_18

Introduction

We usually think of files as those things that contain data and that are stored on some form of storage media such as a magnetic or solid-state drive. And this is true – as far as it goes in a Linux environment.

The Free On-line Dictionary of Computing[1] provides a good definition for "computer file" that I will paraphrase here in a way that refers specifically to Linux files. A computer file is a unit of storage consisting of a single sequence of data with a finite length that is stored on a non-volatile storage medium. Files are stored in directories and are accessed using a file name and an optional path. Files also support various attributes such as permissions and timestamps for creation, last modification, and last access.

Although this definition is basically what I said, it provides more detail about the characteristics that are an intrinsic part of Linux files. I would amend the FOLDOC definition to say that files are *usually* stored on some non-volatile medium. Files can also be stored on volatile media such as virtual filesystems, which we will explore in Volume 2, Chapter 24.

In this chapter we will explore these characteristics, the data meta-structures that provide these capabilities, and more.

Preparation

We did create a few directories and files in Chapter 7, but there are no user files in the ~/Documents directory for us to experiment with during this chapter, so let's create some there.

EXPERIMENT 18-1: PREPARATION

In this experiment we create some new files and a new user to help illustrate some aspects of file permissions. Start this experiment as the student user. Make the PWD the ~/Documents directory. Enter the following command on a single line:

```
[student@studentvm1 Documents]$ for X in `seq -w 20`;do echo "Hello
world" file$X > testfile$X ; touch test$X file$X ; done
```

---

[1] Free On-line Dictionary of Computing, http://foldoc.org/, editor Denis Howe

The seq utility prints a sequence of numbers, in this case from 0 to 20. The back-ticks (`)
around that command cause the results to be expanded into a list that can be used by the
for command. The -w option specifies that all numbers will have the same length, so if the
largest number is two digits in length, the single-digit numbers are padded with zeros so that
1 becomes 01 and so on.

Display a long list of files and display their sizes in human-readable format rather than an
exact byte count:

```
[student@studentvm1 Documents]$ ll -h
total 880K
-rw-rw-r-- 1 student student    0 Dec  4 09:47 file01
-rw-rw-r-- 1 student student    0 Dec  4 09:47 file02
-rw-rw-r-- 1 student student    0 Dec  4 09:47 file03
-rw-rw-r-- 1 student student    0 Dec  4 09:47 file04
-rw-rw-r-- 1 student student    0 Dec  4 09:47 file05
-rw-rw-r-- 1 student student    0 Dec  4 09:47 file06
<snip>
-rw-rw-r-- 1 student student    0 Dec  4 09:47 test18
-rw-rw-r-- 1 student student    0 Dec  4 09:47 test19
-rw-rw-r-- 1 student student    0 Dec  4 09:47 test20
-rw-rw-r-- 1 student student  44K Dec  4 09:47 testfile09
-rw-rw-r-- 1 student student  44K Dec  4 09:47 testfile02
-rw-rw-r-- 1 student student  44K Dec  4 09:47 testfile03
<snip>
-rw-rw-r-- 1 student student  44K Dec  4 09:47 testfile19
-rw-rw-r-- 1 student student  44K Dec  4 09:47 testfile20
```

Now we have a few files to work with. But we will also need another user for testing, so log
into a terminal session as root and add a new user. Using a simple password is fine:

```
[root@studentvm1 ~]# useradd -c "Student user 1" student1
[root@studentvm1 ~]# passwd student1
Changing password for user student1.
New password: <Enter the password>
BAD PASSWORD: The password is shorter than 8 characters
Retype new password: <Enter the password again>
passwd: all authentication tokens updated successfully.
```

Now we are ready.

User Accounts and Security

User accounts are the first line of security on your Linux computer and are used in the Linux world to provide access to the computer, to keep out people who should not have access, and to keep valid users from interfering with each other's data and usage of the computer. We will explore more aspects of user accounts in Chapter 38 of Volume 2.

The security of the computer and the data stored there is based on the user accounts created by the Linux system administrator or some form of centralized authorization system.[2] A user cannot access any resources on a Linux system without logging on with an account ID and password. The administrator creates an account for each authorized user and assigns an initial password.

The attributes of permissions and file ownership are one aspect of security provided by Linux. Each file and directory on a Linux system has an owner and a set of access permissions. Setting the ownership and permissions correctly allows users to access the files that belong to them but not files belonging to others.

File Attributes

The listing of the files created in Experiment 18-1 shows a number of file attributes that are important to security and access management. The file permissions, the number of hard links, the User and Group[3] ownership both shown here as "student," the file size, the date and time it was last modified, and the file name itself are all shown in this listing. There are more attributes that are not displayed in this listing, but we will explore all of them as we proceed through this chapter.

File Ownership

The sample file listing shown in Figure 18-1 was extracted from the listing in Experiment 18-1. It shows the details of a single file. We will use this file to explore the structure and attributes of a file. File ownership is one of the attributes that is part of the Linux file security protocols.

---

[2] Centralized authentication systems are beyond the scope of this course.
[3] I capitalize User, Group, and Other here and many places throughout this course in order to explicitly refer to the ownership classes shown in Figure 18-2.

```
-rw-rw-r-- 1 student student 44K Dec  4 09:47 testfile09
```

Figure 18-1. *A long listing of one of the sample files just created*

There are two owners associated with every file, the User who owns the file and the Group ownership. The user who created the file is always the owner of the file – at least until ownership is changed. In Red Hat–based distributions, each user has their own private group, and files created by them also belong to that group. This is the Red Hat Private Group method and is used to improve security. In many older Unix and some Linux systems, all users, and thus the files they created, belonged to a common group, usually group 100, "users." This meant that all users could, in theory at least, access files belonging to other users, so long as directory permissions allowed it. This is a holdover from a time when data security and privacy on computers was much less of an issue than it is now. This Red Hat Private Group scheme is intended to improve security by reducing the number of users who have access to the files by default to one – the file owner.

So the file in Figure 18-1 is owned by the User student, and the Group ownership is student. The User and Group ownership can be expressed using the notation User.Group.

The root user can always change User and Group ownership – or anything else. The User (owner) of a file can only change the Group ownership under certain circumstances.

There are some standards that we need to consider when adding users and groups. When adding group IDs for things like shared directories and files, I like to choose numbers starting at 5000 and above. This allows space for 4,000 users with identical UID and GID numbers. We will explore UID and GID assignments and standards in Chapter 16 of Volume 2.

Let's explore file ownership and its implications in Experiment 18-2.

EXPERIMENT 18-2: FILE OWNERSHIP

Perform this experiment as the student user. Look at one of the files we created in our
~/Documents directory in Experiment 18-1, file09:

```
[student@studentvm1 Documents]$ ll file09
-rw-r--r-- 1 student student 0 Feb  9 16:17 file09
```

This file, like all of the others in our Documents directory, has the ownership student.student.
Let's try to change it to ownership of student1.student user using the chown (CHange
OWNership) command:

```
[student@studentvm1 Documents]$ chown student1 file09
chown: changing ownership of 'file09': Operation not permitted
```

The student user does not have authority to change the User ownership of a file to any other
user. Now let's try to change the Group ownership. If you are changing the User ownership of
the file and not the Group ownership, it is not necessary to specify the group with the chown
command. We can use the chgrp (CHange GRouP) command to attempt changing the Group
ownership:

```
[student@studentvm1 Documents]$ chgrp student1 file09
chgrp: changing group of 'file09': Operation not permitted
```

Once again we are not authorized to change the ownership on this file. Linux prevents users
from changing the ownership of files to protect us from other users and to protect those other
users from us. The root user can change the ownership of any file.

It looks like the user cannot change the file's User and Group ownership at all. This
is a security feature. It prevents one user from creating files in the name of another
user. But what if I really do want to share a file with someone else? There is one way to
circumvent the ownership issue. Copy the file to /tmp. Let's see how that works.

EXPERIMENT 18-3: SHARING FILES

As the student user, let's first add a bit of data to file09:

```
[student@studentvm1 Documents]$ echo "Hello world." > file09
[student@studentvm1 Documents]$ cat file09
Hello world.
```

Now copy the file to /tmp:

```
[student@studentvm1 Documents]$ cp file09 /tmp
```

Open a terminal session and use the su command to switch user to student1:

```
[student@studentvm1 ~]$ su - student1
Password: <Enter password for student1>
Running /etc/profile
Running /etc/profile.d/myBashConfig.sh
Running /etc/Bashrc
Running /etc/Bashrc
[student1@studentvm1 ~]
```

Now view the contents of the file that is located in /tmp. Then copy the file from /tmp to the student1 home directory and view it again:

```
[student1@studentvm1 ~]$ cat /tmp/file09
Hello world.
[student1@studentvm1 ~]$ cp /tmp/file09 . ; cat file09
Hello world.
```

Why does this work? Let's look at file permissions to find out:

```
[student1@studentvm1 ~]$ ll /tmp/file09 file09
-rw-r--r-- 1 student1 student1 13 Feb 10 09:28 file09
-rw-r--r-- 1 student  student  13 Feb 10 09:26 /tmp/file09
[student1@studentvm1 ~]$
```

File Permissions

The file permissions, also called the file mode, along with file ownership, provide a means of defining which users and groups have specific types of access to files and directories. For now we just look at files and will examine directory permissions later. Figure 18-2 shows the three types of permissions and their representation in symbolic (rwx) and octal (421) formats. Octal is only a bit different from hex – literally. Hex characters are composed of 4 binary bits, and octal is composed of 3 binary bits.

   User, Group, and Other define the classes of users that the permissions affect. The User is the primary owner of the file. So the User student owns all files with User ownership of student. Those files may or may not have Group ownership of student, but in most circumstances they will. So the User permissions define the access rights of the User who "owns" the file. The Group permissions define the access rights of the Group that owns the file, if it is different from the User ownership. And Other is everyone else. All other users fall into the Other category, so access by all other users on the system is defined by the Other permissions.

	User	Group	Other
Permissions	r w x	r w x	r w x
Bits	1 1 1	1 1 1	1 1 1
Octal value	4 2 1	4 2 1	4 2 1

Figure 18-2.   File permission representations and their octal values

   There are three permissions bits for each class, User, Group, and Other. Each bit has a meaning, (R)ead, (W)rite, and e(X)ecute, and a corresponding octal positional value. We can simplify the class notation by using "UGO" either together or separately in commands. These classes are expressed in lowercase in the commands that affect them:

- Read means that the file can be read by members of that class.

- Write means that the file can be written by members of the class.

- Execute means that the file is executable by members of that class.

Using file09 from Experiment 18-3 as our example, the permissions shown for that file in Figure 18-3 should now be easier to decipher. The permissions of rw-rw-r-- (420,420,400, which is equivalent to decimal 664) mean that the student user can read and write the file and it is not executable. The student group can also read and write this file. And all other users can read the file but cannot write to it, which means they cannot alter it in any way.

```
rw-rw-r-- 1 student student 0 Dec  4 09:47 file09
```

Figure 18-3. *The long listing of file09*

You see what is possible here? The file is readable by any user. That means that copying it from the /tmp directory, which is universally accessible, to the student1 home directory by student1 will work so long as the file has the read permission set for Other.

EXPERIMENT 18-4: MAKING FILES PRIVATE

As the user student – the original user – change the permissions on /tmp/file09 to rw-rw---- so that Other does not have permissions to read the file and it improves privacy:

```
[student@studentvm1 ~]$ cd /tmp ; ll file*
-rw-rw-r-- 1 student student 13 Feb 10 09:26 file09
[student@studentvm1 tmp]$ chmod 660 file09 ; ll file*
-rw-rw---- 1 student student 13 Feb 10 09:26 file09
```

Notice that the file is no longer readable by Other. Now as the student1 user, try to read the file:

```
[student1@studentvm1 ~]$ cat /tmp/file09
cat: /tmp/file09: Permission denied
```

Even though the file is located in a directory that is accessible by all users, users other than student no longer have access to the file. They cannot now view its content and they cannot copy it.

In Experiment 18-4 we changed the file permissions using the octal representation of the permissions we wanted, which is the shortest command and so the least amount of typing. How did we get 660 for the permissions? Let's start with the permissions for the User, which is one octal digit.

Each octal digit can be represented by three bits, r,w,x, with the positional values of 4,2,1. So if we want read and write but not execute, that is 110 in binary, which translates to 4+2+0=6. We perform the same operation for the Group ownership. Full read, write, execute translates to 111 in binary, which becomes 4+2+1=7 in octal.

We will discuss file permissions and methods for changing them a bit later in this chapter.

Directory Permissions

Directory permissions are not all that different from file permissions:

- The Read permission on a directory allows access to list the content of the directory.

- Write allows the users of a class to create, change, and delete files in the directory.

- Execute allows the users of a class to make the directory the present working directory (PWD).

There are two additional permissions, called special mode bits, that are used extensively by the system but that are usually functionally invisible to non-root users. These are the setgid and setuid bits. We will use the setgid permission later in this chapter.

Implications of Group Ownership

We still need a way for users to share files with some other users but not all users. This is where groups can provide an answer. Group ownership in Linux is all about security while also being able to allow sharing access to files with other users. One of the Unix legacies that Linux has inherited is file ownership and permissions. This is good but a bit of explanation is in order.

A group is an entity defined in the /etc/group file with a meaningful name, such as "development" or "dev," that lists the user IDs, like "student," of the members of the group. So by making Group ownership of a file to be "development," all members of the development group can access the file based on its Group permissions.

Let's see how this is done in Experiment 18-5 and learn a few other things along the way.

EXPERIMENT 18-5: EXPLORING GROUP OWNERSHIP

This experiment will require working as different users including root. We will create a new user to use for testing and a group for developers. We will use the short version, dev, for the name. We will then create a directory, also called dev, where shared files can be stored and add two of our now three non-root users to the dev group.

Start as root and create the new user. Again, it is fine to use a short password on your VM for these experiments:

```
[root@studentvm1 ~]# useradd -c "Student User 2" student2
[root@studentvm1 ~]# passwd student2
Changing password for user student2.
New password: <Enter new password>
BAD PASSWORD: The password is shorter than 8 characters
Retype new password: <Enter new password>
passwd: all authentication tokens updated successfully.
```

Add the new group. There are some loose standards for group ID numbers, which we will explore in a later chapter, but the bottom line is that we will use GID (group ID) 5000 for this experiment:

```
[root@studentvm1 ~]# groupadd -g 5000 dev
```

We now add two of the existing users to the dev group, student and student1, using the usermod (user modify) tool. The -G option is a list of the groups to which we are adding the user. In this case the list of groups is only one in length, but we could add a user to more than one group at a time:

```
[root@studentvm1 ~]# usermod -G 5000 student
[root@studentvm1 ~]# usermod -G 5000 student1
```

Another option for adding the users to the new group would be to use gpasswd instead of usermod. Either of these methods creates the same result so that both users are added to the dev group:

```
[root@studentvm1 ~]# gpasswd -M student,student1 dev
```

Look at the /etc/group file. The tail command shows the last ten lines of the data stream:

```
[root@studentvm1 ~]# tail /etc/group
vboxsf:x:981:
dnsmasq:x:980:
tcpdump:x:72:
student:x:1000:
screen:x:84:
systemd-timesync:x:979:
dictd:x:978:
student1:x:1001:
student2:x:1002:
dev:x:5000:student,student1
```

As the root user, create the shared directory /home/dev, and set the Group ownership to dev and the permissions to 770 (rwxrwx---), which will prevent users who are not members of the dev group from accessing the directory:

```
[root@studentvm1 ~]# cd /home ; mkdir dev ; ll
total 32
drwxr-xr-x   2 root      root       4096 Feb 10 13:42 dev
drwx------.  2 root      root      16384 Jan 17 07:29 lost+found
drwx------. 21 student   student    4096 Feb 10 06:41 student
drwx------   4 student1  student1   4096 Feb 10 09:28 student1
drwx------   3 student2  student2   4096 Feb 10 13:06 student2
[root@studentvm1 home]# chgrp dev dev ; chmod 770 dev ; ll
total 32
drwxrwx---   2 root      dev        4096 Feb 10 13:42 dev
drwx------.  2 root      root      16384 Jan 17 07:29 lost+found
drwx------. 21 student   student    4096 Feb 10 06:41 student
drwx------   4 student1  student1   4096 Feb 10 09:28 student1
drwx------   3 student2  student2   4096 Feb 10 13:06 student2
```

As the student user, make /home/dev the PWD:

```
[student@studentvm1 ~]$ cd /home/dev
-Bash: cd: /home/dev: Permission denied
```

This fails because the new group membership has not been initialized:

```
[student@studentvm1 ~]$ id
uid=1000(student) gid=1000(student) groups=1000(student)
```

Group memberships are read and set by the shell when it is started in a terminal session or a virtual console. To make this change, you need to exit from all of your terminal sessions, log out, log back in, and start new terminal sessions for the shells to initialize the new group settings. After starting a new shell, verify that the new group has been initialized for your user ID.

Linux only reads the /etc/group file when a login shell is started. The GUI desktop is the login shell, and the terminal emulator sessions that you start on the desktop are not login shells. Remote access using SSH is a login shell as are the virtual consoles. The shells that run in screen sessions are not login shells.

Remember the startup sequences we followed in Chapter 17 of this volume? Login shells run a different set of shell configuration scripts during their startup. Refer to Figure 17-1.

```
[student@studentvm1 ~]$ id
uid=1000(student) gid=1000(student) groups=1000(student),5000(dev)
```

Make /home/dev the PWD and verify that the directory is empty:

```
[student@studentvm1 ~]$ cd /home/dev ; ll -a
total 8
drwxrwx--- 2 root dev  4096 Feb 10 13:42 .
drwxr-xr-x. 7 root root 4096 Feb 10 13:42 ..
```

As the student user, create a file in the /home/dev directory, change the Group ownership to dev, and set permissions to 660 to prevent Other users from having access to the file while allowing access by all members of the dev group:

```
[student@studentvm1 dev]$ echo "Hello World" > file01 ; ll
-rw-r--r-- 1 student dev 12 Feb 10 13:49 file01
[student@studentvm1 dev]$ chgrp dev file01
[student@studentvm1 dev]$ chmod 660 file01 ; ll
total 4
-rw-rw---- 1 student dev 12 Feb 11 09:26 file01
```

Now open a new terminal session and switch user to student1. As the student1 user, make /home/dev the PWD and add some text to the file:

```
[student1@studentvm1 ~]$ cd ../dev ; echo "Hello to you, too" >>
file01 ; cat file01
Hello World
Hello to you, too
```

Now we have a way to share files among users. Even though this file is owned by the student user, it belongs to the dev group so that student1, which is a member of the dev group, can also read and write it.

There is still one more thing we can do to make it even easier. When we created the file in the shared dev directory, it had the group ID that belonged to the user that created it, student, but we changed that to the group dev. We can add the setgid (Set Group ID) bit, or SGID, on the directory, which informs Linux to create files in the /home/dev directory with the GID being the same as the GID of the directory. Set the SGID bit using symbolic notation. It can be done with octal mode but this is easier:

```
[root@studentvm1 home]# chmod g+s dev ; ll
total 36
drwxrws---    2 root     dev       4096 Dec  9 13:09 dev
drwx------.   2 root     root     16384 Aug 13 16:16 lost+found
drwx------.  22 student  student   4096 Dec  9 15:16 student
drwx------    4 student1 student1  4096 Dec  9 12:56 student1
drwx------    4 student2 student2  4096 Dec  9 13:03 student2
[root@studentvm1 home]#
```

The lowercase s in the Group permissions of the dev directory means that both the setgid and execute bits are on, and an uppercase S means that the setgid bit is on but the execute bit is off.

For those who want to try this using octal mode, the octal mode settings we usually use consist of three octal digits, from 0 to 7, as User, Group, and Other sets of permissions. But there is a fourth octal digit that can precede these three more common digits, but if it is not specified, it is ignored. The SGID bit is octal 2 (010 in binary), so we know we want the octal permissions settings to be 2770 on the dev directory. That can be set like this:

```
[root@studentvm1 home]# ll | grep dev ; chmod 2770 dev ; ll | grep dev
drwxrwx---   2 root     dev        4096 Apr  1 13:39 dev
drwxrws---   2 root     dev        4096 Apr  1 13:39 dev
```

As both student and student1 users, make /home/dev the PWD and create some new files. Notice that the files were created with dev as the group owner, so it was not necessary to change it with the **chgrp** command.

In a terminal session, switch user to student2 and make /home/dev the PWD:

```
[student2@studentvm1 ~]$ cd /home/dev
-Bash: cd: /home/dev: Permission denied
[student2@studentvm1 ~]$
```

Access is denied because student2 is not a member of the dev group and the directory permissions do not allow access to the directory by non-members.

We now have an easy way for the users in the group to share files securely. This could be one group of many that share files on a host. Other groups might be accounting, marketing, transportation, test, and so on.

umask

When a user creates a new file using commands like touch or redirecting the output of a command to a file or using an editor like vim, the permissions of the file are -rw-r--r--. Why? Because umask.

The umask is a setting that Linux uses to specify the default permissions of all new files. The umask is set in /etc/profile, one of the bash shell configuration files that we covered in Chapter 17. The umask for root and non-root non-login shells is 022, while the umask for non-root login shells is 002.

The tricky element of umask is that it is a form of reverse logic. It does not specify the bits of the file privileges we want to set to on; it specifies the ones we want to set to off when the file is created.

The execute bit is never set to on for new files. Therefore, the umask setting only applies to the read and write permissions. With a umask of 000, and considering that the execute bit is never set to on for new files, the default permissions of a new file would be rw-rw-rw-, but with the umask 2 bits on for Group and Other (022), the permissions are rw-r-r-- so that Other users and users in the same group can read the file but not delete or change it.

The umask command is used to set the umask value.

EXPERIMENT 18-6: UMASK

This experiment should be performed as the student user. Since we have already seen the permissions on plenty of new files using the default umask, we start by viewing the current umask value:

```
[student@studentvm1 ~]$ umask
0002
```

There are four digits there, and the three right ones are User, Group, and Other. What is the first one? Although this is meaningless for Linux files when using this command, the leading zero can be used in some commands to specify the special mode bits, setgid and setuid as we have just seen. This can be safely ignored when using the umask command. The `info setgid` command can provide a link to more information about these special mode bits.

Change the umask and run a quick test. There is probably already a file01 in your home directory, so we will create the file umask.test as a test of the new umask:

```
[student@studentvm1 ~]$ umask 006 ; umask
0006
[student@studentvm1 ~]$ touch umask.test ; ll umask.test
-rw-rw---- 1 student student 0 Apr  2 08:50 umask.test
[student@studentvm1 ~]$
```

The umask is only set for the shell in which the command is issued. To make it persistent across all new shell sessions and after reboots, it would need to be changed in a script in /etc/profile.d. This is covered in Chapter 17.

The new file was created with permissions that do not allow any access for users in the Other class. Set the umask back to 002.

I have never personally encountered a situation in which changing the umask for any of my Linux systems made sense for me, but I know of situations in which it did for some other users. For example, it might make sense to set the umask to 006 to prevent Other users from any access to the file even when it is located in a commonly accessible directory, as we did in Experiment 18-6. It might also make sense to change it before performing operations on many files in a script so that it would not be necessary to perform a chmod on every file.

Changing File Permissions

You have probably noticed that the methods for setting file and directory permissions are flexible. When setting permissions there are two basic ways of doing so: symbolic and octal numeric. We have used both in setting permissions, but it is necessary to delve a little further into the chmod command to fully understand its limitations as well as the flexibility it provides.

EXPERIMENT 18-7: CHANGING FILE PERMISSIONS

Perform this experiment as the student user. Let's first look at setting permissions using numeric notation. Suppose we want to set a single file's permissions to rw-rw-r. This is simple. Let's use ~/umask.test for this. Verify the current permissions and then set the new ones:

```
[student@studentvm1 ~]$ ll umask.test ; chmod 664 umask.test ; ll
umask.test
-rw-rw---- 1 student student 0 Apr  2 08:50 umask.test
-rw-rw-r-- 1 student student 0 Apr  2 08:50 umask.test
[student@studentvm1 ~]$
```

This method of setting permissions ignores any existing permissions. Regardless of what they were before the command, they are now what was specified in the command. There is no means to change only one or some permissions. This may not be what we want if we need to add a single permission to multiple files.

In order to test this, we need to create some additional files and set some differing permissions on them. Make ~/testdir the PWD:

```
[student@studentvm1 ~]$ cd ~/testdir
[student@studentvm1 testdir]$ for X in `seq -w 100` ; do touch file$X ; done
```

You can list the directory content to verify that the new files all have permissions of rw-rw-r--. If the width of your terminal is 130 columns or more, you can pipe the output like this:

```
[student@studentvm1 testdir]$ ll | column
total 0
-rw-rw---- 1 student student 0 Dec 12 21:56 file051
-rw-rw---- 1 student student 0 Dec 12 21:56 file001
-rw-rw---- 1 student student 0 Dec 12 21:56 file052
```

```
-rw-rw----  1 student student  0 Dec 12 21:56 file002
-rw-rw----  1 student student  0 Dec 12 21:56 file053
-rw-rw----  1 student student  0 Dec 12 21:56 file003
-rw-rw----  1 student student  0 Dec 12 21:56 file054
-rw-rw----  1 student student  0 Dec 12 21:56 file004
-rw-rw----  1 student student  0 Dec 12 21:56 file055
<snip>
```

We could also do something like this to display just the file names and their permissions, which leaves enough space to format the output data stream into columns:

```
[student@studentvm1 testdir]$ ll | awk '{print $1" "$9}' | column
total
-rwxr-xr-x cpuHog                    -rw-r--r--. newfile.txt
drwxr-xr-x. Desktop                  drwxr-xr-x. Pictures
-rw-r--r--. diskusage.txt            drwxr-xr-x. Public
-rw-r--r--. dmesg1.txt               drwxr-xr-x. Templates
-rw-r--r--. dmesg2.txt               drwxrwxr-x testdir
-rw-r--r--. dmesg3.txt               drwxr-xr-x. testdir1
-rw-r--r--. dmesg4.txt               drwxr-xr-x. testdir6
drwxr-xr-x. Documents                drwxr-xr-x. testdir7
drwxr-xr-x. Downloads                -rw-rw-r-- umask.test
drwxr-xr-x. Music                    drwxr-xr-x. Videos
prw-r--r-- mypipe                    -rw-r--r-- zoom_x86_64.rpm
```

The awk command uses the whitespace to delineate the fields in the original data stream from the ll command. We then use variables with a list of the fields we want to print, in this case fields $1, the file permissions, and $9, the file name. Then we pipe the result of that through the column utility to enable better use of the terminal width.

Let's change the permissions on some of these files. First, we change all of them. Be sure to verify the results after each change:

```
[student@studentvm1 testdir]$ chmod 760 * ; ll
```

Now let's add read to Other for a subset of the files. And then a few more changes:

```
[student@studentvm1 testdir]$ chmod 764 file06* ; ll
[student@studentvm1 testdir]$ chmod 764 file0*3 ; ll
[student@studentvm1 testdir]$ chmod 700 file0[2-5][6-7] ; ll
[student@studentvm1 testdir]$ chmod 640 file0[4-7][2-4] ; ll
```

There should be several differing sets of permissions. So far we have mostly been using brute force to change all of the permissions on various files filtered by the file globbing and sets. This is the best we can do using numeric formats for our changes.

Now we become a bit more targeted. Suppose we want to turn on the G (group) execute bit for files file013, file026, file027, file036, file053, and file092. Also, a file cannot be executed if the read bit for the G class is not also set to on, so we need to turn that bit on too. Note that some of these files already have some of these bits set, but that is okay; setting them to the same value again does not cause any problems. We also want to ensure that the write bit is off for all of these files so that users in the same group cannot change the files. We can do this all in one command without changing any of the other permissions on these files or any other files:

```
[student@studentvm1 testdir]$ chmod g+rx,g-w file013 file026 file027
file036 file053 file092
[student@studentvm1 testdir]$ ll | awk '{print $1" "$9}' | column
```

We have used the symbolic mode to both add and remove permissions to and from a list of files having a range of existing permissions that we needed to keep unchanged.

Applying Permissions

Permissions can sometimes be tricky. Given a file with ownership of student.student and the permissions --- rw- rw-, would you expect the student user to be able to read this file? You probably would – I did – but permissions do not work like that.

The permissions are scanned from left to right with the first match in the sequence providing permissions access. In this case, the student user attempts to read the file, but the scan of the permissions finds permissions --- for the User of the file. This means that the User has no access to this file.

EXPERIMENT 18-8: MORE ABOUT PERMISSIONS

As the student user in ~/testdir, change the permissions of file001 to 066 and then try to read it:

```
[student@studentvm1 testdir]$ chmod 066 file001 ; ll file001 ; cat
file001
----rw-rw- 1 student student 0 Dec 12 21:56 file001
cat: file001: Permission denied
```

Despite the fact that Group and Others have read and write access to the file, the User cannot access it. The user can, however, change the permissions back by adding u+rw.

Now as the student user, make /home/dev the PWD and create a file with a bit of content there, set the permissions to 066, and read the file:

```
[student@studentvm1 dev]$ echo "Hello World" > testfile-01.txt ; ll ;
cat testfile-01.txt
total 4
-rw-rw-r-- 1 student dev 12 Apr  2 09:19 testfile-01.txt
Hello World
```

Note that the Group ownership of this file is dev. Then as the student1 user, make /home/dev/ the PWD and read the file:

```
[student1@studentvm1 ~]$ cd /home/dev ; cat testfile-01.txt
Hello World
```

This shows that we can create a file to which the owner has no access but members of a common group (dev in this case) or anyone else can have access to read and write it.

Timestamps

All files and directories are created with three timestamps: access, atime; modify, mtime; and change, ctime. These three timestamps can be used to determine the last time a file was accessed, the permissions or ownership changed, or the content modified.

Note that the time displayed in a long file listing is the mtime, which is the time that a file or directory was last modified. This time in the listing is truncated to the nearest second, but all of the timestamps are maintained to the nanosecond. We will look at this information in more detail in the "File Information" section.

Linux EXT4 files have a relatively new timestamp in their inodes – the Birth time.[4] This records the time the file was created and is the one timestamp that is never changed. This timestamp has been added since the first edition of this course. This is called the btime. The Birth field was present in the output from the stat command, but the data was not stored in the inode.

---

[4] See the man page for inode.

File Meta-structures

All of these file attributes are all stored in the various meta-structures on the storage device. Each file has a directory entry that points to an inode for the file. The inode contains most of the information pertaining to the file including the location of the data on the storage device. We will look in detail at the meta-structures of the EXT4 filesystem, which is the default for many distributions, in Chapter 19 of this volume.

The Directory Entry

The directory entry is very simple. It resides in a directory such as your home directory and contains the name of the file and the pointer to the inode belonging to the file. This pointer is the inode number.

The inode

The inode is more complex than the directory entry because it contains all of the other metadata pertaining to the file. This metadata includes the user and group IDs, timestamps, access permissions, what type of file such as ASCII text or binary executable, pointers to the data on the storage device, and more. Each inode in a filesystem – a partition or logical volume – is identified with a unique inode number. We will discuss the inode in more detail later in this chapter because it is a very important part of the EXT filesystem meta-structure.

File Information

There are a number of different types of files that you can run into in a Linux environment. Linux has some commands to help you determine a great deal of information about files. Most of the information provided by these tools is stored in the file inode.

EXPERIMENT 18-9: EXPLORING FILES

The `file` command tells what type a file is. In this case that ~/.bash_profile file is an ASCII text file:

```
[student@studentvm1 ~]$ file .bash_profile
.bash_profile: ASCII text
```

And this tells us that /bin/ls is a compiled executable binary file that is dynamically linked:

```
[student@studentvm1 ~]$ file /bin/ls
/bin/ls: ELF 64-bit LSB pie executable, x86-64, version 1 (SYSV),
dynamically linked, interpreter /lib64/ld-linux-x86-64.so.2,
BuildID[sha1]=c317b9642d768fb20adb11ab87e59bce8d8abc6e, for GNU/Linux
3.2.0, stripped
```

The `strings` command extracts all of the text strings from any file including binary executables. Use the following command to view the text strings in the ls executable. You may need to pipe the output through the less filter:

```
[student@studentvm1 ~]$ strings /bin/ls
```

The `strings` command produces a lot of output from a binary file like ls. Much of the ASCII plain text is just random text strings that appear in the binary file, but some are actual messages.

The `stat` command provides a great deal of information about a file. The following command shows atime, ctime, and mtime; the file size in bytes and blocks; and its inode, the number of (hard) links, and more:

```
[student@studentvm1 ~]$ stat /bin/ls
  File: /bin/ls
  Size: 142072         Blocks: 280        IO Block: 4096    regular file
Device: 253,1   Inode: 788998     Links: 1
Access: (0755/-rwxr-xr-x) Uid: (    0/   root) Gid: (    0/   root)
Access: 2023-02-12 09:42:45.381755845 -0500
Modify: 2023-01-02 07:55:31.000000000 -0500
Change: 2023-01-17 21:22:49.990032410 -0500
 Birth: 2023-01-17 21:22:49.762032384 -0500
```

The Birth time is also shown.

Look at one of the files in ~/testdir that we just changed the permissions for:

```
[student@studentvm1 testdir]$ stat file013
  File: file013
  Size: 0            Blocks: 0        IO Block: 4096    regular empty file
Device: 253,4    Inode: 2291        Links: 1
Access: (0754/-rwxr-xr--)  Uid: ( 1000/ student)   Gid: ( 1000/ student)
Access: 2023-02-11 15:36:47.469943267 -0500
Modify: 2023-02-11 15:36:47.469943267 -0500
Change: 2023-02-12 09:03:14.730693683 -0500
 Birth: 2023-02-11 15:36:47.469943267 -0500
```

This shows that the ctime (change) records the date and time that the file attributes such as permissions or other data stored in the inode were changed. Now let's change the content by adding some text to the file and check the metadata again:

```
[student@studentvm1 testdir]$ echo "Hello World" > file013 ; stat file013
  File: file013
  Size: 12           Blocks: 8        IO Block: 4096    regular file
Device: 253,4    Inode: 2291        Links: 1
Access: (0754/-rwxr-xr--)  Uid: ( 1000/ student)   Gid: ( 1000/ student)
Access: 2023-02-11 15:36:47.469943267 -0500
Modify: 2023-02-12 09:49:06.908569402 -0500
Change: 2023-02-12 09:49:06.908569402 -0500
 Birth: 2023-02-11 15:36:47.469943267 -0500
```

The mtime has changed because the file content was changed. The number of blocks assigned to the file has changed, and these changes are stored in the inode, so the ctime is changed too. Note that the empty file had zero data blocks assigned to it and, after adding 12 characters, eight blocks have been assigned, which is way more than needed. But this illustrates that file space on the hard dive is preallocated when the file is created in order to help reduce file fragmentation, which can reduce file access efficiency.

Read the data in the file and check the metadata one more time:

```
[student@studentvm1 testdir]$ cat file013 ; stat file013
Hello World
  File: file013
  Size: 12           Blocks: 8        IO Block: 4096    regular file
```

```
Device: 253,4    Inode: 2291         Links: 1
Access: (0754/-rwxr-xr--)  Uid: ( 1000/ student)   Gid: ( 1000/ student)
Access: 2023-02-12 10:01:05.238151167 -0500
Modify: 2023-02-12 09:49:06.908569402 -0500
Change: 2023-02-12 09:49:06.908569402 -0500
 Birth: 2023-02-11 15:36:47.469943267 -0500
```

First, we see the content of the file, and then we can see that this access to the file changed the atime.

Notice that the btime never changes.

Spend some time exploring the results from other files including some of the ones in your home directory and ~/testdir.

Links

Links are an especially interesting feature of Linux filesystems that can make some tasks easier by providing access to files from multiple locations in the filesystem directory tree without the need for typing long pathnames. There are two types of links: hard and soft. The difference between the two types of links is significant, but both types are used to solve similar problems. Both types of links provide multiple directory entries, that is, references, to a single file, but they do it quite differently. Links are powerful and add flexibility to Linux filesystems.

I have found in the past that some application programs required a particular version of a library. When an upgrade to that library replaced the old version, the program would crash with an error specifying the name of the old library that was missing. Usually the only change in the library name was the version number. Acting on a hunch, I simply added a link to the new library but named the link after the old library name. I tried the program again and it worked perfectly. And, okay, the program was a game, and everyone knows the lengths that gamers will go to, to keep their games running.

In fact almost all applications are linked to libraries using a generic name with only a major version number in the link name while the link points to the actual library file that also has a minor version number. In other instances required files have been moved from one directory to another in order to be in compliance with the Linux Filesystem Hierarchical Standard (FHS) that we will learn about in Chapter 19. In this circumstance, links have been provided in the old directories to provide backward compatibility for those programs that have not yet caught up with the new locations. If you do a long listing of the /lib64 directory, you can find many examples of both. A shortened listing can be seen in Figure 18-4.

```
lrwxrwxrwx. 1 root root      36 Dec  8  2016 cracklib_dict.hwm ->
../../usr/share/cracklib/pw_dict.hwm
lrwxrwxrwx. 1 root root      36 Dec  8  2016 cracklib_dict.PWD ->
../../usr/share/cracklib/pw_dict.PWD
lrwxrwxrwx. 1 root root      36 Dec  8  2016 cracklib_dict.pwi ->
../../usr/share/cracklib/pw_dict.pwi
lrwxrwxrwx. 1 root root      27 Jun  9  2016 libaccountsservice.so.0 ->
libaccountsservice.so.0.0.0
-rwxr-xr-x. 1 root root  288456 Jun  9  2016 libaccountsservice.so.0.0.0
lrwxrwxrwx  1 root root      15 May 17 11:47 libacl.so.1 -> libacl.so.1.1.0
-rwxr-xr-x  1 root root   36472 May 17 11:47 libacl.so.1.1.0
lrwxrwxrwx. 1 root root      15 Feb  4  2016 libaio.so.1 -> libaio.so.1.0.1
-rwxr-xr-x. 1 root root    6224 Feb  4  2016 libaio.so.1.0.0
-rwxr-xr-x. 1 root root    6224 Feb  4  2016 libaio.so.1.0.1
lrwxrwxrwx. 1 root root      30 Jan 16 16:39 libakonadi-calendar.so.4 -> libakonadi-
calendar.so.4.14.26
-rwxr-xr-x. 1 root root  816160 Jan 16 16:39 libakonadi-calendar.so.4.14.26
lrwxrwxrwx. 1 root root      29 Jan 16 16:39 libakonadi-contact.so.4 -> libakonadi-
contact.so.4.14.26
```

Figure 18-4. *This very shortened listing of the /lib64 directory contains many examples of the use of symbolic links*

The leftmost character of some of the entries in the long file listing in Figure 18-4 is an "l", which means that this is a soft, or symbolic, link, but the arrow syntax in the file name section is even more noticeable. So, to select one file as an example, libacl.so.1 is the name of the link, and -> libacl.so.1.1.0 points to the actual file. Short listings using ls do not show any of this. On most modern terminals, links are color-coded. This figure does not show hard links, but let's start with hard links as we go deeper.

Hard Links

A hard link is a directory entry that points to the inode for a file. Each file has one inode that contains information about that file including the location of the data belonging to that file. Each inode is referenced by at least one and sometimes more directory entries.

In Figure 18-5 multiple directory entries point to a single inode. These are all hard links. I have abbreviated the locations of three of the directory entries using the tilde (~) convention for the home directory, so that ~ is equivalent to /home/user in this example. Note that the fourth directory entry is in a completely different directory, /home/shared, which represents a location for sharing files between users of the computer.

Figure 18-5 provides a good illustration of the meta-structures that contain the metadata for a file and provide the operating system with the data needed to access the file for reading and writing.

Tip   The inode numbers shown in these experiments will be different on your VM than they are on my VM.

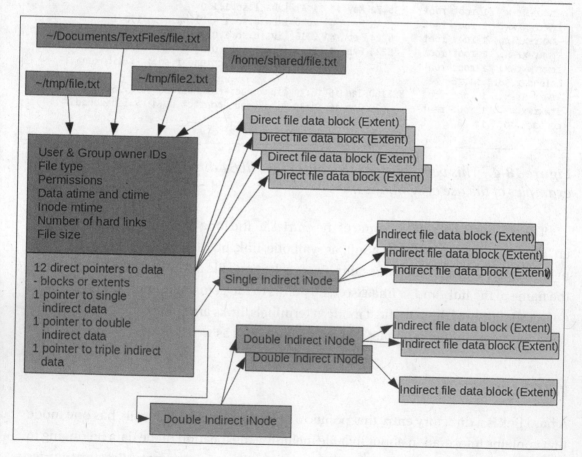

Figure 18-5.   *For hard links, multiple directory entries point to the same inode using the inode number that is unique for the filesystem*

In Figure 18-6 we see from a long listing with the -i option, which lists the inode numbers, that all of these directory entries point to the same inode.

```
[student@studentvm1 ~]$ ll-i Documents/TextFiles/file.txt ~/tmp/file* /home/shared/file.txt
434 -rw-rw-r--4 student student 12 Apr  2 12:32 Documents/TextFiles/file.txt
434 -rw-rw-r--4 student student 12 Apr  2 12:32 /home/shared/file.txt
434 -rw-rw-r--4 student student 12 Apr  2 12:32 /home/student/tmp/file2.txt
434 -rw-rw-r--4 student student 12 Apr  2 12:32 /home/student/tmp/file.txt
```

Figure 18-6. *A long listing of the files shown in Figure 18-5. The inode number of 434 is the first field. All of these directory entries share the same inode*

We will explore this figure in detail in Chapter 19. For now we will learn more about links.

EXPERIMENT 18-10: EXPLORING LINKS

As the student user, make ~/testdir the PWD and delete all of the files contained there:

```
[student@studentvm1 testdir]$ cd ~/testdir ; rm -rf * ; ll
total 0
```

Create a single file with a bit of plain text content and list the directory contents:

```
[student@studentvm1 testdir]$ echo "Hello World" > file001 ; ll
total 4
-rw-rw---- 1 student student 12 Feb 12 11:59 file001
```

Notice the number 1 between the permissions and the ownership. This is the number of hard links to this file. Because there is only one directory entry pointing to this file, there is only one link. Use the stat command to verify this:

```
[student@studentvm1 testdir]$ stat file001
  File: file001
  Size: 12        Blocks: 8        IO Block: 4096    regular file
Device: 253,4   Inode: 2182      Links: 1
Access: (0660/-rw-rw----) Uid: ( 1000/ student)   Gid: ( 1000/ student)
Access: 2023-02-12 11:59:41.942185794 -0500
Modify: 2023-02-12 11:59:41.942185794 -0500
```

```
Change: 2023-02-12 11:59:41.942185794 -0500
 Birth: 2023-02-12 11:59:41.942185794 -0500
```

The inode number for this file on my VM is 157, but it will probably be different on your VM. Now create a hard link to this file. The ln utility defaults to creation of a hard link:

```
[student@studentvm1 testdir]$ ln file001 link1 ; ll
total 8
-rw-rw---- 2 student student 12 Feb 12 11:59 file001
-rw-rw---- 2 student student 12 Feb 12 11:59 link1
```

The link count is now 2 for both directory entries. Display the content of both files and then **stat** them both:

```
[student@studentvm1 testdir]$ cat file001 link1
Hello World
Hello World
[student@studentvm1 testdir]$ stat file001 link1
  File: file001
  Size: 12           Blocks: 8          IO Block: 4096   regular file
Device: 253,4   Inode: 2182         Links: 2
Access: (0660/-rw-rw----) Uid: ( 1000/ student)  Gid: ( 1000/ student)
Access: 2023-02-12 12:06:11.752916155 -0500
Modify: 2023-02-12 11:59:41.942185794 -0500
Change: 2023-02-12 12:04:34.457983455 -0500
 Birth: 2023-02-12 11:59:41.942185794 -0500
  File: link1
  Size: 12           Blocks: 8          IO Block: 4096   regular file
Device: 253,4   Inode: 2182         Links: 2
Access: (0660/-rw-rw----) Uid: ( 1000/ student)  Gid: ( 1000/ student)
Access: 2023-02-12 12:06:11.752916155 -0500
Modify: 2023-02-12 11:59:41.942185794 -0500
Change: 2023-02-12 12:04:34.457983455 -0500
 Birth: 2023-02-12 11:59:41.942185794 -0500
```

All of the metadata for both files is identical including the inode number and the number of links. Create another link in the same directory. It does not matter which existing directory entry we use to create the new link because they both point to the same inode:

```
[student@studentvm1 testdir]$ ln link1 link2 ; ll
total 12
```

```
-rw-rw---- 3 student student 12 Feb 12 11:59 file001
-rw-rw---- 3 student student 12 Feb 12 11:59 link1
-rw-rw---- 3 student student 12 Feb 12 11:59 link2
```

You should **stat** all three of these files to verify that the metadata for them is identical. Let's create a link to this inode in your home directory:

```
[student@studentvm1 testdir]$ ln link1 ~/link3 ; ll ~/link*
-rw-rw---- 4 student student 12 Feb 12 11:59 link3
```

You can see from the listing that we now have four hard links to this file. It is possible to view the inode number with the `ls -li` or `ll -i` command. The number 2182 at the left side of each file listing is the inode number:

```
[student@studentvm1 testdir]$ ll -i
total 12
2182 -rw-rw---- 4 student student 12 Feb 12 11:59 file001
2182 -rw-rw---- 4 student student 12 Feb 12 11:59 link1
2182 -rw rw     4 student student 12 Feb 12 11:59 link2
```

Let's create another link from /tmp/:

```
[student@studentvm1 testdir]$ link file001 /tmp/link4
link: cannot create link '/tmp/link4' to 'file001': Invalid cross-device link
```

This attempt to create a hard link from /tmp to a file in /home fails because these directories are separate filesystems.

Hard links are limited to files contained within a single filesystem. Filesystem is used here in the sense of a partition or logical volume that is mounted on a specified mount point, such as, in this case, /home. This is because inode numbers are unique only within each filesystem and a different filesystem, /var or /opt, for example, will have inodes with the same number as the inode for our file.

Because all of the hard links point to the single inode, which contains the metadata about the file, all of these attributes are part of the file, such as ownership, permissions, and the total number of hard links to the inode, and cannot be different for each hard link. It is one file with one set of attributes. The only attribute that can be different is the file name, which is not contained in the inode. Hard links to a single file/inode that are located in the same directory must have different names due to the fact that there can be no duplicate file names within a single directory.

One of the interesting consequences of hard links is that deleting the actual file inode and data requires deleting all of the links. The problem with this is that it may not be obvious where all of the links are located. A normal file listing does not make this immediately obvious. So we need a way to search for all of the links for a specific file.

Locating Files with Several Hard Links

The find command can locate files with multiple hard links. It can locate all files with a given inode number, which means we can find all of the hard links to a file.

EXPERIMENT 18-11: FINDING HARD LINKS

As root let's look for all files with four hard links. We could also use +4 or -4 to find all files with more or less than four hard links, respectively, but we will look for exactly four. We start the search in the root (/) directory so that the find command will locate all files with four hard links:

```
[root@studentvm1 ~]# find / -type f -links 4
/home/student/link3
/home/student/testdir/link2
/home/student/testdir/file001
/home/student/testdir/link1
/usr/sbin/fsck.ext2
/usr/sbin/mkfs.ext3
/usr/sbin/mke2fs
/usr/sbin/mkfs.ext4
/usr/sbin/e2fsck
/usr/sbin/fsck.ext3
/usr/sbin/mkfs.ext2
/usr/sbin/fsck.ext4
<snip>
```

This shows the hard links we created in Experiment 18-10, as well as some other interesting files such as the programs for creating filesystems like EXT3 and EXT4.

Exploring this a little more, look for the inode numbers of the mkfs files. The -exec option executes the command that follows. The curly braces – {} – in this command substitute the file names found into the ls -li command so that we get a long listing of just the found files.

The -i option displays the inode number. The last part of this command is an escaped semicolon (\;), which is used to terminate the -exec command list. An unescaped semicolon would be used to separate individual commands for the -exec option if there were more:

```
[root@studentvm1 ~]# find / -type f -name mkfs*[0-9] -links 4 -exec ls
-li {} \;
264063 -rwxr-xr-x. 4 root root 136976 Jul 20  2022 /usr/sbin/mkfs.ext2
264063 -rwxr-xr-x. 4 root root 136976 Jul 20  2022 /usr/sbin/mkfs.ext3
264063 -rwxr-xr-x. 4 root root 136976 Jul 20  2022 /usr/sbin/mkfs.ext4
```

All three of these files have the same inode (264063) so that they are really the same file with multiple links. But there are four hard links to this file, so let's find all of them by searching for files with the inode number 264063. Be sure to use the inode number that matches the one for this file on your VM – it will be different from the one shown here:

```
[root@studentvm1 ~]# find /usr -inum 531003
/usr/sbin/mkfs.ext3
/usr/sbin/mke2fs
/usr/sbin/mkfs.ext4
/usr/sbin/mkfs.ext2
```

We could also use the -samefile option to accomplish the same thing without knowing the inode number. This option finds both hard and soft links:

```
[root@studentvm1 ~]# find /usr -samefile /usr/sbin/mkfs.ext3
/usr/sbin/mkfs.ext3
/usr/sbin/mke2fs
/usr/sbin/mkfs.ext4
/usr/sbin/mkfs.ext2
```

The result shows that the name search we were doing previously would not find the fourth link.

Symbolic (Soft) Links

In Experiment 18-10 we found experimentally that hard links do not work across filesystem boundaries. Soft links, also known as symbolic or symlinks, can circumvent that problem. A symlink can be used in most of the same places as a hard link and more.

The difference between a hard link and a soft link is that, while hard links point directly to the inode belonging to the file, soft links point to a directory entry, that is, one of the hard links. Because soft links point to a hard link for the file and not the inode, they are not dependent upon the inode number and can work across filesystems, thus spanning partitions and logical volumes. And, unlike hard links, soft links can point to the directory itself, which is a common use case for soft links.

The downside to this is that if the hard link to which the symlink points is deleted or renamed, the symlink is broken. The symbolic link is still there, but it points to a hard link that no longer exists. Fortunately the **ls** command highlights broken links with flashing white text on a red background in a long listing.

<hr>

EXPERIMENT 18-12: SYMBOLIC LINKS

As the student user in a terminal session, make the ~/testdir directory the PWD. There are three hard links there, so let's create a symlink to one of the hard links and then list the directory:

```
student@studentvm1 testdir]$ ln -s link1 softlink1 ; ll
total 12
-rw-rw---- 4 student student 12 Feb 12 11:59 file001
-rw-rw---- 4 student student 12 Feb 12 11:59 link1
-rw-rw---- 4 student student 12 Feb 12 11:59 link2
lrwxrwxrwx 1 student student  5 Feb 12 12:37 softlink1 -> link1
```

The symbolic link is just a file that contains a pointer to the target file to which it is linked. This can be further tested by the following command:

```
[student@studentvm1 testdir]$ stat softlink1 link1
  File: softlink1 -> link1
  Size: 5              Blocks: 0          IO Block: 4096    symbolic link
Device: 253,4   Inode: 2183       Links: 1
Access: (0777/lrwxrwxrwx) Uid: ( 1000/ student)   Gid: ( 1000/ student)
Access: 2023-02-12 12:37:31.635884495 -0500
Modify: 2023-02-12 12:37:31.633884495 -0500
Change: 2023-02-12 12:37:31.633884495 -0500
 Birth: 2023-02-12 12:37:31.633884495 -0500
  File: link1
  Size: 12             Blocks: 8          IO Block: 4096    regular file
```

```
Device: 253,4    Inode: 2182       Links: 4
Access: (0660/-rw-rw----)  Uid: ( 1000/ student)  Gid: ( 1000/ student)
Access: 2023-02-12 12:06:11.752916155 -0500
Modify: 2023-02-12 11:59:41.942185794 -0500
Change: 2023-02-12 12:09:29.392779392 -0500
 Birth: 2023-02-12 11:59:41.942185794 -0500
```

The first file is the symlink and the second is the hard link. The symlink has a different set of timestamps including and especially a different btime, a different inode number, and even a different size. The hard links are still all the same because they all point to the same inode.

Now we can create a link from /tmp to one of these files and verify the content:

```
[student@studentvm1 testdir]$ cd /tmp ; ln -s ~/testdir/file001
softlink2 ; ll /tmp
total 80
-rw-rw----  1 student student    13 Feb 10 09:26 file09
drwx------. 2 root    root    16384 Jan 17 07:29 lost+found
lrwxrwxrwx  1 student student    29 Feb 12 12:40 softlink2 ->
/home/student/testdir/file001
drwx------  2 student student  4096 Feb  8 14:35 ssh-XXXXXX2UEIbd
drwx------  2 student student  4096 Feb 11 13:29 ssh-XXXXXXhSPk1A
<snip>
[student@studentvm1 tmp]$ cat softlink2
Hello World
```

This enables us to access the file by placing a link of it in /tmp, but, unlike a copy of the file, the current version of the file is always there.

Now let's delete the original file and see what happens:

```
[student@studentvm1 testdir]$ rm file001 ; ll
total 8
-rw-rw---- 3 student student 12 Feb 12 11:59 link1
-rw-rw---- 3 student student 12 Feb 12 11:59 link2
lrwxrwxrwx 1 student student  5 Feb 12 12:37 softlink1 -> link1
```

Notice what happens to the soft link. Deleting the hard link to which the soft link points leaves a broken link in /tmp. On my system the broken link is highlighted in red and the target hard link is flashing.

If the broken link needs to be fixed, you can create another hard link in the same directory with the same name as the old one. If the soft link is no longer needed, it can be deleted with the `rm` command.

The `unlink` command can also be used to delete files and links. It is very simple and has no options as the `rm` command does. Its name does more accurately reflect the underlying process of deletion in that it removes the link – the directory entry – to the file being deleted.

Chapter Summary

This chapter has explored files, directories, and links in detail. We looked at file and directory ownership and permissions, file timestamps, the Red Hat Private Group concept and its security implications, umask for setting the default permissions on new files, and how to obtain information about files. We also created a directory in which users can easily share files with enough security to prevent other users from accessing them.

We learned about file metadata, its locations, and the metadata structures like the directory entry and the file inode. We explored hard and soft links, how they differ, how they relate to the metadata structures, and some uses for them.

Don't forget that permissions and ownership are mostly irrelevant to the root user. The root user can do anything even if that sometimes takes a bit of hacking such as changing permissions.

Exercises

Complete these exercises to finish this chapter:

1. If the student user, who is a member of the ops group, sets the permissions of file09 in the /tmp or other shared directory to 066 and Group ownership to ops, who has what type of access to it and who does not? Explain the logic of this in detail.

2. If the development group uses a shared directory, /home/dev, to share files, what specific permission needs to be set on the dev directory to ensure that files created in that directory are accessible by the entire group without additional intervention?

3. Why are the permissions for your home directory, /home/student, set to 700?

4. For file09 in Exercise 1, how can the student user regain access to the file?

5. Why did we set the shared directory permissions to 770 in Experiment 18-5?

6. What would be different if we set the permissions of the shared directory to 774?

7. If root creates a new file in /home/dev, to what group does it belong?

8. Given that the directory, ~/test, has ownership of student.student and the file permissions are set to --xrwxrwx (177), which of the following tasks can the student user perform? Listing the content of the directory? Creating and deleting files in the directory? Making the directory the PWD?

9. Create a file in a publicly accessible directory such as /tmp and give it permissions so that all users except those belonging to the dev group can access it for read and write. Users in the dev group should have no access at all.

10. Create a file as the student user and set the permissions on a file such that the root user has no access but the student user, who created the file, has full read/write access and Other users can read the file.

11. Which type of link is required when linking from one filesystem to another? Why?

12. The umask for the root user is 022. What are the permissions for new files created by root?

13. Why does a hard link not break if one of the links is moved to another directory in the same filesystem? Demonstrate this.

14. Fix the symlink in /tmp that we broke when we deleted file001.

CHAPTER 19

Filesystems

Objectives

In this chapter you will learn

Three definitions for the term "filesystem"

- The meta-structures of the EXT4 filesystem

- How to obtain information about an EXT4 filesystem

- To resolve problems that prevent a host from booting due to errors in configuration files

- To detect and repair filesystem inconsistencies that might result in data loss

- To describe and use the Linux Filesystem Hierarchical Standard (FHS)

- To create a new partition and install an EXT4 filesystem on it

- Configure /etc/fstab to mount a new partition at boot time

Overview

Every general-purpose computer needs to store data of various types on a hard disk drive (HDD), solid-state drive (SSD), or some equivalent such as a USB memory stick. There are a couple reasons for this. First, RAM loses its contents when the computer is switched off so that everything stored in RAM gets lost. There are non-volatile types of RAM that can maintain the data stored there after power is removed, such as flash RAM that is used in USB memory sticks and solid-state drives (SSDs).

571

© David Both 2023
D. Both, *Using and Administering Linux: Volume 1*, https://doi.org/10.1007/978-1-4842-9618-9_19

The second reason that data needs to be stored on storage devices is that even standard RAM is still more expensive than disk space. Both RAM and disk costs have been dropping rapidly, but RAM still leads the way in terms of cost per byte. A quick calculation of the cost per byte, based on costs for 16GB of RAM vs. a 2TB hard drive, shows that the RAM is about 71 times more expensive per unit than the hard drive. A typical cost for RAM is around $0.0000000043743750 per byte as of this writing.

For a quick historical note to put present RAM costs in perspective, in the very early days of computing, one type of memory was based on dots on a CRT screen. This was very expensive at about $1.00 per bit!

Definitions

You may hear people talk about the terms "filesystems" and "storage" in a number of different and possibly confusing ways. Both words can have multiple meanings, and you may have to discern the correct meaning from the context of a discussion or document.

The terms are defined here as they are used in this course.

Filesystem

I define the various meanings of the word "filesystem" based on how I have observed it being used in different circumstances. Note that, while attempting to conform to standard "official" meanings, my intent is to define the term based on its various usages. This chapter covers all three meanings of the term "filesystem" in a Linux environment:

1. A specific type of data storage format such as EXT3, EXT4, BTRFS, XFS, and so on. Linux supports almost 100 types of filesystems including some very old ones, as well as some of the newest. Each of these filesystem types uses its own metadata structures to define how the data is stored and accessed.

2. The entire Linux hierarchical directory structure starting at the top (/) root directory.

3. A partition or logical volume formatted with a specific type of filesystem that can be mounted on a specified mount point on a Linux filesystem.

Storage

Another set of terms that need to be defined are those relating to persistent data storage hardware:

1. **Storage**: Any hardware device designed for the long-term, non-volatile, storage of data. That is, the data is persistent across reboots and is not lost when power is removed.

2. **Hard drive (HDD/hard disk drive)**: A storage device that uses a spinning disk for persistent data storage.

3. **Solid-state drive (SSD)**: A storage device that uses a form of flash memory for persistent data storage.

Filesystem Functions

Storage filesystems are designed to provide space for non-volatile storage of data, and that brings with it some interesting and inescapable details. There are many other important functions that flow from that requirement.

A filesystem is all of the following:

1. **Data storage**: A structured place to store and retrieve data. This is the primary function of any filesystem.

2. **Namespace**: A naming and organizational methodology that provides rules for naming and structuring data.

3. **Security model**: A scheme for defining access rights.

4. **Application programming interface (API)**: System function calls to manipulate filesystem objects like directories and files.

5. **Implementation**: The software to implement the preceding functions.

All filesystems need to provide a namespace, that is, a naming and organizational methodology. This defines how a file can be named, specifically the length of a file name and the subset of characters that can be used for file names out of the total set of characters available. It also defines the logical structure of the data on a disk, such as the use of directories for organizing files instead of just lumping them all together in a single, huge data space.

Once the namespace has been defined, a metadata structure is necessary to provide the logical foundation for that namespace. This includes the data structures required to support a hierarchical directory structure; structures to determine which blocks of space on the disk are used and which are available; and structures that allow for maintaining the names of the files and directories, information about the files such as their size and times they were created or modified or last accessed, and the location or locations of the data belonging to the file on the disk. Other metadata is used to store high-level information about the subdivisions of the disk such as logical volumes and partitions. This higher-level metadata and the structures it represents contain the information describing the filesystem stored on the drive or partition, but are separate from and independent of the filesystem metadata.

Filesystems also require an application programming interface (API) that provides access to system function calls that manipulate filesystem objects like files and directories. APIs provide for tasks such as creating, moving, and deleting files. It also provides functions that determine things like where a file is placed on a filesystem. Such functions may account for objectives such as speed or minimizing disk fragmentation.

Modern filesystems also provide a security model, which is a scheme for defining access rights to files and directories. The Linux filesystem security model helps ensure that users only have access to their own files and not those of others or the operating system itself.

The final building block is the software required to implement all of these functions. Linux uses a two-part software implementation as a way to improve both system and developer efficiency, which is illustrated in Figure 19-1.

The first part of this two-part implementation is the Linux virtual filesystem. This virtual filesystem provides a single set of commands for the kernel, and developers, to access all types of filesystems. The virtual filesystem software calls the specific device driver required to interface to the various types of local filesystems, such as EXT4 and BTRFS, and to remote filesystems like the Network File System (NFS). The filesystem-specific device drivers are the second part of the implementation. The device driver interprets the standard set of filesystem commands to ones specific to the type of filesystem on the partition or logical volume.

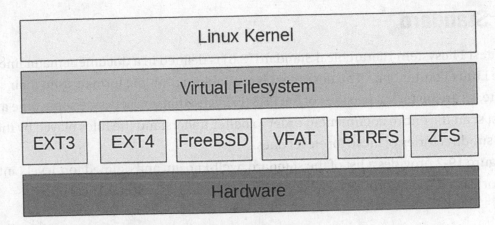

Figure 19-1. *The Linux two-part filesystem structure*

The Linux Filesystem Hierarchical Standard

As a usually very organized Virgo, I like things stored in smaller, organized groups rather than in one big bucket. The use of directories helps me store and then locate the files I want when I want them. Directories are also known as folders because they can be thought of as folders in which files are kept in a sort of physical desktop filing cabinet analogy.

In Linux, and many other operating systems, directories can be structured in a tree-like hierarchy. The Linux directory structure is well defined and documented in the Linux Filesystem Hierarchichal Standard (FHS).[1] This standard has been put in place to ensure that all distributions of Linux are consistent in their directory usage. Such consistency makes writing and maintaining shell and compiled programs easier for SysAdmins because the programs, their configuration files, and their data, if any, should be located in the standard directories.

---

[1] Linux Foundation, *Linux Filesystem Hierarchical Standard*, http://refspecs.linuxfoundation.org/fhs.shtml

The Standard

The latest Filesystem Hierarchical Standard (3.0) is defined in a document maintained by the Linux Foundation.[2] The document is available in multiple formats from their website, as are historical versions of the FHS. I suggest that you set aside some time and at least scan the entire document in order to better understand the roles played by the many subdirectories of these top-level ones.

Figure 19-2 provides a list of the standard, well-known, and defined top-level Linux directories and their purposes. These directories are listed in alphabetical order.

---

[2] The Linux Foundation maintains documents defining many Linux standards. It also sponsors the work of Linus Torvalds.

Directory	Part of /	Description
/ (root filesystem)	Yes	The root filesystem is the top-level directory of the filesystem. It must contain all of the files required to boot the Linux system before other filesystems are mounted. After the system is booted, all other filesystems are mounted on standard, well defined, mount points as subdirectories of the root filesystem.
/bin	Yes	The /bin directory contains user executable files.[3]
/boot	No	Contains the static bootloader and kernel executable and configuration files required to boot a Linux computer.
/dev	Yes	This directory contains the device files for every hardware device attached to the system. These are not device drivers, rather they are files that represent each device on the computer and facilitate access to those devices.
/etc	Yes	Contains a wide variety of system configuration files for the host computer.
/home	No	Home directory storage for user files. Each user has a subdirectory in /home.
/lib	Yes	Contains shared library files that are required to boot the system.
/media	No	A place to mount external removable media devices such as USB thumb drives that may be connected to the host.
/mnt	No	A temporary mountpoint for regular filesystems (as in not removable media) that can be used while the administrator is repairing or working on a filesystem.
/opt	No	Optional files such as vendor supplied application programs should be located here.

Figure 19-2. *The top level of the Linux Filesystem Hierarchical Standard*

---

[3] Note that /bin and /sbin are now just links to /usr/bin and /usr/sbin, respectively. They are no longer generally split into the arbitrary classifications "essential" and "non-essential" as they used to be.

Directory	Part of /	Description
/proc	Virtual	Virtual filesystem used to expose access to internal kernel information and editable tuning parameters.
/root	Yes	This is not the root (/) filesystem. It is the home directory for the root user.
/sbin	Yes	System binary files. These are executables used for system administration.
/selinux	Virtual	This filesystem is only used when SELinux is enabled.
/sys	Virtual	This virtual filesystem contains information about the USB and PCI busses and the devices attached to each.
/tmp	No	Temporary directory. Used by the operating system and many programs to store temporary files. Users may also store files here temporarily. Note that files stored here may be deleted at any time without prior notice.
/usr	No	These are shareable, read only files including executable binaries and libraries, man[ual] files, and other types of documentation.
/usr/local	No	These are typically shell programs or compiled programs and their supporting configuration files that are written locally and used by the SysAdmin or other users of the host.
/var	No	Variable data files are stored here. This can include things like log files, MySQL and other database files, web server data files, email inboxes, and much more.

Figure 19-2. (*continued*)

The directories shown in Figure 19-2 that have a Yes in column 2 are considered to be an integral part of the root filesystem. That is, they cannot be created as a separate filesystem and mounted at startup time. This is because they, specifically their contents, must be present at boot time in order for the system to boot properly. The /media and /mnt directories are part of the root filesystem, but they should never contain any data. Rather, they are simply temporary mount points.

The rest of the directories do not need to be present during the boot sequence, but will be mounted later, during the startup sequence that prepares the host to perform useful work.

Wikipedia also has a good description of the FHS.[4] This standard should be followed as closely as possible to ensure operational and functional consistency. Regardless of the filesystem types, that is, EXT4, XFS, BTRFS, etc., used on a host, this hierarchical directory structure is the same.

Problem Solving

One of the best reasons I can think of for adhering to the Linux FHS is that of making the task of problem solving as easy as possible. Many applications expect things to be in certain places, or they won't work. Where you store your cat pictures and MP3s doesn't matter, but where your system configuration files are located does.

Using the Linux Filesystem Hierarchical Standard promotes consistency and simplicity, which makes problem solving easier. Knowing where to find things in the Linux filesystem directory structure has saved me from endless flailing about on more than just a few occasions.

I find that most of the core utilities, Linux services, and servers provided with the distributions I use are consistent in their usage of the /etc directory and its subdirectories for configuration files. This means that finding a configuration file for a misbehaving program or service supplied by the distribution should be easy.

I typically use a number of the ASCII text files in /etc to configure Sendmail, Apache, DHCP, NFS, NTP, DNS, and more. I always know where to find the files I need to modify for those services, and they are all open and accessible because they are in ASCII text, which makes them readable to both computers and humans.

Using the Filesystem Incorrectly

One situation involving the incorrect usage of the filesystem occurred while I was working as a lab administrator at a large technology company. One of our developers had installed an application in the wrong location, /var. The application was crashing

---

[4]Wikipedia, *Filesystem Hierarchy Standard*, https://en.wikipedia.org/wiki/Filesystem_Hierarchy_Standard

because the /var filesystem was full, and the log files, which were stored in /var/log on that filesystem, could not be appended with new messages that would indicate that the /var filesystem was full due to the lack of space in /var. However, the system remained up and running because the critical / (root) and /tmp filesystems did not fill up. Removing the offending application and reinstalling it in the /opt filesystem, where it was supposed to be, resolved that problem. I also had a little discussion with the developer who did the original installation.

Adhering to the Standard

So how do we as SysAdmins adhere to the Linux FHS? It is actually pretty easy, and there is a hint way back in Figure 19-2. The /usr/local directory is where locally created executables and their configuration files should be stored. By local programs, the FHS means those that we create ourselves as SysAdmins to make our work or the work of other users easier. This includes all of those powerful and versatile shell programs we write. Our programs should be located in /usr/local/bin and the configuration files, if any, in /usr/local/etc. There is also a /var/local directory in which the database files for local programs can be stored.

I have written a fair number of shell programs over the years, and it took me at least five years before I understood the appropriate places to install my own software on host computers. In some cases I had even forgotten where I installed them. In other cases, I installed the configuration files in /etc instead of /usr/local/etc, and my file was overwritten during an upgrade. It took a few hours to track that down the first time it happened.

By adhering to these standards when writing shell programs, it is easier for me to remember where I have installed them. It is also easier for other SysAdmins to find things by searching only the directories in which we as SysAdmins would have installed those programs and their files.

Linux Unified Directory Structure

The Linux filesystem unifies all physical storage devices and partitions into a single directory structure. It all starts at the top – the root (/) directory. All other directories and their subdirectories are located under the single Linux root directory. This means that there is only one single directory tree in which to search for files and programs.

This can work only because a filesystem, such as /home, /tmp, /var, /opt, or /usr, can be created on separate physical storage devices, a different partition, or a different logical volume from the / (root) filesystem and then be mounted on a mountpoint (directory) as part of the root filesystem tree. Even removable drives such as a USB thumb drive or an external USB or an ESATA hard drive will be mounted onto the root filesystem and become an integral part of that directory tree.

One reason to do this is apparent during an upgrade from one version of a Linux distribution to another or changing from one distribution to another. In general, and aside from any upgrade utilities like **dnf-upgrade** in Fedora, it is wise to occasionally reformat the hard drive(s) containing the operating system during an upgrade to positively remove any cruft that has accumulated over time. If /home is part of the root filesystem, it will be reformatted as well and would then have to be restored from a backup. By having /home as a separate filesystem, it will be known to the installation program as a separate filesystem, and formatting of it can be skipped. This can also apply to /var where database, email inbox, website, and other variable user and system data are stored.

You can also be intentional about which files reside on which disks. If you've got a smaller SSD and a large piece of spinning rust, put the important frequently accessed files necessary for booting on the SSD – or your favorite game or whatever. Similarly, don't waste SSD space on archival storage of large files that you rarely access.

As another example, a long time ago, when I was not yet aware of the potential issues surrounding having all of the required Linux directories as part of the / (root) filesystem, I managed to fill up my home directory with a large number of very big files. Since neither the /home directory nor the /tmp directory was a separate filesystem but simply subdirectories of the root filesystem, the entire root filesystem filled up. There was no room left for the operating system to create temporary files or to expand existing data files. At first the application programs started complaining that there was no room to save files, and then the OS itself started to act very strangely. Booting to single-user mode and clearing out the offending files in my home directory allowed me to get going again; I then reinstalled Linux using a pretty standard hierarchical setup and was able to prevent complete system crashes from occurring again.

I once had a situation where a Linux host continued to run, but prevented the user from logging in using the GUI desktop. I was able to log in using the command-line interface (CLI) locally using one of the virtual consoles and remotely using SSH. The problem was that the /tmp filesystem had filled up and some temporary files required by the GUI desktop could not be created at login time. Because the CLI login did not require files to be created in /tmp, the lack of space there did not prevent me from logging in using the CLI. In this case the /tmp directory was a separate filesystem, and there was plenty of space available in the volume group of which the /tmp logical volume was a part. I simply expanded the /tmp logical volume to a size that accommodated my fresh understanding of the amount of temporary file space needed on that host, and the problem was solved. Note that this solution did not require a reboot and as soon as the /tmp filesystem was enlarged the user was able to log into the desktop.

Filesystem Types

Linux supports reading around 100 partition types; it can create and write to only a few of these. But it is possible – and very common – to mount filesystems of different types on the same root filesystem. In this context we are talking about filesystems in terms of the structures and metadata required to store and manage the user data on a partition of a hard drive or a logical volume. The complete list of filesystem partition types recognized by the Linux **fdisk** command is provided in Figure 19-3, so that you can get a feel for the high degree of compatibility that Linux has with very many types of systems.

```
0   Empty              24  NEC DOS            81  Minix / old Lin  bf  Solaris
1   FAT12              27  Hidden NTFS Win    82  Linux swap / So  c1  DRDOS/sec (FAT-
2   XENIX root         39  Plan 9             83  Linux            c4  DRDOS/sec (FAT-
3   XENIX usr          3c  PartitionMagic     84  OS/2 hidden or   c6  DRDOS/sec (FAT-
4   FAT16 <32M         40  Venix 80286        85  Linux extended   c7  Syrinx
5   Extended           41  PPC PReP Boot      86  NTFS volume set  da  Non-FS data
6   FAT16              42  SFS                87  NTFS volume set  db  CP/M / CTOS / .
7   HPFS/NTFS/exFAT    4d  QNX4.x             88  Linux plaintext  de  Dell Utility
8   AIX                4e  QNX4.x 2nd part    8e  Linux LVM        df  BootIt
9   AIX bootable       4f  QNX4.x 3rd part    93  Amoeba           e1  DOS access
a   OS/2 Boot Manag    50  OnTrack DM         94  Amoeba BBT       e3  DOS R/O
b   W95 FAT32          51  OnTrack DM6 Aux    9f  BSD/OS           e4  SpeedStor
c   W95 FAT32 (LBA)    52  CP/M               a0  IBM Thinkpad hi  ea  Rufus alignment
e   W95 FAT16 (LBA)    53  OnTrack DM6 Aux    a5  FreeBSD          eb  BeOS fs
f   W95 Ext'd (LBA)    54  OnTrackDM6         a6  OpenBSD          ee  GPT
10  OPUS               55  EZ-Drive           a7  NeXTSTEP         ef  EFI (FAT-12/16/
11  Hidden FAT12       56  Golden Bow         a8  Darwin UFS       f0  Linux/PA-RISC b
12  Compaq diagnost    5c  Priam Edisk        a9  NetBSD           f1  SpeedStor
14  Hidden FAT16 <3    61  SpeedStor          ab  Darwin boot      f4  SpeedStor
16  Hidden FAT16       63  GNU HURD or Sys    af  HFS / HFS+       f2  DOS secondary
17  Hidden HPFS/NTF    64  Novell Netware     b7  Bsdg fs          fb  VMware VMFS
18  AST SmartSleep     65  Novell Netware     b8  Bsdg swap        fc  VMware VMKCORE
1b  Hidden W95 FAT3    70  DiskSecure Mult    bb  Boot Wizard hid  fd  Linux raid auto
1c  Hidden W95 FAT3    75  PC/IX              bc  Acronis FAT32 L  fe  LANstep
1e  Hidden W95 FAT1    80  Old Minix          be  Solaris boot     ff  BBT
```

Figure 19-3. *The list of filesystems supported by Linux*

The main purpose in supporting the ability to read so many partition types is to allow for compatibility and at least some interoperability with other filesystems. The choices available when creating a new filesystem with Fedora are shown in the following list.

btrfs	**cramfs**	**ext2**
ext3	**ext4**	fat
gfs2	hfsplus	minix
msdos	ntfs	reiserfs
vfat	xfs	

Other Linux distributions support creating different filesystem types. For example, CentOS 6 supports creating only those filesystems highlighted in bold in the preceding list.

Mounting

The term to "mount" a filesystem in Linux refers back to the early days of computing when a reel of tape or removable disk pack would need to be physically mounted on an appropriate drive device. After being physically placed on the drive, the filesystem on the disk pack would be "mounted" by the operating system to make the contents available for access by the OS, application programs, and users.

A mount point is simply an empty directory, like any other, that is created as part of the root filesystem. So, for example, the home filesystem is mounted on the directory /home. Filesystems can be mounted at mount points on non-root filesystems in the directory tree, but this is less common.

The Linux root filesystem is mounted on the root directory (/) very early in the boot sequence. Other filesystems are mounted later, by the Linux startup programs, either **rc** under SystemV or by systemd in newer Linux releases. Mounting of filesystems during the startup process is managed by the /etc/fstab configuration file. An easy way to remember that is that fstab stands for "filesystem table," and it is a list of filesystems that are to be mounted, their designated mount points, and any options that might be needed for specific filesystems.

Filesystems are mounted on an existing directory/mount point using the **mount** command. In general, any directory that is used as a mount point should be empty and not have any other files contained in it. Linux will not prevent users from mounting one filesystem over one that is already there or on a directory that contains files. If you mount a filesystem on an existing directory or filesystem, the original contents will be hidden, and only the content of the newly mounted filesystem will be visible.

The Linux EXT4 Filesystem

Although written for Linux, the EXT filesystem has its roots in the Minix operating system and the Minix filesystem, which predate Linux by about five years, having been first released in 1987. When writing the original Linux kernel, Linus Torvalds needed a filesystem and did not want to write one at that point. So he simply included the Minix filesystem,[5] which had been written by Andrew S. Tanenbaum[6] and which was a part of Tanenbaum's Minix[7] operating system. Minix was a Unix-like operating system written for educational purposes. Its code was freely available and was appropriately licensed to allow Torvald's to include it in his first version of Linux.

Tip   The current default filesystem for Fedora new installations is BTRFS, but EXT4 is still much more widely used, which is why we use it in this course. I think EXT4 is also more appropriate for servers and other systems used for infrastructure, but I know that other SysAdmins have different opinions on this.

The original EXT filesystem[8] (Extended) was written by Rémy Card[9] and released with Linux in 1992 in order to overcome some size limitations of the Minix filesystem. The primary structural changes were to the metadata of the filesystem, which was based on the Unix filesystem, UFS, also known as the Berkeley Fast File System or FFS. The EXT2 filesystem quickly replaced the EXT filesystem; EXT3 and EXT4 followed with additional fixes and features.

---

[5] Wikipedia, *Minix Filesystem*, https://en.wikipedia.org/wiki/MINIX_file_system
[6] Wikipedia, *Andrew S. Tanenbaum*, https://en.wikipedia.org/wiki/Andrew_S._Tanenbaum
[7] Wikipedia, *Minix*, https://en.wikipedia.org/wiki/MINIX
[8] Wikipedia, *Extended Filesystem*, https://en.wikipedia.org/wiki/Extended_file_system
[9] Wikipedia, *Rémy Card*, https://en.wikipedia.org/wiki/Rémy_Card

The EXT4 filesystem has the following meta-structures:

- The space in each EXT4 partition is divided into cylinder groups that allow for more granular management of the data space. In my experience the group size usually amounts to about 8MB.

- Each cylinder group contains the following:

  - A superblock, which contains the metadata that defines the other filesystem structures and locates them on the physical disk assigned to the group.

  - An inode bitmap block that is used to determine which inodes are used and which are free.

  - The inodes that have their own space on the disk. Each inode contains information about one file, including the locations of the data blocks, that is, zones belonging to the file.

  - A zone bitmap to keep track of the used and free data zones.

  - A journal,[10] which records in advance the changes that will be performed to the filesystem and which helps eliminate data loss due to crashes and power failures.

Cylinder Groups

The space in each EXT4 filesystem is divided into cylinder groups that allow for more granular management of the data space. In my experience the group size can vary from about 8MiB for older systems to 34MiB for software versions with newer hosts, larger storage devices, and newer versions of the EXT filesystem. Figure 19-4 shows the basic structure of a cylinder group. The data allocation unit in a cylinder is the block, which is usually 4K in size.

---

[10] Wikipedia, *Journaling file system*, https://en.wikipedia.org/wiki/Journaling_file_system

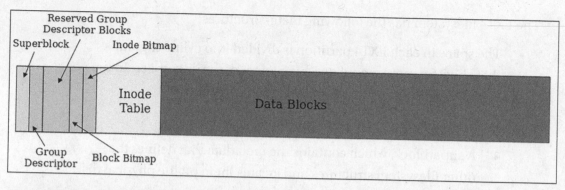

Figure 19-4. *The structure of a cylinder group*

The first block in the cylinder group is a superblock, which contains the metadata that defines the other filesystem structures and locates them on the physical disk. Some of the additional groups in the partition will have backup superblocks, but not all. A damaged superblock can be replaced by using a disk utility such as **dd** to copy the contents of a backup superblock to the primary superblock. It does not happen often, but I have experienced a damaged superblock once many years ago, and I was able to restore its contents using those of one of the backup superblocks. Fortunately I had been foresighted and used the **dumpe2fs** command to dump the descriptor information of the partitions on my system.

Tip   Damaged superblocks are very rare. I have not had one in probably more than 20 years.

Each cylinder group has two types of bitmaps. The inode bitmap is used to determine which inodes are used and which are free within that group. The inodes have their own space, the inode table in each group. Each inode contains information about one file, including the locations of the data blocks belonging to the file. The block bitmap keeps track of the used and free data blocks within the filesystem. On very large filesystems, the group data can run to hundreds of pages in length. The group metadata includes a listing of all of the free data blocks in the group. For both types of bitmaps, one bit represents one specific data zone or one specific inode. If the bit is zero, the zone or inode is free and available for use, while if it is one, the data zone or inode is in use.

Let's take a look at the metadata for the root filesystem of our VMs. The details and values of yours will probably be different from mine.

EXPERIMENT 19-1: EXPLORING THE SUPERBLOCK

Perform this experiment as root. We use the dumpe2fs utility to dump the data from the primary superblock of the root (/) filesystem. You may need to run the output data stream from the dumpe2fs command through the less utility to see it all:

```
[root@studentvm1 ~]# dumpe2fs -h /dev/mapper/fedora_studentvm1-root |
less
dumpe2fs 1.46.5 (30-Dec-2021)
Filesystem volume name:    root
Last mounted on:           /
Filesystem UUID:           7cc97551-57b1-4d2c-b839-0f689d885b64
Filesystem magic number:   0xEF53
Filesystem revision #:     1 (dynamic)
Filesystem features:       has_journal ext_attr resize_inode dir_index
filetype needs_recovery extent 64bit flex_bg sparse_super large_file
huge_file dir_nlink extra_isize metadata_csum
Filesystem flags:          signed_directory_hash
Default mount options:     user_xattr acl
Filesystem state:          clean
Errors behavior:           Continue
Filesystem OS type:        Linux
Inode count:               131072
Block count:               524288
Reserved block count:      26214
Overhead clusters:         26150
Free blocks:               336688
Free inodes:               126045
First block:               0
Block size:                4096
Fragment size:             4096
Group descriptor size:     64
Reserved GDT blocks:       255
Blocks per group:          32768
Fragments per group:       32768
Inodes per group:          8192
Inode blocks per group:    512
Flex block group size:     16
```

Filesystem created:	Tue Jan 17 07:29:41 2023
Last mount time:	Fri Feb 10 02:01:24 2023
Last write time:	Fri Feb 10 02:01:16 2023
Mount count:	40
Maximum mount count:	-1
Last checked:	Tue Jan 17 07:29:41 2023
Check interval:	0 (<none>)
Lifetime writes:	808 MB
Reserved blocks uid:	0 (user root)
Reserved blocks gid:	0 (group root)
First inode:	11
Inode size:	256
Required extra isize:	32
Desired extra isize:	32
Journal inode:	8
Default directory hash:	half_md4
Directory Hash Seed:	2468459f-67d5-404e-a289-afb754043271
Journal backup:	inode blocks
Checksum type:	crc32c
Checksum:	0x29d6ca33
Journal features:	journal_incompat_revoke journal_64bit
journal_checksum_v3	
Total journal size:	64M
Total journal blocks:	16384
Max transaction length:	16384
Fast commit length:	0
Journal sequence:	0x000004c1
Journal start:	1
Journal checksum type:	crc32c
Journal checksum:	0xcc06298d

There is a lot of information here, and what you see on your VM should be similar. There are some specific data that are of special interest.

The first two entries give the filesystem label and the last mountpoint. That makes it easy to see that this is the root (/) filesystem. If your /etc/fstab uses UUIDs to mount one or more partitions, such as /boot, this is that UUID as it is stored in the filesystem's primary superblock.

The current filesystem state is "clean," which means that all of the data has been written from buffers and the journal to the data space and the filesystem is consistent. If the filesystem were not clean, then not all data has been written to the data area of the hard drive yet. Note that this and some other data in the superblock may not be current if the filesystem is mounted.

This also tells us that the filesystem type is "Linux," which is Type 83 as shown in Figure 19-3. This is a non-LVM partition. Type 8e would be a Linux LVM partition.

You can also see the inode and block counts, which tell us how many files and how much total data can be stored on this filesystem. Since each file uses one inode, this filesystem can hold 131,072 files. Along with the block size of 4096 bytes, the total block count of 524,288 gives 2,147,483,648 total bytes of storage, with 107,372,544 bytes in reserved blocks. When a data block is found by various error detection mechanisms to have errors, the data is moved to one of the reserved blocks, and the regular data block is marked as defective and unavailable for future data storage. The number of free blocks tells us that 1,379,074,048 bytes are free and available.

The directory hash and hash seed are used by the HTree[11] directory tree structure implementation to hash directory entries so that they can be easily found during file seek operations. Much of the rest of the superblock information is relatively easy to extract and understand. The man page for EXT4 has some additional information about the filesystem features listed near the top of this output.

Now use the following command to view both the superblock and the group data for this partition:

```
[root@studentvm1 ~]# dumpe2fs /dev/mapper/fedora_studentvm1-root | less
<SNIP>
Group 0: (Blocks 0-32767) csum 0x34a5 [ITABLE_ZEROED]
  Primary superblock at 0, Group descriptors at 1-1
  Reserved GDT blocks at 2-256
  Block bitmap at 257 (+257), csum 0xcb5022c0
  Inode bitmap at 273 (+273), csum 0x30f9d8bd
  Inode table at 289-800 (+289)
```

---

[11] This Wikipedia entry needs a lot of work but can give you a slightly more accurate description of HTree: https://en.wikipedia.org/wiki/HTree

```
    44 free blocks, 3181 free inodes, 588 directories, 3174 unused inodes
    Free blocks: 24544-24575, 32756-32767
    Free inodes: 1126, 2217-2218, 5014-5016, 5018-8192
  Group 1: (Blocks 32768-65535) csum 0x2fd5 [ITABLE_ZEROED]
    Backup superblock at 32768, Group descriptors at 32769-32769
    Reserved GDT blocks at 32770-33024
    Block bitmap at 258 (bg #0 + 258), csum 0x249636e4
    Inode bitmap at 274 (bg #0 + 274), csum 0x7a501695
    Inode table at 801-1312 (bg #0 + 801)
    32511 free blocks, 8189 free inodes, 3 directories, 8188 unused inodes
    Free blocks: 33025-65535
    Free inodes: 8196-16384
  Group 2: (Blocks 65536-98303) csum 0x9ed7 [ITABLE_ZEROED]
    Block bitmap at 259 (bg #0 + 259), csum 0xda4d2287
    Inode bitmap at 275 (bg #0 + 275), csum 0x8ca184e6
    Inode table at 1313-1824 (bg #0 + 1313)
    32768 free blocks, 8190 free inodes, 2 directories, 8190 unused inodes
    Free blocks: 65536-98303
    Free inodes: 16387-24576
<SNIP>
```

I have pruned the output from this command to show data for the first three groups. Each group has its own block and inode bitmaps and an inode table. The listing of free blocks in each group enables the filesystem to easily locate free space in which to store new files or to add to existing ones. If you compare the block number range for the entire group against the free blocks, you will see that the file data is spread through the groups rather than being jammed together starting from the beginning. We will see more about this later in this chapter in the section "Data Allocation Strategies."

Group 2 in the preceding output has no data stored in it because all of the data blocks assigned to this group are free. If you scroll down toward the end of the data for this filesystem, you will see that the remaining groups have no data stored in them either.

The inode

What is an inode? Short for index-node, an inode is one 256-byte block on the disk that stores data about a file. This includes the size of the file; the user IDs of the user and group owners of the file; the file mode, that is, the access permissions; and three timestamps specifying the time and date that the file was last accessed and modified and that the data in the inode itself was last modified.

The inode has been mentioned previously as a key component of the metadata of the Linux EXT filesystems. Figure 19-5 shows the relationship between the inode and the data stored on the hard drive. This diagram is the directory and inode for a single file, which, in this case, is highly fragmented. The EXT filesystems work actively to reduce fragmentation, so it is very unlikely you will ever see a file with this many indirect data blocks or extents. In fact fragmentation is extremely low in EXT filesystems, so most inodes will use only one or two direct data pointers and none of the indirect pointers.

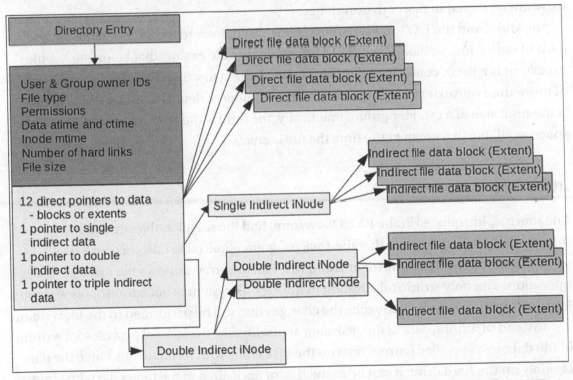

Figure 19-5. *The inode stores information about each file and enables the EXT filesystem to locate all data belonging to it*

The inode does not contain the name of the file as part of its metadata. Access to a file is via the directory entry, which itself is the name of the file and which contains a pointer to the inode. The value of that pointer is the inode number. Each inode in a filesystem has a unique ID number, but inodes in other filesystems on the same computer and even the same hard drive can have the same inode number. This has implications for links that were discussed in Chapter 18. For files that have significant fragmentation, it becomes necessary to have some additional capabilities in the form of indirect nodes. Technically these are not really inodes, so I use the name node here for convenience.

An indirect node is a normal data block in the filesystem that is used only for describing data and not for storage of metadata. Thus, more than 15 entries can be supported. For example, a block size of 4K can support 512 4-byte indirect nodes, thus allowing 12 (direct) + 512 (indirect) = 524 extents for a single file. Double and triple indirect node support is also possible, but files requiring that many extents are unlikely to be encountered in most environments.

In Minix and the EXT1 to EXT3 filesystems, the pointer to the data is in the form of a list of data zones or blocks. For EXT4 the inode lists the extents that belong to the file. An extent is a list of contiguous data blocks that belong to a file. Files may be comprised of more than one extent. The only limit on the number of data blocks in a single extent is the total size of a cylinder group. Practically, the limit is the amount of contiguous free space available in a group at the time the file is created.

Journal

The journal, introduced in the EXT3 filesystem, had the singular objective of overcoming the massive amounts of time that the `fsck` program required to fully recover a disk structure damaged by an improper shutdown that occurred during a file update operation. The only structural addition to the EXT filesystem to accomplish this was the journal,[12] which records in advance the changes that will be performed to the filesystem.

Instead of writing data to the disk data areas directly, the journal provides for writing of file data to a specified journal area on the disk along with its metadata. Once the data is safely on the hard drive, it can be merged in or appended to the target file with almost

---

[12] Wikipedia, *Journaling File System*, https://en.wikipedia.org/wiki/Journaling_file_system

zero chance of losing data. As this data is committed to the data area of the disk, the journal is updated so that the filesystem will still be in a consistent state in the event of a system failure before all of the data in the journal is committed. On the next boot, the filesystem will be checked for inconsistencies, and data remaining in the journal will then be committed to the data areas of the disk to complete the updates to the target file.

Journaling does impact data write performance; however, there are three options available for the journal that allow the user to choose between performance and data integrity and safety. The EXT4 man page has a description of these settings:

- **Journal**: Both metadata and file contents are written to the journal before commit to the main filesystem. This offers the greatest reliability with a performance penalty because the data is written twice.

- **Writeback**: The metadata is written to the journal but the file contents are not. This is a faster option but subject to possible out-of-order writes in which files being appended to during a crash may gain a tail of garbage on the next mount.

- **Ordered**: This option is a bit like writeback, but it forces file contents to be written before associated metadata is marked as committed in the journal. It is an acceptable compromise between reliability and performance and is the default for newly created EXT4 filesystems.

My personal preference is the middle ground because my environments do not require heavy disk write activity, so performance should not normally be an issue. I chose the default, which provides reliability with a bit of a performance hit. This choice can be set in /etc/fstab as a mount option or as a boot parameter by passing the option to the kernel by editing the GRUB kernel options line in /etc/default/grub.

The journaling function reduces the time required to check the hard drive for inconsistencies after a failure from hours or even days to mere minutes at the most. Of course these times may vary significantly depending upon many factors, especially the size and type of drives. I have had many issues over the years that have crashed my systems. The details could fill another chapter, but suffice it to say that most were self-inflicted like kicking out a power plug. Fortunately the EXT journaling filesystems have reduced that bootup recovery time to two or three minutes. In addition, I have never had a problem with lost data since I started using EXT3 with journaling.

The journaling feature of EXT4 may be turned off, and it then functions as an EXT2 filesystem. The journal itself still exists, empty and unused. Simply remount the partition with the mount command using the type parameter to specify EXT2. You may be able to do this from the command line, depending upon which filesystem you are working with, but you can change the type specifier in the /etc/fstab file and then reboot. I strongly recommend against mounting an EXT3 or EXT4 filesystem as EXT2 because of the additional potential for lost data and extended recovery times.

An existing EXT2 filesystem can be upgraded with the addition of a journal using the following command where /dev/sda1 is the drive and partition identifier. Be sure to change the file type specifier in /etc/fstab and remount the partition to have the change take effect:

```
tune2fs -j /dev/sda1
```

This should seldom be necessary because the EXT2 filesystem was superseded by EXT3 with journaling in 2001.[13]

Data Allocation Strategies

The EXT filesystem implements several data allocation strategies that ensure minimal file fragmentation. Reducing fragmentation results in improved filesystem performance.

Data allocation for the EXT4 filesystem is managed using extents. An extent is described by its starting and ending places on the hard drive. This makes it possible to describe very long physically contiguous files in a single inode pointer entry, which can significantly reduce the number of pointers required to describe the location of all the data in larger files. Other allocation strategies have been implemented in EXT4 to further reduce fragmentation.

EXT4 scatters newly created files across the disk so that they are not bunched up in one location at the beginning of the disk as many early PC filesystems such as FAT did. The file allocation algorithms attempt to spread the files as evenly as possible among the cylinder groups and, when fragmentation is necessary, to keep the discontinuous file extents close to the others belonging to the same file to minimize head seek and

---

[13]Wikipedia, *EXT3*, https://en.wikipedia.org/wiki/Ext3

rotational latency as much as possible on HDDs. Additional strategies are used to preallocate extra storage space when a new file is created or when an existing file is extended. This helps ensure that extending the file will not automatically result in its becoming fragmented. New files are never allocated immediately following the end of existing files, which also reduces or prevents fragmentation of the existing files.

Aside from the actual location of the data on the disk, EXT4 uses functional strategies such as delayed allocation to allow the filesystem to collect all of the data being written to the disk before allocating the space to it. This can improve the likelihood that the allocated data space will be contiguous.

Data Fragmentation

For many older PC filesystems such as FAT and all its variants and NTFS, fragmentation has been a significant problem resulting in degraded hard drive performance. Defragmentation became an industry in itself with different brands of defragmentation software that ranged from very effective to only marginally so.

Older storage devices use magnetic disks that rotate at high speed and moving heads to position the data read/write transducers over the correct track. It is this wait for the heads to seek to a specific track and then the wait for the desired data block to be read by the read/write heads that causes the delays when files are fragmented. Although SSDs can experience file fragmentation, there is no performance penalty because, like all solid-state memory, even though SSDs are designed to emulate the function of a hard drive, they do not have the spinning platters and moving heads of a traditional hard drive.

Linux's Extended filesystems use data allocation strategies that help minimize fragmentation of files on the hard drive and reduce the effects of fragmentation when it does occur. You can use the **fsck** command on EXT filesystems to check the total filesystem fragmentation. The following example is to check the home directory of my main workstation, which was only 1.5% fragmented. Jason, my diligent technical reviewer, reports 1.2% fragmentation on his home desktop workstation:

```
fsck -fn /dev/mapper/vg_01-home
```

Let's see how fragmented our VM home directories are.

EXPERIMENT 19-2: FRAGMENTATION

Let's look at the amount of file fragmentation on the hard drive of your VM. Perform this experiment as root.

The `fsck` (filesystem check) command is usually used to repair filesystems after a crash or another incident that may make them inconsistent. It can also be used to report on fragmentation. The -f option forces checking of the filesystem even if it is marked as clean, and the -n option tells `fsck` to not fix problems it finds. This results in a report, hopefully short, of the current state of the filesystem:

```
[root@studentvm1 ~]# fsck -fn /dev/mapper/fedora_studentvm1-home
fsck from util-linux 2.38.1
e2fsck 1.46.5 (30-Dec-2021)
Warning!  /dev/mapper/fedora_studentvm1-home is mounted.
Warning: skipping journal recovery because doing a read-only filesystem
check.
Pass 1: Checking inodes, blocks, and sizes
Pass 2: Checking directory structure
Pass 3: Checking directory connectivity
Pass 4: Checking reference counts
Pass 5: Checking group summary information
Free blocks count wrong (147338, counted=147283).
Fix? no

Free inodes count wrong (128657, counted=128631).
Fix? no

home: 2415/131072 files (1.7% non-contiguous), 376950/524288 blocks
```

Some problems may occasionally be reported such as inconsistencies in the inode or data block counts. This can occur during normal operation on a virtual hard drive just as it can on a physical one. I have on occasion simply powered off the VM without a proper shutdown. It is unlikely that you will have errors like this.

For now, look at the last line of the output from `fsck`. This shows that there are 1.7% non-contiguous blocks, which implies that there is little fragmentation. Jason, technical editor for the first edition of this course, reported 1.9% fragmentation on his studentvm1 host.

The other numbers on this line are rather obscure. After reading the man page for fsck and many online searches, I have found that these numbers are not explicitly defined. I *think* that the first pair means that 2,415 inodes from a total of 131,072 have been used.

Cross-checking with the output of dumpe2fs in Experiment 19-1, the number 131,072 is correct for the total number of inodes, and the free inode count is 126,045, with the difference being 5027. The total block count of 524,288 also matches up as does the difference between that and the free blocks, so we can conclude that my initial assumptions were correct.

Check all of these numbers on your own VM to verify that they are correct.

I once performed some theoretical calculations to determine whether disk defragmentation might result in any noticeable performance improvement. While I did make some assumptions, the disk performance data I used were from a then new 300GB Western Digital hard drive with a 2.0ms track to track seek time. The number of files in this example was the actual number that existed in the filesystem on the day I did the calculation. I did assume that a fairly large amount of the fragmented files would be touched each day, 20%.

Total files	271,794
% Fragmentation	5.00%
Discontinuities	13,590
% fragmented files touched per day (assumption)	20%
Number of additional seeks	2,718
Average seek time	10.90ms
Total additional seek time per day	29.63Sec
Track to Track seek time	2.00ms
Total additional seek time per day	5.44Sec

Figure 19-6. The theoretical effects of fragmentation on disk performance

I have done two calculations for the total additional seek time per day, one based on the track to track seek time, which is the more likely scenario for most files due to the EXT file allocation strategies, and one for the average seek time, which I assumed would make a fair worst-case scenario.

You can see from Figure 19-6 that the impact of fragmentation on a modern EXT filesystem with a hard drive of even modest performance would be minimal and negligible for the vast majority of applications. You can plug the numbers from your environment into your own similar spreadsheet to see what you might expect in the way of performance impact. This type of calculation most likely will not represent actual performance, but it can provide a bit of insight into fragmentation and its theoretical impact on a system. Jason reported noticeable impact from fragmentation with very large files that are very near continually accessed – usually databases – for which the application itself is also reading non-sequentially, meaning there was enough jumping around to begin with that disk I/O was already a limiting factor.

Most of the partitions on my primary workstation are around 1.5% or 1.6% fragmented; I do have one 128GB filesystem on a logical volume (LV) that is 3.3% fragmented. That is with less than 100 very large ISO image files, and I have had to expand the LV several times over the years as it got too full. This resulted in more fragmentation than had I been able to allocate a larger amount of space to the LV in the beginning.

Some application environments require greater assurance of even less fragmentation. The EXT filesystem can be tuned with care by a knowledgeable admin who can adjust the parameters to compensate for specific workload types. This can be done when the filesystem is created or later using the **tune2fs** command. The results of each tuning change should be tested, meticulously recorded, and analyzed to ensure optimum performance for the target environment. In the worst case where performance cannot be improved to desired levels, other filesystem types are available that may be more suitable for a particular workload. And remember that it is common to mix filesystem types on a single host system to match the load placed on each filesystem.

Due to the low amount of fragmentation on most EXT filesystems, it is not necessary to defragment. In any event there is no safe defragmentation tool for EXT filesystems. There are a few tools that allow you to check the fragmentation of an individual file or the fragmentation of the remaining free space in a filesystem. There is one tool, e4defrag, which will defragment a single file, directory, or filesystem as much as the remaining free space will allow. As its name implies, it only works on files in an EXT4 filesystem, and it does have some limitations.

EXPERIMENT 19-3: CHECKING FRAGMENTATION

Perform this experiment as root. Run the following command to check the fragmentation status of the filesystem. I used the /var filesystem because it has the most fragmentation on my VM:

```
[root@studentvm1 ~]# e4defrag -c /dev/mapper/fedora_studentvm1-var
e4defrag 1.46.5 (30-Dec-2021)
<Fragmented files>                               now/best       size/ext
1. /var/log/cron-20230129                          16/1            4 KB
2. /var/log/wtmp                                    26/1            4 KB
3. /var/log/secure-20230122                         13/1            4 KB
4. /var/log/cron-20230205                           10/1            4 KB
5. /var/log/secure-20230129                          7/1            4 KB

 Total/best extents                                4781/2863
 Average size per extent                           137 KB
 Fragmentation score                               9
 [0-30 no problem: 31-55 a little bit fragmented: 56- needs defrag]
 This device (/dev/mapper/fedora_studentvm1-var) does not need
defragmentation.
 Done.
```

This output shows a list of fragmented files, a score, and information about how to interpret that score. It also contains a recommendation about whether to defrag or not. The recommendation here is that defragmentation is not needed.

But let's defrag one of these files just to see what that would look like. Choose a file with the most fragmentation for your test:

```
[root@studentvm1 ~]# e4defrag -v /var/log/wtmp
e4defrag 1.46.5 (30-Dec-2021)
ext4 defragmentation for /var/log/wtmp
[1/1]/var/log/wtmp:     100% extents: 26 -> 1  [ OK ]
 Success:               [1/1]
```

This only took a couple seconds on my VM.

Read the man page for e4defrag for more information on its limitations.

There are no safe tools for defragmenting EXT1, EXT2, and EXT3 filesystems. And, according to its own man page, the **e4defrag** utility is not guaranteed to perform complete defragmentation. It may be able to "reduce" file fragmentation. Based on the inconsistency in its report shown in Experiment 19-3, I am disinclined to use it and, in any event, there is seldom any necessity to do so.

If it does become necessary to perform a complete defragmentation on an EXT filesystem, there is only one method that will work reliably. You must move all of the files from the filesystem to be defragmented, ensuring that they are deleted after being safely copied to another location. If possible, you could then increase the size of the filesystem to help reduce future fragmentation. Then copy the files back onto the target filesystem. Even this does not guarantee that all of the files will be completely defragmented.

Repairing Problems

We can repair problems that cause the host not to boot, such as a misconfigured /etc/fstab file, but in order to do so, the filesystem on which the configuration file being repaired resides must be mounted. That presents a problem if the filesystem in question cannot be mounted during Linux startup. This means that the host must be booted into recovery mode to perform the repairs.

The /etc/fstab File

How does Linux know where to mount the filesystems on the directory tree? The /etc/fstab file defines the filesystems and the mount points on which they are to be mounted. Since I have already mentioned the /etc/fstab as a potential problem, let's look at it to see what it does. Then we will break it in order to see how to fix it.

Figure 19-7 shows the /etc/fstab from our VM, StudentVM1. Your fstab should look almost identical to this one with the exception of the value of the UUID for the boot partition. The function of fstab is to specify the filesystems that should be mounted during startup and the mount points on which they are to be mounted, along with any options that might be necessary. Each filesystem has at least one attribute that we can use to refer to in /etc/fstab in order to identify it to the startup process.

Each of the filesystem line entries in this simple fstab contains six columns of data.

```
#
# /etc/fstab
# Created by anaconda on Tue Jan 17 07:34:13 2023
#
# Accessible filesystems, by reference, are maintained under '/dev/disk/'.
# See man pages fstab(5), findfs(8), mount(8) and/or blkid(8) for more info.
#
# After editing this file, run 'systemctl daemon-reload' to update systemd
# units generated from this file.
#
/dev/mapper/fedora_studentvm1-root /                       ext4      defaults          1 1
UUID=ea7b0db9-9d11-4214-8b9c-73eaedfa7f43 /boot            ext4      defaults          1 2
UUID=4B7A-D235              /boot/efi        vfat   umask=0077,shortname=winnt 0 2
/dev/mapper/fedora_studentvm1-home /home                   ext4      defaults          1 2
/dev/mapper/fedora_studentvm1-tmp /tmp                     ext4      defaults          1 2
/dev/mapper/fedora_studentvm1-usr /usr                     ext4      defaults          1 2
/dev/mapper/fedora_studentvm1-var /var                     ext4      defaults          1 2
/dev/mapper/fedora_studentvm1-test /test                   ext4      defaults          1 2
```

Figure 19-7. *The filesystem table (fstab) for StudentVM1*

The first column is an identifier that identifies the filesystem so that the startup process knows which filesystem to work with in this line. There are multiple ways to identify the filesystem, two of which are shown here. The /boot partition in Figure 19-7 is identified using the UUID, or Universal Unique IDentifier. This is an ID that is guaranteed to be unique so that no other partition can have the same one. The UUID is generated when the filesystem is created and is located in the superblock for the partition.

All of the other partitions on our VMs are identified using the path to the device special files in the /dev directory. Another option would be to use the labels we entered when we created the filesystems during the installation process. A typical entry in fstab would look like that in Figure 19-8.

```
LABEL=boot /boot             ext4      defaults           1 2
```

Figure 19-8. *Using a label to identify the system in /etc/fstab*

The filesystem label is also stored in the partition superblock. Let's change the /boot partition entry in the fstab to use the label we have already created to identify it.

```
┌─────────────────────────────────────────────────────────────────────────────┐
│              EXPERIMENT 19-4: FILESYSTEM LABELS                              │
└─────────────────────────────────────────────────────────────────────────────┘
```

Perform this experiment as root. Be sure to verify the device special ID for the boot partition and then dump the content of the superblock for the /boot partition[14]:

```
[root@studentvm1 ~]# lsblk
NAME                          MAJ:MIN RM   SIZE RO TYPE MOUNTPOINTS
sda                             8:0    0    60G  0 disk
├─sda1                          8:1    0     1M  0 part
├─sda2                          8:2    0     1G  0 part /boot
├─sda3                          8:3    0     1G  0 part /boot/efi
└─sda4                          8:4    0    58G  0 part
  ├─fedora_studentvm1-root    253:0    0     2G  0 lvm  /
  ├─fedora_studentvm1-usr     253:1    0    15G  0 lvm  /usr
  ├─fedora_studentvm1-tmp     253:2    0     5G  0 lvm  /tmp
  ├─fedora_studentvm1-var     253:3    0    10G  0 lvm  /var
  ├─fedora_studentvm1-home    253:4    0     2G  0 lvm  /home
  └─fedora_studentvm1-test    253:5    0   500M  0 lvm  /test
sr0                            11:0    1  50.5M  0 rom
zram0                         252:0    0     8G  0 disk [SWAP]
```

Notice that the sda1 partition has no indication of what it is. We can use the following command to see that it is a BIOS boot partition:

```
[root@studentvm1 ~]# fdisk -l /dev/sda
Disk /dev/sda: 60 GiB, 64424509440 bytes, 125829120 sectors
Disk model: VBOX HARDDISK
Units: sectors of 1 * 512 = 512 bytes
Sector size (logical/physical): 512 bytes / 512 bytes
I/O size (minimum/optimal): 512 bytes / 512 bytes
Disklabel type: gpt
Disk identifier: 864009FC-A0DF-460A-918C-E3BF313E8E03

Device       Start      End   Sectors Size Type
/dev/sda1     2048     4095      2048  1M BIOS boot
/dev/sda2     4096  2101247   2097152  1G Linux filesystem
```

---

[14] Wikipedia, *BIOS boot partition*, https://en.wikipedia.org/wiki/BIOS_boot_partition

```
/dev/sda3  2101248    4198399   2097152   1G EFI System
/dev/sda4  4198400 125827071 121628672  58G Linux LVM
```

The /boot partition is /dev/sda2. If there is no BIOS boot partition, the /boot partition will probably be /dev/sda1. Just be sure you identify the correct partition for this part of the experiment:

```
[root@studentvm1 ~]# dumpe2fs /dev/sda2
dumpe2fs 1.46.5 (30-Dec-2021)
Filesystem volume name:    boot
Last mounted on:           /boot
Filesystem UUID:           ea7b0db9-9d11-4214-8b9c-73eaedfa7f43
<snip>
```

The filesystem volume name is the label. We can test this. Change the label and then check the superblock:

```
[root@studentvm1 ~]# e2label /dev/sda2 MyBoot
[root@studentvm1 ~]# dumpe2fs /dev/sda2 | head
dumpe2fs 1.46.5 (30-Dec-2021)
Filesystem volume name:    MyBoot
Last mounted on:           /boot
Filesystem UUID:           ea7b0db9-9d11-4214-8b9c-73eaedfa7f43
<snip>
```

Notice the filesystem UUID in the superblock is identical to that shown in the /etc/fstab file in Figure 19-7. Use the vim editor to comment out the current entry for the /boot partition and create a new entry using the label. The fstab should now look like this. I have modified it to be a bit more tidy by aligning the columns better:

```
<snip>
#
/dev/mapper/fedora_studentvm1-root /                 ext4   defaults        1 1
# UUID=ea7b0db9-9d11-4214-8b9c-73eaedfa7f43 /boot    ext4   defaults        1 2
LABEL=boot                         /boot             ext4   defaults        1 2
UUID=4B7A-D235                     /boot/efi         vfat   umask=0077,shortname=winnt 0 2
/dev/mapper/fedora_studentvm1-home /home            ext4   defaults        1 2
/dev/mapper/fedora_studentvm1-tmp  /tmp             ext4   defaults        1 2
/dev/mapper/fedora_studentvm1-usr  /usr             ext4   defaults        1 2
/dev/mapper/fedora_studentvm1-var  /var             ext4   defaults        1 2
/dev/mapper/fedora_studentvm1-test /test ext4 defaults 1 2
```

Reboot StudentVM1 to ensure that the change works as expected.

Ooops! It did not.

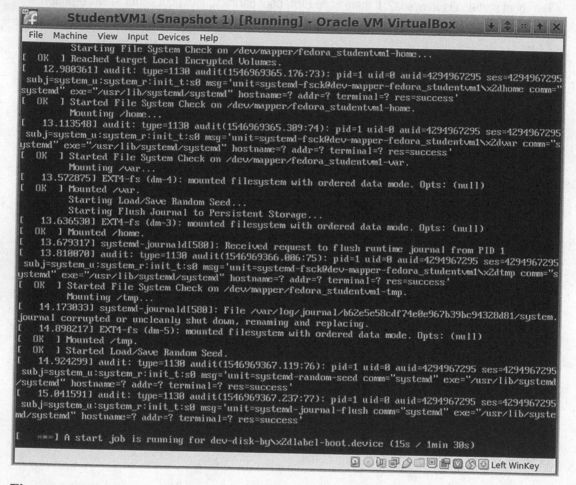

Figure 19-9. *An error occurred during the reboot of StudentVM1 after changing fstab*

If you have followed my instructions carefully, this problem shows up during startup (after boot)[15] with the message shown on the last line in Figure 19-9. This indicates that the boot. device (/dev/sda1) cannot be mounted.

---

[15] See Chapter 16.

Can you think of any reason that might be the case? I can – I intentionally skipped the step of setting the filesystem label from MyBoot back to just boot.

We can wait until the 1-minute and 30-second timeout completes, and then the system, having determined that the filesystem cannot be mounted, will automatically proceed to maintenance mode. Type in your root password and press the **Enter** key to continue.

Verify the current filesystem label, change it to "boot", and then run the mount command:

```
[root@studentvm1 ~]# e2label /dev/sda2
MyBoot
[root@studentvm1 ~]# e2label /dev/sda2 boot
[root@studentvm1 ~]# mount -a
[  188.3880009] EXT4-fs (sda2): mounted filesystem with ordered data mode.
   Quota mode: none.
```

Now bring the system up to the graphical target (similar to runlevel 5):

```
[root@studentvm1 ~]# systemctl isolate graphical.target
```

Note that it was not necessary to reboot to make the repair or to raise the system from the recovery target to the graphical target.

Let's get back to deconstructing the fstab file. The second column in the /etc/fstab file in Figure 19-7 is the mountpoint on which the filesystem identified by the data in column 1 is mounted. These mountpoints are empty directories to which the filesystem is mounted.

The third column specifies the filesystem type, in this case EXT4 for most of the entries. The one different entry in Figure 19-7 is for the swap partition. Figure 19-10 shows an entry for a VFAT device, which is usually how USB memory sticks are formatted. The mountpoint for this device is located at /media/SS-R100.

```
LABEL=SS-R100    /media/SS-R100    vfat    user,noauto,defaults    0 0
```

Figure 19-10. *An fstab entry for a USB memory stick showing some alternate configuration possibilities*

The fourth column of data in the fstab file is a list of options. The mount command has many options, and each option has a default setting. In Figure 19-7 the fourth column of fstab indicates that the filesystem is to be mounted using all defaults.

In Figure 19-10, some of the defaults are overridden. The "user" option means that any user can mount or unmount the filesystem even if another user has already mounted it. The "noauto" option means that this filesystem is not automatically mounted during the Linux startup. It can be manually mounted and unmounted after startup. This is ideal for a removable device like a USB memory stick that may be used for sharing files or transporting them to work on at another location.

The last two columns are of numbers. In Figure 19-7, the entries for /home are 1 and 2, respectively. The first number is used by the dump command, which is one possible option for making backups. The dump command is seldom used for backups any more, so this column is usually ignored. If by some chance someone is still using dump to make backups, a one (1) in this column means to back up this entire filesystem, and a zero means to skip this filesystem.

The last column is also numeric. It specifies the sequence in which fsck is run against filesystems during startup. Zero (0) means do not run fsck on the filesystem. One (1) means to run fsck on this filesystem first. The root partition is always checked first as you can see from the numbers in this column in Figure 19-7.

The rest of the entries in this column have a value of 2, which means that fsck will not begin running against those filesystems until it has finished with checking the root filesystem. Than all of the filesystems that have a value of 2 can be checked in parallel rather than sequentially so that the overall check can be finished sooner.

Although it is generally considered best practice to mount filesystems on mountpoints directly on the / (root) filesystem, it is also possible to use multi-level mountpoints. Figure 19-11 shows what multi-level mounts look like. For example, the /usr filesystem is mounted on the /usr directory. In Figure 19-2 the /usr/local directory is listed. It contains locally created executables, especially scripts in /usr/local/bin and configuration files in /usr/local/etc, as well as libraries, man pages, and more. I have encountered installations where a filesystem, "local", was mounted on /usr. This gives additional flexibility during Linux upgrades because the /usr/local filesystem does not need to be formatted during an upgrade or reinstallation like the rest of the /usr filesystem.

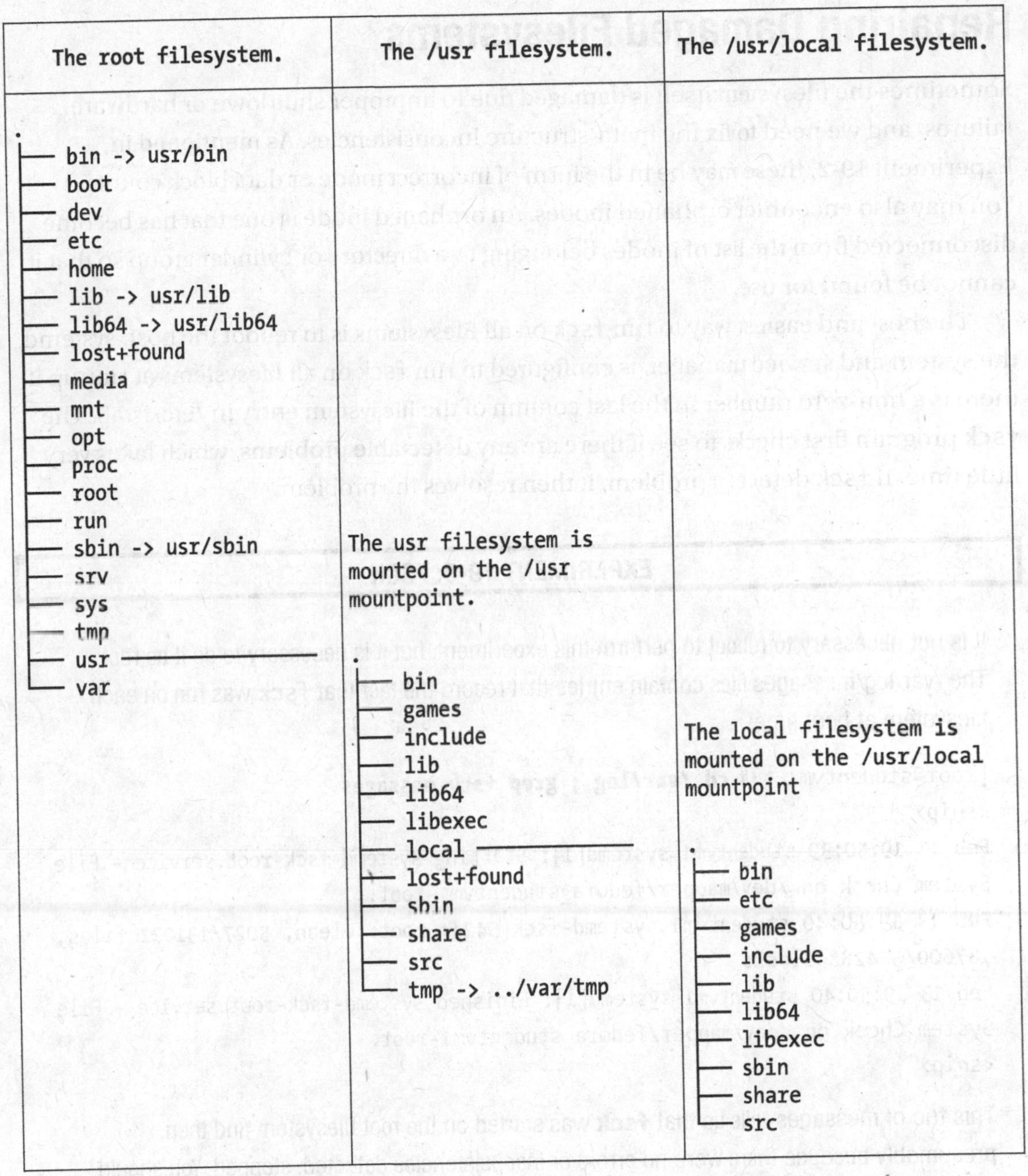

The root filesystem.	The /usr filesystem.	The /usr/local filesystem.
— bin -> usr/bin — boot — dev — etc — home — lib -> usr/lib — lib64 -> usr/lib64 — lost+found — media — mnt — opt — proc — root — run — sbin -> usr/sbin — srv — sys — tmp — usr ──────── — var	The usr filesystem is mounted on the /usr mountpoint. — bin — games — include — lib — lib64 — libexec — local ──────── — lost+found — sbin — share — src — tmp -> ../var/tmp	The local filesystem is mounted on the /usr/local mountpoint — bin — etc — games — include — lib — lib64 — libexec — sbin — share — src

Figure 19-11. *It is possible to do multi-level mounts although this is not considered a good practice. Note that this illustration shows only the top-level directories of each filesystem*

Repairing Damaged Filesystems

Sometimes the filesystem itself is damaged due to improper shutdown or hardware failures, and we need to fix the meta-structure inconsistencies. As mentioned in Experiment 19-2, these may be in the form of incorrect inode or data block counts. You may also encounter orphaned inodes. An orphaned inode is one that has become disconnected from the list of inodes belonging to a directory or cylinder group so that it cannot be found for use.

The best and easiest way to run fsck on all filesystems is to reboot the host. systemd, the system and service manager, is configured to run fsck on all filesystems at startup if there is a non-zero number in the last column of the filesystem entry in /etc/fstab. The fsck program first checks to see if there are any detectable problems, which takes very little time. If fsck detects a problem, it then resolves the problem.

EXPERIMENT 19-5: FSCK

It is not necessary to reboot to perform this experiment, but it is necessary to do it as root. The /var/log/messages files contain entries that record the fact that fsck was run on each filesystem at boot time:

```
[root@studentvm1 ~]# cd /var/log ; grep fsck messages
<snip>
Feb 13 19:50:39 studentvm1 systemd[1]: Starting systemd-fsck-root.service - File
System Check on /dev/mapper/fedora_studentvm1-root...
Feb 13 19:50:40 studentvm1 systemd-fsck[542]: root: clean, 5027/131072 files,
187600/524288 blocks
Feb 13 19:50:40 studentvm1 systemd[1]: Finished systemd-fsck-root.service - File
System Check on /dev/mapper/fedora_studentvm1-root.
<snip>
```

This trio of messages tells us that **fsck** was started on the root filesystem and then, presumably because there were no errors or inconsistencies detected, stopped. You should see messages like these for every filesystem at each boot.

Due to the fact that fsck is run at each startup, there should seldom be reason to run it from the command line. Despite this, we SysAdmins sometimes find the need to do things that "should never be necessary." So there is a way to enter rescue mode and run fsck on most filesystems manually.

Using a Fedora Live USB Device for System Recovery

We cannot access maintenance mode when booting the system if the root filesystem won't mount so we need to find another way to enter maintenance mode, run fsck, or perform another maintenance on the root filesystem. I have managed to bork the fstab file so that the host won't boot.

Recovery Mode Using a Live USB Image

The only way to resolve this problem is to find a way to get into a usable recovery mode. When all else fails, Fedora provides a really cool tool, the same live USB thumb drive that I use to install new instances of Fedora.

Because fsck can't be run on a mounted root filesystem, we need to boot the system without mounting root. The only way to do this is using a live USB device.

EXPERIMENT 19-6: USING A LIVE USB DEVICE FOR RECOVERY

Even if your filesystem is not borked, you should perform this experiment because you will surely need to do this at least several times in your career.

The objective of this experiment is to run fsck on the root partition. We will also do a couple other fun things while we are here.

Power off the VM and verify that it is set to boot first from the "Optical" device. It should have been set that way during creation of the VM. "Mount" the Fedora live USB ISO image on IDE Secondary Device 0 in the Storage configuration page. Boot into the Fedora Xfce live user desktop just as you did to install Fedora.

Open a terminal session and switch to root privilege.

Run lsblk in for reference. I used the results to identify the / root, boot, and efi partitions. In this case there is no efi partition because I did not use UEFI on this VM. The loop[16] devices are used to enable Linux to mount a partition or volume to a virtual mount point in RAM rather than a physical mount point on a physical device:

```
[root@localhost-live ~]# lsblk
NAME                        MAJ:MIN RM  SIZE RO TYPE MOUNTPOINTS
loop0                           7:0  O  1.5G  1 loop
loop1                           7:1  O   6G   1 loop
|-live-rw                     253:0  O   6G   0 dm   /
`-live-base                   253:1  O   6G   1 dm
loop2                           7:2  O  32G   0 loop
`-live-rw                     253:0  O   6G   0 dm   /
sda                             8:0  O  60G   0 disk
|-sda1                          8:1  O   1M   0 part
|-sda2                          8:2  O   1G   0 part
|-sda3                          8:3  O   1G   0 part
`-sda4                          8:4  O  58G   0 part
  |-fedora_studentvm1-tmp     253:2  O   5G   0 lvm
  |-fedora_studentvm1-var     253:3  O  10G   0 lvm
  |-fedora_studentvm1-home    253:4  O   2G   0 lvm
  |-fedora_studentvm1-usr     253:5  O  15G   0 lvm
  |-fedora_studentvm1-root    253:6  O   2G   0 lvm
  `-fedora_studentvm1-test    253:7  O 500M   0 lvm
sr0                            11:0  1  1.6G  0 rom  /run/initramfs/live
zram0                         252:0  O   8G   0 disk [SWAP]
[root@localhost-live ~]#
```

It is not necessary to mount the root partition in order to run the filesystem check (fsck) on it. In fact we are in this situation because filesystems must be unmounted when fsck is run. This protects the filesystem against changes while fsck is performing its recovery operations. That would be bad.

---

[16] See the loop man page.

Run the filesystem check. The -a option tells fsck to automatically fix any problems it encounters. Otherwise, you would need to press the "y" key to repair every problem, and there can be hundreds and even thousands of them on a badly borked filesystem. I know this from experience:

```
[root@localhost-live ~]# fsck -a /dev/mapper/fedora_studentvm1-root
fsck from util-linux 2.38.1
e2fsck 1.46.5 (30-Dec-2021)
root: clean, 5027/131072 files, 187600/524288 blocks
```

That only took a few seconds for my VM, but there were no anomalies that needed repaired.

We have also seen that configuration files can get damaged, and we can use the live USB drive to help us resolve those problems as well. Mount the root partition on the /mnt mount point where we can work on it:

```
root@localhost-live ~]# mount /dev/mapper/fedora_studentvm1-root /mnt
```

Make /mnt/etc the PWD. Remember the VM's root directory is mounted on /mnt. Now use vim to edit fstab:

```
[root@localhost-live etc]# vim fstab
```

It is not necessary to make any changes to this file. But you can now see that it is possible to use the live USB device to perform many types of recovery tasks.

To complete this experiment, exit from vim (Esc-: and then q and press Enter) and power off the VM. Remove the ISO USB image from the "Optical Drive" on the VM's IDE controller.

You can learn more about using the live USB device from an article I wrote for Opensource.com, "How I recovered my Linux system using a Live USB device."[17] That article is about a much more complex recovery than we have explored here.

Finding Lost Files

Files can get lost by the filesystem and by the user. This can also happen during fsck regardless of when or how it is initiated.

---

[17] Both, David, Opensource.com, *How I recovered my Linux system using a Live USB device*, https://opensource.com/article/22/9/recover-linux-system-live-usb

One reason this happens is that the directory entry for the file that points to the file inode is damaged and no longer points to the inode for the file. You would probably see messages about orphaned inodes during startup when this occurs.

These files are not really lost. The `fsck` utility has found the inode, but there is no corresponding directory entry for that file. The `fsck` utility does not know the name of the file or in what directory it was listed. It can recover the file; all it needs to do is make up a name and add the name to a directory along with a pointer to the inode.

But where does it place the directory entry? Look in the lost+found directory of each filesystem to locate recovered files that belong to that filesystem. These lost files are moved to the lost+found directory simply by creating a directory entry for them in lost+found. The file names are seemingly random and give no indication of the types of files they are. You will have to use other tools such as `file`, `stat`, `cat`, and `string` to make some sort of determination so that you can rename the file with a meaningful name and extension and move it to an appropriate directory.

Creating a New Filesystem

I have had many occasions when it has become necessary to create a new filesystem. This can be simply because I need a completely new filesystem for some specific purpose, or it can be due to the need to replace an existing filesystem that is too small or damaged.

This exercise takes you through the process of creating a new partition on an existing hard drive, creating a filesystem and a mountpoint, and mounting the new filesystem. This is a common task, and you should become familiar with how to perform it. In many cases you will do this by adding a new hard drive with plenty of space. In this exercise we will use some space on the virtual hard drive that is left free for exactly this purpose. This exercise is about raw partitions and filesystems and not about using logical volume management. We will cover LVM and adding space to logical volumes in Chapter 20 of Volume 2.

Finding Space

Before we can add a raw partition to our host, we need to identify some available storage space. We currently have a single virtual hard drive available on our VM, /dev/sda. Let's see if there is some space available for a new partition on this device.

EXPERIMENT 19-7: FINDING AVAILABLE STORAGE SPACE

Perform this experiment as root on StudentVM1. If your VM is not running, start it now and log in.

Use the **fdisk** command to determine whether any free space exists on /dev/sda:

```
[root@studentvm1 ~]# fdisk -l /dev/sda
Disk /dev/sda: 60 GiB, 64424509440 bytes, 125829120 sectors
Disk model: VBOX HARDDISK
Units: sectors of 1 * 512 = 512 bytes
Sector size (logical/physical): 512 bytes / 512 bytes
I/O size (minimum/optimal): 512 bytes / 512 bytes
Disklabel type: gpt
Disk identifier: 864009FC-A0DF-460A-918C-E3BF313E8E03

Device       Start       End    Sectors Size Type
/dev/sda1     2048      4095       2048  1M BIOS boot
/dev/sda2     4096   2101247    2097152  1G Linux filesystem
/dev/sda3  2101248   4198399    2097152  1G EFI System
/dev/sda4  4198400 125827071 121628672 58G Linux LVM
[root@studentvm1 ~]#
```

We can do a quick calculation using the number of sectors shown in the preceding data. The first line of output shows the total number of sectors on the device is 125,829,120 and the ending sector of /dev/sda4 is 125827071, which is a difference of 2049 sectors – not nearly enough to create a new partition.

We need another option if we want to add a new partition.

Notice the partition types in the Type column shown in Experiment 19-7. The **fdisk** program does not provide any direct information on the total size of each partition in bytes, but that can be calculated from the available information.

Add a New Virtual Hard Drive

Because the existing virtual hard drive has no room for a new partition, we need to create a new virtual hard drive. This is easy to do with VirtualBox because we added some additional ports to the SATA controller during creation of the VM.

EXPERIMENT 19-8: ADD A NEW VIRTUAL HARD DRIVE

On the physical host desktop, open the VirtualBox Manager if it is not already. Check to see if there is a SATA port available so we can add a new virtual disk drive while the VM is running. We did set the number of SATA ports to 5 in Chapter 4, but verify this anyway.

We can add the new virtual disk device while the VM is up and running. This procedure is equivalent to installing a new hot-plug hard drive in a physical hardware system while it is running. Power on the VM and log into the GUI desktop as the student user.

Open the Storage Settings menu and click the **Adds hard disk** icon as shown in Figure 19-12 to create a new disk device on the SATA controller.

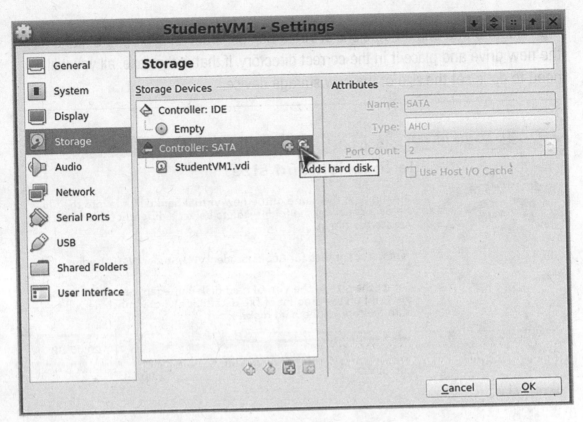

Figure 19-12. *Click the **Adds hard disk** icon to add a new drive to the SATA controller*

Click the **OK** button and then the **Create new disk** button. The next dialog is a choice of hard disk file type. Use the default of VDI, which is a VirtualBox Disk Image. Click the **Next** button. We want this disk to be dynamically allocated per the default, so do not make any changes on this dialog and click **Next** to continue.

Use the dialog in Figure 19-13 to set the virtual disk name to **StudentVM1-1** and the disk size to **20GB**. Click the **Finish** button to create the new virtual hard drive. The new drive now appears in the **Hard Disk Selector** dialog box and is highlighted. Click the **Choose** button to complete the addition of a new virtual drive.

Tip   I found that current versions of VirtualBox generate an appropriate name for the new drive and place it in the correct directory. If that is the case, all you will need to do is set the size of the new storage device.

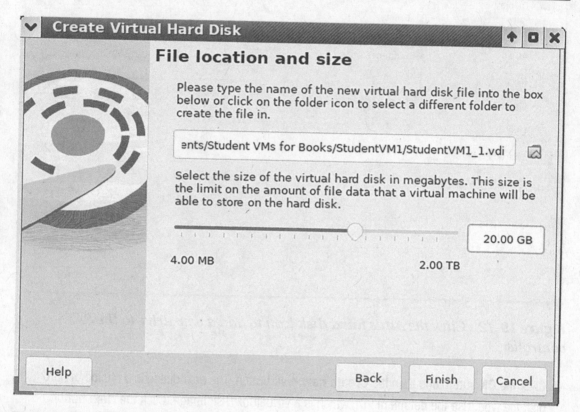

Figure 19-13. *Enter the name of the virtual disk as StudentVM1-1 and set the size to 20GB*

The final result is shown in Figure 19-14, where you can see the new drive.

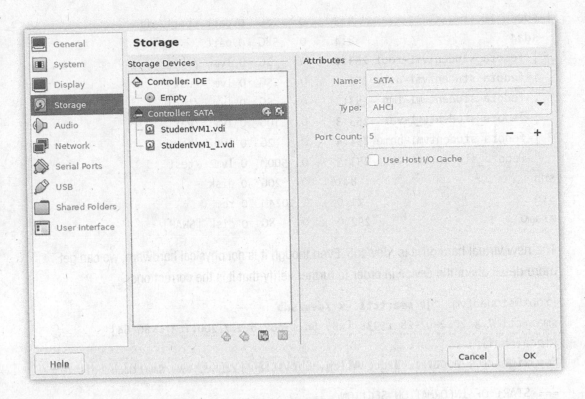

Figure 19-14. *The new storage drive on the SATA controller*

We have now added a second virtual hard drive to the StudentVM1 virtual host.

Now that the new storage drive has been created, we can partition and format the device.

EXPERIMENT 19-9: PREPARING THE NEW STORAGE DRIVE

Open a terminal session and su – to root. Display the list of current storage devices and partitions:

```
[root@studentvm1 ~]# lsblk -i
NAME                    MAJ:MIN RM  SIZE RO TYPE MOUNTPOINTS
sda                     8:0      0   60G  0 disk
|-sda1                  8:1      0    1M  0 part
|-sda2                  8:2      0    1G  0 part /boot
```

```
|-sda3                          8:3    0     1G   0 part  /boot/efi
`-sda4                          8:4    0    58G   0 part
  |-fedora_studentvm1-root 253:0    0     2G   0 lvm   /
  |-fedora_studentvm1-usr  253:1    0    15G   0 lvm   /usr
  |-fedora_studentvm1-tmp  253:2    0     5G   0 lvm   /tmp
  |-fedora_studentvm1-var  253:3    0    10G   0 lvm   /var
  |-fedora_studentvm1-home 253:4    0     2G   0 lvm   /home
  `-fedora_studentvm1-test 253:5    0   500M   0 lvm   /test
sdb                            8:16   0    20G   0 disk
sr0                           11:0    1  1024M   0 rom
zram0                        252:0    0     8G   0 disk [SWAP]
```

The new virtual hard drive is /dev/sdb. Even though it is not physical hardware, we can get more detail about the device in order to further verify that it is the correct one:

```
[root@studentvm1 ~]# smartctl -x /dev/sdb
smartctl 7.3 2022-02-28 r5338 [x86_64-linux-6.1.7-200.fc37.x86_64]
(local build)
Copyright (C) 2002-22, Bruce Allen, Christian Franke, www.smartmontools.org

=== START OF INFORMATION SECTION ===
Device Model:     VBOX HARDDISK
Serial Number:    VB9d500d54-408ea7d6
Firmware Version: 1.0
User Capacity:    21,474,836,480 bytes [21.4 GB]
Sector Size:      512 bytes logical/physical
Device is:        Not in smartctl database 7.3/5319
ATA Version is:   ATA/ATAPI-6 published, ANSI INCITS 361-2002
Local Time is:    Wed Feb 15 12:17:41 2023 EST
SMART support is: Unavailable - device lacks SMART capability.
<SNIP>
```

We have determined that we have a 20GB (virtual) hard drive, /dev/sdb. The next step is to create a partition, format it, and add a partition label.

We use the fdisk utility to create a new partition:

```
[root@studentvm1 ~]# fdisk /dev/sdb
Welcome to fdisk (util-linux 2.32.1).
Changes will remain in memory only, until you decide to write them.
Be careful before using the write command.
```

Device does not contain a recognized partition table.
Created a new DOS disklabel with disk identifier 0xd1acbaf8.

Command (m for help):

Because this device was just created, it has no partition table. Let's create a single new partition of 2GB in size. We do not need a lot of space for this experiment, so the partition can be small. Press the **N** key to begin creation of a new partition:

Command (m for help): **n**
Partition type
    p   primary (0 primary, 0 extended, 4 free)
    e   extended (container for logical partitions)

Enter p to create a primary partition:

Select (default p): **p**

Just press Enter to create this as partition number 1:

Partition number (1-4, default 1): **<Press Enter for the default partition number (1)>**
First sector (2048-41943039, default 2048): **<Press Enter for the default first sector>**
Last sector, +sectors or +size{K,M,G,T,P} (2048-41943039, default 41943039) **+2G**

Created a new partition 1 of type 'Linux' and of size 2 GiB.

Now enter p to print the current partition table:

Command (m for help): **p**
Disk /dev/sdb: 20 GiB, 21474836480 bytes, 41943040 sectors
Disk model: VBOX HARDDISK
Units: sectors of 1 * 512 = 512 bytes
Sector size (logical/physical): 512 bytes / 512 bytes
I/O size (minimum/optimal): 512 bytes / 512 bytes
Disklabel type: dos
Disk identifier: 0xc43a2838

Device	Boot	Start	End	Sectors	Size	Id	Type
/dev/sdb1		2048	4196351	4194304	2G	83	Linux

Press W to write the revised partition table to the disk. The existing partition table, if any, is not altered until the data is written to the disk:

```
Command (m for help): w
The partition table has been altered.
Calling ioctl() to re-read partition table.
Syncing disks.

[root@studentvm1 ~]#
```

Create an EXT4 filesystem on the new partition. This won't take more than a few seconds because of the small size of the partition. By default the EXT4 filesystem fills the partition. It is possible to specify a size smaller than the partition for the size of the filesystem, but that wastes the unused space:

```
[root@studentvm1 ~]# mkfs -t ext4 /dev/sdb1
mke2fs 1.44.3 (10-July-2018)
Creating filesystem with 524288 4k blocks and 131072 inodes
Filesystem UUID: ee831607-5d5c-4d54-b9ba-959720bfdabd
Superblock backups stored on blocks:
        32768, 98304, 163840, 229376, 294912

Allocating group tables: done
Writing inode tables: done
Creating journal (16384 blocks): done
Writing superblocks and filesystem accounting information: done
[root@studentvm1 ~]#
```

Let's add a partition label. This first command verifies that there is no label – thus the blank line:

```
[root@studentvm1 ~]# e2label /dev/sdb1
```

Now we create the label and verify that it has been added:

```
[root@studentvm1 ~]# e2label /dev/sdb1 TestFS
[root@studentvm1 ~]# e2label /dev/sdb1
TestFS
[root@studentvm1 ~]#
```

Create a mountpoint on the filesystem directory tree:

```
[root@studentvm1 ~]# mkdir /TestFS
[root@studentvm1 ~]# ll /
```

Mount the new filesystem:

```
[root@studentvm1 ~]# mount /TestFS/
mount: /TestFS/: can't find in /etc/fstab.
[root@studentvm1 ~]#
```

This error occurred because we did not create an entry for the new filesystem in /etc/fstab.
But let's mount it manually first:

```
[root@studentvm1 ~]# mount -t ext4 /dev/sdb1 /TestFS/
[root@studentvm1 ~]# lsblk -i
NAME                      MAJ:MIN RM  SIZE RO TYPE MOUNTPOINT
sda                           8:0  0   60G  0 disk
|-sda1                        8:1  0    1G  0 part /boot
`-sda2                        8:2  0   59G  0 part
  |-fedora_studentvm1-root 253:0  0    2G  0 lvm  /
  |-fedora_studentvm1-swap 253:1  0    4G  0 lvm  [SWAP]
  |-fedora_studentvm1-usr  253:2  0   15G  0 lvm  /usr
  |-fedora_studentvm1-home 253:3  0    2G  0 lvm  /home
  |-fedora_studentvm1-var  253:4  0   10G  0 lvm  /var
  `-fedora_studentvm1-tmp  253:5  0    5G  0 lvm  /tmp
sdb                          8:16  0   20G  0 disk
`-sdb1                       8:17  0    2G  0 part /TestFS
sr0                         11:0   1 1024M  0 rom
[root@studentvm1 ~]#
```

It is not always necessary to specify the filesystem type as we did here because the mount command is capable of determining the common filesystem types. You may need to do this if the filesystem is one of the more obscure types, but it can't hurt anyway.

Unmount the filesystem:

```
[root@studentvm1 ~]# umount /TestFS
```

Now add the following entry for our new filesystem to the bottom of the /etc/fstab file:

```
/dev/sdb1          /TestFS              ext4    defaults      1 2
```

Now mount the new filesystem:

```
[root@studentvm1 ~]# mount /TestFS
mount: (hint) your fstab has been modified, but systemd still uses
       the old version; use 'systemctl daemon-reload' to reload.

[root@studentvm1 ~]# ll /TestFS/
total 16
drwx------. 2 root root 16384 Jan 14 08:54 lost+found
[root@studentvm1 ~]# lsblk -i
NAME                        MAJ:MIN RM   SIZE RO TYPE MOUNTPOINTS
sda                             8:0   0   60G  0 disk
|-sda1                          8:1   0    1M  0 part
|-sda2                          8:2   0    1G  0 part /boot
|-sda3                          8:3   0    1G  0 part /boot/efi
`-sda4                          8:4   0   58G  0 part
  |-fedora_studentvm1-root  253:0   0    2G  0 lvm  /
  |-fedora_studentvm1-usr   253:1   0   15G  0 lvm  /usr
  |-fedora_studentvm1-tmp   253:2   0    5G  0 lvm  /tmp
  |-fedora_studentvm1-var   253:3   0   10G  0 lvm  /var
  |-fedora_studentvm1-home  253:4   0    2G  0 lvm  /home
  `-fedora_studentvm1-test  253:5   0  500M  0 lvm  /test
sdb                            8:16   0   20G  0 disk
`-sdb1                         8:17   0    2G  0 part /TestFS
sr0                            11:0   1 1024M  0 rom
zram0                         252:0   0    8G  0 disk [SWAP]
```

All of the pertinent data about the filesystem is recorded in fstab, and options specific to this filesystem can be specified as well. For example, we may not want this filesystem to mount automatically at startup, so we would set that option as noauto,defaults.

Unmount the TestFS filesystem:

```
[root@studentvm1 ~]# umount /TestFS
```

Change the line for this new filesystem in /etc/fstab so it looks like the following:

```
/dev/sdb1        /TestFS          ext4    noauto,defaults        1 2
```

Mount the filesystem manually to verify that it works as expected. Now reboot the VM and verify that the /TestFS filesystem does not mount automatically. It should not.

Other Filesystems

There are many filesystems besides EXT4 and its predecessors. Each of these has its own advantages and drawbacks. I have tried several, like XFS, ReiserFS, and BTRFS, but I have found that the EXT filesystems have always been perfect for my needs.

Our student virtual machines will not provide a real test to help determine which filesystem might be better for our needs, but let's create a filesystem with BTRFS just to experiment with.

EXPERIMENT 19-10

Perform this experiment as root. We still have space on the /dev/sdb virtual drive, so add another partition, /dev/sdb2, with a size of 2GB on that drive. Then format the new partition as BTRFS:

```
[root@studentvm1 ~]# fdisk /dev/sdb

Welcome to fdisk (util-linux 2.32.1).
Changes will remain in memory only, until you decide to write them.
Be careful before using the write command.

Command (m for help): n
Partition type
   p   primary (1 primary, 0 extended, 3 free)
   e   extended (container for logical partitions)
Select (default p): <Press Enter for default partition as Primary>
Partition number (2-4, default 2): <Press Enter for default partition
number 2>
First sector (4196352-41943039, default 4196352): <Press Enter for default
first sector>
```

Last sector, +sectors or +size{K,M,G,T,P} (4196352-41943039, default
41943039): **+2G**

Created a new partition 2 of type 'Linux' and of size 2 GiB.

Command (m for help): **p**
Disk /dev/sdb: 20 GiB, 21474836480 bytes, 41943040 sectors
Disk model: VBOX HARDDISK
Units: sectors of 1 * 512 = 512 bytes
Sector size (logical/physical): 512 bytes / 512 bytes
I/O size (minimum/optimal): 512 bytes / 512 bytes
Disklabel type: dos
Disk identifier: 0xc43a2838

Device	Boot	Start	End	Sectors	Size	Id	Type
/dev/sdb1		2048	4196351	4194304	2G	83	Linux
/dev/sdb2		4196352	8390655	4194304	2G	83	Linux

Command (m for help): **w**
The partition table has been altered.
Syncing disks.

[root@studentvm1 ~]# **mkfs -t btrfs /dev/sdb2**
btrfs-progs v4.17.1
See http://btrfs.wiki.kernel.org for more information.

Label:	(null)
UUID:	54c2d286-caa9-4a44-9c12-97600122f0cc
Node size:	16384
Sector size:	4096
Filesystem size:	2.00GiB
Block group profiles:	
Data:	single 8.00MiB
Metadata:	DUP 102.38MiB
System:	DUP 8.00MiB
SSD detected:	no
Incompat features:	extref, skinny-metadata
Number of devices:	1

```
Devices:
  ID      SIZE  PATH
   1    2.00GiB  /dev/sdb2

[root@studentvm1 ~]#
```

Mount the new BTRFS filesystem on the temporary mount point, /mnt. Create or copy some files to /mnt and experiment with it. After you have experimented with this filesystem for a bit, unmount it. We will explore the BTRFS filesystem more in Chapter 34 of Volume 2.

From a functional standpoint, the BTRFS filesystem works the same way as the EXT4 filesystem. They both store data in files using the same inode and allocation structures and strategies, they use directories for file organization, they provide security using the same file attributes, and they use the same file management tools.

Chapter Summary

In this chapter we have looked at the three meanings of the term "filesystem" and explored each in detail. A filesystem can be a system and metadata structure such as EXT4 or BTRFS used to store data on a partition or logical volume of some storage medium, a well-defined, logical structure of directories that establishes an organizational methodology for data storage as set forth in the Linux Filesystem Hierarchical Standard (LFHS), and a unit of data storage as created on a partition or logical volume that may be mounted on a specific, defined directory as part of the LFHS.

These three uses of the term "filesystem" have overlapping meanings, which contributes to potential confusion. This chapter separates and defines the various uses of the term and the application of the term to specific functions and data structures.

Exercises

Perform these exercises to complete this chapter:

1. What information about a file is contained in the inode?

2. What information about a file is contained only in the directory entry?

3. What is the block size in the partitions on StudentVM1?

4. Calculate the size of a cylinder group on all partitions of StudentVM1. Are they all the same?

5. How would you discover filesystem inconsistencies such as orphaned inodes or incorrect counts of free inode and data blocks?

6. Describe the complete process required to resolve filesystem inconsistencies.

7. Where should well-designed application software be installed in the Linux filesystem?

8. When installing locally created scripts, in which directory should the script itself be installed?

9. When installing locally created scripts, in which directory should the configuration files, if any, be installed?

10. We still should have some free space on the second virtual hard drive, /dev/sdb, that we added to the StudentVM1 host. Use 1GB of that to create a new partition with an XFS filesystem on it. Create a mountpoint, /var/mystuff, and configure it to mount automatically on boot. Ensure that it mounts manually and then reboot to verify that it mounts on boot.

11. What happens if we unmount the /TestFS filesystem and create a file in the /TestFS directory, which is a mountpoint for that filesystem? Can the file be created and some content be added and then viewed?

12. What happens to the test file created in the previous exercise when the /TestFS filesystem is mounted?

13. How does the "user" option differ from the "users" option for the **mount** command?

Index

A

Address
 IP, 121, 204, 304, 309
 MAC, 121, 455
Agetty, 508
Alias
 command, 110, 210, 308, 309, 434, 439,
  458, 484, 520, 529–531
 host, 308–310, 531
 user, 309, 310
anaconda system installer
 anaconda, 148, 150, 159,
  251, 467
Apache web server
 Apache, 579
 configuration, 579
ASCII
 plain text, 279, 556
 text, 280, 377, 383, 457, 470, 472, 514,
  555, 556, 579
Authentication, 538

B

Backup
 recovery testing, 70
Bash
 configuration files
  ~/.bash_history, 202
  ~/.bash_logout, 202, 515
  ~/.bash_profile, 202, 515, 517, 521,
   522, 524, 556

~/.bashrc, 202, 290, 515, 517, 522,
 529, 531
/etc/bashrc, 515
/etc/profile, 515, 517, 518, 520, 521,
 523, 524, 549
environment, 64, 430, 513, 514, 521
external commands, 433, 438–440
global configuration directory
 /etc/profile.d, 290, 515, 517–521,
 524, 529, 531, 550
history, 230, 231, 233
internal commands, 430, 433,
 434, 437–440
program, 223, 306, 359, 430, 517, 524
shell options, 430–431
syntax, 22, 209, 433
tab completion, 223
variables, 430, 432, 434, 441, 513, 520
Bash commands
 external, 439
 internal, 437
 ~/.bash_login, 517
Bell Labs, 42, 43, 47, 235, 236
Berkeley Software Distribution (BSD), 44
Binary
 executable, 319, 435, 555, 556
BIOS
 POST, 464, 468
 SMBIOS, 380, 381
Books
 "Just for Fun", 6, 46
 "Linux and the Unix Philosophy", 3, 5, 45

627

© David Both 2023
D. Both, *Using and Administering Linux: Volume 1*, https://doi.org/10.1007/978-1-4842-9618-9

N

O

P, Q

T

V

Command list

Printed in the United States
by Baker & Taylor Publisher Services